JOSEPH ANDREWS

WITH SHAMELA
AND RELATED WRITINGS

AUTHORITATIVE TEXTS
BACKGROUNDS AND SOURCES
CRITICISM

A NORTON CRITICAL EDITION

Henry Fielding
JOSEPH ANDREWS

WITH SHAMELA
AND RELATED WRITINGS

AUTHORITATIVE TEXTS
BACKGROUNDS AND SOURCES
CRITICISM

Edited by

HOMER GOLDBERG

STATE UNIVERSITY OF NEW YORK AT STONY BROOK

W · W · NORTON & COMPANY · New York · London

The text of this book is composed in Electra, with
display type set in Bernhard Modern. Composition by Vail-Ballou.
Manufacturing by The Murray Printing Company.
Book design by Antonina Krass

First Edition

Library of Congress Cataloging-in-Publication Data
Fielding, Henry, 1707–1754.
Joseph Andrews

(Norton critical edition)
Bibliography: p. 495
1. Fielding, Henry, 1707–1754—Criticism and
interpretation. 2. Fielding, Henry, 1707–1754.
History of the adventures of Joseph Andrews.
I. Goldberg, Homer. I. Title.
PR3452.G65 1987 823'.5 86-18074

ISBN 0-393-02422-9
ISBN 0-393-95555-9 pbk.

W. W. Norton & Company, Inc., 500 Fifth Avenue, New York, N.Y. 10110
www.wwnorton.com

W. W. Norton & Company Ltd., Castle House, 75/76 Wells Street,
London W1T 3QT
67890

For Emily and John—and about time

Contents

Editor's Preface   ix

The Text of *Joseph Andrews*   1

The Text of *Shamela*   271

Related Writings

  From *The Champion*
    [Essay on Reputation]   309
    [Essay on Good Nature]   310
    [The Apology for the Clergy]   312
  An Essay on the Knowledge of the Characters of Men   321
  Preface to *The Adventures of David Simple*   331

Backgrounds and Sources

  Samuel Richardson · From *Pamela, or Virtue
    Rewarded*   335
  Conyers Middleton · From the Dedication to *The
    History of the Life of Marcus Tullius Cicero*   340
  Miguel de Cervantes Saavedra · From *The Life
    and Atchievements of the Renown'd Don Quixote*   343
  Paul Scarron · From *Le Roman comique*   359
  Alain-René Lesage · From *Histoire de Gil Blas de
    Santillane*   367
  Pierre Carlet de Chamblain de Marivaux · From
    *Le Paysan parvenu, ou les Memoirs de M * * **   376
  Political and Religious Background   388

Criticism

  CONTEMPORARY RESPONSES AND EARLY CRITICISM
  Letters
    George Cheyne to Samuel Richardson,
      March 9, 1742   395

Thomas Gray to Richard West, April 1742   395

William Shenstone to Richard Graves, 1742   395

William Shenstone to Lady Henrietta Luxborough,
March 22, 1749   396

Elizabeth Carter to Catherine Talbot,
January 1, 1743   396

Samuel Richardson to Lady Dorothy Bradshaigh,
1749   396

Pierre François Guyot Desfontaines · From
Observations sur les ecrits modernes   397

From *The Student*, or, *The Oxford and Cambridge
Monthly Miscellany*, January 20, 1750   398

Sarah Fielding [and Jane Collier?] · [Parson Adams
Not an Object of Ridicule]   398

James Beattie · [The New Comic Romance]   400

William Hazlitt · [A Perfect Piece of Statistics
in Its Kind]   401

MODERN CRITICISM

Mark Spilka · Comic Resolution in Fielding's
Joseph Andrews   404

Dick Taylor, Jr. · Joseph as Hero in *Joseph Andrews*   412

Martin C. Battestin · [Thematic Meaning and
Structure]   427

Sheldon Sacks · [Fielding's Guidance of the Reader's
Attitudes in Book 1, Chapters 1–11]   441

[Wilson's Tale]   456

Morris Golden · [Fielding's Psychology and Its
Relation to Morality]   458

Homer Goldberg · The Reasoning Behind the Form
of *Joseph Andrews*   471

Brian McCrea · Rewriting *Pamela*: Social Change and
Religious Faith in *Joseph Andrews*   484

Selected Bibliography   495

Editor's Preface

Joseph Andrews is a book avowedly written with an eye to other books. While purporting to demonstrate the beneficial influence of the current best-seller it mocked, it proclaimed itself an imitation of Cervantes and traced its lineage back to the "great Original" of Western narrative, Homer. It also claimed affinities to works as diverse as *Telemachus*, the Abbé Fenélon's fictionalized treatise on the proper conduct of princes, the exotic and ribald *Arabian Nights*, and even a work sometimes regarded as the prototype of *Pamela*, Marivaux's *La Vie de Marianne*. Critics have disagreed about the relative significance of these and other possible influences on Fielding's novel and have offered conflicting interpretations of his own prefatory efforts to explain what he was about. Yet the primary emphasis of those remarks is fairly plain. Fielding assumed his readers would understand the work before them was a comic fiction, or, as he called it, "comic Romance." His initial concern in the preface is to legitimate this kind of writing by placing it within a neoclassical taxonomy of literary kinds; the greater part of the argument is directed to defining the comic; and when he resumes the discussion in the second of his "little Volumes" (3.1), the "biographies" he cites as antecedents are predominantly works of comic fiction, chief among them *Don Quixote*.

Fielding came to this subtler imitation of Cervantes from his first student attempt to transplant Quixote fourteen years earlier by a roundabout route. The son of an army officer of aristocratic descent, he attended Eton, where he studied the traditional curriculum of Latin and Greek. When he resumed his classical studies in 1728 at the University of Leyden (where he began the scenes eventually produced as *Don Quixote in England*, 1734), he had already published a burlesque satiric poem and his first theatrical comedy, *Love in Several Masques*, produced by Colley Cibber at the Theatre-Royal. After his education was cut short, probably by a shortage of funds, he pursued an active theatrical career, writing some twenty comedies, farces, burlesques, and satires that were produced between 1730 and 1737, and eventually managing his own company at the Little Theatre, Haymarket. Given his early inclination and frequent success, Fielding might well have continued writing for the theatre if the popularity of his two political satires, *Pasquin* (1736) and *The Historical Register for the Year 1736* (1737), had not provoked the Walpole administration to enact a statute closing down all unlicensed theatres, of which Fielding's was the most prominent. He spent the next two years studying law in the Middle Temple. Then in November 1739, he embarked on another career as part-owner and principal writer of the thrice-weekly antiadministration periodical *The Champion*. After being called to the bar in June 1740, he divided his energies between the law and opposition journalism until the acclaim for *Pamela* and the appearance of its self-congratulatory second edition (February 1741) provoked *Shamela*.

In one sense it was only a short step from *Shamela* to *Joseph Andrews*. It simply involved replacing one device for ridiculing Richardson's pious exemplum—changing the heroine's moral character—with another—changing her sex. But this ostensible second parody was in fact a giant leap into a "new Province of Writing" (*Tom Jones*, 2.1). In the perspective of literary history, Fielding's claim of introducing a "Species of Writing hitherto unattempted in our Language" signifies more than he may have intended; his importation of a foreign "Idea of Romance" proved to be extraordinarily original: the first full-blown English comic novel. If the conception of Fielding's "most glaring" character—an amiable parson-errant viewing the world he encounters through an idiosyncratic transforming vision—derived from Cervantes (with hints from the behavior of his own erudite but absentminded friend, the Reverend William Young), he so brilliantly conceived and vividly realized his creation that Parson Adams soon became a proverbial figure in his own right, the prototype of learned innocence. Experienced as he was in the production of comedy, farce, and satire, nothing in Fielding's theatrical writing prepares us for this or the novel's other memorable character inventions—Lady Booby, Slipslop, Trulliber, or Peter Pounce—or the sustained imagination of its comic incidents. From the preface's formula of "the Discovery of Affectation" as the exclusive source of the ridiculous, one might anticipate a repetitive sequence of simple unmaskings. Instead, Fielding generated an unexpected variety of amusing adventures out of the encounter between his "Character of perfect Simplicity" and a world of vanity and hypocrisy, malice and envy. It has been said that Fielding brought to the novel a sense of form acquired in the theatre; but none of his dramatic pieces posed problems on the scale of those entailed in managing this "more extended and comprehensive" series of actions and interweaving this Quixotic strand with the evolving fortunes of his male Pamela-turned-faithful-lover. If he used some of the same venerable plot devices to resolve this story that he had employed in one of his first plays, *The Author's Farce* (1730), these contrivances are in the service of a more comprehensive shaping of the narrative in whole and part.

The novel's extended framework gave Fielding scope to indulge his satiric bent over a broader range of individual and societal foibles than in any of his plays or essays. Freed from the drama's confinement to dialogue and the first-person burlesque of Pamela's self-absorption, he expanded his essayist's manner into the role of a knowing narrator presiding as a philosophic master of the revels, a role that allowed him to play with the editorial postures and conventions of narration he had observed in his wide reading of ancients and moderns. Many antecedents contributed to Fielding's urbane and amusing narrative manner: what Pope called "Cervantes' serious air," Scarron's facetious byplay, the English tradition of mock-heroics from Butler through Dryden and Pope, the straightfaced ironic analysis perfected by Swift, and Fielding's own habits of critical reflection as a periodical essayist. But again, the synthesis of these diverse elements as the expression of a sustained controlling sensibility was distinctively new. After a dozen years of fairly successful professional writing, something in the specific narrative situation of the novel inspired Fielding to find his truest authorial voice— by turns witty, playful, or earnest, but always genial, assured, and knowledgeable. In addition to augmenting the comic pleasures of the book, through this pervasively intruding narrator he conveyed attitudes and values he had more directly articulated in his essays, thereby guiding and shaping the reader's response to the actions he depicted. Thus he inaugurated the rich mode of third-person narration and commentary he exploited more fully in *Tom Jones*, founding a major tradition of the English novel continued in their individual ways by Jane Austen, Thackeray, Dickens, Trollope, and George Eliot.

The text of *Joseph Andrews* is that of the *Wesleyan Edition of the Works of Henry Fielding*, edited by Martin C. Battestin. Based on a critical analysis of the first four editions that Fielding oversaw in varying degrees, it represents the best-informed reconstruction of his final intention. It relies principally on the significantly revised second edition for the substantive text and the first edition with selectively admitted later variants for spelling, punctuation, capitalization, and typographic features. The latter have been corrected or normalized in minor ways, chiefly in bringing the demarcation of quotations into conformity with modern practice. Otherwise the text appears as it would to Fielding's contemporary readers.

Fielding followed mid-eighteenth-century practice in capitalizing nouns, though not always consistently ("degree" and "Degree" occur within a few lines of the preface, p. 7, for example). He also followed current convention in using italics for proper names and foreign words and phrases; or for simple emphasis ("which should be *rapid* in this Part," p. 187); or for the narrative counterpart of stage directions: "*(and then she burst into a Fit of Tears.)*," p. 24. Occasionally he will italicize direct discourse for no apparent reason, as with Adams's comment on Miss Grave-airs (p. 97), or the sportsman's opening remark to Adams (p. 103). More often he will do so to call attention to some peculiarity or aberration of language, whether it be Adams's archaism ("*smote*," p. 103), his own playful neologism ("*Authoring*," p. 70), Slipslop's "hard Words," or the jargon of bookselling (p. 72), doorkeeping (p. 138), law (p. 43), medicine (p. 50), or hunting (p. 188). This practice is most pointedly demonstrated in the account of the ravisher's beating of Adams (pp. 108–9), where Fielding italicized the several "languages" in the second edition. Elsewhere italics serve to underscore irony, as when we are told Trulliber "was a Parson on *Sundays*" (p. 127, italics added in the second edition), or to convey scorn toward the human hunters who are described as "the *Retinue* who *attended*" their hounds (p. 184, italicized words added in the second edition). More specifically pointed italics are remarked in the notes.

Joseph Andrews would not have flourished as long as it has if its primary pleasures were not accessible to each new generation of readers. But some acquaintance with its literary roots may add to our understanding and appreciation of it. To this end, three kinds of materials are included: writing Fielding parodied (the most notorious scene in *Pamela* and Middleton's Dedication to the *Life of Cicero*), writing that influenced his (excerpts from Cervantes, Scarron, Lesage, and Marivaux), and some of Fielding's own writing germane to the novel or *Shamela*. The latter allows the reader to trace continuities in Fielding's preoccupations and thought but also to consider the differences between his comic and serious treatment of similar concerns. Although the excerpts from Richardson and the continental novelists are a necessarily limited sampling of an extensive body of fiction, these materials should enable the reader to recover some sense of the immediate literary context in which *Shamela* and *Joseph Andrews* were conceived and to compare Fielding's practices with those of his avowed predecessors. An extended note on the political and religious background is intended to provide a coherent context for allusions scattered through the two works.

The notes identify Fielding's numerous references, give eighteenth-century definitions of words whose meaning has changed, and indicate the most significant of Fielding's many revisions. In preparing the notes, I have been helped immeasurably by the work of previous editors, especially, for the novel, J. Paul De Castro's first scholarly edition (1929) and Martin Battestin's Wesleyan Edition; for *Shamela*, the editions of Sheridan Baker, Martin Battestin, and Douglas Brooks; and for the *Essay on the Characters of Men*, Henry Knight Miller. Particular contributions of these and other scholars are acknowledged where appropriate. Knowledgeable readers may discern my additions and occasional corrections. I have tried to make the notes as self-containedly clear and informative as possible without, I hope, distracting readers from enjoying the novel.

In selecting the modern criticism, I have tried to offer a representative but by no means comprehensive sampling of different approaches to the novel. I have chosen critics whose arguments should be accessible to undergraduates. Where excerpting has been necessary, I have tried to present their views as fully and adequately as possible. At variance with each other, these views should not be considered authoritative, but only as persuasive as the evidence of one's own attentive reading of the novel warrants. They are intended to stimulate thought, not foreclose it.

I am grateful to Richmond Hathorn, Judge Arthur Goldberg, Dr. Lester King, and Carol Blum for their patient and helpful responses to my inquiries concerning the classics, the law, eighteenth-century medicine, and French. I also thank my staunch friend Tom Rogers for his thorough critique of the notes. I alone am responsible for any errors. For faithfully typing and retyping before the era of the word processor I thank Carol De Mangin, Kathleen Merle, Irene Greenwood, and, especially, Joanna Kalinowski.

The Text of
JOSEPH ANDREWS

THE
HISTORY
OF THE
ADVENTURES
OF
JOSEPH ANDREWS,
And of his FRIEND
Mr. *ABRAHAM ADAMS.*

Written in Imitation of
The *Manner* of CERVANTES,
Author of *Don Quixote.*

IN TWO VOLUMES.

VOL. I.

LONDON:
Printed for A. MILLAR, over-againſt
St. Clement's Church, in the *Strand.*
M,DCC,XLII.

Preface

As it is possible the mere *English* Reader may have a different Idea of Romance with the Author of these little Volumes;[1] and may consequently expect a kind of Entertainment, not to be found, nor which was even intended, in the following Pages; it may not be improper to premise a few Words concerning this kind of Writing, which I do not remember to have seen hitherto attempted in our Language.

The Epic as well as the Drama is divided into Tragedy and Comedy. *Homer*, who was the Father of this Species of Poetry, gave us a Pattern of both these, tho' that of the latter kind is entirely lost; which *Aristotle* tells us, bore the same relation to Comedy which his *Iliad* bears to Tragedy.[2] And perhaps, that we have no more Instances of it among the Writers of Antiquity, is owing to the Loss of this great Pattern, which, had it survived, would have found its Imitators equally with the other Poems of this great Original.

And farther, as this Poetry may be Tragic or Comic, I will not scruple to say it may be likewise either in Verse or Prose: for tho' it wants one particular, which the Critic enumerates in the constituent Parts of an Epic Poem, namely Metre;[3] yet, when any kind of Writing contains all its other Parts, such as Fable, Action, Characters, Sentiments, and Diction, and is deficient in Metre only; it seems, I think, reasonable to refer it to the Epic; at least, as no Critic hath thought proper to range it under any other Head, nor to assign it a particular Name to itself.

Thus the *Telemachus*[4] of the Arch-Bishop of *Cambray* appears to me of the Epic Kind, as well as the *Odyssey* of *Homer*; indeed, it is much fairer and more reasonable to give it a Name common with that Species from which it differs only in a single Instance, than to confound it with those which it resembles in no other. Such are those voluminous Works

---

1. The five editions of the novel in Fielding's lifetime were each published in two pocket-sized volumes. *Romance*, a term associated with the extravagant genre condemned three paragraphs below, also meant simply an extended narrative prose fiction. The "mere *English* Reader" is one who reads only English, not necessarily a pejorative expression.

2. In *Poetics* 4, Aristotle credits Homer in his *Margites*—a lost comic epic named after its hero, a fool (*margos*)—with transforming personal invective into "a dramatic picture of the Ridiculous," thus outlining "the general forms of Com-

edy" as he had done for Tragedy in the *Iliad* (Bywater trans.).

3. In *Poetics* 24, Aristotle says the epic has the same parts as tragedy (previously defined as plot, character, thought, diction, melody, and spectacle) except for the last two. He uses *fable* and *action* as synonyms for plot.

4. *Les Avantures de Télémaque fils d'Ulysse* (1699), a prose epic by François de Salignac de la Mothe-Fénelon (1651–1715). The two English translations went through about twenty editions between 1699 and 1740.

commonly called *Romances*, namely, *Clelia*, *Cleopatra*, *Astræa*, *Cassandra*, the *Grand Cyrus*,[5] and innumerable others which contain, as I apprehend, very little Instruction or Entertainment.

Now a comic Romance is a comic Epic-Poem in Prose; differing from Comedy, as the serious Epic from Tragedy: its Action being more extended and comprehensive; containing a much larger Circle of Incidents, and introducing a greater Variety of Characters. It differs from the serious Romance in its Fable and Action, in this; that as in the one these are grave and solemn, so in the other they are light and ridiculous: it differs in its Characters, by introducing Persons of inferiour Rank, and consequently of inferiour Manners, whereas the grave Romance, sets the highest before us; lastly in its Sentiments and Diction, by preserving the Ludicrous instead of the Sublime. In the Diction I think, Burlesque itself may be sometimes admitted; of which many Instances will occur in this Work, as in the Descriptions of the Battles, and some other Places, not necessary to be pointed out to the Classical Reader; for whose Entertainment those Parodies or Burlesque Imitations are chiefly calculated.

But tho' we have sometimes admitted this in our Diction, we have carefully excluded it from our Sentiments and Characters: for there it is never properly introduced, unless in Writings of the Burlesque kind, which this is not intended to be. Indeed, no two Species of Writing can differ more widely than the Comic and the Burlesque: for as the latter is ever the Exhibition of what is monstrous and unnatural, and where our Delight, if we examine it, arises from the surprizing Absurdity, as in appropriating the Manners of the highest to the lowest, or *è converso*;[6] so in the former, we should ever confine ourselves strictly to Nature from the just Imitation of which, will flow all the Pleasure we can this way convey to a sensible Reader. And perhaps, there is one Reason, why a Comic Writer should of all others be the least excused for deviating from Nature, since it may not be always so easy for a serious Poet to meet with the Great and the Admirable; but Life every where furnishes an accurate Observer with the Ridiculous.

I have hinted this little, concerning Burlesque; because, I have often heard that Name given to Performances, which have been truly of the Comic kind, from the Author's having sometimes admitted it in his Diction only; which as it is the Dress of Poetry, doth like the Dress of Men establish Characters, (the one of the whole Poem, and the other of the whole Man,) in vulgar Opinion, beyond any of their greater Excellencies: But surely, a certain Drollery in Style, where the Characters and Sentiments are perfectly natural, no more constitutes the Burlesque, than an empty Pomp and Dignity of Words, where every thing else is

5. Huge multivolume French romances by Honoré d'Urfé (*Astrée*, 1607–28); Gauthier de Costes de la Calprenède (*Cassandre*, 1644–50; *Cléopâtre*, 1647–56); and Madeleine de Scudéry (*Artamène ou le Grand Cyrus*, 1649–53; *Clélie*, 1654–60). They endowed their legendary heroes and heroines of antiquity with chivalric manners and the elaborate sentiments of seventeenth-century French courtiers and embroiled them in improbable adventures turning on sexual disguises, surprising discoveries, and miraculous reunions of long-lost lovers. Their translations remained popular in England well into the eighteenth century.

6. Vice versa.

mean and low, can entitle any Performance to the Appellation of the true Sublime.

And I apprehend, my Lord *Shaftesbury's* Opinion of mere Burlesque agrees with mine, when he asserts, 'There is no such Thing to be found in the Writings of the Antients.'[7] But perhaps, I have less Abhorrence than he professes for it: and that not because I have had some little Success on the Stage this way;[8] but rather, as it contributes more to exquisite Mirth and Laughter than any other; and these are probably more wholesome Physic for the Mind, and conduce better to purge away Spleen, Melancholy and ill Affections, than is generally imagined. Nay, I will appeal to common Observation, whether the same Companies are not found more full of Good-Humour and Benevolence, after they have been sweeten'd for two or three Hours with Entertainments of this kind, than when soured by a Tragedy or a grave Lecture.

But to illustrate all this by another Science, in which, perhaps, we shall see the Distinction more clearly and plainly: Let us examine the Works of a Comic History-Painter, with those Performances which the *Italians* call *Caricatura*; where we shall find the true Excellence of the former, to consist in the exactest copying of Nature; insomuch, that a judicious Eye instantly rejects any thing *outré*; any Liberty which the Painter hath taken with the Features of that *Alma Mater.*—Whereas in the *Caricatura* we allow all Licence. Its Aim is to exhibit Monsters, not Men; and all distortions and Exaggerations whatever are within its proper Province.

Now what *Caricatura* is in Painting, Burlesque is in Writing; and in the same manner the Comic Writer and Painter correlate to each other. And here I shall observe, that as in the former, the Painter seems to have the Advantage; so it is in the latter infinitely on the side of the Writer: for the *Monstrous* is much easier to paint than describe, and the *Ridiculous* to describe than paint.

And tho' perhaps this latter Species doth not in either Science so strongly affect and agitate the Muscles as the other; yet it will be owned, I believe, that a more rational and useful Pleasure arises to us from it. He who should call the Ingenious *Hogarth*[9] a Burlesque Painter, would, in my Opinion, do him very little Honour: for sure it is much easier, much less the Subject of Admiration, to paint a Man with a Nose, or any other Feature of a preposterous Size, or to expose him in some absurd or monstrous Attitude, than to express the Affections of Men on

7. Anthony Ashley Cooper, third earl of Shaftesbury (1671–1713), *Sensus Communis; An Essay on the Freedom of Wit and Humour* (1709) 1.5. Shaftesbury regarded burlesque as a corruption of "pleasantry and humour" in reaction to "spiritual tyranny"; hence it was not to be found in the "politer ages," which encouraged free discourse.

8. Although Fielding's name did not appear on the title page until the third edition (March 1743), he evidently expected some readers to know he wrote the novel (see Dr. Cheyne's comment, p.

395). The most popular of his theatrical burlesques, *Tom Thumb* (1730), expanded to *The Tragedy of Tragedies* (1731), parodies elements of more than forty seventeenth- and eighteenth-century tragedies and heroic dramas.

9. Fielding's friend, William Hogarth (1697–1764), the "Comic History-Painter" referred to above, portrayed contemporary vices and foibles in such famous series of paintings and engravings as *The Harlot's Progress* (1732), *The Rake's Progress* (1733–35), and *Marriage à la Mode* (1745).

Canvas. It hath been thought a vast Commendation of a Painter, to say his Figures *seem to breathe*; but surely, it is a much greater and nobler Applause, *that they appear to think*.

But to return—The Ridiculous only, as I have before said, falls within my Province in the present Work.—Nor will some Explanation of this Word be thought impertinent by the Reader, if he considers how wonderfully[1] it hath been mistaken, even by Writers who have profess'd it: for to what but such a Mistake, can we attribute the many Attempts to ridicule the blackest Villanies; and what is yet worse, the most dreadful Calamities? What could exceed the Absurdity of an Author, who should write *the Comedy of* Nero, *with the merry Incident of ripping up his Mother's Belly*;[2] or what would give a greater Shock to Humanity, than an Attempt to expose the Miseries of Poverty and Distress to Ridicule? And yet, the Reader will not want much Learning to suggest such Instances to himself.

Besides, it may seem remarkable, that *Aristotle*, who is so fond and free of Definitions, hath not thought proper to define the Ridiculous. Indeed, where he tells us it is proper to Comedy, he hath remarked that Villany is not its Object:[3] but he hath not, as I remember, positively asserted what is. Nor doth the *Abbé Bellegarde*, who hath writ a Treatise on this Subject,[4] tho' he shews us many Species of it, once trace it to its Fountain.

The only Source of the true Ridiculous (as it appears to me) is Affectation. But tho' it arises from one Spring only, when we consider the infinite Streams into which this one branches, we shall presently cease to admire[5] at the copious Field it affords to an Observer. Now Affectation proceeds from one of these two Causes, Vanity, or Hypocrisy: for as Vanity puts us on affecting false Characters, in order to purchase Applause; so Hypocrisy sets us on an Endeavour to avoid Censure by concealing our Vices under an Appearance of their opposite Virtues. And tho' these two Causes are often confounded, (for there is some Difficulty in distinguishing them) yet, as they proceed from very different Motives, so they are as clearly distinct in their Operations: for indeed, the Affectation which arises from Vanity is nearer to Truth than the other; as it hath not that violent Repugnancy of Nature to struggle with, which that of the Hypocrite hath. It may be likewise noted, that Affectation doth not imply an absolute Negation of those Qualities which are affected: and therefore, tho', when it proceeds from Hypocrisy, it be nearly allied to Deceit; yet when it comes from Vanity only, it partakes

---

1. Astonishingly.
2. When the Roman emperor ordered his mother, Agrippina, killed, she urged her assassins symbolically to stab her womb (Tacitus, *Annals* 14.8). In *The Jacobite's Journal*, March 26, 1748, Fielding refers to a Bartholomew Fair showman "who exhibited the comical Humours of *Nero* ripping up his Mother's Belly," but the episode is apparently his own invention.
3. "The Ridiculous may be defined as a mistake or deformity not productive of pain or harm to others . . ." (*Poetics* 5, Bywater trans.).
4. In *Réflexions sur le ridicule* (1696; trans. 1706), Jean Baptiste Morvan de Bellegarde (1648–1734) uses representative characters to caution his reader against foibles of the polite world. Among the subject headings are Affectation, Foolish Vanity, and Imposture.
5. Wonder.

of the Nature of Ostentation: for instance, the Affectation of Liberality in a vain Man, differs visibly from the same Affection in the Avaricious; for tho' the vain Man is not what he would appear, or hath not the Virtue he affects, to the degree he would be thought to have it; yet it sits less aukwardly on him than on the avaricious Man, who *is* the very Reverse of what he would *seem* to be.

From the Discovery of this Affectation arises the Ridiculous—which always strikes the Reader with Surprize and Pleasure; and that in a higher and stronger Degree when the Affectation arises from Hypocrisy, than when from Vanity: for to discover any one to be the exact Reverse of what he affects, is more surprizing, and consequently more ridiculous, than to find him a little deficient in the Quality he desires the Reputation of. I might observe that our *Ben Johnson*, who of all Men understood the *Ridiculous* the best, hath chiefly used the hypocritical Affectation.

Now from Affectation only, the Misfortunes and Calamities of Life, or the Imperfections of Nature, may become the Objects of Ridicule. Surely he hath a very ill-framed Mind, who can look on Ugliness, Infirmity, or Poverty, as ridiculous in themselves: nor do I believe any Man living who meets a dirty Fellow riding through the Streets in a Cart, is struck with an Idea of the Ridiculous from it; but if he should see the same Figure descend from his Coach and Six, or bolt from his Chair[6] with his Hat under his Arm, he would then begin to laugh, and with justice. In the same manner, were we to enter a poor House, and behold a wretched Family shivering with Cold and languishing with Hunger, it would not incline us to Laughter, (at least we must have very diabolical Natures, if it would:) but should we discover there a Grate, instead of Coals, adorned with Flowers, empty Plate or China Dishes on the Side-board, or any other Affectation of Riches and Finery either on their Persons or in their Furniture; we might then indeed be excused, for ridiculing so fantastical an Appearance. Much less are natural Imperfections the Objects of Derision: but when Ugliness aims at the Applause of Beauty, or Lameness endeavours to display Agility; it is then that these unfortunate Circumstances, which at first moved our Compassion, tend only to raise our Mirth.

The Poet carries this very far;

> *None are for being what they are in Fault,*
> *But for not being what they would be thought.*[7]

Where if the Metre would suffer the Word *Ridiculous* to close the first Line, the Thought would be rather more proper. Great Vices are the proper Objects of our Detestation, smaller Faults of our Pity: but Affectation appears to me the only true Source of the Ridiculous.

---

6. A sedan chair, an enclosed one-passenger vehicle carried between poles by two men.
7. William Congreve (1670–1729), "Of Pleasing; an Epistle to Sir Richard Temple," ll. 63–64. The preceding lines strengthen the link to Fielding's thought and language: "Affect not any thing in Nature's Spite. / Baboons and Apes ridiculous we find; / For what? For ill resembling Human-kind."

But perhaps it may be objected to me, that I have against my own Rules introduced Vices, and of a very black Kind into this Work. To which I shall answer: First, that it is very difficult to pursue a Series of human Actions and keep clear from them. Secondly, That the Vices to be found here, are rather the accidental Consequences of some human Frailty, or Foible, than Causes habitually existing in the Mind. Thirdly, That they are never set forth as the Objects of Ridicule but Detestation. Fourthly, That they are never the principal Figure at that Time on the Scene; and lastly, they never produce the intended Evil.

Having thus distinguished *Joseph Andrews* from the Productions of Romance Writers on the one hand, and Burlesque Writers on the other, and given some few very short Hints (for I intended no more) of this Species of writing;[8] which I have affirmed to be hitherto unattempted in our Language; I shall leave to my good-natur'd Reader to apply my Piece to my Observations, and will detain him no longer than with a Word concerning the Characters of this Work.

And here I solemnly protest, I have no Intention to vilify or asperse any one: for tho' every thing is copied from the Book of Nature, and scarce a Character or Action produced which I have not taken from my own Observations and Experience, yet I have used the utmost Care to obscure the Persons by such different Circumstances, Degrees,[9] and Colours,[1] that it will be impossible to guess at them with any degree of Certainty; and if it ever happens otherwise, it is only where the Failure characterized is so minute, that it is a Foible only which the Party himself may laugh at as well as any other.

As to the Character of *Adams*, as it is the most glaring in the whole, so I conceive it is not to be found in any Book now extant. It is designed a Character of perfect Simplicity; and as the Goodness of his Heart will recommend him to the Good-natur'd; so I hope it will excuse me to the Gentlemen of his Cloth;[2] for whom, while they are worthy of their sacred Order, no Man can possibly have a greater Respect. They will therefore excuse me, notwithstanding the low Adventures in which he is engaged, that I have made him a Clergyman; since no other Office could have given him so many Opportunities of displaying his worthy Inclinations.

---

8. For Fielding's continuation of these "Hints," see his preface to *David Simple*, pp. 331–32 below.

9. Ranks, classes.

1. Appearances.

2. The clergy.

Contents

BOOK I

CHAPTER

I. Of writing Lives in general, and particularly of *Pamela*; with a Word by the bye of *Colley Cibber* and others.   14

II. Of Mr. *Joseph Andrews* his Birth, Parentage, Education, and great Endowments, with a Word or two concerning Ancestors.   16

III. Of Mr. *Abraham Adams* the Curate, Mrs. *Slipslop* the Chambermaid, and others.   18

IV. What happened after their Journey to *London*.   21

V. The Death of Sir *Thomas Booby*, with the affectionate and mournful Behaviour of his Widow, and the great Purity of *Joseph Andrews*.   23

VI. How *Joseph Andrews* writ a Letter to his Sister *Pamela*.   25

VII. Sayings of wise Men. A Dialogue between the Lady and her Maid, and a Panegyric or rather Satire on the Passion of Love, in the sublime Style.   27

VIII. In which, after some very fine Writing, the History goes on, and relates the Interview between the Lady and *Joseph*; where the latter hath set an Example, which we despair of seeing followed by his Sex, in this vicious Age.   30

IX. What passed between the Lady and Mrs. *Slipslop*, in which we prophesy there are some Strokes which every one will not truly comprehend at the first Reading.   34

X. *Joseph* writes another Letter: His Transactions with Mr. *Peter Pounce*, &c. with his Departure from Lady *Booby*.   37

XI. Of several new Matters not expected.   38

XII. Containing many surprizing Adventures, which *Joseph Andrews* met with on the Road, scarce credible to those who have never travelled in a Stage-Coach.   40

XIII. What happened to *Joseph* during his Sickness at the Inn,
with the curious Discourse between him and Mr. *Barnabas* the Parson of the Parish.   45

XIV. Being very full of Adventures, which succeeded each
other at the Inn.   48

XV. Shewing how Mrs. *Tow-wouse* was a little mollified;
and how officious Mr. *Barnabas* and the Surgeon were
to prosecute the Thief: With a Dissertation accounting
for their Zeal; and that of many other Persons not mentioned in this History.   52

XVI. The Escape of the Thief. Mr. *Adams's* Disappointment. The Arrival of two very extraordinary Personages, and the Introduction of Parson *Adams* to Parson
Barnabas.   55

XVII. A pleasant Discourse between the two Parsons and the
Bookseller, which was broke off by an unlucky Accident happening in the Inn, which produced a Dialogue
between Mrs. *Tow-wouse* and her Maid of no gentle
kind.   62

XVIII. The History of *Betty* the Chambermaid, and an Account
of what occasioned the violent Scene in the preceding
Chapter.   67

BOOK II

I. Of Divisions in Authors.   70

II. A surprizing Instance of Mr. *Adams's* short Memory,
with the unfortunate Consequences which it brought
on *Joseph*.   72

III. The Opinion of two Lawyers concerning the same
Gentleman, with Mr. *Adams's* Enquiry into the Religion of his Host.   76

IV. The History of *Leonora*, or the Unfortunate Jilt.   80

V. A dreadful Quarrel which happened at the Inn where
the Company dined, with its bloody Consequences to
Mr. *Adams*.   92

VI. Conclusion of the Unfortunate Jilt.   98

VII. A very short Chapter, in which Parson *Adams* went a
great Way.   102

VIII. A notable Dissertation, by Mr. *Abraham Adams*; wherein that Gentleman appears in a political Light.   104

IX. In which the Gentleman descants on Bravery and heroic Virtue, 'till an unlucky Accident puts an end to the Discourse.   106

X. Giving an Account of the strange Catastrophe of the preceding Adventure, which drew poor *Adams* into fresh Calamities; and who the Woman was who owed the Preservation of her Chastity to his victorious Arm.   110

XI. What happened to them while before the Justice. A Chapter very full of Learning.   113

XII. A very delightful Adventure, as well to the Persons concerned as to the good-natur'd Reader.   118

XIII. A Dissertation concerning high People and low People, with Mrs. *Slipslop's* Departure in no very good Temper of Mind, and the evil Plight in which she left *Adams* and his Company.   122

XIV. An Interview between Parson *Adams* and Parson *Trulliber*.   127

XV. An Adventure, the Consequence of a new Instance which Parson *Adams* gave of his Forgetfulness.   132

XVI. A very curious Adventure, in which Mr. *Adams* gave a much greater Instance of the honest Simplicity of his Heart than of his Experience in the Ways of this World.   134

XVII. A Dialogue between Mr. *Abraham Adams* and his Host, which, by the Disagreement in their Opinions seemed to threaten an unlucky Catastrophe, had it not been timely prevented by the Return of the Lovers.   139

BOOK III

I. Matter prefatory in Praise of *Biography*.   145

II. A Night-Scene, wherein several wonderful Adventures befel *Adams* and his Fellow-Travellers.   149

III. In which the Gentleman relates the History of his Life.   157

IV. A Description of Mr. *Wilson's* Way of Living. The tragical Adventure of the Dog, and other grave Matters.   175

V. A Disputation on Schools, held on the Road between

Mr. *Abraham Adams* and *Joseph*; and a Discovery not unwelcome to them both.   179

VI. Moral Reflections by *Joseph Andrews*, with the Hunting Adventure, and Parson *Adams's* miraculous Escape.   182

VII. A Scene of Roasting very nicely adapted to the present Taste and Times.   190

VIII. Which some Readers will think too short, and others too long.   196

IX. Containing as surprizing and bloody Adventures as can be found in this, or perhaps any other authentic History.   199

X. A Discourse between the Poet and Player; of no other Use in this History, but to divert the Reader.   203

XI. Containing the Exhortations of Parson *Adams* to his Friend in Affliction; calculated for the Instruction and Improvement of the Reader.   206

XII. More Adventures, which we hope will as much please as surprize the Reader.   209

XIII. A curious Dialogue which passed between Mr. *Abraham Adams* and Mr. *Peter Pounce*, better worth reading than all the Works of *Colley Cibber* and many others.   214

BOOK IV

I. The Arrival of Lady *Booby* and the rest at *Booby-Hall*.   217

II. A Dialogue between Mr. *Abraham Adams* and the Lady *Booby*.   220

III. What past between the Lady and Lawyer *Scout*.   222

IV. A short Chapter, but very full of Matter; particularly the Arrival of Mr. *Booby* and his Lady.   225

V. Containing Justice Business; Curious Precedents of Depositions, and other Matters necessary to be perused by all Justices of the Peace and their Clerks.   226

VI. Of which you are desired to read no more than you like.   230

VII. Philosophical Reflections, the like not to be found in any light *French* Romance. Mr. *Booby's* grave Advice to *Joseph*, and *Fanny's* Encounter with a Beau.   234

VIII. A Discourse which happened between Mr. *Adams*, Mrs. *Adams*, *Joseph* and *Fanny*; with some Behaviour of Mr. *Adams*, which will be called by some few Readers, very low, absurd, and unnatural. 240

IX. A Visit which the good Lady *Booby* and her polite Friend paid to the Parson. 246

X. The History of two Friends, which may afford an useful Lesson to all those Persons, who happen to take up their Residence in married Families. 247

XI. In which the History is continued. 251

XII. Where the good-natur'd Reader will see something which will give him no great Pleasure. 253

XIII. The History returning to the Lady *Booby*, gives some Account of the terrible Conflict in her Breast between Love and Pride; with what happened on the present Discovery. 255

XIV. Containing several curious Night-Adventures, in which Mr. *Adams* fell into many Hair-breadth 'Scapes, partly owing to his Goodness, and partly to his Inadvertency. 258

XV. The Arrival of Gaffar and Gammar *Andrews*, with another Person, not much expected; and a perfect Solution of the Difficulties raised by the Pedlar. 262

XVI. Being the last. In which this true History is brought to a happy Conclusion. 266

The History of the Adventures of JOSEPH ANDREWS, and of his Friend Mr. *Abraham Adams*

BOOK I

Chapter I

Of writing Lives in general, and particularly of Pamela; *with a Word by the bye of* Colley Cibber *and others.*

It is a trite but true Observation, that Examples work more forcibly on the Mind than Precepts: And if this be just in what is odious and blameable, it is more strongly so in what is amiable and praise-worthy. Here Emulation most effectually operates upon us, and inspires our Imitation in an irresistible manner. A good Man therefore is a standing Lesson to all his Acquaintance, and of far greater use in that narrow Circle than a good Book.

But as it often happens that the best Men are but little known, and consequently cannot extend the Usefulness of their Examples a great way; the Writer may be called in aid to spread their History farther, and to present the amiable Pictures to those who have not the Happiness of knowing the Originals; and so, by communicating such valuable Patterns to the World, he may perhaps do a more extensive Service to Mankind than the Person whose Life originally afforded the Pattern.

In this Light I have always regarded those Biographers who have recorded the Actions of great and worthy Persons of both Sexes. Not to mention those antient Writers which of late days are little read, being written in obsolete, and, as they are generally thought, unintelligible Languages; such as *Plutarch, Nepos,*[1] and others which I heard of in my

---

1. The Greek Plutarch (ca. A.D. 46–120), the most celebrated biographer of antiquity, and the Roman Cornelius Nepos (ca. 100–25 B.C.) were distinguished by their dominant interest in the moral character of their subjects. Although these and other classical authors were still read in their original tongues in schools like Fielding's Eton, reading the ancients in translation had become acceptable by the early eighteenth century, and because university instruction was at the student's discretion, many graduates knew little Latin and less Greek.

Youth; our own Language affords many of excellent Use and Instruction, finely calculated to sow the Seeds of Virtue in Youth, and very easy to be comprehended by Persons of moderate Capacity. Such are the History of *John* the Great, who, by his brave and heroic Actions against Men of large and athletic Bodies, obtained the glorious Appellation of the Giant-killer; that of an Earl of *Warwick*, whose Christian Name was *Guy*; the Lives of *Argalus* and *Parthenia*, and above all, the History of those seven worthy Personages, the Champions of Christendom.[2] In all these, Delight is mixed with Instruction, and the Reader is almost as much improved as entertained.[3]

But I pass by these and many others, to mention two Books lately published, which represent an admirable Pattern of the Amiable in either Sex. The former of these which deals in Male-virtue, was written by the great Person himself, who lived the Life he hath recorded, and is by many thought to have lived such a Life only in order to write it. The other is communicated to us by an Historian who borrows his Lights, as the common Method is, from authentic Papers and Records.[4] The Reader, I believe, already conjectures, I mean, the Lives of Mr. *Colley Cibber*,[5] and of Mrs.[6] *Pamela Andrews*. How artfully doth the former, by insinuating that he *escaped* being promoted to the highest Stations in Church and State, teach us a Contempt of worldly Grandeur! how strongly doth he inculcate an absolute Submission to our Superiors! Lastly, how completely doth he arm us against so uneasy, so wretched a Passion as the Fear of Shame; how clearly doth he expose the Emptiness and Vanity of that Fantom, Reputation![7]

What the Female Readers are taught by the Memoirs of Mrs. *Andrews*, is so well set forth in the excellent Essays or Letters prefixed to the sec-

2. These were cheap, crudely illustrated little versions of romances and folktales sold by itinerant peddlers to children and persons of limited education: *The History of Jack and the Giants; The History of Guy, Earl of Warwick; The Unfortunate Lovers: The History of Argalus and Parthenia;* and *The Most Famous History of the Seven Champions of Christendom* (i. e., the patron saints of England, Scotland, Wales, Ireland, France, Spain, and Italy).

3. A facetious reference to a traditional definition of the ends of poetry, derived from Horace's *Ars Poetica* 333–47.

4. In *Pamela, or Virtue Rewarded* (1740), Samuel Richardson pretended that he was the "editor" of actual letters and journals of a young serving maid who resists her powerful master's protracted efforts to seduce and rape her and is eventually rewarded by becoming his wife.

5. An *Apology for the Life of Mr. Colley Cibber . . . Written by Himself* appeared in April 1740. An actor, playwright, and theatre manager who became poet laureate in 1730, Cibber (1671–1757) produced and acted in Fielding's first play, *Love in Several Masques* (1728), and staged half a dozen others at Drury Lane in the next few years; but the two men did not stay on good terms, and Fielding had already satirized him in *The Author's Farce* (1734) and *The Historical Register for the*

Year 1736 (1737) before the apologist dismissed Fielding as "a broken Wit" and applauded the legislation that barred him from the stage. For Fielding's ridicule of the *Apology* in *The Champion,* see below, p. 30, n. 3.

6. Mistress, a title applied to unmarried as well as married women.

7. Chapter 3 of the *Apology* recounts Cibber's "several Chances for the Church, the Court, and the Army": if he had been accepted as a scholar at Winchester, his father had hopes of his becoming a bishop; if he had been offered a commission after volunteering in the bloodless Revolution of 1688, he might have become a general; if he had not been stagestruck, he might have received a government appointment. Whether in church or state, he was "afraid of succeeding to the Preferment I sought for" (*Apology,* ed. B. R. S. Fone [Ann Arbor: U of Michigan P, 1968] 46). Fielding also alludes to Cibber's deference to "lawful Power and Dignity" (158) in justifying the Licensing Act (see p. 63, n. 6) against a playwright (Fielding) who would "knock all Distinctions of Mankind on the Head" and incite the mob to laugh at "their Superiors" (156); to his repeated acknowledgments of his own vanity and his defiance of his critics to "make me more ridiculous than Nature has made me" (29); and to his professed unconcern about misrepresentations of his character (30).

ond and subsequent Editions[8] of that Work, that it would be here a needless Repetition. The authentic History with which I now present the public, is an Instance of the great Good that Book is likely to do, and of the Prevalence of Example which I have just observed: since it will appear that it was by keeping the excellent Pattern of his Sister's Virtues before his Eyes, that Mr. *Joseph Andrews* was chiefly enabled to preserve his Purity in the midst of such great Temptations; I shall only add, that this Character of Male-Chastity, tho' doubtless as desirable and becoming in one Part of the human Species, as in the other, is almost the only Virtue which the great Apologist hath not given himself for the sake of giving the Example to his Readers.

Chapter II

Of Mr. Joseph Andrews *his Birth, Parentage, Education, and great Endowments, with a Word or two concerning Ancestors.*

Mr. *Joseph Andrews*, the Hero of our ensuing History, was esteemed to be the only Son of Gaffar and Gammer[1] *Andrews*, and Brother to the illustrious *Pamela*, whose Virtue is at present so famous. As to his Ancestors, we have searched with great Diligence, but little Success: being unable to trace them farther than his Great Grandfather, who, as an elderly Person in the Parish remembers to have heard his Father say, was an excellent Cudgel-player.[2] Whether he had any Ancestors before this, we must leave to the Opinion of our curious Reader, finding nothing of sufficient Certainty to relie on. However, we cannot omit inserting an Epitaph which an ingenious Friend of ours hath communicated.

> *Stay Traveller, for underneath this Pew*
> *Lies fast asleep that merry Man* Andrew;
> *When the last Day's great Sun shall gild the Skies,*
> *Then he shall from his Tomb get up and rise.*
> *Be merry while thou can'st: for surely thou*
> *Shall shortly be as sad as he is now.*

The Words are almost out of the Stone with Antiquity. But it is needless to observe, that *Andrew* here is writ without an s, and is besides a Christian Name. My Friend moreover conjectures this to have been the Founder of that Sect of laughing Philosophers, since called *Merry Andrews*.[3]

To wave therefore a Circumstance, which, tho' mentioned in conformity to the exact Rules of Biography, is not greatly material; I proceed

8. To his original self-congratulatory preface, Richardson added twice as much preliminary praise from correspondents, much of it expounding the moral lessons to be drawn from the story (see p. 33, n. 4). For Fielding's parody of these letters, see below, p. 275.

1. Rustic terms of respect applied to older people of low rank.

2. Cudgel play was a popular contest at country fairs: "the weapon was a stout stick with basket-handguard; he who first drew blood from his adversary's head won the bout" (E. D. Cuming, in *Johnson's England*, ed. A. S. Turberville [Oxford: Clarendon Press, 1933] 1.378).

3. Clowns, buffoons.

to things of more consequence. Indeed it is sufficiently certain, that he had as many Ancestors, as the best Man living; and perhaps, if we look five or six hundred Years backwards, might be related to some Persons of very great Figure at present, whose Ancestors within half the last Century are buried in as great Obscurity. But suppose for Argument's sake we should admit that he had no Ancestors at all, but had sprung up, according to the modern Phrase, out of a Dunghill, as the *Athenians* pretended they themselves did from the Earth,[4] would not this *Autokopros**** have been justly entitled to all the Praise arising from his own Virtues? Would it not be hard, that a Man who hath no Ancestors should therefore be render'd incapable of acquiring Honour, when we see so many who have no Virtues, enjoying the Honour of their Forefathers? At ten Years old (by which Time his Education was advanced to Writing and Reading) he was bound an Apprentice, according to the Statute, to Sir *Thomas Booby*,[5] an Uncle of Mr. *Booby's* by the Father's side. Sir *Thomas* having then an Estate in his own hands, the young *Andrews* was at first employed in what in the Country they call *keeping Birds*. His Office was to perform the Part the Antients assigned to the God *Priapus*,[6] which Deity the Moderns call by the Name of *Jack-o'-Lent*:[7] but his Voice being so extremely musical, that it rather allured the Birds than terrified them, he was soon transplanted from the Fields into the Dog-kennel, where he was placed under the Huntsman, and made what Sportsmen term a *Whipper-in*.[8] For this Place likewise the Sweetness of his Voice disqualified him: the Dogs preferring the Melody of his chiding to all the alluring Notes of the Huntsman, who soon became so incensed at it, that he desired Sir *Thomas* to provide otherwise for him; and constantly laid every Fault the Dogs were at, to the Account of the poor Boy, who was now transplanted to the Stable. Here he soon gave Proofs of Strength and Agility, beyond his Years, and constantly rode the most spirited and vicious Horses to water with an Intrepidity which surprized every one.[9] While he was in this Station, he rode several Races for Sir *Thomas*, and this with such Expertness and Success, that the neighbouring Gentlemen frequently solicited the Knight, to permit little *Joey* (for so he was called) to ride their Matches. The best Gamesters,

---

* In *English*, sprung from a Dunghil.

---

4. Tracing their ancestry to the legendary Cecrops and Erichthonius, who were mothered by Earth, the Ancient Athenians claimed ("pretended") to be *autocthones*, original inhabitants, or, literally, "sprung from the earth."

5. Fielding first supplied this derisive name for Squire B—, Pamela's would-be seducer and eventual husband, in *Shamela*; the term was often applied to country squires by London sophisticates. An act of 1563, commonly known as the Statute of Apprentices, provided that a lad might be apprenticed in husbandry at the age of ten.

6. A Greco-Roman fertility god whose statue, displaying a huge phallus, was placed in gardens, probably originally to foster growth, but by the

time of Virgil to serve as a watchman against thieves and birds (*Georgics* 4.110).

7. Usually designating the dummy target of a Lenten throwing game, in Fielding's West Country this name was also given to a scarecrow (A. C. Humphreys).

8. Someone who keeps the pack of hounds together.

9. After currying and dressing the horse, the groom or stable boy was expected to ride his mount to "some running river or fresh spring a mile or two distant from the stable, and there let him drink" (Thomas Fairfax, *The Complete Sportsman; or, Country Gentleman's Recreation* [1760?] 38).

before they laid their Money, always enquired which Horse little *Joey* was to ride, and the Betts were rather proportioned by the Rider than by the Horse himself; especially after he had scornfully refused a considerable Bribe to play booty[1] on such an Occasion. This extremely raised his Character,[2] and so pleased the Lady *Booby*, that she desired to have him (being now seventeen Years of Age) for her own Foot-boy.

Joey was now preferred from the Stable to attend on his Lady; to go on her Errands, stand behind her Chair, wait at her Tea-table, and carry her Prayer-Book to Church; at which Place, his Voice gave him an Opportunity of distinguishing himself by singing Psalms: he behaved likewise in every other respect so well at divine Service, that it recommended him to the Notice of Mr. *Abraham Adams* the Curate; who took an Opportunity one Day, as he was drinking a Cup of Ale in Sir *Thomas's* Kitchin, to ask the young Man several Questions concerning Religion; with his Answers to which he was wonderfully pleased.

Chapter III

Of Mr. Abraham Adams *the Curate, Mrs.* Slipslop *the Chambermaid, and others.*

Mr. *Abraham Adams* was an excellent Scholar. He was a perfect Master of the *Greek* and *Latin* Languages; to which he added a great Share of Knowledge in the Oriental Tongues, and could read and translate *French, Italian* and *Spanish*. He had applied many Years to the most severe Study, and had treasured up a Fund of Learning rarely to be met with in a University. He was besides a Man of good Sense, good Parts,[1] and good Nature;[2] but was at the same time as entirely ignorant of the Ways of this World, as an Infant just entered into it could possibly be. As he had never any Intention to deceive, so he never suspected such a Design in others. He was generous, friendly and brave to an Excess; but Simplicity was his Characteristic:[3] he did, no more than Mr. *Colley Cibber*, apprehend any such Passions as Malice and Envy to exist in Mankind,[4] which was indeed less remarkable in a Country Parson than in a Gentleman who hath past his Life behind the Scenes, a Place which hath been seldom thought the School of Innocence; and where a very little Observation would have convinced the great Apologist, that those Passions have a real Existence in the human Mind.

His Virtue and his other Qualifications, as they rendered him equal to his Office, so they made him an agreeable and valuable Companion, and had so much endeared and well recommended him to a Bishop, that at the Age of Fifty, he was provided with a handsome Income of

---

1. To throw the race.
2. Reputation.
1. Natural abilities, talents.
2. For Fielding's extended definition of this term, see below, pp. 310–12.
3. Essential or distinctive trait.

4. "My Ignorance, and want of Jealousy [suspicion] of Mankind has been so strong, that it is with Reluctance I even yet believe any Person, I am acquainted with, can be capable of Envy, Malice, or Ingratitude . . ." (Cibber's *Apology* 9).

twenty-three Pounds a Year; which however, he could not make any great Figure with: because he lived in a dear Country, and was a little incumbered with a Wife and six Children.[5]

It was this Gentleman, who, having, as I have said, observed the singular Devotion of young *Andrews*, had found means to question him, concerning several Particulars; as how many Books there were in the New Testament? which were they? how many Chapters they contained? and such like; to all which Mr. *Adams* privately[6] said, he answer'd much better than Sir *Thomas*, or two other neighbouring Justices of the Peace could probably have done.

Mr. *Adams* was wonderfully[7] sollicitous to know at what Time, and by what Opportunity the Youth became acquainted with these Matters: *Joey* told him, that he had very early learnt to read and write by the Goodness of his Father, who, though he had not Interest enough to get him into a Charity School,[8] because a Cousin of his Father's Landlord did not vote on the right side for a Church-warden in a Borough Town, yet had been himself at the Expence of Sixpence a Week for his Learning. He told him likewise, that ever since he was in Sir *Thomas's* Family, he had employed all his Hours of Leisure in reading good Books; that he had read the Bible, the *Whole Duty of Man*, and *Thomas à Kempis*; and that as often as he could, without being perceived, he had studied a great good Book which lay open in the Hall Window, where he had read, *as how the Devil carried away half a Church in Sermon-time, without hurting one of the Congregation*; and *as how a Field of Corn ran away down a Hill with all the Trees upon it, and covered another Man's Meadow*. This sufficiently assured Mr. *Adams*, that the good Book meant could be no other than *Baker's* Chronicle.[9]

The Curate, surprized to find such Instances of Industry and Application in a young Man, who had never met with the least encouragement, asked him, if he did not extremely regret the want of a liberal Education, and the not having been born of Parents, who might have

5. Adams's stipend is near the bottom of the twenty- to fifty-pound scale for licensed curates authorized by an act of 1713.

6. Fielding inserted this word in the fourth edition, to make clear Adams's propriety.

7. Admiringly.

8. From the beginning of the eighteenth century, charity schools, organized by the Society for the Promotion of Christian Knowledge, supported by private benevolence and closely associated with the church, offered free instruction in reading, writing, and arithmetic and some vocational training, with primary emphasis on religion and morality. By 1727, they enrolled nearly thirty thousand boys and girls throughout England. Although these schools were governed by independent trustees, the churchwardens, as the principal temporal officials of their parishes, would be associated with them.

9. *The Whole Duty of Man, laid down in a plain and familiar way for the use of all, but especially the meanest reader* (1658), probably the most popular devotional work of the period, articulated man's duties to God, himself, and his fellow man. *De Imitatio Christi* (translated as *The Imitation of Christ* or *The Christian's Pattern*) by Thomas à Kempis (1380–1471), German Augustine monk, traces the soul's progress from worldly concerns to Christian perfection and union with God. In Sir Richard Baker's *Chronicle of the Kings of England* (1643), the account of each reign concludes with topical summaries. Joseph remembers sensational passages from the category "Casualties" (natural disasters and other extraordinary events), the first in the reign of Henry IV, when the Devil's appearance in an Essex church was accompanied by "a Tempest of Whirl-wind and Thunder" that broke the steeple and demolished the chancel, the second an earthquake in Elizabeth's reign that caused a twenty-acre field complete with trees and sheep to "travel . . . from *Saturday* in the evening, til *Monday* noon."

indulged his Talents and Desire of Knowledge? To which he answered, 'he hoped he had profited somewhat better from the Books he had read, than to lament his Condition in this World. That for his part, he was perfectly content with the State to which he was called, that he should endeavour to improve his Talent, which was all required of him, but not repine at his own Lot, nor envy those of his Betters.'[1] 'Well said, my Lad,' reply'd the Curate, 'and I wish some who have read many more good Books, nay and some who have written good Books themselves, had profited so much by them.'

Adams had no nearer Access to Sir *Thomas*, or my Lady, than through the Waiting-Gentlewoman: For Sir *Thomas* was too apt to estimate Men merely by their Dress, or Fortune; and my Lady was a Woman of Gaiety, who had been bless'd with a Town-Education, and never spoke of any of her Country Neighbours, by any other Appellation than that of *The Brutes*. They both regarded the Curate as a kind of Domestic only, belonging to the Parson of the Parish,[2] who was at this time at variance with the Knight; for the Parson had for many Years lived in a constant State of Civil War, or, which is perhaps as bad, of Civil Law, with Sir *Thomas* himself and the Tenants of his Manor. The Foundation of this Quarrel was a Modus,[3] by setting which aside, an Advantage of several Shillings *per Annum* would have accrued to the Rector: but he had not yet been able to accomplish his Purpose; and had reaped hitherto nothing better from the Suits than the Pleasure (which he used indeed frequently to say was no small one) of reflecting that he had utterly undone many of the poor Tenants, tho' he had at the same time greatly impoverish'd himself.

Mrs. *Slipslop* the Waiting-Gentlewoman, being herself the Daughter of a Curate, preserved some Respect for *Adams*; she professed great Regard for his Learning, and would frequently dispute with him on Points of Theology; but always insisted on a Deference to be paid to her Understanding, as she had been frequently at *London*, and knew more of the world than a Country Parson could pretend to.

She had in these Disputes a particular Advantage over *Adams*: for she was a mighty Affecter of hard Words, which she used in such a manner, that the Parson, who durst not offend her, by calling her Words in question, was frequently at some loss to guess her meaning, and would have been much less puzzled by an *Arabian* Manuscript.

1. Joseph has absorbed the lessons and language of *The Whole Duty of Man*, which enjoins "Contentedness . . . with that condition . . . God hath placed us in, not murmuring and repining at our lot," and, following Matthew 25:14–30, diligence "to improve . . . [the] talents intrusted to us" (1673 ed., ch. 7, pp. 162, 169). It also condemns envy of "persons . . . of some special qualification" for their "wisdom, learning, and the like" and of one's "*betters*" for their "outward advantages of honour, greatness, and the like" (1673 ed., ch. 13, pp. 278, 281).

2. As a curate, Adams, though appointed by the bishop, would be paid by the rector who owned the benefice, or living, and who could summarily dismiss him whenever he chose to resume charge of the parish himself. There were many such absentee incumbents who had little or nothing to do with the spiritual care of their parishes.

3. A *modus decimandi* was a legal arrangement whereby a sum of money replaced payment of tithes in kind. This assured the clerical incumbent of a definite income, but specifying this fixed amount also meant he would profit less as the value of his parishioners' produce increased—hence the rector's effort to have it nullified.

Adams therefore took an Opportunity one day, after a pretty long Discourse with her on the *Essence*, (or, as she pleased to term it, the *Incense*) of Matter, to mention the Case of young *Andrews*; desiring her to recommend him to her Lady as a Youth very susceptible of Learning, and one, whose Instruction in *Latin* he would himself undertake; by which means he might be qualified for a higher Station than that of a Footman: and added, she knew it was in his Master's power easily to provide for him in a better manner. He therefore desired, that the Boy might be left behind under his Care.

'La Mr. *Adams*,' said Mrs. *Slipslop*, 'do you think my Lady will suffer any *Preambles*[4] about any such Matter? She is going to *London* very *concisely*,[5] and I am *confidous* would not leave *Joey* behind her on any account; for he is one of the genteelest young Fellows you may see in a Summer's Day, and I am *confidous* she would as soon think of parting with a Pair of her Grey-Mares: for she values herself as much on one as the other.' *Adams* would have interrupted, but she proceeded: 'And why is *Latin* more *necessitous*[6] for a Footman than a Gentleman? It is very proper that you Clergymen must learn it, because you can't preach without it: but I have heard Gentlemen say in *London*, that it is fit for no body else. I am *confidous* my Lady would be angry with me for mentioning it, and I shall draw myself into no such *Delemy*.' At which words her Lady's Bell rung, and Mr. *Adams* was forced to retire; nor could he gain a second Opportunity with her before their *London* Journey, which happened a few Days afterwards. However, *Andrews* behaved very thankfully and gratefully to him for his intended Kindness, which he told him he never would forget, and at the same time received from the good Man many Admonitions concerning the Regulation of his future Conduct, and his Perseverance in Innocence and Industry.

Chapter IV

What happened after their Journey to London.

No sooner was young *Andrews* arrived at *London*, than he began to scrape an Acquaintance with his party-colour'd Brethren,[1] who endeavour'd to make him despise his former Course of Life. His Hair was cut after the newest Fashion, and became his chief Care. He went abroad with it all the Morning in Papers, and drest it out in the Afternoon; they could not however teach him to game, swear, drink, nor any other genteel Vice the Town abounded with. He applied most of his leisure Hours to Music, in which he greatly improved himself, and became so perfect a Connoisseur in that Art, that he led the Opinion of all the other Footmen at an Opera, and they never condemned or applauded a single

---

4. Proposals. Slipslop's "hard Words" are glossed in the notes when the intended word is not obvious and it is possible to "guess her meaning."
5. Slipslop confuses two meanings of "shortly,"

substituting *briefly* for *soon*.
6. Needy, mistaken for needed.
1. Footmen wore variegated liveries.

Song contrary to his Approbation or Dislike. He was a little too forward in Riots[2] at the Play-Houses and Assemblies; and when he attended his Lady at Church (which was but seldom) he behaved with less seeming[3] Devotion than formerly: however, if he was outwardly a pretty Fellow, his Morals remained entirely uncorrupted, tho' he was at the same time smarter and genteeler, than any of the Beaus in Town, either in or out of Livery.

His Lady, who had often said of him that *Joey* was the handsomest and genteelest Footman in the Kingdom, but that it was pity he wanted Spirit, began now to find that Fault no longer; on the contrary, she was frequently heard to cry out, *Aye, there is some Life in this Fellow*. She plainly saw the Effects which Town-Air hath on the soberest Constitutions. She would now walk out with him into *Hyde-Park* in a Morning, and when tired, which happened almost every Minute, would lean on his Arm, and converse with him in great Familiarity. Whenever she stept out of her Coach she would take him by the Hand, and sometimes, for fear of stumbling, press it very hard; she admitted him to deliver Messages at her Bed-side in a Morning, leered at him at Table, and indulged him in all those innocent Freedoms which Women of Figure may permit without the least sully of their Virtue.

But tho' their Virtue remains unsullied, yet now and then some small Arrows will glance on the Shadow of it, their Reputation; and so it fell out to Lady *Booby*, who happened to be walking Arm in Arm with *Joey* one Morning in *Hyde-Park*, when Lady *Tittle* and Lady *Tattle* came accidentally by in their Coach. *Bless me*, says Lady *Tittle*, *can I believe my Eyes? Is that Lady* Booby? *Surely*, says *Tattle*. *But what makes you surprized? Why is not that her Footman?* reply'd *Tittle*. At which *Tattle* laughed and cryed, *An old Business, I assure you, is it possible you should not have heard it? The whole Town hath known it this half Year*. The Consequence of this Interview was a Whisper through a hundred Visits, which were separately performed by the two Ladies[*] the same Afternoon, and might have had a mischievous Effect, had it not been stopt by two fresh Reputations which were published[4] the Day afterwards, and engrossed the whole Talk of the Town.

But whatever Opinion or Suspicion the scandalous Inclination of Defamers might entertain of Lady *Booby's* innocent Freedoms, it is certain they made no Impression on young *Andrews*, who never offered to encroach beyond the Liberties which his Lady allowed him. A Behav-

---

[*] It may seem an Absurdity that *Tattle* should visit, as she actually did, to spread a known Scandal: but the Reader may reconcile this, by supposing with me, that, notwithstanding what she says, this was her first Acquaintance with it.

---

2. Revelry. After holding seats below for their employers, footmen were admitted free to the upper gallery. When the management of Drury Lane tried to withdraw this privilege in 1737, a riot by three hundred footmen ensued. Assemblies were large social gatherings at which footmen attended upon their masters.
3. Seemly.
4. Exposed to public scrutiny.

iour which she imputed to the violent Respect he preserved for her, and
which served only to heighten a something she began to conceive, and
which the next Chapter will open a little farther.

Chapter V

The Death of Sir Thomas Booby, *with the affectionate and
mournful Behaviour of his Widow, and the great Purity of* Joseph
Andrews.

At this Time, an Accident happened which put a stop to these agreeable Walks, which probably would have soon puffed up the Cheeks of
Fame,[1] and caused her to blow her brazen Trumpet through the Town,
and this was no other than the Death of Sir *Thomas Booby*, who departing this Life, left his disconsolate Lady confined to her House as closely
as if she herself had been attacked by some violent Disease. During the
first six Days the poor Lady admitted none but Mrs. *Slipslop* and three
Female Friends who made a Party at Cards: but on the seventh she
ordered *Joey*, whom for a good Reason we shall hereafter call JOSEPH,[2]
to bring up her Tea-kettle. The Lady being in Bed, called *Joseph* to her,
bad him sit down, and having accidentally laid her hand on his, she
asked him, *if he had never been in Love?* Joseph answered, with some
Confusion, 'it was time enough for one so young as himself to think on
such things.' 'As young as you are,' reply'd the Lady, 'I am convinced
you are no Stranger to that Passion; Come *Joey*,' says she, 'tell me truly,
who is the happy Girl whose Eyes have made a Conquest of you?' *Joseph*
returned, 'that all Women he had ever seen were equally indifferent to
him.' 'O then,' said the Lady, 'you are a general Lover. Indeed you
handsome Fellows, like handsome Women, are very long and difficult
in fixing: but yet you shall never persuade me that your Heart is so
insusceptible of Affection; I rather impute what you say to your Secrecy,
a very commendable Quality, and what I am far from being angry with
you for. Nothing can be more unworthy in a young Man than to betray
any Intimacies with the Ladies.' *Ladies! Madam*, said *Joseph, I am sure
I never had the Impudence to think of any that deserve that Name*. 'Don't
pretend to too much Modesty,' said she, 'for that sometimes may be
impertinent: but pray, answer me this Question, Suppose a Lady should
happen to like you, suppose she should prefer you to all your Sex, and
admit you to the same Familiarities as you might have hoped for, if you
had been born her equal, are you certain that no Vanity could tempt
you to discover her? Answer me honestly, *Joseph*, Have you so much

1. In the *Aeneid* 4.173–97, the goddess Fama
(rumour) eagerly spreads a mixture of truth and
falsehood about Dido's liaison with Aeneas. The
passage, in which she is described as a winged
monster with many eyes, ears, and tongues, was a
crux of neoclassical debate on the use of description in epic.
2. Alluding to his biblical prototype in chastity,
who resists the advances of his master Potiphar's
wife (Genesis 39:7–12).

more Sense and so much more Virtue than you handsome young Fellows generally have, who make no scruple of sacrificing our dear Reputation to your Pride, without considering the great Obligation we lay on you, by our Condescension and Confidence? Can you keep a Secret, my *Joey*?' 'Madam,' says he, 'I hope your Ladyship can't tax me with ever betraying the Secrets of the Family, and I hope, if you was to turn me away, I might have that Character of you.' 'I don't intend to turn you away, *Joey*,' said she, and sighed, 'I am afraid it is not in my power.' She then raised herself a little in her Bed, and discovered one of the whitest Necks that ever was seen; at which *Joseph* blushed. 'La!' says she, in an affected Surprize, 'what am I doing? I have trusted myself with a Man alone, naked in Bed; suppose you should have any wicked Intentions upon my Honour, how should I defend myself?' *Joseph* protested that he never had the least evil Design against her. 'No,' says she, 'perhaps you may not call your Designs wicked, and perhaps they are not so.'—He swore they were not. 'You misunderstand me,' says she, 'I mean if they were against my Honour, they may not be wicked, but the World calls them so. But then, say you, the World will never know any thing of the matter, yet would not that be trusting to your Secrecy? Must not my Reputation be then in your power? Would you not then be my Master?' *Joseph* begged her Ladyship to be comforted, for that he would never imagine the least wicked thing against her, and that he had rather die a thousand Deaths[3] than give her any reason to suspect him. 'Yes,' said she, 'I must have Reason to suspect you. Are you not a Man? and without Vanity I may pretend to some Charms. But perhaps you may fear I should prosecute you; indeed I hope you do, and yet Heaven knows I should never have the Confidence to appear before a Court of Justice, and you know, *Joey*, I am of a forgiving Temper. Tell me *Joey*, don't you think I should forgive you?' 'Indeed Madam,' says *Joseph*, 'I will never do any thing to disoblige your Ladyship.' 'How,' says she, 'do you think it would not disoblige me then? Do you think I would willingly suffer you?' 'I don't understand you, Madam,' says *Joseph*. 'Don't you?' said she, 'then you are either a Fool or pretend to be so, I find I was mistaken in you, so get you down Stairs, and never let me see your Face again: your pretended Innocence cannot impose on me.' 'Madam,' said *Joseph*, 'I would not have your Ladyship think any Evil of me. I have always endeavoured to be a dutiful Servant both to you and my Master.' 'O thou Villain,' answered my Lady, 'Why did'st thou mention the Name of that dear Man, unless to torment me, to bring his precious Memory to my Mind, (*and then she burst into a Fit of Tears.*) Get thee from my Sight, I shall never endure thee more.' At which Words she turned away from him, and *Joseph* retreated from the Room in a most disconsolate Condition, and writ that Letter which the Reader will find in the next Chapter.

---

3. Joseph echoes Pamela's assurance to her apprehensive parents that "I will die a thousand deaths rather than be dishonest any way" (letter 3).

Chapter VI

How Joseph Andrews *writ a Letter to his Sister* Pamela.

To Mrs. *Pamela Andrews*, living with Squire *Booby*.

'Dear Sister,

'Since I received your Letter of your good Lady's Death, we have had a Misfortune of the same kind in our Family. My worthy Master, Sir *Thomas*, died about four Days ago,[1] and what is worse, my poor Lady is certainly gone distracted. None of the Servants expected her to take it so to heart, because they quarrelled almost every day of their Lives: but no more of that, because you know, *Pamela*, I never loved to tell the Secrets of my Master's Family;[2] but to be sure you must have known they never loved one another, and I have heard her Ladyship wish his Honour dead above a thousand times: but no body knows what it is to lose a Friend till they have lost him.[3]

'Don't tell any body what I write, because I should not care to have Folks say I discover[4] what passes in our Family: but if it had not been so great a Lady, I should have thought she had had a mind to me. Dear *Pamela*, don't tell any body: but she ordered me to sit down by her Bedside, when she was in naked Bed; and she held my Hand, and talked exactly as a Lady does to her Sweetheart in a Stage-Play, which I have seen in *Covent-Garden*, while she wanted him to be no better than he should be.[5]

'If Madam be mad, I shall not care for staying long in the Family; so I heartily wish you could get me a Place either at the Squire's, or some other neighbouring Gentleman's, unless it be true that you are going to be married to Parson *Williams*,[6] as Folks talk, and then I should be very willing to be his Clerk: for which you know I am qualified, being able to read, and to set a Psalm.[7]

'I fancy, I shall be discharged very soon; and the Moment I am, unless I hear from you, I shall return to my old Master's Country Seat, if it be

---

1. The previous chapter says this is the seventh day after Sir Thomas's death; the discrepancy may be a sign of Joseph's flustered state. Pamela's troubles begin when the death of her mistress puts her in the power of that lady's lecherous son.

2. Although Pamela writes her parents detailed accounts of her master's attempts on her virtue, she warns them to say nothing to the servant conveying her letters: "For it will be said that I blab every thing" (letter 16). When they weep before him on reading another of her letters, she is piously "sorry . . . [the other servants] have cause to think so evil of my master from any of us" (letter 28). For Fielding's direct attack on this aspect of Richardson's novel in *Shamela*, see below, p. 305.

3. Joseph's sentiment mimics the moral "sentences" interspersed throughout Pamela's narrative: "O how amiable a thing is doing good!" (letter 6); "What blessed things are trials and temptations,

when we have the strength to resist and subdue them!" (letter 17).

4. Reveal.

5. A euphemism, usually applied to a woman, for easy sexual morals. R. F. Brissenden identifies Joseph's reference as act 1, scene 2 of *The London Merchant* (1731) by Fielding's friend George Lillo (see p. 204, n. 7), in which the evil Millwood begins her seduction of the innocent apprentice, George Barnwell, by "laying her hand on his, as by accident." Compare Lady Booby's similar gesture on pp. 23 and 31.

6. To conceal his intentions, Pamela's master writes her parents that he is arranging her marriage to his chaplain, Mr. Williams. Fielding's satiric transformation of this character is a prominent feature of *Shamela*.

7. To start the tune, setting the pitch for the congregation. Each line would be read out by the clerk before being sung.

only to see Parson *Adams*, who is the best Man in the World. *London* is a bad Place, and there is so little good Fellowship, that next-door Neighbours don't know one another. Pray give my Service to all Friends that enquire for me; so I rest

> *Your Loving Brother,*
> Joseph Andrews.'

As soon as *Joseph* had sealed and directed this Letter, he walked down Stairs, where he met Mrs. *Slipslop*, with whom we shall take this Opportunity to bring the Reader a little better acquainted. She was a Maiden Gentlewoman of about Forty-five Years of Age, who having made a small Slip in her Youth had continued a good Maid ever since. She was not at this time remarkably handsome; being very short, and rather too corpulent in Body, and somewhat red, with the Addition of Pimples in the Face. Her Nose was likewise rather too large, and her Eyes too little; nor did she resemble a Cow so much in her Breath, as in two brown Globes which she carried before her; one of her Legs was also a little shorter than the other, which occasioned her to limp as she walked.[8] This fair Creature had long cast the Eyes of Affection on *Joseph*, in which she had not met with quite so good Success as she probably wished, tho' besides the Allurements of her native Charms, she had given him Tea, Sweetmeats, Wine, and many other Delicacies, of which by keeping the Keys, she had the absolute Command. *Joseph* however, had not returned the least Gratitude to all these Favours, not even so much as a Kiss; tho' I would not insinuate she was so easily to be satisfied: for surely then he would have been highly blameable. The truth is, she was arrived at an Age when she thought she might indulge herself in any Liberties with a Man, without the danger of bringing a third Person into the world to betray them. She imagined, that by so long a Self-denial, she had not only made amends for the small Slip of her Youth above hinted at: but had likewise laid up a quantity of Merit to excuse any future Failings. In a word, she resolved to give a loose to her amorous Inclinations, and pay off the Debt of Pleasure which she found she owed herself, as fast as possible.

With these Charms of Person, and in this Disposition of Mind, she encountered poor *Joseph* at the Bottom of the Stairs, and asked him if he would drink a Glass of something good this Morning. *Joseph*, whose Spirits were not a little cast down, very readily and thankfully accepted the Offer; and together they went into a Closet, where having delivered him a full Glass of Ratifia,[9] and desired him to sit down, Mrs. *Slipslop* thus began:

'Sure nothing can be a more simple *Contract* in a Woman, than to place her Affections on a Boy. If I had ever thought it would have been my Fate, I should have wished to die a thousand Deaths rather than live to see that Day. If we like a Man, the lightest Hint *sophisticates*. Whereas a Boy *proposes* upon us to break through all the *Regulations* of Modesty,

---

8. For Slipslop's Cervantean ancestress, see below, p. 352.

9. A liqueur flavored with the fruit or pits of cherries, almonds, peaches, or apricots.

before we can make any *Oppression* upon him.' *Joseph*, who did not understand a Word she said, answered, 'Yes Madam;—' 'Yes Madam!' reply'd Mrs. *Slipslop* with some Warmth, 'Do you intend to *result* my Passion? Is it not enough, ungrateful as you are, to make no Return to all the Favours I have done you: but you must treat me with *Ironing*? Barbarous Monster! how have I deserved that my Passion should be *resulted* and treated with *Ironing*?' 'Madam,' answered *Joseph*, 'I don't understand your hard Words: but I am certain, you have no Occasion to call me ungrateful: for so far from intending you any Wrong, I have always loved you as well as if you had been my own Mother.' 'How, Sirrah!' says Mrs. *Slipslop* in a Rage: 'Your own Mother! Do you *assinuate* that I am old enough to be your Mother? I don't know what a Stripling may think: but I believe a Man would *refer* me to any Green-Sickness[1] silly Girl *whatsomdever*: but I ought to despise you rather than be angry with you, for *referring* the Conversation of Girls to that of a Woman of Sense.' 'Madam,' says *Joseph*, 'I am sure I have always valued the Honour you did me by your Conversation; for I know you are a Woman of Learning.' 'Yes but, *Joseph*,' said she a little softened by the Compliment to her Learning, 'If you had a Value for me, you certainly would have found some Method of shewing it me; for I am *convicted* you must see the Value I have for you. Yes, *Joseph*, my Eyes whether I would or no, must have declared a Passion I cannot conquer.—Oh! *Joseph*!—'

As when a hungry Tygress,[2] who long had traversed the Woods in fruitless search, sees within the Reach of her Claws a Lamb, she prepares to leap on her Prey; or as a voracious Pike, of immense Size, surveys through the liquid Element a Roach or Gudgeon which cannot escape her Jaws, opens them wide to swallow the little Fish: so did Mrs. *Slipslop* prepare to lay her violent amorous Hands on the poor *Joseph*, when luckily her Mistress's Bell rung, and delivered the intended Martyr from her Clutches. She was obliged to leave him abruptly, and defer the Execution of her Purpose to some other Time. We shall therefore return to the Lady *Booby*, and give our Reader some Account of her Behaviour, after she was left by *Joseph* in a Temper of Mind not greatly different from that of the inflamed *Slipslop*.

Chapter VII

Sayings of wise Men. A Dialogue between the Lady and her Maid, and a Panegyric or rather Satire on the Passion of Love, in the sublime Style.

It is the Observation of some antient Sage, whose Name I have forgot, that Passions operate differently on the human Mind, as Diseases on the Body, in proportion to the Strength or Weakness, Soundness or Rottenness of the one and the other.

We hope therefore, a judicious Reader will give himself some Pains

---

1. An anemia incurred by young women about the time of puberty.

2. The first of the burlesque passages referred to in the preface (p. 4).

to observe, what we have so greatly laboured to describe, the different Operations of this Passion of Love in the gentle and cultivated Mind of the Lady *Booby*, from those which it effected in the less polished and coarser Disposition of Mrs. *Slipslop*.

Another Philosopher, whose Name also at present escapes my Memory, hath somewhere said, that Resolutions taken in the Absence of the beloved Object are very apt to vanish in its Presence; on both which wise Sayings the following Chapter may serve as a Comment.

No sooner had *Joseph* left the Room in the Manner we have before related, than the lady, enraged at her Disappointment, began to reflect with Severity on her Conduct. Her Love was now changed to Disdain, which Pride assisted to torment her. She despised herself for the Meanness[1] of her Passion, and *Joseph* for its ill Success. However, she had now got the better of it in her own Opinion, and determined immediately to dismiss the Object. After much tossing and turning in her Bed, and many Soliloquies, which, if we had no better Matter for our Reader, we would give him; she at last rung the Bell as above-mentioned, and was presently attended by Mrs. *Slipslop*, who was not much better pleased with *Joseph*, then the Lady herself.

Slipslop, said Lady *Booby*, *when did you see* Joseph? The poor Woman was so surprized at the unexpected Sound of his Name, at so critical a time, that she had the greatest Difficulty to conceal the Confusion she was under from her Mistress, whom she answered nevertheless, with pretty good Confidence, though not entirely void of Fear of Suspicion, that she had not seen him that Morning. 'I am afraid,' said Lady *Booby*, 'he is a wild young Fellow.' 'That he is,' said *Slipslop*, 'and a wicked one too. To my knowledge he games, drinks, swears and fights eternally: besides he is horribly *indicted* to Wenching.' 'Ay!' said the Lady, 'I never heard that of him.' 'O Madam,' answered the other, 'he is so lewd a Rascal that if your Ladyship keeps him much longer, you will not have one Virgin in your House except myself. And yet I can't conceive what the Wenches see in him, to be so foolishly fond as they are; in my Eyes he is as ugly a Scarecrow as I ever *upheld*.' 'Nay,' said the Lady, 'the Boy is well enough.'—'La Ma'am,' cries *Slipslop*, 'I think him the *ragmaticallest* Fellow in the Family.' 'Sure, *Slipslop*,' says she, 'you are mistaken: but which of the Women do you most suspect?' 'Madam,' says *Slipslop*, 'there is *Betty* the Chamber-Maid, I am almost *convicted*, is with Child by him.' 'Ay!' says the Lady, 'then pray pay her her Wages instantly. I will keep no such Sluts in my Family. And as for *Joseph*, you may discard him too.' 'Would your Ladyship have him paid off immediately?' cries *Slipslop*, 'for perhaps, when *Betty* is gone, he may mend; and really the Boy is a good Servant, and a strong healthy *luscious* Boy enough.' 'This Morning,' answered the Lady with some Vehemence. 'I wish Madam,' cries *Slipslop*, 'your Ladyship would be so good as to try him a little longer.' 'I will not have my Commands disputed,' said the Lady, 'sure you are not fond of him yourself.' 'I Madam?' cries *Slipslop*,

1. Baseness.

reddening, if not blushing, 'I should be sorry to think your Ladyship had any reason to *respect* me of Fondness for a Fellow; and if it be your Pleasure, I shall fulfill it with as much *reluctance* as possible.' 'As little, I suppose you mean,' said the Lady; 'and so about it instantly.' Mrs. *Slipslop* went out, and the Lady had scarce taken two turns before she fell to knocking and ringing with great Violence. *Slipslop*, who did not travel post-haste, soon returned, and was countermanded as to *Joseph*, but ordered to send *Betty* about her Business without delay. She went out a second time with much greater alacrity than before; when the Lady began immediately to accuse herself of Want of Resolution, and to apprehend the Return of her Affection with its pernicious Consequences: she therefore applied herself again to the Bell, and resummoned Mrs. *Slipslop* into her Presence; who again returned, and was told by her Mistress, that she had consider'd better of the Matter, and was absolutely resolved to turn away *Joseph*; which she ordered her to do immediately. *Slipslop*, who knew the Violence of her Lady's Temper, and would not venture her Place for any *Adonis* or *Hercules* in the Universe, left her a third time; which she had no sooner done, than the little God *Cupid*, fearing he had not yet done the Lady's Business, took a fresh Arrow with the sharpest Point out of his Quiver, and shot it directly into her Heart: in other and plainer Language, the Lady's Passion got the better of her Reason. She called back *Slipslop* once more, and told her, she had resolved to see the Boy, and examine him herself; therefore bid her send him up. This wavering in her Mistress's Temper probably put something into the Waiting-Gentlewoman's Head, not necessary to mention to the sagacious Reader.

Lady *Booby* was going to call her back again, but could not prevail with herself. The next Consideration therefore was, how she should behave to *Joseph* when he came in. She resolved to preserve all the Dignity of the Woman of Fashion to her Servant, and to indulge herself in this last view of *Joseph* (for that she was most certainly resolved it should be) at his own Expence, by first insulting, and then discarding him.

O Love, what monstrous Tricks dost thou play with thy Votaries of both Sexes! How dost thou deceive them, and make them deceive themselves! Their Follies are thy Delight! Their Sighs make thee laugh, and their Pangs are thy Merriment!

Not the Great *Rich*, who turns Men into Monkeys, Wheelbarrows, and whatever else best humours his Fancy, hath so strangely metamorphosed the human Shape;[2] nor the Great *Cibber*, who confounds all

---

2. John Rich (1682?–1761), enterprising manager of the theatre at Lincoln's Inn Fields from 1714 and of a new theatre in Covent Garden from 1732, altered the pattern of London theatrical offerings with his afterpieces, interludes, and other popular entertainments. His pantomimes, the rage of the 1720's and a staple of theatrical fare thereafter, combined legends from Ovid's *Metamorphoses* and other classical sources with the low comedy tricks of Harlequin; performing under the stage name of Lun, Rich made this traditional *commedia dell-arte* figure a mute conjurer whose magic wand produced the transformations described. Fielding, the only theatrical manager who refused to stage pantomimes, mocked Rich in *Pasquin* (1736) and *The Champion* and parodied his pantomime on the myth of Phaethon's fatal mishandling of the chariot of his father, the sun (see below, p. 364, n. 7), in *Tumble Down Dick: or, Phaeton in the Suds* (1736). For examples of Rich's spectacular stage effects, see below, p. 295, n. 4.

Number, Gender, and breaks through every Rule of Grammar at his Will, hath so distorted the *English* Language,[3] as thou dost metamorphose and distort the human Senses.

Thou puttest out our Eyes, stoppest up our Ears, and takest away the power of our Nostrils; so that we can neither see the largest Object, hear the loudest Noise, nor smell the most poignant Perfume. Again, when thou pleasest, thou can'st make a Mole-hill appear as a Mountain; a *Jew's*-Harp sound like a Trumpet; and a Dazy smell like a Violet. Thou can'st make Cowardice brave, Avarice generous, Pride humble, and Cruelty tender-hearted. In short, thou turnest the Heart of Man inside-out, as a Juggler doth a Petticoat, and bringest whatsoever pleaseth thee out from it. If there be any one who doubts all this, let him read the next Chapter.

Chapter VIII

In which, after some very fine Writing, the History goes on, and relates the Interview between the Lady and Joseph; *where the latter hath set an Example, which we despair of seeing followed by his Sex, in this vicious Age.*

Now the Rake *Hesperus*[1] had called for his Breeches, and having well rubbed his drowsy Eyes, prepared to dress himself for all Night; by whose Example his Brother Rakes on Earth likewise leave those Beds, in which they had slept away the Day. Now *Thetis* the good Housewife began to put on the Pot in order to regale the good Man *Phœbus*,[2] after his daily Labours were over. In vulgar Language, it was in the Evening when *Joseph* attended his Lady's Orders.

But as it becomes us to preserve the Character of this Lady, who is the Heroine of our Tale; and as we have naturally a wonderful Tenderness for that beautiful Part of the human Species, called the Fair Sex; before we discover too much of her Frailty to our Reader, it will be proper to give him a lively Idea of that vast Temptation, which overcame all the Efforts of a modest and virtuous Mind; and then we humbly hope his Good-nature will rather pity than condemn the Imperfection of human Virtue.

---

3. In *The Champion* for April 22, 1740, Fielding pronounced Cibber an "absolute Master" of English, "for surely he must be absolute Master of that whose Laws he can trample under Feet, and which he can use as he pleases." In the April 29 number, he uses the *Apology* to demonstrate the uselessness of grammar, since Cibber "is generally to be understood without, and . . . is sometimes not to be understood with it." On May 6, he continued to anatomize a "Stile . . . so very singular that one might almost say, '*He hath even a Language to himself*' "; and on May 17, he concluded his assault by trying one "*Col. Apol.*" in the Court of Censorial Inquiry "for the Murder of the *English* Language" with "a certain Weapon

called a Goose-quill." Among the scores of expressions Fielding ridicules are the use of "adept" for "novice," reference to the participle "outdoing" as "the pleasant accusative case," and a description of someone "out of his depth with his simple head above water."

1. The evening star.

2. "The Bright"—Greek epithet for Apollo, the sun god. In ancient mythology, the sea goddess Thetis was wed to Peleus, a mortal, to whom she bore Achilles. Fielding's conceit of the domestic union of these deities was anticipated by Matthew Prior (1664–1721) in his poem "A Better Answer" 17–20.

Nay, the Ladies themselves will, we hope, be induced, by considering the uncommon Variety of charms, which united in this young Man's Person, to bridle their rampant Passion for Chastity, and be at least, as mild as their violent Modesty and Virtue will permit them, in censuring the Conduct of a Woman, who, perhaps, was in her own Disposition as chaste as those pure and sanctified Virgins, who, after a Life innocently spent in the Gaieties of the Town, begin about Fifty to attend twice *per diem*, at the polite Churches and Chapels, to return Thanks for the Grace which preserved them formerly amongst Beaus from Temptations, perhaps less powerful than what now attacked the Lady *Booby*.

Mr. *Joseph Andrews* was now in the one and twentieth Year of his Age. He was of the highest Degree of middle Stature. His Limbs were put together with great Elegance and no less Strength. His Legs and Thighs were formed in the exactest Proportion. His Shoulders were broad and brawny, but yet his Arms hung so easily, that he had all the Symptoms of Strength without the least clumsiness. His Hair was of a nut-brown Colour, and was displayed in wanton [3] Ringlets down his Back. His Forehead was high, his Eyes dark, and as full of Sweetness as of Fire. His Nose a little inclined to the Roman. His Teeth white and even. His Lips full, red, and soft. His Beard was only rough on his Chin and upper Lip; but his Cheeks, in which his Blood glowed, were overspread with a thick Down. His Countenance had a Tenderness joined with a Sensibility [4] inexpressible. Add to this the most perfect Neatness in his Dress, and an Air, which to those who have not seen many Noblemen, would give an Idea of Nobility.

Such was the Person who now appeared before the Lady. She viewed him some time in Silence, and twice or thrice before she spake, changed her Mind as to the manner in which she should begin. At length, she said to him, '*Joseph*, I am sorry to hear such Complaints against you; I am told you behave so rudely to the Maids, that they cannot do their Business in quiet; I mean those who are not wicked enough to hearken to your Solicitations. As to others, they may not, perhaps, call you rude: for there are wicked sluts who make one ashamed of one's own Sex; and are as ready to admit any nauseous Familiarity as Fellows to offer it; nay, there are such in my Family: but they shall not stay in it; that impudent Trollop, who is with Child by you, is discharged by this time.'

As a Person who is struck through the Heart with a Thunderbolt, looks extremely surprised, nay, and perhaps is so too.—Thus the poor *Joseph* received the false Accusation of his Mistress; he blushed and looked confounded, which she misinterpreted to be Symptoms of his Guilt, and thus went on.

'Come hither, *Joseph*: another Mistress might discard you for these Offences; But I have a Compassion for your Youth, and if I could be certain you would be no more guilty—Consider, Child, (*laying her Hand carelessly upon his*) [5] you are a handsome young Fellow, and might do

3. Luxuriant.
4. Sensitivity.

5. See above, p. 25, n. 5.

better; you might make your Fortune—.' 'Madam,' said *Joseph*, 'I do assure your Ladyship, I don't know whether any Maid in the House is Man or Woman—.' 'Oh fie! *Joseph*,' answer'd the Lady, 'don't commit another Crime in denying the Truth. I could pardon the first; but I hate a Lyar.' 'Madam,' cries *Joseph*, 'I hope your Ladyship will not be offended at my asserting my Innocence: for by all that is Sacred, I have never offered more than Kissing.' 'Kissing!' said the Lady, with great Discomposure of Countenance, and more Redness in her Cheeks, than Anger in her Eyes, 'do you call that no Crime? Kissing, *Joseph*, is as a Prologue to a Play. Can I believe a young Fellow of your Age and Complexion will be content with Kissing? No, *Joseph*, there is no Woman who grants that but will grant more, and I am deceived greatly in you, if you would not put her closely to it. What would you think, *Joseph*, if I admitted you to kiss me?' *Joseph* reply'd, 'he would sooner die than have any such Thought.' 'And yet, *Joseph*,' returned she, 'Ladies have admitted their Footmen to such Familiarities; and Footmen, I confess to you, much less deserving them; Fellows without half your Charms: for such might almost excuse the Crime. Tell me, therefore, *Joseph*, if I should admit you to such Freedom, what would you think of me?—tell me freely.' 'Madam,' said *Joseph*, 'I should think your Ladyship condescended a great deal below yourself.' 'Pugh!' said she, 'that I am to answer to myself: but would not you insist on more? Would you be contented with a Kiss? Would not your Inclinations be all on fire rather by such a Favour?' 'Madam,' said *Joseph*, 'if they were, I hope I should be able to controll them, without suffering them to get the better of my Virtue.'—You have heard, Reader, Poets talk of the *Statue of Surprize*;[6] you have heard likewise, or else you have heard very little, how Surprize made one of the Sons of *Crœsus* speak tho' he was dumb.[7] You have seen the Faces, in the Eighteen-penny Gallery, when through the Trap-Door, to soft or no Musick, Mr. *Bridgewater*, Mr. *William Mills*,[8] or some other of ghostly Appearance, hath ascended with a Face all pale with Powder, and a Shirt all bloody with Ribbons; but from none of these, nor from *Phidias*, or *Praxiteles*, if they should return to Life—no, not from the inimitable Pencil of my Friend *Hogarth*,[9] could you receive such an Idea of Surprize, as would have entered in at your Eyes, had they beheld the Lady *Booby*, when those last Words issued out of the Lips of *Joseph*.—'Your Virtue! (said the Lady recovering after a Silence of two

6. Battestin locates instances of this common comparison in Ovid's *Metamorphoses* (3.418–19), Shakespeare's *Richard III* (3.7.25–26), Lewis Theobald's *Persian Princess* (4.2), and Edward Young's *Busiris* (4). Fielding cited Young's stage direction ("—Passion choaks / Their Words, and they're the Statues of Despair") in a mock-scholarly footnote to the *Tragedy of Tragedies* (2.8, n. k) ironically praising dramatists for their "judicious" rendering of "Passions . . . too big for Utterance."

7. According to Herodotus (1.85), when a Persian soldier was about to kill Croesus, king of Lydia, his mute son saved his life by crying out, 'Man, do not kill Croesus!"

8. Roger Bridgewater (d. 1754) frequently appeared as the ghost in *Hamlet*; William Mills (d. 1750) often played Banquo in *Macbeth* and was the ghost of Tom Thumb's father in the *Tragedy of Tragedies*.

9. Fielding associates his friend (see p. 5, n. 9) with two ancient Greeks (Phidias, a fifth-century B.C. painter, sculptor, and architect; and Praxiteles, a sculptor of the next century) traditionally invoked as master artists, though none of their work survives.

Minutes) I shall never survive it. Your Virtue! Intolerable Confidence[1]! have you the Assurance[2] to pretend,[3] that when a Lady demeans herself to throw aside the Rules of Decency, in order to honour you with the highest Favour in her Power, your Virtue should resist her Inclination? That when she had conquer'd her own Virtue, she should find an Obstruction in yours?' 'Madam,' said *Joseph*, 'I can't see why her having no Virtue should be a Reason against my having any. Or why, because I am a Man, or because I am poor, my Virtue must be subservient to her Pleasures.' 'I am out of patience,' cries the Lady: 'Did ever Mortal hear of a Man's Virtue! Did ever the greatest, or the gravest Men pretend to any of this Kind! Will Magistrates who punish Lewdness, or Parsons, who preach against it, make any scruple of committing it? And can a Boy, a Stripling, have the Confidence to talk to his Virtue?' 'Madam,' says *Joseph*, 'that Boy is the Brother of *Pamela*, and would be ashamed, that the Chastity of his Family, which is preserved in her, should be stained in him. If there are such Men as your Ladyship mentions, I am sorry for it, and I wish they had an Opportunity of reading over those Letters, which my Father hath sent me of my Sister *Pamela's*, nor do I doubt but such an Example would amend them.'[4] 'You impudent Villain,' cries the Lady in a Rage, 'Do you insult me with the Follies of my Relation, who hath exposed himself all over the Country upon your Sister's account? a little Vixen, whom I have always wondered my late Lady *John Booby* ever kept in her House. Sirrah! get out of my sight, and prepare to set out this Night, for I will order you your Wages immediately, and you shall be stripped and turned away.—' 'Madam,' says *Joseph*, 'I am sorry I have offended your Ladyship, I am sure I never intended it.' 'Yes, Sirrah,' cries she, 'you have had the Vanity to misconstrue the little innocent Freedom I took in order to try, whether what I had heard was true. O' my Conscience, you have had the Assurance to imagine, I was fond of you myself.' *Joseph* answered, he had only spoke out of Tenderness for his Virtue; at which Words she flew into a violent Passion, and refusing to hear more, ordered him instantly to leave the Room.

He was no sooner gone, than she burst forth into the following Exclamation: 'Whither doth this violent Passion hurry us? What Meannesses do we submit to from its Impulse? Wisely we resist its first and least Approaches; for it is then only we can assure ourselves the Victory. No Woman could ever safely say, *so far only will I go*. Have I not exposed myself to the Refusal of my Footman? I cannot bear the Reflection.' Upon which she applied herself to the Bell, and rung it with infinite more Violence than was necessary; the faithful *Slipslop* attending near

---

1. Presumption.
2. Audacity.
3. Maintain.
4. The editor's preface promises that *Pamela* will "teach . . . the Man of *Passion* how to subdue it; and the Man of *Intrigue*, how . . . to reclaim [reform]." At the end of *Pamela* 1, the editor remarks that gentlemen "may be taught" by the example of the redeemed Squire B—" the inexpressible Difference between the Hazards and Remorse attending a profligate Life, and the Pleasures flowing from virtuous Love, and benevolent Actions."

at hand: To say the truth, she had conceived a Suspicion at her last Interview with her Mistress; and had waited ever since in the Antichamber, having carefully applied her Ears to the Key-Hole during the whole time, that the preceeding Conversation passed between *Joseph* and the Lady.

Chapter IX

What passed between the Lady and Mrs. Slipslop, *in which we prophesy there are some Strokes which every one will not truly comprehend at the first Reading.*

'Slipslop,' said the Lady, 'I find too much Reason to believe all thou hast told me of this wicked *Joseph*; I have determined to part with him instantly; so go you to the Steward, and bid him pay him his Wages.' *Slipslop*, who had preserved hitherto a Distance to her Lady, rather out of Necessity than Inclination, and who thought the Knowledge of this Secret had thrown down all Distinction between them, answered her Mistress very pertly, 'she wished she knew her own Mind; and that she was certain she would call her back again, before she was got half way down stairs.' The Lady replied, 'she had taken a Resolution, and was resolved to keep it.' 'I am sorry for it,' cries *Slipslop*; 'and if I had known you would have punished the poor Lad so severely, you should never have heard a *Particle*[1] of the Matter. Here's a Fuss indeed, about nothing.' 'Nothing!' returned my Lady; 'Do you think I will countenance Lewdness in my House?' 'If you will turn away every Footman,' said *Slipslop*, 'that is a lover of the Sport, you must soon open the Coach-Door yourself, or get a Sett of *Mophrodites* to wait upon you; and I am sure I hated the Sight of them even singing in an Opera.'[2] 'Do as I bid you,' says my Lady, 'and don't shock my Ears with your beastly Language.' 'Marry-come-up,' cries *Slipslop*, 'People's Ears are sometimes the nicest[3] Part about them.'

The Lady, who began to admire[4] the new Style in which her Waiting-Gentlewoman delivered herself, and by the Conclusion of her Speech, suspected somewhat of the Truth, called her back, and desired to know what she meant by that extraordinary degree of Freedom in which she thought proper to indulge her Tongue. 'Freedom!' says *Slipslop*, 'I don't know what you call Freedom, Madam; Servants have Tongues as well as their Mistresses.' 'Yes, and saucy ones too,' answered the Lady: 'but I assure you I shall bear no such Impertinence.' 'Impertinence! I don't know that I am impertinent,' says *Slipslop*. 'Yes indeed you are,' cries my Lady; 'and unless you mend your Manners, this House is no Place for you.' 'Manners!' cries *Slipslop*, 'I never was thought to want Manners

---

1. Particular (detail).
2. Slipslop uses her version of the term *herma-phrodite*, loosely applied to any effeminate man, to refer to the *castrati*, or male sopranos who were the stars of the currently popular Italian opera.

The Italians continued to create sopranos surgically into the nineteenth century.
3. Most fastidious.
4. Wonder at.

nor Modesty neither; and for Places, there are more Places than one; and I know what I know.' 'What do you know, Mistress?' answered the Lady. 'I am not obliged to tell that to every body,' says *Slipslop*, 'any more than I am obliged to keep it a Secret.' 'I desire you would provide yourself,'[5] answered the Lady. 'With all my heart,' replied the Waiting-Gentle-woman; and so departed in a Passion, and slapped the Door after her.

The Lady too plainly perceived that her Waiting-Gentlewoman knew more than she would willingly have had her acquainted with; and this she imputed to *Joseph's* having discovered to her what past at the first Interview. This therefore blew up her Rage against him, and confirmed her in a Resolution of parting with him.

But the dismissing Mrs. *Slipslop* was a Point not so easily to be resolved upon: she had the utmost Tenderness for her Reputation, as she knew on that depended many of the most valuable Blessings of Life; particularly Cards, making Court'sies in public Places, and above all, the Pleasure of demolishing the Reputations of others, in which innocent Amusement she had an extraordinary Delight. She therefore determined to submit to any Insult from a Servant, rather than run a Risque of losing the Title to so many great Privileges.

She therefore sent for her Steward, Mr. *Peter Pounce*; and ordered him to pay *Joseph* his Wages, to strip off his Livery and turn him out of the House that Evening.

She then called *Slipslop* up, and after refreshing her Spirits with a small Cordial which she kept in her Closet, she began in the following manner:

'*Slipslop*, why will you, who know my passionate Temper, attempt to provoke me by your Answers? I am convinced you are an honest Servant, and should be very unwilling to part with you. I believe likewise, you have found me an indulgent Mistress on many Occasions, and have as little Reason on your side to desire a change. I can't help being surprized therefore, that you will take the surest Method to offend me. I mean repeating my Words, which you know I have always detested.'

The prudent Waiting-Gentlewoman, had duly weighed the whole Matter, and found on mature Deliberation, that a good Place in Possession was better than one in Expectation; as she found her Mistress therefore inclined to relent, she thought proper also to put on some small Condescension;[6] which was as readily accepted: and so the Affair was reconciled, all Offences forgiven, and a Present of a Gown and Petticoat made her as an Instance of her Lady's future Favour.

She offered once or twice to speak in favour of *Joseph*: but found her Lady's Heart so obdurate, that she prudently dropt all such Efforts. She considered there were more Footmen in the House, and some as stout Fellows, tho' not quite so handsome as *Joseph*: besides, the Reader hath already seen her tender Advances had not met with the Encouragement she might have reasonably expected. She thought she had thrown away

---

5. Prepare to leave Lady Booby's service.   6. Submission.

a great deal of Sack and Sweet-meats[7] on an ungrateful Rascal; and being a little inclined to the Opinion of that female Sect, who hold one lusty young Fellow to be near as good as another lusty young Fellow, she at last gave up *Joseph* and his Cause, and with a Triumph over her Passion highly commendable, walked off with her Present, and with great Tranquility paid a visit to a Stone-Bottle,[8] which is of sovereign Use to a Philosophical Temper.

She left not her Mistress so easy. The poor Lady could not reflect, without Agony, that her dear Reputation was in the power of her Servants. All her Comfort, as to *Joseph* was, that she hoped he did not understand her Meaning; at least, she could say for herself, she had not plainly express'd any thing to him; and as to Mrs. *Slipslop*, she imagined she could bribe her to Secrecy.

But what hurt her most was, that in reality she had not so entirely conquered her Passion; the little God lay lurking in her Heart, tho' Anger and Disdain so hoodwinked her, that she could not see him. She was a thousand times on the very Brink of revoking the Sentence she had passed against the poor Youth. Love became his Advocate, and whispered many things in his favour. Honour likewise endeavoured to vindicate his Crime, and Pity to mitigate his Punishment; on the other side, Pride and Revenge spoke as loudly against him: and thus the poor Lady was tortured with Perplexity; opposite Passions distracting and tearing her Mind different ways.

So have I seen, in the Hall of *Westminster*, where Serjeant *Bramble* hath been retained on the right Side, and Serjeant *Puzzle* on the left; the Balance of Opinion (so equal were their Fees) alternately incline to either Scale.[9] Now *Bramble* throws in an Argument, and *Puzzle's* Scale strikes the Beam; again, *Bramble* shares the like Fate, overpowered by the Weight of *Puzzle*. Here *Bramble* hits, there *Puzzle* strikes; here one has you, there t'other has you; 'till at last all becomes one Scene of Confusion in the tortured Minds of the Hearers; equal Wagers are laid on the Success, and neither Judge nor Jury can possibly make any thing of the Matter; all Things are so enveloped by the careful Serjeants in Doubt and Obscurity.

Or as it happens in the Conscience, where Honour and Honesty pull one way, and a Bribe and Necessity another.—If it was only our present Business to make Similies, we could produce many more to this Purpose: but a Similie (as well as a Word) to the Wise. We shall therefore see a little after our Hero, for whom the Reader is doubtless in some pain.

---

7. White wine and pastries, fruits, nuts, or candies.
8. Commonly used to store gin or other hard liquor.
9. Westminster Hall, adjacent to the Houses of Parliament, was the site of the chief courts of law from the thirteenth century until 1825. Sergeants were a superior order of barristers. The scales are the traditional emblem of justice.

Chapter X

Joseph writes another Letter: His Transactions with Mr. Peter
Pounce, *&c. with his Departure from Lady* Booby.

The disconsolate *Joseph*, would not have had an Understanding sufficient for the principal Subject of such a Book as this, if he had any
longer misunderstood the Drift of his Mistress; and indeed that he did
not discern it sooner, the Reader will be pleased to apply to an Unwillingness in him to discover what he must condemn in her as a Fault.
Having therefore quitted her Presence, he retired into his own Garret,
and entered himself into an Ejaculation on the numberless Calamities
which attended Beauty, and the Misfortune it was to be handsomer than
one's Neighbours.

He then sat down and addressed himself to his Sister *Pamela*, in the
following Words:

'*Dear Sister* Pamela,
'Hoping you are well, what News have I to tell you! O *Pamela*, my
Mistress is fallen in love with me—That is, what great Folks call falling
in love, she has a mind to ruin me; but I hope, I shall have more Reso-
lution and more Grace[1] than to part with my Virtue to any Lady upon
Earth.

'Mr. *Adams* hath often told me, that Chastity is as great a Virtue in a
Man as in a Woman. He says he never knew any more than his Wife,
and I shall endeavour to follow his Example. Indeed, it is owing entirely
to his excellent Sermons and Advice, together with your Letters, that I
have been able to resist a Temptation, which he says no Man complies
with, but he repents in this World, or is damned for it in the next; and
why should I trust to Repentance on my Death-bed, since I may die in
my sleep? What fine things are good Advice and good Examples! But I
am glad she turned me out of the Chamber as she did: for I had once
almost forgotten every word Parson *Adams* had ever said to me.

'I don't doubt, dear Sister, but you will have Grace to preserve your
Virtue against all Trials; and I beg you earnestly to pray, I may be enabled
to preserve mine: for truly, it is very severely attacked by more than one:
but, I hope I shall copy your Example, and that of *Joseph*, my Name's-
sake;[2] and maintain my Virtue against all Temptations.'

Joseph had not finished his Letter, when he was summoned down
stairs by Mr. *Peter Pounce*, to receive his Wages: for, besides that out of
eight Pounds a Year, he allowed his Father and Mother four, he had
been obliged, in order to furnish himself with musical Instruments, to
apply to the Generosity of the aforesaid *Peter*, who, on urgent Occasions, used to advance the Servants their Wages: not before they were

1. Pamela frequently appeals to Grace (divine   2. See above, p. 23, n. 2.
favor and influence) in her letters.

due, but before they were payable; that is, perhaps, half a Year after they were due, and this at the moderate *Premiums* of fifty *per Cent.* or a little more; by which charitable Methods, together with lending Money to other People, and even to his own Master and Mistress, the honest Man had, from nothing, in a few Years amassed a small Sum of twenty thousand Pounds or thereabouts.[3]

Joseph having received his little Remainder of Wages, and having stript off his Livery, was forced to borrow a Frock and Breeches of one of the Servants: (for he was so beloved in the Family, that they would all have lent him any thing) and being told by *Peter*, that he must not stay a Moment longer in the House, than was necessary to pack up his Linnen,[4] which he easily did in a very narrow Compass; he took a melancholy Leave of his Fellow-Servants, and set out at seven in the Evening.

He had proceeded the length of two or three Streets, before he absolutely determined with himself, whether he should leave the Town that Night, or procuring a Lodging, wait 'till the Morning. At last, the Moon, shining very bright, helped him to come to a Resolution of beginning his Journey immediately, to which likewise he had some other Inducements which the Reader, without being a Conjurer,[5] cannot possibly guess; 'till we have given him those hints, which it may be now proper to open.

Chapter XI

Of several new Matters not expected.

It is an Observation sometimes made, that to indicate our Idea of a simple Fellow, we say, *He is easily to be seen through*: Nor do I believe it a more improper Denotation of a simple Book. Instead of applying this to any particular Performance, we chuse rather to remark the contrary in this History, where the Scene opens itself by small degrees, and he is a sagacious Reader who can see two Chapters before him.

For this reason, we have not hitherto hinted a Matter which now seems necessary to be explained; since it may be wondered at, first, that *Joseph* made such extraordinary haste out of Town, which hath been already shewn; and secondly, which will be now shewn, that instead of proceeding to the Habitation of his Father and Mother, or to his beloved Sister *Pamela*, he chose rather to set out full speed to the Lady *Booby's* Country Seat, which he had left on his Journey to *London*.

Be it known then, that in the same Parish where this Seat stood, there lived a young Girl whom *Joseph* (tho' the best of Sons and Brothers) longed more impatiently to see than his Parents or his Sister. She was a

---

3. Pounce's prototype, Fielding's avaricious neighbor Peter Walter (1664?–1746), who amassed a fortune as steward to the Duke of Newcastle and others, was notorious for lending money to his "betters" at usurious rates. See below, p. 215, n. 4.

4. Shirts, underclothes.

5. Extremely clever.

poor Girl, who had been formerly bred up in Sir *John's*[1] Family; whence
a little before the Journey to *London*, she had been discarded by Mrs.
Slipslop on account of her extraordinary Beauty: for I never could find
any other reason.

This young Creature (who now lived with a Farmer in the Parish) had
been always beloved by *Joseph*, and returned his Affection. She was two
Years only younger than our Hero. They had been acquainted from
their Infancy, and had conceived a very early liking for each other, which
had grown to such a degree of Affection, that Mr. *Adams* had with much
ado prevented them from marrying; and persuaded them to wait, 'till a
few Years Service and Thrift had a little improved their Experience, and
enabled them to live comfortably together.

They followed this good Man's Advice; as indeed his Word was little
less than a Law in his Parish: for as he had shewn his Parishioners by a
uniform Behaviour of thirty-five Years duration, that he had their Good
entirely at heart; so they consulted him on every Occasion, and very
seldom acted contrary to his Opinion.

Nothing can be imagined more tender than was the parting between
these two Lovers. A thousand Sighs heaved the Bosom of *Joseph*; a thousand Tears distilled from the lovely Eyes of *Fanny*, (for that was her
Name.) Tho' her Modesty would only suffer her to admit his eager Kisses,
her violent Love made her more than passive in his Embraces; and she
often pulled him to her Breast with a soft Pressure, which, tho' perhaps
it would not have squeezed an Insect to death, caused more Emotion in
the Heart of *Joseph*, than the closest *Cornish* Hug[2] could have done.

The Reader may perhaps wonder, that so fond a Pair should during a
Twelve-month's Absence never converse with one another; indeed there
was but one Reason which did, or could have prevented them; and this
was, that poor *Fanny* could neither write nor read, nor could she be
prevailed upon to transmit the Delicacies of her tender and chaste Passion, by the Hands of an Amanuensis.

They contented themselves therefore with frequent Enquiries after
each other's Health, with a mutual Confidence in each other's Fidelity,
and the Prospect of their future Happiness.

Having explained these Matters to our Reader, and, as far as possible,
satisfied all his Doubts, we return to honest *Joseph*, whom we left just
set out on his Travels by the Light of the Moon.

Those who have read any Romance or Poetry antient or modern,
must have been informed, that Love hath Wings; by which they are not

---

1. Since Slipslop has the power of dismissal, this
must be the family of Sir Thomas, rather than
that of his kinsman Sir John, in which Pamela
serves. Other uncharacteristic substantive discrep-
ancies occur in this chapter: Adams could not
have been parish priest for thirty-five years if he is
only fifty years old, as indicated on p. 18; and the
innkeeper could not recognize Joseph's livery if it
had been earlier "stript off" as the property of his
employer. Fielding let all these stand and kept
Joseph in livery (see p. 51), although he did
change subsequent references from Sir John to Sir
Thomas (pp. 79, 180) in the second edition.
2. A powerful squeezing hold, or "lock," invented
by the formidable wrestlers of Cornwall and Devon.

to understand, as some young Ladies by mistake have done, that a Lover can fly: the Writers, by this ingenious Allegory, intending to insinuate no more, than that Lovers do not march like Horse-Guards;[3] in short, that they put the best Leg foremost, which our lusty Youth, who could walk with any Man, did so heartily on this Occasion, that within four Hours, he reached a famous House of Hospitality well known to the Western Traveller. It presents you a Lion on the Sign-Post: and the Master, who was christened *Timotheus*, is commonly called plain *Tim*.[4] Some have conceived that he hath particularly chosen the Lion for his Sign, as he doth in Countenance greatly resemble that magnanimous Beast, tho' his Disposition savours more of the Sweetness of the Lamb. He is a Person well received among all sorts of Men, being qualified to render himself agreeable to any; as he is well versed in History and Politicks, hath a smattering in Law and Divinity, cracks a good Jest, and plays wonderfully well on the *French* Horn.

A violent Storm of Hail forced *Joseph* to take Shelter in this Inn, where he remembered Sir *Thomas* had dined in his way to Town. *Joseph* had no sooner seated himself by the Kitchin-Fire, than *Timotheus*, observing his Livery, began to condole[5] the loss of his late Master; who was, he said, his very particular and intimate Acquaintance, with whom he had cracked many a merry Bottle, aye many a dozen in his Time. He then remarked that all those Things were over now, all past, and just as if they had never been; and concluded with an excellent Observation on the Certainty of Death, which his Wife said was indeed very true. A Fellow now arrived at the same Inn with two Horses, one of which he was leading farther down into the Country to meet his Master; these he put into the Stable, and came and took his Place by *Joseph's* Side, who immediately knew him to be the Servant of a neighbouring Gentleman, who used to visit at their House.

This Fellow was likewise forced in by the Storm; for he had Orders to go twenty Miles farther that Evening, and luckily on the same Road which *Joseph* himself intended to take. He therefore embraced this Opportunity of complimenting his Friend with his Master's Horses, (notwithstanding he had received express commands to the contrary) which was readily accepted: and so after they had drank a loving Pot, and the Storm was over, they set out together.

Chapter XII

Containing many surprizing Adventures, which Joseph Andrews *met with on the Road, scarce credible to those who have never travelled in a Stage-Coach.*

Nothing remarkable happened on the Road, 'till their arrival at the Inn, to which the Horses were ordered; whither they came about two in

---

3. In the stately pace of troops ceremonially guarding the monarch and the royal palace.
4. Timothy Harris, host of the Red Lion Inn, Egham, Surrey, southwest of London on the Basingstoke-Salisbury road. Fielding named him among the "Publicans of good Taste" in *Tom Jones* 8.8.
5. Lament.

the Morning. The Moon then shone very bright, and *Joseph* making his Friend a present of a Pint of Wine, and thanking him for the favour of his Horse, notwithstanding all Entreaties to the contrary, proceeded on his Journey on foot.

He had not gone above two Miles, charmed with the hopes of shortly seeing his beloved *Fanny*, when he was met by two Fellows in a narrow Lane, and ordered to stand and deliver.[1] He readily gave them all the Money he had, which was somewhat less than two Pounds; and told them he hoped they would be so generous as to return him a few Shillings, to defray his Charges on his way home.

One of the Ruffians answered with an Oath, *Yes, we'll give you something presently: but first strip and be d—n'd to you.—Strip*, cry'd the other, *or I'll blow your Brains to the Devil. Joseph*, remembring that he had borrowed his Coat and Breeches of a Friend; and that he should be ashamed of making any Excuse for not returning them, reply'd, he hoped they would not insist on his Clothes, which were not worth much; but consider the Coldness of the Night. *You are cold, are you, you Rascal!* says one of the Robbers, *I'll warm you with a Vengeance*; and damning his Eyes, snapt a Pistol[2] at his Head: which he had no sooner done, than the other levelled a Blow at him with his Stick, which *Joseph*, who was expert at Cudgel-playing, caught with his, and returned the Favour so successfully on his Adversary, that he laid him sprawling at his Feet, and at the same Instant received a Blow from behind, with the Butt-end of a Pistol from the other Villain, which felled him to the Ground, and totally deprived him of his Senses.

The Thief, who had been knocked down, had now recovered himself; and both together fell to be-labouring poor *Joseph* with their Sticks, till they were convinced they had put an end to his miserable Being: They then stript him entirely naked, threw him into a Ditch, and departed with their Booty.

The poor Wretch, who lay motionless a long time, just began to recover his Senses as a Stage-Coach came by. The Postillion hearing a Man's Groans, stopt his Horses, and told the Coachman, 'he was certain there was a *dead* Man lying in the Ditch, for he heard him groan.' 'Go on, Sirrah,' says the Coachman, 'we are confounded late, and have no time to look after dead Men.' A Lady, who heard what the Postillion said, and likewise heard the Groan, called eagerly to the Coachman, 'to stop and see what was the matter.' Upon which he bid the Postillion 'alight, and look into the Ditch.' He did so, and returned, 'that there was a Man sitting upright as naked as ever he was born.'—'O *J-sus*,' cry'd the Lady, 'A naked Man! Dear Coachman, drive on and leave him.' Upon this the Gentlemen got out of the Coach; and *Joseph* begged them, 'to have Mercy upon him: For that he had been robbed, and almost beaten to death.' 'Robbed,' cries an old Gentleman; 'Let us make all the haste

---

1. The highwayman's traditional order to his victim ("stand" = halt). The biblical prototype of this episode is the parable of the Good Samaritan,

Luke 10:30–37.

2. Pulled the trigger; flintlocks often failed to fire.

imaginable, or we shall be robbed too.' A young Man, who belonged to the Law answered, 'he wished they had past by without taking any Notice: But that now they might be proved to have been *last in his Company*; if he should die, they might be called to some account for his Murther. He therefore thought it adviseable to save the poor Creature's Life, for their own sakes, if possible; at least, if he died, to prevent the Jury's finding *that they fled for it*.³ He was therefore *of Opinion*, to take the Man into the Coach, and carry him to the next Inn.' The Lady insisted, 'that he should not come into the Coach. That if they lifted him in, she would herself alight: for she had rather stay in that Place to all Eternity, than ride with a naked Man.' The Coachman objected, 'that he could not suffer him to be taken in, unless some body would pay a Shilling for his Carriage the four Miles.' Which the two Gentlemen refused to do; but the Lawyer, who was afraid of some Mischief happening to himself if the Wretch was left behind in that Condition, saying, 'no Man could be too cautious in these Matters, and that he remembred very extraordinary Cases in the Books,' threatned the Coachman, and bid him deny taking him up at his Peril; 'for that if he died, he should be indicted for his Murther, and if he lived, and brought an Action against him, he would willingly take a Brief in it.' These Words had a sensible Effect on the Coachman, who was well acquainted with the Person who spoke them; and the old Gentleman abovementioned, thinking the naked Man would afford him frequent Opportunities of shewing his Wit to the Lady, offered to join with the Company in giving a Mug of Beer for his Fare; till partly alarmed by the Threats of the one, and partly by the Promises of the other, and being perhaps *a little* moved with Compassion at the poor Creature's Condition, who stood bleeding and shivering with the Cold, he at length agreed; and *Joseph* was now advancing to the Coach, where seeing the Lady, who held the Sticks of her Fan before her Eyes, he absolutely refused, miserable as he was, to enter, unless he was furnished with sufficient Covering, to prevent giving the least Offence to Decency. So perfectly modest was this young Man; such mighty Effects had the spotless Example of the amiable *Pamela*, and the excellent sermons of Mr. *Adams* wrought upon him.

Though there were several great Coats about the Coach, it was not easy to get over this Difficulty which *Joseph* had started. The two Gentlemen complained they were cold, and could not spare a Rag; the Man of Wit saying, with a Laugh, *that Charity began at home*; and the Coachman, who had two great Coats spread under him, refused to lend either, lest they should be made bloody; the Lady's Footman desired to be excused for the same Reason, which the Lady herself, notwithstanding her Abhorence of a naked Man, approved: and it is more than probable, poor *Joseph*, who obstinately adhered to his modest Resolution, must have perished, unless the Postillion, (a Lad who hath been since transported for robbing a Hen-roost) had voluntarily stript off a great Coat,

---

3. Flight from a felony was an offense in itself punishable by forfeiture of one's property.

his only Garment, at the same time swearing a great Oath, (for which he was rebuked by the Passengers) 'that he would rather ride in his Shirt all his Life, than suffer a Fellow-Creature to lie in so miserable a Condition.'

Joseph, having put on the great Coat, was lifted into the Coach, which now proceeded on its Journey. He declared himself almost dead with the Cold, which gave the Man of Wit an occasion to ask the Lady, if she could not accommodate him with a Dram.[4] She answered with some Resentment, 'she wondered at his asking her such a Question;' but assured him, 'she never tasted any such thing.'

The Lawyer was enquiring into the Circumstances of the Robbery, when the Coach stopt, and one of the Ruffians, putting a Pistol in, demanded their Money of the Passengers; who readily gave it them; and the Lady, in her Fright, delivered up a little silver Bottle, of about a half-pint Size, which, the Rogue clapping it to his Mouth, and drinking her Health, declared held some of the best *Nantes*[5] he had ever tasted: this the Lady afterwards assured the Company was the Mistake of her Maid, for that she had ordered her to fill the Bottle with *Hungary* Water.[6]

As soon as the Fellows were departed, the Lawyer, who had, it seems, a Case of Pistols in the Seat of the Coach, informed the Company, that if it had been Day-light, and he could have come at his Pistols, he would not have submitted to the Robbery; he likewise set forth, that he had often met Highwaymen when he travelled on horseback, but none ever durst attack him; concluding, that if he had not been more afraid for the Lady than for himself, he should not have now parted with his Money so easily.

As Wit is generally observed to love to reside in empty Pockets;[7] so the Gentleman, whose Ingenuity we have above remark'd, as soon as he had parted with his Money, began to grow wonderfully facetious. He made frequent Allusions to *Adam* and *Eve*, and said many excellent things on Figs and Fig-Leaves; which perhaps gave more Offence to *Joseph* than to any other in the Company.

The Lawyer likewise made several very pretty Jests, without departing from his Profession. He said, 'if *Joseph* and the Lady were alone, he would be the more capable of making a *Conveyance* to her, as his *Affairs* were not *fettered* with any *Incumbrance*; he'd warrant, he soon suffered a *Recovery* by a Writ of *Entry*, which was the proper way to create *Heirs in Tail*; that for his own part, he would engage to make so *firm a Settlement* in a Coach, that there should be no Danger of an *Ejectment*;'[8] with an Inundation of the like Gibbrish, which he continued to vent till the Coach arrived at an Inn, where one Servant-Maid only was up in readiness to attend the Coachman, and furnish him with cold Meat and

4. Strong drink.
5. French brandy.
6. A distillate of rosemary flowers and alcohol, said to have cured the queen of Hungary of paralysis, commonly used as a lotion or remedy for fainting or hysteria.

7. "I'm poor enough to be a Wit" (Congreve, *Love for Love* 1.1); "Love of Wit makes no Man rich" (Thomas Fuller, *Gnomologia*, 1732, no. 3295).
8. The terms of the lawyer's ribaldry are drawn from the law of real property.

a Dram. *Joseph* desired to alight, and that he might have a Bed prepared for him, which the Maid readily promised to perform; and being a good-natur'd Wench, and not so squeamish as the Lady had been, she clapt a large Faggot on the Fire, and furnishing *Joseph* with a great Coat belonging to one of the Hostlers, desired him to sit down and warm himself, whilst she made his Bed. The Coachman, in the mean time, took an Opportunity to call up a Surgeon, who lived within a few Doors: after which, he reminded his Passengers how late they were, and after they had taken Leave of *Joseph*, hurried them off as fast as he could.

The Wench soon got *Joseph* to bed, and promised to use her Interest[9] to borrow him a Shirt; but imagined, as she afterwards said, by his being so bloody, that he must be a dead Man: she ran with all speed to hasten the Surgeon, who was more than half drest, apprehending that the Coach had been overturned and some Gentleman or Lady hurt. As soon as the Wench had informed him at his Window, that it was a poor foot Passenger who had been stripped of all he had, and almost murdered; he chid her for disturbing him so early, slipped off his Clothes again, and very quietly returned to bed and to sleep.

Aurora now began to shew her blooming Cheeks over the Hills, whilst ten Millions of feathered Songsters, in jocund Chorus, repeated Odes a thousand times sweeter than those of our *Laureate*, and sung both *the Day and the Song*;[1] when the Master of the Inn, Mr. *Tow-wouse*, arose, and learning from his Maid an Account of the Robbery, and the Situation of his poor naked Guest, he shook his Head, and cried, *Good-lack-a-day!* and then ordered the Girl to carry him one of his own Shirts.

Mrs. *Tow-wouse* was just awake, and had stretched out her Arms in vain to fold her departed Husband, when the Maid entered the Room. 'Who's there? *Betty*?' 'Yes Madam.' 'Where's your Master?' 'He's without, Madam; he hath sent me for a Shirt to lend a poor naked Man, who hath been robbed and murdered.' 'Touch one, if you dare, you Slut,' said Mrs. *Tow-wouse*, 'your Master is a pretty sort of a Man to take in naked Vagabonds, and clothe them with his own Clothes. I shall have no such Doings.—If you offer to touch any thing, I will throw the Chamber-Pot at your Head. Go, send your Master to me.' 'Yes Madam,' answered *Betty*. As soon as he came in, she thus began: 'What the Devil do you mean by this, Mr. *Tow-wouse*? Am I to buy Shirts to lend to a sett of scabby Rascals?' 'My Dear,' said Mr. *Tow-wouse*, 'this is a poor Wretch.' 'Yes,' says she, 'I know it is a poor Wretch, but what the Devil have we to do with poor Wretches? The Law makes us provide for too many already.[2] We shall have thirty or forty poor Wretches in red Coats

---

9. Influence.
1. An allusion to the refrain of Fielding's parody in *The Historical Register for the Year 1736*, i.1, of one of laureate Cibber's official New Year odes ("Then sing the day, / And sing the song"), which Cibber himself blithely quoted in deprecating his first schoolboy ode in the *Apology*. Fielding also mocked Cibber's poetic ineptitude in *Pasquin* (1736), 2.1, and *The Vernoniad* (1741), n. 54; and *The Grub Street Journal* annually subjected his

odes to satiric annotation and parody.
2. Because of a traditional fear of a standing army as a threat to liberty, there were few permanent military installations in England at this time, and troops were quartered in inns and alehouses, whose proprietors were required by law to supply them food, bed, and beer for the paltry compensation of four pence a day (compare Adams's reckoning, p. 126).

shortly.' 'My Dear,' cries *Tow-wouse*, 'this Man hath been robbed of all he hath.' 'Well then,' says she, 'where's his Money to pay his Reckoning? Why doth not such a Fellow go to an Ale-house?[3] I shall send him packing as soon as I am up, I assure you.' 'My Dear,' said he, 'common Charity won't suffer you to do that.' 'Common Charity, a F—t!' says she, 'Common Charity teaches us to provide for ourselves, and our Families; and I and mine won't be ruined by your Charity, I assure you.' 'Well,' says he, 'my Dear, do as you will when you are up, you know I never contradict you.' 'No,' says she, 'if the Devil was to contradict me, I would make the House too hot to hold him.'

With such like Discourses they consumed nearly half an Hour, whilst *Betty* provided a Shirt from the Hostler, who was one of her Sweethearts, and put it on poor *Joseph*. The Surgeon had likewise at last visited him, had washed and drest his Wounds, and was now come to acquaint Mr. *Tow-wouse*, that his Guest was in such extreme danger of his Life, that he scarce saw any hopes of his Recovery.—'Here's a pretty Kettle of Fish,' cries Mrs. *Tow-wouse*, 'you have brought upon us! We are like to have a Funeral at our own expence.' *Tow-wouse*, (who notwithstanding his Charity, would have given his Vote as freely as he ever did at an Election, that any other House in the Kingdom, should have had quiet Possession of his Guest) answered, 'My Dear, I am not to blame: he was brought hither by the Stage-Coach; and *Betty* had put him to bed before I was stirring.' 'I'll *Betty* her,' says she—At which, with half her Garments on, the other half under her Arm, she sallied out in quest of the unfortunate *Betty*, whilst *Tow-wouse* and the Surgeon went to pay a Visit to poor *Joseph*, and enquire into the Circumstance of this melancholy Affair.

Chapter XIII

What happened to Joseph *during his Sickness at the Inn, with the curious Discourse between him and Mr.* Barnabas *the Parson of the Parish.*

As soon as *Joseph* had communicated a particular History of the Robbery, together with a short Account of himself, and his intended Journey, he asked the Surgeon 'if he apprehended him to be in any Danger:' To which the Surgeon very honestly answered, 'he feared he was; for that his Pulse was very exalted and feverish, and if his Fever should prove more than *Symptomatick*,[1] it would be impossible to save him.' *Joseph*, fetching a deep Sigh, cried, 'Poor *Fanny, I would I could have lived to see thee! but* G—'s *Will be done.'*

The Surgeon then advised him, 'if he had any worldly Affairs to settle, that he would do it as soon as possible; for though he hoped he might

---

3. Inns were set up to lodge and feed travelers; the humbler and less reputable alehouse, primarily a place to drink, sometimes provided makeshift beds for those who could not afford regular accommodations.

1. The doctor fears that Joseph's fever may not be simply a secondary effect of his injury but a primary illness in itself.

recover, yet he thought himself obliged to acquaint him he was in great danger, and if the malign Concoction of his Humours[2] should cause a suscitation of his Fever, he might soon grow delirious, and incapable to make his Will.' Joseph answered, 'that it was impossible for any Creature in the Universe to be in a poorer Condition than himself: for since the Robbery he had not one thing of any kind whatever, which he could call his own.' *I had,* said he, *a poor little Piece of Gold which they took away, that would have been a Comfort to me in all my Afflictions; but surely,* Fanny, *I want nothing to remind me of thee. I have thy dear Image in my Heart, and no Villain can ever tear it thence.*

Joseph desired Paper and Pens to write a Letter, but they were refused him; and he was advised to use all his Endeavours to compose himself. They then left him; and Mr. *Tow-wouse* sent to a Clergyman to come and administer his good Offices to the Soul of poor *Joseph*, since the Surgeon despaired of making any successful Applications to his Body.

Mr. *Barnabas* (for that was the Clergyman's Name)[3] came as soon as sent for, and having first drank a Dish of Tea with the Landlady, and afterwards a Bowl of Punch with the Landlord, he walked up to the Room where *Joseph* lay: but, finding him asleep, returned to take the other Sneaker,[4] which when he had finished, he again crept softly up to the Chamber-Door, and, having opened it, heard the Sick Man talking to himself in the following manner:

'O most adorable *Pamela!* most virtuous Sister, whose Example could alone enable me to withstand all the Temptations of Riches and Beauty, and to preserve my Virtue pure and chaste, for the Arms of my dear *Fanny*, if it had pleased Heaven that I should ever have come unto them. What Riches, or Honours, or Pleasures can make us amends for the Loss of Innocence? Doth not that alone afford us more Consolation, than all worldly Acquisitions? What but Innocence and Virtue could give any Comfort to such a miserable Wretch as I am? Yet these can make me prefer this sick and painful Bed to all the Pleasures I should have found in my Lady's.[5] These can make me face Death without Fear; and though I love my *Fanny* more than ever Man loved a Woman; these

2. The pretended physician in *The Mock Doctor* (1732), Fielding's translation of Molière's *Le Medecin malgré lui*, also invokes "a certain malignity" of "the said humours" (sc. 9). The theory of illness as an imbalance among the body's four cardinal humours, or basic fluids (blood, phlegm, and yellow and black bile), articulated by Hippocrates, fifth-century B.C. Greek physician, and transmitted by Galen (ca. A.D. 129–99), persisted in Fielding's time, though its authority had been significantly eroded by the work of advanced investigators like Herman Boerhaave (1668–1738), who made the University of Leyden an international medical center when Fielding studied there. In Hippocratic theory, *concoction*, the second stage of a disease, is not malign but a wholesome ripening that separates morbid matter from the healthy humours for elimination. "Suscitation" is the surgeon's "hard word" for "rousing."

3. R. F. Brissenden notes that Fielding has, ironically, chosen the name ("which is, being interpreted, The son of consolation"—Acts 4:36) given by the apostles to one who sold his land and gave them the proceeds. "A good man, and full of the Holy Ghost and of faith" (Acts 11:24), he became Paul's companion and fellow preacher.

4. Small bowl of punch.

5. Joseph's reflections follow the tenor of recurrent sentiments in *Pamela*: "what signify all the Riches in the World, with a bad Conscience . . . ? (letter 2); "may I never deserve the least Rag . . . when I forfeit a Title to that Innocence, that I hope will ever be the Pride of my Life; and then I am sure it will be my highest Comfort at my Death, when all the Riches and Pomps of the World will be worse than the vilest Rags that can be worn by Beggars!" (letter 29).

can teach me to resign myself to the Divine Will without repining. O thou delightful charming Creature, if Heaven had indulged thee to my Arms, the poorest, humblest State would have been a Paradise; I could have lived with thee in the lowest Cottage, without envying the Palaces, the Dainties, or the Riches of any Man breathing. But I must leave thee, leave thee for ever, my dearest Angel, I must think of another World, and I heartily pray thou may'st meet Comfort in this.'—*Barnabas* thought he had heard enough; so down stairs he went, and told *Tow-wouse* he could do his Guest no Service: for that he was very light-headed, and had uttered nothing but a Rhapsody of Nonsense all the time he stayed in the Room.

The Surgeon returned in the Afternoon, and found his Patient in a higher Fever, as he said, than when he left him, though not delirious: for notwithstanding Mr. *Barnabas's* Opinion, he had not been once out of his Senses since his arrival at the Inn.

Mr. *Barnabas* was again sent for, and with much difficulty prevailed on to make another Visit. As soon as he entered the Room, he told *Joseph*, 'he was come to pray by him, and to prepare him for another World: In the first place therefore, he hoped he had repented of all his Sins?' *Joseph* answered, 'he hoped he had: but there was one thing which he knew not whether he should call a Sin; if it was, he feared he should die in the Commission of it, and that was the Regret of parting with a young Woman, whom he loved as tenderly as he did his Heartstrings?' *Barnabas* bad him be assured, 'that any Repining at the Divine Will, was one of the greatest Sins he could commit; that he ought to forget all carnal Affections, and think of better things.' *Joseph* said, 'that neither in this World nor the next, he could forget his *Fanny*, and that the Thought, however grievous, of parting from her for ever, was not half so tormenting, as the Fear of what she would suffer when she knew his Misfortune.' *Barnabas* said, 'that such Fears argued a Diffidence[6] and Despondence very criminal; that he must divest himself of all human Passion, and fix his Heart above.' *Joseph* answered, 'that was what he desired to do, and should be obliged to him, if he would enable him to accomplish it.' *Barnabas* replied, 'That must be done by Grace.' *Joseph* besought him to discover how he might attain it. *Barnabas* answered, 'By Prayer and Faith.' He then questioned him concerning his Forgiveness of the Thieves. *Joseph* answered, 'he feared, that was more than he could do: for nothing would give him more Pleasure than to hear they were taken.' 'That,' cries *Barnabas*, 'is for the sake of Justice.' 'Yes,' said *Joseph*, 'but if I was to meet them again, I am afraid I should attack them, and kill them too, if I could.' 'Doubtless,' answered *Barnabas*, 'it is lawful to kill a Thief: but can you say, you forgive them as a Christian ought?' *Joseph* desired to know what that Forgiveness was. 'That is,' answered *Barnabas*, 'to forgive them as—as—it is to forgive them as— in short, it is to forgive them as a Christian.' *Joseph* reply'd, 'he forgave

6. Lack of faith.

them as much as he could.' 'Well, well,' said *Barnabas*, 'that will do.' He then demanded of him, 'if he remembered any more Sins unrepented of; and if he did, he desired him to make haste and repent of them as fast as he could: that they might repeat over a few Prayers together.' *Joseph* answered, 'he could not recollect any great Crimes he had been guilty of, and that those he had committed, he was sincerely sorry for.' *Barnabas* said that was enough, and then proceeded to Prayer with all the expedition he was master of: Some Company then waiting for him below in the Parlour, where the Ingredients for Punch were all in Readiness; but no one would squeeze the Oranges till he came.

Joseph complained he was dry, and desired a little Tea; which *Barnabas* reported to Mrs. *Tow-wouse*, who answered, 'she had just done drinking it, and could not be slopping[7] all day;' but ordered *Betty* to carry him up some Small Beer.[8]

Betty obeyed her Mistress's Commands; but *Joseph*, as soon as he had tasted it, said, he feared it would encrease his Fever, and that he longed very much for Tea: To which the good-natured *Betty* answered, he should have Tea, if there was any in the Land; she accordingly went and bought him some herself, and attended him with it; where we will leave her and *Joseph* together for some time, to entertain the Reader with other matters.

Chapter XIV

Being very full of Adventures, which succeeded each other at the Inn.

It was now the Dusk of the Evening, when a grave Person rode into the Inn, and committing his Horse to the Hostler, went directly into the Kitchin, and having called for a Pipe of Tobacco, took his place by the Fire-side; where several other Persons were likewise assembled.

The Discourse ran altogether on the Robbery which was committed the Night before, and on the poor Wretch, who lay above in the dreadful Condition, in which we have already seen him. Mrs. *Tow-wouse* said, 'she wondered what the devil *Tom Whipwell* meant by bringing such Guests to her House, when there were so many Ale-houses on the Road proper for their Reception? But she assured him, if he died, the Parish should be at the Expence of the Funeral.' She added, 'nothing would serve the Fellow's Turn but Tea, she would assure him.' *Betty*, who was just returned from her charitable Office, answered, she believed he was a Gentleman: for she never saw a finer Skin in her Life. 'Pox on his Skin,' replied Mrs. *Tow-wouse*, 'I suppose, that is all we are like to have for the Reckoning. I desire no such Gentlemen should ever call at the *Dragon*;' (which it seems was the Sign of the Inn.)[1]

---

7. Steeping tea.
8. Weak or inferior brew.
1. Inns and shops attracted trade with large pictorial signboards. "The Green Dragon" and "The George and Dragon" (depicting the legendary victory of England's patron saint) were popular inn signs not usually intended as emblematic of the innkeeper (or, as in this case, his wife).

The Gentleman lately arrived discovered a great deal of Emotion at the Distress of this poor Creature, whom he observed not to be fallen into the most compassionate Hands. And indeed, if Mrs. *Tow-wouse* had given no Utterance to the Sweetness of her Temper, Nature had taken such Pains in her Countenance, that *Hogarth* himself never gave more Expression to a Picture.

Her Person was short, thin, and crooked. Her Forehead projected in the middle, and thence descended in a Declivity to the Top of her Nose, which was sharp and red, and would have hung over her Lips, had not Nature turned up the end of it. Her Lips were two Bits of Skin, which, whenever she spoke, she drew together in a Purse. Her Chin was peeked,[2] and at the upper end of that Skin, which composed her Cheeks, stood two Bones, that almost hid a Pair of small red Eyes. Add to this, a Voice most wonderfully adapted to the Sentiments it was to convey, being both loud and hoarse.

It is not easy to say, whether the Gentleman had conceived a greater Dislike for his Landlady, or Compassion for her unhappy Guest. He enquired very earnestly of the Surgeon, who was now come into the Kitchin, 'whether he had any hopes of his Recovery?' he begged him, to use all possible means towards it, telling him, 'it was the duty of Men of all Professions, to apply their Skill *gratis* for the Relief of the Poor and Necessitous.' The Surgeon answered, 'he should take proper care: but he defied all the Surgeons in *London* to do him any good.' 'Pray, Sir,' said the Gentleman, 'What are his Wounds?'—'Why, do you know any thing of Wounds?' says the Surgeon, (winking upon Mrs. *Tow-wouse*.) 'Sir, I have a small smattering in Surgery,' answered the Gentleman. 'A smattering,—ho, ho, ho!' said the Surgeon, 'I believe it is a smattering indeed.'

The Company were all attentive, expecting to hear the Doctor, who was what they call a dry Fellow, expose the Gentleman.

He began therefore with an Air of Triumph: 'I suppose, Sir, you have travelled.' 'No really, Sir,' said the Gentleman. 'Ho! then you have prac-tised in the Hospitals, perhaps.'—'No, Sir.' 'Hum! not that neither? Whence, Sir, then, if I may be so bold to enquire, have you got your Knowledge in Surgery?' 'Sir,' answered the Gentleman, 'I do not pre-tend to much; but, the little I know I have from Books.' 'Books!' cries the Doctor.—'What, I suppose you have read *Galen* and *Hippocrates*!' 'No, Sir,' said the Gentleman. 'How! you understand Surgery,' answers the Doctor, 'and not read *Galen* and *Hippocrates*!' 'Sir,' cries the other, 'I believe there are many Surgeons who have never read these Authors.' 'I believe so too,' says the Doctor, 'more shame for them: but thanks to my Education: I have them by heart, and very seldom go without them

2. Pointed. Battestin follows the fifth edition, although the four editions reviewed by Fielding read "pecked" (first and second) and "picked" (third and fourth), both variants of "peaked," or tapered to a point. For this meaning of "picked" the OED cites a 1696 description in the *London Gazette* of a man with a "picked Chin," so the third and fourth editions may well reflect Fielding's final intention.

both in my Pocket.' 'They are pretty large Books,' said the Gentleman. 'Aye,' said the Doctor, 'I believe I know how large they are better than you,' (at which he fell a winking, and the whole Company burst into a Laugh.)[3]

The Doctor pursuing his Triumph, asked the Gentleman, 'if he did not understand Physick as well as Surgery.' 'Rather better,' answered the Gentleman. 'Aye, like enough,' cries the Doctor, with a wink. 'Why, I know a little of Physick too.' 'I wish I knew half so much,' said *Towwouse*, 'I'd never wear an Apron again.' 'Why, I believe, Landlord,' cries the Doctor, 'there are few Men, tho' I say it, within twelve Miles of the Place, that handle a Fever better.—V*eniente occurrite Morbo*:[4] That is my Method.—I suppose Brother, you understand *Latin*?' 'A little,' says the Gentleman. 'Aye, and *Greek* now I'll warrant you: *Ton dapomibominos poluflosboio Thalasses.*[5] But I have almost forgot these things, I could have repeated *Homer* by heart once.'—'Efags! the Gentleman has caught a *Traytor*,'[6] says Mrs. *Tow-wouse*; at which they all fell a laughing.

The Gentleman, who had not the least affection for joking, very contentedly suffered the Doctor to enjoy his Victory; which he did with no small Satisfaction: and having sufficiently sounded his Depth, told him, 'he was thoroughly convinced of his great Learning and Abilities; and that he would be obliged to him, if he would let him know his opinion of his Patient's Case above stairs.' 'Sir,' says the Doctor, 'his Case is that of a dead Man.—The Contusion on his Head has *perforated* the *internal Membrane* of the *Occiput*, and *divellicated* that *radical* small *minute* invisible *Nerve*, which *coheres* to the *Pericranium*; and this was attended with a Fever at first *symptomatick*, then *pneumatick*, and he is at length *grown deliruus*, or delirious, as the Vulgar express it.'[7]

3. Although Galen made extensive studies of anatomy and Hippocrates wrote treatises on surgery, most surgeons would be ignorant of these authors, since, unlike physicians, they usually trained as practical apprentices rather than attending university. They were also more likely to acquire their advanced knowledge in hospitals than through travel abroad, a method favored for physicians. The "pretty large Books" were sets of folios larger than telephone books in which the author's collected and selected works were published in Greek and Latin. The doctor may be referring to such modest-sized individual works as Hippocrates' *Aphorisms* or Galen's *Ars Medica*, but given the other signs of his ignorance, he is probably bluffing.

4. "Counteract the oncoming illness," Persius, *Satires* 3.64, referring to the youthful development of bad habits. (*Veniente* should be *venienti*; the substitution in the second edition of *accurite* for the correct *occurite* suggests Fielding intended to display the doctor's inadequate Latin.) This "interventionist" slogan is contradicted by the surgeon's nontreatment of Joseph's injuries, which is more in keeping with the "expectant" Hippocratic method of waiting upon nature's healing powers. "Physick" (medicine) was technically the domain of the physicians, a separate faculty from surgeons.

5. The doctor remembers two recurrent formulaic phrases of Homer and combines them to create a resonant line of nonsense: "then answering him of the loud sounding sea."

6. "Efags" is a dialect corruption of the mild oath "in faith," or "by my faith." To catch a tartar meant "to tackle one who unexpectedly proves to be too formidable" (OED), after the Tartars' reputation for tenacious ferocity. Since Fielding italicized *Traytor*, and let it stand in the second edition while changing "got" to "caught," he probably intended it as Mrs. Tow-wouse's ignorant substitution of a more familiar word.

7. The existence of such invisible nerves was a current hypothesis. The doctor's jargon mingles standard technical terms for the back of the skull (occiput) and the membrane covering the skull bone (pericranium), and a fever that affects the lungs (pneumatic), with some individual embellishments: "divellicated" (torn apart), not to be found in Johnson's *Dictionary*, is used by another incompetent doctor in *Tom Jones* 8.13; "cohere" is misused for "adhere," and "deliruus" for "delirus." Perhaps carried away by his dire prognostic rhetoric, the surgeon belies his own earlier observation that Joseph is not delirious (p. 47).

He was proceeding in this learned manner, when a mighty Noise interrupted him. Some young Fellows in the Neighbourhood had taken one of the Thieves, and were bringing him into the Inn. *Betty* ran up Stairs with this News to *Joseph*; who begged they might search for a little piece of broken Gold, which had a Ribband tied to it, and which he could swear to amongst all the Hoards of the richest Men in the Universe.

Notwithstanding the Fellow's persisting in his Innocence, the Mob were very busy in searching him, and presently, among other things, pulled out the Piece of Gold just mentioned; which *Betty* no sooner saw, then she laid violent hands on it, and conveyed it up to *Joseph*, who received it with raptures of Joy, and hugging it in his Bosom declared, *he could now die contented.*

Within a few Minutes afterwards, came in some other Fellows, with a Bundle which they had found in a Ditch; and which was indeed the Clothes which had been stripped off from *Joseph*, and the other things they had taken from him.

The Gentleman no sooner saw the Coat, then he declared he knew the Livery; and if it had been taken from the poor Creature above stairs, desired he might see him: for that he was very well acquainted with the Family to whom that Livery belonged.

He was accordingly conducted up by *Betty*: but what, Reader, was the surprize on both sides, when he saw *Joseph* was the Person in Bed; and when *Joseph* discovered the Face of his good Friend Mr. *Abraham Adams*.

It would be impertinent to insert a Discourse which chiefly turned on the relation of Matters already well known to the Reader: for as soon as the Curate had satisfied *Joseph* concerning the perfect Health of his *Fanny*, he was on his side very inquisitive into all the Particulars which had produced this unfortunate Accident.

To return therefore to the Kitchin, where a great variety of Company were now assembled from all the Rooms of the House, as well as the Neighbourhood: so much delight do Men take in contemplating the Countenance of a Thief:

Mr. *Tow-wouse* began to rub his Hands with pleasure, at seeing so large an Assembly; who would, he hoped, shortly adjourn into several Apartments, in order to discourse over the Robbery; and drink a Health to all honest Men: but Mrs. *Tow-wouse*, whose Misfortune it was commonly to see things a little perversly, began to rail at those who brought the Fellow into her House; telling her Husband, 'they were very likely to thrive, who kept a House of entertainment for Beggars and Thieves.'

The Mob had now finished their search; and could find nothing about the Captive likely to prove any Evidence: for as to the Clothes, tho' the Mob were very well satisfied with that Proof; yet, as the Surgeon observed, they could not convict him, because they were not found in his Custody; to which *Barnabas* agreed: and added, that these were *Bona Waviata*,[8] and belonged to the Lord of the Manor.

---

8. The legal term for stolen goods discarded by a thief in flight, also known as waifs.

'How,' says the Surgeon, 'do you say these Goods belong to the Lord of the Manor?' 'I do,' cried *Barnabas*. 'Then I deny it,' says the Surgeon. 'What can the Lord of the Manor have to do in the Case? Will any one attempt to persuade me that what a Man finds is not his own?' 'I have heard, (says an old Fellow in the Corner) Justice *Wise-one* say, that if every Man had his right, whatever is found belongs to the King of *London*.' 'That may be true,' says *Barnabas*, 'in some sense: for the Law makes a difference between things stolen, and things found: for a thing may be stolen that never is found; and a thing may be found that never was stolen. Now Goods that are both stolen and found are *Waviata*; and they belong to the Lord of the Manor.' 'So the Lord of the Manor is the Receiver of stolen Goods:' (says the Doctor) at which there was a universal Laugh, being first begun by himself.[9]

While the Prisoner, by persisting in his Innocence, had almost (as there was no Evidence against him) brought over *Barnabas*, the Surgeon, *Tow-wouse*, and several others to his side; *Betty* informed them, that they had over-looked a little Piece of Gold, which she had carried up to the Man in bed; and which he offered to swear to amongst a Million, aye, amongst ten Thousand. This immediately turned the Scale against the Prisoner; and every one now concluded him guilty. It was resolved therefore, to keep him secured that Night, and early in the Morning to carry him before a Justice.

Chapter XV

Shewing how Mrs. Tow-wouse *was a little mollified; and how officious Mr.* Barnabas *and the Surgeon were to prosecute the Thief: With a Dissertation accounting for their Zeal; and that of many other Persons not mentioned in this History.*

Betty told her Mistress, she believed the Man in Bed was a greater Man than they took him for: for besides the extreme Whiteness of his Skin, and the Softness of his Hands; she observed a very great Familiarity between the Gentleman and him; and added, she was certain they were intimate Acquaintance, if not Relations.

This somewhat abated the severity of Mrs. *Tow-wouse's* Countenance. She said, 'God forbid she should not discharge the duty of a Christian, since the poor Gentleman was brought to her House. She had a natural antipathy to Vagabonds: but could pity the Misfortunes of a Christian as soon as another.' *Tow-wouse* said, 'If the Traveller be a Gentleman, tho' he hath no Money about him now, we shall most likely be paid hereafter; so you may begin to score[1] whenever you will.' Mrs.

---

9. Although the doctor "triumphs" here as he did over Adams, Barnabas is on more solid legal ground in stressing that the goods are not only found but stolen. The king's right to stolen goods abandoned in flight (as a penalty to the owner for failing to pursue and apprehend the thief) had in most cases been ceded to the lord of the manor, although the owner's right prevailed if he recovered the goods himself, or if he prosecuted the thief to conviction. The "old Fellow" confuses this special case with the ancient royal prerogative over waifs and strays, a broad range of lost or ownerless goods, and the surgeon misapplies the general principle that property *abandoned* by its owner belongs to the first finder.

1. Keep an account of charges.

Tow-wouse answered, 'Hold your simple Tongue, and don't instruct me in my Business. I am sure I am sorry for the Gentleman's Misfortune with all my heart, and I hope the Villain who hath used him so barbarously will be hanged. *Betty*, go, see what he wants. G— forbid he should want any thing in my House.'[2]

Barnabas, and the Surgeon went up to *Joseph*, to satisfy themselves concerning the piece of Gold. *Joseph* was with difficulty prevailed upon to shew it them; but would by no Entreaties be brought to deliver it out of his own Possession. He, however, attested this to be the same which had been taken from him; and *Betty* was ready to swear to the finding it on the Thief.

The only Difficulty that remained, was how to produce this Gold before the Justice: for as to carrying *Joseph* himself, it seemed impossible; nor was there any greater likelihood of obtaining it from him: for he had fastened it with a Ribband to his Arm, and solemnly vowed, that nothing but irresistible Force should ever separate them; in which Resolution, Mr. *Adams*, clenching a Fist rather less than the Knuckle of an Ox, declared he would support him.

A Dispute arose on this Occasion concerning Evidence, not very necessary to be related here; after which the Surgeon dress'd Mr. *Joseph's* Head; still persisting in the imminent Danger in which his Patient lay: but concluding with a very important Look, 'that he began to have some hopes; that he should send him a *Sanative soporiferous* Draught,[3] and would see him in the Morning.' After which *Barnabas* and he departed, and left Mr. *Joseph* and Mr. *Adams* together.

Adams informed *Joseph* of the occasion of this Journey which he was making to *London*, namely to publish three Volumes of Sermons; being encouraged, he said, by an Advertisement lately set forth by a Society of Booksellers, who proposed to purchase any Copies offered to them at a Price to be settled by two Persons:[4] but tho' he imagined he should get a considerable Sum of Money on this occasion, which his Family were in urgent need of; he protested, 'he would not leave *Joseph* in his present Condition:' finally, he told him, 'he had nine Shillings and three-pence-half-penny[5] in his Pocket, which he was welcome to use as he pleased.'

This Goodness of Parson *Adams* brought Tears into *Joseph's* Eyes; he declared 'he had now a second Reason to desire life, that he might shew his Gratitude to such a Friend.' *Adams* bad him 'be chearful, for that he plainly saw the Surgeon, besides his Ignorance, desired to make a Merit of curing him, tho' the Wounds in his Head, he perceived, were by no means dangerous; that he was convinced he had no Fever, and doubted not but he would be able to travel in a day or two.'

2. This reply was added in the second edition, which may account for the inconsistency within the paragraph concerning the transcription of "God."

3. A sleeping potion.

4. Battestin points out that this advertisement actually appeared in Fielding's *Champion* and other London newspapers during the spring and summer of 1741, though the society's proposal was more circumspect than Adams claims, since their acceptance of the manuscript was contingent upon the recommendation of the same "two Persons of Judgment," one to be named by the author, the other by them. Retail booksellers were also publishers.

5. That is, somewhat more than a week's portion of his annual income.

These Words infused a Spirit into *Joseph*; he said, 'he found himself very sore from the Bruises, but had no reason to think any of his Bones injured, or that he had received any Harm in his Inside; unless that he felt something very odd in his Stomach: but he knew not whether that might not arise from not having eaten one Morsel for above twenty-four Hours.' Being then asked, if he had any Inclination to eat, he answered in the Affirmative; then Parson *Adams* desired him to name what he had the greatest fancy for; whether a poached Egg, or Chicken-broth: he answered, 'he could eat both very well; but that he seemed to have the greatest Appetite for a piece of boiled Beef and Cabbage.'

Adams was pleased with so perfect a Confirmation that he had not the least Fever: but advised him to a lighter Diet, for that Evening. He accordingly eat either a Rabbit or a Fowl, I never could with any tolerable Certainty discover which; after this he was by Mrs. *Tow-wouse's* order conveyed into a better Bed, and equipped with one of her Husband's Shirts.

In the Morning early, *Barnabas* and the Surgeon came to the Inn, in order to see the Thief conveyed before the Justice. They had consumed the whole Night in debating what Measures they should take to produce the Piece of Gold in Evidence against him: for they were both extremely zealous in the Business, tho' neither of them were in the least interested in[6] the Prosecution; neither of them had ever received any private Injury from the Fellow, nor had either of them ever been suspected of loving the Publick well enough, to give them a Sermon or a Dose of Physick for nothing.

To help our Reader therefore as much as possible to account for this Zeal, we must inform him, that as this Parish was so unfortunate as to have no Lawyer in it; there had been a constant Contention between the two Doctors, spiritual and physical, concerning their Abilities in a Science, in which, as neither of them professed it,[7] they had equal Pretensions to dispute each other's Opinions. These Disputes were carried on with great Contempt on both sides, and had almost divided the Parish; Mr. *Tow-wouse* and one half of the Neighbours inclining to the Surgeon, and Mrs. *Tow-wouse* with the other half to the Parson. The Surgeon drew his Knowledge from those inestimable Fountains, called the *Attorney's Pocket-Companion*, and Mr. *Jacob's Law-Tables*; *Barnabas* trusted entirely to *Wood's Institutes*.[8] It happened on this Occasion, as was pretty frequently the Case, that these two learned Men differed about

---

6. Likely to benefit from.

7. Made it his profession.

8. *An Institute of the Laws of England* (1720), by Thomas Wood (1661–1722), the most systematic analysis of the law prior to Blackstone's *Commentaries* (1765–69), was a standard text for students for the bar; according to the sale catalog of Fielding's library, his copy was "*interleaved with MSS. notes of Mr. Fielding.*" The surgeon's authorities had no such scholarly standing. *The Attorney's Pocket Companion* (1733), by John Mallory, was a practical manual of information on the forms and conduct of legal actions; *The Statute-Law Common-plac'd: or a General Table to the Statutes* (1719) was one of more than a dozen compilations by Giles Jacob (1686–1744). In *The Champion* for December 25, 1739, Fielding cited Jacob's works as the source of "a very competent Knowledge of the Law" in arguing ironically that learning is unnecessary and pernicious to the learned professions; but in a later number (February 12, 1739–40), he acknowledged the usefulness to laymen of the *New Law Dictionary* (1729), the most respected and successful of his works.

the sufficiency of Evidence: the Doctor being of opinion, that the Maid's Oath would convict the Prisoner without producing the Gold; the Parson, *è contra, totis viribus*.[9] To display their Parts therefore before the Justice and the Parish was the sole Motive, which we can discover, to this Zeal, which both of them pretended to be for publick Justice.

O Vanity! How little is thy Force acknowledged, or thy Operations discerned? How wantonly dost thou deceive Mankind under different Disguises? Sometimes thou dost wear the Face of Pity, sometimes of Generosity: nay, thou hast the Assurance even to put on those glorious Ornaments which belong only to heroick Virtue. Thou odious, deformed Monster! whom Priests have railed at, Philosophers despised, and Poets ridiculed: Is there a Wretch so abandoned as to own thee for an Acquaintance in publick? yet, how few will refuse to enjoy thee in private? nay, thou art the Pursuit of most Men through their Lives. The greatest Villanies are daily practised to please thee: nor is the meanest[1] Thief below, or the greatest Hero above thy notice. Thy Embraces are often the sole Aim and sole Reward of the private Robbery, and the plundered Province. It is, to pamper up thee, thou Harlot, that we attempt to withdraw from others what we do not want,[2] or to with-hold from them what they do. All our Passions are thy Slaves. Avarice itself is often no more than thy Hand-maid, and even Lust thy Pimp. The Bully Fear like a Coward, flies before thee, and Joy and Grief hide their Heads in thy Presence.

I know thou wilt think, that whilst I abuse thee, I court thee; and that thy Love hath inspired me to write this sarcastical Panegyrick on thee: but thou art deceived, I value thee not of a farthing;[3] nor will it give me any Pain, if thou should'st prevail on the Reader to censure this Digression as errant Nonsense: for know to thy Confusion, that I have introduced thee for no other Purpose than to lengthen out a short Chapter; and so I return to my History.

Chapter XVI

The Escape of the Thief. Mr. Adams's *Disappointment. The Arrival of two very extraordinary Personages, and the Introduction of Parson* Adams *to Parson* Barnabas.

Barnabas and the Surgeon being returned, as we have said, to the Inn, in order to convey the Thief before the Justice, were greatly concerned to find a small Accident had happened which somewhat disconcerted them; and this was no other than the Thief's Escape, who had modestly withdrawn himself by Night, declining all Ostentation, and not chusing, in imitation of some great Men, to distinguish himself at the Expence of being pointed at.

---

9. "With all his strength to the contrary."
1. Lowliest.
2. Need.

3. A quarter penny, the smallest coin—hence, proverbially, of no worth or concern.

When the Company had retired the Evening before, the Thief was detained in a Room where the Constable, and one of the young Fellows who took him, were planted as his Guard. About the second Watch, a general Complaint of Drowth[1] was made both by the Prisoner and his Keepers. Among whom it was at last agreed, that the Constable should remain on Duty, and the young Fellow call up the Tapster; in which Disposition the latter apprehended not the least Danger, as the Constable was well armed, and could besides easily summon him back to his Assistance, if the Prisoner made the least Attempt to gain his Liberty.

The young Fellow had not long left the Room, before it came into the Constable's Head, that the Prisoner might leap on him by surprize, and thereby, preventing him of the use of his Weapons, especially the long Staff in which he chiefly confided, might reduce the Success of a Struggle to an equal Chance. He wisely therefore, to prevent this Inconvenience, slipt out of the Room himself and locked the Door, waiting without with his Staff in his Hand, ready lifted to fell the unhappy Prisoner, if by ill Fortune he should attempt to break out.

But human Life, as hath been discovered by some great Man or other, (for I would by no means be understood to affect the Honour of making any such Discovery) very much resembles a Game at *Chess*:[2] for, as in the latter, while a Gamester is too attentive to secure himself very strongly on one side the Board, he is apt to leave an unguarded Opening on the other; so doth if often happen in Life; and so did it happen on this Occasion: for whilst the cautious Constable with such wonderful Sagacity had possessed himself of the Door, he most unhappily forgot the Window.

The Thief who played on the other side, no sooner perceived this Opening, than he began to move that way; and finding the Passage easy, he took with him the young Fellow's Hat; and without any Ceremony, stepped into the Street, and made the best of his Way.

The young Fellow returning with a double Mug of Strong Beer was a little surprized to find the Constable at the Door: but much more so, when, the Door being opened, he perceived the Prisoner had made his Escape, and which way: he threw down the Beer, and without uttering any thing to the Constable, except a hearty Curse or two, he nimbly leapt out at the Window, and went again in pursuit of his Prey: being very unwilling to lose the Reward which he had assured himself of.[3]

The Constable hath not been discharged of Suspicion on this account: It hath been said, that not being concerned in the taking the Thief, he could not have been entitled to any part of the Reward, if he had been

---

1. Thirst.
2. One such "great Man" is Sancho Panza (*Don Quixote* 2.12); another is Richard Brathwaite (1588?–1673) in *The English Gentleman* (1630). Both use the analogy to make the point that distinctions of office and power are obliterated when the game of life is done and, like the chess pieces, we are all "throwne into a bagge . . .

where there shall be no difference betwixt the greatest and least . . ." (Brathwaite, p. 111).
3. The Crown's reward for the capture and conviction of a highwayman was substantial: forty pounds (nearly double Adams' annual stipend) plus his horse and arms and any money or other goods in his possession not claimed by his victims.

convicted. That the Thief had several Guineas in his Pocket; that it was very unlikely he should have been guilty of such an Oversight. That his Pretence for leaving the Room was absurd: that it was his constant Maxim, that a wise Man never refused Money on any Conditions: That at every Election, he always had sold his Vote to both Parties, &c.

But notwithstanding these and many other such Allegations, I am sufficiently convinced of his Innocence; having been positively assured of it, by those who received their Informations from his own Mouth; which, in the Opinion of some Moderns, is the best and indeed only Evidence.

All the Family were now up, and with many others assembled in the Kitchin, where Mr. *Tow-wouse* was in some Tribulation; the Surgeon having declared, that by Law, he was liable to be indicted for the Thief's Escape, as it was out of his House: He was a little comforted however by Mr. *Barnabas's* Opinion, that as the Escape was by Night, the Indictment would not lie.[4]

Mrs. *Tow-wouse* delivered herself in the following Words: 'Sure never was such a Fool as my Husband! would any other Person living have left a Man in the Custody of such a drunken, drowsy Blockhead as *Tom Suckbribe?*' (which was the Constable's Name) 'and if he could be indicted without any harm to his Wife and Children, I should be glad of it.' (Then the Bell rung in *Joseph's* Room.) 'Why *Betty*, *John Chamberlain*, where the Devil are you all? Have you no Ears, or no Conscience, not to tend the Sick better?—See what the Gentleman wants; why don't you go yourself, Mr. *Tow-wouse?* but any one may die for you; you have no more feeling than a Deal-Board.[5] If a Man lived a Fortnight in your House without spending a Penny, you would never put him in mind of it. See whether he drinks Tea or Coffee for Breakfast.' 'Yes, my Dear,' cry'd *Tow-wouse.* She then asked the Doctor and Mr. *Barnabas* what Morning's Draught they chose, who answered, they had a Pot of *Syderand*,[6] at the Fire; which we will leave them merry over, and return to *Joseph.*

He had rose pretty early this Morning: but tho' his Wounds were far from threatning any danger, he was so sore with the Bruises, that it was impossible for him to think of undertaking a Journey yet; Mr. *Adams* therefore, whose Stock was visibly decreased with the Expences of Supper and Breakfast, and which could not survive that Day's Scoring, began to consider how it was possible to recruit it. At last he cry'd, 'he had luckily hit on a sure Method, and though it would oblige him to return himself home together with *Joseph*, it mattered not much.' He then sent for *Tow-wouse*, and taking him into another Room, told him, 'he wanted to borrow three Guineas, for which he would put ample Security into his Hands.' *Tow-wouse* who expected a Watch or Ring, or something of double the Value, answered, 'he believed he could furnish him.' Upon which *Adams* pointing to his Saddle-Bag told him with a Face and Voice full of Solemnity, 'that there were in that Bag no less than nine Volumes of Manuscript Sermons, as well worth a hundred Pound as a Shilling was worth twelve Pence, and that he would deposite one of the Volumes in his Hands by way of Pledge; not doubting but that he would have the Honesty to return it on his Repayment of the Money: for otherwise he must be a very great loser, seeing that every Volume would at least bring him ten Pounds, as he had been informed by a neighbouring Clergyman in the Country: for, (said he) as to my own part, having never yet dealt in Printing, I do not pretend to ascertain the exact Value of such things.'

Tow-wouse, who was a little surprized at the Pawn, said (and not without some Truth) 'that he was no Judge of the Price of such kinds of Goods; and as for Money, he really was very short.' *Adams* answered, 'certainly he would not scruple to lend him three Guineas, on what was undoubtedly worth at least ten.' The Landlord replied, 'he did not believe he had so much Money in the House, and besides he was to make up a Sum.[7] He was very confident the Books were of much higher Value, and heartily sorry it did not suit him.' He then cry'd out, *Coming Sir!* though no body called, and ran down Stairs without any Fear of breaking his Neck.

Poor *Adams* was extremely dejected at this Disappointment, nor knew he what farther Stratagem to try. He immediately apply'd to his Pipe, his constant Friend and Comfort in his Afflictions; and leaning over the Rails, he devoted himself to Meditation, assisted by the inspiring Fumes of Tobacco.

He had on a Night-Cap drawn over his Wig, and a short great Coat, which half covered his Cassock;[8] a Dress, which added to something comical enough in his Countenance, composed a Figure likely to attract the Eyes of those who were not over-given to Observation.

Whilst he was smoaking his Pipe in this Posture, a Coach and Six, with a numerous Attendance, drove into the Inn. There alighted from the Coach a young Fellow, and a Brace of Pointers, after which another young Fellow leapt from the Box,[9] and shook the former by the hand, and both together with the Dogs were instantly conducted by Mr. *Tow-wouse* into an Apartment; whither as they passed, they entertained themselves with the following short facetious Dialogue.

'You are a pretty Fellow for a Coachman, *Jack!*' says he from the Coach, 'you had almost overturned us just now.' 'Pox[1] take you,' says the Coachman, 'if I had only broke your Neck, it would have been saving somebody else the trouble: but I should have been sorry for the Pointers.' 'Why, you Son of a B——,' answered the other, 'if no body

---

7. He was obligated to pay a certain amount by a certain date.
8. The distinctive long close-fitting black tunic worn by Anglican clergy under their gowns.

9. The tool and equipment case on which the coach driver sat.
1. Syphilis.

could shoot better than you, the Pointers would be of no use.' 'D—n me,' says the Coachman, 'I will shoot with you, five Guineas[2] a Shot.' 'You be hang'd,' says the other, 'for five Guineas you shall shoot at my A—.' 'Done,' says the Coachman, 'I'll pepper you better than ever you was peppered by *Jenny Bouncer*.'[3] 'Pepper your Grand-mother,' says the other, 'here's *Tow-wouse* will let you shoot at him for a Shilling a time.' 'I know his Honour better,' cries *Tow-wouse*, 'I never saw a surer shot at a Partridge. Every Man misses now and then; but if I could shoot half as well as his Honour, I would desire no better Livelihood than I could get by my Gun.' 'Pox on you,' said the Coachman, 'you demolish more Game now than your Head's worth. There's a Bitch, *Tow-wouse*, by G— she never *blinked** a Bird in her Life.' 'I have a Puppy, not a Year old, shall hunt with her for a hundred,' cries the other Gentleman. 'Done,' says the Coachman, 'but you will be pox'd before you make the Bett. If you have a mind for a Bett,' cries the Coachman, 'I will match my spotted Dog with your white Bitch for a hundred, play or pay.'[4] 'Done,' says the other, 'and I'll run *Baldface* against *Slouch* with you for another.' 'No,' cries he from the Box, 'but I'll venture *Miss Jenny* against *Baldface*, or *Hannibal* either.' 'Go to the Devil,' cries he from the Coach, 'I will make every Bett your own way, to be sure! I will match *Hannibal* with *Slouch* for a thousand, if you dare, and I say done first.'[5]

They were now arrived, and the Reader will be very contented to leave them, and repair to the Kitchin, where *Barnabas*, the Surgeon, and an Exciseman were smoking their Pipes over some *Syder-and*, and where the Servants, who attended the two noble Gentleman we have just seen alight, were now arrived.

'Tom,' cries one of the Footmen, 'there's Parson *Adams* smoking his Pipe in the Gallery.' 'Yes,' says *Tom*, 'I pulled off my Hat to him, and the Parson spoke to me.'

'Is the Gentleman a Clergyman then?' says *Barnabas*, (for his Cassock had been tied up when first he arrived.) 'Yes, Sir,' answered the Footman, 'and one there be but few like.' 'Ay,' said *Barnabas*, 'if I had known it sooner, I should have desired his Company; I would always shew a proper Respect for the Cloth; but what say you, Doctor, shall we adjourn into a Room, and invite him to take part of a Bowl of Punch?'

This Proposal was immediately agreed to, and executed; and Parson *Adams* accepting the Invitation; much Civility passed between the two Clergymen, who both declared the great Honour they had for the Cloth. They had not been long together before they entered into a Discourse

---

* To *blink* is a Term used to signify the Dog's passing by a Bird without pointing at it.

---

2. Five pounds and five shillings, almost a fourth of Adams's annual stipend.

3. Playing on two meanings of "pepper"—to pelt with shot, and to infect with venereal disease.

4. A bet requiring the bettor to pay if his contendor does not appear for the match.

5. This cursing conversation had its real life counterparts: "of all the monstrous Absurdities, none seems so shocking as Imprecation. There are a set of Insignificants, who, for want of Capacity, to keep up a Conversation, are continually damning themselves and their Neighbours" (*Gentleman's Magazine*, October 1731).

on small Tithes,[6] which continued a full Hour, without the Doctor or the Exciseman's having one Opportunity to offer a Word.

It was then proposed to begin a general Conversation, and the Exciseman opened up on foreign Affairs: but a Word unluckily dropping from one of them introduced a Dissertation on the Hardships suffered by the inferiour Clergy;[7] which, after a long Duration, concluded with bringing the nine Volumes of Sermons on the Carpet.[8]

Barnabas greatly discouraged poor *Adams*; he said, 'The Age was so wicked, that no body read Sermons: Would you think it, Mr. *Adams*, (said he) I once intended to print a Volume of Sermons myself, and they had the Approbation of two or three Bishops: but what do you think a Bookseller offered me?' 'Twelve Guineas perhaps (cried *Adams*.)' 'Not Twelve Pence, I assure you,' answered *Barnabas*, 'nay the Dog refused me a Concordance in Exchange.—At last, I offered to give him the printing them, for the sake of dedicating them to that very Gentleman who just now drove his own Coach into the Inn, and I assure you, he had the Impudence to refuse my Offer: by which means I lost a good Living,[9] that was afterwards given away in exchange for a Pointer, to one who—but I will not say any thing against the Cloth. So you may guess, Mr. *Adams*, what you are to expect; for if Sermons would have gone down,[1] I believe—I will not be vain: but to be concise with you, three Bishops said, they were the best that ever were writ: but indeed there are a pretty moderate number printed already, and not all sold yet.'—'Pray, Sir,' said *Adams*, 'to what do you think the Numbers may amount?' 'Sir,' answered *Barnabas*, 'a Bookseller told me he believed five thousand Volumes at least.'[2] 'Five thousand!' quoth the Surgeon, 'what can they be writ upon? I remember, when I was a Boy, I used to read one *Tillotson's* Sermons;[3] and I am sure, if a Man practised half so much as is in one of those Sermons, he will go to Heaven.' 'Doctor,' cried *Barnabas*, 'you have a profane way of talking, for which I must reprove you. A Man can never have his Duty too frequently inculcated into him.

---

6. The church's assessment on lesser agricultural products and local industry, as distinguished from the great tithes on the basic grain, fibre, and wood crops.

7. The rank and file of parsons or priests, as distinct from the bishops.

8. Under consideration (from the heavy cloth covering a council table). Fielding changed the number of volumes here from three to nine in the fourth edition, making it consistent with the number on p. 72, but left it at three in his original mention of the sermons on p. 53.

9. The practice of exchanging a laudatory dedication for patronage, begun in the seventeenth century, reached its nadir in the 1730's, when hack writers auctioned their dedications to the highest bidder, often celebrating someone completely unknown to them. In his own "Dedication to the Public" of *The Historical Register for the Year 1736*, Fielding dryly noted "asking leave to dedicate . . . is asking whether you will pay for

your Dedication, and in that sense I believe it understood by both authors and patrons."

1. Found acceptance.

2. As an estimate of the number of titles in print, this is almost certainly an exaggeration, but there were an extraordinary number of sermons published. Battestin cites contemporary indices of nearly ten thousand individual sermons published between 1660 and 1750.

3. John Tillotson (1630–94), archbishop of Canterbury (1691–94), was an extremely popular preacher whose plainspoken sermons expounding a moderate rational optimistic theology that espoused good works and played down original sin (see below, p. 391) were regarded as models of style. Sold posthumously for the great sum of twenty-five hundred guineas, they were published in fourteen volumes between 1696 and 1704; a new twelve-volume edition appeared the same year as the novel.

And as for *Tillotson*, to be sure he was a good Writer, and said things very well: but Comparisons are odious, another Man may write as well as he—I believe there are some of my Sermons,'—and then he apply'd the Candle to his Pipe.—'And I believe there are some of my Discourses,' cries *Adams*, 'which the Bishops would not think totally unworthy of being printed; and I have been informed I might procure a very large Sum (indeed an immense one) on them.' 'I doubt that;' answered *Barnabas*: 'however, if you desire to make some Money of them, perhaps you may sell them by advertising *the Manuscript Sermons of a Clergyman lately deceased, all warranted Originals, and never printed.*[4] And now I think of it, I should be obliged to you, if there be ever a Funeral one among them, to lend it me: for I am this very day to preach a Funeral Sermon, for which I have not penned a Line, though I am to have a double Price.' *Adams* answered, 'he had but one, which he feared would not serve his purpose, being sacred to the Memory of a Magistrate, who had exerted himself very singularly in the Preservation of the Morality of his Neighbours, insomuch, that he had neither Ale-house, nor lewd Woman in the Parish where he lived.'—'No," replied *Barnabas*, 'that will not do quite so well; for the Deceased, upon whose Virtues I am to harangue, was a little too much addicted to Liquor, and publickly kept a Mistress.—I believe I must take a common Sermon, and trust to my Memory to introduce something handsome on him.'—'To your Invention rather, (said the Doctor) your Memory will be apter to put you out: for no Man living remembers any thing good of him.'

With such kind of spiritual Discourse, they emptied the Bowl of Punch, paid their Reckoning, and separated: *Adams* and the Doctor went up to *Joseph*; Parson *Barnabas* departed to celebrate the aforesaid Deceased, and the Exciseman descended into the Cellar to gage the Vessels.[5]

Joseph was now ready to sit down to a Loin of Mutton, and waited for Mr. *Adams*, when he and the Doctor came in. The Doctor having felt his Pulse, and examined his Wounds, declared him much better, which he imputed to *that Sanative soporiferous Draught*, a Medicine, 'whose Virtues,' he said, 'were never to be sufficiently extolled:' And great indeed they must be, if *Joseph* was so much indebted to them as the Doctor imagined, since nothing more than those Effluvia, which escaped the Cork, could have contributed to his Recovery: for the Medicine had stood untouched in the Window ever since its arrival.

Joseph passed that day and the three following with his Friend *Adams*, in which nothing so remarkable happened as the swift Progress of his Recovery. As he had an excellent Habit of Body,[6] his Wounds were now

4. As Barnabas's next remark suggests, such a collection would be attractive to parsons unable or unwilling to compose their own sermons. A very similar advertisement cited by Battestin virtually proclaims this: "A Choice Collection of MANUSCRIPT SERMONS of an eminent Divine lately deceas'd. In this Collection there 'is a Discourse suited for every Sunday in the Year, and an Account when and where preached, which will be warranted Originals" (*Common Sense*, Dec. 13–20, 1740).

5. To regulate the collection of duty on domestic manufactures, the Crown employed inspectors who determined the quantity of produce—in this case, beer and ale brewed on the premises—to be taxed.

6. Physical constitution.

almost healed, and his Bruises gave him so little uneasiness, that he pressed Mr. *Adams* to let him depart, told him he should never be able to return sufficient Thanks for all his Favours; but begged that he might no longer delay his Journey to *London*.

Adams, notwithstanding the Ignorance, as he conceived it, of Mr. *Tow-wouse*, and the Envy (for such he thought it) of Mr. *Barnabas*, had great Expectations from his Sermons: seeing therefore *Joseph* in so good a way, he told him he would agree to his setting out the next Morning in the Stage-Coach, that he believed he should have sufficient after the Reckoning paid, to procure him one Day's Conveyance in it, and afterwards he would be able to get on, on foot, or might be favoured with a lift in some Neighbour's Waggon, especially as there was then to be a Fair in the Town whither the Coach would carry him, to which Numbers from his Parish resorted.—And as to himself, he agreed to proceed to the great City.

They were now walking in the Inn Yard, when a fat, fair, short Person rode in, and alighting from his Horse went directly up to *Barnabas*, who was smoking his Pipe on a Bench. The Parson and the Stranger shook one another very lovingly by the Hand, and went into a Room together.

The Evening now coming on, *Joseph* retired to his Chamber, whither the good *Adams* accompanied him; and took this Opportunity to expatiate on the great Mercies God had lately shewn him, of which he ought not only to have the deepest inward Sense; but likewise to express outward Thankfulness for them. They therefore fell both on their Knees, and spent a considerable time in Prayer and Thanksgiving.

They had just finished, when *Betty* came in and told Mr. *Adams*, Mr. *Barnabas* desired to speak to him on some Business of Consequence below Stairs. *Joseph* desired, if it was likely to detain him long, he would let him know it, that he might go to Bed, which *Adams* promised, and in that Case, they wished one another good Night.

Chapter XVII

A pleasant Discourse between the two Parsons and the Bookseller, which was broke off by an unlucky Accident happening in the Inn, which produced a Dialogue between Mrs. Tow-wouse *and her Maid of no gentle kind.*

As soon as *Adams* came into the Room, Mr. *Barnabas* introduced him to the Stranger, who was, he told him, a Bookseller, and would be as likely to deal with him for his Sermons as any Man whatever.[1] *Adams*, saluting the Stranger, answered *Barnabas*, that he was very much obliged to him, that nothing could be more convenient, for he had no other Business to the Great City, and was heartily desirous of returning with

1. Fielding may have had in mind either of the two prominent booksellers who published *Pamela*. Charles Rivington (1688–1742) brought out many religious works, including one of the earliest sermons of George Whitefield (see n. 3, below). On the other hand, the physical description on the previous page—rare for an incidental character—fits Thomas Osborne (d. 1767).

the young Man who was just recovered of his Misfortune. He then snapt his Fingers (as was usual with him) and took two or three turns about the Room in an Extasy.—And to induce the Bookseller to be as expeditious as possible, as likewise to offer him a better Price for his Commodity, he assured him, their meeting was extremely lucky to himself: for that he had the most pressing Occasion for Money at that time, his own being almost spent, and having a Friend then in the same Inn who was just recovered from some Wounds he had received from Robbers, and was in a most indigent Condition. 'So that nothing,' says he, 'could be so opportune, for the supplying both our Necessities, as my making an immediate Bargain with you.'

As soon as he had seated himself, the Stranger began in these Words, 'Sir, I do not care absolutely to deny engaging in what my Friend Mr. *Barnabas* recommends: but Sermons are mere Drugs.[2] The Trade is so vastly stocked with them, that really unless they come out with the Name of *Whitfield* or *Westley*,[3] or some other such great Man, as a Bishop, or those sort of People, I don't care to touch, unless now it was a Sermon preached on the *30th of January*, or we could say in the Title Page, published at the *earnest Request* of the Congregation, or the Inhabitants:[4] but truly for a dry Piece of Sermons, I had rather be excused; especially as my Hands are so full at present. However, Sir, as Mr. *Barnabas* mentioned them to me, I will, if you please, take the Manuscript with me to Town, and send you my Opinion of it in a very short time.'

'O,' said *Adams*, 'if you desire it, I will read two or three Discourses as a Specimen.' This *Barnabas*, who loved Sermons no better than a Grocer doth Figs, immediately objected to, and advised *Adams* to let the Bookseller have his Sermons; telling him, if he gave him a Direction, he might be certain of a speedy Answer: Adding, he need not scruple trusting them in his Possession. 'No,' said the Bookseller, 'if it was a Play that had been acted twenty Nights together, I believe it would be safe.'[5]

Adams did not at all relish the last Expression; he said, he was sorry to hear Sermons compared to Plays. 'Not by me, I assure you,' cry'd the Bookseller, 'though I don't know whether the licensing Act[6] may not shortly bring them to the same footing: but I have formerly known a hundred Guineas given for a Play—.' 'More shame for those who gave it,' cry'd *Barnabas*. 'Why so?' said the Bookseller, 'for they got hundreds

---

2. Unsellable commodities.
3. The sermons of George Whitefield (1714–70) and John Wesley (1703–91), popular preachers who started the evangelical movement called Methodism, were much in demand. For their doctrines, see below, pp. 391–92.
4. A common way of "puffing" sermons. January 30, the anniversary of the execution of Charles I (1649), was traditionally the occasion for political sermons emphasizing loyalty to the crown.
5. For a new play, an opening run of six to nine nights would be a success; a popular play would

yield a bookseller profits for many years.
6. Under pretext of controlling the excesses and immorality of the stage, Walpole used this law, enacted June 21, 1737, to silence Fielding's satiric attacks on his ministry, in the very successful *Pasquin* (1736) and *The Historical Register for the Year 1736* (1737). It not only required the Lord Chamberlain's prior approval of all plays but closed the Little Theatre in the Haymarket, which Fielding managed, thereby depriving him of his theatrical livelihood.

by it.' 'But is there no difference between conveying good or ill Instructions to Mankind?' said *Adams*; 'would not an honest Mind rather lose Money by the one, than gain it by the other?' 'If you can find any such, I will not be their Hinderance,' answered the Bookseller, 'but I think those Persons who get by preaching Sermons, are the properest to lose by printing them: for my part, the Copy that sells best, will be always the best Copy in my Opinion; I am no Enemy to Sermons but because they don't sell: for I would as soon print one of *Whitfield's*, as any Farce whatever.'

'Whoever prints such Heterodox Stuff, ought to be hanged,' says *Barnabas*. 'Sir,' said he, turning to *Adams*, 'this Fellow's Writings (I know not whether you have seen them) are levelled at the Clergy. He would reduce us to the Example of the Primitive Ages forsooth! and would insinuate to the People, that a Clergyman ought to be always preaching and praying. He pretends to understand the Scripture literally, and would make Mankind believe, that the Poverty and low Estate, which was recommended to the Church in its Infancy, and was only temporary Doctrine adapted to her under Persecution, was to be preserved in her flourishing and established State.[7] Sir, the Principles of *Toland*, *Woolston*, and all the Free-Thinkers, are not calculated to do half the Mischief, as those professed by this Fellow and his Followers.'[8]

'Sir,' answered *Adams*, 'if Mr. *Whitfield* had carried his Doctrine no farther than you mention, I should have remained, as I once was, his Well-Wisher. I am myself as great an Enemy to the Luxury and Splendour of the Clergy as he can be. I do not, more than he, by the flourishing Estate of the Church, understand the Palaces, Equipages, Dress, Furniture, rich Dainties, and vast Fortunes of her Ministers. Surely those things, which savour so strongly of this World, become not the Servants of one who professed his Kingdom was not of it:[9] but when he began to call Nonsense and Enthusiasm to his Aid, and to set up the detestable Doctrine of Faith against good Works,[1] I was his Friend no longer; for

7. For Fielding's views on clerical poverty, see below, p. 318.

8. This title adopted by the late-seventeenth- and early-eighteenth-century advocates of the untrammelled use of reason in religion became an epithet for infidelity (according to Johnson's *Dictionary*, "a libertine; a contumer of religion"). In *Christianity Not Mysterious* (1696), John Toland (1670–1722), disputing the traditional view of faith as a mystery presided over by the priesthood, argued that nothing in the gospel was "contrary to reason, nor above it." He was prosecuted and remained a favorite object of clerical abuse in the ensuing deist controversy over reason and revelation that extended to the time of the novel. Thomas Woolston (1670–1733) carried scriptural criticism to an extreme in his *Discourses on the Miracles of our Saviour* (1727–29), ridiculing them as literally preposterous events meant to be read only as allegories. He was fined and imprisoned for blasphemy. Like other deists, Toland and Woolston "levelled at the Clergy." Toland blamed the corruption of primitive Christianity on "the Craft and

Ambition of *Priests.*" Anticipating Whitefield's denunciation of his worldly clerical brethren, Woolston challenged churchmen to debate "whether the hireling preachers of this age . . . be not worshippers of the Apocalyptic Beast, and ministers of Antichrist" (*A Free Gift to the Clergy*, 1722).

9. Christ to Pilate, John 18:36.

1. The charge of enthusiasm—a misguided belief in the divine inspiration of one's religious opinions—had been brought against Whitefield by Edmund Gibson, the bishop of London in a pastoral letter (see below, p. 276, n. 4) and much more vehemently by the reverend Joseph Trapp in *The Nature, Folly, Sin, and Danger of Being Righteous Overmuch; with a Particular View to Doctrines and Practices of Certain Modern Enthusiasts*, which went through four editions in 1739. For Fielding's earlier references to Trapp's text in *The Champion* and *Shamela*, see below, pp. 288, 316, 318. For Whitefield's preaching of justification by faith rather than works, see below, p. 392.

surely, that Doctrine was coined in Hell, and one would think none but the Devil himself could have the Confidence to preach it. For can any thing be more derogatory to the Honour of God, than for Men to imagine that the All-wise Being will hereafter say to the Good and Virtuous, *Notwithstanding the Purity of thy Life, notwithstanding that constant Rule of Virtue and Goodness in which you walked upon Earth, still as thou did'st not believe every thing in the true Orthodox manner, thy want of Faith shall condemn thee?* Or on the other side, can any Doctrine have a more pernicious Influence on Society than a Persuasion, that it will be a good Plea for the Villain at the last day; *Lord, it is true I never obeyed one of thy Commandments, yet punish me not, for I believe them all?*' 'I suppose, Sir,' said the Bookseller, 'your Sermons are of a different Kind.' 'Ay, Sir,' said *Adams*, 'the contrary, I thank Heaven, is inculcated in almost every Page, or I should belye my own Opinion, which hath always been, that a virtuous and good *Turk*, or Heathen, are more acceptable in the sight of their Creator, than a vicious and wicked Christian, tho' his Faith was as perfectly Orthodox as St. *Paul's* himself.'[2]— 'I wish you Success,' says the Bookseller, 'but must beg to be excused, as my Hands are so very full at present; and indeed I am afraid, you will find a Backwardness in the Trade, to engage in a Book which the Clergy would be certain to cry down,' 'God forbid,' says *Adams*, 'any Books should be propagated which the Clergy would cry down: but if you mean by the Clergy, some few designing factious Men, who have it at Heart to establish some favourite Schemes at the Price of the Liberty of Mankind, and the very Essence of Religion, it is not in the power of such Persons to decry any Book they please; witness that excellent Book called, A *Plain Account of the Nature and End of the Sacrament*; a Book written (if I may venture on the Expression) with the Pen of an Angel, and calculated to restore the true Use of Christianity, and of that Sacred Institution: for what could tend more to the noble Purposes of Religion, than frequent cheerful Meetings among the Members of a Society, in which they should in the Presence of one another, and in the Service of the supreme Being, make Promises of being good, friendly and benevolent to each other? Now this excellent Book was attacked by a Party, but unsuccessfully.'[3] At these Words *Barnabas* fell a ringing with all the Violence imaginable, upon which a Servant attending, he bid him 'bring a Bill immediately: for that he was in Company, for aught he knew, with the Devil himself; and he expected to hear the Alcoran, the *Levi-*

2. It was St. Paul who first proclaimed the doctrine of justification by faith (Acts 13:39; Romans 3:28). For the relation of Adams's view to the current orthodoxy, see below, p. 392.

3. In *A Plain Account of the Nature and End of the Sacrament of the Lord's Supper* (1735), Benjamin Hoadly (1676–1761), bishop of Winchester, restored the communion to what he took to be its "original Simplicity" as defined in the New Testament: a rite of remembrance for Christians gathered to thank their "Absent Saviour" for his sacrifice, to affirm fidelity to his teaching, and "to revive and enlarge our affectionate Union and Sympathy with all other Members of the same Body" (p. 105). This radically demystified view, denying any real spiritual presence of Christ in the bread and wine, diminishing the sacerdotal function of the clergy, and discounting the orthodox view of the sacrament as a special assurance of grace, provoked rejoinders from a broad spectrum of churchmen; for two mentioned in *Shamela*, see below, p. 295, n. 3. For more on Hoadly and the "Party" of "designing factious Men," see below, p. 391.

athan, or *Woolston*[4] commended, if he staid a few Minutes longer.'
Adams desired, 'as he was so much moved at his mentioning a Book,
which he did without apprehending any possibility of Offence, that he
would be so kind to propose any Objections he had to it, which he would
endeavour to answer.' 'I propose Objections!' said *Barnabas*, 'I never
read a Syllable in any such wicked Book; I never saw it in my Life, I
assure you.'—*Adams* was going to answer, when a most hideous Uproar
began in the Inn. Mrs. *Tow-wouse*, Mr. *Tow-wouse*, and *Betty*, all lifting up their Voices together: but Mrs. *Tow-wouse's* Voice, like a Bass
Viol in a Concert, was clearly and distinctly distinguished among the
rest, and was heard to articulate the following Sounds.—'O you damn'd
Villain, is this the Return to all the Care I have taken of your Family?
This the Reward of my Virtue?[5] Is this the manner in which you behave
to one who brought you a Fortune, and preferred you to so many Matches,
all your Betters? To abuse my Bed, my own Bed, with my own Servant:
but I'll maul the Slut, I'll tear her nasty Eyes out; was ever such a pitiful
Dog, to take up with such a mean Trollop? If she had been a Gentlewoman like my self, it had been some excuse, but a beggarly saucy dirty
Servant-Maid. Get you out of my House, you Whore.' To which, she
added another Name, which we do not care to stain our Paper with.—
It was a monosyllable, beginning with a B—, and indeed was the same,
as if she had pronounced the Words, *She-Dog*. Which Term, we shall,
to avoid Offence, use on this Occasion, tho' indeed both the Mistress
and Maid uttered the above-mentioned B—, a Word extremely disgust-
ful to Females of the lower sort. *Betty* had borne all hitherto with Patience,
and had uttered only Lamentations: but the last Appellation stung her to
the Quick, 'I am a Woman as well as yourself,' she roared out, 'and no
She-Dog, and if I have been a little naughty, I am not the first; if I have
been no better than I should be,' cries she sobbing, 'that's no Reason
you should call me out of my Name; my Be—Betters are wo—worse
than me.' 'Huzzy, huzzy,' says Mrs. *Tow-wouse*, 'have you the Impudence to answer me? Did I not catch you, you saucy—' and then again
repeated the terrible word so odious to Female Ears. 'I can't bear that
Name,' answered *Betty*, 'if I have been wicked, I am to answer for it
myself in the other World, but I have done nothing that's unnatural,
and I will go out of your House this Moment: for I will never be called
She-Dog, by any Mistress in *England*.' Mrs. *Tow-wouse* then armed
herself with the Spit: but was prevented from executing any dreadful

4. Barnabas names two works that were anathema
to the church. The *Alcoran (Koran)*, the sacred
book of Islam, radically altered the Old and New
Testaments, reducing Jesus to a forerunner of the
ultimate prophet, Mohammed. In *The Leviathan:
or the Matter, Form, and Power of a Commonwealth, Ecclesiastical and Civil* (1651), Thomas
Hobbes (1588–1679) denied the independent
authority of the church over a realm distinct from
the temporal power, declaring "Christian sover-
eigns . . . the supreme pastors, the only persons
whom Christians now hear speak from God,"
whose dominion over a brutishly self-interested
mankind he attributed solely to His "irresistable
power." After a parliamentary investigation for
"atheism, Blasphemy, and profaneness" (1666),
the book was publicly burned and "Hobbism"
became an epithet for impiety and immorality.
For Woolston, see above, p. 64, n. 8.
5. *Pamela* was widely known by its subtitle, "Virtue Rewarded."

Purpose by Mr. *Adams*, who confined her Arms with the Strength of a Wrist, which *Hercules* would not have been ashamed of. Mr. *Tow-wouse* being caught, as our Lawyers express it, with the Manner,[6] and having no Defence to make, very prudently withdrew himself, and *Betty* committed herself to the Protection of the Hostler, who, though she could not conceive him pleased with what had happened, was in her Opinion rather a gentler Beast than her Mistress.

Mrs. *Tow-wouse*, at the Intercession of Mr. *Adams*, and finding the Enemy vanished, began to compose herself, and at length recovered the usual Serenity of her Temper, in which we will leave her, to open to the Reader the Steps which led to a Catastrophe, common enough, and comical enough too, perhaps in modern History, yet often fatal to the Repose and Well-being of Families, and the Subject of many Tragedies, both in Life and on the Stage.

Chapter XVIII

The History of Betty *the Chambermaid, and an Account of what occasioned the violent Scene in the preceding Chapter.*

Betty, who was the Occasion of all this Hurry,[1] had some good Qualities. She had Good-nature, Generosity and Compassion, but unfortunately her Constitution was composed of those warm Ingredients, which, though the Purity of Courts or Nunneries might have happily controuled them, were by no means able to endure the ticklish Situation of a Chamber-maid at an Inn, who is daily liable to the Solicitations of Lovers of all Complexions, to the dangerous Addresses of fine Gentlemen of the Army, who sometimes are obliged to reside with them a whole Year together, and above all are exposed to the Caresses of Footmen, Stage-Coachmen, and Drawers;[2] all of whom employ the whole Artillery of kissing, flattering, bribing, and every other Weapon which is to be found in the whole Armory of Love, against them.

Betty, who was but one and twenty, had now lived three Years in this dangerous Situation, during which she had escaped pretty well. An Ensign of Foot was the first Person who made any Impression on her Heart; he did indeed raise a Flame in her, which required the Care of a Surgeon to cool.[3]

While she burnt for him, several others burnt for her. Officers of the Army, young Gentlemen travelling the Western Circuit,[4] inoffensive Squires, and some of graver Character were set afire by her Charms!

At length, having perfectly recovered the Effects of her first unhappy Passion, she seemed to have vowed a State of perpetual Chastity. She

---

6. "A Thief taken with the Manner, *i.e.* surprized in the Fact with the Goods upon him"—Fielding's definition in *The Covent Garden Journal*, October 28, 1752.
1. Commotion.
2. Bartenders.

3. The usual treatment for venereal disease was the prescription of mercury compounds.
4. The semiannual itinerary followed by judges and barristers (including Fielding) to conduct the county assizes (superior criminal and civil courts) in Southwestern England.

was long deaf to all the Sufferings of her Lovers, till one day at a neighbouring Fair, the Rhetorick of *John* the Hostler, with a new Straw Hat, and a Pint of Wine, made a second Conquest over her.

She did not however feel any of those Flames on this Occasion, which had been the Consequence of her former Amour; nor indeed those other ill Effects, which prudent young Women very justly apprehend from too absolute an Indulgence to the pressing Endearments of their Lovers. This latter, perhaps was a little owing to her not being entirely constant to *John*, with whom she permitted *Tom Whipwell* the Stage-Coachman, and now and then a handsome young Traveller, to share her Favours.[5]

Mr. *Tow-wouse* had for some time cast the languishing Eyes of Affection on this young Maiden. He had laid hold on every Opportunity of saying tender things to her, squeezing her by the Hand, and sometimes of kissing her Lips: for as the Violence of his Passion had considerably abated to Mrs. *Tow-wouse*; so like Water, which is stopt from its usual Current in one Place, it naturally sought a vent in another. Mrs. *Tow-wouse* is thought to have perceived this Abatement, and probably it added very little to the natural Sweetness of her Temper: for tho' she was as true to her Husband, as the Dial to the Sun, she was rather more desirous of being shone on, as being more capable of feeling his Warmth.

Ever since *Joseph's* arrival, *Betty* had conceived an extraordinary Liking to him, which discovered itself more and more, as he grew better and better; till that fatal Evening, when, as she was warming his Bed, her Passion grew to such a Height, and so perfectly mastered both her Modesty and her Reason, that after many fruitless Hints, and sly Insinuations, she at last threw down the Warming-Pan, and embracing him with great Eagerness, swore he was the handsomest Creature she had ever seen.

Joseph in great Confusion leapt from her, and told her, he was sorry to see a young Woman cast off all Regard to Modesty: but she had gone too far to recede, and grew so very indecent, that *Joseph* was obliged, contrary to his Inclination, to use some Violence to her, and taking her in his Arms, he shut her out of the Room, and locked the Door.

How ought Man to rejoice, that his Chastity is always in his own power, that if he hath sufficient Strength of Mind, he hath always a competent Strength of Body to defend himself: and cannot, like a poor weak Woman, be ravished against his Will.[6]

Betty was in the most violent Agitation at this Disappointment. Rage and Lust pulled her Heart, as with two Strings, two different Ways; one Moment she thought of stabbing *Joseph*, the next, of taking him in her Arms, and devouring him with Kisses; but the latter Passion was far more prevalent. Then she thought of revenging his Refusal on herself: but whilst she was engaged in this Meditation, happily Death presented himself

---

5. The folk belief that intercourse with a variety of men inhibits pregnancy probably derived from the relative infrequency of pregnancy among prostitutes.

6. A reference to *Pamela's* peril in mimicry of her frequent moral exclamations (see above, p. 25, n. 3).

to her in so many Shapes of drowning, hanging, poisoning, &c. that her distracted Mind could resolve on none. In this Perturbation of Spirit, it accidentally occurred to her Memory, that her Master's Bed was not made, she therefore went directly to his Room; where he happened at that time to be engaged at his Bureau. As soon as she saw him, she attempted to retire: but he called her back, and taking her by the hand, squeezed her so tenderly, at the same time whispering so many soft things into her Ears, and, then pressed her so closely with his Kisses, that the vanquished Fair-One, whose Passions were already raised, and which were not so whimsically capricious that one Man only could lay them, though perhaps, she would have rather preferred that one: The vanquished Fair-One quietly submitted, I say, to her Master's Will, who had just attained the Accomplishment of his Bliss, when Mrs. *Towwouse* unexpectedly entered the Room, and caused all that Confusion which we have before seen, and which it is not necessary at present to take any farther Notice of. Since without the Assistance of a single Hint from us, every Reader of any Speculation,[7] or Experience, though not married himself, may easily conjecture, that it concluded with the Discharge of *Betty*, the Submission of Mr. *Tow-wouse*, with some things to be performed on his side by way of Gratitude for his Wife's Goodness in being reconciled to him, with many hearty Promises never to offend any more in the like manner: and lastly, his quietly and contentedly bearing to be reminded of his Transgressions, as a kind of Penance, once or twice a Day, during the Residue of his Life.

7. Perception.

The History of the Adventures of
JOSEPH ANDREWS,
and of his Friend Mr.
Abraham Adams

BOOK II

Chapter I

Of Divisions in Authors.

There are certain Mysteries or Secrets in all Trades from the highest to the lowest, from that of *Prime Ministring* to this of *Authoring*, which are seldom discovered, unless to Members of the same Calling. Among those used by us Gentlemen of the latter Occupation, I take this of dividing our Works into Books and Chapters to be none of the least considerable. Now for want of being truly acquainted with this Secret, common Readers imagine, that by this Art of dividing, we mean only to swell our Works to a much larger Bulk than they would otherwise be extended to. These several Places therefore in our Paper, which are filled with our Books and Chapters, are understood as so much Buckram, Stays, and Stay-tape in a Taylor's Bill, serving only to make up the Sum Total, commonly found at the Bottom of our first Page,[1] and of his last.

But in reality the Case is otherwise, and in this, as well as all other Instances, we consult the Advantage of our Reader, not our own; and indeed many notable Uses arise to him from this Method: for first, those little Spaces between our Chapters may be looked upon as an Inn or Resting-Place, where he may stop and take a Glass, or any other Refreshment, as it pleases him. Nay, our fine[2] Readers will, perhaps, be scarce able to travel farther than through one of them in a Day. As to those vacant Pages which are placed between our Books, they are to be regarded as those Stages, where, in long Journeys, the Traveller stays

---

1. The price of a book was often printed at the bottom of the title page.   2. Delicate.

some time to repose himself, and consider of what he hath seen in the Parts he hath already past through; a Consideration which I take the Liberty to recommend a little to the Reader: for however swift his Capacity may be, I would not advise him to travel through these Pages too fast: for if he doth, he may probably miss the seeing some curious Productions of Nature which will be observed by the slower and more accurate Reader. A Volume without any such Places of Rest resembles the Opening of Wilds or Seas, which tires the Eye and fatigues the Spirit when entered upon.

Secondly, What are the Contents prefixed to every Chapter, but so many Inscriptions over the Gates of Inns (to continue the same Metaphor,) informing the Reader what Entertainment he is to expect, which if he likes not, he may travel on to the next: for in Biography, as we are not tied down to an exact Concatenation equally with other Historians; so a Chapter or two (for Instance this I am now writing) may be often pass'd over without any Injury to the Whole. And in these Inscriptions I have been as faithful as possible, not imitating the celebrated *Montagne*, who promises you one thing and gives you another;[3] nor some Title-Page Authors, who promise a great deal, and produce nothing at all.[4]

There are, besides these more obvious Benefits, several others which our Readers enjoy from this Art of dividing; tho' perhaps most of them too mysterious to be presently understood, by any who are not initiated into the Science of *Authoring*. To mention therefore but one which is most obvious, it prevents spoiling the Beauty of a Book by turning down its Leaves, a Method otherwise necessary to those Readers, who, (tho' they read with great Improvement and Advantage) are apt, when they return to their Study, after half an Hour's Absence, to forget where they left off.

These Divisions have the Sanction of great Antiquity. *Homer* not only divided his great Work into twenty-four Books, (in Compliment perhaps to the twenty-four Letters[5] to which he had very particular Obligations), but, according to the Opinion of some very sagacious Critics, hawked them all separately, delivering only one Book at a Time, (probably by Subscription).[6] He was the first Inventor of the Art which hath so long

3. The *Essais* (1580–88) of Michel Eyquem de Montaigne (1533–92), widely popular and influential in England from the time of John Florio's translation in 1603, often casually digressed from their announced subjects.

4. The title page often provided a preview of the work or the equivalent of a modern dustjacket blurb. For example, the densely printed title page of Defoe's *History of the Remarkable Life of John Sheppard* (1724), exploiting the celebrated thief's recent sensational escape from Newgate, ticks off all the episodes, which are scarcely more developed in the body of the pamphlet. See also the title page of *Shamela*, below, p. 271.

5. Of the Greek alphabet, by which the books of the Homeric poems are designated in their Greek texts. The book divisions are now attributed to a later scribe, possibly Aristarchus, librarian of Alex-

andria in the second century B.C.

6. An allusion to the phenomenally lucrative five-part subscription publication of Pope's *Iliad* (see below, p. 168, n. 9). The ancient tradition that the Homeric epics were assembled from scattered lays in the sixth century B.C. was revived in Rene Rapin's *Observations on the Poems of Homer and Virgil* (John Davies trans., 1672), Thomas Parnell's "Essay on . . . Homer" prefacing Pope's *Iliad* (1715), and *Remarks upon a Late Discourse of Free-Thinking* (1713), by Richard Bentley (1662–1742), who added that Homer sang these "songs" for "small earnings and good cheer." In Fielding's *A Journey from This World to the Next* (1743), Homer, asked if he wrote and sang the *Iliad* in this fashion, refers the narrator to the unity of the poem itself (compare Parson Adams's view, below, p. 154).

lain dormant, of publishing by Numbers, an Art now brought to such Perfection, that even Dictionaries are divided and exhibited piece-meal to the Public; nay, one Bookseller hath (*to encourage Learning and ease the Public*) contrived to give them a Dictionary in this divided Manner for only fifteen Shillings more than it would have cost entire.[7]

Virgil hath given us his Poem in twelve Books, an Argument of his Modesty; for by that doubtless he would insinuate that he pretends to no more than half the Merit of the *Greek*: for the same Reason, our *Milton* went originally no farther than ten; 'till being puffed up by the Praise of his Friends, he put himself on the same footing with the *Roman* Poet.[8]

I shall not however enter so deep into this Matter as some very learned Criticks have done; who have with infinite Labour and acute Discernment discovered what Books are proper for Embellishment, and what require Simplicity only, particularly with regard to Similies, which I think are now generally agreed to become any Book but the first.

I will dismiss this Chapter with the following Observation: That it becomes an Author generally to divide a Book, as it doth a Butcher to joint his Meat, for such Assistance is of great Help to both the Reader and the Carver. And now having indulged myself a little, I will endeavour to indulge the Curiosity of my Reader, who is no doubt impatient to know what he will find in the subsequent Chapters of this Book.

Chapter II

A surprizing Instance of Mr. Adams's *short Memory, with the unfortunate Consequences which it brought on* Joseph.

Mr. *Adams* and *Joseph* were now ready to depart different ways, when an Accident determined the former to return with his Friend, which *Tow-wouse*, Barnabas, and the Bookseller had not been able to do. This Accident was, that those Sermons, which the Parson was travelling to *London* to publish, were, O my good Reader, left behind; what he had mistaken for them in the Saddle-Bags being no other than three Shirts, a pair of Shoes, and some other Necessaries, which Mrs. *Adams*, who thought her Husband would want Shirts more than Sermons on his Journey, had carefully provided him.

This Discovery was now luckily owing to the Presence of *Joseph* at the opening the Saddle-Bags; who having heard his Friend say, he carried with him nine Volumes of Sermons, and not being of that Sect of Phi-

---

7. In the 1730's, booksellers discovered a profitable market in weekly or monthly six-penny or shilling installments of large multivolume works. Among these "number books' were two competing translations of Pierre Bayle's *Dictionaire historique et critique* (1697), and Robert James's *Medicinal Dictionary*. Battestin concludes that James's work—the only dictionary published by a single bookseller (Richardson's friend, Thomas Osborne) and one that gave only five sheets for a shilling instead

of the usual six—is Fielding's specific reference, although only the proposals for it had appeared before the novel was completed. Fielding's italicized parenthesis employs stock language of booksellers' proposals and advertisements.

8. The first edition of *Paradise Lost* (1667) was in ten books; in the second edition (1674), Milton divided the two longest (7 and 10) to produce twelve of nearly equal length.

losophers, who can reduce all the Matter of the World into a Nut-shell, seeing there was no room for them in the Bags, where the Parson had said they were deposited, had the Curiosity to cry out, 'Bless me, Sir, where are your Sermons?' The Parson answer'd, 'There, there, Child, there they are, under my Shirts.' Now it happened that he had taken forth his last Shirt, and the Vehicle remained visibly empty. 'Sure, Sir,' says *Joseph*, 'there is nothing in the Bags.' Upon which *Adams* starting, and testifying some Surprize, cry'd, 'Hey! fie, fie upon it; they are not here sure enough. Ay, they are certainly left behind.'

Joseph was greatly concerned at the Uneasiness which he apprehended his Friend must feel from this Disappointment: he begged him to pursue his Journey, and promised he would himself return with the Books to him, with the utmost Expedition. 'No, thank you, Child,' answered *Adams*, 'it shall not be so. What would it avail me, to tarry in the Great City, unless I had my Discourses with me, which are, *ut ita dicam*, the sole Cause, the *Aitia monotate* of my Peregrination.[1] No, Child, as this Accident hath happened, I am resolved to return back to my Cure, together with you; which indeed my Inclination sufficiently leads me to. This Disappointment may, perhaps, be intended for my Good.' He concluded with a Verse out of *Theocritus*, which signifies no more than, *that sometimes it rains and sometimes the Sun shines.*[2]

Joseph bowed with Obedience, and Thankfulness for the Inclination which the Parson express'd of returning with him; and now the Bill was called for, which, on Examination, amounted within a Shilling to the Sum Mr. *Adams* had in his Pocket. Perhaps the Reader may wonder how he was able to produce a sufficient Sum for so many Days: that he may not be surprized, therefore, it cannot be unnecessary to acquaint him, that he had borrowed a Guinea of a Servant belonging to the Coach and Six, who had been formerly one of his Parishioners, and whose Master, the Owner of the Coach, then lived within three Miles of him: for so good was the Credit of Mr. *Adams*, that even Mr. *Peter* the Lady *Booby*'s Steward, would have lent him a Guinea with very little Security.

Mr. *Adams* discharged the Bill, and they were both setting out, having agreed *to ride and tie*: a Method of Travelling much used by Persons who have but one Horse between them, and is thus performed. The two Travellers set out together, one on horseback, the other on foot: Now as it generally happens that he on horseback out-goes him on foot, the Custom is, that when he arrives at the Distance agreed on, he is to dismount, tie the Horse to some Gate, Tree, Post, or other thing, and then proceed on foot, when the other comes up to the Horse, he unties him, mounts and gallops on, 'till having passed by his Fellow-Traveller,

---

1. The first italicized phrase is Latin ("so to speak"); the second is "sole cause" in Greek.

2. Spoken as comfort to a youth whose love has forsaken him: "Good luck comes with another morn . . . rain one day, shine the next" (*Idyll* 4.42–43, J. M. Edmonds trans.; Loeb Classical Library). Except for Lattimore's *Iliad* and Bywater's

Poetics, all subsequent attributed classical translations are from this series.

In one of his most extensive revisions, Fielding added these two paragraphs and the first clause of the next in the second edition. The next sentence originally began "The Bill was now called for . . ."

he likewise arrives at the Place of tying. And this is that Method of Travelling so much in use among our prudent Ancestors, who knew that Horses had Mouths as well as Legs, and that they could not use the latter, without being at the Expence of suffering the Beasts themselves to use the former. This was the Method in use in those Days: when, instead of a Coach and Six, a Member of Parliament's Lady used to mount a Pillion behind her Husband; and a grave Serjeant at Law condescended to amble to *Westminster* on an easy Pad,[3] with his Clerk kicking his Heels[4] behind him.

Adams was now gone some Minutes, having insisted on *Joseph's* beginning the Journey on horseback, and *Joseph* had his Foot in the Stirrup, when the Hostler presented him a Bill for the Horse's Board during his Residence at the Inn. *Joseph* said Mr. *Adams* had paid all; but this Matter being referred to Mr. *Tow-wouse* was by him decided in favour of the Hostler, and indeed with Truth and Justice: for this was a fresh Instance of that shortness of Memory which did not arise from want of Parts, but that continual Hurry in which Parson *Adams* was always involved.

Joseph was now reduced to a Dilemma which extremely puzzled him. The Sum due for Horse-meat[5] was twelve Shillings, (for *Adams* who had borrowed the Beast of his Clerk, had ordered him to be fed as well as they could feed him) and the Cash in his Pocket amounted to Sixpence, (for *Adams* had divided the last Shilling with him). Now, tho' there have been some ingenious Persons who have contrived to pay twelve Shillings with Sixpence, *Joseph* was not one of them. He had never contracted a Debt in his Life, and was consequently the less ready at an Expedient to extricate himself. *Tow-wouse* was willing to give him Credit 'till next time, to which Mrs. *Tow-wouse* would probably have consented (for such was *Joseph's* Beauty, that it had made some Impression even on that Piece of Flint which that good Woman wore in her Bosom by way of heart). *Joseph* would have found therefore, very likely, the Passage free, had he not, when he honestly discovered the Nakedness of his Pockets, pulled out that little Piece of Gold which we have mentioned before. This caused Mrs. *Tow-wouse's* Eyes to water; she told *Joseph*, she did not conceive a Man could want Money whilst he had Gold in his Pocket. *Joseph* answered, he had such a Value for that little Piece of Gold, that he would not part with it for a hundred times the Riches which the greatest Esquire in the County was worth. 'A pretty Way indeed,' said Mrs. *Tow-wouse*, 'to run in debt, and then refuse to part with your Money, because you have a Value for it. I never knew any Piece of Gold of more Value than as many Shillings as it would change for.' 'Not to preserve my Life from starving, nor to redeem it from a Robber, would I part with this dear Piece,' answered *Joseph*. 'What (says Mrs. *Tow-wouse*) I suppose, it was given you by some vile Trollop, some Miss[6] or other; if it had been the Present of a virtuous Woman, you

---

3. Slow-paced horse.
4. Walking.
5. Fodder.
6. Kept mistress or whore.

would not have had such a Value for it. My Husband is a Fool if he parts with the Horse, without being paid for him.' 'No, no, I can't part with the Horse indeed, till I have the Money,' cried *Tow-wouse*. A Resolution highly commended by a Lawyer then in the Yard, who declared Mr. *Tow-wouse* might justify the Detainer.[7]

As we cannot therefore at present get Mr. *Joseph* out of the Inn, we shall leave him in it, and carry our Reader on after Parson *Adams*, who, his Mind being perfectly at ease, fell into a Contemplation on a Passage in *Æschylus*,[8] which entertained him for three Miles together, without suffering him once to reflect on his Fellow-Traveller.

At length having spun out this Thread, and being now at the Summit of a Hill, he cast his Eyes backwards, and wondered that he could not see any sign of *Joseph*. As he left him ready to mount the Horse, he could not apprehend any Mischief had happened, neither could he suspect that he had miss'd his Way, it being so broad and plain: the only Reason which presented itself to him, was that he had met with an Acquaintance who had prevailed with him to delay some time in Discourse.

He therefore resolved to proceed slowly forwards, not doubting but that he should be shortly overtaken, and soon came to a large Water, which filling the whole Road, he saw no Method of passing unless by wading through, which he accordingly did up to his Middle; but was no sooner got to the other Side, than he perceived, if he had looked over the Hedge, he would have found a Foot-Path capable of conducting him without wetting his Shoes.

His Surprize at *Joseph's* not coming up grew now very troublesome: he began to fear he knew not what, and as he determined, to move no farther; and, if he did not shortly overtake him, to return back; he wished to find a House of publick Entertainment where he might dry his Clothes and refresh himself with a Pint: but seeing no such (for no other Reason than because he did not cast his Eyes a hundred Yards forwards) he sat himself down on a Stile, and pulled out his *Æschylus*.

A Fellow passing presently by, *Adams* asked him, if he could direct him to an Alehouse. The Fellow who had just left it, and perceived the House and Sign to be within sight, thinking he had jeered him, and being of a morose Temper, bad him *follow his Nose and be d—n'd*. *Adams* told him he was a *saucy Jackanapes*; upon which the Fellow turned about angrily: but perceiving *Adams* clench his Fist he thought proper to go on without taking any farther notice.

A Horseman following immediately after, and being asked the same Question, answered, 'Friend, there is one within a Stone's-Throw; I believe you may see it before you.' *Adams* lifting up his Eyes, cry'd, 'I protest and so there is;' and thanking his Informer proceeded directly to it.

7. Legal term for withholding another's possessions. Mrs. Tow-wouse's part in this incident was added in the second edition.
8. First of the three great Greek tragedians. The best known of his surviving plays are *Prometheus Bound* and the *Oresteia* trilogy (*Agamemnon, The Libation Bearers, The Eumenides*).

Chapter III

The Opinion of two Lawyers concerning the same Gentleman, with Mr. Adams's *Enquiry into the Religion of his Host.*

He had just entered the House, had called for his Pint[1] and seated himself, when two Horsemen came to the Door, and fastening their Horses to the Rails, alighted. They said there was a violent Shower of Rain coming on, which they intended to weather there, and went into a little Room by themselves, not perceiving Mr. *Adams.*

One of these immediately asked the other, if he had seen a more comical Adventure a great while? Upon which the other said, 'he doubted whether by Law, the Landlord could justify detaining the Horse for his Corn and Hay.' But the former answered, 'Undoubtedly he can: it is an adjudged Case, and I have known it tried.'

Adams, who tho' he was, as the Reader may suspect, a little inclined to Forgetfulness, never wanted more than a Hint to remind him, overhearing their Discourse, immediately suggested to himself that this was his own Horse, and that he had forgot to pay for him, which upon enquiry, he was certified[2] of by the Gentlemen; who added, that the Horse was likely to have more Rest than Food, unless he was paid for.

The poor Parson resolved to return presently to the Inn, tho' he knew no more than *Joseph,* how to procure his Horse his Liberty: he was however prevailed on to stay under Covert, 'till the Shower which was now very violent, was over.

The three Travellers then sat down together over a Mug of good Beer; when *Adams,* who had observed a Gentleman's House as he passed along the Road, enquired to whom it belonged: one of the Horsemen had no sooner mentioned the Owner's Name, than the other began to revile him in the most opprobrious Terms. The *English* Language scarce affords a single reproachful Word, which he did not vent on this Occasion. He charged him likewise with many particular Facts.[3] He said,—'he no more regarded a Field of Wheat when he was hunting, than he did the High-way; that he had injured several poor Farmers by trampling their Corn[4] under his Horse's Heels; and if any of them begged him with the utmost Submission to refrain, his Horse-whip was always ready to do them justice.' He said, 'that he was the greatest Tyrant to the Neighbours in every other Instance, and would not suffer a Farmer to keep a Gun, tho' he might justify it by Law; and in his own Family so cruel a Master, that he never kept a Servant a Twelve-month. In his Capacity as a Justice,' continued he, 'he behaves so partially, that he commits or acquits just as he is in the humour, without any regard to Truth or Evidence: The Devil may carry any one before him for me; I would rather be tried before some Judges than be a Prosecutor before him: If I had an Estate

---

1. Of ale or beer.
2. Assured.
3. A legal term for acts or, more specifically,

criminal acts.
4. The generic term for any grain crop.

in the Neighbourhood, I would sell it for half the Value, rather than live near him.' *Adams* shook his Head, and said, 'he was sorry such Men were suffered to proceed with Impunity, and that Riches could set any Man above Law.' The Reviler a little after retiring into the Yard, the Gentleman, who had first mentioned his Name to *Adams*, began to assure him, 'that his Companion was a prejudiced Person. It is true,' says he, 'perhaps, that he may have sometimes pursued his Game over a Field of Corn, but he hath always made the Party ample Satisfaction; that so far from tyrannizing over his Neighbours, or taking away their Guns, he himself knew several Farmers not qualified, who not only kept Guns, but killed Game with them.[5] That he was the best of Masters to his Servants, and several of them had grown old in his Service. That he was the best Justice of Peace in the Kingdom, and to his certain knowledge had decided many difficult Points, which were referred to him, with the greatest Equity, and the highest Wisdom. And he verily believed, several Persons would give a Year's Purchase[6] more for an Estate near him, than under the Wings of any other great Man.' He had just finished his Encomium, when his Companion returned and acquainted him the Storm was over. Upon which, they presently mounted their Horses and departed.

Adams, who was in the utmost Anxiety at those different Characters[7] of the same Person, asked his Host if he knew the Gentleman; for he began to imagine they had by mistake been speaking of two several Gentlemen. 'No, no, Master!' answered the Host, a shrewd cunning Fellow, 'I know the Gentleman very well of whom they have been speaking, as I do the Gentlemen who spoke of him. As for riding over other Men's Corn, to my knowledge he hath not been on horseback these two Years. I never heard he did any Injury of that kind; and as to making Reparation, he is not so free of his Money as that comes to neither. Nor did I ever hear of his taking away any Man's Gun; nay, I know several who have Guns in their Houses: but as for killing Game with them, no Man is stricter; and I believe he would ruin any who did. You heard one of the Gentlemen say, he was the worst Master in the World, and the other that he is the best: but as for my own part, I know all his Servants, and never heard from any of them that he was either one or the other.—' 'Aye, aye,' says *Adams*, 'and how doth he behave as a Justice, pray?' 'Faith, Friend,' answered the Host, 'I question whether he is in the Commission:[8] the only Cause I have heard he hath decided a great while, was one between those very two Persons who just went out of this House; and I am sure he determined that justly, for I heard the whole matter.' 'Which did he decide it in favour of?' quoth *Adams*. 'I think I need not answer that Question,' cried the Host, 'after the dif-

---

5. The law restricted killing of game to persons "qualified" by ownership of an estate worth one hundred pounds a year, possession of a ninety-nine year lease on one of one hundred and fifty pounds, or position as son and heir of a "person of high degree." They were entitled to confiscate guns from unqualified persons.

6. Land was priced for sale in multiples of its annual rent or return (purchase).

7. Descriptions.

8. Local magistrates were empowered as the *Commission of the Peace.*

ferent Characters you have heard of him. It is not my Business to contradict Gentlemen, while they are drinking in my House: but I knew neither of them spoke a Syllable of Truth.' 'God forbid! (said *Adams*,) that Men should arrive at such a Pitch of Wickedness, to be-lye the Character of their Neighbour from a little private Affection, or what is infinitely worse, a private Spite. I rather believe we have mistaken them, and they mean two other Persons: for there are many Houses on the Road.' 'Why prithee, Friend,' cries the Host, 'dost thou pretend never to have told a lye in thy Life?' 'Never a malicious one, I am certain,' answered *Adams*; 'nor with a Design to injure the Reputation of any Man living.' 'Pugh, malicious! no, no,' replied the Host; 'not malicious with a Design to hang a Man, or bring him into Trouble: but surely out of love to one's self, one must speak better of a Friend than an Enemy.' 'Out of love to your self, you should confine yourself to Truth,' says *Adams*, 'for by doing otherwise, you injure the noblest Part of yourself, your immortal Soul. I can hardly believe any Man such an Idiot to risque the Loss of that by any trifling Gain, and the greatest Gain in this World is but Dirt in comparison of what shall be revealed hereafter.' Upon which the Host taking up the Cup, with a Smile drank a Health to Hereafter: adding, 'he was for something present.' 'Why,' says *Adams* very gravely, 'Do not you believe another World?' To which the Host answered, 'yes, he was no Atheist.' 'And you believe you have an immortal Soul?' cries *Adams*: He answered, 'God forbid he should not.' 'And Heaven and Hell?' said the Parson. The Host then bid him 'not to prophane: for those were Things not to be mentioned nor thought of but in Church.' *Adams* asked him, 'why he went to Church, if what he learned there had no Influence on his Conduct in Life?' 'I go to Church,' answered the Host, 'to say my Prayers and behave godly.' 'And dost not thou,' cry'd *Adams*, 'believe what thou hearest at Church?' 'Most part of it, Master,' returned the Host. 'And dost not thou then tremble,' cries *Adams*, 'at the Thought of eternal Punishment?' 'As for that, Master,' said he, 'I never once thought about it: but what signifies talking about matters so far off? the Mug is out,[9] shall I draw another?'

Whilst he was gone for that purpose, a Stage-Coach drove up to the Door. The Coachman coming into the House, was asked by the Mistress, what Passengers he had in his Coach? 'A Parcel of *Squinny-gut*[1] B——s, (says he) I have a good mind to overturn them; you won't prevail upon them to drink any thing I assure you.' *Adams* asked him, if he had not seen a young Man on Horse-back on the Road, (describing *Joseph*). 'Aye,' said the Coachman, 'a Gentlewoman in my Coach that is his Acquaintance redeemed him and his Horse; he would have been here before this time, had not the Storm driven him to shelter.' 'God bless her,' said *Adams* in a Rapture; nor could he delay walking out to satisfy himself who this charitable Woman was; but what was his surprize, when he saw his old Acquaintance, Madam *Slipslop*? Her's indeed was not so great, because she had been informed by *Joseph*, that he was on the Road. Very civil were the Salutations on both sides; and Mrs. *Slipslop* rebuked the Hostess for denying the Gentleman to be there when she asked for him: but indeed the poor Woman had not erred designedly: for Mrs. *Slipslop* asked for a Clergyman; and she had unhappily mistaken *Adams* for a Person travelling to a neighbouring Fair with the Thimble and Button,[2] or some other such Operation: for he marched in a swinging[3] great, but short, white Coat with black Buttons, a short Wig, and a Hat, which so far from having a black Hatband, had nothing black about it.[4]

Joseph was now come up, and Mrs. *Slipslop* would have had him quit[5] his Horse to the Parson, and come himself into the Coach: but he absolutely refused, saying he thanked Heaven he was well enough recovered to be very able to ride, and added, he hoped he knew his Duty better than to ride in a Coach while Mr. *Adams* was on horseback.

Mrs. *Slipslop* would have persisted longer, had not a Lady in the Coach put a short End to the Dispute, by refusing to suffer a Fellow in a Livery to ride in the same Coach with herself: so it was at length agreed that *Adams* should fill the vacant Place in the Coach, and *Joseph* should proceed on horseback.

They had not proceeded far before Mrs. *Slipslop*, addressing herself to the Parson, spoke thus: 'There hath been a strange Alteration in our Family, Mr. *Adams*, since Sir *Thomas's* Death.' 'A strange Alteration indeed!' says *Adams*, 'as I gather from some Hints which have dropped from *Joseph*.' 'Aye,' says she, 'I could never have believed it, but the longer one lives in the World, the more one sees. So *Joseph* hath given you Hints.'—'But of what Nature, will always remain a perfect Secret with me,' cries the Parson; 'he forced me to promise before he would communicate any thing. I am indeed concerned to find her Ladyship behave in so unbecoming a manner. I always thought her in the main, a good Lady, and should never have suspected her of Thoughts so unworthy a Christian, and with a young Lad her own Servant.' 'These things are no Secrets to me, I assure you,' cries *Slipslop*; 'and I believe, they will be none any where shortly: for ever since the Boy's Departure she hath behaved more like a mad Woman than any thing else.' 'Truly, I am heartily concerned,' says *Adams*, 'for she was a good sort of a Lady; indeed I have often wished she had attended a little more constantly at the Service, but she hath done a great deal of Good in the Parish.' 'O Mr. *Adams!*' says *Slipslop*, 'People that don't see all, often know nothing. Many Things have been given away in our Family, I do assure you, without her knowledge. I have heard you say in the Pulpit, we ought not to brag: but indeed I can't avoid saying, if she had kept the Keys herself, the Poor would have wanted many a Cordial[6] which I have let them have. As for my late Master, he was as worthy a Man as ever lived,

---

2. Used in the thimblerig, a crooked guessing game like the modern shell game or three-card monte.

3. Whopping.

4. A clergyman usually dressed in black and wore a long coat.

5. Yield.

6. Restorative drink or food.

and would have done infinite Good if he had not been controlled: but he loved a quiet Life, Heavens rest his Soul! I am confident he is there, and enjoys a quiet Life, which some Folks would not allow him here.' *Adams* answered, 'he had never heard this before, and was mistaken, if she herself,' (for he remembered she used to commend her Mistress and blame her Master,) 'had not formerly been of another Opinion.' 'I don't know, (replied she,) what I might once think: but now I am *confidous* Matters are as I tell you: The World will shortly see who hath been deceived; for my part I say nothing, but that it is *wondersome* how some People can carry all things with a grave Face.'

Thus Mr. *Adams* and she discoursed: 'till they came opposite to a great House which stood at some distance from the Road; a Lady in the Coach spying it, cry'd, 'Yonder lives the unfortunate *Leonora*, if one can justly call a Woman unfortunate, whom we must own at the same time guilty, and the Author of her own Calamity.' This was abundantly sufficient to awaken the Curiosity of Mr. *Adams*, as indeed it did that of the whole Company, who jointly solicited the Lady to acquaint them with *Leonora's* History, since it seemed, by what she had said, to contain something remarkable.

The Lady, who was perfectly well bred, did not require many Entreaties, and having only wished their Entertainment might make amends for the Company's Attention, she began in the following manner.

Chapter IV

The History of Leonora, or the Unfortunate Jilt.[1]

Leonora was the Daughter of a Gentleman of Fortune; she was tall and well-shaped, with a Sprightliness in her Countenance, which often attracts beyond more regular Features joined with an insipid Air; nor is this kind of Beauty less apt to deceive than allure; the Good-Humour which it indicates, being often mistaken for Good-Nature,[2] and the Vivacity for true Understanding.

Leonora, who was now at the Age of Eighteen, lived with an Aunt of her's in a Town in the North of *England*. She was an extreme Lover of Gaiety, and very rarely missed a Ball or any other publick Assembly; where she had frequent Opportunities of satisfying a greedy Appetite of Vanity with the Preference which was given her by the Men to almost every other Woman present.

Among many young Fellows who were particular in their Gallantries towards her, *Horatio* soon distinguished himself in her Eyes beyond all his Competitors; she danced with more than ordinary Gaiety when he happened to be her Partner; neither the Fairness of the Evening nor the Musick of the Nightingale, could lengthen her Walk like his Company.

1. The interpolation of independent tales was common in longer fiction from the Greek prose romances of the second century A.D. to the modern "Biographies" Fielding praises in book 3, chapter 1.
2. For Fielding's elaboration of the distinction between these qualities, see below, pp. 324–26.

She affected no longer to understand the Civilities of others; whilst she inclined so attentive an Ear to every Compliment of *Horatio*, that she often smiled even when it was too delicate for her Comprehension.

'Pray, Madam,' says *Adams*, 'who was this Squire *Horatio*?'

Horatio, says the Lady, was a young Gentleman of a good Family, bred to the Law, and had been some few Years called to the Degree of a Barrister.[3] His Face and Person were such as the Generality allowed handsome: but he had a Dignity in his Air very rarely to be seen. His Temper was of the saturnine Complexion,[4] but without the least Taint of Moroseness. He had Wit and Humour with an Inclination to Satire, which he indulged rather too much.

This Gentleman, who had contracted the most violent Passion for *Leonora*, was the last Person who perceived the Probability of its Success. The whole Town had made the Match for him, before he himself had drawn a Confidence from her Actions sufficient to mention his Passion to her; for it was his Opinion, (and perhaps he was there in the right) that it is highly impolitick to talk seriously of Love to a Woman before you have made such a Progress in her Affections, that she herself expects and desires to hear it.

But whatever Diffidence the Fears of a Lover may create, which are apt to magnify every Favour conferred on a Rival, and to see the little Advances towards themselves through the other End of the Perspective;[5] it was impossible that *Horatio's* Passion should so blind his Discernment, as to prevent his conceiving Hopes from the Behavior of *Leonora*; whose Fondness for him was now as visible to an indifferent Person in their Company, as his for her.

'I never knew any of these forward Sluts come to good, (says the Lady, who refused *Joseph's* Entrance into the Coach,) nor shall I wonder at any thing she doth in the Sequel.'

The Lady proceeded in her Story thus: It was in the Midst of a gay Conversation in the Walks one Evening, when *Horatio* whispered *Leonora*, 'that he was desirous to take a Turn or two with her in private; for that he had something to communicate to her of great Consequence.' 'Are you sure it is of Consequence?' said she, smiling.—'I hope,' answered he, 'you will think so too, since the whole future Happiness of my Life must depend on the Event.'[6]

Leonora, who very much suspected what was coming, would have deferred it 'til another Time: but *Horatio*, who had more than half conquered the Difficulty of speaking by the first Motion, was so very importunate, that she at last yielded, and leaving the rest of the Company, they turned aside into an unfrequented Walk.

They had retired far out of the sight of the Company, both maintaining a strict Silence. At last *Horatio* made a full Stop, and taking *Leonora*,

3. One admitted to plead cases in the courts, usually after six or seven years' study in one of the Inns of Court. Fielding was a barrister.
4. In astrology, persons born under the sign of Saturn were thought to have a cold and gloomy temperament.
5. Telescope—i.e., to diminish them.
6. Outcome.

who stood pale and trembling, gently by the Hand, he fetched a deep
Sigh, and then looking on her Eyes with all the Tenderness imaginable,
he cried out in a faltering Accent; 'O *Leonora*! is it necessary for me to
declare to you on what the future Happiness of my Life must be founded!
Must I say, there is something belonging to you which is a Bar to my
Happiness, and which unless you will part with, I must be miserable?'
'What can that be?' replied *Leonora*.—'No wonder,' said he, 'you are
surprized, that I should make an Objection to any thing which is yours,
yet sure you may guess, since it is the only one which the Riches of the
World, if they were mine, should purchase of me.—O it is that which
you must part with, to bestow all the rest! Can *Leonora*, or rather will
she doubt longer?—Let me then whisper it in her Ears,—It is your Name,
Madam. It is by parting with that, by your Condescension to be for ever
mine, which must at once prevent me from being the most miserable,
and will render me the happiest of Mankind.' *Leonora*, covered with
Blushes, and with as angry a Look as she could possibly put on, told
him, 'that had she suspected what his Declaration would have been, he
should not have decoyed her from her Company; that he had so surprized and frighted her, that she begged him to convey her back as quick
as possible;' which he, trembling very near as much as herself, did.

'More Fool he,' cried *Slipslop*, 'it is a sign he knew very little of our
Sect.' 'Truly, Madam,' said *Adams*, 'I think you are in the right, I should
have insisted to know a piece of her Mind, when I had carried matters
so far.' But Mrs. *Grave-airs* desired the Lady to omit all such fulsome
Stuff in her Story: for that it made her sick.

Well then, Madam, to be as concise as possible, said the Lady, many
Weeks had not past after this Interview, before *Horatio* and *Leonora*
were what they call on a good footing together. All Ceremonies except
the last were now over; the Writings were now drawn,[7] and every thing
was in the utmost forwardness preparative to the putting *Horatio* in possession of all his Wishes. I will if you please repeat you a Letter from
each of them which I have got by heart, and which will give you no
small Idea of their Passion on both sides.

Mrs. *Grave-airs* objected to hearing these Letters: but being put to the
Vote, it was carried against her by all the rest in the Coach; Parson
Adams contending for it with the utmost Vehemence.

HORATIO *to* LEONORA

How vain, most adorable Creature, is the Pursuit of Pleasure in the
absence of an Object to which the Mind is entirely devoted, unless it
have some Relation to that Object! I was last Night condemned to the
Society of Men of Wit and Learning, which, however agreeable it might
have formerly been to me, now only gave me a Suspicion that they
imputed my Absence[8] in Conversation to the true Cause. For which
Reason, when your Engagements forbid me the extatic Happiness of

7. The legal papers stipulating the marital prop-   8. Inattention.
erty settlement were prepared.

seeing you, I am always desirous to be alone; since my Sentiments for *Leonora* are so delicate, that I cannot bear the Apprehension of another's prying into those delightful Endearments with which the warm Imagination of a Lover will sometimes indulge him, and which I suspect my Eyes then betray. To fear this Discovery of our Thoughts, may perhaps appear too ridiculous a Nicety to Minds, not susceptible of all the Tendernesses of this delicate Passion. And surely we shall suspect there are few such, when we consider that it requires every human Virtue to exert itself in its full Extent. Since the Beloved whose Happiness it ultimately respects, may give us charming Opportunities of being brave in her Defence, generous to her Wants, compassionate to her Afflictions, grateful to her Kindness, and, in the same manner, of exercising every other Virtue, which he who would not do to any Degree, and that with the utmost Rapture, can never deserve the Name of a Lover: It is therefore with a View to the delicate Modesty of your Mind that I cultivate it so purely in my own, and it is that which will sufficiently suggest to you the Uneasiness I bear from those Liberties which Men to whom the World allow Politeness will sometimes give themselves on these Occasions.

Can I tell you with what Eagerness I expect the Arrival of that blest Day, when I shall experience the Falshood of a common Assertion that the greatest human Happiness consists in Hope? A Doctrine which no Person had ever stronger Reason to believe than myself at present, since none ever tasted such Bliss as fires my Bosom with the Thoughts of spending my future Days with such a Companion, and that every Action of my Life will have the glorious Satisfaction of conducing to your Happiness.

* Leonora *to* Horatio

The Refinement of your Mind has been so evidently proved, by every Word and Action ever since I had first the Pleasure of knowing you, that I thought it impossible my good Opinion of *Horatio* could have been heightened by any additional Proof of Merit. This very Thought was my Amusement when I received your last Letter, which, when I opened, I confess I was surprized to find the delicate Sentiments expressed there, so far exceeded what I thought could come even from you, (altho' I know all the generous Principles human Nature is capable of, are centered in your Breast) that Words cannot paint what I feel on the Reflection, that my Happiness shall be the ultimate End of all your Actions.

Oh *Horatio*! what a Life that must be, where the meanest domestick Cares are sweetened by the pleasing Consideration that the Man on Earth who best deserves, and to whom you are most inclined to give your Affections, is to reap either Profit or Pleasure from all you do! In

* This Letter was written by a young Lady on reading the former.[9]

9. This note, added in the second edition, probably refers to Fielding's sister Sarah (see below, pp. 331 and 398).

such a Case, Toils must be turned into Diversions, and nothing but the unavoidable Inconveniences of Life can make us remember that we are mortal.

If the solitary Turn of your Thoughts, and the Desire of keeping them undiscovered, makes even the Conversation of Men of Wit and Learning tedious to you, what anxious Hours must I spend who am condemn'd by Custom to the Conversation of Women, whose natural Curiosity leads them to pry into all my Thoughts, and whose Envy can never suffer *Horatio's* Heart to be possessed by any one without forcing them into malicious Designs, against the Person who is so happy as to possess it: but indeed, if ever Envy can possibly have any Excuse, or even Alleviation, it is in this Case, where the Good is so great, that it must be equally natural to all to wish it for themselves, nor am I ashamed to own it: and to your Merit, *Horatio*, I am obliged, that prevents my being in that most uneasy of all the Situations I can figure in my Imagination, of being led by Inclination to love the Person whom my own Judgment forces me to condemn.

Matters were in so great forwardness between this fond Couple, that the Day was fixed for their Marriage, and was now within a Fortnight, when the Sessions chanced to be held for that County in a Town about twenty Miles distance from that which is the Scene of our Story. It seems, it is usual for the young Gentlemen of the Bar to repair to these Sessions, not so much for the sake of Profit, as to shew their Parts and learn the Law of the Justices of Peace: for which purpose one of the wisest and gravest of all the Justices is appointed Speaker or Chairman, as they modestly call it, and he reads them a Lecture, and instructs them in the true Knowledge of the Law.

'You are here guilty of a little Mistake,' says *Adams*, 'which if you please I will correct; I have attended at one of these Quarter Sessions, where I observed the Counsel taught the Justices, instead of learning any thing of them.'[1]

It is not very material, said the Lady: hither repaired *Horatio*, who as he hoped by his Profession to advance his Fortune, which was not at present very large, for the sake of his dear *Leonora*, he resolved to spare no Pains, nor lose any Opportunity of improving or advancing himself in it.

The same Afternoon in which he left the Town, as *Leonora* stood at her Window, a Coach and Six passed by: which she declared to be the completest, genteelest, prettiest Equipage she ever saw; adding these

---

1. The Court of Quarter Sessions, the supreme county authority, met at least four times a year. Theoretically, an assembly of all the county's justices of the peace, it was often attended by as few as two or three. Chosen by his fellow justices, the chairman was expected to deliver a "charge" to the grand and petty juries, "the usual method" being "to run over the several articles, or head of crimes, which might become subject to the inquiry" of the juries, as Fielding explained in his own *Charge Deliver'd to the Grand Jury . . . for the City and Liberty of Westminster . . . 1749.* Despite handbooks like Michael Dalton's *Country Justice* (Fielding owned the 1705 and 1715 editions), the minimal qualifications for the office of local justice—allegiance to sovereign and church and possession of a freehold of twenty pounds a year—did produce situations like the one Adams describes.

remarkable Words, *O I am in love with that Equipage!* which, tho' her Friend *Florella* at the time did not greatly regard, she hath since remembered.

In the Evening an Assembly was held, which *Leonora* honoured with her Company: but intended to pay her dear *Horatio* the Compliment of refusing to dance in his Absence.

O Why have not Women as good Resolution to maintain their Vows, as they have often good Inclinations in making them!

The Gentleman who owned the Coach and Six, came to the Assembly. His Clothes were as remarkably fine as his Equipage could be. He soon attracted the Eyes of the Company; all the Smarts,[2] all the Silk Waistcoats with Silver and Gold Edgings, were eclipsed in an instant.

'Madam,' said *Adams*, 'if it be not impertinent, I should be glad to know how this Gentleman was drest.'

Sir, answered the Lady, I have been told, he had on a Cut-Velvet Coat of a Cinnamon Colour, lined with a Pink Satten, embroidered all over with Gold; his Waistcoat, which was Cloth of Silver, was embroidered with Gold likewise. I cannot be particular as to the rest of his Dress: but it was all in the *French* Fashion, for *Bellarmine*, (that was his Name) was just arrived from *Paris*.

This fine Figure did not more entirely engage the Eyes of every Lady in the Assembly, than *Leonora* did his. He had scarce beheld her, but he stood motionless and fixed as a Statue, or at least would have done so, if Good-Breeding had permitted him. However, he carried it so far before he had power to correct himself, that every Person in the Room easily discovered where his Admiration was settled. The other Ladies began to single out their former Partners, all perceiving who would be *Bellarmine*'s Choice; which they however endeavoured, by all possible means, to prevent: Many of them saying to *Leonora*, 'O Madam, I suppose we shan't have the pleasure of seeing you dance To-Night;' and then crying out in *Bellarmine*'s hearing, 'O *Leonora* will not dance, I assure you; her Partner is not here.' One maliciously attempted to prevent her, by sending a disagreeable Fellow to ask her, that so she might be obliged either to dance with him, or sit down: but this Scheme proved abortive.

Leonora saw herself admired by the fine Stranger, and envied by every Woman present. Her little Heart began to flutter within her, and her Head was agitated with a convulsive Motion; she seemed as if she would speak to several of her Acquaintance, but had nothing to say: for as she would not mention her present Triumph, so she could not disengage her Thoughts one moment from the Contemplation of it: She had never tasted any thing like this Happiness. She had before known what it was to torment a single Woman; but to be hated and secretly cursed by a whole Assembly, was a Joy reserved for this blessed Moment. As this vast Profusion of Ecstasy had confounded her Understanding, so there

2. A "cant word" for "a fellow affecting briskness or vivacity" (Johnson's *Dictionary*).

was nothing so foolish as her Behaviour; she played a thousand childish Tricks, distorted her Person into several Shapes, and her Face into several Laughs, without any Reason. In a word, her Carriage was as absurd as her Desires, which were to affect an Insensibility of the Stranger's Admiration, and at the same time a Triumph from that Admiration over every Woman in the Room.

In this Temper of Mind, *Bellarmine*, having enquired who she was, advanced to her, and with a low Bow, begged the Honour of dancing with her, which she with as low a Curt'sy immediately granted. She danced with him all Night, and enjoyed perhaps the highest Pleasure, which she was capable of feeling.

At these Words, *Adams* fetched a deep Groan, which frighted the Ladies, who told him, 'they hoped he was not ill.' He answered, 'he groaned only for the Folly of *Leonora.*'

Leonora retired, (continued the Lady) about Six in the Morning, but not to Rest. She tumbled and tossed in her Bed, with very short Intervals of Sleep, and those entirely filled with Dreams of the Equipage and fine Clothes she had seen, and the Balls, Operas and Ridotto's,[3] which had been the Subject of their Conversation.

In the Afternoon *Bellarmine*, in the dear Coach and Six, came to wait on her. He was indeed charmed with her Person, and was, on Enquiry, so well pleased with the Circumstances of her Father, (for he himself, notwithstanding all his Finery, was not quite so rich as a *Crœsus* or an *Attālus*.) 'Attălus,' says Mr. *Adams*, 'but pray how came you acquainted with these Names?'[4] The Lady smiled at the Question, and proceeded— He was so pleased, I say, that he resolved to make his Addresses to her directly. He did so accordingly, and that with so much Warmth and Briskness, that he quickly baffled her weak Repulses, and obliged the Lady to refer him to her Father, who, she knew, would quickly declare in favour of a Coach and Six.

Thus, what *Horatio* had by Sighs and Tears, Love and Tenderness, been so long obtaining, the *French-English Bellarmine* with Gaiety and Gallantry possessed himself of in an instant. In other words, what Modesty had employed a full Year in raising, Impudence demolished in twenty-four Hours.

Here *Adams* groaned a second time, but the Ladies, who began to smoke him,[5] took no Notice.

From the Opening of the Assembly 'till the End of *Bellarmine's* Visit, *Leonora* had scarce one thought of *Horatio*: but he now began, tho' an unwelcome Guest, to enter into her Mind. She wished she had seen the charming *Bellarmine* and his charming Equipage before Matters had

---

3. A currently fashionable entertainment or social gathering featuring music and dancing, often in masquerade, introduced into England from Italy in 1722.
4. Since women were not usually given a classical education, the lady surprises Adams with the names of ancient kings of legendary wealth. Croesus was king of Lydia in the sixth century B.C. In the second and third centuries, a succession of monarchs named Attalus built Pergamon into the most opulent dominion in Asia Minor, and one of them, bequeathing his possessions to Rome, became a byword for largesse in Latin poetry.
5. To catch on to him.

gone so far. 'Yet, why (says she) should I wish to have seen him before, or what signifies it that I have seen him now? Is not *Horatio* my Lover? almost my Husband? Is he not as handsome, nay handsomer than *Bellarmine*? Aye, but *Bellarmine* is the genteeler and the finer Man; yes, that he must be allowed. Yes, yes, he is that certainly. But did not I no longer ago than yesterday love *Horatio* more than all the World? aye, but yesterday I had not seen *Bellarmine*. But doth not *Horatio* doat on me, and may he not in despair break his Heart if I abandon him? Well, and hath not *Bellarmine* a Heart to break too? Yes, but I promised *Horatio* first; but that was poor *Bellarmine's* Misfortune, if I had seen him first, I should certainly have preferred him. Did not the dear Creature prefer me to every Woman in the Assembly, when every She was laying out for him? When was it in *Horatio's* power to give me such an Instance of Affection? Can he give me an Equipage or any of those Things which *Bellarmine* will make me Mistress of? How vast is the Difference between being the Wife of a poor Counsellor, and the Wife of one of *Bellarmine's* Fortune! If I marry *Horatio*, I shall triumph over no more than one Rival: but by marrying *Bellarmine*, I shall be the Envy of all my Acquaintance. What Happiness![6]—But can I suffer *Horatio* to die? for he hath sworn he cannot survive my Loss: but perhaps he may not die; if he should, can I prevent it? Must I sacrifice my self to him? besides, *Bellarmine* may be as miserable for me to.' She was thus arguing with herself, when some young Ladies called her to the Walks, and a little relieved her Anxiety for the present.

The next Morning *Bellarmine* breakfasted with her in presence of her Aunt, whom he sufficiently informed of his Passion for *Leonora*; he was no sooner withdrawn, than the old Lady began to advise her Niece on this Occasion.—'You see, Child, (says she) what Fortune hath thrown in your way, and I hope you will not withstand your own Preferments.' *Leonora* sighing, 'begged her not to mention any such thing, when she knew her Engagements to *Horatio*.' 'Engagements to a Fig,' cry'd the Aunt, 'you should thank Heaven on your Knees that you have it yet in your power to break them. Will any Woman hesitate a Moment, whether she shall ride in a Coach or walk on Foot all the Days of her Life?—But *Bellarmine* drives six, and *Horatio* not even a Pair.' 'Yes, but, Madam, what will the World say?' answered *Leonora*; 'will not they condemn me?' 'The World is always on the side of Prudence,' cries the Aunt, 'and would surely condemn you if you sacrificed your Interest to any Motive whatever. O, I know the World very well, and you shew your own Ignorance, my Dear, by your Objection. O' my Conscience the World is wiser. I have lived longer in it than you, and I assure you there is not any thing worth our Regard besides Money: nor did I ever know one Person who married from other Considerations, who did not afterwards heartily repent it. Besides, if we examine the two Men, can you prefer a sneaking[7] Fellow, who hath been bred at a University, to a fine Gentle-

6. These two sentences were added in the second edition.   7. Paltry, contemptible.

man just come from his Travels?—All the World must allow *Bellarmine* to be a fine Gentleman, positively a fine Gentleman, and a handsome Man.—' 'Perhaps, Madam, I should not doubt, if I knew how to be handsomely off with the other.' 'O leave that to me,' says the Aunt. 'You know your Father hath not been acquainted with the Affair.[8] Indeed, for my part, I thought it might do well enough, not dreaming of such an Offer: but I'll disengage you, leave me to give the Fellow an Answer. I warrant you shall have no farther Trouble.'

Leonora was at length satisfied with her Aunt's Reasoning; and *Bellarmine* supping with her that Evening, it was agreed he should the next Morning go to her Father and propose the Match, which she consented should be consummated at his Return.

The Aunt retired soon after Supper, and the Lovers being left together, *Bellarmine* began in the following manner: 'Yes, Madam, this Coat I assure you was made at *Paris*, and I defy the best *English* Taylor even to imitate it. There is not one of them can cut, Madam, they can't cut. If you observe how this Skirt is turned, and this Sleeve, a clumsy *English* Rascal can do nothing like it.—Pray how do you like my Liveries?' *Leonora* answered, 'she thought them very pretty.' 'All *French*,' says he, 'I assure you, except the Great Coats;[9] I never trust any thing more than a Great Coat to an *Englishman*; you know one must encourage our own People what one can, especially as, before I had a Place, I was in the Country Interest, he, he, he! but for myself, I would see the dirty Island at the bottom of the Sea, rather than wear a single Rag of *English* Work about me, and I am sure after you have made one Tour to *Paris*, you will be of the same Opinion with regard to your own Clothes. You can't conceive what an Addition a *French* Dress would be to your Beauty; I positively assure you, at the first Opera I saw since I came over, I mistook the *English* Ladies for Chambermaids, he he, he!'[1]

With such sort of polite Discourse did the gay *Bellarmine* entertain his beloved *Leonora*, when the Door opened on a sudden, and *Horatio* entered the Room. Here 'tis impossible to express the Surprize of *Leonora*.

'Poor Woman,' says Mrs. *Slipslop*, 'what a terrible *Quandary*[2] she

8. An apparent inconsistency, since her father would have necessarily been consulted in drawing up the marriage settlement mentioned on p. 82.
9. Overcoats.
1. To protect the woolen industry, England's principal manufacture and primary export, the export of raw wool had been banned since the seventeenth century; but it was smuggled to France in great quantities, and in spite of prohibitive duties on foreign cloth, Paris fashions were in vogue. In the first edition, Bellarmine simply expresses this Francophile taste, which, as Battestin points out, the opposition press vociferously condemned as aggravating the much-lamented decline in the woolen trade that they sought to blame on Walpole's policies. A contemporary reader, mindful of the recent (November 1741)

disclosure that the Court had imported French clothes for the king's birthday, might plausibly associate Bellarmine's attitude with the Court party. In the second edition, after Walpole had resigned, Fielding ironically compounded the satire, attacking those opposition politicians who had entered the government (see below, pp. 389–90) by inserting "especially, as before I had a Place [government appointment], I was in the Country Interest" [the opposition]. For a parallel emendation, see below, p. 110.
2. Evidently italicized as one of Slipslop's "hard words"; Johnson's *Dictionary* called it a "low word," although it had been in literary use since the sixteenth century; Pamela uses it in one of her early letters.

must be in!' 'Not at all,' says Miss *Grave-airs*, 'such Sluts can never be confounded.' 'She must have then more than *Corinthian* Assurance,' said *Adams*; 'ay, more than *Lais* herself.'[3]

A long Silence, continued the Lady, prevailed in the whole Company: If the familiar Entrance of *Horatio* struck the greatest Astonishment into *Bellarmine*, the unexpected Presence of *Bellarmine* no less surprized *Horatio*. At length *Leonora* collecting all the Spirits she was Mistress of, addressed herself to the latter, and pretended to wonder at the Reason of so late a Visit. 'I should, indeed,' answered he, 'have made some Apology for disturbing you at this Hour, had not my finding you in Company assured me I do not break in on your Repose.' *Bellarmine* rose from his Chair, traversed the Room in a Minuet Step, and humm'd an Opera Tune, while *Horatio* advancing to *Leonora* ask'd her in a Whisper, if that Gentleman was not a Relation of her's; to which she answered with a Smile, or rather Sneer, 'No, he is no Relation of mine yet;' adding, 'she could not guess the Meaning of his Question.' *Horatio* told her softly, 'it did not arise from Jealousy.' 'Jealousy!' cries she, 'I assure you;—it would be very strange in a common Acquaintance to give himself any of those Airs.' These Words a little surprized *Horatio*, but before he had time to answer, *Bellarmine* danced up to the Lady, and told her, 'he feared he interrupted some Business between her and the Gentleman.' 'I can have no Business,' said she, 'with the Gentleman, nor any other, which need be any Secret to you.'

'You'll pardon me,' said *Horatio*, 'if I desire to know who this Gentleman is, who is to be intrusted with all our Secrets.' 'You'll know soon enough,' cries *Leonora*, 'but I can't guess what Secrets can ever pass between us of such mighty Consequence.' 'No Madam!' cries *Horatio*, 'I'm sure you would not have me understand you in earnest.' ' 'Tis indifferent to me,' says she, 'how you understand me; but I think so unseasonable a Visit is difficult to be understood at all, at least when People find one engaged, though one's Servants do not deny one,[4] one may expect a well-bred Person should soon take the Hint.' 'Madam,' said *Horatio*, 'I did not imagine any Engagement with a Stranger, as it seems this Gentleman is, would have made my Visit impertinent, or that any such Ceremonies were to be preserved between Persons in our Situation.' 'Sure you are in a Dream,' says she, 'or would persuade me that I am in one. I know no pretensions a common Acquaintance can have to lay aside the Ceremonies of Good-Breeding.' 'Sure,' said he, 'I am in a Dream; for it is impossible I should be really esteemed a common Acquaintance by *Leonora*, after what has passed between us!' 'Passed between us! Do you intend to affront me before this Gentleman?' 'D—n me, affront the Lady,' says *Bellarmine*, cocking his Hat and strut-

---

3. This sentence was added in the second edition. The ancient city of Corinth was known for its licentiousness. Hence "Corinthian brass," originally referring to a fine metal developed there, became an epithet for shamelessness. There were apparently three legendary courtesans named Lais

in fourth- and fifth-century B.C. Corinth whose identities were confused in ancient accounts. Given Leonora's situation, Adams may have in mind the one who flaunted her affair with Diogenes to Aristippus, who was keeping her.

4. See below, p. 138.

ting up to *Horatio*, 'does any Man dare affront this Lady before me, d—n me?' 'Harkee, Sir,' says *Horatio*, 'I would advise you to lay aside that fierce Air; for I am mightily deceived, if this Lady has not a violent Desire to get your Worship a good drubbing.' 'Sir,' said *Bellarmine*, 'I have the Honour to be her Protector, and d—n me, if I understand your Meaning.' 'Sir,' answered *Horatio*, 'she is rather your Protectress: but give yourself no more Airs, for you see I am prepared for you,' (shaking his Whip at him.) 'Oh! *Serviteur tres humble,*' says *Bellarmine*, '*Je Vous entend parfaitement bien.*'[5] At which time the Aunt, who had heard of *Horatio's* Visit, entered the Room and soon satisfied all his Doubts. She convinced him that he was never more awake in his Life, and that nothing more extraordinary had happened in his three days Absence, than a small Alteration in the Affections of *Leonora*: who now burst into Tears, and wondered what Reason she had given him to use her in so barbarous a Manner. *Horatio* desired *Bellarmine* to withdraw with him: but the Ladies prevented it by laying violent Hands on the latter; upon which, the former took his Leave without any great Ceremony, and departed, leaving the Lady with his Rival to consult for his Safety, which *Leonora* feared her Indiscretion might have endangered: but the Aunt comforted her with Assurances, that *Horatio* would not venture his Person against so accomplished a Cavalier as *Bellarmine*, and that being a Lawyer, he would seek Revenge in his own way, and the most they had to apprehend from him was an Action.[6]

They at length therefore agreed to permit *Bellarmine* to retire to his Lodgings, having first settled all Matters relating to the Journey which he was to undertake in the Morning, and their Preparations for the Nuptials at his return.

But alas! as wise Men have observed, the Seat of Valour is not the Countenance, and many a grave and plain Man, will, on a just Provocation, betake himself to that mischievous Metal, cold Iron; while Men of a fiercer Brow, and sometimes with that Emblem of Courage, a Cockade,[7] will more prudently decline it.

Leonora was waked in the Morning, from a Visionary Coach and Six, with the dismal Account, that *Bellarmine* was run through the Body by *Horatio*, that he lay languishing at an Inn, and the Surgeons had declared the Wound mortal. She immediately leap'd out of the Bed, danced about the Room in a frantic manner, tore her Hair and beat her Breast in all the Agonies of Despair; in which sad Condition her Aunt, who likewise arose at the News, found her. The good old Lady applied her utmost Art to comfort her Niece. She told her, 'while there was Life, there was Hope: but that if he should die, her Affliction would be of no service to *Bellarmine*, and would only expose herself, which might probably keep her some time without any future Offer; that as Matters had happened, her wisest way would be to think no more of *Bellarmine*, but to endeavour to regain the Affections of *Horatio*.' 'Speak not to me,' cry'd the

5. "Your very humble servant. I understand you perfectly." 6. Lawsuit. 7. A hat ornament worn by soldiers.

disconsolate *Leonora*, 'is it not owing to me, that poor *Bellarmine* has lost his Life? have not these cursed Charms' (at which Words she looked stedfastly in the Glass,) 'been the Ruin of the most charming Man of this Age? Can I ever bear to contemplate my own Face again?' (with her Eyes still fixed on the Glass.) 'Am I not the Murderess of the finest Gentleman? No other Woman in the Town could have made any Impression on him.'[8] 'Never think of Things passed,' cries the Aunt, 'think of regaining the Affections of *Horatio*.' 'What Reason,' said the Niece, 'have I to hope he would forgive me? no, I have lost him as well as the other, and it was your wicked Advice which was the Occasion of all; you seduced me, contrary to my Inclinations, to abandon poor *Horatio*,' at which Words she burst into Tears; 'you prevailed upon me, whether I would or no, to give up my Affections for him; had it not been for you, *Bellarmine* never would have entered into my Thoughts; had not his Addresses been backed by your Persuasions, they never would have made any Impression on me; I should have defied all the Fortune and Equipage in the World: but it was you, it was you, who got the better of my Youth and Simplicity, and forced me to lose my dear *Horatio* for ever.'

The Aunt was almost borne down with this Torrent of Words, she however rallied all the Strength she could, and drawing her Mouth up in a Purse, began: 'I am not surprised, Niece, at this Ingratitude. Those who advise young Women for their Interest, must always expect such a Return: I am convinced my Brother will thank me for breaking off your Match with *Horatio* at any rate.' 'That may not be in your power yet,' answered *Leonora*; 'tho' it is very ungrateful in you to desire or attempt it, after the Presents you have received from him.' (For indeed true it is, that many Presents, and some pretty valuable ones, had passed from *Horatio* to the old Lady: but as true it is, that *Bellarmine* when he break-fasted with her and her Niece, had complimented her with a Brilliant from his Finger, of much greater Value than all she had touched of the other.)

The Aunt's Gall was on float[9] to reply, when a Servant brought a Letter into the Room; which *Leonora* hearing it came from *Bellarmine*, with great Eagerness opened, and read as follows:

Most Divine Creature,

The Wound which I fear you have heard I received from my Rival, is not like to be so fatal as those shot into my Heart, which have been fired from your Eyes, *tout-brillant*. Those are the only Cannons by which I am to fall: for my Surgeon gives me Hopes of being soon able to attend your *Ruelle*;[1] 'till when, unless you would do me an Honour which I have scarce the *Hardiesse* to think of, your Absence will be the greatest Anguish which can be felt by,

---

8. This sentence was added in the second edition.
9. Flooding; anger was once thought to be stimulated by the secretion of gall.

1. A morning reception in a fashionable lady's bedchamber.

MADAM,
Avec tout le respecte *in the World,*
        Your most Obedient, most Absolute
Devoté,
        Bellarmine'

As soon as *Leonora* perceived such Hopes of *Bellarmine's* Recovery, and that the Gossip Fame had, according to Custom, so enlarged his Danger, she presently abandoned all farther Thoughts of *Horatio,* and was soon reconciled to her Aunt, who received her again into Favour, with a more Christian Forgiveness than we generally meet with. Indeed it is possible she might be a little alarmed at the Hints which her Niece had given her concerning the Presents. She might apprehend such Rumours, should they get abroad, might injure a Reputation, which by frequenting Church twice a day, and preserving the utmost Rigour and Strictness in her Countenance and Behaviour for many Years, she had established.

Leonora's Passion returned now for *Bellarmine* with greater Force after its small Relaxation than ever. She proposed to her Aunt to make him a Visit in his Confinement, which the old Lady, with great and commendable Prudence advised her to decline: 'For,' says she, 'should any Accident intervene to prevent your intended Match, too forward a Behaviour with this Lover may injure you in the Eyes of others. Every Woman 'till she is married ought to consider of and provide against the Possibility of the Affair's breaking off.' *Leonora* said, 'she should be indifferent to whatever might happen in such a Case: for she had now so absolutely placed her Affections on this dear Man (so she called him) that, if it was her misfortune to lose him, she should for ever abandon all Thoughts of Mankind.' She therefore resolved to visit him, notwithstanding all the prudent Advice of her Aunt to the contrary, and that very Afternoon executed her Resolution.

The Lady was proceeding in her Story, when the Coach drove into the Inn where the Company were to dine, sorely to the dissatisfaction of Mr. *Adams,* whose Ears were the most hungry Part about him; he being, as the Reader may perhaps guess, of an insatiable Curiosity, and heartily desirous of hearing the End of this Amour, tho' he professed he could scarce wish Success to a Lady of so inconstant a Disposition.

Chapter V

A dreadful Quarrel which happened at the Inn where the Company dined, with its bloody Consequences to Mr. Adams.

As soon as the Passengers had alighted from the Coach, Mr. *Adams,* as was his Custom, made directly to the Kitchin, where he found *Joseph* sitting by the Fire and the Hostess anointing his Leg: for the Horse which

Mr. *Adams* had borrowed of his Clerk, had so violent a Propensity to kneeling, that one would have thought it had been his Trade as well as his Master's: nor would he always give any notice of such his Intention; he was often found on his Knees, when the Rider least expected it. This Foible however was of no great Inconvenience to the Parson, who was accustomed to it, and as his Legs almost touched the Ground when he bestrode the Beast, had but a little way to fall, and threw himself forward on such Occasions with so much dexterity, that he never received any Mischief; the Horse and he frequently rolling many Paces distance, and afterwards both getting up and meeting as good Friends as ever.

Poor *Joseph*, who had not been used to such kind of Cattle, tho' an excellent Horseman, did not so happily disengage himself: but falling with his Leg under the Beast, received a violent Contusion, to which the good Woman was, as we have said, applying a warm Hand with some camphirated Spirits just at the time when the Parson entered the Kitchin.

He had scarce express'd his Concern for *Joseph's* Misfortune, before the Host likewise entered. He was by no means of Mr. *Tow-wouse's* gentle Disposition, and was indeed perfect Master of his House and every thing in it but his Guests.

This surly Fellow, who always proportioned his Respect to the Appearance of a Traveller, from *God bless your Honour*, down to plain *Coming presently*, observing his Wife on her Knees to a Footman, cried out, without considering his Circumstances, 'What a Pox is the Woman about? why don't you mind the Company in the Coach? Go and ask them what they will have for Dinner?' 'My Dear,' says she, 'you know they can have nothing but what is at the Fire, which will be ready presently; and really the poor young Man's Leg is very much bruised.' At which Words, she fell to chafing more violently than before: the Bell then happening to ring, he damn'd his Wife, and bid her go in to the Company, and not stand rubbing there all day: for he did not believe the young Fellow's Leg was so bad as he pretended; and if it was, within twenty Miles he would find a Surgeon to cut it off. Upon these Words, *Adams* fetched two Strides across the Room; and snapping his Fingers over his Head muttered aloud, 'he would excommunicate such a Wretch for a Farthing: for he believed the Devil had more Humanity.' These Words occasioned a Dialogue between *Adams* and the Host, in which there were two or three sharp Replies, 'till *Joseph* bad the latter know how to behave himself to his Betters. At which the Host, (having first strictly surveyed *Adams*) scornfully repeating the Word *Betters*, flew into a Rage, and telling *Joseph* he was as able to walk out of his House as he had been to walk into it, offered to lay violent Hands on him; which perceiving, *Adams* dealt him so sound a Compliment over his Face with his Fist, that the Blood immediately gushed out of his Nose in a Stream. The Host being unwilling to be outdone in Courtesy, especially by a Person of *Adams's* Figure, returned the Favour with so much Gratitude, that the Parson's Nostrils likewise began to look a little redder than usual. Upon which he again assailed his Antagonist, and with another stroke laid him sprawling on the Floor.

The Hostess, who was a better Wife than so surly a Husband deserved, seeing her Husband all bloody and stretched along, hastened presently to his assistance, or rather to revenge the Blow which to all appearance was the last he would ever receive; when, lo! a Pan full of Hog's-Blood, which unluckily stood on the Dresser,[1] presented itself first to her Hands. She seized it in her Fury, and without any Reflection discharged it into the Parson's Face, and with so good an Aim, that much the greater part first saluted his Countenance, and trickled thence in so large a current down his Beard, and over his Garments, that a more horrible Spectacle was hardly to be seen or even imagined. All which was perceived by Mrs. *Slipslop*, who entered the Kitchin at that Instant. This good Gentlewoman, not being of a Temper so extremely cool and patient as perhaps was required to ask many Questions on this Occasion; flew with great Impetuosity at the Hostess's Cap, which, together with some of her Hair, she plucked from her Head in a moment, giving her at the same time several hearty Cuffs in the Face, which by frequent Practice on the inferiour Servants, she had learned an excellent Knack of delivering with a good Grace. Poor *Joseph* could hardly rise from his Chair; the Parson was employed in wiping the Blood from his Eyes, which had intirely blinded him, and the Landlord was but just beginning to stir, whilst Mrs. *Slipslop* holding down the Landlady's Face with her Left Hand, made so dextrous a use of her Right, that the poor Woman began to roar in a Key,[2] which alarmed all the Company in the Inn.

There happened to be in the Inn at this time, besides the Ladies who arrived in the Stage-Coach, the two Gentlemen who were present at Mr. *Tow-wouse's* when *Joseph* was detained for his Horse's-Meat, and whom we have before mentioned to have stopt at the Alehouse with *Adams*. There was likewise a Gentleman just returned from his Travels to *Italy*; all whom the horrid Outcry of Murther, presently brought into the Kitchin, where the several Combatants were found in the Postures already described.

It was now no difficulty to put an end to the Fray, the Conquerors being satisfied with the Vengeance they had taken, and the Conquered having no Appetite to renew the Fight. The principal Figure, and which engaged the Eyes of all was *Adams*, who was all over covered with Blood, which the whole Company concluded to be his own; and consequently imagined him no longer for this World. But the Host, who had now recovered from his Blow, and was risen from the Ground, soon delivered them from this Apprehension, by damning his Wife, for wasting the Hog's Puddings,[3] and telling her all would have been very well if she had not intermeddled like a B—— as she was; adding, he was very glad the Gentlewoman had paid her, tho' not half what she deserved. The poor Woman had indeed fared much the worst, having, besides the unmerciful Cuffs received, lost a Quantity of Hair which Mrs. *Slipslop* in Triumph held in her left Hand.

The Traveller, addressing himself to Miss *Grave-airs*, desired her not to be frightened: for here had been only a little Boxing, which he said to their *Disgracia* the *English* were *accustomata* to; adding, it must be however a Sight somewhat strange to him, who was just come from *Italy*, the *Italians* not being addicted to the *Cuffardo*, but *Bastonza*, says he. He then went up to *Adams*, and telling him he looked like the Ghost of *Othello*, bid him *not shake his gory Locks at him, for he could not say he did it.*[4] *Adams* very innocently answered, *Sir, I am far from accusing you.* He then returned to the Lady, and cried, 'I find the bloody Gentleman is *uno insipido del nullo senso. Damnata di me*, if I have seen such a *spectaculo* in my way from *Viterbo.*'[5]

One of the Gentlemen having learnt from the Host the Occasion of this Bustle, and being assured by him that *Adams* had struck the first Blow, whispered in his Ear: 'he'd warrant he would *recover.*' 'Recover! Master,' said the Host, smiling: 'Yes, yes, I am not afraid of dying with a Blow or two neither; I am not such a Chicken as that.' 'Pugh!' said the Gentleman, 'I mean you will recover Damages, in that Action which undoubtedly you intend to bring, as soon as a Writ can be returned from *London*;[6] for you look like a Man of too much Spirit and Courage to suffer any one to beat you without bringing your Action against him: He must be a scandalous Fellow indeed, who would put up a Drubbing whilst the Law is open to revenge it; besides, he hath drawn Blood from you and spoiled your Coat, and the Jury will give Damages for that too. An excellent new Coat upon my Word, and now not worth a Shilling!

'I don't care,' continued he, 'to intermeddle in these Cases: but you have a Right to my Evidence; and if I am sworn, I must speak the Truth. I saw you sprawling on the Floor, and the Blood gushing from your Nostrils. You may take your own Opinion; but was I in your Circumstances, every Drop of my Blood should convey an Ounce of Gold into my Pocket: remember I don't advise you to go to Law, but if your Jury were Christians, they must give swinging[7] Damages, that's all.' 'Master,' cry'd the Host, scratching his Head, 'I have no stomach to Law, I thank you. I have seen enough of that in the Parish, where two of my Neighbours have been at Law about a House, 'till they have both lawed themselves into a Goal.'[8] At which Words he turned about, and began to

---

4. A rearrangement of Macbeth's guilty words to the ghost of Banquo, *Macbeth* 3.4.
5. The gentleman's Italian is as dubious as his Shakespeare, consisting mostly of Italianized English ("accustomata" for *abituata*, "Cuffardo" from *cuff*, "disgracia" for *disgrazia*, and "damnato" for *dannato*). He confuses two senses of "dull," substituting *insipido* (tasteless, flat) for *insipiente* (ignorant, foolish); "Bastonza" is his invention for *bastone* (cudgel).
6. To initiate a lawsuit, the plaintiff had to obtain

a writ from the Court of Chancery directing the sheriff of the county to order the defendant's appearance in court.
7. Huge. The gentleman cautiously disavows advising the host to sue because as a lawyer (see title of chapter 3) he is aware that he could be charged with the crime of maintenance, for instigating or encouraging a suit in which he has no interest.
8. Jail; in this case presumably a debtors' prison.

enquire again after his Hog's Puddings, nor would it probably have been a sufficient Excuse for his Wife that she spilt them in his Defence, had not some Awe of the Company, especially of the *Italian* Traveller, who was a Person of great Dignity, with-held his Rage. Whilst one of the above-mentioned Gentlemen was employed, as we have seen him, on the behalf of the Landlord, the other was no less hearty on the side of Mr. *Adams*, whom he advised to bring his Action immediately. He said the Assault of the Wife was in Law the Assault of the Husband; for they were but one Person;[9] and he was liable to pay Damages, which he said must be considerable, where so bloody a Disposition appeared. *Adams* answered, if it was true that they were but one Person he had assaulted the Wife; for he was sorry to own he had struck the Husband the first Blow. 'I am sorry you own it too,' cries the Gentleman; 'for it could not possibly appear to the Court: for here was no Evidence present but the lame Man in the Chair, whom I suppose to be your Friend, and would consequently say nothing but what made for you.' 'How, Sir,' says *Adams*, 'do you take me for a Villain, who would prosecute Revenge in cold Blood, and use unjustifiable Means to obtain it? If you knew me and my Order, I should think you affronted both.' At the word Order, the Gentleman stared, (for he was too bloody to be of any modern Order of Knights,) and turning hastily about, said, every Man knew his own Business.

Matters being now composed, the Company retired to their several Apartments, the two Gentlemen congratulating each other on the Success of their good Offices, in procuring a perfect Reconciliation between the contending Parties; and the Traveller went to his Repast, crying, as the *Italian* Poet says,

> "*Je voi* very well, *que tutta e pace.*
> So send up Dinner, good *Boniface*'[1]

The Coachman began now to grow importunate with his Passengers, whose Entrance into the Coach was retarded by Miss *Grave-airs* insisting, against the Remonstrances of all the rest, that she would not admit a Footman into the Coach: for poor *Joseph* was too lame to mount a Horse. A young Lady, who was, as it seems, an Earl's Grand Daughter, begged it with almost Tears in her Eyes; Mr. *Adams* prayed, and Mrs. *Slipslop* scolded, but all to no purpose. She said, 'she would not demean herself to ride with a Footman: that there were Waggons on the Road: that if the Master of the Coach desired it, she would pay for two Places: but would suffer no such Fellow to come in.' 'Madam,' says *Slipslop*, 'I am sure no one can refuse another coming into a Stage Coach.' 'I don't know, Madam,' says the Lady, 'I am not much used to Stage-Coaches, I seldom travel in them.' 'That may be, Madam,' replied *Slipslop*, 'very

---

9. Under English common law, a wife was immune from punishment for a crime committed in the presence and under the presumed coercion of her husband.

1. The innkeeper in George Farquhar's *The Beaux' Stratagem* (1707), whose name became a generic term for his function.

good People do, and some People's Betters, for aught I know.' Miss *Grave-airs* said, 'Some Folks, might sometimes give their Tongues a liberty, to some People that were their Betters, which did not become them: for her part, she was not used to converse with Servants.' *Slipslop* returned, 'some People kept no Servants to converse with: for her part, she thanked Heaven, she lived in a Family where there were a great many; and had more under her own Command, than any paultry little Gentlewoman in the Kingdom.' Miss *Grave-airs* cry'd, 'she believed, her Mistress would not encourage such Sauciness to her Betters.' 'My Betters,' says *Slipslop*, 'who is my Betters, pray?' 'I am your Betters,' answered Miss *Grave-airs*, 'and I'll acquaint your Mistress.'—At which Mrs. *Slipslop* laughed aloud, and told her, 'her Lady was one of the great Gentry, and such little paultry Gentlewomen, as some Folks who travelled in Stage-Coaches, would not easily come at her.'

This smart Dialogue between some People, and some Folks, was going on at the Coach-Door, when a solemn Person riding into the Inn, and seeing Miss *Grave-airs*, immediately accosted her with, 'Dear Child, how do you?' She presently answered, 'O! Papa, I am glad you have overtaken me.' 'So am I,' answered he: 'for one of our Coaches is just at hand; and there being room for you in it, you shall go no farther in the Stage, unless you desire it.' 'How can you imagine I should desire it?' says she; so bidding *Slipslop*, 'ride with her Fellow, if she pleased;' she took her Father by the Hand, who was just alighted, and walked with him into a Room.

Adams instantly asked the Coachman in a Whisper, if he knew who the Gentleman was? The Coachman answered, he was now a Gentleman, and kept his Horse and Man: 'but Times are altered, Master,' said he, 'I remember, when he was no better born than myself.' 'Aye, aye,' says *Adams*. 'My Father drove the Squire's Coach,' answered he, 'when that very Man rode Postilion; but he is now his Steward, and a great Gentleman.' *Adams* then snapped his Fingers, and cry'd, he thought *she was some such Trollop*.

Adams made haste to acquaint Mrs. *Slipslop* with this good News, as he imagined it; but it found a Reception different from what he expected. That prudent Gentlewoman, who despised the Anger of Miss *Grave-airs*, whilst she conceived her the Daughter of a Gentleman of small Fortune, now she heard her Alliance with the upper Servants of a great Family in her Neighbourhood, began to fear her Interest with the Mistress. She wished she had not carried the Dispute so far, and began to think of endeavouring to reconcile her self to the young Lady before she left the Inn; when luckily, the Scene at *London*, which the Reader can scarce have forgotten, presented itself to her Mind, and comforted her with such Assurance, that she no longer apprehended any Enemy with her Mistress.

Every thing being now adjusted, the Company entered the Coach, which was just on its Departure, when one Lady recollected she had left her Fan, a second her Gloves, a third a Snuff-Box, and a fourth a Smelling-Bottle behind her; to find all which, occasioned some Delay, and much swearing of the Coachman.

As soon as the Coach had left the Inn, the Women all together fell to the Character of Miss *Grave-airs*, whom one of them declared she had suspected to be some low Creature from the beginning of their Journey; and another affirmed had not even the Looks of a Gentlewoman; a third warranted she was no better than she should be,[2] and turning to the Lady who had related the Story in the Coach, said, 'Did you ever hear, Madam, any thing so prudish as her Remarks? Well, deliver me from the Censoriousness of such a Prude.' The fourth added, 'O Madam! all these Creatures are censorious: but for my part, I wonder where the Wretch was bred; indeed I must own I have seldom conversed with these mean[3] kind of People, so that it may appear stranger to me; but to refuse the general Desire of a whole Company, hath something in it so astonishing, that, for my part, I own I should hardly believe it, if my own Ears had not been Witnesses to it.' 'Yes, and so handsome a young Fellow,' cries *Slipslop*, 'the Woman must have no Compassion in her, I believe she is more of a *Turk* than a Christian; I am certain if she had any Christian Woman's Blood in her Veins, the Sight of such a young Fellow must have warm'd it. Indeed there are some wretched, miserable old Objects that turn one's Stomach, I should not wonder if she had refused such a one; I am as nice[4] as herself, and should have cared no more than herself for the Company of *stinking* old Fellows: but hold up thy Head, *Joseph*, thou art none of those, and she who hath no *Compulsion* for thee is a *Myhummetman*, and I will maintain it.' This Conversation made *Joseph* uneasy, as well as the Ladies; who perceiving the Spirits which Mrs. *Slipslop* was in, (for indeed she was not a Cup too low) began to fear the Consequence; one of them therefore desired the Lady to conclude the Story—'Ay Madam,' said *Slipslop*, 'I beg your Ladyship to give us that Story you *commencated* in the Morning,' which Request that well-bred Woman immediately complied with.

Chapter VI

Conclusion of the Unfortunate Jilt.

Leonora having once broke through the Bounds which Custom and Modesty impose on her Sex, soon gave an unbridled Indulgence to her Passion. Her Visits to *Bellarmine* were more constant, as well as longer, than his Surgeon's; in a word, she became absolutely his Nurse, made his Water-gruel, administered him his Medicines, and, notwithstanding the prudent Advice of her Aunt to the contrary, almost intirely resided in her wounded Lover's Apartment.

The Ladies of the Town began to take her Conduct under consideration; it was the Chief Topick of Discourse at their Tea-Tables, and was

2. See above, p. 25, n. 5.
3. Low.

4. Fastidious.

very severely censured by the most part; especially by *Lindamira*, a Lady whose discreet and starch *Carriage*, together with a constant Attendance at Church three times a day, had utterly defeated many malicious Attacks on her own Reputation: for such was the Envy that *Lindamira's* Virtue had attracted, that notwithstanding her own strict Behaviour and strict Enquiry into the Lives of others, she had not been able to escape being the Mark of some Arrows herself, which however did her no Injury; a Blessing perhaps owed by her to the Clergy, who were her chief male Companions, and with two or three of whom she had been barbarously and unjustly calumniated.

'Not so unjustly neither perhaps,' says *Slipslop*, 'for the Clergy are Men as well as other Folks.'

The extreme Delicacy of *Lindamira's* Virtue was cruelly hurt by these Freedoms which *Leonora* allowed herself; she said, 'it was an Affront to her Sex, that she did not imagine it consistent with any Woman's Honour to speak to the Creature, or to be seen in her Company; and that, for her part, she should always refuse to dance at an Assembly with her, for fear of Contamination, by taking her by the Hand.'

But to return to my Story: As soon as *Bellarmine* was recovered, which was somewhat within a Month from his receiving the Wound, he set out, according to Agreement, for *Leonora's* Father's, in order to propose the Match and settle all Matters with him touching Settlements, and the like.

A little before his Arrival, the old Gentleman had received an Intimation of the Affair by the following Letter; which I can repeat *verbatim*, and which they say was written neither by *Leonora* nor her Aunt, tho' it was in a Woman's Hand. The Letter was in these Words:

'*Sir*,

I am sorry to acquaint you that your Daughter *Leonora* hath acted one of the basest, as well as most simple [1] Parts with a young Gentleman to whom she had engaged herself, and whom she hath (pardon the Word) jilted for another of inferiour Fortune, notwithstanding his superiour Figure. You may take what Measures you please on this Occasion; I have performed what I thought my Duty, as I have, tho' unknown to you, a very great Respect for your Family.'

The old Gentleman did not give himself the trouble to answer this kind Epistle, nor did he take any notice of it after he had read it, 'till he saw *Bellarmine*. He was, to say the truth, one of those Fathers who look on Children as an unhappy Consequence of their youthful Pleasures; which as he would have been delighted not to have had attended them, so was he no less pleased with any opportunity to rid himself of the Incumbrance. He pass'd in the World's Language as an exceeding good Father, being not only so rapacious as to rob and plunder all Mankind

1. Foolish.

to the utmost of his power, but even to deny himself the Conveniencies and almost Necessaries of Life; which his Neighbours attributed to a desire of raising immense Fortunes for his Children: but in fact it was not so, he heaped up Money for its own sake only, and looked on his Children as his Rivals, who were to enjoy his beloved Mistress, when he was incapable of possessing her, and which he would have been much more charmed with the Power of carrying along with him: nor had his Children any other Security of being his Heirs, than that the Law would constitute them such without a Will, and that he had not Affection enough for any one living to take the trouble of writing one.

To this Gentleman came *Bellarmine* on the Errand I have mentioned. His Person, his Equipage, his Family and his Estate seemed to the Father to make him an advantageous Match for his Daughter; he therefore very readily accepted his Proposals: but when *Bellarmine* imagined the principal Affair concluded, and began to open the incidental Matters of Fortune; the old Gentleman presently changed his Countenance, saying, 'he resolved never to marry his Daughter on a *Smithfield* Match;[2] that whoever had Love for her to take her, would, when he died, find her Share of his Fortune in his Coffers: but he had seen such Examples of Undutifulness happen from the too early Generosity of Parents, that he had made a Vow never to part with a Shilling whilst he lived.' He commended the Saying of *Solomon*,[3] *he that spareth the Rod, spoileth the Child:* but added, 'he might have likewise asserted, that *he that spareth the Purse, saveth the Child.*' He then ran into a Discourse on the Extravagance of the Youth of the Age; whence he launched into a Dissertation on Horses, and came at length to commend those *Bellarmine* drove. That fine Gentleman, who at another Season would have been well enough pleased to dwell a little on that Subject, was now very eager to resume the Circumstance of Fortune. He said, 'he had a very high value for the young Lady, and would receive her with less than he would any other whatever; but that even his Love to her made some Regard to worldly Matters necessary; for it would be a most distracting Sight for him to see her, when he had the Honour to be her Husband, in less than a Coach and Six.' The old Gentleman answer'd, 'Four will do, Four will do;' and then took a turn from Horses to Extravagance, and from Extravagance to Horses, till he came round to the Equipage again, wither he was no sooner arrived, than *Bellarmine* brought him back to the Point; but all to no purpose, he made his Escape from that Subject in a Minute, till at last the Lover declared, 'that in the present Situation of his Affairs it was impossible for him, though he loved *Leonora* more than *tout le monde,* to marry her without any Fortune.' To which the Father answered, 'he was sorry then his Daughter must lose so valuable a Match; that if he had an Inclination at present, it was not in his power to advance a Shilling: that he had had great Losses and been at great Expences on Projects, which, though he had great Expec-

2. A marriage for money, after the great London cattle market of that name, where one might be cheated in a "Smithfield bargain."
3. Proverbs 13:24.

tation from them, had yet produced him nothing: that he did not know what might happen hereafter, as on the Birth of a Son, or such Accident, but he would make no promise, or enter into any Article: for he would not break his Vow for all the Daughters in the World.'

In short, Ladies, to keep you no longer in suspense, *Bellarmine* having tried every Argument and Persuasion which he could invent,[4] and finding them all ineffectual, at length took his leave, but not in order to return to *Leonora*; he proceeded directly to his own Seat, whence after a few Days stay, he returned to *Paris*, to the great delight of the *French*, and the honour of the *English* Nation.

But as soon as he arrived at his home, he presently dispatched a Messenger, with the following Epistle to *Leonora*.

'*Adorable* and *Charmante*,

I am sorry to have the Honour to tell you I am not the *heureux* Person destined for your divine Arms. Your Papa hath told me so with a *Politesse* not often seen on this side *Paris*. You may perhaps guess his manner of refusing me—*Ah mon Dieu!* You will certainly believe me, Madam, incapable of my self delivering this *triste* Message: Which I intend to try the *French* Air to cure the Consequences of—*Ah jamais! Coeur! Ange!*—*Ah Diable!*—If your Papa obliges you to a Marriage, I hope we shall see you at *Paris*, till when the Wind that flows from thence will be the warmest *dans le Monde*: for it will consist almost entirely of my Sighs. *Adieu, ma Princesse! Ah L'Amour!*

Bellarmine'

I shall not attempt Ladies, to describe *Leonora's* Condition when she received this Letter. It is a Picture of Horrour, which I should have as little pleasure in drawing as you in beholding. She immediately left the Place, where she was the Subject of Conversation and Ridicule, and retired to that House I shewed you when I began the Story, where she hath ever since led a disconsolate Life, and deserves perhaps Pity for her Misfortunes more than our Censure, for a Behaviour to which the Artifices of her Aunt very probably contributed, and to which very young Women are often rendered too liable, by that blameable Levity in the Education of our Sex.

'If I was inclined to pity her,' said a young Lady in the Coach, 'it would be for the Loss of *Horatio*; for I cannot discern any Misfortune in her missing such a Husband as *Bellarmine*.'

'Why I must own,' says *Slipslop*, 'the Gentleman was a little falsehearted: but *howsumever* it was hard to have two Lovers, and get never a Husband at all—But pray, madam, what became of *Ourasho?*'

He remains, said the Lady, still unmarried, and hath applied himself so strictly to his Business, that he hath raised I hear a very considerable Fortune. And what is remarkable, they say, he never hears the name of

---

4. "Think of"; in classical rhetoric, invention is the process of finding arguments.

Leonora without a Sigh, nor hath ever uttered one Syllable to charge her with her ill Conduct towards him.[5]

Chapter VII

A very short Chapter, in which Parson Adams went a great Way.

The Lady having finished her Story received the Thanks of the Company, and now *Joseph* putting his Head out of the Coach, cried out, 'Never believe me, if yonder be not our Parson *Adams* walking along without his Horse.' 'On my Word, and so he is,' says *Slipslop*; 'and as sure as Two-pence, he hath left him behind at the Inn.' Indeed, true it is, the Parson had exhibited a fresh Instance of his Absence of Mind: for he was so pleased with having got *Joseph* into the Coach, that he never once thought of the Beast in the Stable; and finding his Legs as nimble as he desired, he sallied out brandishing a Crabstick, and had kept on before the Coach, mending and slackening his Pace occasionally, so that he had never been much more or less than a Quarter of a Mile distant from it.

Mrs. *Slipslop* desired the Coachman to overtake him, which he attempted, but in vain: for the faster he drove, the faster ran the Parson, often crying out, *Aye, aye, catch me if you can:* 'till at length the Coachman swore he would as soon attempt to drive after a Greyhound; and giving the Parson two or three hearty Curses, he cry'd, 'Softly, softly Boys,' to his Horses, which the civil Beasts immediately obeyed.

But we will be more courteous to our Reader than he was to Mrs. *Slipslop*, and leaving the Coach and its Company to pursue their Journey, we will carry our Reader on after Parson *Adams*, who stretched forwards without once looking behind him, 'till having left the Coach full three Miles in his Rear, he came to a Place, where by keeping the extremest Track to the Right, it was just barely possible for a human Creature to miss his Way. This Track however did he keep, as indeed he had a wonderful Capacity at these kinds of bare Possibilities; and travelling in it about three Miles over the Plain, he arrived at the Summit of a Hill, whence looking a great way backwards, and perceiving no Coach in sight, he sat himself down on the Turf, and pulling out his *Æschylus* determined to wait here for its Arrival.

He had not sat long here, before a Gun going off very near, a little startled him; he looked up, and saw a Gentleman within a hundred Paces taking up a Partridge, which he had just shot.

Adams stood up, and presented a Figure to the Gentleman which

5. In a similar story in *The Champion*, February 7, 1739/40, Fielding sketched what might have been Leonora's fate if she had wed Bellarmine. Amanda, a young widow of means, having declined the proposals of several country gentlemen out of a "foolish Desire . . . of making a Blaze in the World, and enjoying the Triumph of a Crowd of well-dress'd Admirers," becomes "the general Mark of Admiration among the Men, and Envy among the Women" of London society, only to succumb to the "too false, too artful, and too agreeable *Bellarmine*." After a brief country interlude of domestic bliss, her tight-fisted spouse returns to London, leaving her to endure her austere pregnancy "in the Company of an old Aunt, who was every Day throwing in my Teeth, the Folly I had committed in so disadvantageous a Match," while he wastes her fortune "in the Arms of a Strumpet."

would have moved Laughter in many: for his Cassock had just again fallen down below his great Coat, that is to say, it reached his Knees; whereas, the Skirts of his great Coat descended no lower than half way down his Thighs: but the Gentleman's Mirth gave way to his Surprise, at beholding such a Personage in such a Place.

Adams advancing to the Gentleman told him he hoped he had good Sport; to which the other answered, 'Very little.'[1] 'I see, Sir,' says *Adams*, 'you have *smote* one Partridge:' to which the Sportsman made no Reply, but proceeded to charge his Piece.

Whilst the Gun was charging, *Adams* remained in Silence, which he at last broke, by observing that it was a delightful Evening. The Gentleman, who had at first sight conceived a very distasteful Opinion of the Parson, began, on perceiving a Book in his Hand, and smoking[2] likewise the Information of the Cassock, to change his Thoughts, and made a small Advance to Conversation on his side, by saying, *Sir, I suppose you are not one of these Parts?*

Adams immediately told him, No; that he was a Traveller, and invited by the Beauty of the Evening and the Place to repose a little, and amuse himself with reading. 'I may as well repose myself too,' said the Sportsman; 'for I have been out this whole Afternoon, and the Devil a Bird have I seen 'till I came hither.'

'Perhaps then the Game is not very plenty hereabouts,' cries *Adams*. 'No, Sir,' said the Gentleman, 'the Soldiers, who are quartered in the Neighbourhood, have killed it all.'[3] 'It is very probable,' cries *Adams*, 'for Shooting is their Profession.' 'Ay, shooting the Game,' answered the other, 'but I don't see they are so forward to shoot our Enemies. I don't like that Affair of *Carthagena*;[4] if I had been there, I believe I should have done otherguess things, d—n me; what's a Man's Life when his Country demands it; a Man who won't sacrifice his Life for his Country deserves to be hanged, d—n me.' Which Words he spoke with so violent a Gesture, so loud a Voice, so strong an Accent, and so fierce a Countenance, that he might have frightened a Captain of Trained-Bands[5] at the Head of his Company; but Mr. *Adams* was not greatly subject to Fear, he told him intrepidly that he very much approved his Virtue, but disliked his Swearing, and begged him not to addict himself to so bad a Custom; without which he said he might fight as bravely as *Achilles* did.[6] Indeed he was charm'd with this Discourse, he told the Gentleman he would willingly have gone many Miles to have met a Man of his

1. In the five editions published in Fielding's lifetime, this phrase is not in quotation marks and "Very" is not capitalized, so that the phrase describes the sportsman's speech. Battestin added these accidentals to make it his reply.

2. See above, p. 86, n. 5.

3. It was illegal for soldiers or their officers to shoot game without permission of the landowner.

4. In March and April 1741, an expedition of ten thousand troops and thirty warships against this Spanish stronghold in the Caribbean failed disastrously because of the extreme timidity of the inexperienced General Wentworth, who repeat-

edly delayed his attacks until his men fell ill of fever. The opposition capitalized on the fiasco, blaming Walpole for sending a green force abroad while burdening and intimidating the populace with the seasoned army he maintained at home (against possible invasion by the French- and Spanish-supported Jacobite pretender).

5. Civilian militia.

6. In books 20 and 21 of the *Iliad*, prior to his killing of Hector, Achilles cuts a swath through the Trojan army and even battles the river Scamandros.

generous Way of thinking; that if he pleased to sit down, he should be greatly delighted to commune with him: for tho' he was a Clergyman, he would himself be ready, if thereto called, to lay down his Life for his Country.

The Gentleman sat down and *Adams* by him, and then the latter began, as in the following Chapter, a Discourse which we have placed by itself, as it is not only the most curious in this, but perhaps in any other Book.

Chapter VIII

A *notable Dissertation, by Mr.* Abraham Adams; *wherein that Gentleman appears in a political Light.*

'I do assure you, Sir,' says he, taking the Gentleman by the Hand, 'I am heartily glad to meet with a Man of your Kidney: for tho' I am a poor Parson, I will be bold to say, I am an honest Man, and would not do an ill Thing to be made a Bishop: Nay, tho' it hath not fallen in my way to offer so noble a Sacrifice, I have not been without Opportunities of suffering for the sake of my Conscience, I thank Heaven for them: for I have had Relations, tho' I say it, who made some Figure in the World; particularly a Nephew, who was a Shopkeeper, and an Alderman of a Corporation.[1] He was a good Lad, and was under my Care when a Boy, and I believe would do what I bad him to his dying Day. Indeed, it looks like extreme Vanity in me, to affect being a Man of such Consequence, as to have so great an Interest in[2] an Alderman; but others have thought so too, as manifestly appeared by the Rector, whose Curate I formerly was, sending for me on the Approach of an Election, and telling me if I expected to continue in his Cure, that I must bring my Nephew to vote for one Colonel *Courtly*, a Gentleman whom I had never heard Tidings of 'till that Instant. I told the Rector, I had no power over my Nephew's Vote, (God forgive me for such Prevarication!) That I supposed he would give it according to his Conscience, that I would by no means endeavour to influence him to give it otherwise. He told me it was in vain to equivocate: that he knew I had already spoke to him in favour of Esquire *Fickle* my Neighbour, and indeed it was true I had: for it was at a Season when the *Church was in Danger*,[3] and when all good Men expected they knew not what would happen to us all. I then answered boldly, If he thought I had given my Promise, he affronted me, in proposing any Breach of it. Not to be too prolix: I persevered, and so did my Nephew, in the Esquire's Interest, who was chose chiefly through his Means, and so I lost my Curacy. Well, Sir, but do you think the Esquire ever mentioned a Word of the Church? *Ne verbum quidem, ut ita dicam;*[4] within

---

1. Town or borough government.
2. Influence on.
3. This rallying cry of the "high church" Anglicans against toleration of dissenting protestant sects (1705), union with Scotland (1707), or any other perceived threat to the established church was an

antiministerial campaign slogan in the election of 1722. Clergy often electioneered, as the rector does here, for administration ("Court") candidates in the hope of church preferment.
4. "Not even a word, so to speak."

two Years he got a Place,[5] and hath ever since lived in *London*; where I have been informed, (but G— forbid I should believe that) that he never so much as goeth to Church. I remained, Sir, a considerable Time without any Cure, and lived a full Month on one Funeral Sermon, which I preached on the Indisposition of a Clergyman; but this by the Bye. At last, when Mr. *Fickle* got his Place, Colonel *Courtly* stood again; and who should make Interest[6] for him, but Mr. *Fickle* himself: that very identical Mr. *Fickle*, who had formerly told me, the Colonel was an Enemy to both the Church and State, had the Confidence to sollicite my Nephew for him, and the Colonel himself offered me to make me Chaplain to his Regiment, which I refused in favour of Sir *Oliver Hearty*, who told us, he would sacrifice every thing to his Country; and I believe he would, except his Hunting, which he stuck so close to, that in five Years together, he went but twice up to Parliament; and one of those Times, I have been told, never was within sight of the House. However, he was a worthy Man, and the best Friend I ever had: for by his Interest with a Bishop, he got me replaced into my Curacy, and gave me eight Pounds out of his own Pocket to buy me a Gown and Cassock, and furnish my House. He had our Interest while he lived, which was not many Years. On his Death, I had fresh Applications made to me; for all the World knew the Interest I had in my good Nephew, who now was a leading Man in the Corporation; and Sir *Thomas Booby*, buying the Estate which had been Sir *Oliver's*, proposed himself a Candidate. He was then a young Gentleman just come from his Travels,[7] and it did me good to hear him discourse on Affairs, which for my part I knew nothing of. If I had been Master of a thousand Votes, he should have had them all. I engaged my Nephew in his Interest, and he was elected, and a very fine Parliament-Man he was. They tell me he made Speeches of an Hour long; and I have been told very fine ones: but he could never persuade the Parliament to be of his Opinion.—*Non omnia possumus omnes.*[8] He promised me a Living, poor Man; and I believe I should have had it, but an Accident happened; which was, that my Lady had promised it before unknown to him. This indeed I never heard 'till afterwards: for my Nephew, who died about a Month before the Incumbent, always told me I might be assured of it. Since that Time, Sir *Thomas*, poor Man, had always so much Business, that he never could find Leisure to see me. I believe it was partly my Lady's fault too: who did not think my Dress good enough for the Gentry at her Table. However, I must do him the Justice to say, he never was ungrateful; and I have always found his Kitchin, and his Cellar too, open to me; many a time after Service on a *Sunday*, for I preach at four Churches, have I recruited my Spirits with a Glass of his Ale. Since my Nephew's Death, the Corporatioon is in other hands; and I am not a Man of that Consequence I was formerly. I have now no longer any Talents to lay out[9] in the Service

5. Government appointment.
6. Expert influence.
7. See below, p. 191, n. 3

8. "We cannot all do all" (Virgil, *Eclogues* 8.63).
9. An allusion to the parable of the talents, Matthew 25:14–30.

of my Country; and to whom nothing is given, of him can nothing be required.[1] However, on all proper Seasons, such as the Approach of an Election, I throw a suitabble Dash or two into my Sermons; which I have the pleasure to hear is not disagreeable to Sir *Thomas*, and the other honest Gentlemen my Neighbours, who have all promised me these five Years, to procure an Ordination for a Son of mine, who is now near Thirty, hath an infinite Stock of Learning, and is, I thank Heaven, of an unexceptionable Life; tho', as he was never at an University, the Bishop refuses to ordain him.[2] Too much Care cannot indeed be taken in admitting any to the sacred Office; tho' I hope he will never act so as to be a Disgrace to any Order: but will serve his God and his Country to the utmost of his power, as I have endeavoured to do before him; nay, and will lay down his Life whenever called to that purpose. I am sure I have educated him in those Principles; so that I have acquitted my Duty, and shall have nothing to answer for on that account: but I do not distrust him; for he is a good Boy; and if Providence should thow it in his way, to be of as much consequence in a public Light, as his Father once was, I can answer for him, he will use his Talents as honestly as I have done.'

Chapter IX

In which the Gentleman descants on Bravery and heroic Virtue, 'till an unlucky Accident puts an end to the Discourse.

The Gentleman highly commended Mr. *Adams* for his good Resolutions, and told him, 'he hoped his Son would tread in his Steps;' adding, 'that if he would not die for his Country, he would not be worthy to live in it; I'd make no more of shooting a Man that would not die for his Country, than—

'Sir,' said he, 'I have disinherited a Nephew who is in the Army, because he would not exchange his Commission,[1] and go to the *West-Indies*. I believe the Rascal is a Coward, tho' he pretends to be in love forsooth. I would have all such Fellows hanged, Sir, I would have them hanged.' *Adams* answered, 'that would be too severe: That Men did not make themselves; and if Fear had too much Ascendance in the Mind, the Man was rather to be pitied than abhorred: That Reason and Time might teach him to subdue it.' He said, 'a Man might be a Coward at one time, and brave at another. *Homer*,' says he, 'who so well understood and copied Nature, hath taught us this Lesson: for *Paris* fights, and *Hector* runs away:[2] nay, we have a mighty Instance of this in the

---

1. Adams's extrapolation from Luke 12:48: "For unto whomsoever much is given, of him much shall be required."
2. Though customary, a university education was not obligatory for ordination. A bishop had authority to determine the fitness of candidates who had attained the required age of twenty-four, usually by testing their knowledge of classical languages and church doctrine, assessing their piety, and reviewing testimonials to their character.

1. With an officer from another regiment.
2. In the *Iliad*, Paris is berated by Hector for shrinking from single combat with Helen's husband, Menelaos (3.30–45), and for lingering at home while the fighting goes on (6.325–31); yet he later fights fiercely, wounding Diomedes, one of the most formidable Greek heroes (11). Conversely, Hector, the pillar of Troy's defense, finally flees before the charge of the enraged Achilles (22).

History of later Ages, no longer ago, than the 705th Year of *Rome*, when
the Great *Pompey*, who had won so many Battles, and been honoured
with so many Triumphs, and of whose Valour, several Authors, especially *Cicero* and *Paterculus*, have formed such Elogiums; this very *Pompey* left the Battle of *Pharsalia* before he had lost it, and retreated to his
Tent, where he sat like the most pusillanimous Rascal in a Fit of Despair,
and yielded a Victory, which was to determine the Empire of the World,
to *Cæsar*.[3] I am not much travelled in the History of modern Times,
that is to say, these last thousand Years: but those who are, can, I make
no question, furnish you with parallel Instances.' He concluded therefore, that had he taken any such hasty Resolutions against his Nephew,
he hoped he would consider better and retract them. The Gentleman
answered with great Warmth, and talked much of Courage and his
Country, 'till perceiving it grew late, he asked *Adams*, 'what Place he
intended for that Night?' He told him, 'he waited there for the Stage-
Coach.' 'The Stage-Coach! Sir,' said the Gentleman, 'they are all past
by long ago. You may see the last yourself, almost three Miles before
us.' 'I protest and so they are,' cries *Adams*, 'then I must make haste and
follow them.' The Gentleman told him, 'he would hardly be able to
overtake them; and that if he did not know his Way, he would be in
danger of losing himself on the Downs; for it would be presently dark;
and he might ramble about all Night, and perhaps, find himself farther
from his Journey's End in the Morning than he was now. He advised
him therefore to accompany him to his House, which was very little out
of his way,' assuring him, 'that he would find some Country-Fellow in
his Parish, who would conduct him for Sixpence to the City, where he
was going.' *Adams* accepted this Proposal, and on they travelled, the
Gentleman renewing his Discourse on Courage, and the Infamy of not
being ready at all times to sacrifice our Lives to our Country. Night
overtook them much about the same time as they arrived near some
Bushes: whence, on a sudden, they heard the most violent Shrieks imaginable in a female Voice. *Adams* offered[4] to snatch the Gun out of his
Companion's Hand. 'What are you doing?' said he. 'Doing!' says *Adams*,
'I am hastening to the Assistance of the poor Creature whom some Villains are murdering.' 'You are not mad enough, I hope,' says the
Gentleman, trembling: 'Do you consider this Gun is only charged with
Shot, and that the Robbers are most probably furnished with Pistols
loaded with Bullets? This is no Business of ours; let us make as much
haste as possible out of the way, or we may fall into their Hands ourselves.' The Shrieks now encreasing, *Adams* made no Answer, but snapt
his Fingers, and brandishing his Crabstick, made directly to the Place
whence the Voice issued; and the Man of Courage made as much Expe-

---

3. Julius Caesar's defeat of his fellow triumvir
Pompey in the battle of Pharsalia (48 B.C.) established his single rule. Plutarch says that when
Caesar's infantry routed a superior cavalry force
and turned his flank, Pompey walked back to his
tent "like a man bereft of sense . . . who had
utterly forgotten he was Pompey the Great" (*Lives*,

"Pompey," 72, B. Perrin trans.). The "Elogiums"
(eulogies) are in Cicero's speech for the Lex Man-
ilia (66 B.C.), investing Pompey with supreme
command in Asia, and the *Roman History* of C.
Velleius Paterculus, who said it would take many
volumes to do justice to Pompey's greatness (2.29).
4. Attempted.

dition towards his own Home, whither he escaped in a very short time
without once looking behind him: where we will leave him, to contemplate his own Bravery, and to censure the want[5] of it in others; and
return to the good *Adams*, who, on coming up to the Place whence the
Noise proceeded, found a Woman struggling with a Man, who had thrown
her on the Ground, and had almost overpowered her. The great Abilities
of Mr. *Adams* were not necessary to have formed a right Judgment of
this Affair, on the first sight. He did not therefore want the Entreaties of
the poor Wretch to assist her, but lifting up his Crabstick, he immediately levelled a Blow at that Part of the Ravisher's Head, where, according to the Opinion of the Ancients, the Brains of some Persons are
deposited, and which he had undoubtedly let forth, had not Nature,
(who, as wise Men have observed, equips all Creatures with what is most
expedient for them;) taken a provident Care, (as she always doth with
those she intends for Encounters) to make this part of the Head three
times as thick as those of ordinary Men, who are designed to exercise
Talents which are vulgarly called rational, and for whom, as Brains are
necessary, she is obliged to leave some room for them in the Cavity of
the Skull: whereas, those Ingredients being entirely useless to Persons of
the heroic Calling, she hath an Opportunity of thickening the Bone, so
as to make it less subject to any Impression or liable to be cracked or
broken; and indeed, in some who are predestined to the Command of
Armies and Empires, she is supposed sometimes to make that Part perfectly solid.

As a Game-Cock when engaged in amorous Toying with a Hen, if
perchance he espies another Cock at hand, immediately quits his Female,
and opposes himself to his Rival; so did the Ravisher, on the Information
of the Crabstick, immediately leap from the Woman, and hasten to
assail the Man. He had no Weapons but what Nature had furnished
him with. However, he clenched his Fist, and presently darted it at that
Part of *Adams's* Breast where the Heart is lodged. *Adams* staggered at
the Violence of the Blow, when throwing away his Staff, he likewise
clenched that Fist which we have before commemorated, and would
have discharged it full in the Breast of his Antagonist, had he not dex-
terously caught it with his left Hand, at the same time darting his Head,
(which some modern Heroes, of the lower Class, use like the Battering-
Ram of the Ancients, for a Weapon of Offence; another Reason to admire
the Cunningness of Nature, in composing it of those impenetrable
Materials) dashing his Head, I say, into the Stomach of *Adams*, he tumbled him on his Back, and not having any regard to the Laws of Heroism, which would have restrained him from any farther Attack on his
Enemy, 'till he was again on his Legs, he threw himself upon him, and
laying hold on the Ground with his left Hand, he with his right bela-
boured the Body of *Adams* 'till he was weary, and indeed, 'till he concluded (to use the Language of fighting) *that he had done his Business*;

5. Lack.

or, in the Language of Poetry, *that he had sent him to the Shades below*; in plain *English, that he was dead.*

But *Adams*, who was no Chicken,[6] and could bear a drubbing as well as any boxing Champion in the Universe, lay still only to watch his Opportunity; and now perceiving his Antagonist to pant with his Labours, he exerted his utmost Force at once, and with such Success, that he overturned him and became his Superiour; when fixing one of his Knees in his Breast, he cried out in an exulting Voice, *It is my turn now*: and after a few Minutes constant Application, he gave him so dextrous a Blow just under his Chin, that the Fellow no longer retained any Motion, and *Adams* began to fear he had struck him once too often; for he often asserted, 'he should be concerned to have the Blood of even the Wicked upon him.'

Adams got up, and called aloud to the young Woman,—'Be of good cheer, Damsel,' said he, 'you are no longer in danger of your Ravisher, who, I am terribly afraid, lies dead at my Feet; but G— forgive me what I have done in Defence of Innocence.' The poor Wretch, who had been sometime in recovering Strength enough to rise, and had afterwards, during the Engagement, stood trembling, being disabled by Fear, even from running away, hearing her Champion was victorious, came up to him, but not without Apprehensions, even of her Deliverer; which, however, she was soon relieved from, by his courteous Behaviour and gentle Words. They were both standing by the Body, which lay motionless on the Ground, and which *Adams* wished to see stir much more than the Woman did, when he earnestly begged her to tell him 'by what Misfortune she came, at such a time of Night, into so lonely a Place?' She acquainted him, 'she was travelling towards *London*, and had accidentally met with the Person from whom he had delivered her, who told her he was likewise on his Journey to the same Place, and would keep her Company; an Offer which, suspecting no harm, she had accepted; that he told her, they were at a small distance from an Inn where she might take up her Lodging that Evening, and he would show her a nearer way to it than by following the Road. That if she had suspected him (which she did not, he spoke so kindly to her,) being alone on these Downs in the dark, she had no human Means to avoid him; that therefore she put her whole Trust in Providence, and walk'd on, expecting every Moment to arrive at the Inn; when, on a sudden, being come to those Bushes, he desired her to stop, and after some rude Kisses, which she resisted, and some Entreaties, which she rejected, he laid violent hands on her, and was attempting to execute his wicked Will, when, she thanked G—, he timely came up and prevented him.' *Adams* encouraged her for saying, she had put her whole Trust in Providence, and told her 'he doubted not but Providence had sent him to her Deliverance, as a Reward for that Trust. He wished indeed he had not deprived the wicked Wretch of Life, but G—'s Will be done;' he said, 'he hoped

6. Coward.

the Goodness of his Intention would excuse him in the next World, and he trusted in her Evidence to acquit him in this.' He was then silent, and began to consider with himself, whether it would be properer to make his Escape, or to deliver himself into the hands of Justice; which Meditation ended, as the Reader will see in the next Chapter.

Chapter X

Giving an Account of the Strange Catastrophe of the preceding Adventure, which drew poor Adams *into fresh Calamities; and who the Woman was who owed the Preservation of her Chastity to his victorious Arm.*

The Silence of *Adams*, added to the Darkness of the Night, and Loneliness of the Place, struck dreadful Apprehensions into the poor Woman's Mind: She began to fear as great an Enemy in her Deliverer, as he had delivered her from; and as she had not Light enough to discover the Age of *Adams*, and the Benevolence visible in his Countenance, she suspected he had used her as some very honest Men have used their Country; and had rescued her out of the hands of one Rifler, in order to rifle her himself.[1] Such were the Suspicions she drew from his Silence: but indeed they were ill-grounded. He stood over his vanquished Enemy, wisely weighing in his Mind the Objections which might be made to either of the two Methods of proceeding mentioned in the last Chapter, his Judgment sometimes inclining to the one and sometimes to the other; for both seemed to him so equally adviseable, and so equally dangerous, that probably he would have ended his Days, at least two or three of them, on that very Spot, before he had taken any Resolution: At length he lifted up his Eyes, and spied a Light in the distance, to which he instantly addressed himself with *Heus tu, Traveller, heus tu!*[2] He presently heard several Voices, and perceived the Light approaching toward him. The Persons who attended the Light began some to laugh, others to sing, and others to hollow, at which the Woman testified some Fear, (for she had concealed her Suspicions of the Parson himself,) but *Adams* said, 'Be of good cheer, Damsel, and repose thy Trust in the same Providence, which hath hitherto protected thee, and never will forsake the Innocent.' These People who now approached were no other, Reader, than a Set of young Fellows, who came to these Bushes in pursuit of a Diversion which they call *Bird-batting*. This, if thou art ignorant of it (as perhaps if thou hast never travelled beyond *Kensington, Islington, Hackney*, or the *Borough*,[3] thou mayst be) I will inform thee, is performed by holding a large Clap-Net[4] before a Lanthorn, and at the same time, beating the Bushes: for the Birds, when they are disturbed from

---

1. An allusion to the conduct of some leaders of the opposition after Walpole resigned in February 1742 (see below, p. 390). This passage, from the beginning of the chapter to ". . . vanquished Enemy," was added in the second edition.
2. "Ho you!" (Latin).
3. Now in central London, these were then sub-

urbs or rural villages to the west, north, northeast, and south respectively. Fashionable diversions were to be found in Kensington and Islington, and "the Borough" (a common way of referring to the less reputable Borough of Southwark, south of the Thames) was the site of a popular fair.
4. A net that is closed by pulling a string.

their Places of Rest, or Roost, immediately make to the Light, and so are enticed within the Net. *Adams* immediately told them, what had happened, and desired them, 'to hold the Lanthorn to the Face of the Man on the ground, for he feared he had *smote* him fatally.' But indeed his Fears were frivolous, for the Fellow, though he had been stunned by the last Blow he received, had long since recovered his Senses, and finding himself quit of *Adams*, had listened attentively to the Discourse between him and the young Woman; for whose Departure he had patiently waited, that he might likewise withdraw himself, having no longer Hopes of succeeding in his Desires, which were moreover almost as well cooled by Mr. *Adams*, as they could have been by the young Woman herself, had he obtained his utmost Wish. This Fellow, who had a Readiness at improving any Accident, thought he might now play a better part than that of a dead Man; and accordingly, the moment the Candle was held to his Face, he leapt up, and laying hold on *Adams*, cried out, 'No, Villain, I am not dead, though you and your wicked Whore might well think me so, after the barbarous Cruelties you have exercised on me. Gentlemen,' said he, 'you are luckily come to the Assistance of a poor Traveller, who would otherwise have been robbed and murdered by this vile Man and Woman, who led me hither out of my way from the High-Road, and both falling on me have used me as you see.' *Adams* was going to answer, when one of the young Fellows, cry'd, 'D—n them, let's carry them both before the Justice.' The poor Woman began to tremble, and *Adams* lifted up his Voice, but in vain. Three or four of them laid hands on him, and one holding the Lanthorn to his Face, they all agreed, *he had the most villainous Countenance* they ever beheld, and an Attorney's Clerk who was of the Company declared, *he was sure he had remembered him at the Bar*. As to the Woman, her Hair was dishevelled in the Struggle, and her Nose had bled, so that they could not perceive whether she was handsome or ugly: but they said her Fright plainly discovered her Guilt. And searching her Pockets, as they did those of *Adams* for Money, which the Fellow said he had lost, they found in her Pocket a Purse with some Gold in it, which abundantly convinced them, especially as the Fellow offered to swear to it. Mr. *Adams* was found to have no more than one Halfpenny about him. This the Clerk said, 'was a great Presumption that he was an old Offender, by cunningly giving all the Booty to the Woman.' To which all the rest readily assented.

This Accident promising them better Sport, than what they had proposed, they quitted their Intention of catching Birds, and unanimously resolved to proceed to the Justice with the Offenders. Being informed what a desperate Fellow *Adams* was, they tied his Hands behind him, and having hid their Nets among the Bushes, and the Lanthorn being carried before them, they placed the two Prisoners in their Front, and then began their March: *Adams* not only submitting patiently to his own Fate, but comforting and encouraging his Companion under her Sufferings.

Whilst they were on their way, the Clerk informed the rest, that this

Adventure would prove a very beneficial one: for that they would all be entitled to their Proportions of 80 *l.* for apprehending the Robbers.[5] This occasion'd a Contention concerning the Parts which they had severally born in taking them; one insisting, 'he ought to have the greatest Share, for he had first laid his Hands on *Adams;*' another claiming a superior Part for having first held the Lanthorn to the Man's Face, on the Ground, by which, he said, 'The whole was discovered.' The Clerk claimed four fifths of the Reward, for having proposed to search the Prisoners; and likewise the carrying them before the Justice: he said indeed, 'in strict Justice he ought to have the whole.' These Claims however they at last consented to refer to future Decision, but seem'd all to agree that the Clerk was intitled to a Moiety. They then debated what Money should be allotted to the young Fellow, who had been employed only in holding the Nets. He very modestly said, 'that he did not apprehend any large Proportion would fall to his share; but hoped they would allow him something: he desired them to consider, that they had assigned their Nets to his Care, which prevented him from being as forward as any in laying hold of the Robbers, (for so these innocent People were called;) that if he had not occupied the Nets, some other must; concluding however that he should be contented with the smallest Share imaginable, and should think that rather their Bounty than his Merit.' But they were all unanimous in excluding him from any Part whatever, the Clerk particularly swearing, 'if they give him a Shilling, they might do what they pleased with the rest; for he would not concern himself with the Affair.' This Contention was so hot, and so totally engaged the Attention of all the Parties, that a dextrous nimble Thief, had he been in Mr. *Adams's* situation, would have taken care to have given the Justice no Trouble that Evening. Indeed it required not the Art of a *Shepherd*[6] to escape, especially as the Darkness of the Night would have so much befriended him: but *Adams* trusted rather to his Innocence than his Heels, and without thinking of Flight, which was easy, or Resistance (which was impossible, as there were six lusty young Fellows, besides the Villain himself, present) he walked with perfect Resignation the way they thought proper to conduct him.

Adams frequently vented himself in Ejaculations during their Journey; at last poor *Joseph Andrews* occuring to his Mind, he could not refrain sighing forth his Name, which being heard by his Companion in Affliction, she cried, with some Vehemence, 'Sure I should know that Voice, you cannot certainly, Sir, be Mr. *Abraham Adams?*' 'Indeed Damsel,' says he, 'that is my Name; there is something also in your Voice, which persuades me I have heard it before.' 'La, Sir,' says she, 'don't you remember poor *Fanny?*' 'How *Fanny!*' answered *Adams*, 'indeed I very well remember you; what can have brought you hither?' 'I have told you Sir,' replied she, 'I was travelling towards *London*; but I thought you mentioned *Joseph Andrews*, pray what is become of him?'

5. See above, p. 56, n. 3.
6. Jack Sheppard (1702–24), a robber who repeatedly escaped prison, including the most secure cell in Newgate. His exploits were celebrated in a flood of popular literature, including two accounts by Defoe (see above, p. 71, n. 4).

'I left him, Child, this Afternoon,' said *Adams*, 'in the Stage-Coach, in his way towards our Parish, whither he is going to see you.' 'To see me? La, Sir,' answered *Fanny*, 'sure you jeer me; what should he be going to see me for?' 'Can you ask that?' replied *Adams*. 'I hope *Fanny* you are not inconstant; I assure you he deserves much better of you.' 'La! Mr. *Adams*,' said she, 'what is Mr. *Joseph* to me? I am sure I never had any thing to say to him, but as one Fellow-Servant might to another.' 'I am sorry to hear this,' said *Adams*, 'a vertuous Passion for a young Man, is what no Woman need be ashamed of. You either do not tell me Truth, or you are false to a very worthy Man.' *Adams* then told her what had happened at the Inn, to which she listened very attentively; and a Sigh often escaped from her, notwithstanding her utmost Endeavours to the contrary, nor could she prevent herself from asking a thousand Questions, which would have assured any one but *Adams*, who never saw farther into People than they desired to let him, of the Truth of a Passion she endeavoured to conceal. Indeed the Fact was, that this poor Girl having heard of *Joseph's* Misfortune by some of the Servants belonging to the Coach, which we have formerly mentioned to have stopped at the Inn while the poor Youth was confined to his Bed, that instant abandoned the Cow she was milking, and taking with her a little Bundle of Clothes under her Arm, and all the Money she was worth in her own Purse, without consulting any one, immediately set forward, in pursuit of One, whom, notwithstanding her shyness to the Parson, she loved with inexpressible Violence, though with the purest and most delicate Passion. This Shyness therefore, as we trust it will recommend her Character to all our Female Readers, and not greatly surprise such of our Males as are well acquainted with the younger part of the other Sex, we shall not give our selves any trouble to vindicate.

Chapter XI

What happened to them while before the Justice.
A Chapter very full of Learning.

Their Fellow-Travellers were so engaged in the hot Dispute concerning the Division of the Reward for apprehending these innocent People, that they attended very little to their Discourse. They were now arrived at the Justice's House, and sent one of his Servants in to acquaint his Worship, that they had taken two Robbers, and brought them before him. The Justice, who was just returned from a Fox-Chace, and had not yet finished his Dinner, ordered them to carry the Prisoners into the Stable, whither they were attended by all the Servants in the House, and all the People of the Neighbourhood, who flock'd together to see them with as much Curiosity as if there was something uncommon to be seen, or that a Rogue did not look like other People.

The Justice being now in the height of his Mirth and his Cups, bethought himself of the Prisoners, and telling his Company he believed they should have good Sport in their Examination, he ordered them into his Presence. They had no sooner entered the Room, than he began to revile them, saying, 'that Robberies on the Highway were now grown so frequent, that People could not sleep safely in their Beds, and assured them they both should be made Examples of at the ensuing Assizes.' After he had gone on some time in this manner, he was reminded by his Clerk, 'that it would be proper to take the Deposition of the Witnesses against them.' Which he bid him do, and he would light his Pipe in the mean time. Whilst the Clerk was employed in writing down the Depositions of the Fellow who had pretended to be robbed, the Justice employed himself in cracking Jests on poor *Fanny*, in which he was seconded by all the Company at Table. One asked, 'whether she was to be indicted for a *Highwayman!*' Another whispered in her Ear, 'if she had not provided herself a great Belly,[1] he was at her service.' A third said, 'he warranted she was a Relation of *Turpin*.[2] To which one of the Company, a great Wit, shaking his Head and then his Sides, answered, 'he believed she was nearer related to *Turpis*;[3] at which there was an universal Laugh. They were proceeding thus with the poor Girl, when somebody smoaking the Cassock, peeping forth from under the Great Coat of *Adams*, cried out, 'What have we here, a Parson?' 'How, Sirrah,' says the Justice, 'do you go a robbing in the Dress of a Clergyman? let me tell you, your Habit will not entitle you to the *Benefit of the Clergy*.'[4] 'Yes,' said the witty Fellow, 'he will have one Benefit of Clergy, he will be exalted above the Heads of the People,'[5] at which there was a second Laugh. And now the witty Spark, seeing his Jokes take, began to rise in Spirits; and turning to *Adams*, challenged him to *cap* Verses,[6] and provoking him by giving the first Blow, he repeated,

Molle meum levibus cord est vilebile Telis.[7]

Upon which *Adams*, with a Look full of ineffable Contempt, told him, he deserved scourging for his Pronuntiation. The witty Fellow answered, 'What do you deserve, Doctor, for not being able to answer the first time? Why, I'll give you one you Blockhead—with an S?

Si licet, ut fulvum spectatur in igdibus haurum.[8]

---

1. Pregnancy was a ground for commuting or postponing capital punishment; hence it was common for a female offender to "plead her belly."
2. Dick Turpin, a notorious highwayman, had been hanged in 1739.
3. The Latin word for "foul" or "shameful."
4. Under the ancient *privilegium clericale* (familiarly referred to as "clergy"), a person in holy orders (or anyone who could demonstrate the ability to read) could either plead exemption from secular jurisdiction after arraignment or (more commonly) avoid hanging after conviction for certain capital crimes; but by this time highway robbery was among those excluded from this exemption.
5. Church pulpits were elevated, though not as high as the gallows.
6. A schoolboy game in which the competitors must answer a quotation with another beginning with the last letter of the first.

7. A mangled line from Ovid: "*molle meum levibusque cor est violabile telis*" ("Tender is my heart, and easily pierced by the light shaft," *Heroides* 15.79, G. Showerman trans.). Like all the wit's subsequent quotations, it is drawn from the second part (*Brevissima Institutio . . . Grammatices*) of *A Short Introduction of Grammar*, which gives "*levibus*" but not his other alterations. This book, commonly referred to by Fielding and others as "Lily's Grammar," had been a royally decreed textbook in the lower grades for two centuries; hence more than a few of Fielding's contemporary readers might recognize the source of the wit's "learning" as well as its limitations.
8. Another garbling of Ovid: "*scilicet ut fulvum spectatur in ignibus aurum*" ("Certainly as tawny gold is tested in fire," *Tristia* 1.5.25). In the fourth edition, "*igdibus*" is corrected, but Battestin retains it as consistent with the wit's other errors.

'What can'st not with an *M* neither? Thou art a pretty Fellow for a Parson—. Why did'st not steal some of the Parson's *Latin* as well as his Gown?' Another at the Table then answered, 'If he had, you would have been too hard for him; I remember you at the College a very Devil at this Sport, I have seen you catch a fresh Man: for no body that knew you, would engage with you.' 'I have forgot those things now,' cried the Wit, 'I believe I could have done pretty well formerly.—Let's see, what did I end with—an *M* again—ay—

Mars, Bacchus, Apollo, virorum.

I could have done it once.'—'Ah! evil betide you, and so you can now,' said the other, 'no body in this County will undertake you.' *Adams* could hold no longer; 'Friend,' said he, 'I have a Boy not above eight Years old, who would instruct thee, that the last Verse runs thus:

Ut sunt Divorum, Mars, Bacchus, Apollo, virorum.'[9]

'I'll hold thee a Guinea of that,' said the Wit, throwing the Money on the Table.—'And I'll go your halves,[1] ' cries the other. 'Done,' answered *Adams*, but upon applying to his Pocket, he was forced to retract, and own he had no Money about him; which set them all a laughing, and confirmed the Triumph of his Adversary, which was not moderate, any more than the Approbation he met with from the whole Company, who told *Adams* he must go a little longer to School, before he attempted to attack that Gentleman in *Latin*.

The Clerk having finished the Depositions, as well of the Fellow himself, as of those who apprehended the Prisoners, delivered them to the Justice; who having sworn the several Witnesses, without reading a Syllable, ordered his Clerk to make the *Mittimus*.[2]

Adams then said, 'he hoped he should not be condemned unheard.' 'No, no,' cries the Justice, 'you will be asked what you have to say for your self, when you come on your Trial, we are not trying you now; I shall only commit you to Goal: if you can prove your Innocence at *Size*, you will be found *Ignoramus*,[3] and so no Harm done.' 'Is it no Punishment, Sir, for an innocent Man to lie several Months in Goal?' cries *Adams*: 'I beg you would at least hear me before you sign the *Mittimus*.' 'What signifies all you can say?' says the Justice, 'is it not here in black and white against you? I must tell you, you are a very impertinent Fellow, to take up so much of my time.—So make haste with his *Mittimus*.'

9. A line from an instructional jingle early in the *Brevissima Institutio*: "*Propria quae maribus tribuntur, mascula dicas: / Ut sunt Divorum*; Mars, Bacchus, Apollo: virorum; / Ut Cato, Virgilius: fluviorum; ut, Tibris, Orontes: / Mensium; ut, October: ventorum; ut, Notus, Auster.*" ("Proper names that are assigned to the male kind you may call masculines, / As are those of Gods: Mars, Bacchus, Apollo; of men/ Like Cato, Virgil; of rivers, like the Tiber . . . ; / Of months . . . ; of winds. . . .") In *The Mock Doctor* (1732), sc. 9, Fielding's false physician makes the first two lines

pass for medical jargon.
1. Share the bet.
2. A writ committing a suspect to jail ("Goal" in the next paragraph).
3. When a grand jury found insufficient evidence to warrant prosecution, they delivered a writ of *ignoramus* ("we do not know" [any valid ground for trying the person]). "*Size*" is the Justice's colloquial term for the assizes, sessions of the county superior courts that might be held quarterly (see p. 84, n. 1) or semiannually (see p. 67, n. 4).

The Clerk now acquainted the Justice, that among other suspicious things, as a Penknife, &c. found in *Adams's* Pocket, they had discovered a Book written, as he apprehended, in Ciphers: for no one could read a Word in it. 'Ay,' says the Justice, 'this Fellow may be more than a common Robber, he may be in a Plot against the Government.—Produce the Book.' Upon which the poor Manuscript of *Æschylus*, which *Adams* had transcribed with his own Hand, was brought forth; and the Justice looking at it, shook his Head, and turning to the Prisoner, asked the Meaning of those Ciphers. 'Ciphers!' answer'd *Adams*, 'it is a Manuscript of *Æschylus*.' 'Who? who?' said the Justice. *Adams* repeated, '*Æschylus*.' 'That is an outlandish [4] Name,' cried the Clerk. 'A fictitious Name rather, I believe,' said the Justice. One of the Company declared it looked very much like *Greek*. '*Greek*!' said the Justice, 'why 'tis all Writing.' 'Nay,' says the other, 'I don't positively say it is so: for it is a very long time since I have seen any *Greek*. There's one,' says he, turning to the Parson of the Parish, who was present, 'will tell us immediately.' The Parson taking up the Book, and putting on his Spectacles and Gravity together, muttered some Words to himself, and then pronounced aloud—'Ay indeed it is a *Greek* Manuscript, a very fine piece of Antiquity. I make no doubt but it was stolen from the same Clergyman from whom the Rogue took the Cassock.' 'What did the Rascal mean by his *Æschylus*?' says the Justice. 'Pooh!' answered the Doctor with a contemptuous Grin, 'do you think that Fellow knows any thing of this Book? *Æschylus*! ho! ho! ho! I see now what it is.—A Manuscript of one of the Fathers. [5] I know a Nobleman who would give a great deal of Money for such a Piece of Antiquity.—Ay, ay, Question and Answer. The Beginning is the Catechism in *Greek*.—Ay,—Ay,—*Pollaki toi* [6]— What's your Name?'—'Ay, what's your Name?' says the Justice to *Adams*, who answered, 'It is *Æschylus*, and I will maintain it.'—'O it is,' says the Justice; 'make Mr. *Æschylus* his *Mittimus*. I will teach you to banter me with a false Name.' [7]

One of the Company having looked stedfastly at *Adams*, asked him, 'if he did not know Lady *Booby*?' Upon which *Adams* presently calling him to mind, answered in a Rapture, 'O Squire, are you there? I believe you will inform his Worship I am innocent.' 'I can indeed say,' replied the Squire, 'that I am very much surprized to see you in this Situation;' and then addressing himself to the Justice, he said, 'Sir, I assure you Mr. *Adams* is a Clergyman as he appears, and a Gentleman of very good

---

4. Foreign.
5. Christian writers of the first five to eight centuries.
6. "Often you." Battestin and Douglas Brooks suggest that the parson is misreading a phrase from Aeschylus' *Seven Against Thebes* (227), but neither there nor in the two places it occurs in *The Suppliants* (119, 131) is *pollaki* followed by *toi*. While the parson might well mistake the particle *de* that does follow for *toi*, A. R. Humphreys concludes that he is simply parroting a phrase from William Camden's widely used Greek gram-

mar, as the wit does earlier with the Latin grammar. In any case, his fakery extends beyond the language to matters more germane to his calling. "What is your name?" (a reminder of baptismal vows) is the opening of the Anglican catechism, not the work of one of the church fathers but developed in the sixteenth century; since it was designed to prepare children for confirmation, it was written in English.
7. This entire paragraph and the reference to it near the end of the next were added in the second edition.

Character. I wish you would enquire a little farther into this Affair: for I am convinced of his Innocence.' 'Nay,' says the Justice, 'if he is a Gentleman, and you are sure he is innocent, I don't desire to commit him, Not I; I will commit the Woman by herself, and take your Bail for the Gentleman; look into the Book, Clerk, and see how it is to take Bail; come—and make the *Mittimus* for the *Woman* as fast as you can.' 'Sir,' cries *Adams*, 'I assure you she is as innocent as myself.' 'Perhaps,' said the Squire, 'there may be some Mistake; pray let us hear Mr. *Adams's* Relation.' 'With all my heart,' answered the Justice, 'and give the Gentleman a Glass to whet his Whistle before he begins. I know how to behave myself to Gentlemen as well as another. No body can say I have committed a Gentleman since I have been in the Commission.' *Adams* then began the Narrative, in which, though he was very prolix, he was uninterrupted, unless by several *Hums* and *Ha's* of the Justice, and his Desire to repeat those Parts which seemed to him most material. When he had finished; the Justice, who, on what the Squire had said, believed every Syllable of his Story on his bare Affirmation, notwithstanding the Depositions on Oath to the contrary, began to let loose several *Rogues and Rascals* against the Witness, whom he ordered to stand forth, but in vain: the said Witness, long since finding what turn Matters were like to take, had privily withdrawn, without attending the Issue. The Justice now flew into a violent Passion, and was hardly prevailed with not to commit the innocent Fellows, who had been imposed on as well as himself. He swore, 'they had best find out the Fellow who was guilty of Perjury, and bring him before him within two Days; or he would bind them all over to their good Behaviour.'[8] They all promised to use their best Endeavours to that purpose, and were dismissed. Then the Justice insisted, that Mr. *Adams* should sit down and take a Glass with him; and the Parson of the Parish delivered him back the Manuscript without saying a Word; nor would *Adams*, who plainly discerned his Ignorance, expose it. As for *Fanny*, she was, at her own Request, recommended to the Care of a Maid-Servant of the House, who helped her to new dress, and clean herself.

The Company in the Parlour had not been long seated, before they were alarmed with a horrible Uproar from without; where the Persons who had apprehended *Adams* and *Fanny*, had been regaling, according to the Custom of the House, with the Justice's Strong Beer. These were all fallen together by the Ears, and were cuffing each other without any Mercy. The Justice himself sallied out, and with the Dignity of his Presence, soon put an end to the Fray. On his return into the Parlour, he reported, 'that the Occasion of the Quarrel, was no other than a Dispute, to whom, if *Adams* had been convicted, the greater Share of the Reward for apprehending him had belonged.' All the Company laughed at this, except *Adams*, who taking his Pipe from his Mouth fetched a

8. To prevent crimes and misdemeanors, a justice could require any persons "not of good fame" (including "nightwalkers" and "such as keep sus- picious company") to pledge a specified amount of security to be forfeited to the Crown on any future misbehavior.

deep Groan, and said, he was concerned to see so litigious a Temper in Men. That he remembered a Story something like it in one of the Parishes where his Cure lay: 'There was,' continued he, 'a Competition between three young Fellows, for the Place of the Clerk, which I disposed of, to the best of my Abilities, according to Merit: that is, I gave it to him who had the happiest Knack at setting a Psalm.[9] The Clerk was no sooner established in his Place, than a Contention began between the two disappointed Candidates, concerning their Excellence, each contending, on whom, had they two been the only Competitors, my Election would have fallen. This Dispute frequently disturbed the Congregation, and introduced a Discord into the Psalmody, 'till I was forced to silence them both. But alas, the litigious Spirit could not be stifled; and being no longer able to vent itself in singing, it now broke forth in fighting. It produced many Battles, (for they were very near a Match;) and, I believe, would have ended fatally, had not the Death of the Clerk given me an Opportunity to promote one of them to his Place; which presently put an end to the Dispute, and entirely reconciled the contending Parties.' *Adams* then proceeded to make some Philosophical Observations on the Folly of growing warm in Disputes, in which neither Party is interested.[1] He then applied himself vigorously to smoaking; and a long Silence ensued, which was at length broken by the Justice; who began to sing forth his own Praises, and to value himself exceedingly on his nice Discernment in the Cause, which had lately been before him. He was quickly interrupted by Mr. *Adams*, between whom and his Worship a Dispute now arose, whether he ought not, in strictness of Law, to have committed him, the said *Adams*; in which the latter maintained he ought to have been committed, and the Justice as vehemently held he ought not. This had most probably produced a Quarrel, (for both were very violent and positive in their Opinions) had not *Fanny* accidentally heard, that a young Fellow was going from the Justice's House, to the very Inn where the Stage-Coach in which *Joseph* was, put up. Upon this News, she immediately sent for the Parson out of the Parlour. *Adams*, when he found her resolute to go, (tho' she would not own the Reason, but pretended she could not bear to see the Faces of those who had suspected her of such a Crime,) was as fully determined to go with her; he accordingly took leave of the Justice and Company, and so ended a Dispute, in which the Law seemed shamefully to intend to set a Magistrate and a Divine together by the ears.

Chapter XII

A very delightful Adventure, as well to the Persons concerned as to the good-natur'd Reader.

Adams, Fanny, and the Guide set out together, about one in the Morning, the Moon then just being risen. They had not gone above a

---

9. See above, p. 25, n. 7.   1. Has anything tangible at stake.

Mile, before a most violent Storm of Rain obliged them to take shelter in an Inn, or rather Alehouse; where *Adams* immediately procured himself a good Fire, a Toast and Ale,[1] and a Pipe, and began to smoke with great Content, utterly forgetting every thing that had happened.

Fanny sat likewise down by the Fire; but was much more impatient at the Storm. She presently engaged the Eyes of the Host, his Wife, the Maid of the House, and the young Fellow who was their Guide; they all conceived they had never seen any thing half so handsome; and indeed, Reader, if thou art of an amorous Hue, I advise thee to skip over the next Paragraph; which to render our History perfect, we are obliged to set down, humbly hoping, that we may escape the Fate of *Pygmalion*:[2] for if it should happen to us or to thee to be struck with this Picture, we should be perhaps in as helpless a Condition as *Narcissus*; and might say to ourselves, *Quod petis est nusquam*.[3] Or if the finest Features in it should set Lady ———'s Image before our Eyes, we should be still in as bad Situation, and might say to our Desires, *Cœlum ipsum petimus stultitia*.[4]

Fanny was now in the nineteenth Year of her Age; she was tall and delicately shaped; but not one of those slender young Women, who seem rather intended to hang up in the Hall of an Anatomist, than for any other Purpose. On the contrary, she was so plump, that she seemed bursting through her tight Stays, especially in the Part which confined her swelling Breasts. Nor did her Hips want the Assistance of a Hoop to extend them. The exact Shape of her Arms, denoted the Form of those Limbs which she concealed; and tho' they were a little redden'd by her Labour, yet if her Sleeve slipt above her Elbow, or her Handkerchief discovered any part of her Neck, a Whiteness appeared which the finest *Italian* Paint would be unable to reach. Her Hair was of a Chesnut Brown, and Nature had been extremely lavish to her of it, which she had cut, and on *Sundays* used to curl down her Neck in the modern Fashion. Her Forehead was high, her Eye-brows arched, and rather full than otherwise. Her Eyes black and sparkling; her Nose, just inclining to the *Roman*; her Lips red and moist, and her Under-Lip, according to the Opinion of the Ladies, too pouting. Her Teeth were white, but not exactly even. The Small-Pox had left one only Mark on her Chin, which was so large, it might have been mistaken for a Dimple, had not her left Cheek produced one so near a Neighbour to it, that the former served only for a Foil to the latter. Her Complexion was fair, a little injured by the Sun, but overspread with such a Bloom, that the finest Ladies would have exchanged all their White for it: add to these, a Countenance in which tho' she was extremely bashful, a Sensibility appeared almost incredible; and a Sweetness, whenever she smiled, beyond either Imi-

1. Served with the toast in the ale.
2. A legendary king of Cyprus who, according to Ovid's *Metamorphoses*, fell in love with a statue of a woman he created.
3. In Greek legend, Aphrodite, goddess of love, punished Narcissus for spurning a nymph by hav-

ing the handsome youth fall in love with his own reflection. The Latin quotation expressing his frustration ("What you seek is nowhere") is from Ovid's *Metamorphoses* 3.433.
4. "Heaven itself we seek in our folly" (Horace, *Odes* 1.3.38, C. E. Bennett trans.).

tation or Description. To conclude all, she had a natural Gentility, superior to the Acquisition of Art, and which surprized all who beheld her.

This lovely Creature was sitting by the Fire with *Adams*, when her Attention was suddenly engaged by a Voice from an inner Room, which sung the following Song:

The SONG

SAY, Chloe,[5] *where must the Swain stray*
  Who is by thy Beauties undone,
To wash their Remembrance away,
  To what distant Lethe[6] *must run?*
The Wretch who is sentenc'd to die,
  May escape and leave Justice behind;
From his Country perhaps he may fly,
  But O can he fly from his Mind!

O Rapture! unthought of before,
  To be thus of Chloe *possest;*
Nor she, nor no Tyrant's hard Power,
  Her Image can tear from my Breast.
But felt not Narcissus *more Joy,*
  With his Eyes he beheld his lov'd Charms?
Yet what he beheld, the fond Boy
  More eagerly wish'd in his Arms.

How can it thy dear Image be,
  Which fills thus my Bosom with Woe?
Can aught bear Resemblance to thee,
  Which Grief and not Joy can bestow?
This Counterfeit snatch from my Heart,
  Ye Pow'rs, tho' with Torment I rave,
Tho' mortal will prove the fell Smart,
  I then shall find rest in my Grave.

Ah! see, the dear Nymph o'er the Plain,
  Comes smiling and tripping along,
A thousand Loves dance in her Train,
  The Graces around her all throng.
To meet her soft Zephyrus[7] *flies,*
  And wafts all the Sweets from the Flow'rs;
Ah Rogue! whilst he kisses her Eyes,
  More Sweets from her Breath he devours.

My Soul, whilst I gaze, is on fire,
  But her Looks were so tender and kind,
My Hope almost reach'd my Desire,
  And left lame Despair far behind.

---

5. Chloe and Strephon (last stanza) were stock names for lovers in the pastoral tradition.
6. In Greek and roman mythology, souls about to be reincarnated drank the waters of the river Lethe in Hades and forgot their past lives.
7. The personification of the west wind in Greek mythology.

Transported with Madness I flew,
  And eagerly seiz'd on my Bliss;
Her Bosom but half she withdrew,
  But half she refus'd my fond Kiss.

Advances like these made me bold,
  I whisper'd her, Love,—we're alone,
The rest let Immortals unfold,
  No Language can tell but their own.
Ah! Chloe, expiring, I cry'd,
  How long I thy Cruelty bore?
Ah! Strephon, she blushing reply'd,
  You ne'er was so pressing before.

Adams had been ruminating all this Time on a Passage in Æschylus, without attending in the least to the Voice, tho' one of the most melodious that ever was heard; when casting his Eyes on *Fanny,* he cried out, 'Bless us, you look extremely pale.' 'Pale! Mr. *Adams,*' says she, 'O Jesus!' and fell backwards in her Chair. *Adams* jumped up, flung his *Æschylus* into the Fire, and fell a roaring to the People of the House for Help. He soon summoned every one into the Room, and the Songster among the rest: But, O Reader, when this Nightingale, who was no other than *Joseph Andrews* himself, saw his beloved *Fanny* in the Situation we have described her, can'st thou conceive the Agitations of his Mind? If thou can'st not, wave that Meditation to behold his Happiness, when clasping her in his Arms, he found Life and Blood returning into her Cheeks; when he saw her open her beloved Eyes, and heard her with the softest Accent whisper, 'Are you *Joseph Andrews?*' 'Art thou my *Fanny?*' he answered eagerly, and pulling her to his Heart, he imprinted numberless Kisses on her Lips, without considering who were present.

If Prudes are offended at the Lusciousness[8] of this Picture, they may take their Eyes off from it, and survey Parson *Adams* dancing about the Room in a Rapture of Joy. Some Philosophers may perhaps doubt, whether he was not the happiest of the three; for the Goodness of his Heart enjoyed the Blessings which were exulting in the Breasts of both the other two, together with his own.[9] But we shall leave such Disquisitions as too deep for us, to those who are building some favourite Hypotheses, which they will refuse no Metaphysical Rubbish to erect, and support: for our part, we give it clearly on the side of *Joseph,* whose Happiness was not only greater than the Parson's, but of longer Duration: for as soon as the first Tumults of *Adams's* Rapture were over, he cast his Eyes towards the Fire, where *Æschylus* lay expiring; and immediately rescued the poor Remains, to-wit, the Sheepskin Covering of his dear Friend, which was

---

8. Voluptuousness.
9. In *An Inquiry Concerning Virtue, or Merit* (1699; rev. 1711), Shaftesbury argued for the social affections ("participation in the good of others," "sharing contentment and delight") as the principal source of happiness (*Characteristics,* ed. J. M. Robertson [London: 1900] 1.298). His application of "moral arithmetic" to the relations of virtue, vice, and happiness was greatly extended and systematized by Francis Hutcheson (1694–1747) in *An Inquiry into the Original of Our Ideas of Beauty and Virtue* (1725), in which he also claimed *"Benevolence is our greatest Happiness"* (177).

the Work of his own Hands, and had been his inseparable Companion for upwards of thirty Years.

Fanny had no sooner perfectly recovered herself, than she began to restrain the Impetuosity of her Transports; and reflecting on what she had done and suffered in the Presence of so many, she immediately covered with Confusion; and pushing *Joseph* gently from her, she begged him to be quiet: nor would admit of either Kiss or Embrace any longer. Then seeing Mrs. *Slipslop* she curt'sied, and offered to advance to her; but that high Woman would not return her Curt'sies; but casting her Eyes another way, immediately withdrew into another Room, muttering as she went, she wondered *who the Creature was*.

Chapter XIII

A *Dissertation concerning high People and low People, with Mrs.* Slipslop's *Departure in no very good Temper of Mind, and the evil Plight in which she left* Adams *and his Company.*

It will doubtless seem extremely odd to many Readers, that Mrs. *Slipslop*, who had lived several Years in the same House with *Fanny*, should in a short Separation utterly forget her. And indeed the truth is, that she remembered her very well. As we would not willingly therefore, that any thing should appear unnatural in this our History, we will endeavour to explain the Reasons of her Conduct; nor do we doubt being able to satisfy the most curious Reader, that Mrs. *Slipslop* did not in the least deviate from the common Road in this Behaviour; and indeed, had she done otherwise, she must have descended below herself, and would have very justly been liable to Censure.

Be it known then, that the human Species are divided into two sorts of People, to-wit, *High* People and *Low* People. As by High People, I would not be understood to mean Persons literally born higher in their Dimensions than the rest of the Species, nor metaphorically those of exalted Characters or Abilities; so by Low People I cannot be construed to intend the Reverse. High People signify no other than People of Fashion, and low People those of no Fashion. Now this word *Fashion*, hath by long use lost its original Meaning, from which at present it gives us a very different Idea: for I am deceived, if by Persons of Fashion, we do not generally include a Conception of Birth and Accomplishments superior to the Herd of Mankind; whereas in reality, nothing more was originally meant by a Person of Fashion, than a Person who drest himself in the Fashion of the Times; and the Word really and truly signifies no more at this day. Now the World being thus divided into People of Fashion, and People of no Fashion, a fierce Contention arose between them, nor would those of one Party, to avoid Suspicion, be seen publickly to speak to those of the other; tho' they often held a very good Correspondence in private. In this Contention, it is difficult to say which Party succeeded: for whilst the People of Fashion seized several Places to their own use, such as Courts, Assemblies, Operas, Balls, &c. the

People of no Fashion, besides one Royal Place called his Majesty's Bear-Garden,[1] have been in constant Possession of all Hops,[2] Fairs, Revels, &c. Two Places have been agreed to be divided between them, namely the Church and the Play-House; where they segregate themselves from each other in a remarkable Manner: for as the People of Fashion exalt themselves at Church over the Heads of the People of no Fashion; so in the Play-House they abase themselves in the same degree under their Feet.[3] This Distinction I have never met with any one able to account for; it is sufficient, that so far from looking on each other as Brethren in the Christian Language, they seem scarce to regard each other as of the same Species. This the Terms *strange Persons, People one does not know, the Creature, Wretches, Beasts, Brutes,* and many other Appellations evidently demonstrate; which Mrs. *Slipslop* having often heard her Mistress use, thought she had also a Right to use in her turn: and perhaps she was not mistaken; for these two Parties, especially those bordering nearly on each other, to-wit the lowest of the High, and the highest of the Low, often change their Parties according to Place and Time; for those who are People of Fashion in one place, are often People of no Fashion in another: And with regard to Time, it may not be unpleasant to survey the Picture of Dependance like a kind of Ladder; as for instance, early in the Morning arises the Postillion, or some other Boy which great Families no more than great Ships are without, and falls to brushing the Clothes, and cleaning the Shoes of *John* the Footman, who being drest himself, applies his Hands to the same Labours for Mr. *Second-hand* the Squire's Gentleman; the Gentleman in the like manner, a little later in the Day, attends the Squire; the Squire is no sooner equipped, than he attends the Levee of my Lord; which is no sooner over, than my Lord himself is seen at the Levee of the Favourite, who after his Hour of Homage is at an end, appears himself to pay Homage to the Levee of his Sovereign. Nor is there perhaps, in this whole Ladder of Dependance, any one Step at a greater distance from the other, than the first from the second: so that to a Philosopher the Question might only seem whether you would chuse to be a great Man at six in the Morning, or at two in the Afternoon. And yet there are scarce two of these, who do not think the least Familiarity with the Persons below them a Condescension, and if they were to go one Step farther, a Degradation.[4]

1. A tumultous arena for cudgel-playing, prize-fighting, bearbaiting, dogfights and bedevilling animals with fireworks at Hockley-in-the-Hole, an unsavory area near Clerkenwell Green in north central London.

2. Slang for popular dancing parties.

3. The enclosed pews of the gentry were elevated on a platform above the church floor. The front and side boxes of the theatre, favored by persons of quality, and the pit, frequented by wits and beaus, were below the inexpensive upper gallery occupied by apprentices, shopkeepers, and foot-men.

4. My colleague Thomas Rogers suggests that Fielding's "Ladder of Dependance" plays upon the familiar current idea of the Great Chain of Being, expounded or alluded to by Leibniz, Locke, Pope, and Bolingbroke, among others, and in particular its emphasis on the gradation and continuity of species. Thus Addison typically observes of the "Scale [ladder] of Beings" in *The Spectator* 519: "The whole Chasm in Nature, from a Plant to a Man, is filled up with diverse Kinds of Creatures, rising one over another by such a gentle and easie Ascent, that the little Transitions and Deviations from one Species to another are almost insensible." The allusion is also noted by Brian McCrea (see below, p. 489).

And now, Reader, I hope thou wilt pardon this long Digression, which seemed to me necessary to vindicate the great Character of Mrs. *Slip-slop*, from what low People, who have never seen high People, might think an Absurdity: but we who know them, must have daily found very high Persons know us in one Place and not in another, To-day, and not To-morrow; all which, it is difficult to account for, otherwise than I have here endeavour'd; and perhaps, if the Gods, according to the Opinion of some, made Men only to laugh at them, there is no part of our Behaviour which answers the End of our Creation better than this.

But to return to our History: *Adams*, who knew no more of all this than the Cat which sat on the Table, imagining Mrs. *Slipslop*'s Memory had been much worse than it really was, followed her into the next Room, crying out, 'Madam *Slipslop*, here is one of your old Acquaintance: Do but see what a fine Woman she is grown since she left Lady *Booby*'s Service.' 'I think I *reflect* something of her,' answered she with great Dignity, 'But I can't remember all the inferior Servants in our Family.' She then proceeded to satisfy *Adams's* Curiosity, by telling him, 'when she arrived at the Inn, she found a Chaise ready for her; that her Lady being expected very shortly in the Country, she was obliged to make the utmost haste, and in *Commensuration* [5] of *Joseph's* Lameness, she had taken him with her;' and lastly, 'that the excessive V*irulence* of the Storm had driven them into the House where he found them.' After which, she acquainted *Adams* with his having left his Horse, and exprest some Wonder at his having strayed so far out of his Way, and at meeting him, as she said, 'in the Company of that Wench, who she feared was no better than she should be.'

The Horse was no sooner put into *Adams's* Head, but he was immediately driven out by this Reflection on the Character of *Fanny*. He protested, 'he believed there was not a chaster Damsel in the Universe. I heartily wish, I heartily wish,' cry'd he, (snapping his Fingers) 'that all her Betters were as good.' He then proceeded to inform her of the Accident of their meeting; but when he came to mention the Circumstance of delivering her from the Rape, she said, 'she thought him properer for the Army than the Clergy: that it did not become a Clergyman to lay violent Hands on any one, that he should have rather prayed that she might be strengthened.' *Adams* said, 'he was very far from being ashamed of what he had done;' she replied, 'want of Shame was not the *Curry-curistick* of a Clergyman.' This Dialogue might have probably grown warmer, had not *Joseph* opportunely entered the Room, to ask leave of Madam *Slipslop* to introduce *Fanny*: but she positively refused to admit any such Trollops; and told him, 'she would have been burnt before she would have suffered him to get into a Chaise with her; if she had once *respected* him of having his Sluts way-laid on the Road for him,' adding, 'that Mr. *Adams* acted a very pretty Part, and she did not doubt but to see him a Bishop.' He made the best Bow he could, and cried out, 'I

---

5. That is, commiseration; Fielding substituted the next Slipslopism, "*Virulence*," for "Violence" in the second edition.

thank you, Madam, for that Right Reverend Appellation, which I shall take all honest Means to deserve.' 'Very honest Means,' returned she with a Sneer, 'to bring good People together.' At these Words, *Adams* took two or three Strides a-cross the Room, when the Coachman came to inform Mrs. *Slipslop*, 'that the Storm was over, and the Moon shone very bright.' She then sent for *Joseph*, who was sitting without with his *Fanny*; and would have had him gone with her: but he peremptorily refused to leave *Fanny* behind; which threw the good Woman into a violent Rage. She said, 'she would inform her Lady what Doings were carrying on, and did not doubt, but she would rid the Parish of all such People;' and concluded a long Speech full of Bitterness and very hard Words, with some Reflections on the Clergy, not decent to repeat: at last finding *Joseph* unmoveable, she flung herself into the Chaise, casting a Look at *Fanny* as she went, not unlike that which *Cleopatra* gives *Octavia* in the Play.[6] To say the truth, she was most disagreeably disappointed by the Presence of *Fanny*; she had from her first seeing *Joseph* at the Inn, conceived Hopes of something which might have been accomplished at an Alehouse as well as a Palace; indeed it is probable, Mr. *Adams* had rescued more than *Fanny* from the Danger of a Rape that Evening.

When the Chaise had carried off the enraged *Slipslop*; *Adams*, *Joseph*, and *Fanny* assembled over the Fire; where they had a great deal of innocent Chat, pretty enough; but as possibly, it would not be very entertaining to the Reader, we shall hasten to the Morning; only observing that none of them went to bed that Night. *Adams*, when he had smoked three Pipes, took a comfortable Nap in a great Chair, and left the Lovers, whose Eyes were too well employed to permit any Desire of shutting them, to enjoy by themselves during some Hours, an Happiness which none of my Readers, who have never been in love, are capable of the least Conception of, tho' we had as many Tongues as *Homer* desired[7] to describe it with, and which all true Lovers will represent to their own Minds without the least Assistance from us.

Let it suffice then to say, that *Fanny* after a thousand Entreaties at last gave up her whole Soul to *Joseph*, and almost fainting in his Arms, with a Sigh infinitely softer and sweeter too, than any *Arabian* Breeze, she whispered to his Lips, which were then close to hers, 'O *Joseph*, you have won me; I will be yours for ever.' *Joseph*, having thanked her on his Knees, and embraced her with an Eagerness, which she now almost returned, leapt up in a Rapture, and awakened the Parson, earnestly begging him, 'that he would that Instant join their Hands together.' *Adams* rebuked him for his Request, and told him, 'he would by no means consent to any thing contrary to the Forms of the Church, that

---

6. At the end of act 3 of Dryden's *All for Love*, the Egyptian queen confronts Mark Antony's wife, who has temporarily won him back, but it is Octavia who leaves the stage.

7. Homer invokes the muses to describe the Greek hosts before Troy because "I could not tell over the multitude of them nor name them,/not if I had ten tongues and ten mouths . . ." (*Iliad* 2.488–89, R. Lattimore trans.). In his translation, Pope inflated the number to a thousand.

he had no Licence, nor indeed would he advise him to obtain one. That the Church had prescribed a Form, namely the Publication of Banns, with which all good Christians ought to comply, and to the Omission of which, he attributed the many Miseries which befel great Folks in Marriage; concluding, *As many as are joined together otherwise than G—'s Word doth allow, are not joined together by G—, neither is their Matrimony lawful.*[8] *Fanny* agreed with the Parson, saying to *Joseph* with a Blush, 'she assured him she would not consent to any such thing, and that she wondred at his offering it.' In which Resolution she was comforted, and commended by *Adams*; and *Joseph* was obliged to wait patiently till after the third Publication of the Banns, which however, he obtained the Consent of *Fanny* in the presence of *Adams* to put in at their Arrival.

The Sun had been now risen some Hours, when *Joseph* finding his Leg surprisingly recovered, proposed to walk forwards; but when they were all ready to set out, an Accident a little retarded them. This was no other than the Reckoning which amounted to seven Shillings; no great Sum, if we consider the immense Quantity of Ale which Mr. *Adams* poured in. Indeed they had no Objection to the Reasonableness of the Bill, but many to the Probability of paying it; for the Fellow who had taken poor *Fanny*'s Purse, had unluckily forgot to return it. So that the Account stood thus:

Mr. *Adams* and Company D.[9]	0	7	0
In Mr. *Adams*'s Pocket, ——————	0	0	6½
In Mr. *Joseph*'s, ——————————	0	0	0
In Mrs. *Fanny*'s, ——————————	0	0	0
Balance ——————————————	0	6	5½

They stood silent some few Minutes, staring at each other, when *Adams* whipt out on his Toes, and asked the Hostess 'if there was no Clergyman in that Parish?' She answered, 'there was.' 'Is he wealthy?' replied he, to which she likewise answered in the Affirmative. *Adams* then snapping his Fingers returned overjoyed to his Companions, crying out, '*Eureka, Eureka*;'[1] which not being understood, he told them in plain *English* 'they need give themselves no trouble; for he had a Brother in the Parish, who would defray the Reckoning, and that he would just step to his House and fetch the Money, and return to them instantly.'

8. Adams cites the part of the marriage ceremony (in the *Book of Common Prayer*) in which the bride and groom are solemnly enjoined to divulge any known impediments to the marriage (such as consanguinity) substituting "as" for "so" and "joined" for "coupled." The established Anglican marriage procedure called for three previous proclamations of the banns in the parish church or churches of the betrothed to permit disclosure of any such impediments by members of the community. The alternative of obtaining a license to wed from the bishop was an expedient usually reserved to the upper classes. It is the method employed by Pamela's master, to prevent his sister's intervention.

9. "Debtor," the bookkeeping designation for the debit side of an account. The columns are for pounds, shillings, and pence (of which Adams is now said to have six more than he did on p. 111).

1. "I have found it" (printed in Greek letters in the first edition)—Archimedes' supposed exclamation on discovering the principle of specific gravity while stepping into a bath.

Chapter XIV

An Interview between Parson Adams and Parson Trulliber.[1]

Parson *Adams* came to the House of Parson *Trulliber*, whom he found stript into his Waistcoat, with an Apron on, and a Pail in his Hand, just come from serving his Hogs; for Mr. *Trulliber* was a Parson on *Sundays*, but all the other six might more properly be called a Farmer.[2] He occupied a small piece of Land of his own, besides which he rented a considerable deal more. His Wife milked his Cows, managed his Dairy, and followed the Markets with Butter and Eggs. The Hogs fell chiefly to his care, which he carefully waited on at home, and attended to Fairs; on which occasion he was liable to many Jokes, his own Size being with much Ale rendered little inferiour to that of the Beasts he sold. He was indeed one of the largest Men you should see, and could have acted the part of Sir *John Falstaff* without stuffing. Add to this, that the Rotundity of his Belly was considerably increased by the shortness of his Stature, his Shadow ascending very near as far in height when he lay on his Back, as when he stood on his Legs. His Voice was loud and hoarse, and his Accents extremely broad; to complete the whole, he had a Stateliness in his Gate, when he walked, not unlike that of a Goose, only he stalked slower.

Mr. *Trulliber* being informed that somebody wanted to speak with him, immediately slipt off his Apron, and clothed himself in an old Night-Gown,[3] being the Dress in which he always saw his Company at home. His Wife who informed him of Mr. *Adams's* Arrival, had made a small Mistake; for she had told her Husband, 'she believed here was a Man come for some of his Hogs.' This Supposition made Mr. *Trulliber* hasten with the utmost expedition to attend his Guest; he no sooner saw *Adams*, than not in the least doubting the cause of his Errand to be what his Wife had imagined, he told him, 'he was come in very good time; that he expected a Dealer that very Afternoon;' and added, 'they were all pure and fat, and upwards of twenty Score a piece.'[4] *Adams* answered, 'he believed he did not know him.' 'Yes, yes,' cry'd *Trulliber*, 'I have seen you often at *Fair*; why, we have dealt before now mun, I warrant you; yes, yes,' cries he, 'I remember thy Face very well, but won't mention a word more till you have seen them, tho' I have never sold thee a Flitch of such Bacon as is now in the Stye.' Upon which he laid violent Hands on *Adams*, and dragged him into the Hogs-Stye, which was indeed but two Steps from his Parlour Window. They were no sooner arrived there than he cry'd out, 'Do but handle them, step in, Friend, art wel-

1. An apt conflation of the dialect words *trullibub* (guts or a fat person) and *trolubber* (a farm laborer).
2. At the end of chapter 3 of his "Apology for the Clergy" (see below, p. 318), Fielding notes that by an act of Henry VIII clergy are "forbid to take any Lands to farm or to buy or sell in Markets, &c., . . . that nothing might prevent them from dis-

charging their Duties to the Souls of Men" (*The Champion*, April 12, 1740).
3. Dressing gown.
4. That is, over four hundred pounds. "Pure and fat" is the equivalent of our colloquial "nice and fat."

come to handle them whether dost buy or no.' At which words opening
the Gate, he pushed *Adams* into the Pig-Stye, insisting on it, that he
should handle them, before he would talk one word with him. *Adams*,
whose natural Complacence was beyond any artificial, was obliged to
comply before he was suffered to explain himself, and laying hold on
one of their Tails, the unruly Beast gave such a sudden spring, that he
threw poor *Adams* all along in the Mire. *Trulliber* instead of assisting
him to get up, burst into a Laughter, and entring the Stye, said to *Adams*
with some contempt, *Why, dost not know how to handle a Hog?* and
was going to lay hold of one himself; but *Adams*, who thought he had
carried his Complacence far enough, was no sooner on his Legs, than
he escaped out of the Reach of the Animals, and cry'd out, *nihil habeo
cum Porcis:*[5] 'I am a Clergyman, Sir, and am not come to buy Hogs.'
Trulliber answered, 'he was sorry for the Mistake; but that he must blame
his Wife;' adding, 'she was a Fool, and always committed Blunders.' He
then desired him to walk in and clean himself, that he would only fasten
up the Stye and follow him. *Adams* desired to leave to dry his Great
Coat, Wig, and Hat by the Fire, which *Trulliber* granted. Mrs. *Trulliber*
would have brought him a Bason of Water to wash his Face, but her
Husband bid her be quiet like a Fool as she was, or she would commit
more Blunders, and then directed *Adams* to the Pump. While *Adams*
was thus employed, *Trulliber* conceiving no great Respect for the
Appearance of his Guest, fastened the Parlour-Door, and now conducted him into the Kitchin; telling him, he believed a Cup of Drink
would do him no harm, and whispered his Wife to draw a little of the
worst Ale. After a short Silence, *Adams* said, 'I fancy, Sir, you already
perceive me to be a Clergyman.' 'Ay, ay,' cries *Trulliber* grinning; 'I
perceive you have some Cassock; I will not venture to *caale* it a whole
one.' *Adams* answered, 'it was indeed none of the best; but he had the
misfortune to tear it about ten Years ago in passing over a Stile.' Mrs.
Trulliber returning with the Drink, told her Husband 'she fancied the
Gentleman was a Traveller, and that he would be glad to eat a bit.'
Trulliber bid her 'hold her impertinent Tongue;' and asked her 'if Parsons used to travel without Horses?' adding, 'he supposed the Gentleman
had none by his having no Boots on.' 'Yes, Sir, yes,' says *Adams*, 'I have
a Horse, but I have left him behind me.' 'I am glad to hear you have
one,' says *Trulliber*; 'for I assure you, I don't love to see Clergymen on
foot; it is not seemly nor suiting the Dignity of the Cloth.' Here *Trulliber*
made a long Oration on the Dignity of the Cloth (or rather Gown)[6] not
much worth relating, till his Wife had spread the Table and set a Mess
of Porridge on it for his Breakfast. He then said to *Adams*, 'I don't know,
Friend, how you came to *caale* on me; however, as you are here, if you
think proper to eat a Morsel, you may.' *Adams* accepted the Invitation,
and the two Parsons sat down together, Mrs. *Trulliber* waiting behind

5. "I have nothing to do with pigs."
6. Both terms were acceptable designations of the
clergy; Fielding's parenthetical correction is
intended to point up the irony that Trulliber is
delivering these sentiments in his nightgown.

her Husband's Chair, as was, it seems, her custom. *Trulliber* eat[7] heartily, but scarce put any thing in his Mouth without finding fault with his Wife's Cookery. All which the poor Woman bore patiently. Indeed she was so absolute an Admirer of her Husband's Greatness and Importance, of which she had frequent Hints from his own Mouth, that she almost carried her Adoration to an opinion of his Infallibility. To say the truth, the Parson had exercised her more ways than one; and the pious Woman had so well edified by her Husband's Sermons, that she had resolved to receive the good things of this World together with the bad.[8] She had indeed been at first a little contentious; but he had long since got the better, partly by her love for *this*, partly by her fear of *that*, partly by her Religion, partly by the Respect he paid himself, and partly by that which he received from the Parish: She had, in short, absolutely submitted, and now worshipped her Husband as *Sarah* did *Abraham*, calling him (not Lord but) Master.[9] Whilst they were at Table, her Husband gave her a fresh Example of his Greatness; for as she had just delivered a Cup of Ale to *Adams*, he snatched it out of his Hand, and crying out, *I caal'd vurst*, swallowed down the Ale. *Adams* denied it, and it was referred to the Wife, who tho' her Conscience was on the side of *Adams*, durst not give it against her Husband. Upon which he said, 'No, Sir, no, I should not have been so rude to have taken it from you, if you had *caal'd vurst*; but I'd have you know I'm a better Man than to suffer the best He in the Kingdom to drink before me in my own House, when I *caale vurst*.'

As soon as their Breakfast was ended, *Adams* began in the following manner: 'I think, Sir, it is high time to inform you of the business of my Embassy. I am a Traveller, and am passing this way in company with two young People, a Lad and a Damsel, my Parishioners, towards my own Cure: we stopt at a House of Hospitality in the Parish, where they directed me to you, as having the Cure.'—'Tho' I am but a Curate,' says *Trulliber*, 'I believe I am as warm[1] as the Vicar himself, or perhaps the Rector of the next Parish too; I believe I could buy them both.' 'Sir,' cries *Adams*, 'I rejoice thereat. Now, Sir, my Business is, that we are by various Accidents stript of our Money, and are not able to pay our Reckoning, being seven Shillings. I therefore request you to assist me with the Loan of those seven Shillings, and also seven Shillings more, which peradventure I shall return to you; but if not, I am convinced you will joyfully embrace such an Opportunity of laying up a Treasure in a better Place than any this World affords.'[2]

Suppose a Stranger, who entered the Chambers of a Lawyer, being

---

7. Then the past tense form, pronounced "et."
8. The third and subsequent editions read "bad things . . . together with the good," but Battestin finds the earlier inversion of this conventional phrase "in better accord with the irony in this passage."
9. In his first epistle, Peter enjoined wives to submit to their husbands, "even as Sarah obeyed Abraham, calling him Lord" (I Peter 3:6, referring to Genesis 18:12).

1. Well off.
2. Adams recalls the Sermon on the Mount ("Lay not up for yourselves treasures upon earth, where moth and rust doth corrupt . . . but lay up for yourselves treasures in heaven . . . ," Matthew 6:19–20) and Jesus' advice to the rich man ("sell that thou hast, and give to the poor, and thou shalt have treasure in heaven," Matthew 19:21).

imagined a Client, when the Lawyer was preparing his Palm for the Fee, should pull out a Writ against him. Suppose an Apothecary, at the Door of a Chariot containing some great Doctor of eminent Skill, should, instead of Directions to a Patient, present him with a Potion for himself. Suppose a Minister should, instead of a good round Sum, treat my Lord— or Sir—or Esq;—with a good Broomstick. Suppose a civil Companion, or a led Captain[3] should, instead of Virtue, and Honour, and Beauty, and Parts, and Admiration, thunder Vice and Infamy, and Ugliness, and Folly, and Contempt, in his Patron's Ears. Suppose when a Trades-man first carries in his Bill, the Man of Fashion should pay it; or sup-pose, if he did so, the Tradesman should abate what he had overcharged on the Supposition of waiting. In short—suppose what you will, you never can nor will suppose any thing equal to the Astonishment which seiz'd on *Trulliber*, as soon as *Adams* had ended his Speech. A while he rolled his Eyes in Silence, some times surveying *Adams*, then his Wife, then casting them on the Ground, then lifting them to Heaven. At last, he burst forth in the following Accents. 'Sir, I believe I know where to lay my little Treasure up as well as another; I thank G— if I am not so warm as some, I am content; that is a Blessing greater than Riches; and he to whom that is given need ask no more. To be content with a little is greater than to possess the World, which a Man may possess without being so. Lay up my Treasure! what matters where a Man's Treasure is, whose Heart is in the Scriptures?[4] there is the Treasure of a Christian.' At these Words the Water ran from *Adams's* Eyes; and catching *Trulli-ber* by the Hand, in a Rapture, 'Brother,' says he, 'Heavens bless the Accident by which I came to see you; I would have walked many a Mile to have communed with you, and, believe me, I will shortly pay you a second Visit: but my Friends, I fancy, by this time, wonder at my stay, so let me have the Money immediately.' *Trulliber* then put on a stern Look, and cry'd out, 'Thou dost not intend to rob me?' At which the Wife, bursting into Tears, fell on her Knees and roared out, 'O dear Sir, for Heaven's sake don't rob my Master, we are but poor People.' 'Get up for a Fool as thou art, and go about thy Business,' said *Trulliber*, 'dost think the Man will venture his Life? he is a Beggar and no Robber.' 'Very true indeed,' answered *Adams*. 'I wish, with all my heart, the Tithing-Man[5] was here,' cries *Trulliber*, 'I would have thee punished as a Vagabond for thy Impudence. Fourteen Shillings indeed! I won't give thee a Farthing. I believe thou art no more a Clergyman[6] than the

3. The inadequate pay of military officers in peacetime reduced many to obsequious depen-dency on the rich. There is an example in book 3, chapter 7.

4. Trulliber answers Adams with his own echoes of Jesus ("for where your treasure is, there will your heart be also," Matthew 6:12; "A good man out of the good treasure of his heart bringeth forth that which is good," Luke 6:45) and the familiar Old and New Testament preference for the con-tentment of righteous poverty over uneasy wealth ("Better is little with the fear of the Lord, /than great treasure and trouble therewith," Proverbs 15:16).

5. The parish constable.

6. Though it is obviously a pretext to withhold money, Trulliber's suspicion had some basis in fact. As Battestin points out, confidence men were known to "borrow" money in clerical guise.

Woman there, (pointing to his Wife) but if thou art, dost deserve to have thy Gown stript over thy Shoulders, for running about the Country in such a manner.' 'I forgive your Suspicions,' says *Adams*, 'but suppose I am not a Clergyman, I am nevertheless thy Brother, and thou, as a Christian, much more as a Clergyman, art obliged to relieve my Distress.' 'Dost preach to me,' replied *Trulliber*, 'dost pretend to instruct me in my Duty?' 'Ifacks, a good Story,' cries Mrs. *Trulliber*, 'to preach to my Master.' 'Silence, Woman,' cries *Trulliber*; 'I would have thee know, Friend, (addressing himself to *Adams*,) I shall not learn my Duty from such as thee; I know what Charity is, better than to give to Vagabonds.' 'Besides, if we were inclined, the Poors Rate[7] obliges us to give so much Charity,' (cries the Wife.) 'Pugh! thou art a Fool. Poors Reate! hold thy Nonsense,' answered *Trulliber*, and then turning to *Adams*, he told him, 'he would give him nothing.' 'I am sorry,' answered *Adams*, 'that you do know what Charity is, since you practise it no better; I must tell you, if you trust to your Knowledge for your Justification, you will find yourself deceived, tho' you should add Faith to it without good Works.' 'Fellow,' cries *Trulliber*, 'Dost thou speak against Faith in my House? Get out of my Doors, I will no longer remain under the same Roof with a Wretch who speaks wantonly of Faith and the Scriptures.' 'Name not the Scriptures,' says *Adams*. 'How, not name the Scriptures! Do you disbelieve the Scriptures?' cries *Trulliber*. 'No, but you do,' answered *Adams*, 'if I may reason from your Practice: for their Commands are so explicit, and their Rewards and Punishments so immense, that it is impossible a Man should stedfastly believe without obeying. Now, there is no Command more express, no Duty more frequently enjoined than Charity. Whoever therefore is void of Charity, I make no scruple of pronouncing that he is no Christian.'[8] 'I would not advise thee, (says *Trulliber*) to say that I am no Christian. I won't take it of you: for I believe I am as good a Man as thyself;' (and indeed, tho' he was now rather too corpulent for athletic Exercises, he had in his Youth been one of the best Boxers and Cudgel-players in the County.) His Wife seeing him clench his Fist, interposed, and begged him not to fight, but shew himself a true Christian, and take the Law of him.[9] As nothing could provoke *Adams* to strike, but an absolute Assault on himself or his Friend; he smiled at the angry Look and Gestures of *Trulliber*; and telling him, he was sorry to see such Men in Orders, departed without farther Ceremony.

---

7. The tax imposed on residents for relief of the poor of the parish.

8. Adams's views recall Paul's preaching: "And though I have the gift of prophecy, and understand all mysteries, and all knowledge; and though I have all faith, so that I could remove mountains, and have not charity, I am nothing" (I Corinthians 13:2). For Fielding's development of these sentiments in *The Champion*, see below, pp. 315–17.

For the question of justification by faith or works, see below. p. 392.

9. While not asserting that "all going to Law is utterly unchristian," *The Whole Duty of Man* condemned "Suits . . . to defend such an inconsiderable right, as the parting with will do us little or no harm, or which is yet worse, to avenge such a trespass" (1673 ed., ch. 17, p. 392,).

Chapter XV

An Adventure, the Consequence of a new Instance which Parson Adams gave of his Forgetfulness.

When he came back to the Inn, he found *Joseph* and *Fanny* sitting together. They were so far from thinking his Absence long, as he had feared they would, that they never once miss'd or thought of him. Indeed, I have been often assured by both, that they spent these Hours in a most delightful Conversation: but as I never could prevail on either to relate it, so I cannot communicate it to the Reader.

Adams acquainted the Lovers with the ill Success of his Enterprize. They were all greatly confounded, none being able to propose any Method of departing, 'till *Joseph* at last advised calling in the Hostess, and desiring her to trust them; which *Fanny* said she despaired of her doing, as she was one of the sourest-fac'd Women she had ever beheld.

But she was agreeably disappointed; for the Hostess was no sooner asked the Question than she readily agreed; and with a Curt'sy and Smile, wished them a good Journey. However, lest *Fanny's* Skill in Physiognomy should be called in question, we will venture to assign one Reason, which might probably incline her to this Confidence and Good-Humour. When *Adams* said he was going to visit his Brother, he had unwittingly imposed on *Joseph* and *Fanny*; who both believed he had meant his natural Brother, and not his Brother in Divinity; and had so informed the Hostess on her Enquiry after him. Now Mr. *Trulliber* had by his Professions of Piety, by his Gravity, Austerity, Reserve, and the Opinion of his great Wealth, so great an Authority in his Parish, that they all lived in the utmost Fear and Apprehension of him. It was therefore no wonder that the Hostess, who knew it was in his Option whether she should ever sell another Mug of Drink,[1] did not dare to affront his supposed Brother by denying him Credit.

They were now just on their Departure, when *Adams* recollected he had left his Great Coat and Hat at Mr. *Trulliber's*. As he was not desirous of renewing his Visit, the Hostess herself, having no Servant at home, offered to fetch it.

This was an unfortunate Expedient: for the Hostess was soon undeceived in the Opinion she had entertained of *Adams*, whom *Trulliber* abused in the grossest Terms, especially when he heard he had had the Assurance to pretend to be his near Relation.

At her Return therefore, she entirely changed her Note. She said, 'Folks might be ashamed of travelling about and pretending to be what they were not. That Taxes were high, and for her part, she was obliged to pay for what she had; she could not therefore possibly, nor would she trust any body, no not her own Father. That Money was never scarcer,

1. Although the incumbent's certification of good character was not a legal requirement for a public house licensee until 1753, a curate of Trulliber's apparent local power could influence the justices who annually granted or renewed licenses.

and she wanted to make up a Sum.[2] That she expected therefore they should pay their Reckoning before they left the House.'

Adams was now greatly perplexed: but as he knew that he could easily have borrowed such a Sum in his own Parish, and as he knew he would have lent it himself to any Mortal in Distress; so he took fresh Courage, and sallied out all round the Parish, but to no purpose; he returned as pennyless as he went, groaning and lamenting, that it was possible in a Country professing Christianity, for a Wretch to starve in the midst of his Fellow-Creatures who abounded.[3]

Whilst he was gone, the Hostess who stayed as a sort of Guard with *Joseph* and *Fanny* entertained them with the Goodness of Parson *Trulliber*; and indeed he had not only a very good Character, as to other Qualities, in the Neighbourhood, but was reputed a Man of great Charity: for tho' he never gave a Farthing, he had always that Word in his Mouth.[4]

Adams was no sooner returned the second time, than the Storm grew exceeding high, the Hostess declaring among other things, that if they offered to stir without paying her, she would soon overtake them with a Warrant.

Plato or *Aristotle*, or some body else hath said, THAT WHEN THE MOST EXQUISITE CUNNING FAILS, CHANCE OFTEN HITS THE MARK, AND THAT BY MEANS THE LEAST EXPECTED. *Virgil* expresses this very boldly:

> *Turne quod optanti Divûm promittere nemo*
> *Auderet, volvenda Dies en attulit ultro.*[5]

I would quote more great Men if I could: but my Memory not permitting me, I will proceed to exemplify these Observations by the following Instance.

There chanced (for *Adams* had not Cunning enough to contrive it) to be at that time in the Alehouse, a Fellow, who had been formerly a Drummer in an *Irish* Regiment, and now travelled the Country as a Pedlar. This Man having attentively listened to the Discourse of the Hostess, at last took *Adams* aside, and asked him what the Sum was for which they were detained. As soon as he was informed, he sighed and said, 'he was sorry it was so much: for that he had no more than six Shillings and Sixpence in his Pocket, which he would lend them with all his heart.' *Adams* gave a Caper, and cry'd out, 'it would do: for that he had Sixpence himself.' And thus these poor People, who could not engage the Compassion of Riches and Piety, were at length delivered out of their Distress by the Charity of a poor Pedlar.

I shall refer it to my Reader, to make what Observations he pleases on

2. She lacked money to pay an amount due on a specified date.
3. Were rich.
4. The clauses beginning "for" were added in the second edition.
5. "Turnus, that which no god had dared to promise to thy prayers, lo, the circling hour has brought unasked!" (*Aeneid* 9.6–7, H. R. Fairclough trans.). Montaigne (*Essais* 1.34) quotes the capitalized sentiment, from a Greek comedy of Menander (ca. 342–292 B.C.), in an anecdote of a man who threw a stone at a dog and killed his stepmother.

this Incident: it is sufficient for me to inform him, that after *Adams* and his Companions had returned him a thousand Thanks, and told him where he might call to be repaid, they all sallied out of the House without any Complements from their Hostess, or indeed without paying her any; *Adams* declaring, he would take particular Care never to call there again, and she on her side assuring them she wanted no such Guests.

Chapter XVI

A very curious Adventure, in which Mr. Adams gave a much greater Instance of the honest Simplicity of his Heart than of his Experience in the Ways of this World.

Our Travellers had walked about two Miles from that Inn, which they had more reason to have mistaken for a Castle, than Don *Quixote* ever had any of those in which he sojourned;[1] seeing they had met with such Difficulty in escaping out of its Walls; when they came to a Parish, and beheld a Sign of Invitation hanging out. A Gentleman sat smoking a Pipe at the Door; of whom *Adams* enquired the Road, and received so courteous and obliging an Answer, accompanied with so smiling a Countenance, that the good Parson, whose Heart was naturally disposed to Love and Affection, began to ask several other Questions; particularly the Name of the Parish, and who was the Owner of a large House whose Front they then had in prospect. The Gentlemen answered as obligingly as before; and as to the House, acquainted him it was his own. He then proceeded in the following manner: 'Sir, I presume by your Habit you are a Clergyman: and as you are travelling on foot, I suppose a Glass of good Beer will not be disagreeable to you; and I can recommend my Landlord's within, as some of the best in all this County. What say you, will you halt a little and let us take a Pipe together: there is no better Tobacco in the Kingdom?' This Proposal was not displeasing to *Adams*, who had allayed his Thirst that Day, with no better Liquor than what Mrs. *Trulliber's* Cellar had produced; and which was indeed little superior either in Richness or Flavour to that which distilled from those Grains her generous Husband bestowed on his Hogs. Having therefore abundantly thanked the Gentleman for his kind Invitation, and bid *Joseph* and *Fanny* follow him, he entered the Ale-House, where a large Loaf and Cheese and a Pitcher of Beer, which truly answered the Character given of it, being set before them, the three Travellers fell to eating with Appetites infinitely more voracious than are to be found at the most exquisite Eating-Houses in the Parish of *St. James's*.[2]

The Gentleman expressed great Delight in the hearty and chearful Behaviour of *Adams*; and particularly in the Familiarity with which he conversed with *Joseph* and *Fanny*, whom he often called his Children,

1. Much of the action of *Don Quixote*, part 1, takes place in an inn that the mad knight believes is a castle.

2. A fashionable district near the royal residence, St. James's Palace, and Pall Mall, noted for its taverns, chocolate houses, and dining and gambling clubs.

a Term, he explained to mean no more than his Parishioners; saying, he looked on all those whom God had entrusted to his Cure, to stand to him in that Relation. The Gentleman shaking him by the Hand highly applauded those Sentiments. 'They are indeed,' says he, 'the true Principles of a Christian Divine; and I heartily wish they were universal: but on the contrary, I am sorry to say the Parson of our Parish instead of esteeming his poor Parishioners as a part of his Family, seems rather to consider them as not of the same Species with himself. He seldom speaks to any unless some few of the richest of us; nay indeed, he will not move his Hat to the others. I often laugh when I behold him on *Sundays* strutting along the Church-Yard, like a Turky-Cock, through Rows of his Parishioners; who bow to him with as much Submission and are as unregarded as a Sett of servile Courtiers by the proudest Prince in *Christendom*. But if such temporal Pride is ridiculous, surely the spiritual is odious and detestable: if such a puffed up empty human Bladder strutting in princely Robes, justly moves one's Derision; surely in the Habit of a Priest it must raise our Scorn.'

'Doubtless,' answered *Adams*, 'your Opinion is right; but I hope such Examples are rare. The Clergy whom I have the honour to know, maintain a different Behaviour; and you will allow me, Sir, that the Readiness, which too many of the Laity show to contemn the Order, may be one reason of their avoiding too much Humility.' 'Very true indeed,' says the Gentleman; 'I find, Sir, you are a Man of excellent Sense, and am happy in this Opportunity of knowing you: perhaps, our accidental meeting may not be disadvantageous to you neither. At present, I shall only say to you, that the Incumbent of this Living is old and infirm; and that it is in my Gift. Doctor, give me your Hand; and assure yourself of it at his Decease.' *Adams* told him, 'he was never more confounded in his Life, than at his utter Incapacity to make any return to such noble and unmerited Generosity.' 'A mere Trifle, Sir,' cries the Gentleman, 'scarce worth your Acceptance; a little more than three hundred a Year. I wish it was double the Value for your sake.' *Adams* bowed, and cried from the Emotions of his Gratitude; when the other asked him, 'if he was married, or had any Children, besides those in the spiritual Sense he had mentioned.' 'Sir,' replied the Parson, 'I have a Wife and six at your service.' 'That is unlucky,' says the Gentleman; 'for I would otherwise have taken you into my own House as my Chaplain: however, I have another in the Parish, (for the Parsonage House is not good enough) which I will furnish for you. Pray does your Wife understand a Dairy?' 'I can't profess she does,' says *Adams*. 'I am sorry for it,' quoth the Gentleman; 'I would have given you half a dozen Cows, and very good Grounds to have maintained them.' 'Sir,' says *Adams*, in an Ecstacy, 'you are too liberal; indeed you are.' 'Not at all,' cries the Gentleman, 'I esteem Riches only as they give me an opportunity of doing Good; and I never saw one whom I had a greater Inclination to serve.' At which Words he shook him heartily by the Hand, and told him he had sufficient Room in his House to entertain him and his Friends. *Adams* begged

he might give him no such Trouble, that they could be very well accom-
modated in the House where they were; forgetting they had not a Six-
penny Piece among them. The Gentleman would not be denied; and
informing himself how far they were travelling, he said it was too long a
Journey to take on foot, and begged that they would favour him, by
suffering him to lend them a Servant and Horses; adding withal, that if
they would do him the pleasure of their Company only two days, he
would furnish them with his Coach and six. *Adams* turning to *Joseph*,
said, 'How lucky is this Gentleman's goodness to you, who I am afraid
would be scarce able to hold out on your lame Leg,' and then addressing
the Person who made him these liberal Promises, after much bowing,
he cried out, 'Blessed be the Hour which first introduced me to a Man
of your Charity: you are indeed a Christian of the true primitive kind,
and an honour to the Country wherein you live. I would willingly have
taken a Pilgrimage to the holy Land to have beheld you: for the Advantages which we draw from your Goodness, give me little pleasure, in
comparison of what I enjoy for your own sake; when I consider the
Treasures you are by these means laying up for your self in a Country
that passeth not away. We will therefore, most generous Sir, accept your
Goodness, as well the Entertainment you have so kindly offered us at
your House this Evening, as the Accommodation of your Horses To-
morrow Morning.' He then began to search for his Hat, as did *Joseph*
for his; and both they and *Fanny* were in order of Departure, when the
Gentleman stopping short, and seeming to meditate by himself for the
space of about a Minute, exclaimed thus: 'Sure never any thing was so
unlucky; I have forgot that my House-Keeper was gone abroad, and hath
locked up all my Rooms; indeed I would break them open for you, but
shall not be able to furnish you with a Bed; for she hath likewise put
away all my Linnen. I am glad it entered into my Head before I had
given you the Trouble of walking there; besides, I believe you will find
better accommodations here than you expect. Landlord, you can provide good Beds for these People, can't you?' 'Yes and please your Worship,' cries the Host, 'and such as no Lord or Justice of the Peace in the
Kingdom need be ashamed to lie in.' 'I am heartily sorry,' says the
Gentleman, 'for this Disappointment. I am resolved I will never suffer
her to carry away the Keys again.' 'Pray, Sir, let it not make you uneasy,'
cries *Adams*, 'we shall do very well here; and the Loan of your Horses is
a Favour, we shall be incapable of making any Return to.' 'Ay!' said the
Squire, 'the Horses shall attend you here at what Hour in the Morning
you please.' And now after many Civilities too tedious to enumerate,
many Squeezes by the Hand, with most affectionate Looks and Smiles
on each other, and after appointing the Horses at seven the next Morning, the Gentleman took his Leave of them, and departed to his own
House. *Adams* and his Companions returned to the Table, where the
Parson smoaked another Pipe, and then they all retired to Rest.

Mr. *Adams* rose very early and called *Joseph* out of his Bed, between
whom a very fierce Dispute ensued, whether *Fanny* should ride behind

Joseph, or behind the Gentleman's Servant; *Joseph* insisting on it, that he was perfectly recovered, and was as capable of taking care of *Fanny*, as any other Person could be. But *Adams* would not agree to it, and declared he would not trust her behind him; for that he was weaker than he imagined himself to be.

This Dispute continued a long time, and had begun to be very hot, when a Servant arrived from their good Friend, to acquaint them, that he was unfortunately prevented from lending them any Horses; for that his Groom had, unknown to him, put his whole Stable under a Course of Physick.

This Advice presently struck the two Disputants dumb; *Adams* cried out, 'Was ever any thing so unlucky as this poor Gentleman? I protest I am more sorry on his account, than my own. You see, *Joseph*, how this good-natur'd Man is treated by his Servants; one locks up his Linen, another physicks his Horses; and I suppose by his being at this House last Night, the Butler had locked up his Cellar. Bless us! how Good-nature is used in this World! I protest I am more concerned on his account than my own.' 'So am not I,' cries *Joseph*; 'not that I am much troubled about walking on foot; all my Concern is, how we shall get out of the House; unless God sends another Pedlar to redeem us. But certainly, this Gentleman has such an Affection for you, that he would lend you a larger Sum than we owe here; which is not above four or five Shillings.' 'Very true, Child,' answered *Adams*; 'I will write a Letter to him, and will even venture to sollicit him for three Half-Crowns;[3] there will be no harm in having two or three Shillings in our Pockets: as we have full forty Miles to travel, we may possibly have occasion for them.'

Fanny being now risen, *Joseph* paid her a Visit, and left *Adams* to write his Letter; which having finished, he dispatched a Boy with it to the Gentleman, and then seated himself by the Door, lighted his Pipe, and betook himself to Meditation.

The Boy staying longer than seemed to be necessary, *Joseph* who with *Fanny* was now returned to the Parson, expressed some Apprehensions, that the Gentleman's Steward had locked up his Purse too. To which *Adams* answered, 'It might very possibly be; and he should wonder at no Liberties which the Devil might put into the Head of a wicked Servant to take with so worthy a Master:' but added, 'that as the Sum was so small, so noble a Gentleman would be easily able to procure it in the Parish; tho' he had it not in his own Pocket. Indeed,' says he, 'if it was four or five Guineas,[4] or any such large Quantity of Money, it might be a different matter.'

They were now sat down to Breakfast over some Toast and Ale, when the Boy returned; and informed them, that the Gentleman was not at home. 'Very well,' cries *Adams*; 'but why, Child, did you not stay 'till his return? Go back again, my good Boy, and wait for his coming home: he cannot be gone far, as his Horses are all sick; and besides, he had no

---

3. Coins worth two shillings and sixpence each.   4. Coins worth twenty-one shillings each.

Intention to go abroad; for he invited us to spend this Day and To-morrow at his House. Therefore, go back, Child, and tarry 'till his return home.' The Messenger departed, and was back again with great Expe-dition; bringing an Account, that the Gentleman was gone a long Jour-ney, and would not be at home again this Month. At these Words, *Adams* seemed greatly confounded, saying, 'This must be a sudden Accident, as the Sickness or Death of a Relation, or some such unfore-seen Misfortune;' and then turning to *Joseph*, cried, 'I wish you had reminded me to have borrowed this Money last Night.' *Joseph* smiling, answered, 'he was very much deceived, if the Gentleman would not have found some Excuse to avoid lending it. I own,' says he, 'I was never much pleased with his professing so much Kindness for you at first sight: for I have heard the Gentlemen of our Cloth in *London* tell many such Stories of their Masters. But when the Boy brought the Message back of his not being at home, I presently[5] knew what would follow; for when-ever a Man of Fashion doth not care to fulfil his Promises, the Custom is, to order his Servants that he will never be at home to the Person so promised. In *London* they call it *denying him.* I have my self denied Sir *Thomas Booby* above a hundred times; and when the Man hath danced Attendance for about a Month, or sometimes longer, he is acquainted in the end, that the Gentleman is gone out of Town, and could do nothing in the Business.' 'Good Lord!' says *Adams*; 'What Wickedness is there in the Christian World? I profess, almost equal to what I have read of the *Heathens.* But surely, *Joseph*, your Suspicions of this Gentle-man must be unjust; for, what a silly Fellow must he be, who would do the Devil's Work for nothing? and can'st thou tell me any Interest[6] he could possibly propose to himself by deceiving us in his Professions?' 'It is not for me,' answered *Joseph*, 'to give Reasons for what Men do, to a Gentleman of your Learning.' 'You say right,' quoth *Adams*; 'Knowl-edge of Men is only to be learnt from Books, *Plato* and *Seneca* for that;[7] and those are Authors, I am afraid Child, you never read.' 'Not I, Sir, truly,' answered *Joseph*; 'all I know is, it is a Maxim among the Gentle-men of our Cloth, that those Masters who promise the most perform the least; and I have often heard them say, they have found the largest Vailes[8] in those Families, where they were not promised any. But, Sir, instead of considering any farther these Matters, it would be our wisest way to contrive some Method of getting out of this House: for the generous Gentleman, instead of doing us any Service, hath left us the whole Reckoning to pay.' *Adams* was going to answer, when their Host came in; and with a kind of Jeering-Smile said, 'Well, Masters! the Squire hath not sent his Horses for you yet. Laud help me! how easily some

---

5. Immediately.
6. Benefit.
7. Lucius Annaeus Seneca (ca. 4 B.C.–A.D. 65), Roman stoic philosopher, espoused high ethical ideals in his numerous moral treatises and his declamatory tragedies; yet he condoned the mur-der of his patron, the emperor Claudius, and prospered in the dissolute court of his successor, Nero, a disparity of preaching and practice height-ening the irony for Fielding's educated readers of Adams's citation.

8. Tips or gratuities were often more substantial, and reliable, than a servant's wages.

Folks make Promises!' 'How!' says *Adams,* 'have you ever known him do any thing of this kind before?' 'Aye marry have I,' answered the Host; 'it is no business of mine, you know, Sir, to say any thing to a Gentleman to his face: but now he is not here, I will assure you, he hath not his Fellow within the three next Market-Towns. I own, I could not help laughing, when I heard him offer you the Living; for thereby hangs a good Jest. I thought he would have offered you my House next; for one is no more his to dispose of than the other.' At these Words, *Adams* blessing himself, declared, 'he had never read of such a Monster; but what vexes me most,' says he, 'is, that he hath decoyed us into running up a long Debt with you, which we are not able to pay; for we have no Money about us; and what is worse, live at such a distance, that if you should trust us, I am afraid you would lose your Money, for want of our finding any Conveniency of sending it.' 'Trust you, Master!' says the Host, 'that I will with all my heart; I honour the Clergy too much to deny trusting one of them for such a Trifle; besides, I like your fear of never paying me. I have lost many a Debt in my Lifetime; but was promised to be paid them all in a very short time. I will score this Reckoning for the Novelty of it. It is the first I do assure you of its kind. But what say you, Master, shall we have t'other Pot before we part? It will waste but a little Chalk[9] more; and if you never pay me a Shilling, the Loss will not ruin me.' *Adams* liked the Invitation very well; especially as it was delivered with so hearty an Accent.—He shook his Host by the Hand, and thanking him, said, 'he would tarry another Pot, rather for the Pleasure of such worthy Company than for the Liquor;' adding, 'he was glad to find some Christians left in the Kingdom; for that he almost began to suspect that he was sojourning in a Country inhabited only by *Jews* and *Turks.*'

The kind Host produced the Liquor, and *Joseph* with *Fanny* retired into the Garden; where while they solaced themselves with amorous Discourse, *Adams* sat down with his Host; and both filling their Glasses and lighting their Pipes, they began that Dialogue, which the Reader will find in the next Chapter.

Chapter XVII

A Dialogue between Mr. Abraham Adams *and his Host, which, by the Disagreement in their Opinions seemed to threaten an unlucky Catastrophe, had it not been timely prevented by the Return of the Lovers.*

'Sir,' said the Host, 'I assure you, you are not the first to whom our Squire hath promised more than he hath performed. He is so famous for this Practice, that his Word will not be taken for much by those who know him. I remember a young Fellow whom he promised his Parents to make an Exciseman. The poor People, who could ill afford it, bred

---

9. Innkeepers kept accounts on a slate.

their Son to Writing and Accounts, and other Learning, to qualify him for the Place; and the Boy held up his Head above his Condition with these Hopes; nor would he go to plough, nor do any other kind of Work; and went constantly drest as fine as could be, with two clean *Holland*[1] Shirts a Week, and this for several Years; 'till at last he followed the Squire up to *London*, thinking there to mind him of his Promises: but he could never get sight of him. So that being out of Money and Business, he fell into evil Company, and wicked Courses; and in the end came to a Sentence of Transportation,[2] the News of which broke the Mother's Heart. I will tell you another true Story of him: There was a Neighbour of mine, a Farmer, who had two Sons whom he bred up to the Business. Pretty Lads they were; nothing would serve the Squire, but that the youngest must be made a Parson. Upon which, he persuaded the Father to send him to School, promising, that he would afterwards maintain him at the University; and when he was of a proper Age, give him a Living. But after the Lad had been seven Years at School, and his Father brought him to the Squire with a Letter from his Master, that he was fit for the University; the Squire, instead of minding his Promise, or sending him thither at his Expence, only told his Father, that the young Man was a fine Scholar; and it was pity he could not afford to keep him at *Oxford* for four or five Years more, by which Time, if he could get him a Curacy, he might have him ordained.' The Farmer said, 'he was not a Man sufficient to do any such thing.' 'Why then,' answered the Squire; 'I am very sorry you have given him so much Learning; for if he cannot get his living by that, it will rather spoil him for any thing else; and your other Son who can hardly write his Name, will do more at plowing and sowing, and is in a better Condition than he: and indeed so it proved; for the poor Lad not finding Friends to maintain him in his Learning, as he had expected; and being unwilling to work, fell to drinking, though he was a very sober Lad before; and in a short time, partly with Grief, and partly with good Liquor, fell into a Consumption and died. Nay, I can tell you more still: There was another, a young Woman, and the handsomest in all this Neighbourhood, whom he enticed up to *London*, promising to make her a Gentlewoman to one of your Women of Quality: but instead of keeping his Word, we have since heard, after having a Child by her himself, she became a common Whore; then kept a Coffee-House in *Covent-Garden*,[3] and a little after died of the *French* Distemper[4] in a Goal. I could tell you many more Stories: but how do you imagine he served me myself? You must know, Sir, I was bred a Sea-faring Man, and have been many Voyages; 'till at last I came to be Master of a Ship myself, and was in a fair Way of making a Fortune, when I was attacked by one of those cursed *Guarda-Costas*, who took

1. Linen.
2. Convicted felons were often transported to the American colonies, where they were sold as virtual slaves for seven- or fourteen-year terms.
3. While a few of these, notably the Bedford, were celebrated meeting places for wits and authors

frequenting the theatres in this central London district, many were houses of ill repute.
4. Venereal disease, also known, according to local prejudice, as the Castilian pocks, mal de Naples, the German pocks, the Portugese disease, and (among the Turks) the Christian disease.

our Ships before the Beginning of the War;[5] and after a Fight wherein I lost the greater part of my Crew, my Rigging being all demolished, and two Shots received between Wind and Water, I was forced to strike.[6] The Villains carried off my Ship, a Brigantine of 150 Tons, a pretty Creature she was, and put me, a Man, and a Boy, into a little bad Pink,[7] in which with much ado, we at last made *Falmouth*; tho' I believe the *Spaniards* did not imagine she could possibly live a Day at Sea. Upon my return hither, where my Wife who was of this Country then lived, the Squire told me, he was so pleased with the Defence I had made against the Enemy, that he did not fear getting me promoted to a Lieutenancy of a Man of War, if I would accept of it, which I thankfully assured him I would. Well, Sir, two or three Years past, during which, I had many repeated Promises, not only from the Squire but (as he told me) from the Lords of the Admiralty. He never returned from *London*, but I was assured I might be satisfied now, for I was certain of the first Vacancy; and what surprizes me still, when I reflect on it, these Assurances were given me with no less Confidence, after so many Disappointments, than at first. At last, Sir, growing weary and somewhat suspicious after so much delay, I wrote to a Friend in *London*, who I knew had some Acquaintance at the best House in the Admiralty;[8] and desired him to back the Squire's Interest: for indeed, I feared he had sollicited the Affair with more Coldness than he pretended.—And what Answer do you think my Friend sent me?—Truly, Sir, he acquainted me, that the Squire had never mentioned my Name at the Admiralty in his Life; and unless I had much faithfuller Interest, advised me to give over my Pretensions, which I immediately did; and with the Concurrence of my Wife, resolved to set up an Alehouse, where you are heartily welcome: and so my Service to you; and may the Squire, and all such sneaking Rascals go to the Devil together.' 'Oh fie!' says *Adams*; 'Oh fie! He is indeed a wicked Man; but G— will, I hope, turn his Heart to Repentance. Nay, if he could but once see the Meanness[9] of this detestable Vice; would he but once reflect that he is one of the most scandalous as well as pernicious Lyars; sure he must despise himself to so intolerable a degree, that it would be impossible for him to continue a Moment in such a Course. And to confess the Truth, notwithstanding the Baseness of this Character, which he hath too well deserved, he hath in his Countenance sufficient Symptoms of that *bona Indoles*,[1] that Sweetness

5. Between 1713 and 1731, Spanish coast guards in the West Indies seized and pillaged one hundred and eighty British ships suspected of smuggling. One such incident, involving Captain Robert Jenkins and the loss of his ear, became the focal point of opposition agitation leading to the war with Spain (1739–48) initially called the War of Jenkins's Ear.
6. To lower the flag as a sign of surrender, because his ship had been hit at a level that is sometimes submerged, hence taking in water.
7. A term applied to vessels of various sizes, apparently in this case a small flat-bottomed coastal sailer unsuited for the open sea.
8. Presumably the Admiralty Board in Whitehall,

responsible for officers' appointments, rather than one of the subordinate Navy boards overseeing ships and supplies, located elsewhere.
9. Baseness.
1. "Good nature." The irony of Adams's claim might be reinforced for Fielding's classically educated readers by a particular association of this Latin phrase. Cicero hopefully applied it or variants of it to Caesar's heir Octavian in letters (*Ad Atticum* 15.12; *Ad Brutum* 1.3.1; 1.10.3) anticipating Octavian's support for the republican cause against Mark Antony—a few months before the future emperor colluded with Antony to assassinate Cicero.

of Disposition which furnishes out a good Christian.' 'Ah! Master, Master, (says the Host,) if you had travelled as far as I have, and conversed with the many Nations where I have traded, you would not give any Credit to a man's Countenance. Symptoms in his Countenance, quotha! I would look there perhaps to see whether a Man had had the Small-Pox, but for nothing else!' He spoke this with so little regard to the Parson's Observation, that it a good deal nettled him; and taking the Pipe hastily from his Mouth, he thus answered:—'Master of mine, perhaps I have travelled a great deal farther than you without the Assistance of a Ship. Do you imagine sailing by different Cities or Countries is travelling? No.

Cœlum non Animum mutant qui trans mare currunt.[2]

I can go farther in an Afternoon, than you in a Twelve-Month. What, I suppose you have seen the Pillars of *Hercules*, and perhaps the Walls of *Carthage*. Nay, you may have heard *Scylla*, and seen *Charybdis*; you may have entered the Closet where *Archimedes* was found at the taking *Syracuse*.[3] I suppose you have sailed among the *Cyclades*,[4] and passed the famous Streights which take their name from the unfortunate *Helle*, whose Fate is sweetly described by *Apollonius Rhodius*; you have past the very Spot, I conceive, where *Dædalus* fell into that Sea, his waxen Wings being melted by the Sun; you have traversed the *Euxine* Sea, I make no doubt; nay, you may have been on the Banks of the *Caspian*, and called at *Colchis*, to see if there is ever another Golden Fleece.'[5]— 'Not I truly, Master,' answered the Host, 'I never touched at any of these Places.' 'But I have been at all these,' replied *Adams*. 'Then I suppose,' cries the Host, 'you have been at the *East Indies*, for there are no such, I will be sworn, either in the *West* or the *Levant*.' 'Pray where's the *Levant*?' quoth *Adams*, 'that should be in the *East Indies* by right.'[6]— 'O ho! you are a pretty Traveller,' cries the Host, 'and not know the *Levant*. My service to you, Master; you must not talk of these things

2. "They change their clime, not their mind, who rush across the sea" (Horace, *Epistles* 1.11.27, H. R. Fairclough trans.).

3. In the midst of the sack of his native city, the Greek mathematician (ca. 287–212 B.C.) was constructing a mathematical figure when slain by a Roman soldier against the orders of the conquering general who venerated him. The headlands bounding the Straits of Gibraltar (the end of the world in ancient times) were associated with the legendary pillars erected by Hercules in the course of his tenth labor (the Oxen of the Sun). Carthage, site of the opening books of the *Aeneid* and Rome's powerful North African rival, was destroyed in the third Punic War (146 B.C.). Passing safely between the cave of Scylla, a maneating monster with a dreadful bark (hence Adams's "heard Scylla"), and the whirlpool Charybdis, traditionally located in the Straits of Messina, was one of the feats of Odysseus (*Odyssey* 12).

4. A circle of Greek islands in the south Aegean Sea.

5. In Greek legend, the Hellespont (the Dardanelles Straits) derived its name from the young Theban princess who fell there from the winged ram on which she and her brother fled their murderous stepmother. When her brother reached Colchis on the Euxine or Black Sea (not the Caspian), he sacrificed the ram to Zeus. Its golden fleece, guarded by a dragon, became the object of the heroic quest of Jason and the Argonauts, recounted in Apollonius Rhodius' third-century B.C. epic, the *Argonautica*, which also briefly relates Helle's fall. Although Dædalus, the legendary Athenian artificer, fashioned the means of escaping the labyrinth of Minos on Crete, it was his son Icarus who fell because he flew too close to the sun.

6. In its early use, "Levant" referred to the Orient, from the French word for the rising of the sun. The then current edition of Chambers's *Cyclopaedia* says it "signifies any country situate to the east of us." By this time, however, it had also acquired its more specific modern reference to "those coasts of the Mediterranean east of Italy" (Johnson's *Dictionary*), roughly the region Adams is discussing.

with me! you must not tip us[7] the Traveller; it won't go here.' 'Since thou art so dull to misunderstand me still,' quoth *Adams*, 'I will inform thee; the travelling I mean is in Books, the only way of travelling by which any Knowledge is to be acquired. From them I learn what I asserted just now, that Nature generally imprints such a Portraiture of the Mind in the Countenance, that a skilful Physiognomist will rarely be deceived. I presume you have never read the Story of *Socrates* to this purpose, and therefore I will tell it you. A certain Physiognomist asserted of *Socrates*, that he plainly discovered by his Features that he was a Rogue in his Nature. A Character so contrary to the Tenour of all this great Man's Actions, and the generally received Opinion concerning him, incensed the Boys of *Athens* so that they threw Stones at the Physiognomist, and would have demolished him for his Ignorance, had not *Socrates* himself prevented them by confessing the Truth of his Observations, and acknowledging that tho' he corrected his Disposition by Philosophy, he was indeed naturally as inclined to Vice as had been predicated of him.[8] Now, pray resolve me,—How should a Man know this Story, if he had not read it?' 'Well Master,' said the Host, 'and what signifies it whether a Man knows it or no? He who goes abroad as I have done, will always have opportunities enough of knowing the World, without troubling his head with *Socrates*, or any such Fellows.'—'Friend,' cries *Adams*, 'if a Man would sail round the World, and anchor in every Harbour of it, without Learning, he would return home as ignorant as he went out.' 'Lord help you,' answered the Host, 'there was my Boatswain, poor Fellow! he could scarce either write or read, and yet he would navigate a Ship with any Master of a Man of War; and a very pretty knowledge of Trade he had too.' 'Trade,' answered *Adams*, 'as *Aristotle* proves in his first Chapter of Politics, is below a Philosopher, and unnatural as it is managed now.'[9] The Host look'd stedfastly at *Adams*, and after a Minute's silence asked him 'if he was one of the Writers of the *Gazetteers*? for I have heard,' says he, 'they are writ by Parsons.' '*Gazetteers*!' answer'd *Adams*. 'What is that?' 'It is a dirty News-Paper,' replied the Host, 'which hath been given away all over the Nation for these many Years to abuse Trade and honest Men, which I would not suffer to lie on my Table, tho' it hath been offered me for nothing.'[1] 'Not I truly,' said *Adams*, 'I

---

7. Assume the character of.

8. The story is cited in Cicero's *Tusculan Disputations* (4.37.80), as evidence that an "unhealthy . . . soul" is curable. For Fielding's views on physiognomy, see below, pp. 323–27.

9. In the *Politics* 1, Aristotle condemns acquisition of wealth by exchange of goods because it is "not in accordance with nature, but involves men's taking things from one another"; he finds "the theory of such matters" a "liberal study," but "the practical pursuit of them . . . narrowing"; and he cites the ancient astronomer Thales's foresighted creation of a monopoly to show "it is easy for philosophers to be rich if they choose, but this is not what they care about" (1258b–1259a; H. Rackham trans.).

1. *The Daily Gazetteer*, organ of Walpole's ministry set up in 1735, was distributed free throughout the kingdom at Treasury expense. Among its numerous contributors were such clergymen as Henry Bland, dean of Durham (Pope's "gratis-given Bland"—*Dunciad* 1.231); Francis Hare (1671–1740), bishop of Chichester, Walpole's Cambridge tutor and his candidate for archbishop of Canterbury in 1737; and Thomas Newcomb (1682?–1762), incumbent of several benefices and a poet who wrote an ode to Walpole after his fall. The *Gazetteer's* support of Walpole's efforts to avoid war over the Spanish harassment of illicit British West Indies trade (see above, p. 141, n. 5) led the opposition *Craftsman* to accuse it of "daily throwing Dirt at . . . injured and distressed Merchants" (February 11, 1738).

never write any thing but Sermons, and I assure you I am no Enemy to Trade, whilst it is consistent with Honesty; nay, I have always looked on the Tradesman, as a very valuable Member of Society, and perhaps inferior to none but the Man of Learning.' 'No, I believe he is not, nor to him neither,' answered the Host. 'Of what use would Learning be in a Country without Trade? What would all you Parsons do to clothe your Backs and feed your Bellies? Who fetches you your Silks and your Linens, and your Wines, and all the other Necessaries of Life? I speak chiefly with regard to the Sailors.' 'You should say the Extravagancies of Life,' replied the Parson, 'but admit they were the Necessaries, there is something more necessary than Life it self, which is provided by Learning; I mean the Learning of the Clergy. Who clothes you with Piety, Meekness, Humility, Charity, Patience, and all the other Christian Virtues? Who feeds your Souls with the Milk of brotherly Love, and diets them with all the dainty Food of Holiness, which at once cleanses them of all impure carnal Affections, and fattens them with the truly rich Spirit of Grace?—Who doth this?' 'Ay, who indeed!' cries the Host; 'for I do not remember ever to have seen any such Clothing or such Feeding. And so in the mean time, Master, my service to you.' *Adams* was going to answer with some severity, when *Joseph* and *Fanny* returned, and pressed his Departure so eagerly, that he would not refuse them; and so grasping his Crabstick, he took leave of his Host, (neither of them being so well pleased with each other as they had been at their first sitting down together) and with *Joseph* and *Fanny*, who both exprest much Impatience, departed; and now all together renewed their Journey.

The History of the Adventures of
JOSEPH ANDREWS,
and of his Friend Mr. *Abraham Adams*

BOOK III

Chapter I

Matter prefatory in Praise of Biography.

Notwithstanding the Preference which may be vulgarly given to the Authority of those Romance-Writers, who intitle their Books, the History of *England*, the History of *France*, of *Spain*, &c. it is most certain, that Truth is only to be found in the Works of those who celebrate the Lives of Great Men, and are commonly called Biographers, as the others should indeed be termed Topographers or Chorographers: Words which might well mark the Distinction between them; it being the Business of the latter chiefly to describe Countries and Cities, which, with the Assistance of Maps, they do pretty justly, and may be depended upon: But as to the Actions and Characters of Men, their Writings are not quite so authentic, of which there needs no other Proof than those eternal Contradictions, occurring between two Topographers who undertake the History of the same Country: For instance, between my Lord *Clarendon* and Mr. *Whitlock*, between Mr. *Echard* and *Rapin*, and many others;[1]

1. The stormy period of English history between 1640 and 1660 remained a subject of partisan dispute between whig and tory polemicists well into the eighteenth century. Edward Hyde (1609–74), earl of Clarendon, mentor and chief minister of Charles II in the early years of the Restoration, and Bulstrode Whitelock (1605–75), a parliamentary leader and adviser to the Cromwells, wrote their respective histories (*The True Historical Narrative of the Rebellion and Civil Wars in England*, 1702–4; and *Memorials of the English Affairs from the Beginning of the Reign of Charles I to the happy Restoration of King Charles II*, 1682) from the opposed perspectives of the contending royalist and parliamentary parties in the twenty-year struggle. *The History of England* (1707–18) by the tory Laurence Echard (1670?–1730) was succeeded in popularity by Nicholas Tindal's translation (1725–31) of Paul de Rapin Thoyras's *Histoire d'Angleterre*, which, despite scrupulous impartiality and a conclusion condemning both parties, was attacked by Stuart partisans. All these books were in Fielding's library. He may also have known Richard Sarage's poem, "On False Historians. A Satire" (1735), which, citing Echard, mocks the "*Romance* call'd hist'ry" wherein "Contending factions" call the same statesman "angel" or "fiend," since, as Battestin notes, two magazines reprinted it in 1741.

where Facts being set forth in a different Light, every Reader believes as he pleases, and indeed the more judicious and suspicious very justly esteem the whole as no other than a Romance, in which the Writer hath indulged a happy and fertile Invention. But tho' these widely differ in the Narrative of Facts; some ascribing Victory to the one, and others to the other Party: Some representing the same Man as a Rogue, to whom others give a great and honest Character, yet all agree in the Scene where the Fact is supposed to have happened; and where the Person, who is both a Rogue, and an honest Man, lived. Now with us Biographers the Case is different, the Facts we deliver may be relied on, tho' we often mistake the Age and Country wherein they happened: For tho' it may be worth the Examination of Critics, whether the Shepherd *Chrysostom*, who, as *Cervantes* informs us, died for Love of the fair *Marcella*, who hated him, was ever in *Spain*, will any one doubt but that such a silly Fellow hath really existed? Is there in the World such a Sceptic as to disbelieve the Madness of *Cardenio*, the Perfidy of *Ferdinand*, the impertinent Curiosity of *Anselmo*, the Weakness of *Camilla*, the irresolute Friendship of *Lothario*;[2] tho' perhaps as to the Time and Place where those several Persons lived, that good Historian may be deplorably deficient: But the most known Instance of this kind is in the true History of *Gil-Blas*, where the inimitable Biographer hath made a notorious Blunder in the Country of Dr. *Sangrado*, who used his Patients as a Vintner doth his Wine-Vessels, by letting out their Blood, and filling them up with Water. Doth not every one, who is the least versed in Physical[3] History, know that *Spain* was not the Country in which this Doctor lived? The same Writer hath likewise erred in the Country of his Arch-bishop, as well as that of those great Personages whose Understandings were too sublime to taste any thing but Tragedy,[4] and in many others. The same Mistakes may likewise be observed in *Scarron*, the *Arabian Nights*, the History of *Marianne* and *Le Paisan Parvenu*,[5] and perhaps some few other Writers of this Class, whom I have not read, or

2. The story of Chrysostom and Marcella is the first of several love tales introduced in *Don Quixote* (1.2.4–6). Cardenio and Ferdinand are the hero and villain of the principal romantic story interwoven with Quixote's adventures in the second half of part 1. Anselmo, Camilla, and Lothario are the protagonists of the interpolated novella, "The Curious Impertinent," (1.4.6–8), in which the morbidly suspicious Anselmo persists in urging his friend Lothario to test his wife's virtue until he succeeds in cuckolding himself.
3. Medical.
4. In the salon of the Marchioness of Chaves, a self-appointed "Court of Judicature for Productions of Wit," the "best Comedy, or the most diverting Romance, was thought but a very weak Performance, not worthy of any Praise; whereas the least Work if Serious, an Ode, an Eclogue, a Sonnet, was judged as the greatest Effort of Humane Wit" (*Gil Blas*, 1716 trans., 4.8). Dr. Sangrado, the second of Gil Blas's masters, dogmatically

prescribes bleeding and a diet of warm water as a universal remedy, though he admits "I have not often the Satisfaction to cure the Persons that fall into my Hands" (*Gil Blas*, 1716 trans., 2.5). For Gil Blas's encounter with the archibishop of Granada, see below, pp. 368–76.
5. The popular *Arabian Nights Entertainments* (1705–8), translated from the French of Antoine Galland's first European collection of these oriental tales, went through many editions was serialized in *Parker's London News* (1723–25). In the uncompleted *La Vie de Marianne, ou les aventures de Madame la comtesse de —— (1731–41)*, by Pierre Carlet de Chamblain de Marivaux (1688–1763), the worldly narrator recalls her youthful experiences as an orphan beset by a hypocritical older benefactor who tries to seduce her; she also becomes attracted to his nephew, who woos and deserts her. For Marivaux's *Le Paysan parvenu* and Paul Scarron's *Roman comique*, see below, pp. 376–87 and pp. 359–67.

do not at present recollect;[6] for I would by no means be thought to comprehend those Persons of surprising Genius, the Authors of immense Romances, or the modern Novel and *Atalantis* Writers;[7] who without any Assistance from Nature or History, record Persons who never were, or will be, and Facts which never did nor possibly can happen: Whose Heroes are of their own Creation, and their Brains the Chaos whence all their Materials are collected. Not that such Writers deserve no Honour; so far otherwise, that perhaps they merit the highest: for what can be nobler than to be as an Example of the wonderful Extent of human Genius. One may apply to them what *Balzac* says of *Aristotle*, that they are *a second Nature*;[8] for they have no Communication with the first; by which Authors of an inferiour Class, who can not stand alone, are obliged to support themselves as with Crutches; but these of whom I am now speaking, seem to be possessed of *those Stilts*, which the excellent *Voltaire* tells us in his Letters *carry the Genius far off, but with an irregular Pace.*[9] Indeed far out of the sight of the Reader,

Beyond the Realm of Chaos and old Night.[1]

But, to return to the former Class, who are contented to copy Nature, instead of forming Originals from the confused heap of Matter in their own Brains; is not such a Book as that which records the Atchievements of the renowned *Don Quixotte*, more worthy the Name of a History than even *Mariana's*;[2] for whereas the latter is confined to a particular Period of Time, and to a particular Nation; the former is the History of the World in general, at least that Part which is polished by Laws, Arts and Sciences; and of that from the time it was first polished to this day; nay and forwards, as long as it shall so remain.

I shall now proceed to apply these Observations to the Work before us; for indeed I have set them down principally to obviate some Constructions, which the Good-nature of Mankind, who are always forward to see their Friends Virtues recorded, may put to particular parts. I ques-

6. The most likely addition to this select group would be Antoine Furetière (1619–88), whose *Roman bourgeois* (1666), published in English as *Scarron's City Romance* (1671), mocks the pretensions of the "immense Romances" alluded to next and in the preface (see above, p. 4, n. 5).

7. *Secret Memoirs and manners of Several Persons of Quality, of both Sexes. From the New Atalantis, an Island in the Mediterranean* (1709), by Mrs. Mary de la Riviere Manley (1663–1724), purported to be translated from Italian. In fact, it was a scandalous "secret history" slandering contemporary whig notables and courtiers in tales of adultery, seduction, incest, and sexual intrigue, for which its author was arrested. Along with its sequel (see below, p. 295, n. 4), it went through numerous editions and was widely imitated. In this context the term *novel* would specify "a small tale, generally of love" (Johnson's *Dictionary*), a popular genre for numerous hack writers.

8. Jean-Louis Guez de Balzac (1594–1654), aca-

demician and prose stylist, best known for his *Lettres* (1624). Battestin locates the citation in the second of *Deux Discours envoyez à Rome* (1627), where Balzac attributes it to an unnamed philosopher in justification of hyperbole.

9. *Letters Concerning the English Nation* (1733), p. 178 (J. Lockman trans.). Voltaire's reference is to the figurative style of English tragedy.

1. A reworking of Milton's description of the response of the fallen angels to the raising of Satan's banner: "At which the universal Host upsent / A shout that tore Hell's Concave, and beyond / Frighted the Reign of *Chaos* and old Night" (*Paradise Lost* 1.541–43).

2. Juan de Mariana's *Historia general de España* was nearly contemporary with *Don Quixote*, being published in Latin in 1592 and in Spanish in 1601, four years before part 1 of Cervantes's work. Fielding owned a copy of the 1699 English translation.

tion not but several of my Readers will know the Lawyer in the Stage-Coach, the Moment they hear his Voice. It is likewise odds, but the Wit and the Prude meet with some of their Acquaintance, as well as all the rest of my Characters. To prevent therefore any such malicious Applications, I declare here once for all, I describe not Men, but Manners; not an Individual, but a Species. Perhaps it will be answered, Are not the Characters then taken from Life? To which I answer in the Affirmative; nay, I believe I might aver, that I have writ little more than I have seen. The Lawyer is not only alive, but hath been so these 4000 Years, and I hope G— will indulge his Life as many yet to come. He hath not indeed confined himself to one Profession, one Religion, or one Country; but when the first mean selfish Creature appeared on the human Stage, who made Self the Centre of the whole Creation; would give himself no Pain, incur no Danger, advance no Money to assist, or preserve his Fellow-Creatures; then was our Lawyer born; and whilst such a Person as I have described, exists on Earth, so long shall he remain upon it. It is therefore doing him little Honour, to imagine he endeavours to mimick some little obscure Fellow, because he happens to resemble him in one particular Feature, or perhaps in his Profession; whereas his Appearance in the World is calculated for much more general and noble Purposes; not to expose one pitiful Wretch, to the small and contemptible Circle of his Acquaintance; but to hold the Glass to thousands in their Closets, that they may contemplate their Deformity, and endeavour to reduce it, and thus by suffering private Mortification may avoid public Shame. This places the Boundary between, and distinguishes the Satirist from the Libeller; for the former privately corrects the Fault for the Benefit of the Person, like a Parent; the latter publickly exposes the Person himself, as an Example to others, like an Executioner.

There are besides little Circumstances to be considered, as the Drapery of a Picture, which tho' Fashion varies at different Times, the Resemblance of the Countenance is not by those means diminished. Thus, I believe, we may venture to say, Mrs. *Tow-wouse* is coeval with our Lawyer, and tho' perhaps during the Changes, which so long an Existence must have passed through, she may in her Turn have stood behind the Bar at an Inn, I will not scruple to affirm, she hath likewise in the Revolution of Ages sat on a Throne. In short where extreme Turbulency of Temper, Avarice, and an Insensibility of human Misery, with a Degree of Hypocrisy, have united in a female Composition, Mrs. *Tow-wouse* was that Woman; and where a good Inclination eclipsed by a Poverty of Spirit and Understanding, hath glimmer'd forth in a Man, that Man hath been no other than her sneaking Husband.

I shall detain my Reader no longer than to give him one Caution more of an opposite kind: For as in most of our particular Characters we mean not to lash Individuals, but all of the like sort; so in our general Descriptions, we mean not Universals, but would be understood with many Exceptions: For instance, in our Description of high People, we cannot be intended to include such, as whilst they are an Honour to their high Rank, by a well-guided Condescension, make their Superiority as easy[3] as possible, to those whom Fortune chiefly hath placed below them. Of this number I could name a Peer[4] no less elevated by Nature than by Fortune, who whilst he wears the noblest Ensigns of Honour on his Person, bears the truest Stamp of Dignity on his Mind, adorned with Greatness, enriched with Knowledge, and embelished with Genius. I have seen this Man relieve with Generosity, while he hath conversed with Freedom, and be to the same Person a Patron and a Companion. I could name a Commoner[5] raised higher above the Multitude by superior Talents, than is in the power of his Prince to exalt him; whose Behaviour to those he hath obliged is more amiable than the Obligation itself, and who is so great a Master of Affability, that if he could divest himself of an inherent Greatness in his Manner, would often make the lowest of his Acquaintance forget who was the Master of that Palace, in which they are so courteously entertained. These are Pictures which must be, I believe, known: I declare they are taken from the Life, and not intended to exceed it. By those high People therefore whom I have described, I mean a Set of Wretches, who while they are a Disgrace to their Ancestors, whose Honours and Fortunes they inherit, (or perhaps a greater to their Mother, for such Degeneracy is scarce credible) have the Insolence to treat those with disregard, who are at least equal to the Founders of their own Splendor. It is, I fancy, impossible to conceive a Spectacle more worthy of our Indignation, than that of a Fellow who is not only a Blot in the Escutcheon of a great Family, but a Scandal to the human Species, maintaining a supercilious Behaviour to Men who are an Honour to their Nature, and a Disgrace to their Fortune.

And now, Reader, taking these Hints along with you, you may, if you please, proceed to the Sequel of this our true History.

Chapter II

A Night-Scene, wherein several wonderful Adventures befel Adams and his Fellow-Travellers.

It was so late when our Travellers left the Inn or Ale-house, (for it might be called either) that they had not travelled many Miles before

---

3. Unoppressive. To make clear that fortune rather than character distinguished men of different ranks, Fielding reversed his original phrasing ("hath chiefly") in the third edition.
4. Probably Fielding's early patron, Philip Dormer Stanhope, fourth earl of Chesterfield (1694–1773), author of the celebrated *Letters* (1774) to his son. Fielding praised him in similar terms in "An Essay on Conversation," published in his *Miscellanies* (1743).

5. Ralph Allen (1693–1764), who made half a million pounds from the postal system he devised for England and Wales that eliminated the need to route everything through London, became Fielding's patron and friend while he was writing *Joseph Andrews*. The celebration of his hospitality may refer to an extended sojourn at his estate, Prior Park, outside Bath (see below, p. 183, n. 3). The estate and its master are the prototypes of Paradise Hall and Squire Allworthy in *Tom Jones*.

Night overtook them, or met them, which you please.[1] The Reader must excuse me if I am not particular as to the Way they took; for as we are now drawing near the Seat of the *Boobies*; and as that is a ticklish Name, which malicious Persons may apply according to their evil Inclinations to several worthy Country 'Squires, a Race of Men whom we look upon as entirely inoffensive, and for whom we have an adequate Regard, we shall lend no assistance to any such malicious Purposes.

Darkness had now overspread the Hemisphere, when *Fanny* whispered *Joseph*, 'that she begged to rest herself a little, for that she was so tired, she could walk no farther.' *Joseph* immediately prevailed with Parson *Adams*, who was as brisk as a Bee, to stop. He had no sooner seated himself, than he lamented the loss of his dear *Æschylus*; but was a little comforted, when reminded, that if he had it in his possession, he could not see to read.

The Sky was so clouded, that not a Star appeared. It was indeed, according to *Milton*, Darkness visible.[2] This was a Circumstance however very favourable to *Joseph*; for *Fanny*, not suspicious of being overseen by *Adams*, gave a loose to her Passion, which she had never done before; and reclining her Head on his Bosom, threw her Arm carelessly round him, and suffered him to lay his Cheek close to hers. All this infused such Happiness into *Joseph*, that he would not have changed his Turf for the finest Down in the finest Palace in the Universe.

Adams sat at some distance from the Lovers, and being unwilling to disturb them, applied himself to Meditation; in which he had not spent much time, before he discovered a Light at some distance, that seemed approaching towards him. He immediately hailed it, but to his Sorrow and Surprize it stopped for a moment and then disappeared. He then called to *Joseph*, asking him, 'if he had not seen the Light.' *Joseph* answered, 'he had.' 'And did you not mark how it vanished? (returned he) tho' I am not afraid of Ghosts, I do not absolutely disbelieve them.'

He then entered into a Meditation on those unsubstantial Beings, which was soon interrupted, by several Voices which he thought almost at his Elbow, tho' in fact they were not so extremely near. However, he could distinctly hear them agree on the Murther of any one they met. And a little after heard one of them say, 'he had killed a dozen since that day Fortnight.'

Adams now fell on his Knees, and committed himself to the care of Providence; and poor *Fanny*, who likewise heard those terrible Words, embraced *Joseph* so closely, that had not he, whose Ears were also open, been apprehensive on her account, he would have thought no danger which threatned only himself[3] too dear a Price for such Embraces.

Joseph now drew forth his Penknife, and *Adams* having finished his Ejaculations, grasped his Crabstick, his only Weapon, and coming up

1. Despite the narrator's facetious demurrer, it is clear from the first leg of Joseph's journey from London (p. 40, n. 4) that the travelers are heading westward.

2. The description of Hell, *Paradise Lost* 1.63.
3. This qualifying clause was added in the second edition.

to *Joseph* would have had him quit *Fanny*, and place her in their Rear: but his Advice was fruitless, she clung closer to him, not at all regarding the Presence of *Adams*, and in a soothing Voice declared, 'she would die in his Arms.' *Joseph* clasping her with inexpressible Eagerness, whispered her, 'that he preferred Death in hers, to Life out of them.' *Adams* brandishing his Crabstick, said, 'he despised Death as much as any Man,' and then repeated aloud,

> '*Est hic, est animus lucis contemptor, et illum,*
> *Qui vita bene credat emi quo tendis, Honorem.*'[4]

Upon this the Voices ceased for a moment, and then one of them called out, 'D—n you, who is there?' To which *Adams* was prudent enough to make no Reply; and of a sudden he observed half a dozen Lights, which seemed to rise all at once from the Ground, and advance briskly towards him. This he immediately concluded to be an Apparition, and now beginning to conceive that the Voices were of the same kind, he called out, 'In the Name of the L—d what would'st thou have?' He had no sooner spoke, than he heard one of the Voices cry out, 'D—n them, here they come;' and soon after heard several hearty Blows, as if a number of Men had been engaged at Quarterstaff. He was just advancing towards the Place of Combat, when *Joseph* catching him by the Skirts, begged him that they might take the Opportunity of the dark, to convey away *Fanny* from the Danger which threatned her. He presently[5] complied, and *Joseph* lifting up *Fanny*, they all three made the best of their way, and without looking behind them or being overtaken, they had travelled full two Miles, poor *Fanny* not once complaining of being tired; when they saw far off several Lights scattered at a small distance from each other, and at the same time found themselves on the Descent of a very steep Hill. *Adams's* Foot slipping, he instantly disappeared, which greatly frightened both *Joseph* and *Fanny*; indeed, if the Light had permitted them to see it, they would scarce have refrained laughing to see the Parson rolling down the Hill, which he did from top to bottom, without receiving any harm. He then hollowed as loud as he could, to inform them of his safety, and relieve them from the Fears which they had conceived for him. *Joseph* and *Fanny* halted some time, considering what to do; at last they advanced a few Paces, where the Declivity seemed least steep; and then *Joseph* taking his *Fanny* in his Arms, walked firmly down the Hill, without making a false step, and at length landed her at the bottom, where *Adams* soon came to them.

Learn hence, my fair Countrywomen, to consider your own Weakness, and the many Occasions on which the strength of a Man may be useful to you; and duly weighing this, take care, that you match not yourselves with the spindle-shanked Beaus and Petit Maîtres[6] of the Age,

---

4. "Here, here is a soul that scorns the light, and counts that fame, whereto thou strivest, cheaply bought with life," Euryalus's response to his friend Nisus's offer to undertake a dangerous mission (*Aeneid* 9.205–6, H. C. Fairclough trans.). Adams alters Virgil's *istum* to *illum*, another form of "that."

5. Immediately.

6. Fops.

who instead of being able like *Joseph Andrews*, to carry you in lusty Arms through the rugged ways and downhill Steeps of Life, will rather want to support their feeble Limbs with your Strength and Assistance.

Our Travellers now moved forwards, whither the nearest Light presented itself, and having crossed a common Field, they came to a Meadow, whence they seemed to be at a very little distance from the Light, when, to their grief, they arrived at the Banks of a River. *Adams* here made a full stop, and declared he could swim, but doubted how it was possible to get *Fanny* over; to which *Joseph* answered, 'if they walked along its Banks they might be certain of soon finding a Bridge, especially as by the number of Lights they might be assured a Parish was near.' 'Odso, that's true indeed,' said *Adams*, 'I did not think of that.' Accordingly *Joseph*'s Advice being taken, they passed over two Meadows, and came to a little Orchard, which led them to a House. *Fanny* begged of *Joseph* to knock at the Door, assuring him, 'she was so weary that she could hardly stand on her Feet.' *Adams* who was foremost performed this Ceremony, and the Door being immediately opened, a plain kind of a Man appeared at it; *Adams* acquainted him, 'that they had a young Woman with them, who was so tired with her Journey, that he should be much obliged to him, if he would suffer her to come in and rest herself.' The Man, who saw *Fanny* by the Light of the Candle which he held in his Hand, perceiving her innocent and modest Look, and having no Apprehensions from the civil Behaviour of *Adams*, presently answered, that the young Woman was very welcome to rest herself in his House, and so were her Company. He then ushered them into a very decent Room, where his Wife was sitting at a Table; she immediately rose up, and assisted them in setting forth Chairs, and desired them to sit down, which they had no sooner done, than the Man of the House asked them if they would have any thing to refresh themselves with? *Adams* thanked him, and answered, he should be obliged to him for a Cup of his Ale, which was likewise chosen by *Joseph* and *Fanny*. Whilst he was gone to fill a very large Jugg with this Liquor, his Wife told *Fanny* she seemed greatly fatigued, and desired her to take something stronger than Ale; but she refused, with many thanks, saying it was true, she was very much tired, but a little Rest she hoped would restore her. As soon as the Company were all seated, Mr. *Adams*, who had filled himself with Ale, and by publick Permission had lighted his Pipe; turned to the Master of the House, asking him, 'if evil Spirits did not use to walk in that Neighbourhood?' To which receiving no answer, he began to inform him of the Adventure which they had met with on the Downs; nor had he proceeded far in his Story, when somebody knocked very hard at the Door. The Company expressed some Amazement, and *Fanny* and the good Woman turned pale; her Husband went forth, and whilst he was absent, which was some time, they all remained silent looking at one another, and heard several Voices discoursing pretty loudly. *Adams* was fully persuaded that Spirits were abroad, and began to meditate some Exorcisms; *Joseph* a little inclined to the same Opinion: *Fanny* was more afraid of Men, and the good Woman herself began to suspect her Guests, and imagined those without were Rogues belonging to their Gang. At length the Master of the House returned, and laughing, told *Adams* he had discovered his Apparition; that the Murderers were Sheep-stealers, and the twelve Persons murdered were no other than twelve Sheep. Adding that the Shepherds had got the better of them, had secured two, and were proceeding with them to a Justice of Peace. This Account greatly relieved the Fears of the whole Company; but *Adams* muttered to himself, 'he was convinced of the truth of Apparitions for all that.'

They now sat chearfully round the Fire, 'till the Master of the House having surveyed his Guests, and conceiving that the Cassock, which having fallen down, appeared under *Adams's* Great-Coat, and the shabby Livery on *Joseph Andrews*, did not well suit with the Familiarity between them, began to entertain some suspicions, not much to their Advantage: addressing himself therefore to *Adams*, he said, 'he perceived he was a Clergyman by his Dress, and supposed that honest Man was his Footman.' 'Sir,' answered *Adams*, 'I am a Clergyman at your Service; but as to that young Man, whom you have rightly termed honest, he is at present in no body's Service, he never lived in any other Family than that of Lady *Booby*, from whence he was discharged, I assure you, for no Crime.' *Joseph* said, 'he did not wonder the Gentleman was surprized to see one of Mr. *Adams's* Character condescend to so much goodness with a poor Man.' 'Child,' said *Adams*, 'I should be ashamed of my Cloth, if I thought a poor Man, who is honest, below my notice or my familiarity. I know not how those who think otherwise, can profess themselves followers and servants of him who made no distinction, unless, peradventure, by preferring the Poor to the Rich. Sir,' said he, addressing himself to the Gentleman, 'these two poor young People are my Parishioners, and I look on them and love them as my Children. There is something singular enough in their History, but I have not now time to recount it.' The Master of the House, notwithstanding the Simplicity which discovered itself in *Adams*, knew too much of the World to give a hasty Belief to Professions. He was not yet quite certain that *Adams* had any more of the Clergyman in him than his Cassock. To try him therefore further, he asked him, 'if Mr. *Pope* had lately published any thing new?' *Adams* answered, 'he had heard great Commendations of that Poet, but that he had never read, nor knew any of his Works.' 'Ho! ho!' says the Gentleman to himself, 'have I caught you?' 'What,' said he, 'have you never seen his *Homer*?'[7] *Adams* answered, 'he had never read any Translation of the Classicks.' 'Why truly,' reply'd the Gentleman, 'there is a Dignity in the *Greek* Language which I think no modern Tongue can reach.' 'Do you understand *Greek*, Sir?' said *Adams* hastily. 'A little, Sir,' answered the Gentleman. 'Do you know, Sir,' cry'd *Adams*, 'where I can buy an *Æschylus*? an unlucky Misfortune lately happened to mine.' *Æschylus* was beyond the Gentleman, tho' he knew him very

7. Pope's English version of the *Iliad* (1715–20) was the most celebrated literary achievement of the day. His collaborative version of the *Odyssey* appeared in 1725–26.

well by Name; he therefore returning back to *Homer*, asked *Adams* 'what Part of the *Iliad* he thought most excellent.' *Adams* return'd, 'his Question would be properer, what kind of Beauty was the chief in Poetry, for that *Homer* was equally excellent in them all.

'And indeed,' continued he, 'what *Cicero* says of a complete Orator, may well be applied to a great Poet; *He ought to comprehend all Perfections.*[8] *Homer* did this in the most excellent degree; it is not without Reason therefore that the Philosopher,[9] in the 22d Chapter of his Poeticks, mentions him by no other Appellation than that of *The Poet*:[2] He was the Father of the Drama, as well as the Epic: Not of Tragedy only, but of Comedy also; for his *Margites*, which is deplorably lost, bore, says *Aristotle*, the same Analogy to Comedy, as his *Odyssey* and *Iliad* to Tragedy.[1] To him therefore we owe *Aristophanes*, as well as *Euripides*, *Sophocles*, and my poor *Æschylus*. But if you please we will confine ourselves (at least for the present) to the *Iliad*, his noblest Work; tho' neither *Aristotle*, nor *Horace* give it the Preference, as I remember, to the *Odyssey*. First then as to his Subject, can any thing be more simple, and at the same time more noble? He is rightly praised by the first of those judicious Critics, for not chusing the whole War,[2] which, tho' he says, it hath a compleat Beginning and End, would have been too great for the Understanding to comprehend at one View. I have therefore often wondered why so correct a Writer as *Horace* should in his Epistle to *Lollius* call him the *Trojani Belli Scriptorem.*[3] Secondly, his Action, termed by *Aristotle Pragmaton Systasis*;[4] is it possible for the Mind of Man to conceive an Idea of such perfect Unity, and at the same time so replete with Greatness? And here I must observe what I do not remember to have seen noted by any, the *Harmotton*,[5] that agreement of his Action to his Subject: For as the Subject is Anger, how agreeable is his Action, which is War? from which every Incident arises, and to which every Episode immediately relates. Thirdly, His Manners, which *Aristotle* places second in his Description of the several Parts of Tragedy, and which he says are included in the Action;[6] I am at a loss whether I should rather admire the Exactness of his Judgment in the nice[7] Distinction, or the Immensity of his Imagination in their Variety. For, as to the former of these, how accurately is the sedate, injured Resentment of *Achilles* distinguished from the hot insulting Passion of *Agamemnon*?

8. "No man can be an orator complete in all points of merit, who has not attained a knowledge of all important subjects and arts" (*De Oratore* 1. 6, E. W. Sutton trans.).

9. An epithet for Aristotle since the middle ages, reflecting his dominance of pre-Enlightenment learning.

1. *Poetics* 4. Compare the second paragraph of Fielding's preface.

2. *Poetics* 23.

3. "Author of the Trojan War" (*Epistles* 1.2).

4. "Combination of the incidents," or plot (*Poetics* 6).

5. "Appropriateness" or "propriety." Aristotle applies the term to character (*Poetics* 15) and diction (*Poetics* 22).

6. Throughout the period, critics employed the term *manners* for Aristotle's *ethos*, or character. Adams may have in mind Aristotle's argument that the characters exist "for the sake of the action" (6) or his specification of the character of the protagonist as part of the formula for the tragic plot (13). In his discourse, he follows the conventional neoclassical order of topics derived from Aristotle's "several Parts of Tragedy": Plot, Character, Thought, Diction, Melody, and Spectacle.

7. Subtle.

How widely doth the brutal Courage of *Ajax* differ from the amiable Bravery of *Diomedes*; and the Wisdom of *Nestor*, which is the Result of long Reflection and Experience, from the Cunning of *Ulysses*, the Effect of Art and Subtilty only? If we consider their Variety, we may cry out with *Aristotle* in his 24th Chapter, that no Part of this divine Poem is destitute of Manners.[8] Indeed I might affirm, that there is scarce a Character in human Nature untouched in some part or other. And as there is no Passion which he is not able to describe, so is there none in his Reader which he cannot raise. If he hath any superior Excellence to the rest, I have been inclined to fancy it is in the Pathetick. I am sure I never read with dry Eyes, the two Episodes, where *Andromache* is introduced, in the former lamenting the Danger, and in the latter the Death of *Hector*.[9] The Images are so extremely tender in these, that I am convinced, the Poet had the worthiest and best Heart imaginable. Nor can I help observing how short *Sophocles* falls of the Beauties of the Original, in that Imitation of the dissuasive Speech of *Andromache*, which he hath put into the Mouth of *Tecmessa*.[1] And yet *Sophocles* was the greatest Genius who ever wrote Tragedy, nor have any of his Successors in that Art, that is to say, neither *Euripides* nor *Seneca* the Tragedian[2] been able to come near him. As to his Sentiments and Diction, I need say nothing; the former are particularly remarkable for the utmost Perfection on that Head, namely Propriety; and as to the latter, *Aristotle*, whom doubtless you have read over and over, is very diffuse.[3] I shall mention but one thing more, which that great Critic in his Division of Tragedy calls *Opsis*,[4] or the Scenery, and which is as proper to the Epic as to the Drama, with this difference, that in the former it falls to the share of the Poet, and in the latter to that of the Painter. But did ever Painter imagine a Scene like that in the 13th and 14th Iliads? where the Reader sees at one View the Prospect of *Troy*, with the Army drawn up before it; the *Grecian* Army, Camp, and Fleet, *Jupiter* sitting on Mount *Ida*, with his Head wrapt in a Cloud, and a Thunderbolt in his Hand looking towards *Thrace*; *Neptune*[5] driving through the Sea, which divides on each side to permit his Passage, and then seating himself on Mount *Samos*: The Heavens opened, and the Deities all seated on their Thrones. This is Sublime! This is Poetry!' *Adams* then rapt out a hundred *Greek* Verses,

8. Aristotle praises Homer (without specifying the *Iliad*) for limiting his role as narrator and introducing dramatic characters "no one of them characterless, but each with distinctive characteristics" (Bywater trans.).

9. *Iliad* 6.405–39, where his wife tries to dissuade Hector from re-entering the battle, and either 22.475–514, where she first learns of his death, or 24.723–45, where she mourns with Hecuba and Helen over his body.

1. In Sophocles' tragedy, *Ajax* 485–524, Tecmessa, the hero's captive wife, tries to dissuade him from killing himself for shame on discovering he has attacked sheep and cattle while out of his mind. Like Andromache, she recounts her unhappy

life, stressing her absolute dependence on him, and invokes his pity for her and their son; but she also charges him with ingratitude for her favors.

2. See above, p. 138, n. 7; Adams specifies "the Tragedian" to distinguish him from his father "the Rhetorician." Comparison of Homer with the tragedians was added in the second edition.

3. Aristotle devotes three chapters to poetic language, but does not amplify his claim that Homer's diction surpasses all others (24).

4. Usually translated "spectacle," the sixth of Aristotle's analytic parts of tragedy.

5. Adams gives Zeus and Poseidon their Roman names.

and with such a Voice, Emphasis and Action, that he almost frighten'd the Women; and as for the Gentleman, he was so far from entertaining any further suspicion of *Adams*, that he now doubted whether he had not a Bishop in his House.[6] He ran into the most extravagant Encomiums on his Learning, and the Goodness of his Heart began to dilate to all the Strangers. He said he had great Compassion for the poor young Woman, who looked pale and faint with her Journey; and in truth he conceived a much higher Opinion of her Quality than it deserved. He said, he was sorry he could not accommodate them all: But if they were contented with his Fire-side, he would sit up with the Men, and the young Woman might, if she pleased, partake his Wife's Bed, which he advis'd her to; for that they must walk upwards of a Mile to any House of Entertainment, and that not very good neither. *Adams*, who liked his Seat, his Ale, his Tobacco and his Company, persuaded *Fanny* to accept this kind Proposal, in which Sollicitation he was seconded by *Joseph*. Nor was she very difficultly prevailed on; for she had slept little the last Night, and not at all the preceding, so that Love itself was scarce able to keep her Eyes open any longer. The Offer therefore being kindly accepted, the good Woman produced every thing eatable in her House on the Table, and the Guests being heartily invited, as heartily regaled themselves, especially Parson *Adams*. As to the other two, they were Examples of the Truth of that physical[7] Observation, that Love, like other sweet Things, is no Whetter of the Stomach.

Supper was no sooner ended, than *Fanny* at her own Request retired, and the good Woman bore her Company. The Man of the House, *Adams* and *Joseph*, who would modestly have withdrawn, had not the Gentleman insisted on the contrary, drew round the Fire-side, where *Adams*, (to use his own Words) replenished his Pipe, and the Gentleman produced a Bottle of excellent Beer, being the best Liquor in his House.

The modest Behaviour of *Joseph*, with the Gracefulness of his Person, the Character which *Adams* gave of him, and the Friendship he seemed to entertain for him, began to work on the Gentleman's Affections, and raised in him a Curiosity to know the Singularity which *Adams* had mentioned in his History. This Curiosity *Adams* was no sooner informed of, than with *Joseph*'s Consent, he agreed to gratify it, and accordingly related all he knew, with as much Tenderness as was possible for the Character of Lady *Booby*; and concluded with the long, faithful and mutual Passion between him and *Fanny*, not concealing the Meanness of her Birth and Education. These latter Circumstances entirely cured a Jealousy[8] which had lately risen in the Gentleman's Mind, that *Fanny* was the Daughter of some Person of Fashion, and that *Joseph* had run away with her, and *Adams* was concerned in the Plot. He was now enamour'd of his Guests, drank their Healths with great Cheerfulness, and return'd many Thanks to *Adams*, who had spent much Breath; for he was a circumstantial Teller of a Story.

6. For the Cervantean prototype of this incident, see below, pp. 356–58.

7. Medical.
8. Suspicion.

Adams told him it was now in his power to return that Favour; for his extraordinary Goodness, as well as that Fund of Literature he was Master of,* which he did not expect to find under such a Roof, had raised in him more Curiosity than he had ever known. 'Therefore,' said he, 'if it be not too troublesome, Sir, your History, if you please.'

The Gentleman answered, he could not refuse him what he had so much Right to insist on; and after some of the common Apologies, which are the usual Preface to a Story, he thus began.

Chapter III

In which the Gentleman relates the History of his Life.

Sir, I am descended of a good Family, and was born a Gentleman. My Education was liberal, and at a public School,[1] in which I proceeded so far as to become Master of the *Latin*, and to be tolerably versed in the *Greek* Language. My Father died when I was sixteen, and left me Master of myself. He bequeathed me a moderate Fortune, which he intended I should not receive till I attained the Age of twenty-five: For he constantly asserted that was full early enough to give up any Man entirely to the Guidance of his own Discretion. However, as this Intention was so obscurely worded in his Will, that the Lawyers advised me to contest the Point with my Trustees, I own I paid so little Regard to the Inclinations of my dead Father, which were sufficiently certain to me, that I followed their Advice, and soon succeeded: For the Trustees did not contest the Matter very obstinately on their side. 'Sir,' said *Adams*, 'May I crave the Favour of your Name?' The Gentleman answer'd, 'his Name was *Wilson*,' and then proceeded.

I stay'd a very little while at School after his Death; for being a forward Youth, I was extremely impatient to be in the World: For which I thought

---

*The Author hath by some been represented to have made a Blunder here: For *Adams* had indeed shewn some Learning, (say they) perhaps all the Author had; but the Gentleman hath shewn none, unless his Approbation of Mr. *Adams* be such: But surely it would be preposterous in him to call it so. I have however, notwithstanding this Criticism which I am told came from the Mouth of a great Orator,[9] in a public Coffee-House, left this Blunder as it stood in the first Edition. I will not have the Vanity to apply to any thing in this Work, the Observation which M. *Dacier* makes in her Preface to her *Aristophanes*. *Je tiens pour une Maxime constante qu'une Beauté médiocre plait plus generalement qu'une Beauté sans défaut*.[1] Mr. *Congreve* hath made such another Blunder in his *Love for Love*, where *Tattle* tells Miss *Prue*, *She should admire him as much for the Beauty he commends in her, as if he himself was possest of it*.[2]

---

9. For a likely candidate, see p. 184, n. 5.
1. "It is my invariable maxim that a middling beauty is more generally pleasing than a faultless one," Mme. Anne Lefevre Dacier (1654–1720), preface to her translation, *Le Plutus et les Nuées d'Aristophane* (Paris: 1684).
2. In act 2, scene 2, Tattle, "a half-witted Beau," teaching Miss Prue, "a silly, awkward Country Girl," to respond to a lover by lying as "all well-bred Persons" do, says "you must think your self more Charming than I speak you:—And like me, for the Beauty which I say you have, as much as

if I had it my self." Fielding added this note in the second edition.
1. At this time the public schools—so called because they were endowed foundations for the public benefit, as opposed to private institutions run for profit—consisted chiefly of such venerable boys' boarding schools as Eton, Winchester, Westminster, and Harrow. In their traditional curriculum, a "liberal" education, i.e., one "becoming a gentleman," in Dr. Johnson's definition, was mainly instruction in Latin and Greek.

my Parts, Knowledge, and Manhood thoroughly qualified me. And to this early Introduction into Life, without a Guide, I impute all my future Misfortunes; for besides the obvious Mischiefs which attend this, there is one which hath not been so generally observed. The first Impression which Mankind receives of you, will be very difficult to eradicate. How unhappy, therefore, must it be to fix your Character[2] in Life, before you can possibly know its Value, or weigh the Consequences of those Actions which are to establish your future Reputation?

A little under seventeen I left my School and went to *London*, with no more than six Pounds in my Pocket. A great Sum as I then conceived; and which I was afterwards surprized to find so soon consumed.

The Character I was ambitious of attaining, was that of a fine Gentleman; the first Requisites to which, I apprehended were to be supplied by a Taylor, a Periwig-maker, and some few more Tradesmen, who deal in furnishing out the human Body. Notwithstanding the Lowness of my Purse, I found Credit with them more easily than I expected, and was soon equipped to my Wish. This I own then agreeably surprized me; but I have since learn'd, that it is a Maxim among many Tradesmen at the polite End of the Town to deal as largely[3] as they can, reckon[4] as high as they can, and arrest as soon as they can.

The next Qualifications, namely Dancing, Fencing, Riding the great Horse,[5] and Musick, came into my head; but as they required Expence and Time, I comforted myself, with regard to Dancing, that I had learned a little in my Youth, and could walk a Minuet genteelly enough; as to Fencing, I thought my Good-Humour would preserve me from the Danger of a Quarrel; as to the Horse, I hoped it would not be thought of; and for Musick, I imagined I could easily acquire the Reputation of it; for I had heard some of my School-fellows pretend to Knowledge in Operas, without being able to sing or play on the Fiddle.

Knowledge of the Town seemed another Ingredient; this I thought I should arrive at by frequenting publick Places. Accordingly I paid constant Attendance to them all; by which means I was soon Master of the fashionable Phrases, learn'd to cry up the fashionable Diversions, and knew the Names and Faces of the most fashionable Men and Women.

Nothing now seemed to remain but an Intrigue, which I was resolved to have immediately; I mean the Reputation of it; and indeed I was so successful, that in a very short time I had half a dozen with the finest Women in Town.

At these Words *Adams* fetched a deep Groan, and then blessing himself, cry'd out, *Good Lord! What wicked Times these are?*

Not so wicked as you imagine, continued the Gentleman; for I assure you, they were all Vestal Virgins for any thing which I knew to the contrary. The Reputation of Intriguing with them was all I sought, and

2. Reputation.
3. Freely.
4. Charge.
5. "Those persons who professed the science of arms were obliged to learn the art of managing their horses, in conformity to certain rules and principles; and hence came the expression of learning to ride the great horse" (Richard Berenger, *The History and Art of Horsemanship* [1771] 1.170.).

was what I arriv'd at: and perhaps I only flattered myself even in that; for very probably the Persons to whom I shewed their Billets, knew as well as I, that they were Counterfeits, and that I had written them to myself.

'WRITE *Letters to yourself!*' said *Adams* staring!

O Sir, answered the Gentleman, *It is the very Error of the Times*. Half our modern Plays have one of these Characters in them.[6] It is incredible the Pains I have taken, and the absurd Methods I employed to traduce the Character of Women of Distinction. When another had spoken in Raptures of any one, I have answered, 'D—n her, she! We shall have her at H——d's[7] very soon.' When he hath reply'd, 'he thought her virtuous,' I have answered, 'Ay, thou wilt always think a Woman virtuous, till she is in the Streets, but you and I, *Jack* or *Tom*, (turning to another in Company) know better.' At which I have drawn a Paper out of my Pocket, perhaps a Taylor's Bill, and kissed it, crying at the same time, *By Gad I was once fond of her*.

'Proceed, if you please, but do not swear any more,' said *Adams*.

Sir, said the Gentleman, I ask your Pardon. Well, Sir, in this Course of Life I continued full three Years,—'What Course of Life?' answered *Adams*; 'I do not remember you have yet mentioned any.'—Your Remark is just, said the Gentleman smiling, I should rather have said, in this Course of doing nothing. I remember some time afterwards I wrote the Journal of one Day, which would serve, I believe, as well for any other, during the whole Time; I will endeavour to repeat it to you.

In the Morning I arose, took my great Stick, and walked out in my green Frock with my Hair in Papers, (*a Groan from* Adams) and sauntered about till ten.

Went to the Auction; told Lady ——— she had a dirty Face; laughed heartily at something Captain ——— said; I can't remember what, for I did not very well hear it; whispered Lord ———; bowed to the Duke of ——— ; and was going to bid for a Snuff-box; but did not, for fear I should have had it.

From 2 to 4, drest myself.	A Groan.
4 to 6, dined.	A Groan.
6 to 8, Coffee-house.	
8 to 9, *Drury-Lane* Play-house.	
9 to 10, *Lincoln's-Inn-Fields*.[8]	
10 to 12, Drawing-Room.	A great Groan.

6. In Congreve's *The Way of the World* (1700), the would-be rake Petulant is known to leave a letter for himself (1.1). Closer analogues occur in Fielding's *The Old Debauchees* (1732), where old Jourdain confesses ruining an innocent woman's reputation by showing a letter from her written by himself (1.9); section 2 of Swift's *Tale of a Tub* (1704); and *Gil Blas* (3.8). Battestin thinks Fielding's capitalization is a private jest at Adams's supposed model, his neighbor and friend, the Reverend William Young (1702?–1757). According to a contemporary report, the absentminded Young was caught in an attempt to obtain himself leave from his duties when he presented his patron a pretended letter of invitation unopened.

7. Mother Haywood's, a fashionable brothel in Covent Garden.

8. Site of Rich's theatre (see above, p. 29, n. 2) from 1714 to 1732, an area where, according to the Act of 1733 authorizing its improvement, "many wicked and disorderly persons have frequented . . . enticing young persons into gaming, idleness, and other vicious courses."

At all which Places nothing happened worth Remark. At which *Adams* said with some Vehemence, 'Sir, this is below the Life of an Animal, hardly above Vegetation; and I am surprized what could lead a Man of your Sense into it.' What leads us into more Follies than you imagine, Doctor, answered the Gentleman; Vanity: For as contemptible a Creature as I was, and I assure you, yourself cannot have more Contempt for such a Wretch than I now have, I then admir'd myself, and should have despised a Person of your present Appearance (you will pardon me) with all your Learning, and those excellent Qualities which I have remarked in you. *Adams* bowed, and begged him to proceed. After I had continued two Years in this Course of Life, said the Gentleman, an Accident happened which obliged me to change the Scene. As I was one day at *St. James's* Coffee-house,[9] making very free with the Character of a young Lady of Quality, an Officer of the Guards who was present, thought proper to give me the lye. I answered, I might possibly be mistaken; but I intended to tell no more than the Truth. To which he made no Reply, but by a scornful Sneer. After this I observed a strange Coldness in all my Acquaintance; none of them spoke to me first, and very few returned me even the Civility of a Bow. The Company I used to dine with, left me out, and within a Week I found myself in as much Solitude at *St. James's*, as if I had been in a Desart. An honest elderly Man, with a great Hat and long Sword, at last told me, he had a Compassion for my Youth, and therefore advised me to shew the World I was not such a Rascal as they thought me to be. I did not at first understand him: But he explained himself, and ended with telling me, if I would write a Challenge to the Captain, he would out of pure Charity go to him with it. 'A very charitable Person truly!' cried *Adams*. I desired till the next Day, continued the Gentleman, to consider on it, and retiring to my Lodgings, I weighed the Consequences on both sides as fairly as I could. On the one, I saw the Risk of this Alternative, either losing my own Life, or having on my hands the Blood of a Man with whom I was not in the least angry. I soon determined that the Good which appeared on the other, was not worth this Hazard. I therefore resolved to quit the Scene, and presently retired to the *Temple*,[1] where I took Chambers. Here I soon got a fresh Set of Acquaintance, who knew nothing of what had happened to me. Indeed they were not greatly to my Approbation; for the Beaus of the *Temple* are only the Shadows of the others. They are the Affectation of Affectation. The Vanity of these is still more ridiculous, if possible, than of the others. Here I met with smart Fellows who drank with Lords they did not know, and intrigued with Women they never saw. *Covent-Garden* was now the farthest Stretch of my Ambition, where I shone forth in the Balconies at the Play-houses, visited Whores, made Love to Orange-Wenches, and damned Plays. This Career was

9. A fashionable haunt of Guards officers and whigs near St. James's Palace and Pall Mall.
1. A complex of buildings between Fleet Street and the Thames near the center of the old City of London inhabited by lawyers and students of the law. Fielding studied law at the Middle Temple, one of the two Inns of Court there, from 1737 to 1739.

soon put a stop to by my Surgeon, who convinced me of the Necessity of confining myself to my Room for a Month.[2] At the End of which, having had Leisure to reflect, I resolved to quit all further Conversation with Beaus and Smarts of every kind, and to avoid, if possible, any Occasion of returning to this Place of Confinement. 'I think,' said *Adams*, 'the Advice of a Month's Retirement and Reflection was very proper; but I should rather have expected it from a Divine than a Surgeon.' The Gentleman smiled at *Adams's* Simplicity, and without explaining himself farther on such an odious Subject went on thus: I was no sooner perfectly restored to Health, than I found my Passion for Women, which I was afraid to satisfy as I had done, made me very uneasy; I determined therefore to keep a Mistress. Nor was I long before I fixed my Choice on a young Woman, who had before been kept by two Gentlemen, and to whom I was recommended by a celebrated Bawd. I took her home to my Chambers, and made her a Settlement, during Cohabitation. This would perhaps have been very ill paid: However, she did not suffer me to be perplexed on that account; for before Quarterday,[3] I found her at my Chambers in too familiar Conversation with a young Fellow who was drest like an Officer, but was indeed a City[4] Apprentice. Instead of excusing her Inconstancy, she rapped out half a dozen Oaths, and snapping her Fingers at me, swore she scorned to confine herself to the best Man in *England*. Upon this we parted, and the same Bawd presently provided her another Keeper. I was not so much concerned at our Separation, as I found within a Day or two I had Reason to be for our Meeting: For I was obliged to pay a second Visit to my Surgeon. I was now forced to do Penance for some Weeks, during which Time I contracted an Acquaintance with a beautiful young Girl, the Daughter of a Gentleman, who after having been forty Years in the Army, and in all the Campaigns under the Duke of *Marlborough*, died a Lieutenant on Half-Pay;[5] and had left a Widow with this only Child, in very distrest Circumstances: they had only a small Pension from the Government, with what little the Daughter could add to it by her Work; for she had great Excellence at her Needle. This Girl was, at my first Acquaintance with her, sollicited in Marriage by a young Fellow in good Circumstances. He was Apprentice to a Linen-draper,[6] and had a little Fortune sufficient to set up his Trade. The Mother was greatly pleased with this Match, as indeed she had sufficient Reason. However, I soon prevented it. I represented him in so low a Light to his Mistress, and made so good

2. Rest was commonly prescribed for venereal disease.
3. One of four days (Lady Day, March 25; Midsummer Day, June 24; Michaelmas, September 29; and Christmas) designated for quarterly payments of rent, or in this case maintenance.
4. The mercantile center of London, so called because it lies within the ancient boundaries.
5. Evidently he remained at this second lowest officer rank because he could not afford to purchase a commission at a higher rank (see below, p. 236, n. 2). In the time of Queen Anne, a few

years earlier, a half-pay lieutenant earned two shillings a day, or thirty-six pounds a year; in 1730, the *total* amount requested as pensions for widows of officers who died on the half-pay list was fifteen hundred pounds. John Churchill, first duke of Marlborough (1650–1722), whom Fielding admired and under whom his father served as a captain, was rewarded for his celebrated victories over the French (1702–11) by the queen's gift of an estate and the publicly funded construction of Blenheim Palace.
6. A retail cloth merchant.

an Use of Flattery, Promises, and Presents, that, not to dwell longer on this Subject than is necessary, I prevailed with the poor Girl, and convey'd her away from her Mother! In a word, I debauched her.—(At which Words, *Adams* started up, fetch'd three Strides cross the Room, and then replaced himself in his Chair.) You are not more affected with this Part of my Story than myself: I assure you it will never be sufficiently repented of in my own Opinion: But if you already detest it, how much more will your Indignation be raised when you hear the fatal Consequences of this barbarous, this villainous Action? If you please therefore, I will here desist.—'By no means,' cries *Adams*, 'Go on, I beseech you, and Heaven grant you may sincerely repent of this and many other things you have related.'—I was now, continued the Gentleman, as happy as the Possession of a fine young Creature, who had a good Education, and was endued with many agreeable Qualities, could make me. We liv'd some Months with vast Fondness together, without any Company or Conversation more than we found in one another: But this could not continue always; and tho' I still preserved a great Affection for her, I began more and more to want the Relief of other Company, and consequently to leave her by degrees, at last, whole Days to herself. She failed not to testify some Uneasiness on these Occasions, and complained of the melancholy Life she led; to remedy which, I introduced her into the Acquaintance of some other kept Mistresses, with whom she used to play at Cards, and frequent Plays and other Diversions. She had not liv'd long in this Intimacy, before I perceived a visible Alteration in her Behaviour; all her Modesty and Innocence vanished by degrees, till her Mind became thoroughly tainted. She affected the Company of Rakes, gave herself all manner of Airs, was never easy but abroad, or when she had a Party at my Chambers. She was rapacious of Money, extravagant to Excess, loose in her Conversation; and if ever I demurred to any of her Demands, Oaths, Tears, and Fits, were the immediate Consequences. As the first Raptures of Fondness were long since over, this Behaviour soon estranged my Affections from her; I began to reflect with pleasure that she was not my Wife, and to conceive an Intention of parting with her, of which having given her a Hint, she took care to prevent me the Pains of turning her out of doors, and accordingly departed herself, having first broken open my Escrutore, and taken with her all she could find, to the Amount of about 200 *l*. In the first Heat of my Resentment, I resolved to pursue her with all the Vengeance of the Law: But as she had the good Luck to escape me during that Ferment, my Passion afterwards cooled, and having reflected that I had been the first Aggressor, and had done her an Injury for which I could make her no Reparation, by robbing her of the Innocence of her Mind; and hearing at the same time that the poor old Woman her Mother had broke her Heart, on her Daughter's Elopement from her, I, concluding myself her Murderer ('As you very well might,' cries *Adams*, with a Groan;) was pleased that God Almighty had taken this Method of punishing me, and resolved quietly to submit to the Loss. Indeed I could wish I had never heard more of the poor Creature, who became in the end an abandoned

Profligate; and after being some Years a common Prostitute, at last ended her miserable Life in *Newgate*.[7]—Here the Gentleman fetch'd a deep Sigh, which Mr. *Adams* echo'd very loudly, and both continued silent looking on each other for some Minutes. At last the Gentleman proceeded thus: I had been perfectly constant to this Girl, during the whole Time I kept her: But she had scarce departed before I discovered more Marks of her Infidelity to me, than the Loss of my Money. In short, I was forced to make a third Visit to my Surgeon, out of whose hands I did not get a hasty Discharge.

I now forswore all future Dealings with the Sex, complained loudly that the Pleasure did not compensate the Pain, and railed at the beautiful Creatures, in as gross Language as *Juvenal* himself formerly reviled them in.[8] I looked on all the Town-Harlots with a Detestation not easy to be conceived, their Persons appeared to me as painted Palaces inhabited by Disease and Death: Nor could their Beauty make them more desirable Objects in my Eyes, than Gilding could make me covet a Pill, or golden Plates a Coffin. But tho' I was no longer the absolute Slave, I found some Reasons to own myself still the Subject of Love. My Hatred for Women decreased daily; and I am not positive but Time might have betrayed me again to some common Harlot, had I not been secured by a Passion for the charming *Saphira*; which having once entered upon, made a violent Progress in my Heart. *Saphira* was Wife to a Man of Fashion and Gallantry, and one who seemed, I own, every way worthy of her Affections, which however he had not the Reputation of having. She was indeed a *Coquette achevée*.[9] 'Pray Sir,' says *Adams*, 'What is a Coquette? I have met with the Word in *French* Authors, but never could assign any Idea to it. I believe it is the same with *une Sotte*, Anglicé *a Fool*.' Sir, answer'd the Gentleman, perhaps you are not much mistaken: but as it is a particular kind of Folly, I will endeavour to describe it. Were all Creatures to be ranked in the Order of Creation, according to their Usefulness, I know few Animals that would not take place of a Coquette; nor indeed hath this Creature much Pretence to any thing beyond Instinct: for tho' sometimes we might imagine it was animated by the Passion of Vanity, yet far the greater part of its Actions fall beneath even that low Motive; For instance, several absurd Gestures and Tricks, infinitely more foolish than what can be observed in the most ridiculous Birds and Beasts, and which would persuade the Beholder that the silly Wretch was aiming at our Contempt. Indeed its Characteristick is Affectation, and this led and governed by Whim only: for as Beauty, Wisdom, Wit, Good-nature, Politeness and Health are sometimes affected by this Creature; so are Ugliness, Folly, Nonsense, Ill-nature, Ill-breeding and Sickness likewise put on by it in their Turn. Its Life is one constant Lye,

---

7. The principal London prison.
8. In his savage *Satire VI*, the Roman satirist Juvenal (fl. A.D. 98–128) flayed the female sex, emphasizing their depraved sexual appetites and infidelities. His "gross Language" may be illustrated by the description of a high-living matron who drinks excessively, then "brings it all up again and souses the floors with the washings of her inside" (429, G. G. Ramsey, trans.). Fielding published a youthful adaptation of part of this poem ("the Revenge taken by an injured Lover") in his *Miscellanies* (1743).
9. An accomplished flirt.

and the only Rule by which you can form any Judgment of them is, that they are never what they seem. If it was possible for a Coquette to love (as it is not, for if ever it attains this Passion, the Coquette ceases instantly) it would wear the Face of Indifference if not of hatred to the beloved Object; you may therefore be assured, when they endeavour to persuade you of their liking, that they are indifferent to you at least. And indeed this was the Case of my *Saphira*, who no sooner saw me in the number of her Admirers, than she gave me what is commonly called Encouragement; she would often look at me, and when she perceived me meet her Eyes, would instantly take them off, discovering at the same time as much Surprize and Emotion as possible. These Arts failed not of the Success she intended; and as I grew more particular[1] to her than the rest of her Admirers, she advanced in proportion more directly to me than to the others. She affected the low Voice, Whisper, Lisp, Sigh, Start, Laugh, and many other Indications of Passion, which daily deceive thousands. When I play'd at Whisk[2] with her, she would look earnestly at me, and at the same time lose Deal or revoke; then burst into a ridiculous Laugh, and cry, 'La! I can't imagine what I was thinking of.' To detain you no longer, after I had gone through a sufficient Course of Gallantry, as I thought, and was thoroughly convinced I had raised a violent Passion in my Mistress; I sought an Opportunity of coming to an Eclaircissement[3] with her. She avoided this as much as possible, however great Assiduity at length presented me one. I will not describe all the Particulars of this Interview; let it suffice, that when she could no longer pretend not to see my Drift, she first affected a violent Surprize, and immediately after as violent a Passion: She wondered what I had seen in her Conduct, which could induce me to affront her in this manner: And breaking from me the first Moment she could, told me, I had no other way to escape the Consequence of her Resentment, than by never seeing, or at least speaking to her more. I was not contented with this Answer; I still pursued her, but to no purpose, and was at length convinced that her Husband had the sole Possession of her Person, and that neither he nor any other had made any Impression on her Heart. I was taken off from following this *Ignis Fatuus*[4] by some Advances which were made me by the Wife of a Citizen,[5] who tho' neither very young nor handsome, was yet too agreeable to be rejected by my amorous Constitution. I accordingly soon satisfy'd her, that she had not cast away her Hints on a barren or cold Soil; on the contrary, they instantly produced her an eager and desiring Lover. Nor did she give me any Reason to complain; she met the Warmth she had raised with equal Ardour. I had no longer a Coquette to deal with, but one who was wiser than to prostitute the noble Passion of Love to the ridiculous Lust of Vanity. We

1. Specially attentive.
2. An early spelling of whist, prototype of bridge. A player revoked when he or she failed to follow suit while holding cards in that suit; the penalty was two tricks. A player might lose deal by dealing the wrong number of cards or failing to turn up the final card to determine the trump suit.
3. A vogue word for an open understanding.
4. "Foolish fire," commonly called will-o'-the-wisp, a capricious phosphorescent light, produced by marsh gas, that misled travelers.
5. "A man of trade, not a gentleman" (Johnson's *Dictionary* [see above, p. 161, n. 4]).

presently understood one another; and as the Pleasures we sought lay in a mutual Gratification, we soon found and enjoyed them. I thought myself at first greatly happy in the possession of this new Mistress, whose Fondness would have quickly surfeited a more sickly Appetite, but it had a different Effect on mine; she carried my Passion higher by it than Youth or Beauty had been able: But my Happiness could not long continue uninterrupted. The Apprehensions we lay under from the Jealousy of her Husband, gave us great Uneasiness. 'Poor Wretch! I pity him,' cry'd *Adams*. He did indeed deserve it, said the Gentleman, for he loved his Wife with great Tenderness, and I assure you it is a great Satisfaction to me that I was not the Man who first seduced her Affections from him. These Apprehensions appeared also too well grounded; for in the End he discovered us, and procur'd Witnesses of our Caresses. He then prosecuted me at Law, and recovered 3000 *l.* Damages,[6] which much distressed my Fortune to pay: and what was worse, his Wife being divorced, came upon my hands. I led a very uneasy Life with her; for besides that my Passion was now much abated, her excessive Jealousy was very troublesome. At length Death delivered me from an Inconvenience, which the Consideration of my having been the Author of her Misfortunes, would never suffer me to take any other Method of discarding.

I now bad adieu to Love, and resolved to pursue other less dangerous and expensive Pleasures. I fell into the Acquaintance of a Set of jolly Companions, who slept all Day and drank all Night: Fellows who might rather be said to consume Time than to live. Their best Conversation was nothing but Noise: Singing, Hollowing, Wrangling, Drinking, Toasting, Sp—wing,[7] Smoking, were the chief Ingredients of our Entertainment. And yet bad as these were, they were more tolerable than our graver Scenes, which were either excessive tedious Narratives of dull common Matters of Fact, or hot Disputes about trifling Matters, which commonly ended in a Wager. This Way of Life the first serious Reflection put a period to, and I became Member of a Club frequented by young Men of great Abilities. The Bottle was now only called in to the Assistance of our Conversation, which rolled on the deepest Points of Philosophy. These Gentlemen were engaged in a Search after Truth, in the Pursuit of which they threw aside all the Prejudices of Education,[8] and governed themselves only by the infallible Guide of Human Reason. This great Guide, after having shewn them the Falshood of that very antient but simple[9] Tenet, that there is such a Being as a Deity in the Universe, helped them to establish in his stead a certain *Rule of Right*, by adhering to which they all arrived at the utmost Purity of Morals. Reflection made me as much delighted with this Society, as it had taught me to despise and detest the former. I began now to esteem

6. For adultery, for which a husband could bring civil suit.
7. Spewing (vomiting).
8. A phrase widely used by moral and religious writers of the time, but particularly associated with John Toland (see above, p. 64, n. 8), Anthony Collins (1676–1729), and other Freethinkers, who regarded such unexamined inherited beliefs as an impediment to rational inquiry and true understanding. Collins led one of the earliest freethinking clubs at the Grecian Coffee House in the Strand in 1712, a few years before Wilson's experience.
9. Naive.

myself a Being of a higher Order than I had ever before conceived, and was the more charmed with this Rule of Right, as I really found in my own Nature nothing repugnant to it. I held in utter Contempt all Persons who wanted any other Inducement to Virtue besides her intrinsick Beauty and Excellence;[1] and had so high an Opinion of my present Companions, with regard to their Morality, that I would have trusted them with whatever was nearest and dearest to me. Whilst I was engaged in this delightful Dream, two or three Accidents happen'd successively, which at first much surprized me. For, one of our greatest Philosophers, or *Rule of Right-men* withdrew himself from us, taking with him the Wife of one of his most intimate Friends. Secondly, Another of the same Society left the Club without remembring to take leave of his Bail.[2] A third having borrowed a Sum of Money of me, for which I received no Security, when I asked him to repay it, absolutely denied the Loan. These several Practices, so inconsistent with our golden Rule, made me begin to suspect its Infallibility; but when I communicated my Thoughts to one of the Club, he said 'there was nothing absolutely good or evil in itself; that Actions were denominated good or bad by the Circumstances of the Agent. That possibly the Man who ran away with his Neighbour's Wife might be one of very good Inclinations, but over-prevailed on by the Violence of an unruly Passion, and in other Particulars might be a very worthy Member of Society: That if the Beauty of any Woman created in him an Uneasiness, he had a Right from Nature to relieve himself;'[3] with many other things, which I then detested so much, that I.

---

1. The club's principles are a satiric exaggeration of the "natural religion" espoused by liberal churchmen as well as the deists they denounced. The prominent theologian Samuel Clarke (1675–1729), whom Fielding admired, maintained that the "Law of Nature . . . founded in the eternal Reason of things" commands "the natural Assent of all Mens unprejudiced Reason to the Rule of Right and Equity" without consideration of reward or punishment but solely because "Virtue and Goodness are truly amiable, and to be chosen for their own sakes and intrinsick worth" (*A Discourse Concerning the Unchangeable Obligations of Natural Religion and the Truth and Certainty of the Christian Revelation*, 1706, pp. 106–7, 113). But these ideas were probably most commonly associated with Shaftesbury (see above, p. 5, n. 7). Although he argued that "the perfection . . . of virtue must be owing to the belief of a God," he maintained that without it numans have a "natural and just sense of right and wrong" and "real . . . love towards equity and right for its own sake, and on account of its own natural beauty and worth" (*An Inquiry Concerning Virtue or Merit* [1699, rev. 1711] 1.3.3, and 1.3.1; in *Characteristics* 1.280, 258, 259). Wilson's contempt alludes to Shaftesbury's argument for the superiority of disinterested voluntary "obedience to the rule of right" ("the only true and liberal service" to God) over selfish concern for eternal reward and punishment, which he conceded might be beneficial "among the vulgar" and those whom "wrong thought" leads to vice (*The Moralists* [1709] 2.3;

Miscellaneous Reflections [1711] 3.2; *Inquiry* 1.3; in *Characteristics* 2.56, 265; 1. 270).

2. Apparently another member who has put up some financial surety that his friend will continue to attend regularly and pay his share of the club's expenses.

3. This defense is a patchwork of ideas and phrases wrenched from their qualifying contexts in Shaftesbury (who saw a function for religion in stemming "the violence of . . . passion" that might undermine an otherwise "good temper" [*Characteristics* I.270]) and two writers with radically less benign conceptions of human nature. Hobbes (see p. 66, n. 4) defined the Right of Nature as "the liberty each man hath, to use his own power, as he will himself, for the preservation of his own nature" (*Leviathan*, ed. M. Oakeshott [London: B. Blackwell, 1960] 1.14.84). He claimed "every man has a right to everything; even to one another's body," but only in that "war of every one against every one," which he defined as man's natural state *prior to civil society* (85). Hobbes's thesis that "nothing [is] simply and absolutely" good or evil, these terms being "used with relation to the person that useth them" *until a* "common rule" is imposed by civil authority (1. 6. 32) was unconditionally extended by Bernard Mandeville (1670–1733): "things are only Good and Evil in reference to something else. . . . What pleases us is good . . . and by this Rule every Man wishes well for himself. . . with little Respect to his Neighbour" (*The Fable of the Bees*, ed. F. B. Kaye [Oxford: Clarendon Press, 1924] 1.367).

took Leave of the Society that very Evening, and never returned to it
again. Being now reduced to a State of Solitude, which I did not like, I
became a great Frequenter of the Play-houses, which indeed was always
my favourite Diversion, and most Evenings past away two or three Hours
behind the Scenes, where I met with several Poets,[4] with whom I made
Engagements at the Taverns. Some of the Players were likewise of our
Parties. At these Meetings we were generally entertain'd by the Poets
with reading their Performances, and by the Players with repeating their
Parts: Upon which Occasions, I observed the Gentleman who furnished
our Entertainment, was commonly the best pleased of the Company;
who, tho' they were pretty civil to him to his Face, seldom failed to take
the first Opportunity of his Absence to ridicule him. Now I made some
Remarks,[5] which probably are too obvious to be worth relating. 'Sir,'
says Adams, 'your Remarks if you please.' First then, says he, I concluded that the general Observation, that Wits are most inclined to Vanity, is not true. Men are equally vain of Riches, Strength, Beauty,
Honours, &c. But, these appear of themselves to the Eyes of the Beholders, whereas the poor Wit is obliged to produce his Performance to shew
you his Perfection, and on his Readiness to do this that vulgar opinion I
have before mentioned is grounded: But doth not the Person who expends
vast Sums in the Furniture of his House, or the Ornaments of his Person, who consumes much Time, and employs great Pains in dressing
himself, or who thinks himself paid for Self-Denial, Labour, or even
Villany by a Title or a Ribbon, sacrifice as much to Vanity as the poor
Wit, who is desirous to read you his Poem or his Play? My second Remark
was, that Vanity is the worst of Passions, and more apt to contaminate
the Mind than any other: For as Selfishness is much more general than
we please to allow it, so it is natural to hate and envy those who stand
between us and the Good we desire. Now in Lust and Ambition these
are few; and even in Avarice we find many who are no Obstacles to our
Pursuits; but the vain Man seeks Pre-eminence; and every thing which
is excellent or praise-worthy in another, renders him the Mark of his
Antipathy. Adams now began to fumble in his Pockets, and soon cried
out, 'O la! I have it not about me.'—Upon this the Gentleman asking
him what he was searching for, he said he searched after a Sermon,
which he thought his Master-piece, against Vanity. 'Fie upon it, fie
upon it, cries he, 'why do I ever leave that Sermon out of my Pocket? I
wish it was within five Miles, I would willingly fetch it, to read it to
you.' The Gentleman answered, that there was no need, for he was
cured of the Passion. 'And for that very Reason,' quoth Adams, 'I would
read it, for I am confident you would admire it: Indeed, I have never
been a greater Enemy to any Passion than that silly one of Vanity.' The
Gentleman smiled, and proceeded—From this Society I easily past to
that of the Gamesters, where nothing remarkable happened, but the
finishing my Fortune, which those Gentlemen soon helped me to the
End of. This opened Scenes of Life hitherto unknown; Poverty and Dis-

4. Playwrights.
5. Observations, in the sense of noticing, not commenting.

tress with their horrid Train of Duns, Attorneys, Bailiffs,[6] haunted me
Day and Night. My Clothes grew shabby, my Credit bad, my Friends
and Acquaintance of all kinds cold. In this Situation the strangest Thought
imaginable came into my Head; and what was this, but to write a Play?
for I had sufficient Leisure; Fear of Bailiffs confined me every Day to
my Room; and having always had a little Inclination and something of
a Genius that way, I set myself to work, and within few Months produced a Piece of five Acts, which was accepted of at the Theatre. I
remembered to have formerly taken Tickets of other Poets for their Benefits long before the Appearance of their Performances,[7] and resolving
to follow a Precedent, which was so well suited to my present Circumstances; I immediately provided myself with a large Number of little
Papers. Happy indeed would be the State of Poetry, would these Tickets
pass current at the Bakehouse, the Ale-House, and the Chandler's-Shop:
But alas! far otherwise; no Taylor will take them in Payment for Buckram, Stays, Stay-tape; nor no Bailiff for Civility-Money.[8] They are indeed
no more than a Passport to beg with, a Certificate that the Owner wants
five Shillings, which induces well-disposed Christians to Charity. I now
experienced what is worse than Poverty, or rather what is the worst Consequence of Poverty, I mean Attendance and Dependance on the Great.
Many a Morning have I waited Hours in the cold Parlours of Men of
Quality, where after seeing the lowest Rascals in Lace and Embroidery,
the Pimps and Buffoons in Fashion admitted, I have been sometimes
told on sending in my Name, that my Lord could not possibly see me
this Morning: A sufficient Assurance that I should never more get entrance
into that House. Sometimes I have been at last admitted, and the great
Man hath thought proper to excuse himself, by telling me he was *tied
up*. 'Tied up,' says *Adams*, 'pray what's that?' Sir, says the Gentleman,
the Profit which Booksellers allowed Authors for the best Works, was so
very small, that certain Men of Birth and Fortune some Years ago, who
were the Patrons of Wit and Learning, thought fit to encourage them
farther, by entring into voluntary Subscriptions for their Encouragement. Thus *Prior*, *Rowe*, *Pope*, and some other Men of Genius, received
large Sums for their Labours from the Public.[9] This seemed so easy a
Method of getting Money, that many of the lowest Scriblers of the Times
ventured to publish their Works in the same Way; and many had the

6. These three terms recapitulate the creditor's
successive measures for recovery, ending with arrest
for debt.
7. The playwright received the profits of the third,
sixth, and ninth performances, if the play ran that
long; but he also had to guarantee to cover the
theatre's expenses for the first of these. Hence
authors often sold tickets to their first benefit night
in advance of the production.
8. A tip to assure favored treatment under arrest.
9. Nicholas Rowe's *Tragedy of Jane Shore* (1714),
Matthew Prior's *Poems on Several Occasions* (1719),
and Pope's *Iliad* (1715–20) and *Odyssey* (1725–
26) were published by subscription. Pope and Prior

earning respectively perhaps as much as nine
thousand and forty-two hundred pounds. This
mode of publication was advantageous to the author
because subscribers usually paid half the purchase
price in advance and the author could contract
directly with a printer, thus retaining the bookseller's share of the profits. The abuses and incessant
solicitations Wilson describes below eventually
brought the practice into such disrepute that War-
burton, advertising his edition of Pope's works in
1751, avowed he had "not, for the sake of profit,
suffered the Author's name to be made cheap by a
subscription."

Assurance to take in Subscriptions for what was not writ, nor ever intended. Subscriptions in this manner growing infinite, and a kind of Tax on the Public; some Persons finding it not so easy a Task to discern good from bad Authors, or to know what Genius was worthy Encouragement, and what was not, to prevent the Expence of Subscribing to so many, invented a Method to excuse themselves from all Subscriptions whatever; and this was to receive a small Sum of Money in consideration of giving a large one if ever they subscribed; which many have done, and many more have pretended to have done, in order to silence all Sollicitation. The same Method was likewise taken with Playhouse Tickets, which were no less a public Grievance; and this is what they call being *tied up* from subscribing. 'I can't say but the Term is apt enough, and somewhat typical,' said *Adams*; 'for a Man of large Fortune, who ties himself up, as you call it, from the Encouragement of Men of Merit, ought to be tied up in reality.' Well, Sir, says the Gentleman, to return to my Story. Sometimes I have received a Guinea from a Man of Quality, given with as ill a Grace as Alms are generally to the meanest Beggar, and purchased too with as much Time spent in Attendance, as, if it had been spent in honest Industry, might have brought me more Profit with infinitely more Satisfaction. After about two Months spent in this disagreeable way with the utmost Mortification, when I was pluming my Hopes on the Prospect of a plentiful Harvest from my Play, upon applying to the Prompter to know when it came into Rehearsal, he informed me he had received Orders from the Managers to return me the Play again; for that they could not possibly act it that Season; but if I would take it and revise it against the next, they would be glad to see it again. I snatch'd it from him with great Indignation, and retired to my Room, where I threw myself on the Bed in a Fit of Despair—'You should rather have thrown yourself on your Knees,' says *Adams*; 'for Despair is sinful.' As soon, continued the Gentleman, as I had indulged the first Tumult of my Passion, I began to consider coolly what Course I should take, in a Situation without Friends, Money, Credit or Reputation of any kind. After revolving many things in my Mind, I could see no other Possibility of furnishing myself with the miserable Necessaries of Life than to retire to a Garret near the *Temple*, and commence Hackney-writer to the Lawyers; for which I was well qualify'd, being an excellent Penman. This Purpose I resolved on, and immediately put it in execution. I had an Acquaintance with an Attorney who had formerly transacted Affairs for me, and to him I applied: But instead of furnishing me with any Business, he laugh'd at my Undertaking, and told me 'he was afraid I should turn his Deeds into Plays, and he should expect to see them on the Stage.' Not to tire you with Instances of this kind from others, I found that *Plato* himself did not hold Poets in greater Abhorrence [1] than these Men of business do. Whenever I durst venture to a Coffee-house, which

---

1. In books 2, 3, and 10 of *The Republic*, Socrates argues that even the works of Homer are deleterious to the moral education of the guardians of his ideal state, because they defame gods and heroes, confuse images with reality, and corrupt the soul of the reader.

was on *Sundays* only,[2] a Whisper ran round the Room, which was constantly attended with a Sneer—*That's Poet Wilson*: for I know not whether you have observed it, but there is a Malignity in the Nature of Man, which when not weeded out, or at least covered by a good Education and Politeness, delights in making another uneasy or dissatisfied with himself. This abundantly appears in all Assemblies, except those which are filled by People of Fashion, and especially among the younger People of both Sexes, whose Birth and Fortunes place them just without the polite Circles; I mean the lower Class of the Gentry, and the higher of the mercantile World, who are in reality the worst bred part of Mankind. Well, Sir, whilst I continued in this miserable State, with scarce sufficient Business to keep me from starving, the Reputation of a Poet being my Bane, I accidentally became acquainted with a Bookseller, who told me 'it was a Pity a Man of my Learning and Genius should be obliged to such a Method of getting his Livelihood; that he had a Compassion for me, and if I would engage with him, he would undertake to provide handsomely for me.' A Man in my Circumstances, as he very well knew, had no Choice. I accordingly accepted his Proposal with his Conditions, which were none of the most favourable, and fell to translating with all my Might. I had no longer reason to lament the want of Business; for he furnished me with so much, that in half a Year I almost writ myself blind. I likewise contracted a Distemper by my sedentary Life, in which no part of my Body was exercised but my right Arm, which rendered me incapable of writing for a long time. This unluckily happening to delay the Publication of a Work, and my last Performance not having sold well, the Bookseller declined any further Engagement, and aspersed me to his Brethren as a careless, idle Fellow. I had however, by having half-work'd and half-starv'd myself to death during the Time I was in his Service, saved a few Guineas, with which I bought a Lottery-Ticket,[3] resolving to throw myself into Fortune's Lap, and try if she would make me amends for the Injuries she had done me at the Gaming-Table. This Purchase being made left me almost pennyless; when, as if I had not been sufficiently miserable, a Bailiff in Woman's Clothes got Admittance to my Chamber, whither he was directed by the Bookseller. He arrested me at my Taylor's Suit, for thirty-five Pounds; a Sum for which I could not procure Bail, and was therefore conveyed to his House, where I was locked up in an upper Chamber. I had now neither Health (for I was scarce recovered from my Indisposition) Liberty, Money, or Friends; and had abandoned all Hopes, and even the Desire of Life. 'But this could not last long,' said *Adams*, 'for doubtless the Taylor released you the moment he was truly acquainted with your Affairs; and knew that your Circumstances would not permit you to pay him.' Oh, Sir,

2. An Act for the better Observation of the Lords Day (1677) banned the serving on Sunday of any "writt, Processe, warrant order judgement or decree" except for treason, felony, or breach of the peace.
3. The government exploited the current passion for gambling to fund public works, selling eighty thousand tickets annually, most of which were bought up by profiteers who sold fractions to the poor. Fielding ridiculed these jobbers and their gullible victims in his farce *The Lottery* (1732).

answered the Gentleman, he knew that before he arrested me; nay, he knew that nothing but Incapacity could prevent me paying my Debts; for I had been his Customer many Years, had spent vast Sums of Money with him, and had always paid most punctually in my prosperous Days: But when I reminded him of this, with Assurances that if he would not molest my Endeavours, I would pay him all the Money I could, by my utmost Labour and Industry, procure, reserving only what was sufficient to preserve me alive: He answered, His Patience was worn out; that I had put him off from time to time; that he wanted the Money; that he had put it into a Lawyer's hands; and if I did not pay him immediately, or find Security, I must lie in Goal and expect no Mercy.[4] 'He may expect Mercy,' cries *Adams* starting from his Chair, 'where he will find none. How can such a Wretch repeat the Lord's Prayer, where the Word which is translated, I know not for what Reason, *Trespasses*, is in the Original *Debts*?[5] And as surely as we do not forgive others their Debts when they are unable to pay them; so surely shall we ourselves be unforgiven, when we are in no condition of paying.' He ceased, and the Gentleman proceeded. While I was in this deplorable Situation a former Acquaintance, to whom I had communicated my Lottery-Ticket, found me out, and making me a Visit with great Delight in his Countenance, shook me heartily by the Hand, and wished me Joy of my good Fortune: 'For,' says he, 'your Ticket is come up a Prize of 3000 *l*.' *Adams* snapt his Fingers at these Words in an Ecstasy of Joy; which however did not continue long: For the Gentleman thus proceeded. Alas! Sir, this was only a Trick of Fortune to sink me the deeper: For I had disposed of this Lottery-Ticket two Days before to a Relation, who refused lending me a Shilling without it, in order to procure myself Bread.[6] As soon as my Friend was acquainted with my unfortunate Sale, he began to revile me, and remind me of all the ill Conduct and Miscarriages of my Life. He said, 'I was one whom Fortune could not save, if she would; that I was now ruined without any Hopes of Retrieval, nor must expect any Pity from my Friends; that it would be extreme Weakness to compassionate the Misfortunes of a Man who ran headlong to his own Destruction.' He then painted to me in as lively Colours as he was able, the Happiness I should have now enjoyed, had I not foolishly disposed of my Ticket. I urg'd the Plea of Necessity: But he made no Answer to that, and began

4. Presuming every man solvent, the law empowered a creditor to imprison his debtor; if the debt exceeded two pounds, he could be jailed indefinitely. The first comprehensive census of English and Welsh prisons (1776) showed nearly two-thirds of the inmates to be debtors. As Battestin notes, Fielding repeatedly condemned this practice in his novels and periodical essays, but despite his outcries and those of Dr. Johnson, efforts to reform the system did not succeed until well into the nineteenth century.

5. Adams points to the discrepancy between the version of the prayer carried over from the pre-reformation Latin service in the *Book of Common Prayer* ("And forgive us our trespasses, As we forgive them that trespass against us") and the gospels' version (Matthew 6:12; Luke 11:4). Where the Authorized (King James) Version of Matthew does use *trespasses*, in the lines following the prayer (6:14–15), which Adams next paraphrases ("but if ye forgive not men their trespasses, neither will your Father forgive your trespasses"), the Greek reads *transgression* and not, as earlier, *debts*.

6. Jailers were not obligated to feed prisoners. Although an imprisoned debtor was legally entitled to fourpence a day subsistence, he was at the mercy of his creditor, who could refuse to pay this sum without fear of prosecution.

again to revile me, till I could bear it no longer, and desired him to
finish his Visit. I soon exchanged the Bailiff's House for a Prison; where,
as I had not Money sufficient to procure me a separate Apartment, I was
crouded in with a great number of miserable Wretches, in common with
whom I was destitute of every Convenience of Life, even that which all
the Brutes enjoy, wholesome Air.[7] In these dreadful Circumstances I
applied by Letter to several of my old Acquaintance, and such to whom
I had formerly lent Money without any great Prospect of its being returned,
for their Assistance; but in vain. An Excuse instead of a Denial was the
gentlest Answer I received.—Whilst I languished in a Condition too
horrible to be described, and which in a Land of Humanity, and, what
is much more Christianity, seems a strange Punishment for a little Inadvertency and Indiscretion. Whilst I was in this Condition, a Fellow came
into the Prison, and enquiring me out deliver'd me the following Letter:

Sir,

*My Father, to whom you sold your Ticket in the last Lottery, died the
same Day in which it came up a Prize, as you have possibly heard, and
left me sole Heiress of all his Fortune. I am so much touched with your
present Circumstances, and the Uneasiness you must feel at having been
driven to dispose of what might have made you happy, that I must desire
your Acceptance of the inclosed, and am*

Your humble Servant,
Harriet Hearty

And what do you think was inclosed? 'I don't know,' cried *Adams*:
'Not less than a Guinea, I hope.'—Sir, it was a Bank-Note for 200 *l.*—
'200 *l.*!' says *Adams*, in a Rapture.—No less, I assure you, answered the
Gentleman; a Sum I was not half so delighted with, as with the dear
Name of the generous Girl that sent it me; and who was not only the
best, but the handsomest Creature in the Universe; and for whom I had
long had a Passion, which I never durst disclose to her. I kiss'd her Name
a thousand times, my Eyes overflowing with Tenderness and Gratitude,
I repeated—. But not to detain you with these Raptures, I immediately
acquired my Liberty, and having paid all my Debts, departed with upwards
of fifty Pounds in my Pocket, to thank my kind Deliverer. She happened
to be then out of Town, a Circumstance which, upon Reflection, pleased
me; for by that means I had an Opportunity to appear before her in a
more decent Dress. At her Return to Town within a Day or two, I threw
myself at her Feet with the most ardent Acknowledgments, which she
rejected with an unfeigned Greatness of Mind, and told me, I could not
oblige her more than by never mentioning, or if possible, thinking on a
Circumstance which must bring to my Mind an Accident that might be
grievous to me to think on. She proceeded thus: 'What I have done is in
my own eyes a Trifle, and perhaps infinitely less than would have become

---

7. Prison quarters were divided into a "masterside," where prisoners might rent private rooms, and a
"commonside," which was often below ground or without windows. "Brutes" = animals.

me to do. And if you think of engaging in any Business, where a larger Sum may be serviceable to you, I shall not be over-rigid, either as to the Security or Interest.' I endeavoured to express all the Gratitude in my power to this Profusion of Goodness, tho' perhaps it was my Enemy, and began to afflict my Mind with more Agonies, than all the Miseries I had underwent; it affected me with severer Reflections than Poverty, Distress, and Prisons united had been able to make me feel: For, Sir, these Acts and Professions of Kindness, which were sufficient to have raised in a good Heart the most violent Passion of Friendship to one of the same, or to Age and Ugliness in a different Sex, came to me from a Woman, a young and beautiful Woman, one whose Perfections I had long known; and for whom I had long conceived a violent Passion, tho' with a Despair, which made me endeavour rather to curb and conceal, than to nourish or acquaint her with it. In short, they came upon me united with Beauty, Softness, and Tenderness, such bewitching Smiles.— O Mr. *Adams*, in that Moment, I lost myself, and forgetting our different Situations, nor considering what Return I was making to her Goodness, by desiring her who had given me so much, to bestow her All, I laid gently hold on her Hand, and conveying it to my Lips, I prest it with inconceivable Ardour; then lifting up my swimming Eyes, I saw her Face and Neck overspread with one Blush; she offered to withdraw her Hand, yet not so as to deliver it from mine, tho' I held it with the gentlest Force. We both stood trembling, her Eyes cast on the ground, and mine stedfastly fixed on her. Good G——, what was then the Condition of my Soul! burning with Love, Desire, Admiration, Gratitude, and every tender Passion, all bent on one charming Object. Passion at last got the better of both Reason and Respect, and softly letting go her Hand, I offered madly to clasp her in my Arms; when a little recovering herself, she started from me, asking me with some Shew of Anger, 'if she had any Reason to expect this Treatment from me.' I then fell prostrate before her, and told her, 'if I had offended, my Life was absolutely in her power, which I would in any manner lose for her sake. Nay, Madam, (said I) you shall not be so ready to punish me, as I to suffer. I own my Guilt. I detest the Reflection that I would have sacrificed your Happiness to mine. Believe me, I sincerely repent my Ingratitude, yet believe me too, it was my Passion, my unbounded Passion for you, which hurried me so far; I have loved you long and tenderly; and the Goodness you have shewn me, hath innocently weighed down a Wretch undone before. Acquit me of all mean mercenary Views, and before I take my Leave of you for ever, which I am resolved instantly to do, believe me, that Fortune could have raised me to no height to which I could not have gladly lifted you. O curst be Fortune.'—'Do not,' says she, interrupting me with the sweetest Voice, 'Do not curse Fortune, since she hath made me happy, and if she hath put your Happiness in my power, I have told you, you shall ask nothing in Reason which I will refuse.' 'Madam,' said I, 'you mistake me if you imagine, as you seem, my Happiness is in the power of Fortune now. You have obliged me too much already; if I have any Wish, it is for some blest Accident, by which I may contribute with my Life to the least Augmentation of your Felicity. As for my self, the only Happiness I can ever have, will be hearing of your's; and if Fortune will make that complete, I will forgive her all her Wrongs to me.' 'You may, indeed,' answered she, smiling, 'For your own Happiness must be included in mine. I have long known your Worth; nay, I must confess,' said she, blushing, 'I have long discovered that Passion for me you profess, notwithstanding those Endeavours which I am convinced were unaffected, to conceal it; and if all I can give with Reason will not suffice,—take Reason away,—and now I believe you cannot ask me what I will deny.'—She uttered these Words with a Sweetness not to be imagined. I immediately started, my Blood which lay freezing at my Heart, rushed tumultuously through every Vein. I stood for a Moment silent, then flying to her, I caught her in my Arms, no longer resisting,—and softly told her, she must give me then herself.—O Sir,—Can I describe her Look? She remained silent and almost motionless several Minutes. At last, recovering herself a little, she insisted on my leaving her, and in such a manner that I instantly obeyed: You may imagine, however, I soon saw her again.—But I ask pardon, I fear I have detained you too long in relating the Particulars of the former Interview. 'So far otherwise,' said *Adams*, licking his Lips, 'that I could willingly hear it over again.' Well, Sir, continued the Gentleman, to be as concise as possible, within a Week she consented to make me the happiest of Mankind. We were married shortly after; and when I came to examine the Circumstances of my Wife's Fortune; (which I do assure you I was not presently at Leisure enough to do) I found it amounted to about six thousand Pounds, most part of which lay in Effects; for her Father had been a Wine-Merchant, and she seemed willing, if I liked it, that I should carry on the same Trade. I readily and too inconsiderately undertook it: For not having been bred up to the Secrets of the Business, and endeavouring to deal with the utmost Honesty and Uprightness, I soon found our Fortune in a declining Way, and my Trade decreasing by little and little: For my Wines which I never adulterated after their Importation, and were sold as neat as they came over, were universally decried by the Vintners, to whom I could not allow them quite as cheap as those who gained double the Profit by a less Price.[8] I soon began to despair of improving our Fortune by these means; nor was I at all easy at the Visits and Familiarity of many who had been my Acquaintance in my Prosperity, but denied, and shunned me in my Adversity, and now very forwardly renewed their Acquaintance with me. In short, I had sufficiently seen, that the Pleasures of the World are chiefly Folly, and the Business of it mostly Knavery; and both, nothing better than Vanity: The Men of Pleasure tearing one another to pieces, from the Emulation of spending Money, and the Men of Business from Envy in getting it. My Happiness consisted entirely in my Wife, whom I loved with an

---

8. Wine was often diluted with cider or water. "Vintners" = innkeepers.

inexpressible Fondness, which was perfectly returned; and my Prospects[9] were no other than to provide for our growing Family; for she was now big of her second Child; I therefore took an Opportunity to ask her Opinion of entering into a retired Life, which after hearing my Reasons, and perceiving my Affection for it, she readily embraced. We soon put our small Fortune, now reduced under three thousand Pounds, into Money, with part of which we purchased this little Place, whither we retired soon after her Delivery, from a World full of Bustle, Noise, Hatred, Envy, and Ingratitude, to Ease, Quiet, and Love. We have here liv'd almost twenty Years, with little other Conversation than our own, most of the Neighbourhood taking us for very strange People; the Squire of the Parish representing me as a Madman, and the Parson as a Presbyterian; because I will not hunt with the one, nor drink with the other.[1] 'Sir,' says *Adams*, 'Fortune hath I think paid you all her Debts in this sweet Retirement.' Sir, replied the Gentleman, I am thankful to the great Author of all Things for the Blessings I here enjoy. I have the best of Wives, and three pretty Children, for whom I have the true Tenderness of a Parent; but no Blessings are pure in this World. Within three Years of my Arrival here I lost my eldest Son. (*Here he sighed bitterly.*) 'Sir,' says *Adams*, 'we must submit to Providence, and consider Death is common to all.' We must submit, indeed, answered the Gentleman; and if he had died, I could have borne the Loss with Patience: But alas! Sir, he was stolen away from my Door by some wicked travelling People whom they call *Gipsies*; nor could I ever with the most diligent Search recover him. Poor Child! he had the sweetest Look, the exact Picture of his Mother; at which some Tears unwittingly dropt from his Eyes, as did likewise from those of *Adams*, who always sympathized with his Friends on those Occasions. Thus, Sir, said the Gentleman, I have finished my Story, in which if I have been too particular, I ask your Pardon; and now, if you please, I will fetch you another Bottle; which Proposal the Parson thankfully accepted.

Chapter IV

A *Description of Mr.* Wilson's *Way of Living. The tragical Adventure of the Dog, and other grave Matters.*

The Gentleman returned with the Bottle, and *Adams* and he sat some time silent, when the former started up and cried, 'No, *that* won't do.' The Gentleman enquired into his Meaning; he answered, 'he had been considering that it was possible the late famous King *Theodore*[1] might

9. Aims.
1. While not teetotalers, Presbyterians, like other dissenters, severely condemned drunkenness.
1. "Late" = recently. Theodore Etienne von Neuhof (1686–1756), a high-living international intriguer, was made king of Corsica in 1736 by nationalists seeking independence from Genoa.

Ousted by the Genoese and French in 1738, he came to England, which had supported his bid for the throne; after being imprisoned for debt, he was taken up in the highest circles. *The Champion* exploited the popular sentimental concern for his supposed misfortunes in its attack on Walpole's restrained foreign policy.

have been that very Son whom he lost;' but added, 'that his Age could not answer that Imagination. However,' says he, 'G— disposes all things for the best, and very probably he may be some Great Man, or Duke, and may one day or other revisit you in that Capacity.' The Gentleman answered, he should know him amongst ten thousand, for he had a Mark on his left Breast, of a Strawberry, which his Mother had given him by longing for that Fruit.[2]

That beautiful young Lady, the *Morning*, now rose from her Bed, and with a Countenance blooming with fresh Youth and Sprightliness, like Miss * ———, with soft Dews hanging on her pouting Lips, began to take her early Walk over the eastern Hills; and presently after, that gallant Person the Sun stole softly from his Wife's Chamber to pay his Addresses to her; when the Gentleman ask'd his Guest if he would walk forth and survey his little Garden, which he readily agreed to, and *Joseph* at the same time awaking from a Sleep in which he had been two Hours buried, went with them. No Parterres, no Fountains, no Statues embellished this little Garden.[3] Its only Ornament was a short Walk, shaded on each side by a Filbert Hedge, with a small Alcove at one end, whither in hot Weather the Gentleman and his Wife used to retire and divert themselves with their Children, who played in the Walk before them: But tho' Vanity had no Votary in this little Spot, here was variety of Fruit, and every thing useful for the Kitchin, which was abundantly sufficient to catch the Admiration of *Adams*, who told the Gentleman he had certainly a good Gardener. Sir, answered he, that Gardener is now before you; whatever you see here, is the Work solely of my own Hands. Whilst I am providing Necessaries for my Table, I likewise procure myself an Appetite for them. In fair Seasons I seldom pass less than six Hours of the twenty-four in this Place, where I am not idle, and by these means I have been able to preserve my Health ever since my Arrival here without Assistance from Physick. Hither I generally repair at the Dawn, and exercise myself whilst my Wife dresses her Children, and prepares our Breakfast, after which we are seldom asunder during the residue of the Day; for when the Weather will not permit them to accompany me here, I am usually within with them; for I am neither ashamed of conversing with my Wife, nor of playing with my Children: to say the Truth, I do not perceive that Inferiority of Understanding which the Levity of Rakes, the Dulness of Men of Business, or the Austerity of the Learned would persuade us of in Women. As for my Woman, I declare I have found none of my own Sex capable of making juster Observations on Life, or of delivering them more agreeably; nor do I believe any one possessed of a faithfuller or braver Friend. And sure as

---

* *Whoever the Reader pleases.*

---

2. According to folk belief, failure to satisfy a pregnant woman's craving for a particular food (usually fruit out of season) would produce a representative birthmark on the infant.

3. At this time these features of the formal garden were giving way to a craze for picturesque landscaping imitative of paintings. Wilson's functional simplicity eschews both the old and new fashions.

this Friendship is sweetened with more Delicacy and Tenderness, so is it confirmed by dearer Pledges than can attend the closest male Alliance: For what Union can be so fast, as our common Interest in the Fruits of our Embraces? Perhaps, Sir, you are not yourself a Father; if you are not, be assured you cannot conceive the Delight I have in my Little-Ones. Would you not despise me, if you saw me stretched on the Ground, and my Children playing round me? 'I should reverence the Sight,' quoth *Adams*, 'I myself am now the Father of six, and have been of eleven, and I can say I never scourged a Child of my own, unless as his School-master, and then have felt every Stroke on my own Posteriors. And as to what you say concerning Women, I have often lamented my own Wife did not understand *Greek*.'—The Gentleman smiled, and answered, he would not be apprehended to insinuate that his own had an Understanding above the Care of her Family, on the contrary, says he, my *Harriet* I assure you is a notable House-wife, and the House-keepers of few Gentlemen understand Cookery or Confectionary better; but these are Arts which she hath no great Occasion for now: however, the Wine you commended so much last Night at Supper, was of her own making, as is indeed all the Liquor in my House, except my Beer, which falls to my Province. ('And I assure you it is as excellent,' quoth *Adams*, 'as ever I tasted.') We formerly kept a Maid-Servant, but since my Girls have been growing up, she is unwilling to indulge them in Idleness; for as the Fortunes I shall give them will be very small, we intend not to breed them above the Rank they are likely to fill hereafter, nor to teach them to despise or ruin a plain Husband. Indeed I could wish a Man of my own Temper, and a retired Life, might fall to their Lot: for I have experienced that calm serene Happiness which is seated in Content, is inconsistent with the Hurry and Bustle of the World. He was proceeding thus, when the Little Things, being just risen, ran eagerly towards him, and asked him Blessing: They were shy to the Strangers, but the eldest acquainted her Father that her Mother and the young Gentlewoman were up, and that Breakfast was ready. They all went in, where the Gentleman was surprized at the Beauty of *Fanny*, who had now recovered herself from her Fatigue, and was entirely clean drest; for the Rogues who had taken away her Purse, had left her her Bundle. But if he was so much amazed at the Beauty of this young Creature, his Guests were no less charmed at the Tenderness which appeared in the Behaviour of Husband and Wife to each other, and to their Children, and at the dutiful and affectionate Behaviour of these to their Parents. These Instances pleased the well-disposed Mind of *Adams* equally with the Readiness which they exprest to oblige their Guests, and their Forwardness to offer them the best of every thing in their House; and what delighted him still more, was an Instance or two of their Charity: for whilst they were at Breakfast, the good Woman was called forth to assist her sick Neighbour, which she did with some Cordials made for the public Use; and the good Man went into his Garden at the same time, to supply another with something which he wanted thence, for they had nothing which those who wanted it were not welcome to. These good People were in the utmost Cheerfulness, when they heard the Report of a Gun, and immediately afterwards a little Dog, the Favourite of the eldest Daughter, came limping in all bloody, and laid himself at his Mistress's Feet: The poor Girl, who was about eleven Years old,[4] burst into Tears at the sight, and presently one of the Neighbours came in and informed them, that the young Squire, the Son of the Lord of the Manor, had shot him as he past by, swearing at the same time he would prosecute the Master of him for keeping a Spaniel; for that he had given Notice he would not suffer one in the Parish. The Dog, whom his Mistress had taken into her Lap, died in a few Minutes, licking her Hand. She exprest great Agony at his Loss, and the other Children began to cry for their Sister's Misfortune, nor could *Fanny* herself refrain. Whilst the Father and Mother attempted to comfort her, *Adams* grasped his Crab Stick, and would have sallied out after the Squire, had not *Joseph* with-held him. He could not however bridle his Tongue—He pronounced the Word *Rascal* with great Emphasis, and he deserved to be hanged more than a Highwayman, and wish'd he had the scourging him. The Mother took her Child, lamenting and carrying the dead Favourite in her Arms out of the Room, when the Gentleman said, this was the second time this Squire had endeavoured to kill the little Wretch, and had wounded him smartly once before, adding, he could have no Motive but Ill-nature; for the little thing, which was not near as big as one's Fist, had never been twenty Yards from the House in the six Years his Daughter had had it. He said he had done nothing to deserve this Usage: but his Father had too great a Fortune to contend with. That he was as absolute as any Tyrant in the Universe, and had killed all the Dogs, and taken away all the Guns in the Neighbourhood, and not only that, but he trampled down Hedges, and rode over Corn and Gardens, with no more Regard than if they were the Highway.[5] 'I wish I could catch him in my Garden,' said *Adams*; 'tho' I would rather forgive him riding through my House than such all ill-natur'd Act as this.'

The Cheerfulness of their Conversation being interrupted by this Accident, in which the Guests could be of no service to their kind Entertainer, and as the Mother was taken up in administring Consolation to the poor Girl, whose Disposition was too good hastily to forget the sudden Loss of her little Favourite, which had been fondling with her a few Minutes before; and as *Joseph* and *Fanny* were impatient to get home and begin those previous Ceremonies to their Happiness which *Adams* had insisted on, they now offered to take their Leave. The Gentleman

---

4. The age of this child, defined on the previous page as "the eldest" of Wilson's "Little Things," seems to be inconsistent with the earlier information (p. 175) that Mrs. Wilson delivered her second child before moving to the country "almost twenty Years" earlier, since in recounting his fortunes Wilson mentions the loss of no child but the eldest son.

5. Although the Game Laws authorized confiscation of guns and dogs from those not qualified by property to hunt (see above, pp. 77, n. 5), Wilson, who does not hunt (p. 175), appears qualified, and the stricture would not apply to a lapdog. On some estates, the lord of the manor had the right to hunt freely over leased, cultivated, and occupied land.

importuned them much to stay Dinner: but when he found their Eagerness to depart, he summoned his Wife, and accordingly having performed all the usual Ceremonies of Bows and Curtsies, more pleasant to be seen then to be related, they took their Leave, the Gentleman and his Wife heartily wishing them a good Journey, and they as heartily thanking them for their kind Entertainment. They then departed, *Adams* declaring that this was the Manner in which the People had lived in the Golden Age.[6]

Chapter V

A Disputation on Schools, held on the Road between Mr. Abraham Adams *and* Joseph; *and a Discovery not unwelcome to them both.*

Our Travellers having well refreshed themselves at the Gentleman's House, *Joseph* and *Fanny* with Sleep, and Mr. *Abraham Adams* with Ale and Tobacco, renewed their Journey with great Alacrity; and, pursuing the Road in which they were directed, travelled many Miles before they met with any Adventure worth relating. In this Interval, we shall present our Readers with a very curious Discourse, as we apprehend it, concerning public Schools, which pass'd between Mr. *Joseph Andrews* and Mr. *Abraham Adams.*

They had not gone far, before *Adams* calling to *Joseph*, asked him if he had attended to the Gentleman's Story; he answered, 'to all the former Part.' 'And don't you think,' says he, 'he was a very unhappy Man in his Youth?' 'A very unhappy Man indeed,' answered the other. '*Joseph*,' cries *Adams*, screwing up his Mouth, 'I have found it; I have discovered the Cause of all the Misfortunes which befel him. A public School, *Joseph*, was the Cause of all the Calamities which he afterwards suffered. Public Schools are the Nurseries of all Vice and Immorality. All the wicked Fellows whom I remember at the University were bred at them.— Ah Lord! I can remember as well as if it was but yesterday, a Knot of them; they called them King's Scholars,[1] I forget why—very wicked Fellows! *Joseph*, you may thank the Lord you were not bred at a public School, you would never have preserved your Virtue as you have. The first Care I always take, is of a Boy's Morals, I had rather he should be a Blockhead than an Atheist or a Presbyterian.[2] What is all the Learning

6. In ancient Greek poetry, the legendary first age, before the reign of Zeus, when men lived in peace and comfort and the earth freely provided all their needs.
1. So named because they were supported by the foundation of a public school established by royal charter or funded by royal endowment. Once selected for a school like Eton, Winchester, or Westminster, these scholars were reasonably assured of continuing as such in university, since Eton and Winchester controlled all the fellowships and scholarships at King's College, Cambridge, and New College, Oxford, respectively, and West-

minster maintained scholars at both universities. Adams's impression may reflect the current prevalence of favoritism and corruption in the admission of scholars and their advancement to university. His view of the public schools echoes a common concern, articulated by John Locke in *Some Thoughts Concerning Education* (1693).
2. Presbyterians may have been somewhat less rigorous than other dissenters in disciplining wayward communicants, but Adams probably has in mind their recent increasing deviation from the orthodox doctrine of the trinity and their academies' reputation for heterodoxy.

of the World compared to his immortal Soul? What shall a Man take in exchange for his Soul? But the Masters of great Schools trouble themselves about no such thing. I have known a Lad of eighteen at the University, who hath not been able to say his Catechism; but for my own part, I always scourged a Lad sooner for missing that than any other Lesson. Believe me, Child, all that Gentleman's Misfortunes arose from his being educated at a public School.'

'It doth not become me,' answer'd *Joseph*, 'to dispute any thing, Sir, with you, especially a matter of this kind; for to be sure you must be allowed by all the World to be the best Teacher of a School in all our County.' 'Yes, that,' says *Adams*, 'I believe, is granted me; that I may without much Vanity pretend to—nay I believe I may go to the next County too—but *gloriari non est meum*.'[3]—'However, Sir, as you are pleased to bid me speak,' says *Joseph*, 'you know, my late Master, Sir *Thomas Booby*, was bred at a public School, and he was the finest Gentleman in all the Neighbourhood. And I have often heard him say, if he had a hundred Boys he would breed them all at the same Place. It was his Opinion, and I have often heard him deliver it, that a Boy taken from a public School, and carried into the World, will learn more in one Year there, than one of a private Education will in five. He used to say, the School itself initiated him a great way, (I remember that was his very Expression) for great Schools are little Societies, where a Boy of any Observation may see in Epitome what he will afterwards find in the World at large.' '*Hinc illæ lachrymæ*;[4] for that very Reason,' quoth *Adams*, 'I prefer a private School, where Boys may be kept in Innocence and Ignorance: for, according to that fine Passage in the Play of *Cato*, the only *English* Tragedy I ever read,

> *If Knowledge of the World must make Men Villains,*
> *May* Juba *ever live in Ignorance.*[5]

Who would not rather preserve the Purity of his Child, than wish him to attain the whole Circle of Arts and Sciences; which, by the bye, he may learn in the Classes of a private School? for I would not be vain, but I esteem myself to be second to none, *nulli secundum*, in teaching these things; so that a Lad may have as much Learning in a private as in a public Education.' 'And with Submission,' answered *Joseph*, 'he may get as much Vice, witness several Country Gentlemen, who were educated within five Miles of their own Houses, and are as wicked as if they had known the World from their Infancy. I remember when I was in the Stable, if a young Horse was vicious in his Nature, no Correction would make him otherwise; I take it to be equally the same among Men: if a Boy be of a mischievous wicked Inclination, no School, tho' ever so private, will ever make him good; on the contrary, if he be of a righteous Temper, you may trust him to *London*, or wherever else you please, he

---

3. "It is not my custom to boast."
4. "Hence those tears" (Horace, *Epistles* 1.19. 41, quoting a stock phrase).

5. Joseph Addison, *Cato* (1713) 2.5. In the play the second half of the first line reads" "makes Man perfidious."

will be in no danger of being corrupted. Besides, I have often heard my
Master say, that the Discipline practised in public Schools was much
better than that in private.'—'You talk like a Jackanapes,' says *Adams*,
'and so did your Master. Discipline indeed! because one Man scourges
twenty or thirty Boys more in a Morning than another, is he therefore a
better Disciplinarian? I do presume to confer[6] in this Point with all who
have taught from *Chiron's*[7] time to this Day; and, if I was Master of six
Boys only, I would preserve as good Discipline amongst them as the
Master of the greatest School in the World. I say nothing, young Man;
remember, I say nothing; but if Sir *Thomas* himself had been educated
nearer home, and under the Tuition of somebody, remember, I name
nobody, it might have been better for him—but his Father must institute
him in the Knowledge of the World. *Nemo mortalium omnibus horis
sapit.*'[8] *Joseph* seeing him run on in this manner asked pardon many
times, assuring him he had no Intention to offend. 'I believe you had
not, Child,' said he, 'and I am not angry with you: but for maintaining
good Discipline in a School; for this,—' And then he ran on as before,
named all the Masters who are recorded in old Books, and preferred
himself to them all. Indeed if this good Man had an Enthusiasm, or
what the Vulgar call a Blind-side, it was this: He thought a Schoolmaster
the greatest Character in the World, and himself the greatest of all
Schoolmasters, neither of which Points he would have given up to *Alexander the Great* at the Head of his Army.

  Adams continued his Subject till they came to one of the beautifullest
Spots of Ground in the Universe. It was a kind of natural Amphitheatre,
formed by the winding of a small Rivulet, which was planted with thick
Woods, and the Trees rose gradually above each other by the natural
Ascent of the Ground they stood on; which Ascent, as they hid with
their Boughs, they seemed to have been disposed by the Design of the
most skillful Planter. The Soil was spread with a Verdure which no Paint
could imitate, and the whole Place might have raised romantic Ideas in
elder Minds than those of *Joseph* and *Fanny*, without the Assistance of
Love.

  Here they arrived about Noon, and *Joseph* proposed to *Adams* that
they should rest a while in this delightful Place, and refresh themselves
with some Provisions which the Good-nature of Mrs. *Wilson* had provided them with. *Adams* made no Objection to the Proposal, so down
they sat, and pulling out a cold Fowl, and a Bottle of Wine, they made
a Repast with a Cheerfulness which might have attracted the Envy of
more splendid Tables. I should not omit, that they found among their
Provision a little Paper, containing a piece of Gold, which *Adams* imagining had been put there by mistake, would have returned back, to restore
it; but he was at last convinced by *Joseph*, that Mr. *Wilson* had taken this

6. Conform.

7. In Greek legend, a centaur of divine descent
who tutored Asclepius (the god of medicine),
Achilles, and Jason, leader of the Argonauts.

8. "None among mortals is wise all the time"
(Pliny, *Natural History* 7.40.131, H. Rackham
trans).

handsome way of furnishing them with a Supply for their Journey, on his having related the Distress which they had been in, when they were relieved by the Generosity of the Pedlar. *Adams* said, he was glad to see such an Instance of Goodness, not so much for the Conveniency which it brought them, as for the sake of the Doer, whose Reward would be great in Heaven.[9] He likewise comforted himself with a Reflection, that he should shortly have an Opportunity of returning it him; for the Gentleman was within a Week to make a Journey into *Somersetshire*, to pass through *Adams's* Parish, and had faithfully promised to call on him: A Circumstance which we thought too immaterial to mention before; but which those who have as great an Affection for that Gentleman as ourselves will rejoice at, as it may give them Hopes of seeing him again. Then *Joseph* made a Speech on Charity, which the Reader, if he is so disposed, may see in the next Chapter; for we scorn to betray him into any such Reading, without first giving him Warning.

Chapter VI

Moral Reflections by Joseph Andrews, *with the Hunting Adventure, and Parson* Adams's *miraculous Escape.*

'I have often wondered, Sir,' said *Joseph*, 'to observe so few Instances of Charity among Mankind; for tho' the Goodness of a Man's Heart did not incline him to relieve the Distresses of his Fellow-Creatures, methinks the Desire of Honour should move him to it. What inspires a Man to build fine Houses, to purchase fine Furniture, Pictures, Clothes, and other things at a great Expence, but an Ambition to be respected more than other People? Now would not one great Act of Charity, one Instance of redeeming a poor Family from all the Miseries of Poverty, restoring an unfortunate Tradesman by a Sum of Money to the means of procuring a Livelihood by his Industry, discharging an undone Debtor from his Debts or a Goal, or any such like Example of Goodness, create a Man more Honour and Respect than he could acquire by the finest House, Furniture, Pictures or Clothes that were ever beheld? For not only the Object himself, who was thus relieved, but all who heard the Name of such a Person must, I imagine, reverence him infinitely more than the Possessor of all those other things: which when we so admire, we rather praise the Builder, the Workman, the Painter, the Laceman, the Taylor, and the rest, by whose Ingenuity they are produced, than the Person who by his Money makes them his own. For my own part, when I have waited behind my Lady in a Room hung with fine Pictures, while I have been looking at them I have never once thought of their Owner, nor hath any one else, as I ever observed; for when it hath been asked whose Picture that was, it was never once answered, the Master's of the House, but *Ammyconni, Paul Varnish, Hannibal Scratchi,* or

---

9. Adams's phrasing corresponds most closely to Matthew 5:12 and Luke 6:23, but the stipulation of heavenly reward for disinterested charitable acts like Wilson's is found in Luke 6:35.

Hogarthi,[1] which I suppose were the Names of the Painters: but if it was asked, who redeemed such a one out of Prison? who lent such a ruined Tradesman Money to set up? who cloathed that Family of poor small Children? it is very plain, what must be the Answer. And besides, these great Folks are mistaken, if they imagine they get any Honour at all by these means; for I do not remember I ever was with my Lady at any House where she commended the House or Furniture, but I have heard her at her return home make sport and jeer at whatever she had before commended: and I have been told by other Gentlemen in Livery, that it is the same in their Families: but I defy the wisest Man in the World to turn a true good Action into Ridicule.[2] I defy him to do it. He who should endeavour it, would be laughed at himself, instead of making others laugh. Nobody scarce doth any Good, yet they all agree in praising those who do. Indeed it is strange that all Men should consent in commending Goodness, and no Man endeavour to deserve that Commendation; whilst, on the contrary, all rail at Wickedness, and all are as eager to be what they abuse. This I know not the Reason of, but it is as plain as Daylight to those who converse in the World, as I have done these three Years.' 'Are all the great Folks wicked then?' says *Fanny*. 'To be sure there are some Exceptions,' answered *Joseph*. 'Some Gentlemen of our Cloth report charitable Actions done by their Lords and Masters, and I have heard 'Squire *Pope*, the great Poet, at my Lady's Table, tell Stories of a Man that lived at a Place called *Ross*, and another at the *Bath*, one *Al—Al—*I forget his Name, but it is in the Book of Verses.[3] This Gentleman hath built up a stately House too, which the 'Squire likes very well; but his Charity is seen farther than his House, tho' it stands on a Hill, ay, and brings him more Honour too. It was his Charity that put him in the Book, where the 'Squire says he puts all those who deserve it; and to be sure, as he lives among all the great People, if there were any such, he would know them.'—This was all of Mr. *Joseph Andrews's* Speech which I could get him to recollect, which I have delivered as near as was possible in his own Words, with a very small Embellishment. But I believe the Reader hath not been a little surprized at the long Silence of Parson *Adams*, especially as so many Occasions offer'd themselves to exert his Curiosity and Observation. The truth is, he was fast asleep, and had so been from the beginning of the preceding Narrative: and indeed if the Reader considers that so many Hours had

1. Jacopo Amigoni (1675–1752), Venetian painter of historical pictures, lived in England from 1730 to 1739. Paolo Veronese (1528–88) and Annibale Carraci (1560–1609) were Italian Renaissance masters. Fielding compliments his friend Hogarth by association with these monumental painters. "Scratchi" is Fielding's improvement on the first edition's "Scarachi."
2. Joseph echoes Shaftesbury's *Sensus Communis; an Essay on the Freedom of Wit and Humour* 4.1: "One may defy the world to turn real bravery or generosity into ridicule" (*Characteristics* 1.86).

3. Ralph Allen (see p. 149, n. 5). Pope paid tribute to his charity in the *Epilogue to the Satires* (1738), dialogue 1, 135–36; he had sojourned at his "stately House," probably in Fielding's company, a few months before the publication of the novel (see Battestin, *Philological Quarterly* 42: 235–39). Pope also eulogized John Kyrle (1637–1724), better known as "the Man of Ross" for his lifetime of philanthropy in that Herefordshire town, in the third of his *Moral Essays*, the *Epistle to Bathurst: of the Use of Riches* 250–90.

past since he had closed his Eyes,[4] he will not wonder at his Repose, tho' even *Henley* himself, or as great an Orator (if any such be) had been in his *Rostrum* or Tub before him.[5]

Joseph, who, whilst he was speaking, had continued in one Attitude, with his Head reclining on one side, and his Eyes cast on the Ground, no sooner perceived, on looking up, the Position of *Adams*, who was stretched on his Back, and snored louder than the usual braying of the Animal with long Ears; than he turned towards *Fanny*, and taking her by the Hand, began a Dalliance, which, tho' consistent with the purest Innocence and Decency, neither he would have attempted, nor she permitted before any Witness. Whilst they amused themselves in this harmless and delightful manner, they heard a Pack of Hounds approaching in full Cry towards them, and presently afterwards saw a Hare pop forth from the Wood, and crossing the Water, land within a few Yards of them in the Meadows. The Hare was no sooner on Shore, than it seated itself on its hinder Legs, and listened to the Sound of the Pursuers. *Fanny* was wonderfully pleased with the little Wretch, and eagerly longed to have it in her Arms, that she might preserve it from the Dangers which seemed to threaten it: but the rational part of the Creation do not always aptly distinguish their Friends from their Foes; what wonder then if this silly Creature, the moment it beheld her, fled from the Friend who would have protected it, and traversing the Meadows again, past the little Rivulet on the opposite side. It was however so spent and weak, that it fell down twice or thrice in its way. This affected the tender Heart of *Fanny*, who exclaimed with Tears in her Eyes against the Barbarity of worrying a poor innocent defenceless Animal out of its Life, and putting it to the extremest Torture for Diversion. She had not much time to make Reflections of this kind, for on a sudden the Hounds rushed through the Wood, which resounded with their Throats, and the Throats of their *Retinue*, who *attended* on them on horseback. The Dogs now past the Rivulet, and pursued the Footsteps of the Hare; five Horsemen attempted to leap over, three of whom succeeded, and two were in the Attempt thrown from their Saddles into the Water; their Companions and their own Horses too proceeded after their Sport, and left their Friends and Riders to invoke the Assistance of Fortune, or employ the more active means of Strength and Agility for their Deliverance. *Joseph* how-

4. In the second edition "so many Hours" replaced the original "two Nights," for which Fielding apologized in a prefatory note to the first edition: "Among other Errors, the Reader is desired to excuse this: That in the Second Volume, Mr. *Adams*, is, by mistake, mentioned to have sat up two subsequent Nights; when in reality, a Night of Rest intervened" (as recorded on p. 136).

5. John Henley (1692–1756) resigned his posts in the Church of England in 1726 to set up an 'Oratory' for the revival of "the Primitive Church," where he preached and lectured to paying audiences on religious and secular topics for thirty years. From 1730 to 1741 he also served Walpole as editor of the pro–ministerial weekly, the *Hyp*

Doctor. His theatrical elocution, eccentric self-advertisement, and bizarre mingling of buffoonery and solemnity made "Orator" Henley a standing butt of derision. In the *Dunciad* (1728), Pope called the Oratory's elevated and adorned lectern "Henley's gilt Tub" (2.2)—tub being the common derogatory term for a dissenting preacher's pulpit. Fielding's italicizing of *Rostrum* (a term then usually restricted to its original referent, the speaker's platform in the ancient Roman forum) may mock Henley's claim to be the "Restorer of ancient Eloquence" or, more directly, his pretentious application of the term to his pulpit in the self-justifying pamphlet, *Milk for Babes* (1729).

ever was not so unconcerned on this Occasion; he left *Fanny* for a moment to herself, and ran to the Gentlemen, who were immediately on their Legs, shaking their Ears, and easily with the help of his Hand attained the Bank, (for the Rivulet was not at all deep) and without staying to thank their kind Assister, ran dripping across the Meadow, calling to their Brother Sportsmen to stop their Horses: but they heard them not.

The Hounds were now very little behind their poor reeling, staggering Prey, which fainting almost at every Step, crawled through the Wood, and had almost got round to the Place where *Fanny* stood, when it was overtaken by its Enemies; and being driven out of the Covert was caught, and instantly tore to pieces before *Fanny's* Face, who was unable to assist it with any Aid more powerful than Pity; nor could she prevail on *Joseph*, who had been himself a Sportsman in his Youth, to attempt any thing contrary to the Laws of Hunting, in favour of the Hare, which he said was killed fairly.

The Hare was caught within a Yard or two of *Adams*, who lay asleep at some distance from the Lovers, and the Hounds in devouring it, and pulling it backwards and forwards, had drawn it so close to him, that some of them (by Mistake perhaps for the Hare's Skin) laid hold of the Skirts of his Cassock; others at the same time applying their Teeth to his Wig, which he had with a Handkerchief fastened to his Head, they began to pull him about; and had not the Motion of his Body had more effect on him than seemed to be wrought by the Noise, they must certainly have tasted his Flesh, which delicious Flavour might have been fatal to him: But being roused by these Tuggings, he instantly awaked, and with a Jerk delivering his Head from his Wig, he with most admirable Dexterity recovered his Legs, which now seemed the only Members he could entrust his Safety to. Having therefore escaped likewise from at least a third Part of his Cassock, which he willingly left as his *Exuviæ*[6] or Spoils to the Enemy, he fled with the utmost speed he could summon to his Assistance. Nor let this be any Detraction from the Bravery of his Character; let the Number of the Enemies, and the Surprize in which he was taken, be considered; and if there be any Modern so outragiously brave, that he cannot admit of Flight in any Circumstance whatever, I say (but I whisper that softly, and I solemnly declare, without any Intention of giving Offence to any brave Man in the Nation) I say, or rather I whisper that he is an ignorant Fellow, and hath never read *Homer* nor *Virgil*, nor knows he any thing of *Hector* or *Turnus*;[7] nay, he is unacquainted with the History of some great Men living, who, tho' as brave as Lions, ay, as Tigers, have run away the Lord knows how far, and the Lord knows why, to the Surprize of their Friends, and the Entertainment of their Enemies. But if Persons of such heroick Disposition are a little offended at the Behaviour of *Adams*, we assure them they shall be as much pleased with what we shall immediately relate of *Joseph*

6. Literally "that which is taken off"—thus armor and weapons stripped from the dead.

7. In the conclusion of the *Aeneid*, Turnus, the fiery leader of the native Italian tribes, flees before Aeneas as Hector does before Achilles in the *Iliad* (see above, p. 106, n. 2).

Andrews. The Master of the Pack was just arrived, or, as the Sportsmen call it, *Come in*, when *Adams* set out, as we have before mentioned. This Gentleman was generally said to be a great Lover of Humour; but not to mince the matter, especially as we are upon this Subject, he was a great *Hunter of Men*: indeed he had hitherto followed the Sport only with Dogs of his own Species; for he kept two or three Couple of barking Curs for that Use only. However, as he thought he had now found a Man nimble enough, he was willing to indulge himself with other Sport, and accordingly crying out, *Stole away*,[8] encouraged the Hounds to pursue Mr. *Adams*, swearing it was the largest Jack Hare he ever saw; at the same time hallooing and hooping as if a conquered Foe was flying before him; in which he was imitated by these two or three Couple of Human, or rather two-leg'd Curs on horseback which we have mentioned before.

Now thou, whoever thou art, whether a Muse, or by what other Name soever thou chusest to be called, who presidest over Biography, and hast inspired all the Writers of Lives in these our Times: Thou who didst infuse such wonderful Humour into the Pen of immortal *Gulliver*,[9] who hast carefully guided the Judgment, whilst thou hast exalted the nervous manly Style of thy *Mallet*:[1] Thou who hadst no Hand in that Dedication, and Preface, or the Translations which thou wouldst willingly have struck out of the Life of *Cicero*:[2] Lastly, Thou who without the Assistance of the least Spice of Literature, and even against his Inclination, hast, in some Pages of his Book, forced *Colley Cibber* to write *English*;[3] do thou assist me in what I find myself unequal to. Do thou introduce on the Plain, the young, the gay, the brave *Joseph Andrews*, whilst Men shall view him with Admiration and Envy; tender Virgins with Love and anxious Concern for his Safety.

No sooner did *Joseph Andrews* perceive the Distress of his Friend, when first the quick-scenting Dogs attacked him, than he grasped his Cudgel in his right Hand, a Cudgel which his Father had of his Grandfather, to whom a mighty strong Man of *Kent* had given it for a Present in that Day, when he broke three Heads on the Stage.[4] It was a Cudgel

---

8. In hunting jargon, the signal that the animal has left its lair and gained a start on its pursuers.

9. Fielding imitated *Gulliver's Travels* in thirteen extracts from "The Voyages of Mr. Job Vinegar" in *The Champion* from March to October 1740, and later eulogized Swift as "a Genius . . . ranked among the first" in the world, who "possessed the Talents of a Lucian, a Rabelais, and a Cervantes, and in his Works exceeded them all" (*The True Patriot*, November 5, 1745).

1. David Mallet (1705–65), Scottish playwright and opposition writer, whose *Life of Francis Bacon* was published in 1740 by Fielding's bookseller, Andrew Millar.

2. *The History of the Life of Marcus Tullius Cicero* (1741), by Conyers Middleton (1683–1750), disputatious Cambridge librarian, attracted much attention and nearly two thousand subscribers.

Fielding parodied its fulsome dedication (reprinted below, pp. 340–43) in *Shamela*. Middleton's preface dismissed *Observations on the Life of Cicero* (1731) by Fielding's patron and friend George Lyttelton as an enjoyable "little piece" radically inadequate in comprehending its subject. There he also describes the difficulty of translating the numerous Ciceronian passages he has "woven into the text as genuine parts of it" with that "splendour of style, as well as sentiment necessary to support the idea of a fine writer."

3. See above, p. 30, n. 3.

4. This part of the passage burlesques the genealogy of Agamemnon's sceptre (*Iliad* 2.102–8), satirically mimicked earlier by Pope in *The Rape of the Lock* 5.89–96. William Joy, known as "Samson, the strong man of Kent," performed feats of strength at the turn of the century.

of mighty Strength and wonderful Art, made by one of Mr. *Deard's* best Workmen,[5] whom no other Artificer can equal; and who hath made all those Sticks which the Beaus have lately walked with about the Park in a Morning: But this was far his Master-piece; on its Head was engraved a Nose and Chin, which might have been mistaken for a Pair of Nut-crackers.[6] The Learned have imagined it designed to represent the *Gorgon*: but it was in fact copied from the Face of a certain long *English* Baronet[7] of infinite Wit, Humour, and Gravity. He did intend to have engraved here many Histories: As the first Night of Captain *B——'s* Play, where you would have seen Criticks in Embroidery transplanted from the Boxes to the Pit, whose ancient Inhabitants were exalted to the Galleries, where they played on Catcalls.[8] He did intend to have painted an Auction-Room, where Mr. *Cock* would have appeared aloft in his Pulpit, trumpeting forth the Praises of a *China* Bason; and with Astonishment wondering that *Nobody bids more for that fine, that superb——* He did intend to have engraved many other things, but was forced to leave all out for want of room.[9]

No sooner had *Joseph* grasped this Cudgel in his Hands, than Lightning darted from his Eyes; and the heroick Youth, swift of Foot,[1] ran with the utmost speed to his Friend's assistance. He overtook him just as *Rockwood* had laid hold of the Skirt of his Cassock, which being torn hung to the ground. Reader, we would make a Simile on this Occasion, but for two Reasons: The first is, it would interrupt the Description, which should be *rapid* in this Part; but that doth not weigh much, many

5. William Deard (d. 1761) owned a fashionable jewelry and toy shop.

6. Throughout the century, the handles of walking sticks were elaborately worked and ornamented, but the specific reference is to a fashion introduced ten years earlier: "Polite young gentlemen at the Court end of town now carry large oaken sticks with great heads and ugly faces carved on them" (a 1731 report cited by Talbot Hughes in *Johnson's England* 1.393). The park is St. James's near the palace.

7. Fielding inserted "long" in the second edition to target tall and thin Sir Thomas Robinson (1700?–1777), an excise commissioner known as "long Sir Thomas" to distinguish him from his squat namesake in Walpole's foreign service. An amateur architect and assiduous flatterer of the great, he consumed a large fortune in improving his estate at Rokeby, Yorkshire, and providing lavish London entertainments for the fashionable world who derided him for his tedious verbosity and excess of polite formalities.

8. Squealing instruments commonly used to "boo" a performance. The noisy rejection of this comedy, *The Modish Couple* (1732), for which Fielding wrote the epilogue, may have been provoked by a scene deriding noisy playhouse critics or by factional hostility to its author or authors. Charles Bodens (d. 1753), guards officer, minor court functionary and notorious pimp for the Prince of

Wales, was almost certainly not the real author. One contemporary account assigns the play to Lord Hervey (see p. 245, n. 2) and the Prince of Wales, another to the Reverend James Miller. On opening night the pit (traditionally the territory of the raucous vulgar and at this time the domain of damning wits) was packed with the putative author's fellow courtiers (the "Criticks in Embroidery"), who, according to one report, carried clubs to discourage hecklers. Nevertheless, those in the galleries, whether displaced critics or opposition hirelings, sounded their catcalls throughout the performance.

9. Christopher Cock, called Christopher Hen and played by an actress in Fielding's *Historical Register for the Year 1736* (1737), ran one of several fashionable auction rooms. The description of the cudgel burlesques Homer's description of the shield of Achilles (*Iliad* 18.478–607). The prototype of Fielding's artificer of gewgaws, Hephaestos, the Greek god of fire, depicts an extraordinary panorama including the earth, sea, and heavens and eight elaborately detailed scenes of city life, warfare, and agriculture. Fielding's repeated "He did intend" mimics Homer's laconic introduction of each successive embellishment of the apparently limitless shield with "Therein he wrought . . ." or "Therein he set. . . ."

1. Homeric epithet for Achilles throughout the *Iliad*.

Precedents occurring for such an Interruption[2]: The second, and much the greater Reason is, that we could find no Simile adequate to our Purpose: For indeed, what Instance could we bring to set before our Reader's Eyes at once the Idea of Friendship, Courage, Youth, Beauty, Strength, and Swiftness; all which blazed in the Person of *Joseph Andrews*. Let those therefore that describe Lions and Tigers, and Heroes fiercer than both, raise their Poems or Plays with the Simile of *Joseph Andrews*, who is himself above the reach of any Simile.

Now *Rockwood* had laid fast hold on the Parson's Skirts, and stopt his Flight; which *Joseph* no sooner perceived, than he levelled his Cudgel at his Head, and laid him sprawling. *Jowler* and *Ringwood* then fell on his Great-Coat, and had undoubtedly brought him to the Ground, had not *Joseph*, collecting all his Force given *Jowler* such a Rap on the Back, that quitting his Hold he ran howling over the Plain: A harder Fate remained for thee, O *Ringwood*. *Ringwood* the best Hound that ever pursued a Hare, who never threw his Tongue but where the Scent was undoubtedly true; good at *trailing*; and *sure in a Highway*, no *Babler*, no *Over-runner*, respected by the whole Pack: For, whenever he opened, they knew the Game was at hand.[3] He fell by the Stroke of *Joseph*. *Thunder*, and *Plunder*, and *Wonder*, and *Blunder*, were the next Victims of his Wrath, and measured their Lengths on the Ground. Then *Fairmaid*, a Bitch which Mr. *John Temple*[4] had bred up in his House, and fed at his own Table, and lately sent the Squire fifty Miles for a Present, ran fiercely at *Joseph*, and bit him by the Leg; no Dog was ever fiercer than she, being descended from an *Amazonian* Breed, and had worried[5] Bulls in her own Country, but now waged an unequal Fight; and had shared the Fate of those we have mentioned before, had not *Diana* (the Reader may believe it or not, as he pleases) in that Instant interposed, and in the Shape of the Huntsman snatched her Favourite up in her Arms.[6]

The Parson now faced about, and with his Crab Stick felled many to Earth, and scattered others, till he was attacked by *Cæsar* and pulled to

---

2. In the fierce battle of *Iliad* 11, there are five such similes (113–21; 155–62; 474–83; 492–97; 547–64), and Virgil employs three in Aeneas's climactic combat with Turnus (*Aeneid* 12.715–24, 749–59, 908–14). Fielding may have in mind St. Evremond's criticism of Virgil for this practice and Dryden's defense: "his similitudes in general . . . are not placed . . . in the heat of any action, but commonly in its declining" (Dedication of the *Aeneis*, 1697).

3. A good hound would give cry ("throw his tongue," "open") only when he came upon a fresh scent, and in following that scent ("trailing") would not run past ("over-run") the hare's evasive turns. A "babler," who barked indiscriminately, would be cut from the pack.

4. De Castro identifies him as the Hon. John Temple, Esq. (1680–1752/53?), an admirer of

Fielding's plays whose estate at Moor Park, Surrey, would be the right distance from the scene.

5. Seized by the throat.

6. Diana (the Greek Artemis), virgin goddess of the hunt, is usually depicted accompanied by dogs. Divine intervention in human form to rescue a favorite is a commonplace of classical epic (compare *Iliad* 3.380–82, and 5.311–17, where Aphrodite rescues Paris and then Aeneas). Battestin (*Studies in Bibliography* 36 [1983]: 102, 107 n.10) sees this passage as parodying Ovid's catalog of Actaeon's dogs who attack him when he is transformed into a stag by Diana (*Metamorphoses* 3.206–25). Fielding's account also burlesques Homer's circumstantial depiction of Achilles' whirlwind destruction of ten Greek warriors (*Iliad* 20.455–89).

the Ground; then *Joseph* flew to his Rescue, and with such Might fell on the Victor, that, O eternal Blot to his Name! *Cæsar* ran yelping away.

The Battle now raged with the most dreadful Violence, when lo the Huntsman, a Man of Years and Dignity, lifted his Voice, and called his Hounds from the Fight; telling them, in a Language they understood, that it was in vain to contend longer; for that Fate had decreed the Victory to their Enemies.

Thus far the Muse hath with her usual Dignity related this prodigious Battle, a Battle we apprehend never equalled by any Poet, Romance or Life-writer whatever, and having brought it to a Conclusion she ceased; we shall therefore proceed in our ordinary Style with the Continuation of this History. The Squire and his Companions, whom the Figure of *Adams* and the Gallantry of *Joseph* had at first thrown into a violent Fit of Laughter, and who had hitherto beheld the Engagement with more Delight than any Chace, Shooting-match, Race, Cock-fighting, Bull or Bear-baiting had ever given them, began now to apprehend the Danger of their Hounds, many of which lay sprawling in the Fields. The Squire therefore having first called his Friends about him, as Guards for Safety of his Person, rode manfully up to the Combatants, and summoning all the Terror he was Master of, into his Countenance, demanded with an authoritative Voice of *Joseph*, what he meant by assaulting his Dogs in that Manner. *Joseph* answered with great Intrepidity, that they had first fallen on his Friend; and if they had belonged to the greatest Man in the Kingdom, he would have treated them in the same Way; for whilst his Veins contained a single Drop of Blood, he would not stand idle by, and see that Gentleman (*pointing to* Adams) abused either by Man or Beast; and having so said, both he and *Adams* brandished their wooden Weapons, and put themselves into such a Posture, that the Squire and his Company thought proper to preponderate,[7] before they offered to revenge the Cause of their four-footed Allies.

At this Instant *Fanny*, whom the Apprehension of *Joseph*'s Danger had alarmed so much, that forgetting her own she had made the utmost Expedition, came up. The Squire and all the Horsemen were so surprized with her Beauty, that they immediately fixed both their Eyes and Thoughts solely on her, every one declaring he had never seen so charming a Creature. Neither Mirth nor Anger engaged them a Moment longer; but all sat in silent Amaze. The Huntsman only was free from her Attraction, who was busy in cutting the Ears of the Dogs,[8] and endeavouring to recover them to Life: in which he succeeded so well, that only two of no great Note remained slaughtered on the Field of Action. Upon this the Huntsman declared, 'twas well it was no worse; for his part he could not blame the Gentleman, and wondered his Master would

7. Consider beforehand.
8. Bleeding was prescribed for various ills in dogs, as in humans.

encourage the Dogs to hunt *Christians*; that it was the surest way to spoil them, to make them follow V*ermin*[9] instead of sticking to a Hare.'

The Squire being informed of the little Mischief that had been done; and perhaps having more Mischief of another kind in his Head, accosted Mr. *Adams* with a more favourable Aspect than before: he told him he was sorry for what had happened; that he had endeavoured all he could to prevent it, the Moment he was acquainted with his Cloth, and greatly commended the Courage of his Servant; for so he imagined *Joseph* to be. He then invited Mr. *Adams* to Dinner, and desired the young Woman might come with him. *Adams* refused a long while; but the Invitation was repeated with so much Earnestness and Courtesy, that at length he was forced to accept it. His Wig and Hat, and other Spoils of the Field, being gathered together by *Joseph*, (for otherwise probably they would have been forgotten;) he put himself into the best Order he could; and then the Horse and Foot moved forward in the same Pace towards the Squire's House, which stood at a very little distance.

Whilst they were on the Road, the lovely *Fanny* attracted the Eyes of all; they endeavoured to outvie one another in Encomiums on her Beauty; which the Reader will pardon my not relating, as they had not any thing new or uncommon in them: So must he likewise my not setting down the many curious Jests which were made on *Adams*, some of them declaring that Parson-hunting was the best Sport in the World: Others commending his standing at Bay, which they said he had done as well as any Badger; with such like Merriment, which tho' it would ill become the Dignity of this History, afforded much Laughter and Diversion to the Squire, and his facetious Companions.

Chapter VII

A Scene of Roasting very nicely adapted to the present Taste and Times.[1]

They arrived at the Squire's House just as his Dinner was ready. A little Dispute arose on the account of *Fanny*, whom the Squire who was a Batchelor, was desirous to place at his own Table; but she would not consent, nor would Mr. *Adams* permit her to be parted from *Joseph*: so that she was at length with him consigned over to the Kitchin, where the Servants were ordered to make him drunk; a Favour which was likewise intended for *Adams*: which Design being executed, the Squire

---

9. A broad term designating foxes, weasels, and badgers as well as rodents and snakes. The fox did not supplant the hare as the hunt's favorite game until later in the century.

1. In the leading article in *The Champion* for March 13, 1739/40, Fielding attacked "a certain Diversion called Roasting . . . in some Vogue with the polite Part of the World." Tracing the pleasure of such hostile ridicule to "a great Deformity of Nature, which delights in the Mis-

eries and Misfortunes of Mankind, or . . . a Pride which we take in comparing the Blemishes of others with our own Perfections," he noted that "the most inoffensive Peculiarity often exposes a Man of Sense and Virtue, to the Ridicule of those who are in every Degree his Inferiors," adding that "the generality of Roasters be of this kind, and the Buffoons they use such as may be very aptly call'd Turnspits, the lowest and most despicable of their Kind."

thought he should easily accomplish, what he had, when he first saw her, intended to perpetrate with *Fanny*.

It may not be improper, before we proceed farther to open a little the Character of this Gentleman, and that of his Friends. The Master of this House then was a Man of a very considerable Fortune; a Batchelor, as we have said, and about forty Years of Age: He had been educated (if we may here use that Expression) in the Country, and at his own Home, under the Care of his Mother and a Tutor,[2] who had Orders never to correct him nor to compel him to learn more than he liked, which it seems was very little, and that only in his Childhood; for from the Age of fifteen he addicted himself entirely to Hunting and other rural Amusements, for which his Mother took care to equip him with Horses, Hounds, and all other Necessaries: and his Tutor endeavouring to ingratiate himself with his young Pupil, who would, he knew, be able handsomely to provide for him, became his Companion, not only at these Exercises, but likewise over a Bottle, which the young Squire had a very early Relish for. At the Age of twenty, his Mother began to think she had not fulfilled the Duty of a Parent; she therefore resolved to persuade her Son, if possible, to that which she imagined would well supply all that he might have learned at a publick School or University. This is what they commonly call *Travelling*; which, with the help of the Tutor who was fixed on to attend him, she easily succeeded in. He made in three Years the Tour of *Europe*, as they term it,[3] and returned home, well furnish'd with *French* Clothes, Phrases and Servants, with a hearty Contempt for his own Country; especially what had any Savour of the plain Spirit and Honesty of our Ancestors. His Mother greatly applauded herself at his Return; and now being Master of his own Fortune, he soon procured himself a Seat in Parliament, and was in the common Opinion one of the finest Gentlemen of his Age: But what distinguished him chiefly, was a strange Delight which he took in every thing which is ridiculous, odious, and absurd in his own Species; so that he never chose a Companion without one or more of these Ingredients, and those who were marked by Nature in the most eminent Degree with them, were most his Favourites: if he ever found a Man who either had not or endeavoured to conceal these Imperfections, he took great pleasure in inventing Methods of forcing him into Absurdities, which were not natural to him, or in drawing forth and exposing those that were; for which purpose he was always provided with a Set of Fellows whom we have before called Curs; and who did indeed no great Honour to the Canine Kind: Their Business was to hunt out and display every thing that had any Savour of the above mentioned Qualities, and especially in the grav-

---

2. In Richardson's sequel to *Pamela*, the heroine selects this method for her children, after extensive reflection on Locke's warning about the corrupting public school (see above, p. 179, n. 1).

3. The Grand Tour, usually confined to Italy and France, and lasting a year or more, was supposed to provide a young gentleman with a cultivated knowledge of foreign languages, customs, politics, and art. Fielding's low opinion of this alternative to university, then at the height of its fashion, is reflected in his portraits of Bellarmine (2.4–6) and the Italianate traveller (2.5) as well as this "Hunter of Men."

est and best Characters: But if they failed in their Search, they were to turn even Virtue and Wisdom themselves into Ridicule for the Diversion of their Master and Feeder. The Gentlemen of Curlike Disposition, who were now at his House, and whom he had brought with him from *London*, were an old Half-pay Officer, a Player, a dull Poet, a Quack Doctor, a scraping Fidler, and a lame *German* Dancing-Master.

As soon as Dinner was served, while Mr.*Adams* was saying Grace, the Captain conveyed his Chair from behind him; so that when he endeavoured to seat himself, he fell down on the Ground; and thus compleated Joke the first, to the great Entertainment of the whole Company. The second Joke was performed by the Poet, who sat next him on the other side, and took an Opportunity, while poor *Adams* was respectfully drinking to the Master of the House, to overturn a Plate of Soup into his Breeches; which, with the many Apologies he made, and the Parson's gentle Answers, caused much Mirth in the Company. Joke the third was served up by one of the Waiting-men, who had been ordered to convey a Quantity of Gin into Mr. *Adams's* Ale, which he declaring to be the best Liquor he ever drank, but rather too rich of the Malt, contributed again to their Laughter. Mr. *Adams*, from whom we had most of this Relation, could not recollect all the Jests of this kind practised on him, which the inoffensive Disposition of his own Heart made him slow in discovering; and indeed, had it not been for the Information which we received from a Servant of the Family, this Part of our History, which we take to be none of the least curious, must have been deplorably imperfect; tho' we must own it probable, that some more Jokes were (as they call it) *cracked* during their Dinner; but we have by no means been able to come at the Knowledge of them. When Dinner was removed, the Poet began to repeat some Verses, which he said were made *extempore*. The following is a Copy of them, procured with the greatest difficulty.

An extempore *Poem on Parson* Adams.

> *Did ever Mortal such a Parson view;*
> *His Cassock old, his Wig not over-new?*
> *Well might the Hounds have him for Fox mistaken,*
> *In Smell more like to that, than rusty*[4] *Bacon.* *
> *But would it not make any Mortal stare,*
> *To see this Parson taken for a Hare?*
> *Could* Phœbus *err thus grossly, even he*
> *For a good Player might have taken thee.*

At which Words the Bard whip'd off the Player's Wig, and received the Approbation of the Company, rather perhaps for the Dexterity of his Hand than his Head. The Player, instead of retorting the Jest on the

---

* All Hounds that will hunt Fox or other Vermin, will hunt a Piece of rusty Bacon trailed on the Ground.

---

4. Rancid.

Poet, began to display his Talents on the same Subject. He repeated many Scraps of Wit out of Plays, reflecting on the whole Body of the Clergy, which were received with great Acclamations by all present. It was now the Dancing-Master's Turn to exhibit his Talents; he therefore addressing himself to *Adams* in broken *English*, told him, 'he was a Man ver well made for de Dance, and he suppose by his Walk, dat he had learn of some great Master. He said it was ver pretty Quality in Clergyman to dance;' and concluded with desiring him to dance a Minuet, telling him, 'his Cassock would serve for Petticoats; and that he would himself be his Partner.' At which Words, without waiting for an Answer, he pulled out his Gloves, and the Fiddler was preparing his Fiddle. The Company all offered the Dancing-Master Wagers that the Parson outdanced him, which he refused, saying, 'he believed so too; for he had never seen any Man in his Life who looked de Dance so well as de Gentleman:' He then stepped forwards to take *Adams* by the Hand, which the latter hastily withdrew, and at the same time clenching his Fist, advised him not to carry the Jest too far, for he would not endure being put upon. The Dancing-master no sooner saw the Fist than he prudently retired out of it's reach, and stood aloof mimicking *Adams*, whose Eyes were fixed on him, not guessing what he was at, but to avoid his laying hold on him, which he had once attempted. In the mean while, the Captain perceiving an Opportunity pinned a Cracker or Devil to the Cassock, and then lighted it with their little smoaking Candle. *Adams* being a Stranger to this Sport, and believing he had been blown up in reality, started from his Chair, and jumped about the Room, to the infinite Joy of the Beholders, who declared he was the best Dancer in the Universe. As soon as the Devil had done tormenting him, and he had a little recovered his Confusion, he returned to the Table, standing up in the Posture of one who intended to make a Speech. They all cried out, *Hear him, Hear him*; and he then spoke in the following manner: 'Sir, I am sorry to see one to whom Providence hath been so bountiful in bestowing his Favours, make so ill and ungrateful a Return for them; for tho' you have not insulted me yourself, it is visible you have delighted in those that do it, nor have once discouraged the many Rudenesses which have been shewn towards me; indeed towards yourself, if you rightly understood them; for I am your Guest, and by the Laws of Hospitality entitled to your Protection. One Gentleman hath thought proper to produce some Poetry upon me, of which I shall only say, that I had rather be the Subject than the Composer. He hath pleased to treat me with Disrespect as a Parson; I apprehend my Order is not the Object of Scorn, nor that I can become so, unless by being a Disgrace to it, which I hope Poverty will never be called. Another Gentleman indeed hath repeated some Sentences, where the Order itself is mentioned with Contempt. He says they are taken from Plays. I am sure such Plays are a Scandal to the Government which permits them, and cursed will be the Nation where they are represented. How others have treated me, I need not observe; they themselves, when they reflect, must allow the Behaviour to be as improper to my Years as to my Cloth. You found me, Sir, travelling with two of my Parishioners, (I omit your Hounds falling on me; for I have quite forgiven it, whether it proceeded from the Wantonness or Negligence of the Huntsman,) my Appearance might very well persuade you that your Invitation was an Act of Charity, tho' in reality we were well provided; yes, Sir, if we had had an hundred Miles to travel, we had sufficient to bear our Expences in a noble manner.' (At which Words he produced the half Guinea which was found in the Basket.) 'I do not shew you this out of Ostentation of Riches, but to convince you I speak Truth. Your seating me at your Table was an Honour which I did not ambitiously affect; when I was here, I endeavoured to behave towards you with the utmost Respect; if I have failed, it was not with Design, nor could I, certainly, so far be guilty as to deserve the Insults I have suffered. If they were meant therefore either to my Order or my Poverty (and you see I am not very poor) the Shame doth not lie at my door, and I heartily pray, that the Sin may be averted from your's.' He thus finished, and received a general Clap from the whole Company. Then the Gentleman of the House told him, 'he was sorry for what had happened; that he could not accuse him of any Share in it: That the Verses were, as himself had well observed, so bad, that he might easily answer them; and for the Serpent,[5] it was undoubtedly a very great Affront done him by the Dancing-Master, for which if he well thrashed him, as he deserved, (the Gentleman said) he should be very much pleased to see it;' (in which probably he spoke Truth.) *Adams* answered, 'whoever had done it, it was not his Profession to punish him that way; but for the Person whom he had accused, I am a Witness, (says he) of his Innocence, for I had my Eye on him all the while. Whoever he was, God forgive him, and bestow on him a little more Sense as well as Humanity.' The Captain answer'd with a surly Look and Accent, 'that he hoped he did not mean to reflect on him; d—n him, he had as much *Imanity* as another, and if any Man said he had not, he would convince him of his Mistake by cutting his Throat.' *Adams* smiling, said, 'he believed he had spoke right by Accident.' To which the Captain returned, 'What do you mean by my speaking right? if you was not a Parson, I would not take these Words; but your Gown protects you. If any Man who wears a Sword had said so much, I had pulled him by the Nose before this.' *Adams* replied, 'if he attempted any Rudeness to his Person, he would not find any Protection for himself in his Gown;' and clenching his Fist, declared he had threshed many a stouter Man. The Gentleman did all he could to encourage this warlike Disposition in *Adams*, and was in hopes to have produced a Battle: But he was disappointed; for the Captain made no other Answer than, 'It is very well you are a Parson,' and so drinking off a Bumper to old Mother Church, ended the Dispute.

Then the Doctor, who had hitherto been silent, and who was the gravest, but most mischievous Dog of all, in a very pompous Speech

5. A firecracker of that shape.

highly applauded what *Adams* had said; and as much discommended the Behaviour to him; he proceeded to Encomiums on the Church and Poverty; and lastly recommended Forgiveness of what had past to *Adams*, who immediately answered, 'that every thing was forgiven;' and in the Warmth of his Goodness he filled a Bumper of strong Beer, (a Liquor he preferred to Wine) and drank a Health to the whole Company, shaking the Captain and the Poet heartily by the Hand, and addressing himself with great Respect to the Doctor; who indeed had not laughed outwardly at any thing that past, as he had a perfect Command of his Muscles, and could laugh inwardly without betraying the least Symptoms in his Countenance. The Doctor now began a second formal Speech, in which he declaimed against all Levity of Conversation; and what is usually called Mirth. He said, 'there were Amusements fitted for Persons of all Ages and Degrees, from the Rattle to the discussing a Point of Philosophy, and that Men discovered themselves in nothing more than in the Choice of their Amusements; for,' says he, 'as it must greatly raise our Expectation of the future Conduct in Life of Boys, whom in their tender Years we perceive instead of Taw[6] or Balls, or other childish Playthings, to chuse, at their Leisure-Hours, to exercise their Genius in Contentions of Wit, Learning, and such like; so must it inspire one with equal Contempt of a Man, if we should discover him playing at Taw or other childish Play.' *Adams* highly commended the Doctor's Opinion, and said, 'he had often wondered at some Passages in ancient Authors, where *Scipio, Lælius,* and other great Men were represented to have passed many Hours in Amusements of the most trifling kind.'[7] The Doctor reply'd, 'he had by him an old *Greek* Manuscript where a favourite Diversion of *Socrates* was recorded.' 'Ay,' says the Parson eagerly, 'I should be most infinitely obliged to you for the Favour of perusing it.' The Doctor promised to send it him, and farther said, 'that he believed he could describe it. I think,' says he, 'as near as I can remember, it was this. There was a Throne erected, on one side of which sat a King, and on the other a Queen, with their Guards and Attendants ranged on both sides; to them was introduced an Ambassador, which Part *Socrates* always used to perform himself; and when he was led up to the Footsteps of the Throne, he addressed himself to the Monarchs in some grave Speech, full of Virtue and Goodness, and Morality, and such like. After which, he was seated between the King and Queen, and royally entertained. This I think was the chief part.—Perhaps I may have forgot some Particulars; for it is long since I read it.' *Adams* said, 'it was indeed a Diversion worthy the Relaxation of so great a Man; and thought something resembling it should be instituted among our great Men, instead of Cards and other idle Pass-time, in which he was informed they trifled away too much of their Lives.' He added, 'the Christian Religion was a nobler

6. Marbles.
7. Scipio Aemilianus, called Scipio Africanus Minor (ca. 185–129 B.C.), twice elected consul, destroyer of Carthage, and regarded by Cicero as the greatest Roman, was a patron to writers, including his close friend, Gaius Laelius (b. ca. 186 B.C.), also a consul and an orator famed for his wisdom. A character in Cicero's dialogue, *De Oratore* (2.6), remarks that on country holidays they became boys again, descending to collecting seashells and other trifling pastimes.

Subject for these Speeches than any *Socrates* could have invented.' The Gentleman of the House approved what Mr. *Adams* said, and declared, 'he was resolved to perform the Ceremony this very Evening.' To which the Doctor objected, as no one was prepared with a Speech, 'Unless,' said he, (turning to *Adams* with a Gravity of Countenance which would have deceived a more knowing Man) 'you have a Sermon about you, Doctor.'—'Sir,' says *Adams*, 'I never travel without one, for fear what may happen.' He was easily prevailed on by his worthy Friend, as he now called the Doctor, to undertake the Part of the Ambassador; so that the Gentleman sent immediate Orders to have the Throne erected; which was performed before they had drank two Bottles: And perhaps the Reader will hereafter have no great reason to admire the Nimbleness of the Servants. Indeed, to confess the Truth, the Throne was no more than this; there was a great Tub of Water provided, on each side of which were placed two Stools raised higher than the Surface of the Tub, and over the Whole was laid a Blanket; on these Stools were placed the King and Queen, namely, the Master of the House, and the Captain. And now the Ambassador was introduced, between the Poet and the Doctor, who having read his Sermon to the great Entertainment of all present, was led up to his Place, and seated between their Majesties. They immediately rose up, when the Blanket wanting its Supports at either end, gave way, and soused *Adams* over Head and Ears in the Water; the Captain made his Escape, but unluckily the Gentleman himself not being as nimble as he ought, *Adams* caught hold of him before he descended from his Throne, and pulled him in with him, to the entire secret Satisfaction of all the Company. *Adams* after ducking the Squire twice or thrice leapt out of the Tub, and looked sharp for the Doctor, whom he would certainly have convey'd to the same Place of Honour; but he had wisely withdrawn: he then searched for his Crabstick, and having found that, as well as his Fellow-Travellers, he declared he would not stay a moment longer in such a House. He then departed, without taking leave of his Host, whom he had exacted a more severe Revenge on, than he intended: For as he did not use sufficient care to dry himself in time, he caught a Cold by the Accident, which threw him into a Fever, that had like to have cost him his Life.[8]

Chapter VIII

Which some Readers will think too short, and others too long.[1]

Adams, and *Joseph*, who was no less enraged than his Friend at the Treatment he met with, went out with their Sticks in their Hands; and

8. The same prank was played on the French philosopher Montesquieu a dozen years earlier by John, duke of Montague (1688?–1749), an incorrigible practical joker. In "An Essay on Conversation" published in his *Miscellanies* (1743), Fielding condemned "that Kind of Raillery . . . which is concerned in tossing Men out of their Chairs, tumbling them into Water, or any of those handi-craft Jokes which are exercised on those notable Persons, commonly known by the Name of Buffoons; who are contented to feed their Belly at the Price of their Br—ch, and to carry off the Wine and the P—ss of a Great Man together" (ed. H. K. Miller [Wesleyan Edition, 1972] 1.150). See also p. 326 below.

1. According to their religious affiliation.

carried off *Fanny*, notwithstanding the Opposition of the Servants, who did all, without proceeding to Violence, in their power to detain them. They walked as fast as they could, not so much from any Apprehension of being pursued, as that Mr. *Adams* might by Exercise prevent any harm from the Water. The Gentleman who had given such Orders to his Servants concerning *Fanny*, that he did not in the least fear her getting away, no sooner heard that she was gone, than he began to rave, and immediately dispatched several with Orders, either to bring her back, or never return. The Poet, the Player, and all but the Dancing-master and Doctor went on this Errand.

The Night was very dark, in which our Friends began their Journey; however they made such Expedition, that they soon arrived at an Inn, which was at seven Miles Distance. Here they unanimously consented to pass the Evening, Mr. *Adams* being now as dry as he was before he had set out on his Embassy.

This Inn, which indeed we might call an Ale-house, had not the Words, *The New Inn*, been writ on the Sign, afforded them no better Provision than Bread and Cheese, and Ale; on which, however they made a very comfortable Meal; for Hunger is better than a *French* Cook.[2]

They had no sooner supped, than *Adams* returning Thanks to the Almighty for his Food, declared he had eat his homely Commons, with much greater Satisfaction than his splendid Dinner, and exprest great Contempt for the Folly of Mankind, who sacrificed their Hopes of Heaven to the Acquisition of vast Wealth, since so much Comfort was to be found in the humblest State and the lowest Provision. 'Very true, Sir,' says a grave Man who sat smoking his Pipe by the Fire, and who was a Traveller as well as himself. 'I have often been as much surprized as you are, when I consider the Value which Mankind in general set on Riches, since every day's Experience shews us how little is in their power; for what indeed truly desirable can they bestow on us? Can they give Beauty to the Deformed, Strength to the Weak, or Health to the Infirm? Surely if they could, we should not see so many ill-favoured Faces haunting the Assemblies of the Great, nor would such numbers of feeble Wretches languish in their Coaches and Palaces. No, not the Wealth of a Kingdom can purchase any Paint, to dress pale Ugliness in the Bloom of that young Maiden, nor any Drugs to equip Disease with the Vigour of that young Man. Do not Riches bring us Sollicitude instead of Rest, Envy instead of Affection, and Danger instead of Safety? Can they prolong their own Possession, or lengthen his Days who enjoys them? So far otherwise, that the Sloth, the Luxury, the Care which attend them, shorten the Lives of Millions, and bring them with Pain and Misery, to an untimely Grave. Where then is their Value, if they can neither embellish, or strengthen our Forms, sweeten or prolong our Lives? Again—Can they adorn the Mind more than the Body? Do they not rather swell the Heart with Vanity, puff up the Cheeks with Pride, shut our Ears to every Call of Virtue, and our Bowels to every Motive of

---

2. "There's no Sauce in the World like Hunger" (Sancho Panza in *Don Quixote* 2.5).

Compassion!' 'Give me your Hand, Brother,' said *Adams* in a Rapture;
'for I suppose you are a Clergyman.' 'No truly,' answered the other,
(indeed he was a Priest of the Church of *Rome*; but those who understand our Laws will not wonder he was not over-ready to own it.)[3]
'Whatever you are,' cried *Adams*, 'you have spoken my Sentiments: I
believe I have preached every Syllable of your Speech twenty times over:
For it hath always appeared to me easier for a Cable Rope (which by the
way is the true rendering of that Word we have translated *Camel*) to go
through the Eye of a Needle, than for a rich Man to get into the Kingdom of Heaven.'[4] 'That, Sir,' said the other, 'will be easily granted you
by Divines, and is deplorably true: But as the Prospect of our Good at a
distance doth not so forcibly affect us, it might be of some Service to
Mankind to be made thoroughly sensible, which I think they might be
with very little serious Attention, that even the Blessings of this World,
are not to be purchased with Riches. A Doctrine in my Opinion, not
only metaphysically, but if I may so say, mathematically demonstrable;
and which I have been always so perfectly convinced of, that I have a
Contempt for nothing so much as for Gold.' *Adams* now began a long
Discourse; but as most which he said occurs among many Authors, who
have treated this Subject, I shall omit inserting it. During its Continuance *Joseph* and *Fanny* retired to Rest, and the Host likewise left the
Room. When the *English* Parson had concluded, the *Romish* resumed
the Discourse, which he continued with great Bitterness and Invective;
and at last ended by desiring *Adams* to lend him eighteen Pence to pay
his Reckoning; promising, if he never paid him, he might be assured of
his Prayers. The good Man answered, that eighteen Pence would be too
little to carry him any very long Journey; that he had half a Guinea in
his Pocket, which he would divide with him. He then fell to searching
his Pockets, but could find no Money: For indeed the Company with
whom he dined, had past one Jest upon him which we did not then
enumerate, and had picked his Pocket of all that Treasure which he had
so ostentatiously produced.

'Bless me,' cry'd *Adams*, 'I have certainly lost it, I can never have
spent it. Sir, as I am a Christian I had a whole half Guinea in my Pocket
this Morning, and have not now a single Halfpenny of it left. Sure the
Devil must have taken it from me.' 'Sir,' answered the Priest smiling,
'You need make no Excuses; if you are not willing to lend me the Money,
I am contented.' 'Sir,' cries *Adams*, 'if I had the greatest Sum in the
World; ay, if I had ten Pounds about me, I would bestow it all to rescue
any Christian from Distress. I am more vexed at my Loss on your account
than my own. Was ever any thing so unlucky? because I have no Money
in my Pocket, I shall be suspected to be no Christian.' 'I am more unlucky,'

3. Though rarely enforced at this time, legislation
enacted in 1669 penalized a Roman Catholic
priest for celebrating mass with a two hundred–
pound fine, and he could be charged with high
treason.
4. Adams substitutes Greek *kamilon* (rope, ship's

cable) for *kamelon* (camel) in Matthew 19:24.
Plausible as it is, there is little textual support for
this emendation and biblical scholars have noted
the comparable use of large animals in other
ancient texts.

quoth the other, 'if you are as generous as you say: For really a Crown would have made me happy, and conveyed me in plenty to the Place I am going, which is not above twenty Miles off, and where I can arrive by tomorrow Night. I assure you I am not accustomed to travel Penny-less. I am but just arrived in *England*, and we were forced by a Storm in our Passage to throw all we had overboard. I don't suspect but this Fellow will take my Word for the Trifle I owe him; but I hate to appear so mean[5] as to confess myself without a Shilling to such People: For these, and indeed too many others know little Difference in their Estimation between a Beggar and a Thief.' However, he thought he should deal better with the Host that Evening than the next Morning; he therefore resolved to set out immediately, notwithstanding the Darkness; and accordingly as soon as the Host returned he communicated to him the Situation of his Affairs; upon which the Host scratching his Head, answered, 'Why, I do not know, Master, if it be so, and you have no Money, I must trust I think, tho' I had rather always have ready Money if I could; but, marry, you look like so honest a Gentleman, that I don't fear your paying me, if it was twenty times as much.' The Priest made no Reply, but taking leave of him and *Adams*, as fast as he could, not without Confusion, and perhaps with some Distrust of *Adams's* Sincerity, departed.

He was no sooner gone than the Host fell a shaking his Head, and declared if he had suspected the Fellow had no Money, he would not have drawn him a single Drop of Drink; saying, he despaired of ever seeing his Face again; for that he looked like a confounded Rogue. 'Rabbit[6] the Fellow,' cries he, 'I thought by his talking so much about Riches, that he had a hundred Pounds at least in his Pocket.' *Adams* chid him for his Suspicions, which he said were not becoming a Christian; and then without reflecting on his Loss, or considering how he himself should depart in the Morning, he retired to a very homely Bed, as his Companions had before; however, Health and Fatigue gave them a sweeter Repose than is often in the power of Velvet and Down to bestow.

Chapter IX

Containing as surprizing and bloody Adventures as can be found in this, or perhaps any other authentic History.

It was almost Morning when *Joseph Andrews*, whose Eyes the Thoughts of his dear *Fanny* had opened, as he lay fondly meditating on that lovely Creature, heard a violent knocking at the Door over which he lay; he presently jumped out of Bed, and opening the Window, was asked if there were no Travellers in the House; and presently by another Voice, If two Men and a young Woman had not taken up their Lodgings there that Night. Tho' he knew not the Voices, he began to entertain a Suspicion of the Truth; for indeed he had received some Information from

5. Poor.   6. "Drat" or "darn."

one of the Servants of the Squire's House, of his Design; and answered in the Negative. One of the Servants who knew the Host well, called out to him by his Name, just as he had opened another Window, and asked him the same Question; to which he answered in the Affirmative. 'O ho!' said another; 'Have we found you?' And ordered the Host to come down and open his Door. *Fanny*, who was as wakeful as *Joseph*, no sooner heard all this, than she leap'd from her Bed, and hastily putting on her Gown and Petticoats, ran as fast as possible to *Joseph's* Room, who then was almost drest; he immediately let her in, and embracing her with the most passionate Tenderness, bid her fear nothing: For he would die in her Defence. 'Is that a Reason why I should not fear,' says she, 'when I should lose what is dearer to me than the whole World?' *Joseph* then kissing her Hand, said he could almost thank the Occasion which had exorted from her a Tenderness she would never indulge him with before. He then ran and waked his Bedfellow *Adams*, who was yet fast asleep, notwithstanding many Calls from *Joseph*: But was no sooner made sensible of their Danger than he leaped from his Bed, without considering the Presence of *Fanny*, who hastily turned her Face from him, and enjoyed a double Benefit from the dark, which as it would have prevented any Offence to an Innocence less pure, or a Modesty less delicate, so it concealed even those Blushes which were raised in her.

Adams had soon put on all his Clothes but his Breeches, which in the Hurry he forgot; however, they were pretty well supplied[1] by the length of his other Garments: And now the House-Door being opened, the Captain, the Poet, the Player, and three Servants came in. The Captain told the Host, that two Fellows who were in his House had run away with a young Woman, and desired to know in which Room she lay. The Host, who presently[2] believed the Story, directed them, and instantly the Captain and Poet, jostling one another, ran up. The Poet, who was the nimblest, entering the Chamber first, searched the Bed and every other part, but to no purpose; the Bird was flown, as the impatient Reader, who might otherwise have been in pain for her, was before advertised.[3] They then enquired where the Men lay, and were approaching the Chamber, when *Joseph* roared out in a loud Voice, that he would shoot the first Man who offered to attack the Door. The Captain enquired what Fire-Arms they had; to which the Host answered, he believed they had none; nay, he was almost convinced of it: For he had heard one ask the other in the Evening, what they should have done, if they had been overtaken when they had no Arms; to which the other answered, they would have defended themselves with their Sticks as long as they were able, and G— would assist a just Cause. This satisfied the Captain, but not the Poet, who prudently retreated down Stairs, saying it was his Business to record great Actions, and not to do them. The Captain was

1. Substituted for.
2. Immediately.
3. Notified.

no sooner well satisfied that there were no Fire-Arms, than bidding Defiance to Gunpowder, and swearing he loved the Smell of it, he ordered the Servants to follow him, and marching boldly up, immediately attempted to force the Door, which the Servants soon helped him to accomplish. When it was opened, they discovered the Enemy drawn up three deep; *Adams* in the Front, and *Fanny* in the Rear. The Captain told *Adams*, that if they would go all back to the House again, they should be civilly treated: but unless they consented, he had Orders to carry the young Lady with him, whom there was great Reason to believe they had stolen from her Parents; for notwithstanding her Disguise, her Air, which she could not conceal, sufficiently discovered her Birth to be infinitely superiour to theirs. *Fanny* bursting into Tears, solemnly assured him he was mistaken; that she was a poor helpless Foundling, and had no Relation in the World which she knew of; and throwing herself on her Knees, begged that he would not attempt to take her from her Friends, who she was convinced would die before they would lose her, which *Adams* confirmed with Words not far from amounting to an Oath. The Captain swore he had no leisure to talk, and bidding them thank themselves for what happened, he ordered the Servants to fall on, at the same time endeavouring to pass by *Adams* in order to lay hold on *Fanny*; but the Parson interrupting him, received a Blow from one of them, which without considering whence it came, he returned to the Captain, and gave him so dextrous a Knock in that part of the Stomach which is vulgarly called the Pit, that he staggered some Paces backwards. The Captain, who was not accustomed to this kind of play, and who wisely apprehended the Consequence of such another Blow, two of them seeming to him equal to a Thrust through the Body, drew forth his Hanger,[4] as *Adams* approached him, and was levelling a Blow at his Head, which would probably have silenced the Preacher for ever, had not *Joseph* in that Instant lifted up a certain huge Stone Pot of the Chamber with one Hand, which six Beaus could not have lifted with both,[5] and discharged it, together with the Contents, full in the Captain's Face. The uplifted Hanger dropped from his Hand, and he fell prostrate on the Floor *with a lumpish Noise, and his Halfpence rattled in his Pocket*;[6] the red Liquour which his Veins contained, and the white Liquor which the Pot contained, ran in one Stream down his Face and his Clothes. Nor had *Adams* quite escaped, some of the Water having in its Passage shed its Honours on his Head, and began to trickle down the Wrinkles or rather Furrows of his Cheeks, when one of the Servants snatching a Mop out of a Pail of Water which had already done its Duty in washing the House,

4. Short sword.

5. Compare *Iliad* 5.302–4, where Diomedes ". . . in his hand caught / up a stone, a huge thing which no two men could carry / such as men are now . . ." (R. Lattimore trans.); and Virgil's amplification in the *Aeneid* 12.896–902, where Turnus casts a stone that "scarce twice six chosen men could uplift upon their shoulders, men of such frames as earth now begets" (H. R. Fairclough trans.).

6. Fielding's italics highlight his burlesque of a formula repeated with variations throughout the *Iliad*: "He fell, thunderously, and his armour clattered upon him" (R. Lattimore trans.).

pushed it in the Parson's Face; yet could not he bear him down; for the Parson wresting the Mop from the Fellow with one Hand, with the other brought his Enemy as low as the Earth, having given him a Stroke over that part of the Face, where, in some Men of Pleasure, the natural and artificial Noses are conjoined.[7]

Hitherto Fortune seemed to incline the Victory on the Travellers side, when, according to her Custom, she began to shew the Fickleness of her Disposition: for now the Host entering the Field, or rather Chamber, of Battle, flew directly at *Joseph*, and darting his Head into his Stomach (for he was a stout Fellow, and an expert Boxer)[8] almost staggered him; but *Joseph* stepping one Leg back, did with his left Hand so chuck him under the Chin that he reeled. The Youth was pursuing his Blow with his right Hand, when he received from one of the Servants such a Stroke with a Cudgel on his Temples, that it instantly deprived him of Sense, and he measured his Length on the Ground.

Fanny rent the Air with her Cries, and *Adams* was coming to the assistance of *Joseph*: but the two Serving-Men and the Host now fell on him, and soon subdued him, tho' he fought like a Madman, and looked so black with the Impressions he had received from the Mop, that *Don Quixotte* would certainly have taken him for an inchanted *Moor*.[9] But now follows the most tragical Part; for the Captain was risen again, and seeing *Joseph* on the Floor, and *Adams* secured, he instantly laid hold on *Fanny*, and with the Assistance of the Poet and Player, who hearing the Battle was over, were now come up, dragged her, crying and tearing her Hair, from the Sight of her *Joseph*, and with a perfect Deafness to all her Entreaties, carried her down Stairs by Violence, and fastened her on the Player's Horse; and the Captain mounting his own, and leading that on which this poor miserable Wretch was, departed without any more Consideration of her Cries than a Butcher hath of those of a Lamb; for indeed his Thoughts were only entertained with the Degree of Favour which he promised himself from the Squire on the Success of this Adventure.

The Servants who were ordered to secure *Adams* and *Joseph* as safe as possible, that the 'Squire might receive no Interruption to his Design on poor *Fanny*, immediately by the Poet's Advice tied *Adams* to one of the Bed-posts, as they did *Joseph* on the other side, as soon as they could bring him to himself; and then leaving them together, back to back, and desiring the Host not to set them at liberty, nor go near them till he had farther Orders, they departed towards their Master; but happened to take a different Road from that which the Captain had fallen into.

---

7. Another burlesque of Homer's manner (e.g., ". . . caught Aineias in the hip, in the place where the hip-bone/turns inside the thigh . . . ," *Iliad* 5.305–6, R. Lattimore trans.), alluding to a cosmetic repair for decay of the septum caused by untreated venereal disease.

8. Butting was an accepted boxing tactic until declared a foul (along with biting, kicking, and gouging) by the London Prize Ring Rules of 1838.
9. In *Don Quixote* 1.3.3, the knight attributes a midnight drubbing to an invisible enchanted moor. For the incident, see below, pp. 353–56.

Chapter X

A Discourse between the Poet and Player; of no other Use in this History, but to divert the Reader.

Before we proceed any farther in this Tragedy, we shall leave Mr. *Joseph* and Mr. *Adams* to themselves, and imitate the wise Conductors of the Stage; who in the midst of a grave Action entertain you with some excellent piece of Satire or Humour called a Dance. Which Piece indeed is therefore danced, and not spoke, as it is delivered to the Audience by Persons whose thinking Faculty is by most People held to lie in their Heels; and to whom, as well as Heroes, who think with their Hands, Nature hath only given Heads for the sake of Conformity, and as they are of use in Dancing, to hang their Hats on.[1]

The Poet addressing the Player, proceeded thus: 'As I was saying' (for they had been at this Discourse all the time of the Engagement, above Stairs) 'the Reason you have no good new Plays is evident; it is from your Discouragement of Authors. Gentlemen will not write, Sir, they will not write without the Expectation of Fame or Profit, or perhaps both. Plays are like Trees which will not grow without Nourishment; but like Mushrooms, they shoot up spontaneously, as it were, in a rich Soil. The Muses, like Vines, may be pruned, but not with a Hatchet. The Town, like a peevish Child, knows not what it desires, and is always best pleased with a Rattle. A Farce-Writer hath indeed some Chance for Success; but they have lost all Taste for the Sublime. Tho' I believe one Reason of their Depravity is the Badness of the Actors. If a Man writes like an Angel, Sir, those Fellows know not how to give a Sentiment Utterance.' 'Not so fast,' says the Player, 'the modern Actors are as good at least as their Authors, nay, they come nearer their illustrious Predecessors, and I expect a *Booth* on the Stage again, sooner than a *Shakespear* or an *Otway*;[2] and indeed I may turn your Observation against you, and with Truth say, that the Reason no Authors are encouraged, is because we have no good new Plays.' 'I have not affirmed the contrary,' said the Poet, 'but I am surprized you grow so warm; you cannot imagine yourself interested[3] in this Dispute, I hope you have a better Opinion of my Taste, than to apprehend I squinted at yourself. No, Sir, if we had six such Actors as you, we should soon rival the *Bettertons* and *Sandfords*[4]

1. Introduced after the Restoration to entertain audiences between acts of even the most serious tragedies (there were no intermissions), dancing, often by foreigners, became a demanded staple of all the theatres by the 1720's. Fielding excluded it when he managed the Little Theatre in the Haymarket.
2. Barton Booth (1681–1733), the most popular tragedian of his day, distinguished himself in Addison's *Cato* (1713) and also excelled as Hotspur, Brutus, and Othello and as the ghost in *Hamlet*. Thomas Otway (1652–1685), best known for *The Orphan* (1680) and *Venice Preserved* (1682), was regarded in the eighteenth century as a tragedian "next to Shakespeare" (Goldsmith, *The Bee*, November 24, 1759).
3. Concerned.
4. Thomas Betterton (1635?–1710), the greatest actor of the Restoration and Booth's mentor, excelled in both tragedy and comedy. His colleague Samuel Sandford, who appeared in numerous roles between 1661 and 1699, was celebrated for his portrayal of villains.

of former Times; for, without a Compliment[5] to you, I think it impossible for any one to have excelled you in most of your Parts. Nay, it is solemn Truth, and I have heard many, and all great Judges, express as much; and you will pardon me if I tell you, I think every time I have seen you lately, you have constantly acquired some new Excellence, like a Snowball. You have deceived me in my Estimation of Perfection, and have outdone what I thought inimitable.' 'You are as little interested,' answer'd the Player, 'in what I have said of other Poets; for d—n me, if there are not manly Strokes, ay whole Scenes, in your last Tragedy, which at least equal *Shakespear*. There is a Delicacy of Sentiment, a Dignity of Expression in it, which I will own many of our Gentlemen did not do adequate Justice to. To confess the Truth, they are bad enough, and I pity an Author who is present at the Murder of his Works.'—'Nay, it is but seldom that it can happen,' returned the Poet, 'the Works of most modern Authors, like dead-born Children, cannot be murdered. It is such wretched half-begotten, half-writ, lifeless, spiritless, low, groveling Stuff, that I almost pity the Actor who is oblig'd to get it by heart, which must be as difficult to remember as Words in a Language you don't understand.' 'I am sure,' said the Player, 'if the Sentences have little Meaning when they are writ, when they are spoken they have less. I know scarce one who ever lays an Emphasis right, and much less adapts his Action to his Character. I have seen a tender Lover in an Attitude of fighting with his Mistress, and a brave Hero suing to his Enemy with his Sword in his Hand—I don't care to abuse my Profession, but rot me if in my Heart I am not inclined to the Poet's Side.' 'It is rather generous in you than just,' said the Poet; 'and tho' I hate to speak ill of any Person's Production; nay I never do it, nor will—but yet to do Justice to the Actors, what could *Booth* or *Betterton* have made of such horrible Stuff as *Fenton's Mariamne*, *Frowd's Philotas*, or *Mallet's Eurydice*,[6] or those low, dirty, last Dying-Speeches, which a Fellow in the City or *Wapping*, your *Dillo* or *Lillo*, what was his Name, called Tragedies?'[7]—'Very well, Sir,' says the Player, 'and pray what do you think of such Fellows as *Quin* and *Delane*, or that face-making Puppy young *Cibber*, that ill-looked Dog *Macklin*, or that saucy Slut Mrs. *Clive*?[8]

5. "An . . . expression of civility, usually understood to include some hypocrisy, and to mean less than it declares" (Johnson's *Dictionary*).

6. The poet echoes Colley Cibber's opinion of *Mariamne*, by Elijah Fenton (1683–1730); after he rejected the tragedy at Drury Lane, it succeeded at Rich's theatre in 1722–23, earning Fenton nearly one thousand pounds. Like *Eurydice* (1731), a popular heroic tragedy by David Mallet (see above, p. 186, n. 1), it was cited derisively in Fielding's *Tragedy of Tragedies* (1731). The less successful *Philotas* (1731) by Philip Frowde (d. 1738) was a "classical" tragedy of love versus duty in the manner of Dryden.

7. Fielding's friend George Lillo (1693–1739) was a jeweler turned dramatist—hence the poet's disdainful reference to the City and Wapping, a

commercial warehouse area. His best known play, *The London Merchant* (1731), was frequently acted in the decade preceding the novel (see above, p. 25, n. 5); Fielding staged the less successful *Fatal Curiosity* (1736) in his Haymarket Theatre. In both plays Lillo forsook the conventional "high" subjects of tragedy to demonstrate the retribution awaiting humble persons tempted to crime, ending with the remorseful reflections of the condemned or dying protagonist.

8. Of these celebrated players of the day, all but Delane acted in Fielding's plays. James Quin (1693–1766) was then at the height of his fame as the successor to Betterton and Booth; Dennis Delane (d. 1750), Irish tragedian, was playing Richard III at Drury Lane shortly before publication of the novel. Although he ridiculed Colley

What work would they make with your *Shakespeares, Otways* and *Lees*? How would those harmonious Lines of the last come from their Tongues?

> *—No more; for I disdain*
> *All Pomp when thou art by—far be the Noise*
> *Of Kings and Crowns from us, whose gentle Souls*
> *Our kinder Fates have steer'd another way.*
> *Free as the Forest Birds we'll pair together,*
> *Without rememb'ring who our Fathers were:*
> *Fly to the Arbors, Grots and flowry Meads,*
> *There in soft Murmurs interchange our Souls,*
> *Together drink the Crystal of the Stream,*
> *Or taste the yellow Fruit which Autumn yields.*
> *And when the golden Evening calls us home,*
> *Wing to our downy Nests and sleep till Morn.*[9]

'Or how would this Disdain of *Otway*,

> *Who'd be that foolish, sordid thing, call'd Man?*[1]

'Hold, hold, hold,' said the Poet, 'Do repeat that tender Speech in the third Act of my Play which you made such a Figure in.'—'I would willingly,' said the Player, 'but I have forgot it.'—'Ay, you was not quite perfect enough in it when you play'd it,' cries the Poet, 'or you would have had such an Applause as was never given on the Stage; an Applause I was extremely concerned for your losing.'—'Sure,' says the Player, 'if I remember, that was hiss'd more than any Passage in the whole Play.'—'Ay your speaking it was hiss'd,' said the Poet. 'My speaking it!' said the Player.—'I mean your not speaking it,' said the Poet. 'You was out,[2] and then they hiss'd.'—'They hiss'd, and then I was out, if I remember,' answer'd the Player; 'and I must say this for myself, that the whole Audience allowed I did your Part Justice, so don't lay the Damnation of your Play to my account.' 'I don't know what you mean by Damnation,' reply'd the Poet. 'Why you know it was acted but one Night,' cried the Player. 'No,' said the Poet, 'you and the whole Town know I had Enemies; the Pit were all my Enemies, Fellows that would cut my Throat, if the Fear of Hanging did not restrain them. All Taylors, Sir, all Taylors.'—'Why should the Taylors be so angry with you?' cries the Player. 'I suppose you don't employ so many in making your Clothes.' 'I admit

---

Cibber's son Theophilus (1703–58) in his inherited managerial role in a 1734 revision of *The Author's Farce*, Fielding praised this talented comedian's lead performance in *The Mock Doctor* (1732). His sometime rival Charles Macklin (1697?–1797), exploiting his long craggy face, had just created a sensation with his naturalistic treatment of the traditionally comic Shylock as a fierce villain (1741). Catherine "Kitty" Clive, nee Raftor (1711–85), popular actress and singer, was a great favorite of Fielding, who praised her in the dedication to *The Intriguing Chambermaid* (1734) not only for her talents but for "acting in real life the part of the best wife, the best daughter, the best

sister, and the best friend."

9. *Theodosius: or The Force of Love* (1680), 2.1, by Nathaniel Lee (1653?–1692). (The player substitutes "Crowns" for Lee's "Courts," "Fates" for "Stars," "There" for "And" and "Nests" for "Nest.") Lee's ranting tragedies remained popular well into the eighteenth century, and Fielding made several of them—but not *Theodosius*—targets of his parody in *The Tragedy of Tragedies* (1731).

1. *The Orphan: or, The Unhappy Marriage* (1680), 1.1. Fielding transposes "Foolish" and "sordid" and adds the commas.

2. At a loss for words.

your Jest,' answered the Poet, 'but you remember the Affair as well as myself; you know there was a Party in the Pit and Upper-Gallery, would not suffer it to be given out again; tho' much, ay infinitely, the Majority, all the Boxes in particular, were desirous of it; nay, most of the Ladies swore they never would come to the House till it was acted again— Indeed I must own their Policy[3] was good, in not letting it be given out a second time; for the Rascals knew if it had gone a second Night, it would have run fifty: for if ever there was Distress in a Tragedy—I am not fond of my own Performance; but if I should tell you what the best Judges said of it—Nor was it entirely owing to my Enemies neither, that it did not succeed on the Stage as well as it hath since among the polite Readers; for you can't say it had Justice done it by the Performers.'—'I think,' answer'd the Player, 'the Performers did the Distress of it Justice; for I am sure we were in Distress enough, who were pelted with Oranges[4] all the last Act; we all imagined it would have been the last Act of our Lives.'

The Poet, whose Fury was now raised, had just attempted to answer, when they were interrupted, and an end put to their Discourse by an Accident; which, if the Reader is impatient to know, he must skip over the next Chapter, which is a sort of Counterpart to this, and contains some of the best and gravest Matters in the whole Book, being a Discourse between Parson *Abraham Adams* and Mr. *Joseph Andrews*.

Chapter XI

Containing the Exhortations of Parson Adams *to his Friend in Affliction; calculated for the Instruction and Improvement of the Reader.*

Joseph no sooner came perfectly to himself, than perceiving his Mistress gone, he bewailed her Loss with Groans, which would have pierced any Heart but those which are possessed by some People, and are made of a certain Composition not unlike Flint in its Hardness and other Properties; for you may strike Fire from them which will dart through the Eyes, but they can never distil one Drop of Water the same way. His own, poor Youth, was of a softer Composition; and at those Words, *O my dear* Fanny! *O my Love! shall I never, never see thee more?* his Eyes overflowed with Tears, which would have become any but a Hero. In a word, his Despair was more easy to be conceived than related.—

Mr. *Adams*, after many Groans, sitting with his Back to *Joseph,* began thus in a sorrowful Tone: 'You cannot imagine, my good Child, that I entirely blame these first Agonies of your Grief; for, when Misfortunes attack us by Surprize, it must require infinitely more Learning than you are master of to resist them: but it is the Business of a Man and a Chris-

---

3. Strategy.
4. Oranges were regularly sold in the theatre, and audiences were often disorderly. When a French troupe reopened the Haymarket Theatre in 1738 after Fielding's company had been banned by the Licensing Act, they were driven from the stage by a hail of apples and potatoes sold by the dozen at the door.

tian to summon Reason as quickly as he can to his Aid; and she will presently teach him Patience and Submission. Be comforted, therefore, Child, I say be comforted. It is true you have lost the prettiest, kindest, loveliest, sweetest young Woman: One with whom you might have expected to have lived in Happiness, Virtue and Innocence. By whom you might have promised yourself many little Darlings, who would have been the Delight of your Youth, and the Comfort of your Age. You have not only lost her, but have reason to fear the utmost Violence which Lust and Power can inflict upon her. Now indeed you may easily raise Ideas of Horror, which might drive you to Despair.'[1]—'O I shall run mad,' cries *Joseph*, 'O that I could but command my Hands to tear my Eyes out and my Flesh off.'—'If you would use them to such Purposes, I am glad you can't,' answer'd *Adams*. 'I have stated your Misfortune as strong as I possibly can; but on the other side, you are to consider you are a Christian, that no Accident happens to us without the Divine Permission, and that it is the Duty of a Man, much more of a Christian, to submit. We did not make ourselves; but the same Power which made us, rules over us, and we are absolutely at his Disposal; he may do with us what he pleases, nor have we any Right to complain. A second Reason against our Complaint is our Ignorance; for as we know not future Events, so neither can we tell to what Purpose any Accident tends; and that which at first threatens us with Evil, may in the end produce our Good. I should indeed have said our Ignorance is twofold (but I have not at present time to divide properly)[2] for as we know not to what purpose any Event is ultimately directed; so neither can we affirm from what Cause it originally sprung. You are a Man, and consequently a Sinner; and this may be a Punishment to you for your Sins; indeed in this Sense it may be esteemed as a Good, yea as the greatest Good, which satisfies the Anger of Heaven, and averts that Wrath which cannot continue without our Destruction. Thirdly, Our Impotency of relieving ourselves, demonstrates the Folly and Absurdity of our Complaints: for whom do we resist? or against whom do we complain, but a Power from whose Shafts no Armour can guard us, no Speed can fly? A Power which leaves us no Hope, but in Submission.'—'O Sir,' cried *Joseph*, 'all this is very true, and very fine; and I could hear you all day, if I was not so grieved at Heart as now I am.' 'Would you take Physick,' says *Adams*, 'when you are well, and refuse it when you are sick? Is not Comfort to be administred to the Afflicted and not to those who rejoice, or those who are at ease?'—'O you have not spoken one Word of Comfort to me yet,'

---

1. "Ideas" = images. In an essay "Of the Remedy of Affliction for the Loss of Our Friends," published the following year, Fielding took exception to the traditional notion that the bereaved console himself with recollection of his loved one: "What is all this less than being Self-Tormentors, and playing with Affliction?" (*Miscellanies*, ed. H. K. Miller [Wesleyan Edition, 1972] 1.219). He also stipulates that philosophic and religious arguments of consolation such as Adams applies

should not be attempted until some time after the loss, "the first Emotions of our Grief" being "so far irresistible, that they are not to be instantly and absolutely overcome" (218).

2. That is, to analyze his subject into topics and order his discourse accordingly. Compare the ordering of the Roman priest's speech, pp. 197–98 above and Adams's discourse to Joseph, p. 241 below.

returned *Joseph*. 'No!' cries *Adams*, 'What am I then doing? what can I say to comfort you?'—'O tell me,' cries *Joseph*, 'that *Fanny* will escape back to my Arms, that they shall again inclose that lovely Creature, with all her Sweetness, all her untainted Innocence about her.'—'Why perhaps you may,' cries *Adams*; 'but I can't promise you what's to come. You must with perfect Resignation wait the Event; if she be restored to you again, it is your Duty to be thankful, and so it is if she be not: *Joseph*, if you are wise and truly know your own Interest, you will peaceably and quietly submit to all the Dispensations of Providence; being thoroughly assured, that all the Misfortunes, how great soever, which happen to the Righteous, happen to them for their own Good.[3]—Nay, it is not your Interest only, but your duty to abstain from immoderate Grief; which if you indulge, you are not worthy the Name of a Christian.'—He spoke these last Words with an Accent a little severer than usual; upon which *Joseph* begged him not to be angry, saying he mistook him, if he thought he denied it was his Duty; for he had known that long ago. 'What signifies knowing your Duty, if you do not perform it?' answer'd *Adams*. 'Your Knowledge encreases your Guilt—O *Joseph*, I never thought you had this Stubbornness in your Mind.' *Joseph* replied, 'he fancied he misunderstood him, which I assure you,' says he, 'you do, if you imagine I endeavour to grieve; upon my Soul I don't.' *Adams* rebuked him for swearing, and then proceeded to enlarge on the Folly of Grief, telling him, all the wise Men and Philosophers, even among the Heathens, had written against it, quoting several Passages from *Seneca*,[4] and the *Consolation*, which tho' it was not *Cicero's*, was, he said, as good almost as any of his Works,[5] and concluded all by hinting, that immoderate Grief in this Case might incense that Power which alone could restore him his *Fanny*. This Reason, or indeed rather the Idea which it raised of the Restoration of his Mistress, had more effect than all which the Parson had said before; and for a moment abated his Agonies: but when his Fears sufficiently set before his Eyes the Danger that poor Creature was in, his Grief returned again with repeated Violence, nor could *Adams* in the least asswage it; tho' it may be doubted in his Behalf, whether *Socrates* himself could have prevailed any better.

They remained some time in silence; and Groans and Sighs issued from them both, at length *Joseph* burst out into the following Soliloquy:

> *Yes, I will bear my Sorrows like a Man,*
> *But I must also feel them as a Man.*
> *I cannot but remember such things were,*
> *And were most dear to me—*[6]

3. This long sentence was added in the second edition, replacing "The Doctrine I teach you is a certain Security—nay. . . ."

4. Seneca (see above, p. 138, n. 7) was an abundant source on this topic, having addressed three dialogues to particular occasions of grief and devoted three of the moral epistles to his friend Lucilius to it, as well as composing a dialogue *De Providentia*.

5. Adams concurs with the view of Conyers Middleton (see above, p. 186, n. 2) and other scholars that the text of the *Consolation*, which appeared in the sixteenth century, is not Cicero's lost treatise on the death of his daughter.

6. The last three lines approximate Macduff's lament for his murdered family (*Macbeth* 4.3.221–23).

Adams asked him what Stuff that was he repeated?—To which he answer'd, they were some Lines he had gotten by heart out of a Play.—'Ay, there is nothing but Heathenism to be learn'd from Plays,' reply'd he—'I never heard of any Plays fit for a Christian to read, but *Cato* and the *Conscious Lovers*;[7] and I must own in the latter there are some things almost solemn enough for a Sermon.' But we shall now leave them a little, and enquire after the Subject of their Conversation.

Chapter XII

More Adventures, which we hope will as much please as surprize the Reader.

Neither the facetious Dialogue which pass'd between the Poet and Player, nor the grave and truly solemn Discourse of Mr. *Adams*, will, we conceive, make the Reader sufficient Amends for the Anxiety which he must have felt on the account of poor *Fanny*, whom we left in so deplorable a Condition. We shall therefore now proceed to the Relation of what happened to that beautiful and innocent Virgin, after she fell into the wicked Hands of the Captain.

The Man of War having convey'd his charming Prize out of the Inn a little before Day, made the utmost Expedition in his power towards the Squire's House, where this delicate Creature was to be offered up a Sacrifice to the Lust of a Ravisher. He was not only deaf to all her Bewailings and Entreaties on the Road, but accosted her Ears with Impurities, which, having been never before accustomed to them, she happily for herself very little understood. At last he changed this Note, and attempted to sooth and mollify her, by setting forth the Splendor and Luxury which would be her Fortune with a Man who would have the Inclination, and Power too, to give her whatever her utmost Wishes could desire; and told her he doubted not but she would soon look kinder on him, as the Instrument of her Happiness, and despise that pitiful Fellow, whom her Ignorance only could make her fond of. She answered, She knew not whom he meant, she never was fond of any pitiful Fellow. 'Are you affronted, Madam,' says he, 'at my calling him so? but what better can be said of one in a Livery, notwithstanding your Fondness for him?' She returned, That she did not understand him, that the Man had been her Fellow-Servant, and she believed was as honest a Creature as any alive; but as for Fondness for Men[1]—'I warrant ye,' cries the Captain, 'we shall find means to persuade you to be fond; and I advise you to yield to gentle ones; for you may be assured that it is not in your power by any Struggles whatever to preserve your Virginity two Hours

---

7. Like Addison's *Cato* (cited by Adams on p. 180), Richard Steele's solemn comedy *The Conscious Lovers* (1722), is filled with elevating moral sentiments; its hero and heroine are exemplars of Christian humanity.

1. Fanny's answer was quite different in the first

edition: "the Riches of the World could not make her amends for the Loss of him; nor would she be persuaded to exchange him for the greatest Prince upon Earth." In the next sentence, "to be fond" was inserted in the second edition to accommodate the new response.

longer. It will be your Interest to consent; for the 'Squire will be much
kinder to you if he enjoys you willingly than by force.'—At which Words
she began to call aloud for Assistance (for it was now open Day) but
finding none, she lifted her Eyes to Heaven, and supplicated the Divine
Assistance to preserve her Innocence. The Captain told her, if she persisted in her Vociferation, he would find a means of stopping her Mouth.
And now the poor Wretch perceiving no Hopes of Succour, abandoned
herself to Despair, and sighing out the Name of *Joseph, Joseph!* a River
of Tears ran down her lovely Cheeks, and wet the Handkerchief which
covered her Bosom. A Horseman now appeared in the Road, upon which
the Captain threatened her violently if she complained; however, the
moment they approached each other, she begged him with the utmost
Earnestness to relieve a distressed Creature, who was in the hands of a
Ravisher. The Fellow stopt at those Words; but the Captain assured him
it was his Wife, and that he was carrying her home from her Adulterer.
Which so satisfied the Fellow, who was an old one, (and perhaps a
married one too) that he wished him a good Journey, and rode on. He
was no sooner past, than the Captain abused her violently for breaking
his Commands, and threaten'd to gagg her; when two more Horsemen,
armed with Pistols, came into the Road just before them. She again
sollicited their Assistance; and the Captain told the same Story as before.
Upon which one said to the other—'That's a charming Wench! *Jack;* I
wish I had been in the Fellow's Place whoever he is.' But the other,
instead of answering him, cried out eagerly, 'Zounds, I know her:' and
then turning to her said, 'Sure you are not *Fanny Goodwill?*'—'Indeed,
indeed I am,' she cry'd—'O *John*, I know you now—Heaven hath sent
you to my Assistance, to deliver me from this wicked Man, who is carrying me away for his vile Purposes—O for G—'s sake rescue me from
him.' A fierce Dialogue immediately ensued between the Captain and
these two Men, who being both armed with Pistols, and the Chariot
which they attended being now arrived, the Captain saw both Force and
Stratagem were vain, and endeavoured to make his Escape; in which
however he could not succeed. The Gentleman who rode in the Chariot, ordered it to stop, and with an Air of Authority examined into the
Merits of the Cause; of which being advertised[2] by *Fanny*, whose Credit
was confirmed by the Fellow who knew her, he ordered the Captain,
who was all bloody from his Encounter at the Inn, to be conveyed as a
Prisoner behind the Chariot, and very gallantly took *Fanny* into it; for,
to say the truth, this Gentleman (who was no other than the celebrated
Mr. *Peter Pounce*, and who preceded the Lady *Booby* only a few Miles,
by setting out earlier in the Morning) was a very gallant Person, and
loved a pretty Girl better than any thing, besides his own Money, or the
Money of other People.

The Chariot now proceeded towards the Inn, which as *Fanny* was

---

2. Informed.

informed lay in their way, and where it arrived at that very time while
the Poet and Player were disputing below Stairs, and *Adams* and *Joseph*
were discoursing back to back above: just at that Period to which we
brought them both in the two preceding Chapters, the Chariot stopt at
the Door, and in an instant *Fanny* leaping from it, ran up to her *Joseph*.—
O Reader, conceive if thou canst, the Joy which fired the Breasts of these
Lovers on this Meeting; and, if thy own Heart doth not sympathetically
assist thee in this Conception, I pity thee sincerely from my own: for let
the hard-hearted Villain know this, that there is a Pleasure in a tender
Sensation beyond any which he is capable of tasting.

Peter being informed by *Fanny* of the Presence of *Adams*, stopt to see
him, and receive his Homage; for, as *Peter* was an Hypocrite, a sort of
People whom Mr. *Adams* never saw through, the one paid that Respect
to his seeming Goodness which the other believed to be paid to his
Riches; hence Mr. *Adams* was so much his Favourite, that he once lent
him four Pounds thirteen Shillings and Sixpence, to prevent his going
to Goal, on no greater Security than a Bond and Judgment,[3] which
probably he would have made no use of, tho' the Money had not been
(as it was) paid exactly at the time.

It is not perhaps easy to describe the Figure of *Adams*; he had risen in
such a violent Hurry, that he had on neither Breeches nor Stockings;
nor had he taken from his Head a red spotted Handkerchief, which by
Night bound his Wig, that was turned inside out, around his Head. He
had on his torn Cassock, and his Great-Coat; but as the remainder of
his Cassock hung down below his Great-Coat; so did a small Strip of
white, or rather whitish Linnen appear below that; to which we may add
the several Colours which appeared on his Face, where a long Piss-burnt
Beard, served to retain the Liquor of the Stone Pot, and that of a blacker
hue which distilled from the Mop.—This Figure, which *Fanny* had
delivered from his Captivity, was no sooner spied by *Peter*, than it disordered the composed Gravity of his Muscles; however he advised him
immediately to make himself clean, nor would accept his Homage in
that Pickle.

The Poet and Player no sooner saw the Captain in Captivity, than
they began to consider of their own Safety, of which Flight presented
itself as the only means; they therefore both of them mounted the Poet's
Horse, and made the most expeditious Retreat in their power.

The Host, who well knew Mr. *Pounce* and the Lady *Booby's* Livery,
was not a little surprized at this change of the Scene, nor was his Confusion much helped by his Wife, who was now just risen, and having
heard from him the Account of what had past, comforted him with a
decent Number of Fools and Blockheads, asked him why he did not
consult her, and told him he would never leave following the nonsensical Dictates of his own Numscull, till she and her Family were ruined.

3. A legal instrument assigning the property of the borrower to the lender if the loan was not repaid on
time.

Joseph being informed of the Captain's Arrival, and seeing his *Fanny* now in Safety, quitted her a moment, and running down stairs, went directly to him, and stripping off his Coat challenged him to fight; but the Captain refused, saying he did not understand Boxing. He then grasped a Cudgel in one Hand, and catching the Captain by the Collar with the other, gave him a most severe Drubbing, and ended with telling him, he had now had some Revenge for what his dear *Fanny* had suffered.

When Mr. *Pounce* had a little regaled himself with some Provision which he had in his Chariot, and Mr. *Adams* had put on the best Appearance his Clothes would allow him, *Pounce* ordered the Captain into his Presence; for he said he was guilty of Felony, and the next Justice of Peace should commit him: but the Servants (whose Appetite for Revenge is soon satisfied) being sufficiently contented with the Drubbing which *Joseph* had inflicted on him, and which was indeed of no very moderate kind, had suffered him to go off, which he did, threatening a severe Revenge against *Joseph*, which I have never heard he thought proper to take.

The Mistress of the House made her voluntary Appearance before Mr. *Pounce*, and with a thousand Curt'sies told him, 'she hoped his Honour would pardon her Husband, who was a very *nonsense* Man, for the sake of his poor Family; that indeed if he could be ruined alone, she should be very willing of it, *for because as why*, his Worship very well knew he deserved it: but she had three poor small Children, who were not capable to get their own Living; and if her Husband was sent to Goal, they must all come to the Parish;[4] for she was a poor weak Woman, continually a breeding, and had no time to work for them. She therefore hoped his Honour would take it into his Worship's Consideration, and forgive her Husband this time; for she was sure he never intended any Harm to Man, Woman, or Child; and if it was not for that Block-Head of his own, the Man in some things was well enough; for she had had three Children by him in less than three Years, and was almost ready to cry out the fourth time.' She would have proceeded in this manner much longer, had not *Peter* stopt her Tongue, by telling her he had nothing to say to her Husband, nor her neither. So, as *Adams* and the rest had assured her of Forgiveness, she cried and curt'sied out of the Room.

Mr. *Pounce* was desirous that *Fanny* should continue her Journey with him in the Chariot,[5] but she absolutely refused, saying she would ride behind *Joseph*, on a Horse which one of Lady *Booby's* Servants had equipped him with. But alas! when the Horse appeared, it was found to be no other than that identical Beast which Mr. *Adams* had left behind him at the Inn, and which these honest Fellows who knew him had redeemed. Indeed whatever Horse they had provided for *Joseph*, they

---

4. Become dependents of the parish, under the provision of the Poor Law—the equivalent of being "on welfare."
5. Most of the remainder of this chapter, from

here to "the whole Procession" in the last sentence, was added in the second edition, constituting the longest revision of the novel.

would have prevailed with him to mount none, no not even to ride before his beloved *Fanny*, till the Parson was supplied; much less would he deprive his Friend of the Beast which belonged to him, and which he knew the moment he saw, tho' *Adams* did not: however, when he was reminded of the Affair, and told that they had brought the Horse with them which he left behind, he answered—*Bless me! and so I did.*

Adams was very desirous that *Joseph* and *Fanny* should mount this Horse, and declared he could very easily walk home. 'If I walked alone,' says he, 'I would wage a Shilling, that the *Pedestrian*[6] out-stripped the *Equestrian* Travellers: but as I intend to take the Company of a Pipe, peradventure I may be an Hour later.' One of the Servants whispered *Joseph* to take him at his Word, and suffer the old Put[7] to walk if he would: This Proposal was answered with an angry Look and a peremptory Refusal by *Joseph*, who catching *Fanny* up in his Arms, aver'd he would rather carry her home in that manner, than take away Mr. *Adams's* Horse, and permit him to walk on foot.

Perhaps, Reader, thou hast seen a Contest between two Gentlemen, or two Ladies quickly decided, tho' they have both asserted they would not eat such a nice Morsel, and each insisted on the other's accepting it; but in reality both were very desirous to swallow it themselves. Do not therefore conclude hence, that this Dispute would have come to a speedy Decision: for here both Parties were heartily in earnest, and it is very probable, they would have remained in the Inn-yard to this day, had not the good *Peter Pounce* put a stop to it; for finding he had no longer hopes of satisfying his old Appetite with *Fanny*, and being desirous of having some one to whom he might communicate his Grandeur, he told the Parson he would convey him home in his Chariot. This Favour was by *Adams*, with many Bows and Acknowledgments, accepted, tho' he afterwards said, 'he ascended the Chariot rather that he might not offend, than from any Desire of riding in it, for that in his heart he preferred the *Pedestrian* even to the *Vehicular* Expedition.' All matters being now settled, the Chariot in which rode *Adams* and *Pounce* moved forwards; and *Joseph* having borrowed a Pillion from the Host, *Fanny* had just seated herself thereon, and had laid hold on the Girdle which her Lover wore for that purpose, when the wise Beast, who concluded that one at a time was sufficient, that two to one were odds, &c. discovered much Uneasiness at this double Load, and began to consider his hinder as his Fore-legs, moving the direct contrary way to that which is called forwards. Nor could *Joseph* with all his Horsemanship persuade him to advance: but without having any regard to the lovely Part of the lovely Girl which was on his Back, he used such Agitations, that had not one of the Men come immediately to her Assistance, she had in plain *English* tumbled backwards on the Ground. This Inconvenience was presently remedied by an Exchange of Horses, and then *Fanny* being again placed

---

6. Fielding's italics indicate Adams's pedantic latinism; this word does not occur in Johnson's *Dictionary*, and its earliest use to mean "walking" cited in the OED is 1791.

7. Clod.

on her Pillion, on a better natured, and somewhat a better fed Beast, the Parson's's Horse finding he had no longer Odds to contend with, agreed to march, and the whole Procession set forward for *Booby-Hall*, where they arrived in a few Hours without any thing remarkable happening on the Road, unless it was a curious Dialogue between the Parson and the Steward; which, to use the Language of a late Apologist, a Pattern to all Biographers, *waits for the Reader in the next Chapter*.[8]

Chapter XIII

A curious Dialogue which passed between Mr. Abraham Adams *and Mr.* Peter Pounce, *better worth reading than all the Works of* Colley Cibber *and many others*.

The Chariot had not proceeded far, before Mr. *Adams* observed it was a very fine Day. 'Ay, and a very fine Country too,' answered *Pounce*. 'I should think so more,' returned *Adams*, 'if I had not lately travelled over the *Downs*, which I take to exceed this and all other Prospects in the Universe.' 'A fig for Prospects,' answered *Pounce*, 'one Acre here is worth ten there; and for my own part, I have no Delight in the Prospect of any Land but my own.' 'Sir,' said *Adams*, 'you can indulge yourself with many fine Prospects of that kind.' 'I thank God I have a little,' replied the other, 'with which I am content, and envy no Man: I have a little, Mr. *Adams*, with which I do as much good as I can.' *Adams* answered, that Riches without Charity were nothing worth; for that they were only a Blessing to him who made them a Blessing to others. 'You and I,' said *Peter*, 'have different Notions of Charity. I own, as it is generally used, I do not like the Word, nor do I think it becomes one of us Gentlemen; it is a mean Parsonlike Quality; tho' I would not infer many Parsons have it neither.' 'Sir,' said *Adams*, 'my Definition of Charity is a generous Disposition to relieve the Distressed.'[1] 'There is something in that Definition,' answered *Peter*, 'which I like well enough; it is, as you say, a Disposition—and does not so much consist in the Act as in the Disposition to do it; but alas, Mr. *Adams*, Who are meant by the Distressed? Believe me, the Distresses of Mankind are mostly imaginary, and it would be rather Folly than Goodness to relieve them.' 'Sure, Sir,' replied *Adams*, 'Hunger and Thirst, Cold and Nakedness, and other Distresses which attend the Poor, can never be said to be imaginary Evils.' 'How can any Man complain of Hunger,' said *Peter*, 'in a Country where such excellent Sallads are to be gathered in almost every Field? or of Thirst, where every River and Stream produces such delicious Potations? And as for Cold and Nakedness, they are Evils introduced by Luxury and Custom. A Man naturally wants Clothes no more than a Horse or any other Animal, and there are whole Nations who go without them: but these

---

8. At the end of chapter 4 of the *Apology*, Cibber announces that he will develop his contemplated "Dissertation upon Theatrical Action" through the "several Vehicles" of particular actors' profiles,

"which you will find waiting in the next Chapter, to carry you . . . the rest of the Journey. . . ."
1. For Fielding's essay on the subject in *The Champion*, see pp. 315–18.

are things perhaps which you, who do not know the World—' 'You will pardon me, Sir,' returned *Adams*; 'I have read of the *Gymnosophists.*'[2] 'A plague of your *Jehosaphats*,' cried *Peter*; 'the greatest Fault in our Constitution is the Provision made for the Poor, except that perhaps made for some others.[3] Sir, I have not an Estate which doth not contribute almost as much again to the Poor as to the Land-Tax, and I do assure you I expect to come myself to the Parish in the end.' To which *Adams* giving a dissenting Smile, *Peter* thus proceeded: 'I fancy, Mr. *Adams*, you are one of those who imagine I am a Lump of Money; for there are many who I fancy believe that not only my Pockets, but my whole Clothes, are lined with Bank-Bills; but I assure you, you are all mistaken: I am not the Man the World esteems me. If I can hold my Head above Water, it is all I can. I have injured myself by purchasing. I have been too liberal of my Money. Indeed I fear my Heir will find my Affairs in a worse Situation than they are reputed to be. Ah! he will have reason to wish I had loved Money more, and Land less.[4] Pray, my good Neighbour, where should I have that Quantity of Riches the World is so liberal to bestow on me? Where could I possibly, without I had stole it, acquire such a Treasure?' 'Why truly,' says *Adams*, 'I have been always of your Opinion; I have wondered as well as yourself with what Confidence they could report such things of you, which have to me appeared as mere Impossibilities; for you know, Sir, and I have often heard you say it, that your Wealth is of your own Acquisition, and can it be credible that in your short time you should have amassed such a heap of Treasure as these People will have you worth? Indeed had you inherited an Estate like Sir *Thomas Booby*, which had descended in your Family for many Generations, they might have had a colour for their Assertions.' 'Why, what do they say I am worth?' cries *Peter* with a malicious Sneer. 'Sir,' answered *Adams*, 'I have heard some aver you are not worth less than twenty thousand Pounds.'[5] At which *Peter* frowned. 'Nay, sir,' said *Adams*, 'you ask me only the Opinion of others, for my own part I have always denied it, nor did I ever believe you could possibly be worth half that Sum.' 'However, Mr. *Adams*,' said he, squeezing him by the Hand, 'I would not sell them all I am worth for double that Sum; and as to what you believe, or they believe, I care not a Fig, no not a Fart. I am not poor because you think me so, nor because you attempt to undervalue me in the Country. I know the Envy of Mankind very well, but I thank Heaven I am above them. It is true my Wealth is of my own Acquisition. I have not an Estate like Sir *Thomas Booby*, that hath descended in my Family through many Generations; but I know the Heirs of such

2. The Greek name ("naked philosophers") for an ancient Hindu ascetic sect who regarded food and clothing as impediments to pure thought. Adams might have read of them in the *Geographica* of Strabo (ca. 64 B.C.–A.D. 19). Pounce substitutes the name of the righteous king of Judah (1 Kings 22:2–50; 2 Chronicles 17–20).

3. That is, the clergy, whom a landowner like Pounce would be required to pay substantial tithes to support.

4. Fielding satirized the penchant of Peter Walter (see above, p. 38, n. 3) for real estate in *The Champion*, May 31, 1740, as Pope had in the *Epistle to Bathurst* (1733); Pope likened him to Didius, a Roman lawyer who purchased the Empire at auction from the Praetorian Guard.

5. This conforms with the narrator's estimate of Peter's wealth (p. 38).

Estates who are forced to travel about the Country like some People in torn Cassocks, and might be glad to accept of a pitiful Curacy for what I know. Yes, Sir, as shabby Fellows as yourself, whom no Man of my Figure, without that Vice of Good-nature about him, would suffer to ride in a Chariot with him.' 'Sir,' said *Adams*, 'I value not your Chariot of a Rush[6]; and if I had known you had intended to affront me, I would have walked to the World's End on foot ere I would have accepted a place in it. However, Sir, I will soon rid you of that Inconvenience,' and so saying, he opened the Chariot-Door without calling to the Coachman, and leapt out into the Highway, forgetting to take his Hat along with him; which however Mr. *Pounce* threw after him with great violence. *Joseph* and *Fanny* stopt to bear him Company the rest of the way, which was not above a Mile.

6. At all.

The History of the Adventures of JOSEPH ANDREWS, and of his Friend Mr. *Abraham Adams*

BOOK IV

Chapter I

The Arrival of Lady Booby *and the rest at* Booby-Hall.

The Coach and Six, in which Lady *Booby* rode, overtook the other Travellers as they entered the Parish. She no sooner saw *Joseph*, than her Cheeks glow'd with red, and immediately after became as totally pale. She had in her Surprize almost stopt her Coach; but recollected herself timely enough to prevent it. She entered the Parish amidst the ringing of Bells, and the Acclamations of the Poor, who were rejoiced to see their Patroness returned after so long an Absence, during which time all her Rents had been drafted to *London*, without a Shilling being spent among them, which tended not a little to their utter impoverishing; for if the Court would be severely missed in such a City as *London*, how much more must the Absence of a Person of great Fortune be felt in a little Country Village, for whose Inhabitants such a Family finds a constant Employment and Supply; and with the Offalls [1] of whose Table the infirm, aged, and infant Poor are abundantly fed, with a Generosity which hath scarce a visible Effect on their Benefactor's Pockets?

But if their Interest inspired so publick a Joy into every Countenance, how much more forcibly did the Affection which they bore Parson *Adams* operate upon all who beheld his Return. They flocked about him like dutiful Children round an indulgent Parent, and vyed with each other in Demonstrations of Duty and Love. The Parson on his side shook every one by the Hand, enquiring heartily after the Healths of all that

---

1. Refuse.

were absent, of their Children and Relations, and exprest a Satisfaction in his Face, which nothing but Benevolence made happy by its Objects could infuse.

Nor, did *Joseph* and *Fanny* want hearty Welcome from all who saw them. In short, no three Persons could be more kindly received, as indeed none ever more deserved to be universally beloved.

Adams carried his Fellow-Travellers home to his House, where he insisted on their partaking whatever his Wife, whom with his Children he found in Health and Joy, could provide. Where we shall leave them, enjoying perfect Happiness over a homely Meal, to view Scenes of greater Splendor but infinitely less Bliss.

Our more intelligent Readers will doubtless suspect by this second Appearance of Lady *Booby* on the Stage, that all was not ended by the Dismission of *Joseph*; and to be honest with them, they are in the right; the Arrow had pierced deeper than she imagined; nor was the Wound so easily to be cured. The Removal of the Object soon cooled her Rage, but it had a different Effect on her Love; that departed with his Person; but this remained lurking in her Mind with his Image. Restless, inter-rupted Slumbers, and confused horrible Dreams were her Portion the first Night. In the Morning, Fancy painted her a more delicious Scene; but to delude, not delight her: for before she could reach the promised Happiness, it vanished, and left her to curse, not bless the Vision.

She started from her Sleep, her Imagination being all on fire with the Phantom, when her Eyes accidentally glancing towards the Spot where yesterday the real *Joseph* had stood, that little Circumstance raised his Idea[2] in the liveliest Colours in her Memory. Each Look, each Word, each Gesture rushed back on her Mind with Charms which all his Cold-ness could not abate. Nay, she imputed that to his Youth, his Folly, his Awe, his Religion, to every thing, but what would instantly have pro-duced Contempt, want of Passion for the Sex; or, that which would have roused her Hatred, want of Liking to her.

Reflection then hurried her farther, and told her she must[3] see this beautiful Youth no more, nay, suggested to her, that she herself had dismissed him for no other Fault, than probably that ·of too violent an Awe and Respect for herself; and which she ought rather to have esteemed a Merit, the Effects of which were besides so easily and surely to have been removed; she then blamed, she cursed the hasty Rashness of her Temper; her Fury was vented all on herself, and *Joseph* appeared inno-cent in her Eyes. Her Passion at length grew so violent that it forced her on seeking Relief, and now she thought of recalling him: But Pride for-bad that, Pride which soon drove all softer Passions from her Soul, and represented to her the Meanness of him she was fond of. That Thought soon began to obscure his Beauties; Contempt succeeded next, and then Disdain, which presently introduced her Hatred of the Creature who had given her so much Uneasiness. These Enemies of *Joseph* had no

2. Image.   3. "Could," not "should."

sooner taken Possession of her Mind, than they insinuated to her a thousand things in his Disfavour; every thing but Dislike of her Person; a Thought, which as it would have been intolerable to her, she checked the moment it endeavoured to arise. Revenge came now to her Assistance; and she considered her Dismission of him stript, and without a Character,[4] with the utmost Pleasure. She rioted in the several kinds of Misery, which her Imagination suggested to her, might be his Fate; and with a Smile composed of Anger, Mirth, and Scorn, viewed him in the Rags in which her Fancy had drest him.

Mrs. *Slipslop* being summoned, attended her Mistress, who had now in her own Opinion totally subdued this Passion. Whilst she was dressing, she asked if that Fellow had been turned away according to her Orders. *Slipslop* answered, she had told her Ladyship so, (as indeed she had)—'And how did he behave?' replied the Lady. 'Truly Madam,' cries *Slipslop*, 'in such a manner that *infected* every body who saw him. The poor Lad had but little Wages to receive: for he constantly allowed his Father and Mother half his Income; so that when your Ladyship's Livery was stript off, he had not wherewithal to buy a Coat, and must have gone naked, if one of the Footmen had not *incommodated* him with one; and whilst he was standing in his Shirt, (and to say truth, he was an *amorous*[5] Figure) being told your Ladyship would not give him a Character, he sighed, and said he had done nothing willingly to offend; that for his part he should always give your Ladyship a good Character where-ever he went; and he pray'd God to bless you; for you was the best of Ladies, tho' his Enemies had set you against him: I wish you had not turned him away; for I believe you have not a faithfuller Servant in the House.'—'How came you then,' replied the Lady, 'to advise me to turn him away?' 'I, Madam,' said *Slipslop*, 'I am sure you will do me the Justice to say, I did all in my power to prevent it; but I saw your Ladyship was angry; and it is not the business of us upper Servants to *hintorfear* on those occasions.'—'And was it not you, audacious Wretch,' cried the Lady, 'who made me angry? Was it not your Tittle-tattle, in which I believe you belyed the poor Fellow, which incensed me against him? He may thank you for all that hath happened; and so may I for the Loss of a good Servant, and one who probably had more Merit than all of you. Poor Fellow! I am charmed with his Goodness to his Parents. Why did not you tell me of that, but suffer me to dismiss so good a Creature without a Character? I see the Reason of your whole Behaviour now as well as your Complaint; you was jealous of the Wenches.' 'I jealous!' said *Slipslop*, 'I assure you I look upon myself as his Betters; I am not Meat for a Footman I hope.' These Words threw the Lady into a violent Passion, and she sent *Slipslop* from her Presence, who departed tossing her Nose and crying, 'Marry come up! there are some People more jealous than I, I believe.' Her Lady affected not to hear the Words, tho' in reality she did, and understood them too. Now ensued a second Con-

---

4. Reference.
5. Fielding substituted this Slipslopism for "lovely" in the second edition.

flict, so like the former, that it might savour of Repetition to relate it minutely. It may suffice to say, that Lady *Booby* found good Reason to doubt whether she had so absolutely conquered her Passion, as she had flattered herself; and in order to accomplish it quite, took a Resolution more common than wise, to retire immediately into the Country. The Reader hath long ago seen the Arrival of Mrs. *Slipslop*, whom no Pertness could make her Mistress resolve to part with; lately, that of Mr. *Pounce*, her Fore-runners; and lastly, that of the Lady herself.

The Morning after her Arrival being *Sunday*, she went to Church, to the great Surprize of every body, who wondered to see her Ladyship, being no very constant Churchwoman, there so suddenly upon her Journey. *Joseph* was likewise there; and I have heard it was remarked, that she fixed her Eyes on him much more than on the Parson; but this I believe to be only a malicious Rumour. When the Prayers were ended Mr. *Adams* stood up, and with a loud Voice pronounced: *I publish the Banns of Marriage between* Joseph Andrews *and* Frances Goodwill, *both of this Parish,* &c. Whether this had any Effect on Lady *Booby* or no, who was then in her Pew, which the Congregation could not see into,[6] I could never discover: But certain it is, that in about a quarter of an Hour she stood up, and directed her Eyes to that part of the Church where the Women sat, and persisted in looking that way during the Remainder of the Sermon, in so scrutinizing a manner, and with so angry a Countenance, that most of the Women were afraid she was offended at them.[7]

The moment she returned home, she sent for *Slipslop* into her Chamber, and told her, she wondered what that impudent Fellow *Joseph* did in that Parish? Upon which *Slipslop* gave her an Account of her meeting *Adams* with him on the Road, and likewise the Adventure with *Fanny*. At the Relation of which, the Lady often changed her Countenance; and when she had heard all, she ordered Mr. *Adams* into her Presence, to whom she behaved as the Reader will see in the next Chapter.

Chapter II

A *Dialogue between Mr.* Abraham Adams *and the Lady* Booby.

Mr. *Adams* was not far off; for he was drinking her Ladyship's Health below in a Cup of her Ale. He no sooner came before her, than she began in the following manner: 'I wonder, Sir, after the many great Obligations you have had to this Family,' (with all which the Reader hath, in the Course of this History, been minutely acquainted) 'that you will ungratefully show any Respect to a Fellow who hath been turned out of it for his Misdeeds. Nor doth it, I can tell you, Sir, become a Man of your Character, to run about the Country with an idle Fellow and Wench. Indeed, as for the Girl, I know no harm of her. *Slipslop* tells me she was formerly bred up in my House, and behaved as she ought, till she hankered after this Fellow, and he spoiled her. Nay, she

---

6. The gentry's proprietary pews were high-backed compartments, often enclosed by curtains.

7. Segregated seating for women survived in some country churches.

may still perhaps do very well, if he will let her alone. You are therefore doing a monstrous thing, in endeavouring to procure a Match between these two People, which will be to the Ruin of them both.'—'Madam,' says *Adams*, 'if your Ladyship will but hear me speak, I protest I never heard any harm of Mr. *Joseph Andrews*; if I had, I should have corrected him for it: For I never have, nor will encourage the Faults of those under my Cure. As for the young Woman, I assure your Ladyship I have as good an Opinion of her as your Ladyship yourself, or any other can have. She is the sweetest-tempered, honestest, worthiest, young Creature; indeed as to her Beauty, I do not commend her on that account, tho' all Men allow she is the handsomest Woman, Gentle or Simple, that ever appeared in the Parish.' 'You are very impertinent,' says she, 'to talk such fulsome Stuff to me. It is mighty becoming truly in a Clergyman to trouble himself about handsome Women, and you are a delicate Judge of Beauty, no doubt. A Man who hath lived all his Life in such a Parish as this, is a rare Judge of Beauty. Ridiculous! Beauty indeed,—a Country Wench a Beauty.—I shall be sick whenever I hear Beauty mentioned again.—And so this Wench is to stock the Parish with Beauties, I hope.—But, Sir, our Poor is numerous enough already; I will have no more Vagabonds settled here.' 'Madam,' says *Adams*, 'your Ladyship is offended with me, I protest without any Reason. This Couple were desirous to consummate long ago, and I dissuaded them from it; nay, I may venture to say, I believe, I was the sole Cause of their delaying it.' 'Well,' says she, 'and you did very wisely and honestly too, notwithstanding she is the greatest Beauty in the Parish.'[1]—'And now, Madam,' continued he, 'I only perform my Office to Mr. *Joseph*.'—'Pray don't Mister such Fellows to me,' cries the Lady. 'He,' said the Parson, 'with the Consent of *Fanny*, before my Face, put in the Banns.'—'Yes,' answered the Lady, 'I suppose the Slut is forward enough; *Slipslop* tells me how her Head runs on Fellows; that is one of her Beauties, I suppose. But if they have put in the Banns, I desire you will publish them no more without my Orders.' 'Madam,' cries *Adams*, 'if any one puts in sufficient Caution, and assigns a proper Reason against them, I am willing to surcease.'[2]—'I tell you a Reason,' says she, 'he is a Vagabond, and he shall not settle here, and bring a Nest of Beggars into the Parish; it will make us but little Amends that they will be Beauties.' 'Madam,' answered *Adams*, 'with the utmost Submission to your Ladyship, I have been informed by Lawyer *Scout*, that any Person who serves a Year, gains a Settlement[3] in the Parish where he serves.' 'Lawyer *Scout*,'

---

1. Early in *Pamela*, Squire B——'s aristocratic neighbors are curious to see his servant girl, who "we understand . . . is the greatest beauty in the county" (letter 23).

2. Desist.

3. The Act of Settlements (1662) enabled a parish to protect itself against wandering indigents by forcibly removing anyone "likely to be chargeable to the Parish" who could not meet the legal conditions for settlement, or legal residence, and thus entitlement to relief from the parish under

the Poor Law. Service for a year was one of the means of gaining a settlement stipulated in an act of 1693. Lady Booby's intervention had its real-life counterparts: "the forced and expensive way of relieving the Poor has put many gentlemen and parishes upon contriving all possible methods of lessening their number, particularly by discouraging and sometimes binding poor persons from marrying" (Thomas Alcock, *Observations on the Defects of the Poor Laws*, 1752).

replied the Lady, 'is an impudent Coxcomb; I will have no Lawyer *Scout*
interfere with me. I repeat to you again, I will have no more Incum-
brances brought on us; so I desire you will proceed no farther.' 'Madam,'
returned *Adams*, 'I would obey your Ladyship in every thing that is
lawful; but surely the Parties being poor is no Reason against their marrying. G—d forbid there should be any such Law. The Poor have little
Share enough of this World already; it would be barbarous indeed to
deny them the common Privileges, and innocent Enjoyments which
Nature indulges to the animal Creation.' 'Since you understand yourself
no better,' cries the Lady, 'nor the Respect due from such as you to a
Woman of my Distinction, than to affront my Ears by such loose Discourse, I shall mention but one short Word; It is my Orders to you, that
you publish these Banns no more; and if you dare, I will recommend it
to your Master, the Doctor, to discard you from his Service. I will, Sir,
notwithstanding your poor Family; and then you and the greatest Beauty
in the Parish may go and beg together.' 'Madam,' answered *Adams*, 'I
know not what your Ladyship means by the Terms *Master* and *Service*.
I am in the Service of a Master who will never discard me for doing my
Duty: And if the Doctor (for indeed I have never been able to pay for a
Licence)[4] thinks proper to turn me out from my Cure, G— will provide
me, I hope, another. At least, my Family as well as myself have Hands;
and he will prosper, I doubt not, our Endeavours to get our Bread honestly with them. Whilst my Conscience is pure, I shall never fear what
Man can do unto me.'—'I condemn my Humility,' said the Lady, 'for
demeaning myself to converse with you so long. I shall take other Measures; for I see you are a Confederate with them. But the sooner you
leave me, the better; and I shall give Orders that my Doors may no
longer be open to you, I will suffer no Parsons who run about the Country with Beauties to be entertained here.'—'Madam,' said *Adams*, 'I shall
enter into no Person's Doors against their Will: But I am assured, when
you have enquired farther into this matter, you will applaud, not blame
my Proceeding; and so I humbly take my leave;' which he did with many
Bows, or at least many Attempts at a Bow.

Chapter III

What past between the Lady and Lawyer Scout.

In the Afternoon the Lady sent for Mr. *Scout*, whom she attacked
most violently for intermeddling with her Servants, which he denied,
and indeed with Truth; for he had only asserted accidentally, and perhaps rightly, that a Year's Service gained a Settlement; and so far he
owned he might have formerly informed the Parson, and believed it was
Law. 'I am resolved,' said the Lady, 'to have no discarded Servants of

---

4. Adams's failure to obtain a license to preach
from the bishop who appointed him to his cure
was not as unusual as the lengthy duration of his
appointment (p. 39). Even if they could afford it,
the insecurity of their tenure made many curates
chary of paying eighteen shillings to three pounds
for a license that might expire at any time with the
termination of their current appointment.

mine settled here; and so, if this be your Law, I shall send to another
Lawyer.' *Scout* said, 'if she sent to a hundred Lawyers, not one nor all
of them could alter the Law. The utmost that was in the power of a
Lawyer, was to prevent the Law's taking effect; and that he himself could
do for her Ladyship as well as any other: And I believe,' says he, 'Madam,
your Ladyship not being conversant in these Matters hath mistaken a
Difference: For I asserted only, that a Man who served a Year was settled. Now there is a material Difference between being settled in Law
and settled in Fact; and as I affirmed generally he was settled, and Law
is preferable to Fact, my Settlement must be understood in Law, and
not in Fact! And suppose, Madam, we admit he was settled in Law,
what use will they make of it, how doth that relate to Fact? He is not
settled in Fact; and if he be not settled in Fact, he is not an Inhabitant;
and if he is not an Inhabitant, he is not of this Parish; and then undoubtedly he ought not to be published here; for Mr. *Adams* hath told me
your Ladyship's Pleasure, and the Reason, which is a very good one, to
prevent burdening us with the Poor, we have too many already; and I
think we ought to have an Act to hang or transport half of them. If we
can prove in Evidence, that he is not settled in Fact, it is another matter.[1] What I said to Mr. *Adams*, was on a Supposition that he was settled
in Fact; and indeed if that was the Case, I should doubt.'—'Don't tell
me your *Facts* and your *ifs*,' said the Lady, 'I don't understand your
Gibberish: You take too much upon you, and are very impertinent in
pretending to direct in this Parish, and you shall be taught better, I
assure you, you shall. But as to the Wench, I am resolved she shall not
settle here; I will not suffer such Beauties as these to produce Children
for us to keep.'—'Beauties indeed! your Ladyship is pleased to be merry,'—
answered *Scout*.—'Mr. *Adams* described her so to me,' said the Lady.
'—Pray what sort of Dowdy is it, Mr. *Scout*?'—'the ugliest Creature
almost I ever beheld, a poor dirty Drab,[2] your Ladyship never saw such
a Wretch.'—'Well but, dear Mr. *Scout*, let her be what she will,—these
ugly Women will bring Children you know; so that we must prevent the
Marriage.'—'True, Madam,' replied *Scout*, 'for the subsequent Marriage co-operating with the Law, will carry Law into Fact. When a Man
is married, he is settled in Fact; and then he is not removeable.[3] I will
see Mr. *Adams*, and I make no doubt of prevailing with him. His only

1. Scout misapplies the basic legal distinction
between questions of law and questions of fact to
propound the legally unsound strategy of depriving
Joseph of his earned *right* to a settlement by
claiming he has not actually "settled down" in the
parish. *The Clergyman's Vade Mecum*, a popular
legal handbook, cautioned the inexperienced parson against attempts to prevent persons marrying
because they are poor or lack legal settlement.
"The Curate is not to stop his proceeding, because
any peevish or pragmatical [meddling] Person . . .
pretends to forbid him. Poverty is no more an
Impediment of Marriage, than Riches. . . . And I
see no reason to doubt, but that the Banns may be
publish'd, and Marriage be solemniz'd betwixt two

Persons that do at present *abide*, or *sojourn* within
a Parish, tho' they may not be fix'd Inhabitants,
according to *the Acts for Settling the Poor*" (Second Edition, 1707, pp. 163–64).
2. Slut.
3. Battestin supports Scout's opinion, citing *Jacob's
Law Dictionary* (see above, p. 54, n. 8) to the
effect that a man who married even before he
attained a legal settlement was immune from
removal; but in her study of *The English Poor in
the Eighteenth Century* (1926; London: Routledge
and Kegan Paul, 1964), Dorothy Marshall shows
that in rural areas at this time married couples
were the most frequent subjects of removal actions
(pp. 164–65).

Objection is doubtless that he shall lose his Fee: But that being once made easy, as it shall be, I am confident no farther Objection will remain. No, no, it is impossible: but your Ladyship can't discommend his Unwillingness to depart from his Fee. Every Man ought to have a proper Value for his Fee. As to the matter in question, if your Ladyship pleases to employ me in it, I will venture to promise you Success. The Laws of this Land are not so vulgar, to permit a mean Fellow to contend with one of your Ladyship's Fortune. We have one sure Card, which is to carry him before Justice *Frolick*, who, upon hearing your Ladyship's Name, will commit him without any farther Questions. As for the dirty Slut, we shall have nothing to do with her: for if we get rid of the Fellow, the ugly Jade will—' 'Take what Measures you please, good Mr. *Scout*,' answered the Lady, 'but I wish you could rid the Parish of both; for *Slipslop* tells me such Stories of this Wench, that I abhor the Thoughts of her; and tho' you say she is such an ugly Slut, yet you know, dear Mr. *Scout*, these forward Creatures who run after Men, will always find some as forward as themselves: So that, to prevent the Increase of Beggars, we must get rid of her.'—'Your Ladyship is very much in the right,' answered *Scout*, 'but I am afraid the Law is a little deficient in giving us any such Power of Prevention; however the Justice will stretch it as far as he is able, to oblige your Ladyship. To say truth, it is a great Blessing to the Country that he is in the Commission; for he hath taken several Poor off our hands, that the Law would never lay hold on. I know some Justices who make as much of committing a Man to *Bridewell*[4] as his Lordship at *Size* would of hanging him: But it would do a Man good to see his Worship our Justice commit a Fellow to *Bridewell*; he takes so much pleasure in it: And when once we ha' un there, we seldom hear any more o' un. He's either starved or eat up by Vermin in a Month's time.'—Here the Arrival of a Visitor put an end to the Conversation, and Mr. *Scout* having undertaken the Cause, and promised it Success, departed.

This *Scout* was one of those Fellows who without any Knowledge of the Law, or being bred to it, take upon them, in defiance of an Act of Parliament,[5] to act as Lawyers in the Country, and are called so. They are the Pests of Society, and a Scandal to a Profession, to which indeed

---

4. Vagrants and the idle poor were committed with petty criminals to Bridewell Hospital, a London workhouse that gave its name to the category of such "correctional" institutions. In "An Enquiry into the Causes of the Late Increase of Robbers" (1751), Fielding condemned these "seminaries of idleness, and common sewers of nastiness and disease," and in "A Proposal for Making an Effectual Provision for the Poor" (1753), he called for their replacement by modern institutions in which paupers would be put to useful work and segregated from criminal influences.

5. In response to complaints about such pettifoggers, "An Act for the Better Regulation of Attorneys and Solicitors" (1729) levied a fifty-pound fine against anyone practicing in any of the courts it specified without being duly sworn and formally enrolled in that court by a judge or judges who certified his professional qualifications. To qualify, an applicant had to serve a five-year clerkship with an admitted attorney. (Attorneys were authorized to conduct most legal business but the actual pleading of cases, which was reserved for barristers [p. 81, n. 3] schooled in one of the Inns of Court.) The regulation was extended to the county courts in 1739, but it was not applied to the Quarter Sessions until 1749, so Scout and his like could continue to "act as Lawyers in the Country" with impunity.

they do not belong; and which owes to such kind of Rascallions the Ill-will which weak Persons bear towards it. With this Fellow, to whom a little before she would not have condescended to have spoken, did a certain Passion for *Joseph*, and the Jealousy and Disdain of poor innocent *Fanny*, betray the Lady *Booby*, into a familiar Discourse, in which she inadvertently confirmed many Hints, with which *Slipslop*, whose Gallant he was, had pre-acquainted him; and whence he had taken an Opportunity to assert those severe Falshoods of little *Fanny*, which possibly the Reader might not have been well able to account for, if we had not thought proper to give him this Information.

Chapter IV

A *short Chapter, but very full of Matter; particularly the Arrival of Mr.* Booby *and his Lady.*

All that Night and the next Day, the Lady *Booby* past with the utmost Anxiety; her Mind was distracted, and her Soul tossed up and down by many turbulent and opposite Passions. She loved, hated, pitied, scorned, admired, despised the same Person by Fits, which changed in a very short Interval. On *Tuesday* Morning, which happened to be a Holiday, she went to Church, where, to her surprize, Mr. *Adams* published the Banns again with as audible a Voice as before. It was lucky for her, that as there was no Sermon, she had an immediate Opportunity of returning home, to vent her Rage, which she could not have concealed from the Congregation five Minutes; indeed it was not then very numerous, the Assembly consisting of no more than *Adams*, his Clerk, his Wife, the Lady, and one of her Servants. At her Return she met *Slipslop*, who accosted her in these Words:—'O Meam, what doth your Ladyship think? To be sure Lawyer *Scout* hath carried *Joseph* and *Fanny* both before the Justice. All the Parish are in Tears, and say they will certainly be hanged: For no body knows what it is for.'—'I suppose they deserve it,' says the Lady. 'What dost thou mention such Wretches to me?'—'O dear Madam,' answer'd *Slipslop*, 'is it not a pity such a *graceless* young Man should die a *virulent* Death? I hope the Judge will take *Commensuration* on his Youth. As for *Fanny*, I don't think it signifies much what becomes of her; and if poor *Joseph* hath done any thing, I could venture to swear she *traduced* him to it: Few Men ever come to *fragrant* Punishment, but by those nasty Creatures who are a Scandal to our *Sect*.' The Lady was no more pleased at this News, after a moment's Reflection, than *Slipslop* herself: For tho' she wished *Fanny* far enough, she did not desire the Removal of *Joseph*, especially with her. She was puzzled how to act, or what to say on this Occasion, when a Coach and six drove into the Court, and a Servant acquainted her with the Arrival of her Nephew *Booby* and his Lady. She ordered them to be conducted into a Drawing-Room, whither she presently repaired, having composed her Countenance as well as she could; and being a little satisfied that the Wedding would by these means be at least interrupted [1]; and that she should have an Opportunity to execute any Resolution she might take, for which she saw herself provided with an excellent Instrument in *Scout*.

The Lady *Booby* apprehended her Servant had made a Mistake, when he mentioned Mr. *Booby's* Lady; for she had never heard of his Marriage: but how great was her Surprize, when at her entering the Room, her Nephew presented his Wife to her, saying, 'Madam, this is that charming *Pamela*, of whom I am convinced you have heard so much.' The Lady received her with more Civility than he expected; indeed with the utmost: For she was perfectly polite, nor had any Vice Inconsistent with Good-breeding. They past some little time in ordinary Discourse, when a Servant came and whispered Mr. *Booby*, who presently told the Ladies he must desert them a little on some Business of Consequence; and as their Discourse during his Absence would afford little Improvement or Entertainment to the Reader, we will leave them for a while to attend Mr. *Booby*. [2]

Chapter V

Containing Justice Business; Curious Precedents of Depositions, and other Matters necessary to be perused by all Justices of the Peace and their Clerks.

The young Squire and his Lady were no sooner alighted from their Coach, than the Servants began to enquire after Mr. *Joseph*, from whom they said their Lady had not heard a Word to her great Surprize, since he had left Lady *Booby's*. Upon this they were instantly informed of what had lately happened, with which they hastily acquainted their Master, who took an immediate Resolution to go himself, and endeavour to restore his *Pamela* her Brother, before she even knew she had lost him.

The Justice, before whom the Criminals were carried, and who lived within a short Mile of the Lady's House, was luckily Mr. *Booby's* Acquaintance, by his having an Estate in his Neighbourhood. Ordering therefore his Horses to his Coach, he set out for the Judgment-Seat, and arriv'd when the Justice had almost finished his Business. He was conducted into a Hall, where he was acquainted that his Worship would wait on him in a moment; for he had only a Man and a Woman to commit to *Bridewell* first. As he was now convinced he had not a Minute to lose, he insisted on the Servants introducing him directly into the Room where the Justice was then executing his Office, as he called it. Being brought thither, and the first Compliments being past between the Squire and his Worship, the former asked the latter what Crime those two young People had been guilty of. 'No great Crime,' answered the Justice. 'I have only ordered them to *Bridewell* for a Month.' 'But

1. That is, the process of publishing the banns leading to the marriage would be interrupted.

2. A dig at *Pamela's* unremitting focus on the exemplary actions and thoughts of its heroine.

what is their Crime?' repeated the Squire. 'Larceny, an't please your Honour,' said *Scout*. 'Ay,' says the Justice, 'a kind of felonious larcenous thing. I believe I must order them a little Correction too, a little Stripping and Whipping.' (Poor *Fanny*, who had hitherto supported all with the thoughts of her *Joseph's* Company, trembled at that Sound; but indeed without reason, for none but the Devil himself would have executed such a Sentence on her.) 'Still,' said the Squire, 'I am ignorant of the Crime, the Fact I mean.' 'Why, there it is in Peaper,' answered the Justice, shewing him a Deposition, which in the Absence of his Clerk he had writ himself, of which we have with great difficulty procured an authentick Copy; and here it follows *verbatim et literatim*.[1]

> The *Depusition of* James Scout, *Layer, and* Thomas Trotter, *Yeoman, taken befor mee, on of his Magesty's Justasses of the Piece for* Zumersetshire.

'These Deponants saith, and first *Thomas Trotter* for himself saith, that on the   of this instant *October*, being Sabbath-Day, betwin the Ours of 2 and 4 in the afternoon, he zeed *Joseph Andrews* and *Francis Goodwill* walk akross a certane Felde belunging to Layer *Scout*, and out of the Path which ledes thru the said Felde, and there he zede *Joseph Andrews* with a Nife cut one Hassel-Twig, of the value, as he believes, of 3 half pence, or thereabouts; and he saith, that the said *Francis Goodwill* was likewise walking on the Grass out of the said Path in the said Felde, and did receive and karry in her Hand the said Twig, and so was cumfarting, eading and abatting to the said *Joseph* therein. And the said *James Scout* for himself says, that he verily believes the said Twig to be his own proper Twig, *&c.*'

'Jesu!' said the Squire, 'would you commit two Persons to *Bridewell* for a Twig?' 'Yes,' said the Lawyer, 'and with great Lenity too; for if we had called it a young Tree they would have been both hanged.'—'Harkee, (says the Justice, taking aside the Squire) I should not have been so severe on this Occasion, but Lady *Booby* desires to get them out of the Parish; so Lawyer *Scout* will give the Constable Orders to let them run away, if they please; but it seems they intend to marry together, and the Lady hath no other means, as they are legally settled there, to prevent their bringing an Incumbrance on her own Parish.' 'Well,' said the Squire, 'I will take care my Aunt shall be satisfied in this Point; and likewise I promise you, *Joseph* here shall never be any Incumbrance on her. I shall be oblig'd to you therefore, if, instead of *Bridewell*, you will commit them to my Custody.'—'O to be sure, Sir, if you desire it,' answer'd the Justice; and without more ado, *Joseph* and *Fanny* were delivered over to Squire *Booby*, whom *Joseph* very well knew; but little ghest how nearly he was related to him. The Justice burnt his *Mittimus*. The Constable was sent about his Business. The Lawyer made no Complaint for want

---

1. Word for word and letter for letter.

of Justice, and the Prisoners, with exulting Hearts, gave a thousand Thanks to his Honour Mr. *Booby*, who did not intend their Obligations to him should cease here; for ordering his Man to produce a Cloakbag which he had caused to be brought from Lady *Booby's* on purpose, he desired the Justice that he might have *Joseph* with him into a Room; where ordering his Servant to take out a Suit of his own Clothes, with Linnen and other Necessaries, he left *Joseph* to dress himself, who not yet knowing the Cause of all this Civility, excused his accepting such a Favour, as long as decently he could. Whilst *Joseph* was dressing, the Squire repaired to the Justice, whom he found talking with *Fanny*; for during the Examination she had lopped her Hat over her Eyes, which were also bathed in Tears, and had by that means concealed from his Worship what might perhaps have rendered the Arrival of Mr. *Booby* unnecessary, at least for herself. The Justice no sooner saw her Countenance cleared up, and her bright Eyes shining through her Tears, than he secretly cursed himself for having once thought of *Bridewell* for her. He would willingly have sent his own Wife thither, to have had *Fanny* in her place. And conceiving almost at the same instant Desires and Schemes to accomplish them, he employed the Minutes whilst the Squire was absent with *Joseph*, in assuring her how sorry he was for having treated her so roughly before he knew her Merit; and told her, that since Lady *Booby* was unwilling that she should settle in her Parish, she was heartily welcome to his, where he promised her his Protection, adding, that he would take *Joseph* and her into his own Family, if she liked it; which Assurance he confirmed with a Squeeze by the Hand. She thanked him very kindly, and said, 'she would acquaint *Joseph* with the Offer, which he would certainly be glad to accept; for the Lady *Booby* was angry with them both; tho' she did not know either had done any thing to offend her: but imputed it to Madam *Slipslop*, who had always been her Enemy.'

The Squire now returned, and prevented any farther Continuance of this Conversation; and the Justice out of a pretended Respect to his Guest, but in reality from an Apprehension of a Rival; (for he knew nothing of his Marriage,) ordered *Fanny* into the Kitchin, whither she gladly retired; nor did the Squire, who declined the Trouble of explaining the whole matter, oppose it.

It would be unnecessary, if I was able, which indeed I am not, to relate the Conversation between these two Gentlemen, which rolled, as I have been informed, entirely on the Subject of Horse-racing. *Joseph* was soon drest in the plainest Dress he could find, which was a blue Coat and Breeches, with a Gold Edging, and a red Waistcoat with the same; and as this Suit, which was rather too large for the Squire, exactly fitted him; so he became it so well, and looked so genteel, that no Person would have doubted its being as well adapted to his Quality as his Shape; nor have suspected, as one might when my Lord—, or Sir—, or Mr.— appear in Lace or Embroidery, that the Taylor's Man wore those Clothes home on his Back, which he should have carried under his Arm.

The Squire now took leave of the Justice, and calling for *Fanny*, made her and *Joseph*, against their Wills, get into the Coach with him, which he then ordered to drive to Lady *Booby's*.—It had moved a few Yards only, when the Squire asked *Joseph*, if he knew who that Man was crossing the Field; for, added he, 'I never saw one take such Strides before.' *Joseph* answered eagerly, 'O Sir, it is Parson *Adams*.'—'O la, indeed, and so it is,' said *Fanny*; 'poor Man he is coming to do what he could for us. Well, he is the worthiest best natur'd Creature.'—'Ay,' said *Joseph*, 'God bless him; for there is not such another in the Universe.'— 'The best Creature living sure,' cries *Fanny*. 'Is he?' says the Squire, 'then I am resolved to have the best Creature living in my Coach,' and so saying he ordered it to stop, whilst *Joseph* at his Request hollowed to the Parson, who well knowing his Voice, made all the haste imaginable, and soon came up with them; he was desired by the Master, who could scarce refrain from Laughter at his Figure, to mount into the Coach, which he with many Thanks refused, saying he could walk by its side, and he'd warrant he kept up with it; but he was at length over-prevailed on. The Squire now acquainted *Joseph* with his Marriage; but he might have spared himself that Labour; for his Servant, whilst *Joseph* was dressing, had performed that Office before. He continued to express the vast Happiness he enjoyed in his Sister, and the Value he had for all who belonged to her. *Joseph* made many Bows, and exprest as many Acknowledgments; and Parson *Adams*, who now first perceived *Joseph's* new Apparel, burst into Tears with Joy, and fell to rubbing his Hands and snapping his Fingers, as if he had been mad.

They were now arrived at the Lady *Booby's*, and the Squire desiring them to wait a moment in the Court, walked in to his Aunt, and calling her out from his Wife, acquainted her with *Joseph's* Arrival; saying, 'Madam, as I have married a virtuous and worthy Woman, I am resolved to own her Relations, and shew them all a proper Respect; I shall think myself therefore infinitely obliged to all mine, who will do the same. It is true, her Brother hath been your Servant; but he is now become my Brother; and I have one Happiness, that neither his Character, his Behaviour or Appearance give me any reason to be ashamed of calling him so. In short, he is now below, drest like a Gentleman, in which Light I intend he shall hereafter be seen; and you will oblige me beyond Expression, if you will admit him to be of our Party; for I know it will give great Pleasure to my Wife, tho' she will not mention it.'

This was a stroke of Fortune beyond the Lady *Booby's* Hopes or Expectation; she answered him eagerly, 'Nephew, you know how easily I am prevailed on to do any thing which *Joseph Andrews* desires—Phoo, I mean which you desire me, and as he is now your Relation, I cannot refuse to entertain him as such.' The Squire told her, he knew his Obligation to her for her Compliance, and going three Steps, returned and told her—he had one more Favour, which he believed she would easily grant, as she had accorded him the former. 'There is a young Woman—' 'Nephew,' says she, 'don't let my Good-nature make you desire, as is too commonly the Case, to impose on me. Nor think, because

I have with so much Condescension agreed to suffer your Brother-in-law to come to my Table, that I will submit to the Company of all my own Servants, and all the dirty Trollops in the Country.' 'Madam,' answer'd the Squire, 'I believe you never saw this young Creature. I never beheld such Sweetness and Innocence joined with such Beauty, and withal so genteel.' 'Upon my Soul, I won't admit her,' reply'd the Lady in a Passion; 'the whole World shan't prevail on me, I resent even the Desire as an Affront, and—' The Squire, who knew her Inflexibility, interrupted her, by asking Pardon, and promising not to mention it more. He then returned to *Joseph*, and she to *Pamela*. He took *Joseph* aside and told him, he would carry him to his Sister; but could not prevail as yet for *Fanny*. *Joseph* begged that he might see his Sister alone, and then be with his *Fanny*; but the Squire knowing the Pleasure his Wife would have in her Brother's Company, would not admit it, telling *Joseph* there would be nothing in so short an Absence from *Fanny*, whilst he was assured of her Safety; adding, he hoped he could not so easily quit a Sister whom he had not seen so long, and who so tenderly loved him— *Joseph* immediately complied; for indeed no Brother could love a Sister more; and recommending *Fanny*, who rejoiced that she was not to go before Lady *Booby*, to the Care of Mr. *Adams*, he attended the Squire up stairs, whilst *Fanny* repaired with the Parson to his House, where she thought herself secure of a kind Reception.

Chapter VI

Of which you are desired to read no more than you like.

The Meeting between *Joseph* and *Pamela* was not without Tears of Joy on both sides; and their Embraces were full of Tenderness and Affection. They were however regarded with much more Pleasure by the Nephew than by the Aunt, to whose Flame they were Fewel only; and this was increased by the Addition of Dress, which was indeed not wanted to set off the lively Colours in which Nature had drawn Health, Strength, Comeliness, and Youth. In the Afternoon *Joseph*, at their Request, entertained them with the Account of his Adventures, nor could Lady *Booby* conceal her Dissatisfaction at those Parts in which *Fanny* was concerned, especially when Mr. *Booby* launched forth into such rapturous Praises of her Beauty. She said, applying to her Niece, that she wondered her Nephew, who had pretended to marry for Love, should think such a Subject proper to amuse his Wife with: adding, that for her part, she should be jealous of a Husband who spoke so warmly in praise of another Woman. *Pamela* answer'd, indeed she thought she had cause; but it was an Instance of Mr. *Booby*'s aptness to see more Beauty in Women than they were Mistresses of. At which Words both the Women fixed their Eyes on two Looking-Glasses; and Lady *Booby* replied that Men were in the general very ill Judges of Beauty; and then whilst both contemplated only their own Faces, they paid a cross Compliment to each other's Charms. When the Hour of Rest approached, which the Lady of the House deferred as long as decently she could, she informed *Joseph* (whom for the future we shall call Mr. *Joseph*, he having as good a Title to that Appellation as many others, I mean that incontested one of good Clothes) that she had ordered a Bed to be provided for him; he declined this Favour to his utmost; for his Heart had long been with his *Fanny*; but she insisted on his accepting it, alledging that the Parish had no proper Accommodation for such a Person, as he was now to esteem himself. The Squire and his Lady both joining with her, Mr. *Joseph* was at last forced to give over his Design of visiting *Fanny* that Evening, who on her side as impatiently expected him till Midnight, when in complacence to Mr. *Adams's* Family, who had sat up two Hours out of Respect to her, she retired to Bed, but not to sleep; the Thoughts of her Love kept her waking, and his not returning according to his Promise, filled her with Uneasiness; of which however she could not assign any other Cause than merely that of being absent from him.

Mr. *Joseph* rose early in the Morning, and visited her in whom his Soul delighted. She no sooner heard his Voice in the Parson's Parlour, than she leapt from her Bed, and dressing herself in a few Minutes, went down to him. They past two Hours with inexpressible Happiness together, and then having appointed *Monday*, by Mr. *Adams's* permission, for their Marriage, Mr. *Joseph* returned according to his Promise, to Breakfast at the Lady *Booby's*, with whose Behaviour since the Evening we shall now acquaint the Reader.

She was no sooner retired to her Chamber than she asked *Slipslop* what she thought of this wonderful Creature her Nephew had married. 'Madam?' said *Slipslop*, not yet sufficiently understanding what Answer she was to make. 'I ask you,' answer'd the Lady, 'what you think of the Dowdy, my Niece I think I am to call her?' *Slipslop*, wanting no further Hint, began to pull her to pieces, and so miserably defaced her, that it would have been impossible for any one to have know the Person. The Lady gave her all the Assistance she could, and ended with saying—'I think, *Slipslop*, you have done her Justice; but yet, bad as she is, she is an Angel compared to this *Fanny*.' *Slipslop* then fell on *Fanny*, whom she hack'd and hew'd in the like barbarous manner, concluding with an Observation that there was always something in those low-life Creatures which must eternally distinguish them from their Betters. 'Really,' said the Lady, 'I think there is one Exception to your Rule, I am certain you may ghess who I mean.'—'Not I, upon my word, Madam,' said *Slipslop*.—'I mean a young Fellow; sure you are the dullest Wretch,' said the Lady.—'O la, I am indeed—Yes truly, Madam, he is an *Accession*,' answer'd *Slipslop*.—'Ay, is he not, *Slipslop*?' returned the Lady. 'Is he not so genteel that a Prince might without a Blush acknowledge him for his Son. His Behaviour is such that would not shame the best Education. He borrows from his Station a Condescension in every thing to his Superiours, yet unattended by that mean Servility which is called Good-Behaviour in such Persons. Every thing he doth hath no mark of the base Motive of Fear, but visibly shews some Respect and Gratitude, and carries with it the Persuasion of Love—And then for his Virtues; such Piety to his Parents, such tender Affection to his Sister, such Integrity in his Friendship, such Bravery, such Goodness, that if he had been born a Gentleman, his Wife would have possest the most invaluable Blessing.'—'To be sure, Ma'am,' says *Slipslop*.—'But as he is,' answered the Lady, 'if he had a thousand more good Qualities, it must render a Woman of Fashion contemptible even to be suspected of thinking of him, yes I should despise myself for such a Thought.' 'To be sure, Ma'am,' said *Slipslop*. 'And why to be sure?' reply'd the Lady, 'thou art always one's Echo. Is he not more worthy of Affection than a dirty Country Clown, tho' born of a Family as old as the Flood, or an idle worthless Rake, or little puisny[1] Beau of Quality? And yet these we must condemn ourselves to, in order to avoid the Censure of the World; to shun the Contempt of others, we must ally ourselves to those we despise; we must prefer Birth, Title and Fortune to real Merit. It is a Tyranny of Custom, a Tyranny we must comply with: For we People of Fashion are the Slaves of Custom.'—'Marry come up!' said *Slipslop*, who now well knew which Party to take, 'if I was a Woman of your Ladyship's Fortune and Quality, I would be a Slave to no body.'—'Me,' said the Lady, 'I am speaking, if a young Woman of Fashion who had seen nothing of the World should happen to like such a Fellow.—Me indeed; I hope thou dost not imagine—' 'No, Ma'am, to be sure,' cried *Slipslop*.—'No! what no?' cried the Lady. 'Thou art always ready to answer, before thou hast heard one. So far I must allow he is a charming Fellow. Me indeed! No, *Slipslop*, all Thoughts of Men are over with me.—I have lost a Husband, who—but if I should reflect, I should run mad.—My future Ease must depend upon Forgetfulness. *Slipslop*, let me hear some of thy Nonsense to turn my Thoughts another way. What dost thou think of Mr. *Andrews*?' 'Why I think,' says *Slipslop*, 'he is the handsomest most properest Man I ever saw; and if I was a Lady of the greatest Degree, it would be well for some Folks. Your Ladyship may talk of Custom if you please; but I am *confidous* there is no more Comparison between young Mr. *Andrews*, and most of the young Gentlemen who come to your Ladyship's House in *London*; a Parcel of *Whipper-snapper* Sparks: I would sooner marry our old Parson *Adams*. Never tell me what People say, whilst I am happy in the Arms of him I love. Some Folks rail against other Folks, because other Folks have what some Folks would be glad of.'—'And so,' answered the Lady, 'if you was a Woman of Condition, you would really marry Mr. *Andrews*?'—'Yes, I assure your Ladyship,' replied *Slipslop*, 'if he would have me.'—'Fool, Idiot,' cries the Lady, 'if he would have a Woman of Fashion! Is that a Question?' 'No truly, Madam,' said *Slipslop*, 'I believe it would be none, if *Fanny* was out of the way; and I am *confidous* if I was in your Ladyship's Place, and liked Mr. *Joseph Andrews*, she should not stay in the Parish a moment. I am

1. Puny.

sure Lawyer *Scout* would send her packing, if your Ladyship would but say the word.' This last Speech of *Slipslop* raised a Tempest in the Mind of her Mistress. She feared *Scout* had betrayed her, or rather that she had betrayed herself. After some Silence and a double Change of her Complexion; first to pale and then to red, she thus spoke: 'I am astonished at the Liberty you give your Tongue. Would you insinuate, that I employed *Scout* against this Wench, on the account of the Fellow?' 'La Ma'am,' said *Slipslop*, frighted out of her Wits. 'I *assassinate* such a Thing!' 'I think you dare not,' answered the Lady, 'I believe my Conduct may defy Malice itself to assert so cursed a Slander. If I had ever discovered[2] any Wantonness, any Lightness in my Behaviour: If I had followed the Example of some whom thou hast I believe seen, in allowing myself indecent Liberties, even with a Husband: but the dear Man who is gone (*here she began to sob*) was he alive again, (*then she produced Tears*) could not upbraid me with any one Act of Tenderness or Passion. No, *Slipslop*, all the time I cohabited with him, he never obtained even a Kiss from me, without my expressing Reluctance in the granting it. I am sure he himself never suspected how much I loved him.—Since his Death, thou knowest, tho' it is almost six Weeks (it wants but a Day) ago,[3] I have not admitted one Visitor, till this Fool my Nephew arrived. I have confined myself quite to one Party of Friends.—And can such a Conduct as this fear to be arraigned? To be accused not only of a Passion which I have always despised; but of fixing it on such an Object, a Creature so much beneath my Notice.'—'Upon my word, Ma'am,' says *Slipslop*, 'I do not understand your Ladyship, nor know I any thing of the matter.'—'I believe indeed thou dost not understand me.—Those are Delicacies which exist only in superior Minds; thy coarse Ideas cannot comprehend them. Thou art a low Creature, of the *Andrews* Breed, a Reptile of a lower Order, a Weed that grows in the common Garden of the Creation.'—'I assure your Ladyship," says *Slipslop*, whose Passions were almost of as high an Order as her Lady's, 'I have no more to do with *Common Garden*[4] than other Folks. Really, your Ladyship talks of Servants as if they were not born of the Christian *Specious*. Servants have Flesh and Blood as well as Quality; and Mr. *Andrews* himself is a Proof that they have as good, if not better. And for my own Part, I can't perceive my *Dears*[*] are coarser than other People's; and I am sure, if Mr. *Andrews* was a *Dear* of mine, I should not be ashamed of him in company with Gentlemen; for whoever hath seen him in his new Clothes, must confess he looks as much like a Gentleman as any body. Coarse, quotha![5] I can't bear to hear the poor young Fellow run down neither; for I will say this, I never heard him say an ill Word of any body in his

[*] Meaning perhaps Ideas.

---

2. Shown.

3. The actual elapsed time is half that. For a detailed chronology of the novel, see F. Homes Dudden, *Henry Fielding: His Life, Works, and Times* (1952; Hamden: Archon Books, 1966) 1.

342–50.

4. Covent Garden, so called after the many "common women" (whores) who trafficked there.

5. "Says he" (indeed).

Life. I am sure his Coarseness doth not lie in his Heart; for he is the best-natur'd Man in the World; and as for his Skin, it is no coarser than other People's, I am sure. His Bosom when a Boy was as white as driven Snow; and where it is not covered with Hairs, is so still. Ifaukins![6] if I was Mrs. *Andrews*, with a hundred a Year, I should not envy the best She who wears a Head. A Woman that could not be happy with such a Man, ought never to be so: For if he can't make a Woman happy, I never yet beheld the Man who could. I say again I wish I was a great Lady for his sake, I believe when I had made a Gentleman of him, he'd behave so, that no body should *deprecate*[7] what I had done; and I fancy few would venture to tell him he was no Gentleman to his Face, nor to mine neither.' At which Words, taking up the Candles, she asked her Mistress, who had been some time in her Bed, if she had any farther Commands; who mildly answered she had none; and telling her, she was a comical Creature, bid her Good-night.

Chapter VII

Philosophical Reflections, the like not to be found in any light French *Romance.* Mr. Booby's *grave Advice to* Joseph, *and* Fanny's *Encounter with a Beau.*

Habit, my good Reader, hath so vast a Prevalence over the human Mind, that there is scarce any thing too strange or too strong to be asserted of it. The Story of the Miser, who from long accustoming to cheat others, came at last to cheat himself, and with great Delight and Triumph, picked his own Pocket of a Guinea, to convey to his Hoard, is not impossible or improbable. In like manner, it fares with the Practisers of Deceit, who from having long deceived their Acquaintance, gain at last a Power of deceiving themselves, and acquire that very Opinion (however false) of their own Abilities, Excellencies and Virtues, into which they have for Years perhaps endeavoured to betray their Neighbours. Now, Reader, to apply this Observation to my present Purpose, thou must know, that as the Passion generally called Love, exercises most of the Talents of the Female or fair World; so in this they now and then discover a small Inclination to Deceit; for which thou wilt not be angry with the beautiful Creatures, when thou hast considered, that at the Age of seven or something earlier, Miss is instructed by her Mother, that Master is a very monstrous kind of Animal, who will, if she suffers him to come too near her, infallibly eat her up, and grind her to pieces. That so far from kissing or toying with him of her own accord, she must not admit him to kiss or toy with her. And lastly, that she must never have any Affection towards him; for if she should, all her Friends in Petticoats would esteem her a Traitress, point at her, and hunt her out of their Society. These

---

6. Dialect form of "In Faith" (truthfully).
7. A prophetic Slipslopism substituted for the correct "discommend" in the second edition. The word did not yet have its modern meaning of "disapprove" but meant "pray mercy or deliverance from," "avert" or "remove."

Impressions being first received, are farther and deeper inculcated by their School-mistresses and Companions; so that by the Age of Ten they have contracted such a Dread and Abhorrence of the above named Monster, that whenever they see him, they fly from him as the innocent Hare doth from the Greyhound. Hence to the Age of fourteen or fifteen, they entertain a mighty Antipathy to Master; they resolve and frequently profess that they will never have any commerce with him, and entertain fond Hopes of passing their Lives out of his reach, of the Possibility of which they have so visible an Example in their good Maiden Aunt. But when they arrive at this Period, and have now past their second Climacteric,[1] when their Wisdom grown riper, begins to see a little farther; and from almost daily falling in Master's way, to apprehend the great Difficulty of keeping out of it; and when they observe him look often at them, and sometimes very eagerly and earnestly too, (for the Monster seldom takes any notice of them till at this Age) they then begin to think of their Danger; and as they perceive they cannot easily avoid him, the wiser Part bethink themselves of providing by other Means for their Security. They endeavour by all the Methods they can invent to render themselves so amiable in his Eyes, that he may have no Inclination to hurt them; in which they generally succeed so well, that his Eyes, by frequent languishing, soon lessen their Idea of his Fierceness, and so far abate their Fears, that they venture to parley with him; and when they perceive him so different from what he hath been described, all Gentleness, Softness, Kindness, Tenderness, Fondness, their dreadful Apprehensions vanish in a moment; and now (it being usual with the human Mind to skip from one Extreme to its Opposite, as easily, and almost as suddenly, as a Bird from one Bough to another;) Love instantly succeeds to Fear: But as it happens to Persons, who have in their Infancy been thoroughly frightned with certain no Persons called Ghosts, that they retain their Dread of those Beings, after they are convinced that there are no such things; so these young Ladies, tho' they no longer apprehend devouring, cannot so entirely shake off all that hath been instilled into them; they still entertain the Idea of that Censure which was so strongly imprinted on their tender Minds, to which the Declarations of Abhorrence they every day hear from their Companions greatly contribute. To avoid this Censure therefore, is now their only care; for which purpose they still pretend the same Aversion to the Monster: And the more they love him, the more ardently they counterfeit the Antipathy. By the continual and constant Practice of which Deceit on others, they at length impose on themselves, and really believe they hate what they love. Thus indeed it happened to Lady *Booby*, who loved *Joseph* long before she knew it; and now loved him much more than she suspected. She had indeed, from the time of his Sister's Arrival in the Quality of her Niece; and from the Instant she viewed him in the Dress and Character of a Gentleman,

1. According to a belief at least as ancient as Pythagoras (sixth century B.C.), the critical periods of a person's life occurred at seven year intervals; the second of these, age fourteen, marked the beginning of pubescence.

began to conceive secretly a Design which Love had concealed from herself, 'till a Dream betrayed it to her.

She had no sooner risen that she sent for her Nephew; when he came to her, after many Compliments on his Choice, she told him, 'he might perceive in her Condescension to admit her own Servant to her Table, that she looked on the Family of *Andrews* as his Relations, and indeed her's; that as he had married into such a Family, it became him to endeavour by all Methods to raise it as much as possible; at length she advised him to use all his Art to dissuade *Joseph* from his intended Match, which would still enlarge their Relation to Meanness and Poverty; concluding, that by a Commission in the Army,[2] or some other genteel Employment, he might soon put young Mr. *Andrews* on the foot of a Gentleman; and that being once done, his Accomplishments might quickly gain him an Alliance, which would not be to their Discredit.'

Her Nephew heartily embraced this Proposal; and finding Mr. *Joseph* with his Wife, at his Return to her Chamber, he immediately began thus: 'My Love to my dear *Pamela*, Brother, will extend to all her Relations; nor shall I shew them less Respect than if I had married into the Family of a Duke. I hope I have given you some early Testimonies of this, and shall continue to give you daily more. You will excuse me therefore, Brother, if my Concern for your Interest makes me mention what may be, perhaps, disagreeable to you to hear: But I must insist upon it, that if you have any Value for my Alliance or my Friendship, you will decline any Thoughts of engaging farther with a Girl, who is, as you are a Relation of mine, so much beneath you. I know there may be at first some Difficulty in your Compliance, but that will daily diminish; and you will in the end sincerely thank me for my Advice. I own, indeed, the Girl is handsome: But Beauty alone is a poor Ingredient, and will make but an uncomfortable Marriage.' 'Sir,' said *Joseph*, 'I assure you her Beauty is her least Perfection; nor do I know a Virtue which that young Creature is not possest of.' 'As to her Virtues,' answered Mr. *Booby*, 'you can be yet but a slender Judge of them: But if she had never so many, you will find her Equal in these among her Superiors in Birth and Fortune, which now you are to esteem on a footing with yourself; at least I will take care they shall shortly be so, unless you prevent me by degrading yourself with such a Match, a Match I have hardly patience to think of; and which would break the Hearts of your Parents, who now rejoice in the Expectation of seeing you make a Figure in the World.' 'I know not,' replied *Joseph*, 'that my Parents have any power over my Inclinations; nor am I obliged to sacrifice my Happiness to their Whim or Ambition: Besides, I shall be very sorry to see that the unexpected Advancement of my Sister, should so suddenly inspire them with this wicked Pride, and make them despise their Equals, I am resolved on no account to quit my dear *Fanny*, no, tho' I could raise her as high above

2. An army regiment was like a corporation in which the officers owned shares according to their rank. In the time of Queen Anne, about thirty years earlier, a commission at the lowest rank of ensign could be purchased for two hundred to five hundred pounds, depending on the regiment.

her present Station as you have raised my Sister.' 'Your Sister, as well as myself,' said *Booby*, 'are greatly obliged to you for the Comparison: But, Sir, she is not worthy to be compared in Beauty to my *Pamela*; nor hath she half her Merit. And besides, Sir, as you civilly throw my Marriage with your Sister in my Teeth, I must teach you the wide Difference between us; my Fortune enabled me to please myself; and it would have been as overgrown a Folly in me to have omitted it, as in you to do it.' 'My Fortune enables me to please myself likewise,' said *Joseph*; 'for all my Pleasure is centred in *Fanny*, and whilst I have Health, I shall be able to support her with my Labour in that Station to which she was born, and with which she is content.' 'Brother,' said *Pamela*, 'Mr. *Booby* advises you as a Friend; and, no doubt, my Papa and Mamma will be of his Opinion, and will have great reason to be angry with you for destroying what his Goodness hath done, and throwing down our Family again, after he hath raised it. It would become you better, Brother, to pray for the Assistance of Grace[3] against such a Passion, than to indulge it.'— 'Sure, Sister, you are not in earnest; I am sure she is your Equal at least.'—'She was my Equal,' answered *Pamela*, 'but I am no longer *Pamela Andrews*, I am now this Gentleman's Lady, and as such am above her—I hope I shall never behave with an unbecoming Pride; but at the same time I shall always endeavour to know myself, and question not the Assistance of Grace to that purpose.' They were now summoned to Breakfast, and thus ended their Discourse for the present, very little to the Satisfaction of any of the Parties.

Fanny was now walking in an Avenue at some distance from the House, where *Joseph* had promised to take the first Opportunity of coming to her. She had not a Shilling in the World, and had subsisted ever since her Return entirely on the Charity of Parson *Adams*. A young Gentleman attended by many Servants, came up to her, and asked her if that was not the Lady *Booby's* House before him? This indeed he well knew; but had framed the Question for no other Reason than to make her look up and discover if her Face was equal to the Delicacy of her Shape. He no sooner saw it, than he was struck with Amazement. He stopt his Horse, and swore she was the most beautiful Creature he ever beheld. Then instantly alighting, and delivering his Horse to his Servant, he rapt out half a dozen Oaths that he would kiss her; to which she at first submitted, begging he would not be rude: but he was not satisfied with the Civility of a Salute, nor even with the rudest Attack he could make on her Lips, but caught her in his Arms and endeavoured to kiss her Breasts, which with all her Strength she resisted; and as our Spark was not of the *Herculean* Race, with some difficulty prevented. The young Gentleman being soon out of breath in the Struggle, quitted her, and remounting his Horse called one of his Servants to him, whom he ordered to stay behind with her, and make her any Offers whatever, to prevail on her to return home with him in the Evening; and to assure

3. See above, p. 37, n. 1.

her he would take her into Keeping. He then rode on with his other
Servants, and arrived at the Lady's House, to whom he was a distant
Relation, and was come to pay a Visit.

The trusty Fellow, who was employ'd in an Office he had been long
accustomed to, discharged his Part with all the Fidelity and Dexterity
imaginable; but to no purpose. She was entirely deaf to his Offers, and
rejected them with the utmost Disdain. At last the Pimp, who had perhaps more warm Blood about him than his Master, began to sollicit for
himself; he told her, tho' he was a Servant, he was a Man of some
Fortune, which he would make her Mistress of—and this without any
Insult to her Virtue, for that he would marry her. She answer'd, if his
Master himself, or the greatest Lord in the Land would marry her, she
would refuse him. At last being weary with Persuasions, and on fire with
Charms which would have almost kindled a Flame in the Bosom of an
antient Philosopher, or modern Divine, he fastened his Horse to the
Ground, and attacked her with much more Force than the Gentleman
had exerted. Poor *Fanny* would not have been able to resist his Rudeness
any long time, but the Deity who presides over chaste Love sent her
Joseph to her Assistance. He no sooner came within sight, and perceived
her struggling with a Man, than like a Cannon-Ball, or like Lightning,
or any thing that is swifter, if any thing be, he ran towards her, and
coming up just as the Ravisher had torn her Handkerchief from her
Breast, before his Lips had touched that Seat of Innocence and Bliss, he
dealt him so lusty a Blow in that part of his Neck which a Rope would
have become with the utmost Propriety, that the Fellow staggered backwards, and perceiving he had to do with something rougher than the
little, tender, trembling Hand of *Fanny*, he quitted her, and turning
about saw his Rival, with Fire flashing from his Eyes, again ready to
assail him; and indeed before he could well defend himself or return the
first Blow, he received a second, which had it fallen on that part of the
Stomach to which it was directed, would have been probably the last he
would have had any Occasion for; but the Ravisher lifting up his Hand,
drove the Blow upwards to his Mouth, whence it dislodged three of his
Teeth; and now not conceiving any extraordinary Affection for the Beauty
of *Joseph's* Person, nor being extremely pleased with this method of Sal-
utation, he collected all his Force, and aimed a Blow at *Joseph's* Breast,
which he artfully parry'd with one Fist, so that it lost its Force entirely
in Air. And stepping one Foot backward, he darted his Fist so fiercely at
his Enemy, that had he not caught it in his Hand (for he was a Boxer of
no inferior Fame) it must have tumbled him on the Ground. And now
the Ravisher meditated another Blow, which he aimed at that part of the
Breast where the Heart is lodged, *Joseph* did not catch it as before, yet so
prevented[4] its Aim, that it fell directly on his Nose, but with abated
Force. *Joseph* then moving both Fist and Foot forwards at the same time,
threw his Head so dextrously into the Stomach of the Ravisher, that he

4. Baffled.

fell a lifeless Lump on the Field, where he lay many Minutes breathless and motionless.

When *Fanny* saw her *Joseph* receive a Blow in his Face, and Blood running in a Stream from him, she began to tear her Hair, and invoke all human and divine Power to his Assistance. She was not, however, long under this Affliction, before *Joseph* having conquered his Enemy, ran to her, and assured her he was not hurt; she then instantly fell on her Knees and thanked G——, that he had made *Joseph* the means of her Rescue, and at the same time preserved him from being injured in attempting it. She offered with her Handkerchief to wipe his Blood from his Face; but he seeing his Rival attempting to recover his Legs, turned to him and asked him if he had enough; to which the other answer'd he had; for he believed he had fought with the Devil, instead of a Man, and loosening his Horse, said he should not have attempted the Wench if he had known she had been so well provided for.

Fanny now begged *Joseph* to return with her to Parson *Adams*, and to promise that he would leave her no more; these were Propositions so agreeable to *Joseph*, that had he heard them he would have given an immediate Assent: but indeed his Eyes were now his only Sense; for you may remember, Reader, that the Ravisher had tore her Handkerchief from *Fanny's* Neck, by which he had discovered [5] such a Sight; that *Joseph* hath declared all the Statues he ever beheld were so much inferiour to it in Beauty, that it was more capable of converting a Man into a Statue, than of being imitated by the greatest Master of that Art. This modest Creature, whom no Warmth in Summer could ever induce to expose her Charms to the wanton Sun, a Modesty to which perhaps they owed their inconceivable Whiteness, had stood many Minutes bare-necked in the Presence of *Joseph*, before her Apprehension of his Danger, and the Horror of seeing his Blood would suffer her once to reflect on what concerned herself; till at last, when the Cause of her Concern had vanished, an Admiration at his Silence, together with observing the fixed Position of his Eyes, produced an Idea in the lovely Maid, which brought more Blood into her Face than had flowed from *Joseph's* Nostrils. The snowy Hue of her Bosom was likewise exchanged to Vermillion at the instant when she clapped her Handkerchief round her Neck. *Joseph* saw the Uneasiness she suffered, and immediately removed his Eyes from an Object, in surveying which he had felt the greatest Delight which the Organs of Sight were capable of conveying to his Soul. So great was his Fear of offending her, and so truly did his Passion for her deserve the noble Name of Love.

Fanny being recovered from her Confusion, which was almost equalled by what *Joseph* had felt from observing it, again mention'd her Request; this was instantly and gladly complied with, and together they crossed two or three Fields, which brought them to the Habitation of Mr. *Adams*.

5. Disclosed.

Chapter VIII

A Discourse which happened between Mr. Adams, Mrs. Adams, Joseph and Fanny; with some Behaviour of Mr. Adams, which will be called by some few Readers, very low, absurd, and unnatural.

The Parson and his Wife had just ended a long Dispute when the Lovers came to the Door. Indeed this young Couple had been the Subject of the Dispute; for Mrs. *Adams* was one of those prudent People who never do any thing to injure their Families, or perhaps one of those good Mothers who would even stretch their Conscience to serve their Children. She had long entertained hopes of seeing her eldest Daughter succeed Mrs. *Slipslop*, and of making her second Son an Exciseman by Lady *Booby's* Interest. These were Expectations she could not endure the Thoughts of quitting, and was therefore very uneasy to see her Husband so resolute to oppose the Lady's Intention in *Fanny's* Affair. She told him, 'it behoved every Man to take the first Care of his Family; that he had a Wife and six Children, the maintaining and providing for whom would be Business enough for him without intermeddling in other Folks Affairs; that he had always preached up Submission to Superiours, and would do ill to give an Example of the contrary Behaviour in his own Conduct; that if Lady *Booby* did wrong, she must answer for it herself, and the Sin would not lie at their Door; that *Fanny* had been a Servant, and bred up in the Lady's own Family, and consequently she must have known more of her than they did, and it was very improbable if she had behaved herself well, that the Lady would have been so bitterly her Enemy; that perhaps he was too much inclined to think well of her because she was handsome, but handsome Women were often no better than they should be; that G—made ugly Women as well as handsome ones, and that if a Woman had Virtue, it signified nothing whether she had Beauty or no.' For all which Reasons she concluded, he should oblige the Lady and stop the future Publication of the Banns: but all these excellent Arguments had no effect on the Parson, who persisted in doing his Duty without regarding the Consequence it might have on his worldly Interest; he endeavoured to answer her as well as he could, to which she had just finished her Reply, (for she had always the last Word every where but at Church) when *Joseph* and *Fanny* entered their Kitchin, where the Parson and his Wife then sat at Breakfast over some Bacon and Cabbage. There was a Coldness in the Civility of Mrs. *Adams*, which Persons of accurate Speculation[1] might have observed, but escaped her present Guests; indeed it was a good deal covered by the Heartiness of *Adams*, who no sooner heard that *Fanny* had neither eat nor drank that Morning, than he presented her a Bone of Bacon[2] he had just been gnawing, being the only Remains of his Provision, and then ran nimbly to the Tap, and produced a Mug of small Beer, which he called Ale, however

---

1. Perception.   2. A term applied generically to pork.

it was the best in his House. *Joseph* addressing himself to the Parson, told him the Discourse which had past between Squire *Booby*, his Sister and himself, concerning *Fanny*: he then acquainted him with the Dangers whence he had rescued her, and communicated some Apprehensions on her account. He concluded, that he should never have an easy Moment till *Fanny* was absolutely his, and begged that he might be suffered to fetch a Licence, saying, he could easily borrow the Money. The Parson answered, that he had already given his Sentiments concerning a Licence, and that a very few Days would make it unnecessary. '*Joseph*,' says he, 'I wish this Haste doth not arise rather from your Impatience than your Fear: but as it certainly springs from one of these Causes, I will examine both. Of each of these therefore in their Turn; and first, for the first of these, namely, Impatience. Now, Child, I must inform you, that if in your purposed Marriage with this young Woman, you have no Intention but the Indulgence of carnal Appetites, you are guilty of a very heinous Sin. Marriage was ordained for nobler Purposes, as you will learn when you hear the Service provided on that Occasion read to you. Nay perhaps, if you are a good Lad, I shall give you a Sermon *gratis*, wherein I shall demonstrate how little Regard ought to be had to the Flesh on such Occasions. The Text will be, Child, *Matthew* the 5th, and Part of the 28th Verse, *Whosoever looketh on a Woman so as to lust after her*. The latter Part I shall omit, as foreign to my Purpose.[3] Indeed all such brutal Lusts and Affections are to be greatly subdued, if not totally eradicated, before the Vessel can be said to be consecrated to Honour. To marry with a View of gratifying those Inclinations is a Prostitution of that holy Ceremony, and must entail a Curse on all who so lightly undertake it. If, therefore, this Haste arises from Impatience, you are to correct, and not give way to it. Now as to the second Head which I proposed to speak to, namely, Fear. It argues a Diffidence highly criminal of that Power in which alone we should put our Trust, seeing we may be well assured that he is able not only to defeat the Designs of our Enemies, but even to turn their Hearts. Instead of taking therefore any unjustifiable or desperate means to rid ourselves of Fear, we should resort to Prayer only on these Occasions, and we may be then certain of obtaining what is best for us. When any Accident threatens us, we are not to despair, nor when it overtakes us, to grieve; we must submit in all things to the Will of Providence, and not set our Affections so much on any thing here, as not to be able to quit it without Reluctance. You are a young Man, and can know but little of this World; I am older, and have seen a great deal. All Passions are criminal in their Excess, and even Love itself, if it is not subservient to our Duty, may render us blind to it. Had *Abraham* so loved his Son *Isaac*,[4] as to refuse

3. Adams omits the context, which makes it clear that Jesus' preaching is not against conjugal sex: "Ye have heard that it was said by them of old time, Thou shalt not commit adultery: but I say unto you, That whosoever looketh on a woman to lust after her hath committed adultery with her already in his heart" (Matthew 5:27–28). His offer of the free sermon and specification of the text were added in the second edition.

4. To test Abraham's devotion, God commanded him to sacrifice his son Isaac, which he was about to do when God intervened (Genesis 22:1–18).

the Sacrifice required, is there any of us who would not condemn him? *Joseph*, I know your many good Qualities, and value you for them: but as I am to render an Account of your Soul, which is committed to my Cure,[5] I cannot see any Fault without reminding you of it. You are too much inclined to Passion, Child, and have set your Affections so absolutely on this young Woman, that if G—required her at your hands, I fear you would reluctantly part with her. Now believe me, no Christian ought so to set his Heart on any Person or Thing in this World, but that whenever it shall be required or taken from him in any manner by Divine Providence, he may be able, peaceably, quietly, and contentedly to resign it.' At which Words one came hastily in and acquainted Mr. *Adams* that his youngest Son was drowned. He stood silent a moment, and soon began to stamp about the Room and deplore his Loss with the bitterest Agony. *Joseph*, who was overwhelmed with Concern likewise, recovered himself sufficiently to endeavour to comfort the Parson; in which Attempt he used many Arguments that he had at several times remember'd out of his own Discourses both in private and publick, (for he was a great Enemy to the Passions, and preached nothing more than the Conquest of them by Reason and Grace) but he was not at leisure now to hearken to his Advice. 'Child, Child,' said he, 'do not go about Impossibilities. Had it been any other of my Children I could have born it with patience; but my little Prattler, the Darling and Comfort of my old Age—the little Wretch to be snatched out of Life just at his Entrance into it; the sweetest, best-temper'd Boy, who never did a thing to offend me. It was but this Morning I gave him his first Lesson in *Quæ Genus*.[6] This was the very Book he learnt, poor Child! it is of no further use to thee now. He would have made the best Scholar, and have been an Ornament to the Church—such Parts and such Goodness never met in one so young.' 'And the handsomest Lad too,' says Mrs. *Adams*, recovering from a Swoon in *Fanny's* Arms.—'My poor *Jacky*,[7] shall I never see thee more?' cries the Parson.—'Yes, surely,' says *Joseph*, 'and in a better Place, you will meet again never to part more.'—I believe the Parson did not hear these Words, for he paid little regard to them, but went on lamenting whilst the Tears trickled down into his Bosom. At last he cry'd out, 'Where is my little Darling?' and was sallying out, when to his great Surprize and Joy, in which I hope the Reader will sympathize, he met his Son in a wet Condition indeed, but alive, and running towards him. The Person who brought the News of his Misfortune, had been a little too eager, as People sometimes are, from I believe no very good Principle, to relate ill News; and seeing him fall into the River, instead of running to his Assistance, directly ran to acquaint his Father of a Fate which he had concluded to be inevitable, but whence the Child was relieved by the same poor Pedlar who had relieved his Father before from a less Distress.

5. Spiritual care.

6. The opening words of the section on genders of irregular nouns in Lily's Grammar (see above, p. 114, n. 7): "*Quae genus aut flexum variant* . . ." (Those which change their gender or declension . . .).

7. Fielding let the inconsistency between this and the subsequent name, Dick, stand through five editions.

The Parson's Joy was now as extravagant as his Grief had been before; he kissed and embraced his Son a thousand times, and danced about the Room like one frantick; but as soon as he discovered the Face of his old Friend the Pedlar, and heard the fresh Obligation he had to him, what were his Sensations? not those which two Courtiers feel in one another's Embraces; not those with which a great Man receives the vile, treacherous Engines of his wicked Purposes; not those with which a worthless younger Brother wishes his elder Joy of a Son, or a Man congratulates his Rival on his obtaining a Mistress, a Place,[8] or an Honour.—No, Reader, he felt the Ebullition, the Overflowings of a full, honest, open Heart towards the Person who had conferred a real Obligation, and of which if thou can'st not conceive an Idea within, I will not vainly endeavour to assist thee.

When these Tumults were over, the Parson taking *Joseph* aside, proceeded thus—'No, *Joseph*, do not give too much way to thy Passions, if thou dost expect Happiness.'—The Patience of *Joseph*, nor perhaps of *Job*, could bear no longer; he interrupted the Parson, saying, 'it was easier to give Advice than take it, nor did he perceive he could so entirely conquer himself, when he apprehended he had lost his Son, or when he found him recover'd.—'Boy,' reply'd *Adams,* raising his Voice, 'it doth not become green Heads to advise grey Hairs—Thou art ignorant of the Tenderness of fatherly Affection; when thou art a Father thou wilt be capable then only of knowing what a Father can feel. No Man is obliged to Impossibilities, and the Loss of a Child is one of those great Trials where our Grief may be allowed to become immoderate.' 'Well, Sir,' cries *Joseph*, 'and if I love a Mistress as well as you your Child, surely her Loss would grieve me equally.' 'Yes, but such Love is Foolishness, and wrong in itself, and ought to be conquered,' answered *Adams*, 'it savours too much of the Flesh.' 'Sure, Sir,' says *Joseph*, 'it is not sinful to love my Wife, no not even to doat on her to Distraction!' 'Indeed but it is,' says *Adams*. 'Every Man ought to love his Wife, no doubt; we are commanded so to do; but we ought to love her with Moderation and Discretion.'[9]—'I am afraid I shall be guilty of some Sin, in spight of all my Endeavours,' says *Joseph*; 'for I shall love without any Moderation, I am sure.'—'You talk foolishly and childishly,' cries *Adams*. 'Indeed,' says Mrs. *Adams*, who had listened to the latter part of their Conversation, 'you talk more foolishly yourself. I hope, my Dear, you will never preach any such Doctrine as that Husbands can love their Wives too well. If I knew you had such a Sermon in the House, I am sure I would burn it; and I declare if I had not been convinced you had loved me as well as you could, I can answer for myself I should have hated and despised you. Marry come up! Fine Doctrine indeed! A Wife hath a Right to insist on her Husband's loving her as much as ever he can: And

---

8. Government appointment. The son of the elder brother would supplant the younger brother as heir to the estate.
9. There is no hint of moderation or discretion in the preaching of Paul to which Adams probably refers: "Husbands, love your wives, even as Christ also loved the church, and gave himself for it" (Ephesians 5:25).

he is a sinful Villain who doth not. Doth he not promise to love her, and to comfort her, and to cherish her, and all that? I am sure I remember it all, as well as if I repeated it over but Yesterday, and shall never forget it. Besides, I am certain you do not preach as you practise; for you have been a loving and a cherishing Husband to me, that's the truth on't; and why you should endeavour to put such wicked Nonsense into this young Man's Head, I cannot devise. Don't hearken to him, Mr. *Joseph*, be as good a Husband as you are able, and love your Wife with all your Body and Soul too.' Here a violent Rap at the Door put an end to their Discourse, and produced a Scene which the Reader will find in the next Chapter.

Chapter IX

A Visit which the good Lady Booby and her polite Friend paid to the Parson.

The Lady *Booby* had no sooner had an Account from the Gentleman of his meeting a wonderful Beauty near her House, and perceived the Raptures with which he spoke of her, than immediately concluding it must be *Fanny*, she began to meditate a Design of bringing them better acquainted; and to entertain Hopes that the fine Clothes, Presents and Promises of this Youth, would prevail on her to abandon *Joseph*: She therefore proposed to her Company a Walk in the Fields before Dinner, when she led them towards Mr. *Adams's* House; and as she approached it, told them, if they pleased she would divert them with one of the most ridiculous Sights they had ever seen, which was an old foolish Parson, who, she said laughing, kept a Wife and six Brats on a Salary of about twenty Pounds a Year; adding, that there was not such another ragged Family in the Parish. They all readily agreed to this Visit, and arrived whilst Mrs. *Adams* was declaiming, as in the last Chapter. Beau *Didapper*, which was the Name of the young Gentleman we have seen riding towards Lady *Booby's*, with his Cane mimicked the Rap of a *London* Footman at the Door. The People within; namely, *Adams*, his Wife, and three Children, *Joseph*, *Fanny*, and the Pedlar, were all thrown into Confusion by this Knock; but *Adams* went directly to the Door, which being opened, the Lady *Booby* and her Company walked in, and were received by the Parson with about two hundred Bows; and by his Wife with as many Curt'sies; the latter telling the Lady, 'she was ashamed to be seen in such a Pickle, and that her House was in such a Litter: But that if she had expected such an Honour from her Ladyship, she should have found her in a better manner.' The Parson made no Apologies, tho' he was in his Half-Cassock and a Flannel Night-Cap. He said, 'they were heartily welcome to his poor Cottage,' and turning to Mr. *Didapper*, cried out, *Non mea renidet in Domo Lacunar.*[1] The Beau answered,

---

1. "No panelled ceiling gleams in my home" (a contraction of Horace, *Odes* 2.18.1–2).

'he did not understand *Welch*;' at which the Parson stared, and made no Reply.

Mr. *Didapper*, or Beau *Didapper*, was a young Gentleman of about four Foot five Inches in height. He wore his own Hair, tho' the Scarcity of it might have given him sufficient Excuse for a Periwig. His Face was thin and pale: The Shape of his Body and Legs none of the best; for he had very narrow Shoulders, and no Calf; and his Gait might more properly be called hopping than walking. The Qualifications of his Mind were well adapted to his Person. We shall handle them first negatively. He was not entirely ignorant: For he could talk a little *French*, and sing two or three *Italian* Songs: He had lived too much in the World to be bashful, and too much at Court to be proud: He seemed not much inclined to Avarice; for he was profuse in his Expences: Nor had he all the Features of Prodigality; for he never gave a Shilling:—No Hater of Women; for he always dangled after them; yet so little subject to Lust, that he had, among those who knew him best, the Character of great Moderation in his Pleasures. No Drinker of Wine; nor so addicted to Passion, but that a hot Word or two from an Adversary made him immediately cool.

Now, to give him only a Dash or two on the affirmative Side: 'Tho' he was born to an immense Fortune, he chose, for the pitiful and dirty Consideration of a Place of little consequence, to depend entirely on the Will of a Fellow, whom they call a Great-Man; who treated him with the utmost Disrespect, and exacted of him a plenary Obedience to his Commands; which he implicitly submitted to, at the Expence of his Conscience, his Honour, and of his Country; in which he had himself so very large a Share.'[2] And to finish his Character, 'As he was entirely well satisfied with his own Person and Parts, so he was very apt to ridicule and laugh at any Imperfection in another.'[3] Such was the little Person or rather Thing[4] that hopped after Lady *Booby* into Mr. *Adams's* Kitchin.

The Parson and his Company retreated from the Chimneyside, where

---

2. Battestin (*Philological Quarterly* 42: 226–41) has identified the original of Beau Didapper as John, Lord Hervey (1696–1743), faithful associate of Walpole (often called "the Great Man"). From 1730 to 1740 his "Place" was vice chamberlain to the King's Household, in charge of domestic management and protocol. In *The Grub Street Opera* (1731), Fielding made him a servile groom to Walpole's conniving butler ("When did Robin ask me what I have not done?" 1.9). Battestin notes other allusive strokes in the portrait: Hervey was slight and delicate, affected French in his conversation, was derided for his halting Latin, had extramarital affairs but drank no alcohol, and followed a strict regimen of diet, exercise, and rest. The suggestion of cowardice at the end of the preceding paragraph belies his resolute conduct in challenging and duelling Pulteney (see pp. 388–90), although opposition pamphlets derided his performance.

Fielding's quotation marks set off his satiric

conversion of Conyers Middleton's praise of Hervey in the dedication of his *Life of Cicero* (see below, pp. 342–43), which he had previously parodied in *Shamela* (see below, pp. 273–74). Didapper (the name of a beau in *Tatler* 67) incorporates "Dapper," a name his enemies applied to Hervey, within the name of a small water bird noted for its bottom-diving.

3. In response to Pope's satiric attacks, Hervey and Lady Mary Wortley Montague (1689–1762) made fun of his physical deformity in *Verses Address'd to the Imitator of the First Satire of the Second Book of Horace* (1733). This sentence, as Battestin notes, is a condensed paraphrastic allusion to two passages in Pope's reply, *A Letter to a Noble Lord* (privately circulated in 1733).

4. In his best-known attack on Hervey, in the figure of Sporus in *An Epistle to Dr. Arbuthnot* (1735), Pope described him as "that Thing of silk" (305).

they had been seated, to give room to the Lady and hers. Instead of
returning any of the Curt'sies or extraordinary Civility of Mrs. *Adams*,
the Lady turning to Mr. *Booby*, cried out, '*Quelle Bête! Quel Animal!*'
And presently after discovering *Fanny* (for she did not need the Circumstance of her standing by *Joseph* to assure the Identity of her Person) she
asked the Beau, 'whether he did not think her a pretty Girl?'—'Begad,
Madam,' answered he, ''tis the very same I met.' 'I did not imagine,'
replied the Lady, 'you had so good a Taste.' 'Because I never liked you,
I warrant,' cries the Beau. 'Ridiculous!' said she, 'you know you was
always my Aversion.' 'I would never mention Aversion,' answered the
Beau, 'with that Face*; dear Lady *Booby*, wash your Face before you
mention Aversion, I beseech you.' He then laughed and turned about
to coquette it with *Fanny*.

Mrs. *Adams* had been all this time begging and praying the Ladies to
sit down, a Favour which she at last obtained. The little Boy to whom
the Accident had happened, still keeping his Place by the Fire, was chid
by his Mother for not being more mannerly: But Lady *Booby* took his
part, and commending his Beauty, told the Parson he was his very Picture. She then seeing a Book in his Hand, asked, 'if he could read?'
'Yes,' cried *Adams*, 'a little *Latin*, Madam, he is just got into *Quæ
Genus*.'—'A Fig for *quere genius*,' answered she, 'let me hear him read
a little *English*.'—'*Lege, Dick, Lege*,' said *Adams*: But the Boy made no
Answer, till he saw the Parson knit his Brows; and then cried, 'I don't
understand you, Father.' 'How, Boy,' says *Adams*, 'What doth *Lego* make
in the imperative Mood? *Legito*, doth it not?' 'Yes,' answered *Dick*.—
'And what besides?' says the Father. '*Lege*,' quoth the Son, after some
hesitation. 'A good Boy,' says the Father: 'And now, Child, What is the
English of *Lego*?'—To which the Boy, after long puzzling, answered, he
could not tell. 'How,' cries *Adams* in a Passion,—'What hath the Water
washed away your Learning? Why, what is *Latin* for the *English* Verb
read? Consider before you speak.'—The Child considered some time,
and then the Parson cried twice or thrice, '*Le—, Le—.*'—*Dick* answered,
'*Lego*.'—'Very well;—and then, what is the *English*,' says the Parson,
'of the Verb *Lego*?'—'To read,' cried *Dick*.—'Very well,' said the Parson,
'a good Boy, you can do well, if you will take pains.—I assure your
Ladyship he is not much above eight Years old, and is out of his *Propria
quæ Maribus*[6] already.—Come, *Dick*, read to her Ladyship;'—which
she again desiring, in order to give the Beau Time and Opportunity with
Fanny, *Dick* began as in the following Chapter.

---

*Lest this should appear unnatural to some Readers, we think proper to acquaint them, that it is taken
verbatim from very polite Conversation.[5]

---

5. Battestin notes a similar remark by the rakish
Captain Toupee in response to Lady Loverule's
suggestion that he let her win some money from
him at dice in Vanbrugh's unfinished comedy, *A
Journey to London* (1728), 4.1. In Swift's *Polite
Conversation* (1728), a collection of "polite . . .

repartees . . . and rejoinders" "now used at *Court*,
and in the *Best Companies*," Miss Notable tells
Mr. Neverout, "don't ask Questions with a dirty
Face" (second conversation).
6. See above, p. 242, n. 6.

Chapter X

The History of two Friends, which may afford an useful Lesson to all those Persons, who happen to take up thier Residence in married Families.

Leonard and *Paul* were two Friends.'—'Pronounce it *Lennard*, Child,' cry'd the Parson.—'Pray, Mr. *Adams*,' says Lady *Booby*, 'let your Son read without Interruption.' *Dick* then proceeded. '*Lennard* and *Paul* were two Friends, who having been educated together at the same School, commenced a Friendship which they preserved a long time for each other. It was so deeply fixed in both their Minds, that a long Absence, during which they had maintained no Correspondence, did not eradicate nor lessen it: But it revived in all its Force at their first Meeting, which was not till after fifteen Years Absence, most of which Time *Lennard* had spent in the *East-Indi-es*.'—'Pronounce it short *Indies*,' says *Adams*.—'Pray, Sir, be quiet,' says the Lady.—The Boy repeated—'in the *East-Indies*, whilst *Paul* had served his King and Country in the Army. In which different Services, they had found such different Success, that *Lennard* was now married, and retired with a Fortune of thirty thousand Pound; and *Paul* was arrived to the Degree of a Lieutenant of Foot; and was not worth a single Shilling.

'The Regiment in which *Paul* was stationed, happened to be ordered into Quarters, within a small distance from the Estate which *Lennard* had purchased; and where he was settled. This latter, who was now become a Country Gentleman and a Justice of Peace, came to attend the Quarter-Sessions,[1] in the Town where his old Friend was quartered, soon after his Arrival. Some Affair in which a Soldier was concerned, occasioned *Paul* to attend the Justices. Manhood, and Time, and the Change of Climate had so much altered *Lennard*, that *Paul* did not immediately recollect the Features of his old Acquaintance: But it was otherwise with *Lennard*. He knew *Paul* the moment he saw him; nor could he contain himself from quitting the Bench, and running hastily to embrace him. *Paul* stood at first a little surprized; but had soon sufficient Information from his Friend, whom he no sooner remembred, than he returned his Embrace with a Passion which made many of the Spectators laugh, and gave to some few a much higher and more agreeable Sensation.

'Not to detain the Reader with minute Circumstances, *Lennard* insisted on his Friend's returning with him to his House that Evening; which Request was complied with, and Leave for a Month's Absence for *Paul*, obtained of the commanding Officer.

'If it was possible for any Circumstance to give any addition to the Happiness which *Paul* proposed in this Visit, he received that additional Pleasure, by finding on his Arrival at his Friend's House, that his Lady

1. See above, p. 84, n. 1.

was an old Acquaintance which he had formerly contracted at his Quarters; and who had always appeared to be of a most agreeable Temper. A Character she had ever maintained among her Intimates, being of that number, every Individual of which is called quite the best sort of Woman in the World.

'But good as this Lady was, she was still a Woman; that is to say, an Angel and not an Angel—' 'You must mistake, Child,' cries the Parson, 'for you read Nonsense.' 'It is so in the Book,' answered the Son. Mr. *Adams* was then silenc'd by Authority, and *Dick* proceeded—'For tho' her Person was of that kind to which Men attribute the Name of Angel, yet in her Mind she was perfectly Woman. Of which a great degree of Obstinacy gave the most remarkable, and perhaps most pernicious Instance.

'A Day or two past after *Paul's* Arrival before any Instances of this appear'd; but it was impossible to conceal it long. Both she and her Husband soon lost all Apprehension from their Friend's Presence, and fell to their Disputes with as much Vigour as ever. These were still pursued with the utmost Ardour and Eagerness, however trifling the Causes were whence they first arose. Nay, however incredible it may seem, the little Consequence of the matter in Debate was frequently given as a Reason for the Fierceness of the Contention, as thus: *If you loved me, sure you would never dispute with me such a Trifle as this.* The Answer to which is very obvious; for the Argument would hold equally on both sides, and was constantly retorted with some Addition, as—*I am sure I have much more Reason to say so, who am in the right.* During all these Disputes, *Paul* always kept strict Silence, and preserved an even Countenance without shewing the least visible Inclination to either Party. One day, however, when Madam had left the Room in a violent Fury, *Leonard* could not refrain from referring his Cause to his Friend. Was ever any thing so unreasonable, says he, as this Woman? What shall I do with her? I doat on her to Distraction; nor have I any Cause to complain of more than this Obstinacy in her Temper; whatever she asserts she will maintain against all the Reason and Conviction[2] in the World. Pray give me your Advice.—First, says *Paul*, I will give my Opinion, which is flatly that you are in the wrong; for supposing she is in the wrong, was the Subject of your Contention anywise material? What signified it whether you was married in a red or yellow Waistcoat? for that was your Dispute. Now suppose she was mistaken, as you love her you say so tenderly, and I believe she deserves it, would it not have been wiser to have yielded, tho' you certainly knew yourself in the right, than to give either her or yourself any Uneasiness? For my own part, if ever I marry, I am resolved to enter into an Agreement with my Wife, that in all Disputes (especially about Trifles) that Party who is most convinced they are right, shall always surrender the Victory: by which means we shall both be forward to give up the Cause. I own, said *Lennard*, my

2. Proof.

dear Friend, shaking him by the Hand, there is great Truth and Reason in what you say; and I will for the future endeavour to follow your Advice. They soon after broke up the Conversation, and *Lennard* going to his Wife, asked her pardon, and told her his Friend had convinced him he had been in the wrong. She immediately began a vast Encomium on *Paul*, in which he seconded her, and both agreed he was the worthiest and wisest Man upon Earth. When next they met, which was at Supper, tho' she had promised not to mention what her husband told her, she could not forbear casting the kindest and most affectionate Looks on *Paul*, and asked him with the sweetest Voice, whether she should help him to some Potted-Woodcock?—Potted Partridge, my Dear, you mean, says the Husband. My Dear, says she, I ask your Friend if he will eat any potted Woodcock; and I'm sure I must know, who potted it. I think I should know too, who shot them, reply'd the Husband, and I am convinced I have not seen a Woodcock this Year; however, tho' I know I am in the right I submit, and the potted Partridge is potted Woodcock, if you desire to have it so. It is equal to me, says she, whether it is one or the other; but you would persuade one out of one's Senses; to be sure you are always in the right in your own Opinion; but your Friend I believe knows which he is eating. *Paul* answered nothing, and the Dispute continued as usual the greatest part of the Evening. The next Morning the Lady accidentally meeting *Paul*, and being convinced he was her Friend, and of her side, accosted him thus:—I am certain, Sir, you have long since wonder'd at the Unreasonableness of my Husband. He is indeed in other respects a good sort of Man; but so positive, that no Woman but one of my complying Temper could possible live with him. Why last Night now, was ever any Creature so unreasonable?—I am certain you must condemn him—Pray answer me, was he not in the wrong? *Paul*, after a short Silence, spoke as follows: I am sorry, Madam, that as Good-manners obliges me to answer against my Will, so an Adherence to Truth forces me to declare myself of a different Opinion. To be plain and honest, you was entirely in the wrong; the Cause I own not worth disputing, but the Bird was undoubtedly a Partridge. O Sir, reply'd the Lady, I cannot possibly help your Taste.—Madam, returned *Paul*, that is very little material; for had it been otherwise, a Husband might have expected Submission.—Indeed! Sir, says she, I assure you!— Yes, Madam, cry'd he, he might from a Person of your excellent Understanding; and pardon me for saying such a Condescension would have shewn a Superiority of Sense even to your Husband himself.—But, dear Sir, said she, why should I submit when I am in the right?—For that very Reason, answer'd he, it would be the greatest Instance of Affection imaginable: for can any thing be a greater Object of our Compassion than a Person we love, in the wrong? Ay, but I should endeavour, said she, to set him right. Pardon me, Madam, answered *Paul*, I will apply to your own Experience, if you ever found your Arguments had that effect. The more our Judgments err, the less we are willing to own it: for my own part, I have always observed the Persons who maintain the worst

side in any Contest, are the warmest. Why, says she, I must confess
there is Truth in what you say, and I will endeavour to practice it. The
Husband then coming in, *Paul* departed. And *Lennard* approaching his
Wife with an Air of Good-humour, told her he was sorry for their foolish
Dispute the last Night: but he was now convinced of his Error. She
answered smiling, she believed she owed his Condescension to his Complacence;[3] that she was ashamed to think a Word had past on so silly an
Occasion, especially as she was satisfy'd she had been mistaken. A little
Contention followed, but with the utmost Goodwill to each other, and
was concluded by her asserting that *Paul* had thoroughly convinced her
she had been in the wrong. Upon which they both united in the Praises
of their common Friend.

'*Paul* now past his time with great Satisfaction; these Disputes being
much less frequent as well as shorter than usual: but the Devil, or some
unlucky Accident in which perhaps the Devil had no hand, shortly put
an end to his Happiness. He was now eternally the private Referee of
every Difference; in which after having perfectly as he thought established the Doctrine of Submission, he never scrupled to assure both
privately that they were in the right in every Argument, as before he had
followed the contrary Method. One day a violent Litigation happened
in his Absence, and both Parties agreed to refer it to his Decision. The
Husband professing himself sure the Decision would be in his favour,
the Wife answer'd, he might be mistaken; for she believed his Friend
was convinced how seldom she was to blame—and that if he knew all.—
The Husband reply'd—My Dear, I have no desire of any Retrospect, but
I believe if you knew all too, you would not imagine my Friend so
entirely on your side. Nay, says she, since you provoke me, I will mention one Instance. You may remember our Dispute about sending *Jacky*
to School in cold Weather, which Point I gave up to you from mere
Compassion, knowing myself to be in the right, and *Paul* himself told
me afterwards, he thought me so. My Dear, replied the Husband, I will
not scruple[4] your Veracity; but I assure you solemnly, on my applying
to him, he gave it absolutely on my side, and said he would have acted
in the same manner. They then proceeded to produce numberless other
Instances, in all which *Paul* had, on Vows of Secrecy, given his Opinion
on both sides. In the Conclusion, both believing each other, they fell
severely on the Treachery of *Paul*, and agreed that he had been the
occasion of almost every Dispute which had fallen out between them.
They then became extremely loving, and so full of Condescension on
both sides, that they vyed with each other in censuring their own Conduct, and jointly vented their Indignation on *Paul*, whom the Wife,
fearing a bloody Consequence, earnestly entreated her Husband to suffer
quietly to depart the next Day, which was the time fixed for his Return
to Quarters, and then drop his Acquaintance.

'However ungenerous this Behaviour in *Lennard* may be esteemed,

3. Desire to please.   4. Doubt.

his Wife obtained a Promise from him (tho' with difficulty) to follow her Advice; but they both exprest such unusual Coldness that day to *Paul*, that he, who was quick of Apprehension, taking *Lennard* aside, prest him so home, that he at last discovered the Secret. *Paul* acknowledged the Truth, but told him the Design with which he had done it—To which the other answered, he would have acted more friendly to have let him into the whole Design; for that he might have assured himself of his Secrecy. *Paul* reply'd, with some Indignation, he had given him a sufficient Proof how capable he was of concealing a Secret from his Wife. *Lennard* returned with some Warmth—He had more reason to upbraid him, for that he had caused most of the Quarrels between them by his strange Conduct, and might (if they had not discovered the Affair to each other) have been the Occasion of their Separation. *Paul* then said—' But something now happened, which put a stop to *Dick's* Reading, and of which we shall treat in the next Chapter.

Chapter XI

In which the History is continued.

Joseph Andrews had borne with great Uneasiness the Impertinence of Beau *Didapper* to *Fanny*, who had been talking pretty freely to her, and offering her Settlements[1]; but the Respect to the Company had restrained him from interfering, whilst the Beau confined himself to the Use of his Tongue only; but the said Beau watching an Opportunity whilst the Ladies Eyes were disposed another way, offered a Rudeness to her with his Hands; which *Joseph* no sooner perceived than he presented him with so sound a Box on the Ear, that it conveyed him several Paces from where he stood. The Ladies immediately skreamed out, rose from their Chairs, and the Beau, as soon as he recovered himself, drew his Hanger, which *Adams* observing, snatched up the Lid of a Pot in his left hand, and covering himself with it as with a Shield without any Weapon of Offence in his other Hand, stept in before *Joseph*, and exposed himself to the enraged Beau, who threatened such Perdition and Destruction, that it frighted the Women, who were all got in a huddle together, out of their Wits; even to hear his Denunciations of Vengeance. *Joseph* was of a different Complexion,[2] and begged *Adams* to let his Rival come on; for he had a good Cudgel in his Hand, and did not fear him. *Fanny* now fainted into Mrs. *Adams's* Arms, and the whole Room was in Confusion, when Mr. *Booby* passing by *Adams*, who lay snug under the Pot-Lid, came up to *Didapper*, and insisted on his sheathing the Hanger, promising he should have Satisfaction; which *Joseph* declared he would give him, and fight him at any Weapon whatever. The Beau now sheathed his Hanger, and taking out a Pocket-Glass, and vowing Vengeance all the Time, re-adjusted his Hair; the Parson deposited his Shield, and

1. Contractual payments to be made in return for her becoming his kept mistress (see above, p. 161).

2. Temperament.

Joseph running to *Fanny*, soon brought her back to Life. Lady *Booby* chid *Joseph* for his Insult on *Didapper*; but he answered he would have attacked an Army in the same Cause. 'What Cause?' said the Lady. 'Madam,' answered *Joseph*, 'he was rude to that young Woman.'—'What,' says the Lady, 'I suppose he would have kissed the Wench; and is a Gentleman to be struck for such an Offer? I must tell you, *Joseph*, these Airs do not become you.'—'Madam,' said Mr. *Booby*, 'I saw the whole Affair, and I do not commend my Brother; for I cannot perceive why he should take upon him to be this Girl's Champion.'—'I can commend him,' says *Adams*, 'he is a brave Lad; and it becomes any Man to be the Champion of the Innocent; and he must be the basest Coward, who would not vindicate a Woman with whom he is on the Brink of Marriage.'—'Sir,' says Mr. *Booby*, 'my Brother is not a proper Match for such a young Woman as this.'—'No,' says Lady *Booby*, 'nor do you, Mr. *Adams*, act in your proper Character, by encouraging any such Doings; and I am very much surprized you should concern yourself in it. I think your Wife and Family your properer Care.'—'Indeed, Madam, your Ladyship says very true,' answered Mrs. *Adams*, 'he talks a pack of Nonsense, that the whole Parish are his Children. I am sure I don't understand what he means by it; it would make some Women suspect he had gone astray: but I acquit him of that; I can read Scripture as well as he; and I never found that the Parson was obliged to provide for other Folks Children; and besides he is but a poor Curate, and hath little enough, as your Ladyship knows, for me and mine.'—'You say very well, Mrs. *Adams*,' quoth the Lady *Booby*, who had not spoke a Word to her before, 'you seem to be a very sensible Woman; and I assure you, your Husband is acting a very foolish Part, and opposing his own Interest; seeing my Nephew is violently set against this Match: and indeed I can't blame him; it is by no means one suitable to our Family.' In this manner the Lady proceeded with Mrs. *Adams*, whilst the Beau hopped about the Room, shaking his Head; partly from Pain, and partly from Anger; and *Pamela* was chiding *Fanny* for her Assurance,[3] in aiming at such a Match as her Brother.—Poor *Fanny* answered only with her Tears, which had long since begun to wet her Handkerchief; which *Joseph* perceiving, took her by the Arm, and wrapping it in his, carried her off, swearing he would own no Relation to any one who was an Enemy to her he lov'd more than all the World. He went out with *Fanny* under his left Arm, brandishing a Cudgel in his right, and neither Mr. *Booby* nor the Beau thought proper to oppose him. Lady *Booby* and her company made a very short stay behind him; for the Lady's Bell now summoned them to dress; for which they had just time before Dinner.

Adams seemed now very much dejected, which his Wife perceiving, began to apply some matrimonial Balsam. She told him he had Reason to be concerned; for that he had probably ruined his Family with his foolish Tricks: But perhaps he was grieved for the Loss of his two Children, *Joseph* and *Fanny*. His eldest Daughter went on:—'Indeed Father,

---

3. Presumption.

it is very hard to bring Strangers here to eat your Children's Bread out of their Mouths.—You have kept them ever since they came home; and for any thing I see to the contrary may keep them a Month longer: Are you obliged to give her Meat, tho'f she was never so handsome? But I don't see she is so much handsomer than other People. If People were to be kept for their Beauty, she would scarce fare better than her Neighbours, I believe.—As for Mr. *Joseph*, I have nothing to say, he is a young Man of honest Principles, and will pay some time or another for what he hath: But for the Girl,—Why doth she not return to her Place she ran away from? I would not give such a Vagabond Slut a Halfpenny, tho' I had a Million of Money; no, tho' she was starving.' 'Indeed but I would,' cries little *Dick*; 'and Father, rather than poor *Fanny* shall be starved, I will give her all this Bread and Cheese.'—(*Offering what he held in his Hand.*)—*Adams* smiled on the Boy, and told him he rejoiced to see he was a Christian; and that if he had a Halfpenny in his Pocket he would have given it him; telling him, it was his Duty to look upon all his Neighbours as his Brothers and Sisters, and love them accordingly. 'Yes, Papa,' says he, 'I love her better than my Sisters; for she is handsomer than any of them.' 'Is she so, Saucebox?' says the Sister, giving him a Box on the Ear, which the Father would probably have resented, had not *Joseph*, *Fanny*, and the Pedlar, at that Instant, returned together.—*Adams* bid his Wife prepare some Food for their Dinner; she said, 'truly she could not, she had something else to do.' *Adams* rebuked her for disputing his Commands, and quoted many Texts of Scripture to prove, *that the Husband is the Head of the Wife, and she is to submit and obey.*[4] The Wife answered, 'it was Blasphemy to talk Scripture out of Church; that such things were very proper to be said in the Pulpit: but that it was prophane to talk them in common Discourse.' *Joseph* told Mr. *Adams* 'he was not come with any Design to give him or Mrs. *Adams* any trouble; but to desire the Favour of all their Company to the *George* (an Alehouse in the Parish,) where he had bespoke a Piece of Bacon and Greens for their Dinner.' Mrs. *Adams*, who was a very good sort of Woman, only rather too strict in Œconomicks,[5] readily accepted this Invitation, as did the Parson himself by her Example; and away they all walked together, not omitting little *Dick*, to whom *Joseph* gave a Shilling, when he heard of his intended Liberality to *Fanny*.

Chapter XII

Where the good-natur'd Reader will see something which will give him no great Pleasure.

The Pedlar had been very inquisitive from the time he had first heard that the great House in this Parish belonged to the Lady *Booby*; and had learnt that she was the Widow of Sir *Thomas*, and that Sir *Thomas* had

---

4. "Wives, submit yourselves unto your own husbands, as unto the Lord. For the husband is the head of the wife, even as Christ is the head of the church" (Ephesians 5:22–23). Similar sentiments are found in I Peter 3:1 and Colossians 3:18.

5. Household management; the term retained this limited meaning and Latin spelling until the nineteenth century.

bought *Fanny*, at about the Age of three or four Years, of a travelling
Woman; and now their homely but hearty Meal was ended, he told
Fanny, he believed he could acquaint her with her Parents. The whole
Company, especially she herself, started at this Offer of the Pedlar's.—
He then proceeded thus, while they all lent their strictest Attention:
'Tho' I am now contented with this humble way of getting my Liveli-
hood, I was formerly a Gentleman; for so all those of my Profession are
called. In a word, I was a Drummer in an *Irish* Regiment of Foot. Whilst
I was in this honourable Station, I attended an Officer of our Regiment
into *England* a recruiting. In our March from *Bristol* to *Froome* (for
since the Decay of the Woollen Trade, the clothing Towns have furnished the Army with a great number of Recruits)[1] we overtook on the
Road a Woman who seemed to be about thirty Years old, or thereabouts, not very handsome; but well enough for a Soldier. As we came
up to her, she mended her Pace, and falling into Discourse with our
Ladies (for every Man of the Party, namely, a Serjeant, two private Men,
and a Drum, were provided with their Woman, except myself) she continued to travel on with us. I perceiving she must fall to my Lot, advanced
presently to her, made Love to her in our military way, and quickly
succeeded to my Wishes. We struck a Bargain within a Mile, and lived
together as Man and Wife to her dying Day.'—'I suppose,' says *Adams*
interrupting him, 'you were married with a Licence: For I don't see how
you could contrive to have the Banns published while you were marching from Place to Place.'—'No, Sir,' said the Pedlar, 'we took a Licence
to go to Bed together, without any Banns.'—'Ay, ay,' said the Parson,
'*ex Necessitate*, a Licence may be allowable enough; but surely, surely,
the other is the more regular and eligible Way.'—The Pedlar proceeded
thus, 'She returned with me to our Regiment, and removed with us from
Quarters to Quarters, till at last, whilst we lay at *Galloway*, she fell ill of
a Fever, and died. When she was on her Death-bed she called me to
her, and crying bitterly, declared she could not depart this World without discovering a Secret to me, which she said was the only Sin which
sat heavy on her Heart. She said she had formerly travelled in a Company of Gipsies, who had made a Practice of stealing away Children;[2]
that for her own part, she had been only once guilty of the Crime; which
she said she lamented more than all the rest of her Sins, since probably
it might have occasioned the Death of the Parents: For, added she, it is
almost impossible to describe the Beauty of the young Creature, which
was about a Year and half old when I kidnapped it. We kept her (for she
was a Girl) above two Years in our Company, when I sold her myself
for three Guineas to Sir *Thomas Booby* in *Somersetshire*. Now, you know

---

1. Because of widespread smuggling of raw wool
to France, a developing preference for East Anglia
worsteds, and the rise of the more efficient Yorkshire industry, the once premier West Country
broadcloth manufactury had been in recession
since the 1720's. The peddler anachronistically
alludes to wholesale enlistments for the war that
began in 1739 from the distressed ancient Somer-
set wool center of Frome, near Bath.
2. Gypsy bands often took in other itinerants and
vagabonds. They were widely believed to steal
infants, though few cases have been documented,
most notably the brief abduction of Adam Smith,
the future political economist, in 1726.

whether there are any more of that Name in this County.'—'Yes,' says *Adams*, 'there are several *Boobys* who are Squires; but I believe no Baronet now alive, besides it answers so exactly in every Point there is no room for Doubt; but you have forgot to tell us the Parents from whom the Child was stolen.'—'Their Name,' answered the Pedlar, 'was *Andrews*. They lived about thirty Miles from the Squire; and she told me, that I might be sure to find them out by one Circumstance; for that they had a Daughter of a very strange Name, *Paměla* or *Paměla*; some pronounced it one way, and some the other.'[3] *Fanny*, who had changed Colour at the first mention of the Name, now fainted away, *Joseph* turned pale, and poor *Dicky* began to roar; the Parson fell on his Knees and ejaculated many Thanksgivings that this Discovery had been made before the dreadful Sin of Incest was committed; and the Pedlar was struck with Amazement, not being able to account for all this Confusion, the Cause of which was presently opened by the Parson's Daughter, who was the only unconcerned Person; (for the Mother was chaffing *Fanny's* Temples, and taking the utmost care of her) and indeed *Fanny* was the only Creature whom the Daughter would not have pitied in her Situation; wherein, tho' we compassionate her ourselves, we shall leave her for a little while, and pay a short Visit to Lady *Booby*.

Chapter XIII

The History returning to the Lady Booby, *gives some Account of the terrible Conflict in her Breast between Love and Pride; with what happened on the present Discovery.*

The Lady sat down with her Company to Dinner: but eat nothing. As soon as her Cloth was removed, she whispered *Pamela*, that she was taken a little ill, and desired her to entertain her Husband and Beau *Didapper*. She then went up into her Chamber, sent for *Slipslop*, threw herself on the Bed, in the Agonies of Love, Rage, and Despair; nor could she conceal these boiling Passions longer, without bursting. *Slipslop* now approached her Bed, and asked how her Ladyship did; but instead of revealing her Disorder, as she intended, she entered into a long Encomium on the Beauty and Virtues of *Joseph Andrews*; ending at last with expressing her Concern, that so much Tenderness should be thrown away on so despicable an Object as *Fanny*. *Slipslop* well knowing how to humour her Mistress's Frenzy, proceeded to repeat, with Exaggeration if possible, all her Mistress had said, and concluded with a Wish, that *Joseph* had been a Gentleman, and that she could see her Lady in the Arms of such a Husband. The Lady then started from the Bed, and taking a Turn or two cross the Room, cry'd out with a deep Sigh,—*Sure*

---

3. A hit at the improbably exotic name of the humble farmer's daughter, taken from a heroine of Sir Philip Sidney's *Arcadia* (1590), and the current uncertainty of its pronunciation. Richardson accented the first syllable, but the second pronunciation, grounded in the name's Greek derivation (signifying "all sweetness"), was more classical. Pope scanned it thus in his "Epistle to Miss Blount, with the Works of Voiture" (1712), l. 49.

he would make any Woman happy.—'Your Ladyship,' says she, 'would be the happiest Woman in the World with him.—A fig for Custom and Nonsense. What *vails* what People say? Shall I be afraid of eating Sweet-meats, because People may say I have a sweet Tooth? If I had a mind to marry a Man, all the World should not hinder me. Your Ladyship hath no Parents to *tutelar* your *Infections*; besides he is of your Ladyship's Family now, and as good a Gentleman as any in the Country; and why should not a Woman follow her Mind as well as a Man? Why should not your Ladyship marry the Brother, as well as your Nephew the Sister? I am sure, if it was a *fragrant* Crime I would not persuade your Ladyship to it.'—'But, dear *Slipslop*,' answered the Lady, 'if I could prevail on myself to commit such a Weakness, there is that cursed *Fanny* in the way, whom the Idiot, O how I hate and despise him—' 'She, a little ugly Mynx,' cries *Slipslop*, 'leave her to me.—I suppose your Ladyship hath heard of *Joseph's fitting* with one of Mr. *Didapper's* Servants about her; and his Master hath ordered them to carry her away by force this Evening. I'll take care they shall not want Assistance. I was talking with his Gentleman, who was below just when your Ladyship sent for me.'—'Go back,' says the Lady *Booby*, 'this Instant; for I expect Mr. *Didapper* will soon be going. Do all you can; for I am resolved this Wench shall not be in our Family; I will endeavour to return to the Company; but let me know as soon as she is carried off.' *Slipslop* went away, and her Mistress began to arraign her own Conduct in the following Manner:

'What am I doing? How do I suffer this Passion to creep imperceptibly upon me! How many Days are past since I could have submitted to ask myself the Question?—Marry a Footman! Distraction! Can I afterwards bear the Eyes of my Acquaintance? But I can retire from them; retire with one in whom I propose more Happiness than the World without him can give me! Retire—to feed continually on Beauties, which my inflamed Imagination sickens with eagerly gazing on; to satisfy every Appetite, every Desire, with their utmost Wish.—Ha! and do I doat thus on a Footman! I despise, I detest my Passion.—Yet why? Is he not generous, gentle, kind?—Kind to whom? to the meanest Wretch, a Creature below my Consideration. Doth he not?—Yes, he doth prefer her; curse his Beauties, and the little low Heart that possesses them; which can basely descend to this despicable Wench, and be ungratefully deaf to all the Honours I do him.—And can I then love this Monster? No, I will tear his Image from my Bosom, tread on him, spurn him. I will have those pitiful Charms which now I despise, mangled in my sight; for I will not suffer the little Jade I hate to riot in the Beauties I contemn. No, tho' I despise him myself; tho' I would spurn him from my Feet, was he to languish at them, no other should taste the Happiness I scorn. Why do I say Happiness? To me it would be Misery.—To sacrifice my Reputation, my Character, my Rank in Life, to the Indulgence of a mean and a vile Appetite.—How I detest the Thought! How much more exquisite is the Pleasure resulting from the Reflection of Virtue and Prudence, than the faint Relish of what flows from Vice and Folly! Whither did I suffer this improper, this mad Passion to hurry me, only by neglect-ing to summon the Aids of Reason to my Assistance? Reason, which hath now set before me my Desires in their proper Colours, and imme-diately helped me to expel them. Yes, I thank Heaven and my Pride, I have now perfectly conquered this unworthy Passion; and if there was no Obstacle in its way, my Pride would disdain any Pleasures which could be the Consequence of so base, so mean, so vulgar—' *Slipslop* returned at this Instant in a violent Hurry, and with the utmost Eager-ness, cry'd out,—O, Madam, I have strange News. *Tom* the Footman is just come from the *George*; where it seems *Joseph* and the rest of them are a *jinketting*;[1] and he says, there is a strange Man who hath discovered that *Fanny* and *Joseph* are Brother and Sister.'—'How, *Slipslop*,' cries the Lady in a Surprize.—'I had not time, Madam,' cries *Slipslop*, 'to enquire about *Particles*, but *Tom* says, it is most certainly true.'

This unexpected Account entirely obliterated all those admirable Reflections which the supreme Power of Reason had so wisely made just before. In short, when Despair, which had more share in producing the Resolutions of Hatred we have seen taken, began to retreat, the Lady hesitated a Moment, and then forgetting all the Purport of her Solilo-quy, dismissed her Woman again, with Orders to bid *Tom* attend her in the Parlour, whither she now hastened to acquaint *Pamela* with the News. *Pamela* said, she could not believe it: For she had never heard that her Mother had lost any Child, or that she had ever had any more than *Joseph* and herself. The Lady flew into a violent Rage with her, and talked of Upstarts and disowning Relations, who had so lately been on a level with her. *Pamela* made no answer: But her husband, taking up her Cause, severely reprimanded his Aunt for her Behaviour to his Wife; he told her, if it had been earlier in the Evening, she should not have staid a Moment longer in her House; that he was convinced, if this young Woman could be proved her Sister, she would readily embrace her as such; and he himself would do the same: He then desired the Fellow might be sent for, and the young Woman with him; which Lady *Booby* immediately ordered, and thinking proper to make some Apology to *Pamela* for what she had said, it was readily accepted, and all things reconciled.

The Pedlar now attended, as did *Fanny*, and *Joseph* who would not quit her; the Parson likewise was induced, not only by Curiosity, of which he had no small Portion, but by his Duty, as he apprehended, to follow them: for he continued all the way to exhort them, who were now breaking their Hearts, to offer up Thanksgivings, and be joyful for so miraculous an Escape.

When they arrived at *Booby-Hall*, they were presently called into the Parlour, where the Pedlar repeated the same Story he had told before, and insisted on the Truth of every Circumstance; so that all who heard him were extremely well satisfied of the Truth, except *Pamela*, who

---

1. Partying (junketing).

imagined, as she had never heard either of her Parents mention such an Accident, that it must be certainly false; and except the Lady *Booby*, who suspected the Falshood of the Story, from her ardent Desire that it should be true; and *Joseph* who feared its Truth, from his earnest Wishes that it might prove false.

Mr. *Booby* now desired them all to suspend their Curiosity and absolute Belief or Disbelief, till the next Morning, when he expected old Mr. *Andrews* and his Wife to fetch himself and *Pamela* home in his Coach, and then they might be certain of perfectly knowing the Truth or Falshood of this Relation; in which he said, as there were many strong Circumstances to induce their Credit, so he could not perceive any Interest the Pedlar could have in inventing it, or in endeavouring to impose such a Falshood on them.

The Lady *Booby*, who was very little used to such Company, entertained them all, *viz.* Her Nephew, his Wife, her Brother and Sister, the Beau, and the Parson, with great Good-humour at her own Table. As to the Pedlar, she ordered him to be made as welcome as possible, by her Servants. All the Company in the Parlour, except the disappointed Lovers, who sat sullen and silent, were full of Mirth: For Mr. *Booby* had prevailed on *Joseph* to ask Mr. *Didapper's* pardon; with which he was perfectly satisfied. Many Jokes past between the Beau and the Parson, chiefly on each other's Dress; these afforded much Diversion to the Company. *Pamela* chid her Brother *Joseph* for the Concern which he exprest at discovering a new Sister. She said, if he loved *Fanny* as he ought, with a pure Affection, he had no Reason to lament being related to her.—Upon which *Adams* began to discourse on *Platonic* Love; whence he made a quick Transition to the Joys in the next World, and concluded with strongly asserting that there was no such thing as Pleasure in this. At which *Pamela* and her Husband smiled on one another.

This happy Pair proposing to retire (for no other Person gave the least Symptom of desiring Rest) they all repaired to several Beds provided for them in the same House; nor was *Adams* himself suffered to go home, it being a stormy Night. *Fanny* indeed often begged she might go home with the Parson; but her Stay was so strongly insisted on, that she at last, by *Joseph's* Advice, consented.

Chapter XIV

Containing several curious Night-Adventures,[1] *in which Mr.* Adams *fell into many Hair-breadth 'Scapes, partly owing to his Goodness, and partly to his Inadvertency.*

About an Hour after they had all separated (it being now past three in the Morning) Beau *Didapper*, whose Passion for *Fanny* permitted him not to close his Eyes, but had employed his Imagination in Contrivances how to satisfy his Desires, at last hit on a Method by which he hoped to

---

1. For the prototype of this episode in *Don Quixote*, see below, pp. 352–56.

effect it. He had ordered his Servant to bring him word where *Fanny* lay, and had received his Information; he therefore arose, put on his Breeches and Nightgown, and stole softly along the Gallery which led to her Apartment; and being come to the Door, as he imagined it, he opened it with the least Noise possible, and entered the Chamber. A Savour now invaded his Nostrils which he did not expect in the Room of so sweet a young Creature, and which might have probably had no good effect on a cooler Lover. However, he groped out the Bed with difficulty; for there was not a Glimpse of Light, and opening the Curtains,[2] he whispered in *Joseph's* Voice (for he was an excellent Mimick) '*Fanny*, my Angel, I am come to inform thee that I have discovered the Falshood of the Story we last Night heard. I am no longer thy Brother, but thy Lover; nor will I be delayed the Enjoyment of thee one Moment longer. You have sufficient Assurances of my Constancy not to doubt my marrying you, and it would be want of Love to deny me the possession of thy Charms.'—So saying, he disencumbered himself from the little Clothes he had on, and leaping into Bed, embraced his Angel, as he conceived her, with great Rapture. If he was surprized at receiving no Answer, he was no less pleased to find his Hug returned with equal Ardour. He remained not long in this sweet Confusion; for both he and his Paramour presently discovered their Error. Indeed it was no other than the accomplished *Slipslop* whom he had engaged; but tho' she immediately knew the Person whom she had mistaken for *Joseph*, he was at a loss to guess at the Representative of *Fanny*. He had so little seen or taken notice of this Gentlewoman, that Light itself would have afforded him no Assistance in his conjecture. Beau *Didapper* no sooner had perceived his Mistake, than he attempted to escape from the Bed with much greater Haste than he had made to it; but the watchful *Slipslop* prevented him. For that prudent Woman being disappointed of those delicious Offerings which her Fancy had promised her Pleasure, resolved to make an immediate Sacrifice to her Virtue. Indeed she wanted an Opportunity to heal some Wounds which her late Conduct had, she feared, given her Reputation; and as she had a wonderful Presence of Mind, she conceived the Person of the unfortunate Beau to be luckily thrown in her way to restore her Lady's Opinion of her impregnable Chastity. At that instant therefore, when he offered to leap from the Bed, she caught fast hold of his Shirt, at the same time roaring out. 'O thou Villain! who hast attacked my Chastity, and I believe ruined me in my Sleep; I will swear a Rape against thee, I will prosecute thee with the utmost Vengeance.' The Beau attempted to get loose, but she held him fast, and when he struggled, she cry'd out, 'Murther! Murther! Rape! Robbery! Ruin!' At which Words Parson *Adams*, who lay in the next Chamber, wakeful and meditating on the Pedlar's Discovery, jumped out of Bed, and without staying to put a rag of Clothes on, hastened into the Apartment whence the Cries proceeded. He made directly to the

---

2. Beds were canopied and curtained for privacy and warmth. Mimicry was one of Lord Hervey's talents.

Bed in the dark, where laying hold of the Beau's Skin (for *Slipslop* had torn his Shirt almost off) and finding his Skin extremely soft, and hearing him in a low Voice begging *Slipslop* to let him go, he no longer doubted but this was the young Woman in danger of ravishing, and immediately falling on the Bed, and laying hold on *Slipslop's* Chin, where he found a rough Beard, his Belief was confirmed; he therefore rescued the Beau, who presently made his Escape, and then turning towards *Slipslop*, receiv'd such a Cuff on his Chops, that his Wrath kindling instantly, he offered to return the Favour so stoutly, that had poor *Slipslop* received the Fist, which in the dark past by her and fell on the Pillow, she would most probably have given up the Ghost.—*Adams* missing his Blow, fell directly on *Slipslop*, who cuffed and scratched as well as she could; nor was he behind-hand with her, in his Endeavours, but happily the Darkness of the Night befriended her—She then cry'd she was a Woman; but *Adams* answered she was rather the Devil, and if she was, he would grapple with him; and being again irritated by another Stroke on his Chops, he gave her such a Remembrance in the Guts, that she began to roar loud enough to be heard all over the House. *Adams* then seizing her by the Hair (for her Double-clout had fallen off in the Scuffle) pinned her Head down to the Bolster, and then both called for lights together. The Lady *Booby*, who was as wakeful as any of her Guests, had been alarmed from the beginning; and, being a Woman of a bold Spirit, she slipt on a Nightgown, Petticoat and Slippers, and taking a Candle, which always burnt in her Chamber, in her Hand, she walked undauntedly to *Slipslop's* Room; where she entred just at the instant as *Adams* had discovered, by the two Mountains which *Slipslop* carried before her, that he was concerned with a Female. He then concluded her to be a Witch, and said he fancied those Breasts gave suck to a Legion of Devils. *Slipslop* seeing Lady *Booby* enter the Room, cried, *Help! or I am ravished*, with a most audible Voice, and *Adams* perceiving the Light, turned hastily and saw the Lady (as she did him) just as she came to the Feet of the Bed, nor did her Modesty, when she found the naked[3] Condition of *Adams*, suffer her to approach farther.—She then began to revile the Parson as the wickedest of all Men, and particularly railed at his Impudence in chusing her House for the Scene of his Debaucheries, and her own Woman for the Object of his Bestiality. Poor *Adams* had before discovered the Countenance of his Bedfellow, and now first recollecting he was naked, he was no less confounded than Lady *Booby* herself, and immediately whipt under the Bed-clothes, whence the chaste *Slipslop* endeavoured in vain to shut him out. Then putting forth his Head on which, by way of Ornament, he wore a Flannel Nightcap, he protested his Innocence, and asked ten thousand Pardons of Mrs. *Slipslop* for the Blows he had struck her, vowing he had mistaken her for a Witch. Lady *Booby* then, casting her Eyes on the Ground, observed something sparkle with great Lustre, which, when she had taken it up, appeared to be a very fine pair of diamond Buttons for the Sleeves.

3. Wearing only a nightshirt (see below, p. 262).

A little farther she saw lie the Sleeve itself of a Shirt with laced Ruffles. 'Heyday!' says she, 'what is the meaning of this?'—'O, Madam,' says *Slipslop*, 'I don't know what hath happened, I have been so terrified. Here may have been a dozen Men in the Room.' 'To whom belongs this laced Shirt and Jewels?' says the Lady.—Undoubtedly,' cries the Parson, 'to the young Gentleman whom I mistook for a Woman on coming into the Room, whence proceeded all the subsequent Mistakes; for if I had suspected him for a Man, I would have seized him had he been another *Hercules*, tho' indeed he seems rather to resemble *Hylas*.'[4] He then gave an Account of the Reason of his rising from Bed, and the rest, till the Lady came into the Room; at which, and the Figures of *Slipslop* and her Gallant, whose Heads only were visible at the opposite corners of the Bed, she could not refrain from Laughter, nor did *Slipslop* persist in accusing the Parson of any Motions toward a Rape. The Lady therefore desired him to return to his Bed as soon as she was departed, and then ordering *Slipslop* to rise and attend her in her own Room, she returned herself thither. When she was gone, *Adams* renewed his Petitions for Pardon to Mrs. *Slipslop*, who with a most Christian Temper not only forgave, but began to move with much Curtesy towards him, which he taking as a Hint to be gone, immediately quitted the Bed, and made the best of his way towards his own; but unluckily instead of turning to the right, he turned to the left, and went to the Apartment where *Fanny* lay, who (as the Reader may remember) had not slept a wink the preceding Night, and who was so hagged out with what had happen'd to her in the Day, that notwithstanding all Thoughts of her *Joseph*, she was fallen into so profound a Sleep, that all the Noise in the adjoining Room had not been able to disturb her. *Adams* groped out the bed, and turning the Clothes down softly, a Custom Mrs. *Adams* had long accustomed him to, crept in, and deposited his Carcase on the Bedpost, a Place which that good Woman had always assigned him.

As the Cat or Lapdog of some lovely Nymph for whom ten thousand Lovers languish, lies quietly by the side of the charming Maid, and ignorant of the Scene of Delight on which they repose meditates the future Capture of a Mouse, or Surprizal of a Plate of Bread and Butter: so *Adams*, lay by the side of *Fanny*, ignorant of the Paradise to which he was so near, nor could the Emanation of Sweets which flowed from her Breath, overpower the Fumes of Tobacco which played in the Parson's Nostrils. And now Sleep had not overtaken the good Man, when *Joseph*, who had secretly appointed *Fanny* to come to her at the break of Day, rapped softly at the Chamber-Door, which when he had repeated twice, *Adams* cry'd, *Come in, whoever you are. Joseph* thought he had mistaken the Door, tho' she had given him the most exact Directions; however, knowing his Friend's Voice, he opened it, and saw some female Vestments lying on a Chair. *Fanny* waking at the same instant, and stretching out her hand on *Adams's* Beard, she cry'd out,—'O Heavens!

---

4. The beauty of Hercules' favorite page, Hylas, cost him his life when infatuated water nymphs drew him into their spring. Hervey, the bisexual prototype of Didapper, was mocked by Pope and others as a "lady-lord" and "master-miss."

where am I?' 'Bless me! where am I?' said the Parson. Then *Fanny*
skreamed, *Adams* leapt out of Bed, and *Joseph* stood, as the Tragedians
call it, like the *Statue of Surprize.*[5] '*How came she into my Room?*' cry'd
Adams. '*How came you into hers?*' cry'd *Joseph*, in an Astonishment. 'I
know nothing of the matter,' answered *Adams*, 'but that she is a Vestal
for me. As I am a Christian, I know not whether she is a Man or Woman.
He is an Infidel who doth not believe in Witchcraft. They as surely exist
now as in the Days of *Saul.*[6] My Clothes are bewitched away too, and
Fanny's brought into their place.' For he still insisted he was in his own
Apartment; but *Fanny* denied it vehemently, and said his attempting to
persuade *Joseph* of such a Falshood, convinced her of his wicked Designs.
'How!' said *Joseph*, in a Rage, 'Hath he offered any Rudeness to you?'—
She answered, she could not accuse him of any more than villainously
stealing to Bed to her, which she thought Rudeness sufficient, and what
no Man would do without a wicked Intention. *Joseph's* great Opinion of
Adams was not easily to be staggered, and when he heard from *Fanny*
that no Harm had happened, he grew a little cooler; yet still he was
confounded, and as he knew the House, and that the Women's Apartments were on this side Mrs. *Slipslop's* Room, and the Men's on the
other, he was convinced that he was in *Fanny's* Chamber. Assuring
Adams, therefore, of this Truth, he begged him to give some Account
how he came there. *Adams* then, standing in his Shirt, which did not
offend *Fanny* as the Curtains of the Bed were drawn, related all that had
happened, and when he had ended, *Joseph* told him, it was plain he had
mistaken, by turning to the right instead of the left. 'Odso!' cries *Adams*,
'that's true, as sure as Sixpence, you have hit on the very thing.' He then
traversed the Room, rubbing his Hands, and begged *Fanny's* pardon,
assuring her he did not know whether she was Man or Woman. That
innocent Creature firmly believing all he said, told him, she was no
longer angry, and begged *Joseph* to conduct him into his own Apartment, where he should stay himself, till she had put her Clothes on.
Joseph and *Adams* accordingly departed, and the latter soon was convinced of the Mistake he had committed; however, whilst he was dressing himself, he often asserted he believed in the Power of Witchcraft
notwithstanding, and did not see how a Christian could deny it.[7]

Chapter XV

The Arrival of Gaffar and Gammar Andrews, *with another Person,
not much expected; and a perfect Solution of the Difficulties raised
by the Pedlar.*

As soon as *Fanny* was drest, *Joseph* returned to her, and they had a
long Conversation together, the Conclusion of which was, that if they

5. See above, p. 32, n. 6.
6. Saul employed the Witch of Endor to summon
the spirit of the dead prophet Samuel (I Samuel
28:7–25).
7. By this time, few educated Englishmen would
have agreed with Adams. In his *Essay on Witch-*

craft (1718), the Reverend (later Bishop) Francis
Hutchinson described it as a delusion. No one
had been tried for this offense since 1712, and the
laws enacted against it under Elizabeth and James
I were quietly repealed in 1736.

found themselves to be really Brother and Sister, they vowed a perpetual Celibacy, and to live together all their days, and indulge a *Platonick* Friendship for each other.

The Company were all very merry at Breakfast, and *Joseph* and *Fanny* rather more cheerful than the preceding Night. The Lady *Booby* produced the Diamond Button, which the Beau most readily owned, and alledged that he was very subject to walk in his Sleep. Indeed he was far from being ashamed of his Amour, and rather endeavoured to insinuate that more than was really true had past between him and the fair *Slipslop*.

Their Tea was scarce over, when News came of the Arrival of old Mr. *Andrews* and his Wife. They were immediately introduced and kindly received by the Lady *Booby*, whose Heart went now pit-a-pat, as did those of *Joseph* and *Fanny*. They felt perhaps little less Anxiety in this Interval than Œdipus himself whilst his Fate was revealing.[1]

Mr. *Booby* first open'd the Cause, by informing the old Gentleman that he had a Child in the Company more than he knew of, and taking *Fanny* by the Hand, told him, this was that Daughter of his who had been stolen away by Gypsies in her Infancy. Mr. *Andrews*, after expressing some Astonishment, assured his Honour that he had never lost a Daughter by Gypsies, nor ever had any other Children than *Joseph* and *Pamela*. These Words were a Cordial to the two Lovers; but had a different effect on Lady *Booby*. She ordered the Pedlar to be called, who recounted his Story as he had done before.—At the end of which, old Mrs. *Andrews* running to *Fanny*, embraced her, crying out, *She is, she is my Child*. The Company were all amazed at this Disagreement between the Man and his Wife; and the Blood had now forsaken the Cheeks of the Lovers, when the old Woman turning to her Husband, who was more surprized than all the rest, and having a little recovered her own Spirits, delivered herself as follows. 'You may remember, my Dear, when you went a Serjeant to *Gibraltar* you left me big with Child, you staid abroad you know upwards of three Years. In your Absence I was brought to bed, I verily believe of this Daughter, whom I am sure I have reason to remember, for I suckled her at this very Breast till the Day she was stolen from me. One Afternoon, when the Child was about a Year, or a Year and half old, or thereabouts, two Gipsy Women came to the Door, and offered to tell my Fortune. One of them had a Child in her Lap; I shewed them my Hand, and desired to know if you was ever to come home again, which I remember as well as if it was but yesterday, they faithfully promised me you should—I left the Girl in the Cradle, and went to draw them a Cup of Liquor, the best I had; when I returned with the Pot (I am sure I was not absent longer than whilst I am telling it to you) the Women were gone. I was afraid they had stolen something, and looked and looked, but to no purpose, and Heaven knows I had very little for them to steal. At last hearing the Child cry in the Cradle, I went

1. In Sophocles' *Oedipus Rex*, the tragedy reaches its climax with the arrival of the old herdsman from whom Oedipus learns his true parentage and hence discovers he has murdered his father and married his mother.

to take it up—but O *the living!*[2] how was I surprized to find, instead of
my own Girl that I had put into the Cradle, who was as fine a fat thriving
Child as you shall see in a Summer's Day, a poor sickly Boy, that did
not seem to have an Hour to live. I ran out, pulling my Hair off, and
crying like any mad after the Women, but never could hear a Word of
them from that Day to this. When I came back, the poor Infant (which
is our *Joseph* there, as stout as he now stands) lifted up its Eyes upon me
so piteously, that to be sure, notwithstanding my Passion, I could not
find in my heart to do it any mischief. A Neighbour of mine happening
to come in at the same time, and hearing the Case, advised me to take
care of this poor Child, and G— would perhaps one day restore me my
own. Upon which I took the Child up, and suckled it to be sure, all the
World as if it had been born of my own natural Body. And as true as I
am alive, in a little time I loved the Boy all to nothing as if it had been
my own Girl.—Well, as I was saying, Times growing very hard, I having
two Children, and nothing but my own Work, which was little enough,
G— knows, to maintain them, was obliged to ask Relief of the Parish;
but instead of giving it me, they removed me, by Justices Warrants,[3]
fifteen Miles to the Place where I now live, where I had not been long
settled before you came home. *Joseph* (for that was the Name I gave him
myself—the Lord knows whether he was baptized or no, or by what
Name) *Joseph*, I say, seemed to me to be about five Years old when you
returned; for I believe he is two or three Years older than our Daughter
here; (for I am thoroughly convinced she is the same) and when you saw
him you said he was a chopping[4] Boy, without ever minding his Age;
and so I seeing you did not suspect any thing of the matter, thought I
might e'en as well keep it to myself, for fear you should not love him as
well as I did. And all this is veritably true, and I will take my Oath of it
before any Justice in the Kingdom.'

The Pedlar, who had been summoned by the Order of Lady *Booby*,
listened with the utmost Attention to Gammar *Andrews's* Story, and
when she had finished, asked her if the supposititious Child had no
Mark on its Breast? To which she answered, 'Yes, he had as fine a Strawberry as ever grew in a Garden.' This *Joseph* acknowledged, and unbut-
toning his Coat, at the Intercession of the Company, shewed to them.
'Well,' says Gaffar *Andrews*, who was a comical sly old Fellow, and very
likely desired to have no more Children than he could keep,[5] 'you have
proved, I think, very plainly that this Boy doth not belong to us; but how
are you certain that the Girl is ours?' The Parson then brought the Pedlar
forward, and desired him to repeat the Story which he had communicated to him the preceding Day at the Alehouse; which he complied

---

2. A truncated and therefore innocuous version
of the oath "Oh the living God!"
3. Evidently Andrews had not gained a settlement
(p. 221, n. 3) in the parish where he left his
family; as a soldier, he would be barred by law
from obtaining one. Mrs. Andrews was relatively
fortunate, since she could have been legally

removed as "likely to be chargeable to the Parish"
as soon as her husband left the country. Removal
was by order of two justices, to the place of last
legal settlement.
4. Big and strong.
5. Support.

with, and related what the Reader, as well as Mr. *Adams*, hath seen before. He then confirmed, from his Wife's Report, all the Circumstances of the Exchange, and of the Strawberry on *Joseph's* Breast. At the Repetition of the Word *Strawberry*, *Adams*, who had seen it without any Emotion, started, and cry'd, *Bless me! something comes into my Head.* But before he had time to bring any thing out, a Servant called him forth. When he was gone, the Pedlar assured *Joseph*, that his Parents were Persons of much greater Circumstances than those he had hitherto mistaken for such; for that he had been stolen from a Gentleman's House, by those whom they call Gypsies, and had been kept by them during a whole Year, when looking on him as in a dying Condition, they had exchanged him for the other healthier Child, in the manner before related. He said, as to the Name of his Father, his Wife had either never known or forgot it; but that she had acquainted him he lived about forty Miles from the Place where the Exchange had been made, and which way, promising to spare no Pains in endeavouring with him to discover the Place.

But Fortune, which seldom doth good or ill, or makes Men happy or miserable by halves, resolved to spare him this Labour. The Reader may please to recollect, that Mr. *Wilson* had intended a Journey to the West, in which he was to pass through Mr. *Adams's* Parish, and had promised to call on him. He was now arrived at the Lady *Booby's* Gates for that purpose, being directed thither from the Parson's House, and had sent in the Servant whom we have above seen call Mr. *Adams* forth. This had no sooner mentioned the Discovery of a stolen Child, and had uttered the word *Strawberry*, than Mr. Wilson, with Wildness in his Looks, and the utmost Eagerness in his Words, begged to be shev.ed into the Room, where he entered without the least Regard to any of the Company but *Joseph*, and embracing him with a Complexion all pale and trembling, desired to see the Mark on his Breast; the Parson followed him capering, rubbing his Hands, and crying out, *Hic est quem quæris, inventus est,* &c.[6] *Joseph* complied with the Request of Mr. *Wilson*, who no sooner saw the Mark, than abandoning himself to the most extravagant Rapture of Passion, he embraced *Joseph*, with inexpressible Extasy, and cried out in Tears of Joy, *I have discovered my Son, I have him again in my Arms.* *Joseph* was not sufficiently apprized yet, to taste the same Delight with his Father, (for so in reality he was;) however, he returned some Warmth to his Embraces: But he no sooner perceived from his Father's Account, the Agreement of every Circumstance, of Person, Time, and Place, than he threw himself at his Feet, and embracing his Knees, with Tears begged his Blessing, which was given with much Affection, and received with such Respect, mixed with such Tenderness on both sides, that it affected all present: But none so much as Lady *Booby*, who left the Room in an Agony, which was but too much perceived, and not very charitably accounted for by some of the Company.

6. "Here is whom you seek; he is found." Removing the bar to lovers' happiness by a final discovery of birth through a sign or token was a cliché of Roman comedy and Greek romance.

Chapter XVI

Being the last. In which this true History is brought to a happy Conclusion.

Fanny was very little behind her *Joseph*, in the Duty she exprest towards her Parents; and the Joy she evidenced in discovering them. Gammar *Andrews* kiss'd her, and said she was heartily glad to see her: But for her part she could never love any one better than *Joseph*. Gaffar *Andrews* testified no remarkable Emotion, he blessed and kissed her, but complained bitterly, that he wanted his Pipe, not having had a Whiff that Morning.

Mr. *Booby*, who knew nothing of his aunt's Fondness, imputed her abrupt Departure to her Pride, and Disdain of the Family into which he was married; he was therefore desirous to be gone with the utmost Celerity: And now, having congratulated Mr. *Wilson* and *Joseph* on the Discovery, he saluted *Fanny*, called her Sister, and introduced her as such to *Pamela*, who behaved with great Decency on the Occasion.

He now sent a Message to his Aunt, who returned, that she wished him a good Journey; but was too disordered to see any Company: He therefore prepared to set out, having invited Mr. *Wilson* to his House, and *Pamela* and *Joseph* both so insisted on his complying, that he at last consented, having first obtained a Messenger from Mr. *Booby*, to acquaint his Wife with the News; which, as he knew it would render her completely happy, he could not prevail on himself to delay a moment in acquainting her with.

The Company were ranged in this manner. The two old People with their two Daughters rode in the Coach, the Squire, Mr. *Wilson*, *Joseph*, Parson *Adams*, and the Pedlar proceeded on Horseback.

In their way *Joseph* informed his Father of his intended Match with *Fanny*; to which, tho' he expressed some Reluctance at first, on the Eagerness of his Son's Instances he consented, saying if she was so good a Creature as she appeared, and he described her, he thought the Disadvantages of Birth and Fortune might be compensated. He however insisted on the Match being deferred till he had seen his Mother; in which *Joseph* perceiving him positive, with great Duty obeyed him, to the great delight of Parson *Adams*, who by these means saw an Opportunity of fulfilling the Church Forms, and marrying his Parishoners without a Licence.

Mr. *Adams* greatly exulting on this Occasion, (for such Ceremonies were Matters of no small moment with him) accidentally gave Spurs to his Horse, which the generous Beast disdaining, for he was high of Mettle, and had been used to more expert Riders than the Gentleman who at present bestrode him: for whose Horsemanship he had perhaps some Contempt, immediately ran away full speed, and played so many antic Tricks, that he tumbled the Parson from his Back; which *Joseph* perceiving, came to his Relief. This Accident afforded infinite Merriment to the Servants, and no less frighted poor *Fanny*, who beheld him as he past by the Coach; but the Mirth of the one, and Terror of the other were soon determined,[1] when the Parson declared he had received no Damage.

The Horse having freed himself from his unworthy Rider, as he probably thought him, proceeded to make the best of his way: but was stopped by a Gentleman and his Servants, who were travelling the opposite way; and were now at a little distance from the Coach. They soon met; and as one of the Servants delivered *Adams* his Horse, his Master hailed him, and *Adams* looking up, presently recollected he was the Justice of Peace before whom he and *Fanny* had made their Appearance. The Parson presently saluted him very kindly; and the Justice informed him, that he had found the Fellow who attempted to swear against him and the young Woman the very next day, and had committed him to *Salisbury* Goal, where he was charged with many Robberies.

Many Compliments having past between the Parson and the Justice, the latter proceeded on his Journey, and the former having with some disdain refused *Joseph's* Offer of changing Horses; and declared he was as able a Horseman as any in the Kingdom, re-mounted his Beast; and now the Company again proceeded, and happily arrived at their Journey's End, Mr. *Adams* by good Luck, rather than by good Riding, escaping a second Fall.

The Company arriving at Mr. *Booby's* House, were all received by him in the most courteous, and entertained in the most splendid manner, after the Custom of the old *English* Hospitality, which is still preserved in some very few Families in the remote Parts of *England*. They all past that Day with the utmost Satisfaction; it being perhaps impossible to find any Set of People more solidly and sincerely happy. *Joseph* and *Fanny* found means to be alone upwards of two Hours, which were the shortest but the sweetest imaginable.

In the Morning, Mr. *Wilson* proposed to his Son to make a Visit with him to his Mother; which, notwithstanding his dutiful Inclinations, and a longing Desire he had to see her, a little concerned him as he must be obliged to leave his *Fanny*: But the Goodness of Mr. *Booby* relieved him; for he proposed to send his own Coach and six for Mrs. *Wilson*, whom *Pamela* so very earnestly invited, that Mr. *Wilson* at length agreed with the Entreaties of Mr. *Booby* and *Joseph*, and suffered the Coach to go empty for his Wife.

On *Saturday* Night the Coach return'd with Mrs. *Wilson*, who added one more to this happy Assembly. The Reader may imagine much better and quicker too than I can describe, the many Embraces and Tears of Joy which succeeded her Arrival. It is sufficient to say, she was easily prevailed with to follow her Husband's Example, in consenting to the Match.

On *Sunday* Mr. *Adams* performed the Service at the Squire's Parish Church, the Curate of which very kindly exchanged Duty, and rode twenty Miles to the Lady *Booby's* Parish, so to do; being particularly

1. Ended.

charged not to omit publishing the Banns, being the third and last Time.

At length the happy Day arrived, which was to put *Joseph* in the possession of all his Wishes. He arose and drest himself in a neat, but plain Suit of Mr. *Booby's*, which exactly fitted him; for he refused all Finery; as did *Fanny* likewise, who could be prevailed on by *Pamela* to attire herself in nothing richer than a white Dimity Night-Gown.[2] Her Shift indeed, which *Pamela* presented her, was of the finest Kind, and had an Edging of Lace round the Bosom; she likewise equipped her with a Pair of fine white Thread Stockings, which were all she would accept; for she wore one of her own short round-ear'd Caps, and over it a little Straw Hat, lined with Cherry-coloured Silk, and tied with a Cherry-coloured Ribbon. In this Dress she came forth from her Chamber, blushing, and breathing Sweets; and was by *Joseph*, whose Eyes sparkled Fire, led to Church, the whole Family attending, where Mr. *Adams* performed the Ceremony; at which nothing was so remarkable, as the extraordinary and unaffected Modesty of *Fanny*, unless the true Christian Piety of *Adams*, who publickly rebuked Mr. *Booby* and *Pamela* for laughing in so sacred a Place, and so solemn an Occasion. Our Parson would have done no less to the highest Prince on Earth: For tho' he paid all Submission and Deference to his Superiors in other Matters, where the least Spice of Religion intervened, he immediately lost all Respect of Persons. It was his Maxim, That he was a Servant of the Highest, and could not, without departing from his Duty, give up the least Article of his Honour, or of his Cause, to the greatest earthly Potentate. Indeed he always asserted, that Mr. *Adams* at Church with his Surplice on, and Mr. *Adams* without that Ornament, in any other place, were two very different Persons.

When the Church Rites were over, *Joseph* led his blooming Bride back to Mr. *Booby's* (for the Distance was so very little, they did not think proper to use a Coach) the whole Company attended them likewise on foot; and now a most magnificent Entertainment was provided, at which Parson *Adams* demonstrated an Appetite surprizing, as well as surpassing every one present. Indeed the only Persons who betrayed any Deficiency on this Occasion were those on whose account the Feast was provided. They pampered their Imaginations with the much more exquisite Repast which the Approach of Night promised them; the Thoughts of which filled both their Minds, tho' with different Sensations; the one all Desire, while the other had her Wishes tempered with Fears.

At length, after a Day past with the utmost Merriment, corrected by the strictest Decency; in which, however, Parson *Adams*, being well filled with Ale and Pudding, had given a Loose to more Facetiousness than was usual to him: The happy, the blest Moment arrived, when *Fanny* retired with her Mother, her Mother-in-law, and her Sister. She was soon undrest; for she had no Jewels to deposite in their Caskets, nor fine Laces to fold with the nicest Exactness. Undressing to her was properly discovering, not putting off Ornaments: For as all her Charms were

2. Evening dress.

the Gifts of Nature, she could divest herself of none. How, Reader, shall I give thee an adequate Idea of this lovely young Creature! the Bloom of Roses and Lillies might a little illustrate her Complexion, or their Smell her Sweetness: but to comprehend her entirely, conceive Youth, Health, Bloom, Beauty, Neatness, and Innocence in her Bridal-Bed; conceive all these in their utmost Perfection, and you may place the charming *Fanny's* Picture before your Eyes.

Joseph no sooner heard she was in Bed, than he fled with the utmost Eagerness to her. A Minute carried him into her Arms, where we shall leave this happy Couple to enjoy the private Rewards of their Constancy; Rewards so great and sweet, that I apprehend *Joseph* neither envied the noblest Duke, nor *Fanny* the finest Duchess that Night.

The third Day, Mr. *Wilson* and his Wife, with their Son and Daughter returned home; where they now live together in a State of Bliss scarce ever equalled. Mr. *Booby* hath with unprecedented Generosity given *Fanny* a Fortune of two thousand Pound, which *Joseph* hath laid out in a little Estate in the same Parish with his Father, which he now occupies, (his Father having stock'd it for him;) and *Fanny* presides, with most excellent Management in his Dairy; where, however, she is not at present very able to bustle much, being, as Mr. *Wilson* informs me in his last Letter, extremely big with her first Child.

Mr. *Booby* hath presented Mr. *Adams* with a Living of one hundred and thirty Pounds a Year. He at first refused it, resolving not to quit his Parishioners, with whom he hath lived so long: But on recollecting he might keep a Curate at this Living, he hath been lately inducted into it.[3]

The Pedlar, besides several handsome Presents both from Mr. *Wilson* and Mr. *Booby*, is, by the latter's Interest made an Excise-man; a Trust which he discharges with such Justice, that he is greatly beloved in his Neighbourhood.

As for the Lady *Booby*, she returned to *London* in a few days, where a young Captain of Dragoons, together with eternal Parties at Cards, soon obliterated the Memory of *Joseph*.

Joseph remains blest with his *Fanny*, whom he doats on with the utmost Tenderness, which is all returned on her side. The Happiness of this Couple is a perpetual Fountain of Pleasure to their fond Parents; and what is particularly remarkable, he declares he will imitate them in their Retirement; nor will be prevailed on by any Booksellers, or their Authors, to make his Appearance in *High-Life*.[4]

---

3. Fielding extended Adams's life beyond the novel. In the introduction to *A Journey from This World to the Next* (1743), he endorses this supposedly found manuscript; letters from him furnish the leading articles in Fielding's journals, *The True Patriot* (December 17, 1745, and January 28, 1746) and *The Jacobite's Journal* (July 9, 1748); and at the end of *Tom Jones* (1749) he replaces the hero's enemy, Parson Thwackum, in the establishment of the beneficent Squire Allworthy as tutor to Tom's children.

4. In May 1741, the bookseller Richard Chandler, one of Fielding's partners in *The Champion*, published *Pamela's Conduct in High Life* by John Kelly. Richardson attacked the spurious sequel in a running newspaper battle while preparing his own announced sequel. Meanwhile a serial continuation evidently intended to pass for his, *Pamela in High Life: or, Virtue Rewarded*, began to appear in September. Richardson's third and fourth volumes, depicting Pamela in her altered state, appeared in December 1741.

The Text of
SHAMELA

A N

A P O L O G Y

F O R   T H E

L   I   F   E

O F

Mrs. SHAMELA ANDREWS.

In which, the many notorious FALSHOODS and
MISREPRESENTATIONS of a Book called

P   A   M   E   L   A,

Are expofed and refuted; and all the matchlefs
ARTS of that young Politician, fet in a true and
juft Light.

Together with

A full Account of all that paffed between her
and Parfon *Arthur Williams*; whofe Character is
reprefented in a manner fomething different from
that which he bears in *PAMELA.* The
whole being exact Copies of authentick Papers
delivered to the Editor.

Neceffary to be had in all FAMILIES.[1]

By Mr. *CONNY KEYBER.*[2]

L O N D O N:

Printed for A. DODD, at the *Peacock,* without *Temple-bar.*
M. DCC. XLI.

---

1. Fielding mockingly alters a sentiment from the
first commendatory letter prefixed to *Pamela* ("it
will be found worthy a Place . . . in all Families")
to mimic the familiar title page caption ("Necessary For All Families") of *The Whole Duty of Man*
(see above, p. 19, n. 9).
2. A compound name referring to the authors of
two recently published lives: the Reverend Conyers Middleton (see above, p. 186, n. 2), whose
long-awaited *Life of Cicero* had appeared two
months earlier, and Colley Cibber (see above, p.
15, n. 5). "Conny" (pronounced "cunny"), a slang
word for gull or dupe, also had a sexual meaning.
"Keyber," a common derisive name for Cibber
previously employed by Fielding, alluded to his
Danish ancestry.

[Although Fielding never acknowledged it as his own, *Shamela* is now generally accepted as his work. (The most comprehensive review of the evidence for Fielding's authorship is Charles Woods, "Fielding and the Authorship of *Shamela*," *Philological Quarterly* 25 [1946]: 248–72). The text is that of the second edition, in which Fielding evidently made minor corrections. Apparent printer's errors have been silently corrected, quotation marks modernized, and a few clarifying punctuation marks added.

The parody employs *Pamela's* principal characters (though the virtuous Mrs. Jervis is equated with the vicious Mrs. Jewkes and the other characters are comparably debased) and it follows the general outline of the greater part of Richardson's story. The abduction to Lincolnshire, the two bedroom assaults, the master's proposed settlement of two hundred and fifty pounds per annum on his would-be mistress, Parson Williams's arrest for debt (after trying to help Pamela escape), and the master's capitulating letter of recall to the heroine he has sent away are all in the original. Pamela is also introduced by Mrs. Jervis to her master dressed as a country girl, and she hides in a woodshed after staging a drowning as part of an escape plan, seriously contemplating suicide when the escape route is barred. Other particular references to *Pamela* are cited in the notes.]

To Miss *Fanny*, &c.[3]

MADAM,

It will be naturally expected, that when I write the Life of *Shamela*, I should dedicate it to some young Lady, whose Wit and Beauty might be the proper Subject of a Comparison with the Heroine of my Piece. This, those, who see I have done it in prefixing your Name to my Work, will much more confirmedly expect me to do; and, indeed, your Character would enable me to run some Length into a Parallel, tho' you, nor any one else, are at all like the matchless *Shamela*.

You see, Madam, I have some Value for your Good-nature, when in a Dedication, which is properly a Panegyrick, I speak against, not for you; but I remember it is a Life which I am presenting you, and why should I expose my Veracity to any Hazard in the Front of the Work,

3. "Lord Fanny" was Pope's derogatory name for Lord Hervey (see p. 245, n. 2), to whom Middleton dedicated his *Life of Cicero*. Fielding's "Etc." mocks Middleton's formality ("To the Right Honourable John Lord Hervey, Lord Keeper of His Majesty's Privy Seal"), but in conjunction with "Fanny," it may also have been intended to convey a sexual innuendo (see below, p. 276, n. 5). Appreciation of Fielding's parody may be heightened by comparing the corresponding passages in the original, reprinted below, pp. 340–43.

considering what I have done in the Body. Indeed, I wish it was possible to write a Dedication, and get any thing by it, without one Word of Flattery; but since it is not, come on, and I hope to shew my Delicacy at least in the Compliments I intend to pay you.

First, then, Madam, I must tell the World, that you have tickled up and brightned many Strokes in this Work by your Pencil.

Secondly, You have intimately conversed with me, one of the greatest Wits and Scholars of my Age.

Thirdly, You keep very good Hours, and frequently spend an useful Day before others begin to enjoy it. This I will take my Oath on; for I am admitted to your Presence in a Morning before other People's Servants are up; when I have constantly found you reading in good Books; and if ever I have drawn you upon me, I have always felt you very heavy.

Fourthly, You have a Virtue which enables you to rise early and study hard, and that is, forbearing to over-eat yourself, and this in spite of all the luscious Temptations of Puddings and Custards, exciting the Brute (as Dr. *Woodward* calls it)[4] to rebel. This is a Virtue which I can greatly admire, though I much question whether I could imitate it.

Fifthly, A Circumstance greatly to your Honour, that by means of your extraordinary Merit and Beauty; you was carried into the Ball-Room at the *Bath*, by the discerning Mr. *Nash*;[5] before the Age that other young Ladies generally arrived at that Honour, and while your Mamma herself existed in her perfect Bloom. Here you was observed in Dancing to balance your Body exactly, and to weigh every Motion with the exact and equal Measure of Time and Tune; and though you sometimes made a false Step, by leaning too much to one Side; yet every body said you would one Time or other, dance perfectly well, and uprightly.

Sixthly, I cannot forbear mentioning those pretty little Sonnets, and sprightly Compositions, which though they came from you with so much Ease, might be mentioned to the Praise of a great or grave Character.

And now, Madam, I have done with you; it only remains to pay my Acknowledgments to an Author, whose Stile I have exactly followed in this Life, it being the properest for Biography. The Reader, I believe, easily guesses, I mean *Euclid's Elements*;[6] it was *Euclid* who taught me to write. It is you, Madam, who pay me for Writing. Therefore I am to both,

> *A most Obedient, and*
> *obliged humble Servant,*
> CONNY KEYBER.

4. In *The State of Physic and of Diseases* (1718), John Woodward (1665–1728), antiquarian, physician, and Fellow of the Royal Society, attributed social discontent, immorality, and atheism to rich and spicy foreign food and drink.

5. Richard "Beau" Nash (1674–1762), gambler and man about town, first organized the social activities at the health resort of Bath in 1705, presiding thereafter as master of ceremonies at its Assembly. Fielding satirically substitutes this tem-

ple of fashionable recreation for Middleton's reference to the House of Commons, to which Hervey was elected at the age of twenty-eight in 1725. In describing Hervey as weighing "every Motion with the exact and equal Measure of Time and Tune . . . though . . . leaning too much to one Side," he is suggesting that he voted in accordance with the prevailing political winds, and in particular, the wishes of Walpole, whom he served loyally.

6. Educated readers would recall that Euclid's

Letters to the Editor.

The EDITOR to Himself.[7]

Dear S I R,

However you came by the excellent *Shamela*, out with it, without Fear or Favour, Dedication and all; believe me, it will go through many Editions, be translated into all Languages, read in all Nations and Ages, and to say a bold Word, it will do more good than the C——y have done harm in the World.[8]

I am, Sir,
Sincerely your Well-wisher,
YOURSELF.

John Puff, Esq; to the EDITOR.

S I R,

  I have read your *Shamela* through and through, and a most inimitable Performance it is. Who is he, what is he that could write so excellent a Book?[9] he must be doubtless most agreeable to the Age, and to *his Honour*[1] himself; for he is able to draw every thing to Perfection but Virtue. Whoever the Author be, he hath one of the worst and most fashionable Hearts in the World, and I would recommend to him, in his next Performance, to undertake the Life of *his Honour*. For he who drew the Character of Parson *Williams*, is equal to the Task; nay he seems to have little more to do than to pull off the Parson's Gown, and *that* which makes him so agreeable to *Shamela*, and the Cap will fit.

I am, Sir,
Your humble Servant,
JOHN PUFF.[2]

Elements (the basis of geometry schoolbooks then as now) is not a sustained prose discourse but a sequence of bare logical demonstrations of propositions that, in the words of a modern translator, "leave something to be desired in point of clearness and precision" (*The Thirteen Books of Euclid's Elements,* trans. Sir Thomas L. Heath, 2nd ed. [Cambridge: Cambridge UP, 1925] 1.248). Some sense of their "style" may be conveyed by Heath's illustrative literal translation for the non-Greek reader: "On the same straight line there shall not be constructed two other straight lines equal, each to each, to the same two straight lines (terminating) at different points on the same side, having the same extremities as the original straight line" (259).

7. Although the laudatory letters prefixed to *Pamela* were not by Richardson, he did write an encomiastic preface in his pretended role of editor, concluding disingenuously "an *Editor* may reasonably be supposed to judge with an Impartiality which is rarely to be met with in an *Author* towards his own Works."

8. It was widely reported that Pope had said *Pamela* "will do more good than a great many of the new sermons." Fielding's "out with it" burlesques one of Richardson's prefatory correspondents: "I can't conceive why you should hesitate a Moment as to the Publication of this very natural and uncommon Piece. I could wish to see it out in its own native Simplicity. . . ."

9. "Yet, I confess, there is *One,* in the World, of whom I think with still greater Respect, than of *Pamela*; and that is of the wonderful AUTHOR of *Pamela*.—Pray, Who is he, Dear Sir? and where, and how, has he been able to hide, hitherto, such an encircling and all-mastering Spirit?"—from a letter prefixed to the second edition of *Pamela*.

1. A common derisive term for Walpole. The next clause mimics another passage from the letter cited in the preceding note: "mis-measuring *other* Minds, by *His Own,* he can draw Every thing, to Perfection, but *Wickedness.*"

2. "A cant Word for the Applause that Writers or Book sellers give their own Books, Etc. to promote their Sale" (*London Magazine,* May 1732).

Note, Reader, several other COMMENDATORY LETTERS and COPIES of VERSES will be prepared against the NEXT EDITION.[3]

An
APOLOGY
For the Life of
Mrs. Shamela Andrews.

Parson TICKLETEXT *to Parson* OLIVER.

Rev. S I R,

Herewith I transmit you a Copy of sweet, dear, pretty *Pamela*, a little Book which this Winter hath produced; of which, I make no doubt, you have already heard mention from some of your Neighbouring Clergy; for we have made it our common Business here, not only to cry it up, but to preach it up likewise: The Pulpit, as well as the Coffee-house, hath resounded with its Praise, and it is expected shortly, that his L——p will recommend it in a ——— Letter to our whole Body.[4]

And this Example, I am confident, will be imitated by all our Cloth in the Country: For besides speaking well of a Brother, in the Character of the Reverend Mr. *Williams*, the useful and truly religious Doctrine of *Grace* is every where inculcated.[5]

This Book is the "SOUL of *Religion*, Good-Breeding, Discretion, Good-Nature, Wit, Fancy, Fine Thought, and Morality. There is an Ease, a natural Air, a dignified Simplicity, and MEASURED FULLNESS in it, that RESEMBLING LIFE, OUT-GLOWS IT. The Author hath reconciled the *pleasing* to the *proper*; the Thought is every where exactly cloathed by the Expression; and becomes its Dress as *roundly* and as close as *Pamela* her Country Habit; or *as she doth her no Habit*, when modest Beauty seeks to hide itself, by casting off the Pride of Ornament, and displays itself without any Covering;" which it frequently doth in this admirable Work, and presents Images to the Reader, which the coldest Zealot cannot read without Emotion.

For my own Part (and, I believe, I may say the same of all the Clergy of my Acquaintance) "I have done nothing but read it to others, and

---

3. See above, p. 16, n. 8.

4. Dr. Benjamin Slocock recommended the novel from the pulpit at St. Saviour's. Three pastoral letters against deism published between 1728 and 1731 by his Lordship Edmund Gibson (1669–1748), bishop of London and Walpole's closest clerical adviser, attracted wide attention, including a parody in the opposition's *Craftsman* (Nov. 16, 1728) and inclusion (as a butter wrapper) in plate 3 of Hogarth's celebrated *A Harlot's Progress*. Another pastoral letter, published in 1739, three years after he broke with Walpole, attacked the enthusiasm of the Methodists, extensively citing Whitefield's *Journals*, so it is not likely that Fielding thought he would subscribe to the religious views praised by Tickletext.

5. See above, p. 37, n. 1. In the next three paragraphs, the quoted passages and the authorial queries preceding the last of these are repeated virtually verbatim from the prefatory matter to the second edition of *Pamela*, though not in the order in which they occur there (the second and third sentences of the first paragraph were originally in praise of the simplicity of the author's style). Besides his own typographical emphases within these quoted passages, Fielding adds only "or as she doth her no Habit," "get thee gone," "in which thou wilt find nothing like thyself," and, most tellingly, in place of "innocent story," the ribald "Etc.," a slang term for female genitalia.

hear others again read it to me, ever since it came into my Hands; and I find I am like to do nothing else, for I know not how long yet to come: because if I lay the Book down *it comes after me*. When it has dwelt all Day long upon the Ear, it takes Possession all Night of the Fancy. It hath Witchcraft in every Page of it."—Oh! I feel an Emotion even while I am relating this: Methinks I see *Pamela* at this Instant, with all the Pride of Ornament cast off.

"Little Book, charming *Pamala*, get thee gone; face the World, in which thou wilt find nothing like thyself." Happy would it be for Mankind, if all other Books were burnt, that we might do nothing but read thee all Day, and dream of thee all Night. Thou alone art sufficient to teach us as much Morality as we want. Dost thou not teach us to pray, to sing Psalms, and to honour the Clergy?[6] Are not these the whole Duty of Man?[7] Forgive me, O Author of *Pamela*, mentioning the Name of a Book so unequal to thine: But, now I think of it, who is the Author, where is he, what is he, that hath hitherto been able to hide such an encircling, all-mastering Spirit, "he possesses every Quality that Art could have charm'd by: yet hath lent it to and concealed it in Nature. The Comprehensiveness of his Imagination must be truly prodigious! It has stretched out this diminutive mere Grain of Mustard seed (a poor Girl's little, &c.) into a Resemblance of that Heaven, which the best of good Books has compared it to."[8]

To be short, this Book will live to the Age of the Patriarchs,[9] and like them will carry on the good Work many hundreds of Years hence, among our Posterity, who will not HESITATE their Esteem with Restraint. If the *Romans* granted Exemptions to Men who begat a *few* Children for the Republick, what Distinction (if Policy and we should ever be reconciled) should we find to reward this Father of Millions, which are to owe Formation to the future Effect of his Influence.—I feel another Emotion.[1]

As soon as you have read this yourself five or six Times over (which may possibly happen within a Week) I desire you would give it to my little God-Daughter, as a Present from me. This being the only Education we intend henceforth to give our Daughters. And pray let your Servant-Maids read it over, or read it to them. Both your self and the neighbouring Clergy, will supply yourselves for the Pulpit from the Booksellers, as soon as the fourth Edition is published.[2] I am,

Sir,

Your most humble Servant,

THO. TICKLETEXT.

6. See below, p. 288 n. 2.

7. See above, p. 19 n. 9.

8. Matthew 13:31–32—"The kingdom of heaven is like to a grain of mustard seed, which a man took, and sowed in his field: which indeed is the least of all seeds: but when it is grown, it is the greatest among herbs, and becometh a tree, so that the birds of the air come and lodge in the branches thereof."

9. That is, nearly a thousand years, from the longevity of Methusaleh, Noah, and others in Genesis.

1. This paragraph closely follows passages from one of *Pamela's* prefatory letters. Fielding's capitalization of "hesitate" may be in mockery of this eccentric phrasing in the original. The original version of the second sentence reads: ". . . this *Father, of Millions*, of MINDS, which we are to owe new Formation. . . ." The last sentence is Fielding's addition.

2. The third edition of *Pamela* appeared March 12, 1741, three weeks before the publication of *Shamela*; the fourth was published on May 5.

Parson OLIVER *to Parson* TICKLETEXT.

Rev. SIR,

I received the Favour of yours with the inclosed Book, and really must own myself sorry, to see the Report I have heard of an epidemical Phrenzy now raging in Town, confirmed in the Person of my Friend.

If I had not known your Hand, I should, from the Sentiments and Stile of the Letter, have imagined it to have come from the Author of the famous Apology, which was sent me last Summer; and on my reading the remarkable Paragraph of *measured Fulness, that resembling Life out-glows it,* to a young Baronet, he cry'd out, C—*ly* C—*b—r* by G—.[3] But I have since observed, that this, as well as many other Expressions in your Letter, was borrowed from those remarkable Epistles, which the Author, or the Editor hath prefix'd to the second Edition which you send me of his Book.

Is it possible that you or any of your Function can be in earnest, or think the Cause of Religion, or Morality, can want such slender Support? God forbid they should. As for Honour to the Clergy, I am sorry to see them so solicitous about it; for if worldly Honour be meant, it is what their Predecessors in the pure and primitive Age, never had or sought. Indeed the secure Satisfaction of a good Conscience, the Approbation of the Wise and Good, (which never were or will be the Generality of Mankind) and the extatick Pleasure of contemplating, that their Ways are acceptable to the Great Creator of the Universe, will always attend those, who really deserve these Blessings: But for worldly Honours, they are often the Purchase of Force and Fraud, we sometimes see them in an eminent Degree possessed by Men, who are notorious for Luxury, Pride, Cruelty, Treachery, and the most abandoned Prostitution; Wretches who are ready to invent and maintain Schemes repugnant to the Interest, the Liberty, and the Happiness of Mankind, not to supply their Necessities, or even Conveniencies, but to pamper their Avarice and Ambition.[4] And if this be the Road to worldly Honours, God forbid the Clergy should be even suspected of walking in it.

The History of *Pamela* I was acquainted with long before I received it from you, from my Neighbourhood to the Scene of Action. Indeed I was in hopes that young Woman would have contented herself with the Good-fortune she hath attained; and rather suffered her little Arts to have been forgotten than have revived their Remembrance, and endeavoured by perverting and misrepresenting Facts to be thought to deserve what she now enjoys: for though we do not imagine her the Author of the Narrative itself, yet we must suppose the Instructions were given by her, as well as the Reward, to the Composer. Who that is, though you so earnestly require of me, I shall leave you to guess from that *Cicero-*

---

3. Colley Cibber (see above, p. 15, n. 5).

4. Compare Parson Adams's reference to the "Schemes" of "A Few Designing Factious Men," p. 65 above.

nian Eloquence, with which the Work abounds; and that excellent Knack of making every Character amiable, which he lays his hands on. [5]

But before I send you some Papers relating to this Matter, which will set *Pamela* and some others in a very different Light, than that in which they appear in the printed Book, I must beg leave to make some few Remarks on the Book itself, and its Tendency, (admitting it to be a true Relation,) towards improving Morality, or doing any good, either to the present Age, or Posterity: which when I have done, I shall, I flatter myself, stand excused from delivering it, either into the hands of my Daughter, or my Servant-Maid.

The Instruction which it conveys to Servant-Maids, is, I think, very plainly this, To look out for their Masters as sharp as they can. The Consequences of which will be, besides Neglect of their Business, and the using all manner of Means to come at Ornaments of their Persons, that if the Master is not a Fool, they will be debauched by him; and if he is a Fool, they will marry him. [6] Neither of which, I apprehend, my good Friend, we desire should be the Case of our Sons.

And notwithstanding our Author's Professions of Modesty, which in my Youth I have heard at the Beginning of an Epilogue, [7] I cannot agree that my Daughter should entertain herself with some of his Pictures; which I do not expect to be contemplated without Emotion, unless by one of my Age and Temper, who can see the Girl lie on her Back, with one Arm round Mrs. *Jewkes* and the other round the Squire, naked in Bed, with his Hand on her Breasts, &c. with as much Indifference as I read any other Page in the whole Novel. [8] But surely this, and some other Descriptions, will not be put into the hands of his Daughter by any wise Man, though I believe it will be difficult for him to keep them from her; especially if the Clergy in Town have cried and preached it up as you say.

But, my Friend, the whole Narrative is such a Misrepresentation of Facts, such a Perversion of Truth, as you will, I am perswaded, agree, as soon as you have perused the Papers I now inclose to you, that I hope you or some other well-disposed Person, will communicate these Papers to the Publick, that this little Jade may not impose on the World, as she hath on her Master.

The true name of this Wench was SHAMELA, and not *Pamela*, as she stiles herself. Her Father had in his Youth the Misfortune to appear in no good Light at the *Old-Bailey*; he afterwards served in the Capacity of a Drummer in one of the *Scotch* Regiments in the *Dutch* Service; where being drummed out, he came over to *England*, and turned Informer against several Persons on the late Gin-Act; and becoming acquainted

5. An apparent reference to Conyers Middleton, whose "amiable" characterization of Lord Hervey and avowed emulation of Cicero's style are mocked in Fielding's dedication.
6. One of the prefatory letters to *Pamela* concludes: "the *moral Meaning* of PAMELA'S Good-fortune, far from tempting young Gentlemen to marry *such* Maids as are found in their Families, is, by teaching Maids to *deserve to be Mistresses*, to stir up Mistresses *to support their Distinction*."
7. That is, presumably, after one of the licentious comedies of the previous age.
8. The scene in question is reprinted below, pp. 335–40.

with an Hostler at an Inn, where a *Scotch* Gentleman's Horses stood, he hath at last by his Interest obtain'd a pretty snug Place in the *Custom-house*. Her Mother sold Oranges in the Play-House; and whether she was married to her Father or no, I never could learn.[9]

After this short Introduction, the rest of her History will appear in the following Letters, which I assure you are authentick.

Letter I.

SHAMELA ANDREWS *to Mrs.* HENRIETTA MARIA HONORA ANDREWS *at her Lodgings at the* FAN *and* PEPPER-BOX *in* DRURY-LANE.[1]

Dear Mamma,

This comes to acquaint you, that I shall set out in the Waggon on *Monday*, desiring you to commodate me with a Ludgin, as near you as possible, in *Coulstin's-Court*, or *Wild-Street*, or somewhere there-abouts;[2] pray let it be handsome, and not above two Stories high: For Parson *Williams* hath promised to visit me when he comes to Town, and I have got a good many fine Cloaths of the Old Put[3] my Mistress's, who died a wil ago; and I beleve Mrs. *Jervis* will come along with me, for she says she would like to keep a House somewhere about *Short's-Gardens*, or towards *Queen-Street*; and if there was convenience for a *Bannio*,[4] she should like it the better; but that she will settle herself when she comes to Town.—*O! How I long to be in the Balconey at the Old House*[5]—so no more at present from

Your affectionate Daughter,

SHAMELA.

Letter II.

SHAMELA ANDREWS *to* HENRIETTA MARIA HONORA ANDREWS.

Dear Mamma,

O what News, since I writ my last! the young Squire hath been here, and as sure as a Gun he hath taken a Fancy to me; *Pamela*, says he, (for

9. Fielding tars Richardson's "poor but honest" rural folk with disreputability: the Old Bailey was the principal criminal court in London; the Scotch regiments had remained in the pay of the Dutch even when the latter were at war with England (1665–67; 1672–74); the prohibitive taxation and licensing fees of the Gin Act (1736), enacted to stem the epidemic of drunkenness produced by cheap gin, proved so unpopular and ineffectual that the act was repealed in 1743—its informers were despised and sometimes physically abused; in this time of widespread smuggling, the customs office, less closely supervised than the internal excise, offered many opportunities for shakedowns and bribery; the women who sold oranges in theatres were often prostitutes.

1. "Appropriating the manners of the highest to the lowest," Fielding names Shamela's mother after Charles I's Catholic queen. Her lodging sign suggests a disreputable house, "pepper" being slang for venereal infection.

2. All the streets and locations mentioned were in the vicinity of Drury Lane, an area whose reputation may be inferred from Pope's remark (in a letter to Cromwell, March 18, 1708) that one might find solace for a lost love with a "Wild Street or Drury Lane Damsel."

3. Fool.

4. For *bagnio* ("bath" in Italian). Equivalent to the modern Turkish bath, it was often enough employed as a house of assignation to earn the secondary meaning of "a brothel." Subsequent references to a "House . . . fit for the Business" suggest that this is what Mrs. Jervis has in mind.

5. The Theatre Royal in Drury Lane, built in 1663, and redesigned by Christopher Wren in 1674 after being destroyed by fire. Shamela's exclamation parodies Pamela's yearnings for her parents' humble cottage (". . . dream that I am with you, in my dear, dear, happy Loft once more," letter 16).

so I am called here) you was a great Favourite of your late Mistress's; yes, an't please your Honour, says I; and I believe you deserved it, says he; thank your Honour for your good Opinion, says I; and then he took me by the Hand, and I pretended to be shy: Laud, says I, Sir, I hope you don't intend to be rude; no, says he, my Dear, and then he kissed me, 'till he took away my Breath—and I pretended to be Angry, and to get away, and then he kissed me again, and breathed very short, and looked very silly; and by Ill-Luck Mrs. *Jervis* came in, and had like to have spoiled Sport.—*How troublesome is such Interruption!* You shall hear now soon, for I shall not come away yet, so I rest,

Your affectionate Daughter,

SHAMELA.

Letter III.
HENRIETTA MARIA HONORA ANDREWS *to* SHAMELA ANDREWS.

Dear Sham,

Your last Letter hath put me into a great hurry of Spirits, for you have a very difficult Part to act. I hope you will remember your Slip with Parson *Williams*, and not be guilty of any more such Folly. Truly, a Girl who hath once known what is what, is in the highest Degree inexcusable if she respects her *Digressions*[6], but a Hint of this is sufficient. When Mrs. *Jervis* thinks of coming to Town, I believe I can procure her a good House, and fit for the Business; so I am,

Your affectionate Mother,

HENRIETTA MARIA HONORA ANDREWS.

Letter IV.
SHAMELA ANDREWS *to* HENRIETTA MARIA HONORA ANDREWS.

Marry come up, good Madam, the Mother had never looked into the Oven for her Daughter, if she had not been there herself. I shall never have done if you upbraid me with having had a small One by *Arthur Williams*, when you yourself—but I say no more. *O! What fine Times when the Kettle calls the Pot.* Let me do what I will, I say my Prayers as often as another, and I read in good Books, as often as I have Leisure; and Parson *Williams* says, that will make amends.—So no more, but I rest

Your afflicted Daughter,

S——

Letter V.
HENRIETTA MARIA HONORA ANDREWS *to* SHAMELA ANDREWS

Dear Child,

Why will you give such way to your Passion? How could you imagine I should be such a Simpleton, as to upbraid thee with being thy Mother's

6. Sheridan Baker plausibly suggests that this is Mrs. Andrews's Slipslopian garbling of "repeats her transgressions"; but in view of the fact that she utters only one other malapropism ("Poluteness," letter 8) and correctly uses harder words than "respect" or "repeats," the phrase may also be interpreted as her affected (and archaic) way of saying "gives in to her wayward inclinations."

own Daughter! When I advised you not to be guilty of Folly, I meant no more than that you should take care to be well paid before-hand, and not trust to Promises, which a Man seldom keeps, after he hath had his wicked Will. And seeing you have a rich Fool to deal with, your not making a good Market will be the more inexcusable; indeed, with such Gentlemen as Parson *Williams*, there is more to be said; for they have nothing to give, and are commonly otherwise the best Sort of Men. I am glad to hear you read good Books, pray continue so to do. I have inclosed you one of Mr. *Whitefield*'s Sermons, and also the Dealings[7] with him, and am

> *Your affectionate Mother,*
> HENRIETTA MARIA, &c.

Letter VI.
SHAMELA ANDREWS *to* HENRIETTA MARIA HONORA ANDREWS.

O Madam, I have strange Things to tell you! As I was reading in that charming Book about the Dealings, in comes my Master—to be sure he is a precious One. *Pamela*, says he, what Book is that, I warrant you *Rochester*'s Poems.[8]—No, forsooth, says I, as pertly as I could; why how now Saucy Chops, Boldface, says he—Mighty pretty Words, says I, pert again.—Yes (says he) you are a d——d, impudent, stinking, cursed, confounded Jade, and I have a great Mind to kick your A——. You, kiss—says I. A-gad, says he, and so I will; with that he caught me in his Arms, and kissed me till he made my Face all over Fire. Now this served purely you know, to put upon the Fool for Anger. O! What precious Fools Men are! And so I flung from him in a mighty Rage, and pretended as how I would go out at the Door; but when I came to the End of the Room, I stood still, and my Master cryed out, Hussy, Slut, Saucebox, Boldface, come hither— Yes to be sure, says I; why don't you come, says he; what should I come for, says I; if you don't come to me, I'll come to you, says he; I shan't come to you I assure you, says I. Upon which he run up, caught me in his Arms, and flung me upon a Chair, and began to offer to touch my Under-Petticoat. Sir, says I, you had better not offer to be rude; well, says he, no more I won't then; and away he went out of the Room. I was so mad to be sure I could have cry'd.

Oh what a prodigious Vexation it is to a Woman to be made a Fool of.

Mrs. *Jervis* who had been without, harkening, now came to me. She burst into a violent Laugh the Moment she came in. Well, says she, as soon as she could speak, I have Reason to bless myself that I am an Old Woman. Ah Child! if you had known the Jolly Blades of my Age, you would not have been left in the lurch in this manner. Dear Mrs. *Jervis*, says I, don't laugh at one; and to be sure I was a little angry with her.—

---

7. A *Short Account of God's Dealings with the Reverend Mr. George Whitefield* (1740) is the Methodist preacher's account of his early years, his temptations, his struggles with Satan, and his spiritual awakening.

8. The poems of John Wilmot, earl of Rochester (1647–80), were notorious for their frank sexual references and celebration of libertinism.

Come, says she, my dear Honeysuckle, I have one Game to play for you; he shall see you in Bed; he shall, my little Rosebud, he shall see those pretty, little, white, round, panting ———— and offer'd to pull off my Handkerchief.—Fie, Mrs. *Jervis*, says I, you make me blush, and upon my Fackins,[9] I believe she did: She went on thus. I know the Squire likes you, and notwithstanding the Aukwardness of his Proceeding, I am convinced hath some hot Blood in his Veins, which will not let him rest, 'till he hath communicated some of his Warmth to thee my little Angel; I heard him last Night at our Door, trying if it was open, now to-night I will take care it shall be so; I warrant that he makes the second Trial; which if he doth, he shall find us ready to receive him. I will at first counterfeit Sleep, and after a Swoon; so that he will have you naked in his Possession: and then if you are disappointed, a Plague of all young Squires, say I.—And so, Mrs. *Jervis*, says I, you would have me yield myself to him, would you; you would have me be a second Time a Fool for nothing. Thank you for that, Mrs. *Jervis*. For nothing! marry forbid, says she, you know he hath large Sums of Money, besides abundance of fine Things; and do you think, when you have inflamed him, by giving his Hand a Liberty with that charming Person; and that you know he may easily think he obtains against your Will, he will not give any thing to come at all—. This will not do, Mrs. *Jervis*, answered I. I have heard my Mamma say, (and so you know, Madam, I have) that in her Youth, Fellows have often taken away in the Morning, what they gave over Night. No, Mrs. *Jervis*, nothing under a regular taking into Keeping, a settled Settlement, for me, and all my Heirs, all my whole Lifetime, shall do the Business — or else crosslegged, is the Word, faith, with *Sham*; and then I snapt my Fingers.

Thursday Night, Twelve o'Clock.

Mrs. *Jervis* and I are just in Bed, and the Door unlocked; if my Master should come—Odsbobs![1] I hear him just coming in at the Door. You see I write in the present Tense, as Parson *Williams* says. Well, he is in Bed between us, we both shamming a Sleep, he steals his Hand into my Bosom, which I, as if in my Sleep, press close to me with mine, and then pretend to awake.—I no sooner see him, but I scream out to Mrs. *Jervis*, she feigns likewise but just to come to herself; we both begin, she to becall, and I to bescratch very liberally. After having made a pretty free Use of my Fingers, without any great Regard to the Parts I attack'd, I counterfeit a Swoon. Mrs. *Jervis* then cries out, O, Sir, what have you done, you have murthered poor *Pamela*: she is gone, she is gone.—

O what a Difficulty it is to keep one's Countenance, when a violent Laugh desires to burst forth.

The poor Booby frightned out of his Wits, jumped out of Bed, and, in his Shirt, sat down by my Bed-Side, pale and trembling, for the Moon shone, and I kept my Eyes wide open, and pretended to fix them in my

---

9. Dialect form of "Upon my Faith."   1. Dialect euphemism for the oath "God's body."

Head. Mrs. *Jervis* apply'd Lavender Water, and Hartshorn,[2] and this, for a full half Hour; when thinking I had carried it on long enough, and being likewise unable to continue the Sport any longer, I began by Degrees to come to my self.

The Squire who had sat all this while speechless, and was almost really in that Condition, which I feigned, the Moment he saw me give Symptoms of recovering my Senses, fell down on his Knees; and O *Pamela*, cryed he, can you forgive me, my injured Maid? by Heaven, I know not whether you are a Man or a Woman, unless by your swelling Breasts.[3] Will you promise to forgive me: I forgive you! D—n you (says I) and d—n you, says he, if you come to that. I wish I had never seen your bold Face, saucy Sow, and so went out of the Room.

O what a silly Fellow is a bashful young Lover!

He was no sooner out of hearing, as we thought, than we both burst into a violent Laugh. Well, says Mrs. *Jervis*, I never saw any thing better acted than your Part: But I wish you may not have discouraged him from any future Attempt; especially since his Passions are so cool, that you could prevent his Hands going further than your Bosom. Hang him, answer'd I, he is not quite so cold as that I assure you; our Hands, on neither side, were idle in the Scuffle, nor have left us any Doubt of each other as to that matter.

Friday Morning.

My Master sent for Mrs. *Jervis*, as soon as he was up, and bid her give an Account of the Plate and Linnen in her Care; and told her, he was resolved that both she and the little Gipsy (I'll assure him) should set out together. Mrs. *Jervis* made him a saucy Answer; which any Servant of Spirit, you know, would, tho' it should be one's Ruin; and came immediately in Tears to me, crying, she had lost her Place on my Account, and that she should be forced to take to a House, as I mentioned before; and that she hoped I would, at least, make her all the amends in my power, for her Loss on my Account, and come to her House whenever I was sent for. Never fear, says I, I'll warrant we are not so near being turned away, as you imagine; and, i'cod,[4] now it comes into my Head, I have a Fetch for him, and you shall assist me in it. But it being now late, and my Letter pretty long, no more at present from

Your Dutiful Daughter,

Shamela.

Letter VII.
Mrs. Lucretia Jervis *to* Henrietta Maria Honora Andrews.

Madam,

Miss *Sham* being set out in a Hurry for my Master's House in *Lincoln-shire*, desired me to acquaint you with the Success of her Stratagem,

---

2. Fainting remedies: a distillate of lavender flowers, and spirits of ammonia.
3. After his second bedroom assault, reprinted below on pp. 335–40, Squire B—— assures Pamela, " 'I know not . . . beyond this lovely Bosom, your Sex.' "
4. A mild oath, equivalent to "egad."

which was to dress herself in the plain Neatness of a Farmer's Daughter, for she before wore the Cloaths of my late Mistress, and to be introduced by me as a Stranger to her Master. To say the Truth, she became the Dress extremely, and if I was to keep a House a thousand Years, I would never desire a prettier Wench in it.

As soon as my Master saw her, he immediately threw his Arms round her Neck, and smothered her with Kisses (for indeed he hath but very little to say for himself to a Woman.) He swore that *Pamela* was an ugly Slut, (pardon, dear Madam, the Coarseness of the Expression) compared to such divine Excellence. He added, he would turn *Pamela* away immediately, and take this new Girl, whom he thought to be one of his Tenant's Daughters, in her Room.

Miss *Sham* smiled at these Words, and so did your humble Servant, which he perceiving, looked very earnestly at your fair Daughter, and discovered the Cheat.

How, *Pamela*, says he, is it you? I thought, Sir, said Miss, after what had happened, you would have known me in any Dress. No, Hussy, says he, but after what hath happened, I should know thee out of any Dress from all thy Sex. He then was what we Women call rude, when done in the Presence of others; but it seems it is not the first time, and Miss defended herself with great Strength and Spirit.

The Squire, who thinks her a pure Virgin, and who knows nothing of my Character, resolved to send her into *Lincolnshire*, on Pretence of conveying her home; where our old Friend *Nanny Jewkes* is Housekeeper, and where Miss had her small one by Parson *Williams* about a Year ago. This is a Piece of News communicated to us by *Robin* Coachman, who is intrusted by his Master to carry on this Affair privately for him: But we hang together, I believe, as well as any Family of Servants in the Nation.

You will, I believe, Madam, wonder that the Squire, who doth not want Generosity, should never have mentioned a Settlement all this while, I believe it slips his Memory: But it will not be long forgot[5], no doubt: For, as I am convinced the young Lady will do nothing unbecoming your Daughter, nor ever admit him to taste her Charms, without something sure and handsome before-hand; so, I am certain, the Squire will never rest till they have danced *Adam* and *Eve*'s kissing Dance together. Your Daughter set out Yesterday Morning, and told me, as soon as she arrived, you might depend on hearing from her.

Be pleased to make my Compliments acceptable to Mrs. *Davis* and Mrs. *Silvester*, and Mrs. *Jolly*, and all Friends, and permit me the Honour, Madam, to be with the utmost Sincerity,

> *Your most Obedient,*
> *Humble Servant,*
> Lucretia Jervis.

If the Squire should continue his Displeasure against me, so as to insist on the Warning he hath given me, you will see me soon, and I

---

5. A. R. Humphreys's emendation of "first," a previously undetected compositor's error.

will lodge in the same House with you, if you have room, till I can
provide for my self to my Liking.

Letter VIII.
Henrietta Maria Honora Andrews *to* Lucretia Jervis.

Madam,

I received the Favour of your Letter, and I find you have not forgot
your usual Poluteness, which you learned when you was in keeping with
a Lord.

I am very much obliged to you for your Care of my Daughter, am
glad to hear she hath taken such good Resolutions, and hope she will
have sufficient Grace to maintain them.

All Friends are well, and remember to you. You will excuse the
Shortness of this Scroll; for I have sprained my right Hand, with boxing
three new made Officers. — Tho' to my Comfort, I beat them all. I rest,

Your Friend and Servant,

Henrietta, &c.

Letter IX.
Shamela Andrews *to* Henrietta Maria Honora Andrews.

Dear Mamma,

I suppose Mrs. *Jervis* acquainted you with what past 'till I left *Bedfordshire;* whence I am after a very pleasant Journey arrived in *Lincolnshire,*
with your old Acquaintance Mrs. *Jewkes,* who formerly helped Parson
Williams to me; and now designs I see, to sell me to my Master; thank
her for that; she will find two Words go to that Bargain.

The Day after my Arrival here, I received a Letter from Mr. *Williams,*
and as you have often desired to see one from him, I have inclosed it to
you; it is, I think, the finest I ever received from that charming Man,
and full of a great deal of Learning.

*O! What a brave Thing it is to be a Schollard, and to be able to talk
Latin.*

Parson Williams *to* Pamela Andrews.

Mrs. Pamela,

Having learnt by means of my Clerk, who Yesternight visited the Rev^d.
Mr. *Peters* with my Commands, that you are returned into this County,
I purposed to have saluted your fair Hands this Day towards Even: But
am obliged to sojourn this Night at a neighbouring Clergyman's; where
we are to pierce a Virgin Barrel of Ale, in a Cup of which I shall not be
unmindful to celebrate your Health.

I hope you have remembered your Promise, to bring me a leaden
Canister of Tobacco (the Saffron Cut) for in Troth, this Country at pres-

ent affords nothing worthy the replenishing a Tube[6] with.—Some I tasted the other Day at an Alehouse, gave me the Heart-Burn, tho' I filled no oftner than five Times.

I was greatly concerned to learn, that your late Lady left you nothing, tho' I cannot say the Tidings much surprized me: For I am too intimately acquainted with the Family; (myself, Father, and Grandfather having been successive Incumbents on the same Cure, which you know is in their Gift) I say, I am too well acquainted with them to expect much from their Generosity. They are in Verity, as worthless a Family as any other whatever. The young Gentleman I am informed, is a perfect Reprobate; that he hath an *Ingenium Versatile*[7] to every Species of Vice, which, indeed, no one can much wonder at, who animadverts on that want of Respect to the Clergy, which was observable in him when a Child, I remember when he was at the Age of Eleven only, he met my Father without either pulling off his Hat, or riding out of the way. Indeed, a Contempt of the Clergy is the fashionable Vice of the Times;[8] but left such Wretches know, they cannot hate, detest, and despise us, half so much as we do them.

However, I have prevailed on myself to write a civil Letter to your Master, as there is a Probability of his being shortly in a Capacity of rendring me a Piece of Service; my good Friend and Neighbour the Rev^d. Mr. *Squeeze-Tithe* being, as I am informed by one whom I have employed to attend for that Purpose, very near his Dissolution.[9]

You see, sweet Mrs. *Pamela*, the Confidence with which I dictate these Things to you; whom after those Endearments which have passed between us, I must in some Respects estimate as my Wife: For tho' the Omission of the Service was a Sin; yet, as I have told you, it was a venial One, of which I have truly repented, as I hope you have; and also that you have continued the wholesome Office of reading good Books, and are improved in your Psalmody, of which I shall have a speedy Trial: For I purpose to give you a Sermon next *Sunday*, and shall spend the Evening with you, in Pleasures, which tho' not strictly innocent, are however to be purged away by frequent and sincere Repentance. I am,

> *Sweet Mrs.* Pamela,
> *Your faithful Servant,*
> ARTHUR WILLIAMS.

You find, Mamma, what a charming way he hath of Writing, and yet I assure you, that is not the most charming thing belonging to him: For, tho' he doth not put any Dears, and Sweets, and Loves into his Letters, yet he says a thousand of them: For he can be as fond of a Woman, as any Man living.

---

6. Pipe.
7. Versatile genius.
8. For Fielding's serious remarks on this, see pp. 312–14; 318–20.

9. Williams hopes to acquire a second clerical benefice or living that is at the disposal of Squire Booby.

Sure Women are great Fools, when they prefer a laced Coat to the Clergy, whom it is our Duty to honour and respect.

Well, on *Sunday* Parson *Williams* came, according to his Promise, and an excellent Sermon he preached; his Text was, *Be not Righteous over much;*[1] and, indeed, he handled it in a very fine way; he shewed us that the Bible doth not require too much Goodness of us, and that People very often call things Goodness that are not so. That to go to Church, and to pray, and to sing Psalms, and to honour the Clergy, and to repent, is true Religion; and 'tis not doing good to one another, for that is one of the greatest Sins we can commit, when we don't do it for the sake of Religion.[2] That those People who talk of Vartue and Morality, are the wickedest of all Persons. That 'tis not what we do, but what we believe, that must save us, and a great many other good Things; I wish I could remember them all.

As soon as Church was over, he came to the Squire's House, and drank Tea with Mrs. *Jewkes* and me; after which Mrs. *Jewkes* went out and left us together for an Hour and half — Oh! he is a charming Man.

After Supper he went Home, and then Mrs. *Jewkes* began to catechize me, about my Familiarity with him. I see she wants him herself. Then she proceeded to tell me what an Honour my Master did me in liking me, and that it was both an inexcusable Folly and Pride in me, to pretend to refuse him any Favour. Pray, Madam, says I, consider I am a poor Girl, and have nothing but my Modesty to trust to. If I part with that, what will become of me. Methinks, says she, you are not so mighty modest when you are with Parson *Williams*; I have observed you gloat at one another, in a Manner that hath made me blush. I assure you, I shall let the Squire know what sort of Man he is; you may do your Will, says I, as long as he hath a Vote for Pallamant-Men, the Squire dares do nothing to offend him; and you will only shew that you are jealous of him, and that's all. How now, Mynx, says she; Mynx! No more Mynx than yourself, says I; with that she hit me a Slap on the Shoulder; and I flew at her and scratched her Face, i'cod, 'till she went crying out of the Room; so no more at present, from

Your Dutiful Daughter,
SHAMELA.

---

1. This text (Ecclesiastes 7:16), which Williams twists into a counsel of moral laxity, was applied in its generally understood antisanctimonial sense to Pamela's too frequent invocation of "the sacred Name" of God by a critical correspondent in Richardson's introduction to the second edition. It was more widely known as the burden of an attack on the Methodists and Whitefield in particular (see above, p. 64, n. 1).

2. As Whitefield emphasized in his sermons, the thirteenth of the Church of England's Articles of Religion stipulates that "Works done before the grace of Christ, and the Inspiration of his Spirit, are not pleasant to God, forasmuch as they spring not of faith in Jesus Christ . . . for that they are not done as God hath willed and commanded them to be done, we doubt not but they have the nature of sin." In addition to espousing salvation through faith rather than works, Williams's sermon also echoes Whitefield's *Short Account* ("I now began to pray and sing psalms thrice every day") and parodies his frequent condemnation of the "Ministers of the Church of England" who "entertain their People with Lectures of mere Morality" (see below, pp. 391–92).

Letter X.
SHAMELA ANDREWS *to* HENRIETTA MARIA HONORA ANDREWS.

O Mamma! Rare News! As soon as I was up this Morning, a Letter was brought me from the Squire, of which I send you a Copy.

Squire BOOBY *to* PAMELA.

Dear Creature,

I hope you are not angry with me for the Deceit put upon you, in conveying you to *Lincolnshire*, when you imagined yourself going to *London*. Indeed, my dear *Pamela*, I cannot live without you; and will very shortly come down and convince you, that my Designs are better than you imagine, and such as you may with Honour comply with. I am,

> *My Dear Creature,*
> *Your doating Lover,*
> BOOBY.

Now, Mamma, what think you?—For my own Part, I am convinced he will marry me, and faith so he shall. O! Bless me! I shall be Mrs. *Booby*, and be Mistress of a great Estate, and have a dozen Coaches and Six, and a fine House at *London*, and another at *Bath*, and Servants, and Jewels, and Plate, and go to Plays, and Opera's, and Court; and do what I will, and spend what I will. But, poor Parson *Williams*! Well; and can't I see Parson *Williams*, as well after Marriage as before: For I shall never care a Farthing for my Husband. No, I hate and despise him of all Things.

Well, as soon as I had read my Letter, in came Mrs. *Jewkes*. You see, Madam, says she, I carry the Marks of your Passion about me; but I have received Order from my Master to be civil to you, and I must obey him: For he is the best Man in the World, notwithstanding your Treatment of him. My Treatment of him; Madam, says I? Yes, says she, your Insensibility to the Honour he intends you, of making you his Mistress. I would have you to know, Madam, I would not be Mistress to the greatest King, no nor Lord in the Universe. I value my Vartue more than I do any thing my Master can give me; and so we talked a full Hour and a half, about my Vartue; and I was afraid at first, she had heard something about the Bantling, but I find she hath not; tho' she is as jealous, and suspicious, as old Scratch.[3]

In the Afternoon, I stole into the Garden to meet Mr. *Williams*; I found him at the Place of his Appointment, and we staid in a kind of Arbour, till it was quite dark. He was very angry when I told him what Mrs. *Jewkes* had threatned — Let him refuse me the Living, says he, if he dares, I will vote for the other Party; and not only so, but will expose

3. The devil.

him all over the Country. I owe him 150 £. indeed, but I don't care for that; by that time the Election is past, I shall be able to plead the *Statue of Lamentations*. [4]

I could have stayed with the dear Man forever, but when it grew dark, he told me, he was to meet the neighbouring Clergy, to finish the Barrel of Ale they had tapped the other Day, and believed they should not part till three or four in the Morning — So he left me, and I promised to be penitent, and go on with my reading in good Books.

As soon as he was gone, I bethought myself, what Excuse I should make to Mrs. *Jewkes*, and it came into my Head to pretend as how I intended to drown myself; so I stript off one of my Petticoats, and threw it into the Canal [5]; and then I went and hid myself in the Coal-hole, where I lay all Night; and comforted myself with repeating over some Psalms, and other good things, which I had got by heart.

In the Morning Mrs. *Jewkes* and all the Servants were frighted out of their Wits, thinking I had run away; and not devising how they should answer it to their Master. They searched all the likeliest Places they could think of for me, and at last saw my Petticoat floating in the Pond. Then they got a Drag-Net, imagining I was drowned, and intending to drag me out; but at last *Moll* Cook coming for some Coals, discovered me lying all along in no very good Pickle. Bless me! Mrs. *Pamela*, says she, what can be the Meaning of this? I don't know, says I, help me up, and I will go in to Breakfast, for indeed I am very hungry. Mrs. *Jewkes* came in immediately, and was so rejoyced to find me alive, that she asked with great Good-Humour, where I had been? and how my Petticoat came into the Pond. I answered, I believed the Devil had put it into my Head to drown my self; but it was a Fib; for I never saw the Devil in my Life, nor I don't believe he hath any thing to do with me.

So much for this Matter. As soon as I had breakfasted, a Coach and Six came to the Door, and who should be in it but my Master.

I immediately run up into my Room, and stript, and washed, and drest my self as well as I could, and put on my prettiest round-ear'd Cap, and pulled down my Stays, to shew as much as I could of my Bosom, (for Parson *Williams* says, that is the most beautiful part of a Woman) and then I practised over all my Airs before the Glass, and then I sat down and read a Chapter in the Whole Duty of Man.

Then Mrs. *Jewkes* came to me and told me, my Master wanted me below, and says she, Don't behave like a Fool; No, thinks I to my self, I believe I shall find Wit enough for my Master and you too.

So down goes me I into the Parlour to him. *Pamela*, says he, the Moment I came in, you see I cannot stay long from you, which I think is a sufficient Proof of the Violence of my Passion. Yes, Sir, says I, I see your Honour intends to ruin me, that nothing but the Destruction of my Vartue will content you.

O *what a charming Word that is, rest his Soul who first invented it.*

---

4. The Statute of Limitations (1623) disallowed legal action for repayment of a debt after six years.   5. An ornamental watercourse.

How can you say I would ruin you, answered the Squire, when you shall not ask any thing which I will not grant you. If that be true, says I, good your Honour, let me go home to my poor but honest Parents;[6] that is all I have to ask, and do not ruin a poor Maiden, who is resolved to carry her Vartue to the Grave with her.

Hussy, says he, don't provoke me, don't provoke me, I say. You are absolutely in my power, and if you won't let me lie with you by fair Means, I will by Force. O la, Sir, says I, I don't understand your paw[7] Words.—Very pretty Treatment indeed, says he, to say I use paw Words; Hussy, Gipsie, Hypocrite, Saucebox, Boldface, get out of my Sight, or I will lend you such a Kick in the ——— I don't care to repeat the Word, but he meant my hinder part. I was offering to go away, for I was half afraid, when he called me back, and took me round the Neck and kissed me, and then bid me go about my Business.

I went directly into my Room, where Mrs. *Jewkes* came to me soon afterwards. So Madam, says she, you have left my Master below in a fine Pet, he hath threshed two or three of his Men already: It is might pretty that all his Servants are to be punished for your Impertinence.

Harkee, Madam, says I, don't you affront me, for if you do, d—n me (I am sure I have repented for using such a Word) if I am not revenged.

How sweet is Revenge: Sure the Sermon Book is in the Right, in calling it the sweetest Morsel the Devil ever dropped into the Mouth of a Sinner.[8]

Mrs. *Jewkes* remembered the Smart of my Nails too well to go farther, and so we sat down and talked about my Vartue till Dinner-time, and then I was sent for to wait on my Master. I took care to be often caught looking at him, and then I always turn'd away my Eyes, and pretended to be ashamed. As soon as the Cloth was removed, he put a Bumper of Champagne into my Hand, and bid me drink ——— O la I can't name the Health. Parson *Williams* may well say he is a wicked Man.

Mrs. *Jewkes* took a Glass and drank the dear *Monysyllable*[9] I don't understand that Word, but I believe it is baudy. I then drank towards his Honour's good Pleasure. Ay, Hussy, says he, you can give me Pleasure if you will; Sir, says I, I shall be always glad to do what is in my power, and so I pretended not to know what he meant. Then he took me into his Lap.—O Mamma, I could tell you something if I would—and he kissed me—and I said I won't be slobber'd about so, so I won't; and he bid me get out out of the Room for a saucy Baggage, and said he had a good mind to spit in my Face.

Sure no Man ever took such a Method to gain a Woman's Heart.

I had not been long in my Chamber before Mrs. *Jewkes* came to me, and told me, my Master would not see me any more that Evening, that is, if he can help it; for, added she, I easily perceive the great Ascendant

---

6. A refrain of Pamela.

7. Obscene. Squire B—— calls Pamela all the following names and "slut" as well.

8. An allusion to a passage from the sermons of Dr. Robert South (1633–1716): "Revenge is certainly the most luscious morsel that the devil can put into the sinner's mouth." An admirer of South's wit, Fielding had previously employed the saying in *The Mock Doctor* (1732) and in *The Champion* for February 2, 1740.

9. A polite slang way of referring to the vulgar name for the female pudendum.

you have over him; and to confess the Truth, I don't doubt but you will shortly be my Mistress.

What, says I, dear Mrs. *Jewkes*, what do you say? Don't flatter a poor Girl, it is impossible his Honour can have any honourable Design upon me. And so we talked of honourable Designs till Supper-time. And Mrs. *Jewkes* and I supped together upon a hot buttered Apple-Pie; and about ten o'Clock we went to Bed.

We had not been a Bed half an Hour, when my Master came pit a pat into the Room in his Shirt as before. I pretended not to hear him, and Mrs. *Jewkes* laid hold of one Arm, and he pulled down the Bedcloaths and came into Bed on the other Side, and took my other Arm and laid it under him, and fell a kissing one of my Breasts as if he would have devoured it; I was then forced to awake, and began to struggle with him, Mrs. *Jewkes* crying why don't you do it? I have one Arm secure, if you can't deal with the rest I am sorry for you. He was as rude as possible to me; but I remembered, Mamma, the Instructions you gave me to avoid being ravished, and followed them, which soon brought him to Terms, and he promised me, on quitting my hold, that he would leave the Bed.

O Parson Williams, *how little are all the Men in the World compared to thee.*

My Master was as good as his Word; upon which Mrs. *Jewkes* said, O Sir, I see you know very little of our *Sect*,[1] by parting so easily from the Blessing when you was so near it. No, Mrs. *Jewkes*, answered he, I am very glad no more hath happened, I would not have injured *Pamela* for the World. And to-morrow Morning perhaps she may hear of something to her Advantage. This she may be certain of, that I will never take her by Force, and then he left the Room.

What think you now, Mrs. *Pamela*, says Mrs. *Jewkes*, are you not yet persuaded my Master hath honourable Designs? I think he hath given no great Proof of them to-night, said I. Your Experience I find is not great, says she, but I am convinced you will shortly be my Mistress, and then what will become of poor me.

With such sort of Discourse we both fell asleep. Next Morning early my Master sent for me, and after kissing me, gave a Paper into my Hand which he bid me read; I did so, and found it to be a Proposal for settling 250 £. a Year on me, besides several other advantagious Offers, as Presents of Money and other things. Well, *Pamela*, said he, what Answer do you make me to this. Sir, said I, I value my Vartue more than all the World, and I had rather be the poorest Man's Wife, than the richest Man's Whore. You are a Simpleton, said he; That may be, and yet I may have as much Wit as some Folks, cry'd I; meaning me, I suppose, said he; every Man knows himself best, says I. Hussy, says he, get out of the Room, and let me see your saucy Face no more, for I find I am in more Danger than you are, and therefore it shall be my Business to avoid

1. Sex.

you as much as I can; and it shall be mine, thinks I, at every turn to throw my self in your way. So I went out, and as I parted, I heard him sigh and say he was bewitched.

Mrs. *Jewkes* hath been with me since, and she assures me she is convinced I shall shortly be Mistress of the Family, and she really behaves to me, as if she already thought me so. I am resolved now to aim at it. I thought once of making a little Fortune by my Person. I now intend to make a great one by my Vartue. So asking Pardon for this long Scroll, I am,

Your dutiful Daughter,

SHAMELA.

Letter XI.

HENRIETTA MARIA HONORA ANDREWS *to* SHAMELA ANDREWS.

Dear Sham,

I received your last Letter with infinite Pleasure, and am convinced it will be your own Fault if you are not married to your Master, and I would advise you now to take no less Terms. But, my dear Child, I am afraid of one Rock only, That Parson *Williams*, I wish he was out of the Way. A Woman never commits Folly but with such Sort of Men, as by many Hints in the Letters I collect him to be: but, consider, my dear Child, you will hereafter have Opportunities sufficient to indulge yourself with Parson *Williams*, or any other you like. My Advice therefore to you is, that you would avoid seeing him any more till the Knot is tied. Remember the first Lesson I taught you, that a married Woman injures only her Husband, but a single Woman herself. I am, in hopes of seeing you a great Lady,

Your affectionate Mother,

HENRIETTA MARIA, &c.

The following Letter seems to have been written before *Shamela* received the last from her Mother.

Letter XII.

SHAMELA ANDREWS *to* HENRIETTA MARIA HONORA ANDREWS.

Dear Mamma,

I Little feared when I sent away my last that all my Hopes would be so soon frustrated; but I am certain you will blame Fortune and not me. To proceed then. About two Hours after I had left the Squire, he sent for me into the Parlour. *Pamela*, said he, and takes me gently by the hand, will you walk with me in the Garden; yes, Sir, says I, and pretended to tremble; but I hope your Honour will not be rude. Indeed, says he, you have nothing to fear from me, and I have something to tell you, which if it doth not please you, cannot offend. We walked out together, and he began thus, *Pamela*, will you tell me Truth? Doth the

Resistance you make to my Attempts proceed from Vartue only, or have I not some Rival in thy dear Bosom who might be more successful? Sir, says I, I do assure you I never had a thought of any Man in the World. How, says he, not of Parson *Williams!* Parson *Williams*, says I, is the last Man upon Earth; and if I was a Dutchess, and your Honour was to make your Addresses to me, you would have no reason to be jealous of any Rival, especially such a Fellow as Parson *Williams*. If ever I had a Liking, I am sure—but I am not worthy of you one Way, and no Riches should ever bribe me the other. My Dear, says he, you are worthy of every Thing, and suppose I should lay aside all Considerations of Fortune, and disregard the Censure of the World, and marry you. O Sir, says I, I am sure you can have no such Thoughts, you cannot demean your self so low. Upon my Soul, I am in earnest, says he,—O Pardon me, Sir, says I, you can't persuade me of this. How Mistress, says he, in a violent Rage, do you give me the Lie? Hussy, I have a great mind to box your saucy Ears, but I am resolved I will never put it in your power to affront me again, and therefore I desire you to prepare your self for your Journey this Instant. You deserve no better Vehicle than a Cart; however, for once you shall have a Chariot, and it shall be ready for you within this half Hour; and so he flung from me in a Fury.

What a foolish Thing it is for a Woman to dally too long with her Lover's Desires; how many have owed their being old Maids to their holding out too long.

Mrs. *Jewkes* came me to presently, and told me, I must make ready with all the Expedition imaginable, for that my Master had ordered the Chariot, and that if I was not prepared to go in it, I should be turned out of Doors, and left to find my way Home on Foot. This startled me a little, yet I resolved, whether in the right or wrong, not to submit nor ask Pardon: For that know you, Mamma, you never could your self bring me to from my Childhood: Besides, I thought he would be no more able to master his Passion for me now, than he had been hitherto; and if he sent two Horses away with me, I concluded he would send four to fetch me back. So, truly, I resolved to brazen it out, and with all the Spirit I could muster up, I told Mrs. *Jewkes* I was vastly pleased with the News she brought me; that no one ever went more readily than I should, from a Place where my Vartue had been in continual Danger. That as for my Master, he might easily get those who were fit for his Purpose; but, for my Part, I preferred my Vartue to all Rakes whatever— And for his Promises, and his Offers to me, I don't value them of a Fig—Not of a Fig, Mrs. *Jewkes*; and then I snapt my Fingers.

Mrs. *Jewkes* went in with me, and helped me to pack up my little All, which was soon done; being no more than two Day-Caps, two Night-Caps, five Shifts, one Sham,[2] a Hoop, a Quilted-Petticoat, two Flannel-Petticoats, two pair of Stockings, one odd one, a pair of lac'd Shoes, a

2. A dickey or false sleeve. Pamela makes a similar inventory of the "little bundle" of clothing she plans to take home, distinguishing this "companion of my poverty, and . . . witness of my honesty" from the "wicked bundle" of presents from her master that she will leave behind (letter 39).

short flowered Apron, a lac'd Neck-Handkerchief, one Clog, and almost
another, and some few Books: as, *A full Answer to a plain and true
Account*, &c.[3] *The Whole Duty of Man*, with only the Duty to one's
Neighbour, torn out. The Third Volume of the *Atalantis*. *Venus in the
Cloyster: Or, the Nun in her Smock*. *God's Dealings with Mr. Whitefield*. *Orfus and Eurydice*.[4] Some Sermon-Books; and two or three Plays,
with their Titles, and Part of the first Act torn off.

So as soon as we had put all this into a Bundle, the Chariot was ready,
and I took leave of all the Servants, and particularly Mrs. *Jewkes*, who
pretended, I believe, to be more sorry to part with me than she was; and
then crying out with an Air of Indifference, my Service to my Master,
when he condescends to enquire after me, I flung my self into the Chariot, and bid *Robin* drive on.

We had not gone far, before a Man on Horseback, riding full Speed,
overtook us, and coming up to the Side of the Chariot, threw a Letter
into the Window, and then departed without uttering a single Syllable.

I immediately knew the Hand of my dear *Williams*, and was somewhat surprized, tho' I did not apprehend the Contents to be so terrible,
as by the following exact Copy you will find them.

Parson WILLIAMS to PAMELA.

Dear Mrs. Pamela,

That Disrespect for the Clergy, which I have formerly noted to you
in that Villain your Master, hath now broke forth in a manifest Fact.[5] I
was proceeding to my Neighbour *Spruce*'s Church, where I purposed to
preach a Funeral Sermon, on the Death of Mr. *John Gage*, the Excise-

---

3. Probably Thomas Bowyer's *A True Account of
the Nature, end, and efficacy of the Sacrament of
the Lord's Supper; being a full answer to the Plain
Account* . . . (1736), one of the attacks on Hoadly's *Plain Account* (p. 65, n. 3). Whitefield's *Short
Account* (p. 282, n. 7) also condemned Hoadly's
view of communion.
4. Of the "three great branches" into which *The
Whole Duty of Man* is divided—the duty to God,
to ourselves, and to our neighbor—Shamela, in
keeping with the self-serving bias of her religion,
lacks "only" the last, which occupies half the
volume. This truncation is consistent with her
enthusiasm for Whitefield, who had recently
denounced the popular devotional book for its
emphasis on good works.
   In specifying the "Third Volume" of the *New
Atalantis* (see above, p. 147, n. 7), *Memoirs of
Europe, Towards the Close of the Eighth Century
. . . done into English by the Translator of the
New Atalantis* (1710), Fielding may have invited
a derisive comparison between *Pamela* and the
first episode of that notorious work, in which a
young nobleman falls in love with a merchant's
adolescent daughter who is beautiful and passionate, but feebleminded. After a titillating sequence
in which he nearly joins her in following the
"Dictates of Nature," he faces Squire B——'s

perplexity—how to "ease my Passion, preserve my
Vertue, and not dishonour my Family" by "a
Marriage with the Daughter of a *Bourgoise*." He
contemplates marrying the girl; but in the end
avoids B——'s fate, for "her *Mind* was a Rock
upon which my Resolution struck: *Love* with all
his *Omnipotence* cou'd never carry me *over* that
Difficulty."
   Venus in the Cloyster (1724) was an erotic tale
originally translated from the French in 1683. Its
republication led to the prosecution of its unscrupulous publisher, Edmund Curll.
   Orpheus and Eurydice (1740), a popular pantomime by Lewis Theobald (1688–1744), Shakespeare editor and original "hero" of Pope's *Dunciad*,
was staged by his friend Rich (p. 29, n. 9). Its
success derived from the dances, musical interludes, and Rich's spectacular effects (e.g., "while
he is playing, the barren mountain changes by
degrees into a pleasant hill. Trees arise and form a
bower over the head of Orpheus") amplifying the
thin scenario of five hundred doggerel lines in
Shamela's library. In *The Champion*, Fielding had
ridiculed its popularity (February 21, 1739/40) and
its reliance on spectacle: "among other very beautiful Scenes, we were diverted with several Prospects of Hell" (May 24, 1740).
5. Criminal act.

man; when I was met by two Persons who are, it seems, Sheriffs Officers, and arrested for the 150 £. which your Master had lent me; and unless I can find Bail within these few Days, of which I see no likelihood, I shall be carried to Goal. This accounts for my not having visited you these two Days; which you might assure yourself, I should not have fail'd, if the *Potestas*[6] had not been wanting. If you can by any means prevail on your Master to release me, I beseech you so to do, not scrupling any thing for Righteousness sake. I hear he is just arrived in this Country, I have herewith sent him a Letter, of which I transmit you a Copy. So with Prayers for your Success, I subscribe myself

> *Your affectionate Friend,*
> Arthur Williams.

Parson Williams *to Squire* Booby.

Honoured Sir,

I am justly surprized to feel so heavy a Weight of your Displeasure, without being conscious of the least Demerit towards so good and generous a Patron, as I have ever found you: For my own Part, I can truly say,

> *Nil conscire sibi nullæ pallescere culpæ.*[7]

And therefore, as this Proceeding is so contrary to your usual Goodness, which I have often experienced, and more especially in the Loan of this Money for which I am now arrested; I cannot avoid thinking some malicious Persons have insinuated false Suggestions against me; intending thereby, to eradicate those Seeds of Affection which I have hardly travailed to sowe in your Heart, and which promised to produce such excellent Fruit. If I have any ways offended you, Sir, be graciously pleased to let me know it, and likewise to point out to me, the Means whereby I may reinstate myself in your Favour: For next to him, whom the Great themselves must bow down before, I know none to whom I shall bend with more Lowliness than your Honour. Permit me to subscribe myself,

> *Honoured Sir,*
> *Your most obedient, and most obliged,*
> *And most dutiful humble Servant,*
> Arthur Williams.

The Fate of poor Mr. *Williams* shocked me more than my own: For, as the *Beggar's Opera* says, *Nothing moves one so much as a great Man in Distress.*[8] And to see a Man of his Learning forced to submit so low, to one whom I have often heard him say, he despises, is, I think, a most

---

6. Power.
7. "To have no guilt at heart, no wrongdoing to turn us pale" (Horace, *Epistles* 1.1.61, H. C. Fairclough trans.). Ironically, Fielding draws Williams's sentiment from a letter Horace addresses to *his* patron, Maecenas, stressing the superiority of virtue to riches or popular acclaim. The original reads nulla culpa.
8. In John Gay's popular satiric ballad opera (1728), Lucy Lockit utters this mock-heroic sentiment as her philandering lover, the highwayman Macheath, is about to be hanged (3.15).

affecting Circumstance. I write all this to you, Dear Mamma, at the Inn where I lie this first Night, and as I shall send it immediately, by the Post, it will be in Town a little before me.—Don't let my coming away vex you: For, as my Master will be in Town in a few Days, I shall have an Opportunity of seeing him; and let the worst come to the worst, I shall be sure of my Settlement at last. Which is all, from

Your dutiful Daughter,

SHAMELA,

P.S. Just as I was going to send this away a Letter is come from my Master, desiring me to return, with a large Number of Promises.—I have him now as sure as a Gun, as you will perceive by the Letter itself, which I have inclosed to you.

This Letter is unhappily lost, as well as the next which *Shamela* wrote, and which contained an Account of all the Proceedings previous to her Marriage.[9] The only remaining one which I could preserve, seems to have been written about a Week after the Ceremony was perform'd, and is as follows:

SHAMELA BOOBY *to* HENRIETTA MARIA HONORA ANDREWS.

Madam,

In my last I left off at our sitting down to Supper on our Wedding Night,* where I behaved with as much Bashfulness as the purest Virgin in the World could have done. The most difficult Task for me was to blush; however, by holding my Breath, and squeezing my Cheeks with my Handkerchief, I did pretty well. My Husband was extreamly eager and impatient to have Supper removed, after which he gave me leave to retire into my Closet for a Quarter of an Hour, which was very agreeable to me; for I employed that time in writing to Mr. *Williams*, who, as I informed you in my last, is released, and presented to the Living, upon the Death of the last Parson. Well, at last I went to Bed, and my Husband soon leap'd in after me; where I shall only assure you, I acted my Part in such a manner, that no Bridegroom was ever better satisfied with his Bride's Virginity. And to confess the Truth, I might have been well enough satisfied too, if I had never been acquainted with Parson *Williams*.

---

* This was the Letter which is lost.

---

9. Fielding thus derisively deletes a full fourth of Richardson's narrative. More than half of this consists of Pamela's daily and then hourly countdown of the week before the wedding, culminating in an 11:00 P.M. wedding night journal entry in which she commits herself "to the Mercies of the Almighty who has led me through so many strange scenes of Terror and Affrightment, to this happy, yet awful Moment." She resumes her journal the following evening with an exclamation anticipatory of *Shamela*: "O How this dear, excellent Man indulges me in every thing!"

O what regard Men who marry Widows should have to the Qualifications of their former Husbands.

We did not rise the next Morning till eleven, and then we sat down to Breakfast; I eat two Slices of Bread and Butter, and drank three Dishes of Tea, with a good deal of Sugar, and we both look'd very silly. After Breakfast we drest our selves, he in a blue Camblet Coat, very richly lac'd, and Breeches of the same; with a Paduasoy[1] Waistcoat, laced with Silver; and I, in one of my Mistress's Gowns. I will have finer when I come to Town. We then took a Walk in the Garden, and he kissed me several Times, and made me a Present of 100 Guineas, which I gave away before Night to the Servants, twenty to one, and ten to another, and so on.

We eat[2] a very hearty Dinner, and about eight in the Evening went to Bed again. He is prodigiously fond of me; but I don't like him half so well as my dear *Williams.* The next Morning we rose earlier, and I asked him for another hundred Guineas, and he gave them me. I sent fifty to Parson *Williams,* and the rest I gave away, two Guineas to a Beggar, and three to a Man riding along the Road, and the rest to other People. I long to be in *London* that I may have an Opportunity of laying some out, as well as giving away. I believe I shall buy every thing I see. What signifies having Money if one doth not spend it.

The next Day, as soon as I was up, I asked him for another Hundred. Why, my Dear, says he, I don't grudge you any thing, but how was it possible for you to lay out the other two Hundred here. La! Sir, says I, I hope I am not obliged to give you an Account of every Shilling; Troth, that will be being your Servant still. I assure you, I married you with no such view, besides did not you tell me I should be Mistress of your Estate? And I will be too. For tho' I brought no Fortune, I am as much your Wife as if I had brought a Million—yes, but, my Dear, says he, if you had brought a Million, you would spend it all at this rate; besides, what will your Expences be in *London*, if they are so great here. Truly, says I, Sir, I shall live like other Ladies of my Fashion; and if you think, because I was a Servant, that I shall be contented to be governed as you please, I will shew you, you are mistaken. If you had not cared to marry me, you might have let it alone. I did not ask you, nor I did not court you. Madam, says he, I don't value a hundred Guineas to oblige you; but this is a Spirit which I did not expect in you, nor did I ever see any Symptoms of it before. O but Times are altered now, I am your Lady, Sir; yes to my Sorrow, says he, I am afraid—and I am afraid to my Sorrow too: For if you begin to use me in this manner already, I reckon you will beat me before a Month's at an end. I am sure if you did, it would injure me less than this barbarous Treatment; upon which I burst into Tears, and pretended to fall into a Fit. This frighted him out of his wits, and he called up the Servants. Mrs. *Jewkes* immediately came in, and she and another of the Maids fell heartily to rubbing my Temples,

1. A popular corded silk fabric; camblet (or camblet) was a plushy fabric of silk mixed with wool or angora.
2. See above, p. 129, n. 7.

and holding Smelling-Bottles to my Nose. Mrs. *Jewkes* told him she fear'd I should never recover, upon which he began to beat his Breasts, and cried out, O my dearest Angel, curse on my passionate Temper, I have destroy'd her, I have destroy'd her!—would she had spent my whole Estate rather than this had happened. Speak to me, my Love, I will melt myself into Gold for thy Pleasure. At last having pretty well tired my self with counterfeiting, and imagining I had continu'd long enough for my purpose in the sham Fit, I began to move my Eyes, to loosen my Teeth, and to open my Hands, which Mr. *Booby* no sooner perceived than he embraced and kissed me with the eagerest Extacy, asked my Pardon on his Knees for what I had suffered through his Folly and Perverseness, and without more Questions fetched me the Money. I fancy I have effectually prevented any farther Refusals or Inquiry into my Expences. It would be hard indeed, that a Woman who marries a Man only for his Money, should be debarred from spending it.

Well, after all things were quiet, we sat down to Breakfast, yet I resolved not to smile once, nor to say one good-natured, or good-humoured Word on any Account.

Nothing can be more prudent in a Wife, than a sullen Backwardness to Reconciliation; it makes a Husband fearful of offending by the Length of his Punishment.

When we were drest, the Coach was by my Desire ordered for an Airing, which we took in it. A long Silence prevailed on both Sides, tho' he constantly squeezed my Hand, and kissed me, and used other Familiarities, which I peevishly permitted. At last, I opened my Mouth first.— And so, says I, you are sorry you are married;—Pray, my Dear, says he, forget what I said in a Passion. Passion, says I, is apter to discover our Thoughts than to teach us to counterfeit. Well, says he, whether you will believe me or no, I solemnly vow, I would not change thee for the richest Woman in the Universe. No, I warrant you, says I; and yet you could refuse me a nasty hundred Pound. At these very Words, I saw Mr. *Williams* riding as fast as he could across a Field; and I looked out, and saw a Lease[3] of Greyhounds coursing a Hare, which they presently killed, and I saw him alight, and take it from them.

My Husband ordered *Robin* to drive towards him, and looked horribly out of humour, which I presently imputed to Jealousy. So I began with him first; for that is the wisest way. La, Sir, says I; what makes you look so Angry and Grim? Doth the sight of Mr. *Williams* give you all this Uneasiness? I am sure, I would never have married a Woman of whom I had so bad an Opinion, that I must be uneasy at every Fellow she looks at. My Dear, answer'd he, you injure me extremely, you was not in my Thoughts, nor, indeed, could be, while they were covered by so morose a Countenance; I am justly angry with that Parson, whose Family hath been raised from the Dunghill by ours; and who hath received from me twenty Kindnesses, and yet is not contented to destroy the Game in all

3. For *leash*, meaning a set of three.

other Places, which I freely give him leave to do; but hath the Impudence to pursue a few Hares, which I am desirous to preserve, round about this little Coppice. Look, my Dear, pray look; says he; I believe he is going to turn Higler.[4] To confess the Truth, he had no less than three ty'd up behind his Horse, and a fourth he held in his Hand.

Pshaw, says I, I wish all the Hares in the Country were d——d (the Parson himself chid me afterwards for using the Word, tho' it was in his Service.) Here's a Fuss, indeed, about a nasty little pitiful Creature, that is not half so useful as a Cat. You shall not persuade me, that a Man of your Understanding, would quarrel with a Clergyman for such a Trifle. No, no, I am the Hare, for whom poor Parson *Williams* is persecuted; and Jealousy is the Motive. If you had married one of your Quality Ladies, she would have had Lovers by dozens, she would so; but because you have taken a Servant-Maid, forsooth! you are jealous if she but looks (and then I began to Water) at a poor P—a—a—rson in his Pu—u—u—lpit, and then out burst a Flood of Tears.

My Dear, said he, for Heaven's sake dry your Eyes, and don't let him be a Witness of your Tears, which I should be sorry to think might be imputed to my Unkindness; I have already given you some Proofs that I am not jealous of this Parson; I will now give you a very strong one: For I will mount my Horse, and you shall take *Williams* into the Coach. You may be sure, this Motion[5] pleased me, yet I pretended to make as light of it as possible, and told him, I was sorry his Behaviour had made some such glaring Instance, necessary to the perfect clearing my Character.

He soon came up to Mr. *Williams*, who had attempted to ride off, but was prevented by one of our Horsemen, whom my Husband sent to stop him. When we met, my Husband asked him how he did with a very good-humoured Air, and told him he perceived he had found good Sport that Morning. He answered pretty moderate, Sir; for that he had found the three Hares tied on to the Saddle dead in a Ditch (winking on me at the same time) and added he was sorry there was such a Rot[6] among them.

Well, says Mr. *Booby*, if you please, Mr. *Williams*, you shall come in and ride with my Wife. For my own part, I will mount on Horseback; for it is fine Weather, and besides, it doth not become me to loll in a Chariot, whilst a Clergyman rides on Horseback.

At which Words, Mr. *Booby* leap'd out, and Mr. *Williams* leap'd in, in an Instant, telling my Husband as he mounted, he was glad to see such a Reformation, and that if he continued his Respect to the Clergy, he might assure himself of Blessings from above.

It was now that the Airing began to grow pleasant to me. Mr. *Williams*, who never had but one Fault, *viz.* that he generally smells of Tobacco, was now perfectly sweet; for he had for two Days together enjoined himself as a Penance, not to smoke till he had kissed my Lips.

4. An itinerant seller or barterer of game, poultry, or produce.

5. Proposal.
6. Liver disease.

I will loosen you from that Obligation, says I, and observing my Husband looking another way, I gave him a charming Kiss, and then he asked me Questions concerning my Wedding-night; this actually made me blush: I vow I did not think it had been in him.

As he went along, he began to discourse very learnedly, and told me the Flesh and the Spirit were two distinct Matters, which had not the least relation to each other. That all immaterial Substances (those were his very Words)[7] such as Love, Desire, and so forth, were guided by the Spirit: But fine Houses, large Estates, Coaches, and dainty Entertainments were the Product of the Flesh. Therefore, says he, my Dear, you have two Husbands, one the Object of your Love, and to satisfy your Desire; the other the Object of your Necessity, and to furnish you with those other Conveniencies. (I am sure I remember every Word, for he repeated it three Times; O he is very good whenever I desire him to repeat a thing to me three times he always doth it!) as then the Spirit is preferable to the Flesh, so am I preferable to your other Husband, to whom I am antecedent in Time likewise. I say these things, my Dear, (said he) to satisfie your Conscience. A Fig for my Conscience, said I, when shall I meet you again in the Garden?

My Husband now rode up to the Chariot, and asked us how we did— I hate the Sight of him. Mr. *Williams* answered, very well, at your Service. They then talked of the Weather, and other things, I wished him gone again, every Minute; but all in vain, I had no more Opportunity of conversing with Mr. *Williams*.

Well; at Dinner Mr. *Booby* was very civil to Mr. *Williams*, and told him he was sorry for what had happened, and would make him sufficient Amends, if in his power, and desired him to accept of a Note for fifty Pounds; which he was so *good* to receive, notwithstanding all that had past; and told Mr. *Booby*, he hop'd he would be forgiven, and that he would pray for him.

We make a charming Fool of him, i'fackins;[8] Times are finely altered, I have entirely got the better of him, and am resolved never to give him his Humour.

O how foolish it is in a Woman, who hath once got the Reins into her own Hand, ever to quit them again.

After Dinner Mr. *Williams* drank the Church *et cætera*; and smiled on me; when my Husband's Turn came, he drank *et cætera*[9] and the Church; for which he was very severely rebuked by Mr. *Williams*; it being a high Crime, it seems, to name any thing before the Church. I

7. Williams sophistically exploits the scriptural opposition of flesh and spirit (Romans 8:1–17; Galatians 5:16–24) and Descartes's differentiation of the physical and mental realms. Although both Descartes and Locke postulated an immaterial substance at work in thought, and subsequent writers employed this phrase, the more immediate target of this derisive reference is probably George Cheyne's *Philosophical Conjectures on the Original Animal Body* (1740), which defined "the *Spirit*" as "the immaterial Substance" (42) informing and perpetually in conflict with the "Matter and Substance of the original first-created Animal Body" (6). Fielding had previously cited passages from this work and Dr. Cheyne's *Essay on the Regimen of the Diet* as unintelligible jargon in *The Champion* for May 17 and June 12, 1740.

8. In faith.

9. See above, p. 276, n. 5.

do not know what *Et cetera* is, but I believe it is something concerning chusing Pallament Men; for I asked if it was not a Health to Mr. *Booby's* Borough, and Mr. *Williams* with a hearty Laugh answered, Yes, Yes, it is his Borough we mean.

I slipt out as soon as I could, hoping Mr. *Williams* would finish the Squire, as I have heard him say he could easily do, and come to me; but it happened quite otherwise, for in about half an Hour, *Booby* came to me, and told me he had left Mr. *Williams*, the Mayor of his Borough, and two or three Aldermen heartily at it, and asked me if I would go hear *Williams* sing a Catch, which, added he, he doth to a Miracle.

Every Opportunity of seeing my dear *Williams*, was agreeable to me, which indeed I scarce had at this time; for when we returned, the whole Corporation[1] were got together, and the Room was in a Cloud of Tobacco; Parson *Williams* was at the upper End of the Table, and he hath pure round cherry Cheeks, and his Face look'd all the World to nothing like the Sun in a Fog. If the Sun had a Pipe in his Mouth, there would be no Difference.

I began now to grow uneasy, apprehending I should have no more of Mr. *Williams's* Company that Evening, and not at all caring for my Husband, I advised him to sit down and drink for his Country with the rest of the Company; but he refused, and desired me to give him some Tea; swearing nothing made him so sick, as to hear a Parcel of Scoundrels, roaring forth the Principles of honest Men over their Cups, when, says he, I know most of them are such empty Blockheads, that they don't know their right Hand from their left; and that Fellow there, who hath talked so much of *Shipping*, at the left Side of the Parson, in whom they all place a Confidence, if I don't take care, will sell them to my Adversary.[2]

I don't know why I mention this Stuff to you; for I am sure I know nothing about *Pollitricks*, more than Parson *Williams* tells me; who says that the Court-side are in the right on't, and that every Christian ought to be on the same with the Bishops.[3]

When we had finished our Tea, we walked in the Garden till it was dark, and then my Husband proposed, instead of returning to the Company, (which I desired, that I might see Parson *Williams* again,) to sup in another Room by our selves, which, for fear of making him jealous, and considering too, that Parson *Williams* would be pretty far gone, I was obliged to consent to.

O! what a devilish thing it is, for a Woman to be obliged to go to bed

---

1. See above, p. 104, n. 1.
2. An allusion to a recent parliamentary disaster for the opposition. Six weeks before the publication of *Shamela*, a motion to remove Walpole failed overwhelmingly when many Tories deserted the opposition. Some of them actually voted against the motion, but the departure before the vote of veteran Jacobite leader William Shippen (1673–1743) and thirty-four followers caused more comment. The widely respected and incorruptible,

though not always sober, Shippen (who sat with other opposition leaders on the left of the Speaker) was suspected by some of taking a bribe. Sheridan Baker points out that Walpole's son Horace wrote "Shippen" here in the margin of his copy.
3. Through the judicious exercise of the crown's power to appoint bishops, Walpole had assembled an episcopal bench in the House of Lords predominantly allied with his administration on "the Court-side."

to a spindle-shanked young Squire, she doth not like, when there is a jolly Parson in the same House she is fond of.

In the Morning I grew very peevish, and in the Dumps, notwithstanding all he could say or do to please me. I exclaimed against the Priviledge of Husbands, and vowed I would not be pulled and tumbled about. At last he hit on the only Method, which could have brought me into Humour, and proposed to me a Journey to *London*, within a few Days. This you may easily guess pleased me; for besides the Desire which I have of shewing my self forth, of buying fine Cloaths, Jewels, Coaches, Houses, and ten thousand other fine things, Parson *Williams* is, it seems going thither too, to be *instuted.*[4]

O! what a charming Journey I shall have; for I hope to keep the dear Man in the Chariot with me all the way; and that foolish Booby (for that is the Name Mr. Williams *hath set him) will ride on Horseback.*

So as I shall have an Opportunity of seeing you so shortly, I think I will mention no more Matters to you now. O I had like to have forgot one very material thing; which is that it will look horribly, for a Lady of my Quality and Fashion, to own such a Woman as you for my Mother. Therefore we must meet in private only, and if you will never claim me, nor mention me to any one, I will always allow you what is very handsome. Parson *Williams* hath greatly advised me in this; and says, he thinks I should do very well to lay out twenty Pounds, and set you up in a little Chandler's Shop: but you must remember all my Favours to you will depend on your Secrecy; for I am positively resolved, I will not be known to be your Daughter; and if you tell any one so, I shall deny it with all my Might, which Parson *Williams* says, I may do with a safe Conscience, being now a married Woman. So I rest

Your humble Servant,

SHAMELA.

P. S. The strangest Fancy hath enter'd into my Booby's Head, that can be imagined. He is resolved to have a Book made about him and me; he proposed it to Mr. *Williams*, and offered him a Reward for his Pains; but he says he never writ any thing of that kind, but will recommend my Husband, when he comes to Town, to a Parson *who does that Sort of Business for Folks*, one who can make my Husband, and me, and Parson *Williams*, to be all great People; for he *can make black white*, it seems. Well, but they say my Name is to be altered, Mr. *Williams*, says the first Syllabub hath too comical a Sound, so it is to be changed into *Pamela*; I own I can't imagine what can be said; for to be sure I shan't confess any of my Secrets to them, and so I whispered Parson *Williams* about that, who answered me, I need not give my self any Trouble; for the Gentleman *who writes Lives*, never asked more than a few Names of his Customers, and that he made all the rest out of his own Head; you mistake, Child, said he, if you apprehend any Truths are to be delivered. So far on the contrary, if you had not been acquainted

---

4. Williams has succeeded in obtaining the living at Squire Booby's disposal and is to be *instituted* in his spiritual office by the Bishop.

with the Name, you would not have known it to be your own History. I
have seen a *Piece of his Performance*, where the Person, whose Life was
written, could he have risen from the Dead again, would not have even
suspected he had been aimed at, unless by the Title of the Book, which
was superscribed with his Name.[5] Well, all these Matters are strange to
me, yet I can't help laughing to think I shall see my self in a printed
Book.

So much for Mrs. *Shamela*, or *Pamela*, which I have taken Pains to
transcribe from the Originals, sent down by her Mother in a Rage, at
the Proposal in her last Letter. The Originals themselves are in my hands,
and shall be communicated to you, if you think proper to make them
publick; and certainly they will have their Use. The Character of *Shamela*, will make young Gentlemen wary how they take the most fatal
Step both to themselves and Families, by youthful, hasty and improper
Matches; indeed, they may assure themselves, that all such Prospects of
Happiness are vain and delusive, and that they sacrifice all the solid
Comforts of their Lives, to a very transient Satisfaction of a Passion,
which how hot so ever it be, will be soon cooled; and when cooled, will
afford them nothing but Repentance.

Can any thing be more miserable, than to be despised by the whole
World, and that must certainly be the Consequence; to be despised by
the Person obliged, which it is more than probable will be the Consequence, and of which, we see an Instance in *Shamela*; and lastly to
despise one's self, which must be the Result of any Reflection on so weak
and unworthy a Choice.

As to the Character of Parson *Williams*, I am sorry it is a true one.
Indeed those who do not know him, will hardly believe it so; but what
Scandal doth it throw on the Order to have one bad Member, unless
they endeavour to screen and protect him? In him you see a Picture of
almost every Vice exposed in nauseous and odious Colours; and if a
Clergyman would ask me by what Pattern he should form himself, I
would say, Be the reverse of *Williams*:[6] So far therefore he may be of
use to the Clergy themselves, and though God forbid there should be
many *Williams's* amongst them, you and I are too honest to pretend,
that the Body wants no Reformation.

To say the Truth, I think no greater Instance of the contrary can be
given than that which appears in your Letter. The confederating to cry
up a nonsensical ridiculous Book, (I believe the most extensively so of
any ever yet published,) and to be so weak and so wicked as to pretend
to make it a Matter of Religion; whereas so far from having any moral
Tendency, the Book is by no means innocent: For,

5. Sheridan Baker's conclusion that this is the
Life of Cicero and the parson who writes lives is
Middleton conforms to Parson Oliver's earlier
identification of *Pamela*'s supposed author (see
above, p. 279, n. 5). But *Cicero* was Middleton's
sole biographical subject, and Charles Woods has
suggested this may refer to the Reverend Thomas
Birch (1705–66) who wrote hundreds of pedestrian
lives for the English edition of Bayle's *Dictionary*
(1734–41).
6. Compare Fielding's "general Picture" of "what
a Clergyman is not" in *The Champion*, below, p.
319.

First, There are many lascivious Images in it, very improper to be laid before the Youth of either Sex.[7]

2dly, Young Gentlemen are here taught, that to marry their Mother's Chambermaids, and to indulge the Passion of Lust, at the Expence of Reason and Common Sense, is an Act of Religion, Virtue, and Honour; and, indeed the surest Road to Happiness.[8]

3dly, All Chambermaids are strictly enjoyned to look out after their Masters; they are taught to use little Arts to that purpose: And lastly, are countenanced in Impertinence to their Superiors, and in betraying the Secrets of Families.

4thly, In the Character of Mrs. *Jewkes* Vice is rewarded; whence every Housekeeper may learn the Usefulness of pimping and bawding for her Master.

5thly, In Parson *Williams*, who is represented as a faultless Character, we see a busy Fellow, intermeddling with the private Affairs of his Patron, whom he is very ungratefully forward to expose and condemn on every Occasion.[9]

Many more Objections might, if I had Time or Inclination, be made to this Book; but I apprehend, what hath been said is sufficient to persuade you of the use which may arise from publishing an Antidote to this Poison. I have therefore sent you the Copies of these Papers, and if you have Leisure to communicate them to the Press, I will transmit you the Originals, tho' I assure you, the Copies are exact.

I shall only add, that there is not the least Foundation for any thing which is said of Lady *Davers*, or any of the other Ladies; all that is merely to be imputed to the Invention of the Biographer. I have particularly enquired after Lady *Davers*, and dont hear Mr. *Booby* hath such a Relation, or that there is indeed any such Person existing.[1] I am,

> *Dear Sir,*
> *Most faithfully and respectfully,*
> *Your humble Servant,*
>
> J. OLIVER.

---

7. *Pamela*'s title page addressed it to "the YOUTH of BOTH SEXES" and proclaimed it "entirely divested of all those Images, which . . . tend to *inflame* the Minds they should *instruct*." At the end of the book, Richardson specified the "application of its most material incidents" to each kind of reader, from "such as are born to large fortunes" to "the *Lower Servants*."

8. One of Richardson's prefatory correspondents anticipates the objection that "Mothers, or Grandmothers, in all Families of affluent Fortune . . . [may fear] that the Example of a Gentleman so amiable as Mr. B - - - may be follow'd, by . . . *their* Sons with too blind and unreflecting a Readiness. . . . because *every belov'd* Maid will be PAMELA, in a Judgment obscur'd by her Influence."

9. Richardson had cited the "odious Character" of *Jewkes* to "Upper Servants" as an example of "what to avoid," but a critical correspondent thought the married Pamela "ought, for Example sake, to have discharg'd" her. Richardson praised the original Parson Williams's intercession for Pamela in the face of his patron's displeasure as a demonstration to the clergy that they will in the long run be "even *more* valued for a Conduct that gave Offense while the Violence of Passion lasted, than if they had merely stooped to flatter or sooth the Vices of the Great."

1. Lady Davers, Squire B——'s proud sister, who savagely excoriates Pamela as a scheming upstart in a lengthy melodramatic scene late in the novel, is eventually converted to admiration of her sister-in-law's virtue. Fielding may again have taken his cue from the "Introduction" to Richardson's second edition, where the objection that "the Passions of Lady Davers . . . are carried too high, and above Nature" is answered by the offer to point out "a Dozen or two of *Quality Originals*, from whom (with Exception perhaps of her *Wit*) one wou'd swear the Author had taken her Copy."

Parson TICKLETEXT *to Parson* OLIVER.

Dear S I R,

I have read over the History of *Shamela*, as it appears in those authentick Copies you favour'd me with, and am very much ashamed of the Character,[2] which I was hastily prevailed on to give that Book. I am equally angry with the pert Jade herself, and with the Author of her Life: For I scarce know yet to whom I chiefly owe an Imposition, which hath been so general, that if Numbers could defend me from Shame, I should have no Reason to apprehend it.

As I have your implied Leave to publish, what you so kindly sent me, I shall not wait for the Originals, as you assure me the Copies are exact, and as I am really impatient to do what I think a serviceable Act of Justice to the World.

Finding by the End of her last Letter, that the little Hussy was in Town, I made it pretty much my Business to enquire after her, but with no effect hitherto: As soon as I succeed in this Enquiry, you shall hear what Discoveries I can learn. You will pardon the Shortness of this Letter, as you shall be troubled with a much longer very soon: And believe me,

> *Dear Sir,*
> *Your most faithful Servant,*
> THO. TICKLETEXT.

P. S. Since I writ, I have a certain Account, that Mr. *Booby* hath caught his Wife in bed with *Williams*; hath turned her off, and is prosecuting him in the spiritual Court.[3]

F I N I S.

2. Recommendation.
3. The ecclesiastical courts had jurisdiction over moral offenses of the clergy.

RELATED WRITINGS

FROM *THE CHAMPION* †

[Essay on Reputation]

March 4, 1739/40

* * *

Tho' Virtue and Wisdom be in Reality the Opposites to Folly and Vice, they are not so in Appearance. Indeed, it requires a nicer Eye to Distinguish them, than is commonly believed. The two latter are continually industrious to disguise themselves, and wear the Habits of the former. They know their native Deformity and endeavour to conceal it; which the World, always judging by the Outside, easily suffers them to accomplish. Actions of the worst Nature have, by the Assistance of false Glosses, been accompanied with Honour, and Men have often arrived at the highest Fame by deserving the highest Infamy; which, when we consider the general Incapacity of Mankind, we shall be so far from being astonish'd at, that we shall rather think it Matter of Wonder, that they have ever judged right. True Virtue is of a retired and quiet Nature, content with herself, not at all busied in courting the Acclamations of the Crowd; she is plain and sober in her Habit, sure of her innate Worth, and therefore neglects to adorn herself with those gaudy Colours, which catch the Eyes of the giddy Multitude. Vice, on the contrary, is of a noisy and boistrous Disposition, despising herself, and jealous [1] of the Contempt of others, always meditating how she may acquire the Applause of the World, gay and fluttering in her Appearance, certain of her own ill Features, and therefore careful by all the Tricks of Art to impose on and engage the Affections of her Beholders.—Thus accomplished, how can the latter fail to please, and the former to be slighted!

* * *

* * * There is a Consciousness in true Merit, which renders a Man careless of the Reception it meets with. He disdains to fly to little Arts to inform the World of what it wants only Judgment to discover of itself. He is rather studious to deserve than acquire Praise. Whereas, the Man of a contrary Character is always forward to acquaint others with his Deserts. He is not desirous of Virtue itself, but only the Reputation of it, therefore is more solicitous to carry Virtue in his Countenance than

---

† Fielding was editor and part owner of *The Champion; or, British Mercury* (later subtitled *Evening Advertiser*), an organ of the opposition to Walpole's ministry, from its first issue, November 15, 1739, to June 1741. The thrice weekly periodical was professedly the work of Captain Hercules Vinegar, "Censor of Great Britain" and "Champion of Virtue, Honour, and Patriotism," aided by members of his fictional family. The text is that of the 1741 collected reprint. A few printer's errors have been silently corrected.
1. Fearful.

in his Heart; whence it often comes to pass, that the worst of Men have imposed on the World, and enjoyed the highest Degree of Reputation, while those of the greatest Worth have been slighted and despised.

*   *   *

[Essay on Good Nature]

March 27, 1740

*   *   *

Good-nature is a Delight in the Happiness of Mankind, and a Concern at their Misery, with a Desire, as much as possible, to procure the former, and avert the latter; and this, with a constant Regard to Desert.

Good-nature is not that Weakness which, without Distinction, affects both the Virtuous and the Base, and equally laments the punishment of Villainy,with the Disappointment of Merit; for as this amiable Quality respects the whole, so it must give up the Particular, to the Good of the General.

It is not that Cowardice which prevents us from repelling or resenting an Injury; for it doth not divest us of Humanity, and like Charity, tho' it doth not end, may at least begin at Home.

From these Propositions, the Truth of which will not, I believe, be denied, unless for the Sake of Argument, I draw the following Conclusions.

That those who include Folly and Cowardice, as the certain Ingredients of Good-nature, compound their Idea of Good-nature of very different Simples from those who exclude them.

That as Good-nature requires a distinguishing Faculty, which is another Word for Judgment, and is perhaps the sole Boundary between Wisdom and Folly; it is impossible for a Fool, who hath no distinguishing Faculty, to be good-natured.

That as Good-nature, which is the chief if not only Quality in the Mind of Man in the least tending that Way, doth not forbid the avenging an Injury, Christianity hath taught us something beyond what the Religion of Nature and Philosophy could arrive at; and consequently, that it is not *as old as the Creation*,[2] nor is Revelation useless with Regard to Morality, if it had taught us no more than this excellent Doctrine, which, if generally followed, would make Mankind much happier, as well as better than they are.

That to be averse to, and repine at the Punishment of Vice and Villainy, is not the Mark of Good nature but Folly; on the contrary, to

---

2. In *Christianity as old as the Creation; or the Gospel a Republication of the Religion of Nature* (1730), Matthew Tindal maintained that God in his beneficence must have made the basic tenets of true religion available to all men through the use of their reason and questioned the unique authority of the Bible as the revelation of God's will. A major statement of the deist position, the work was severely attacked by orthodox Christian writers.

bring a *real* and *great* Criminal to Justice, is, perhaps, the best-natured Office we can perform to Society, and the Prosecutor, the Juryman, the Judge and the Hangman himself may do their Duty without injuring this Character; nay, the last Office, if properly employed, may be in Truth the best natured, as well as the highest Post of Honour in the Kingdom.

That there is no Parodox or Repugnancy in that Character given of the excellent Earl of *Dorset*: That he was *The best good Man with the worst natured Muse.*[3] For Satire on Vice or vicious Men, tho' never so pointed, is no more a Sign of Ill-nature than it would be to crush a Serpent, or destroy a wild Beast. If the Mind be only tainted with one particular Vice, this is but a Potion given to our Disease; and tho' it may be attended with some Pain in the Operation, the Satirist is to be regarded as our Physician, not our Enemy; but if the Mind be totally corrupted, if it subsists a Nusance and Infection only to others, such a Man, I am sure, hath little Reason to complain that the Satirist attacks him instead of the Executioner, and while he lives the Pest and Curse of his Country, may very easily and quietly sit down contented with being laughed at.

Lastly, that as Good-nature is a Delight in the Happiness of Mankind, every good-natured Man will do his utmost to contribute to the Happiness of each Individual; and consequently that every Man who is not a Villain, if he loves not the good-natured Man, is guilty of Ingratitude.

This is that amiable Quality, which, like the Sun, gilds over all our other Virtues; this it is, which enables us to pass through all the Offices and Stations of Life with real Merit. This only makes the dutiful Son, the affectionate Brother, the tender Husband, the indulgent Father, the kind Master, the faithful Friend, and the firm Patriot. This makes us gentle without Fear, humble without Hopes, and charitable without Ostentation, and extends the Power, Knowledge, Strength, and Riches of Individuals to the Good of the Whole. It is (as Shakspeare calls it)[4] the Milk, or rather the Cream of Human Nature, and whoever is possessed of this Perfection should be pitied, not hated for the Want of any other. Whereas all other Virtues without some Tincture of this, may be well called *Splendida Peccata*;[5] for the richer, stronger, more powerful, or more knowing an ill-natured Man is, the greater Mischiefs he will perpetrate; it is Ill-nature, with these qualities, which hath fettered and harrassed Mankind; hath erected the Tyrant's Throne, hath let loose the Conqueror's two-edged Sword, and the Priest's two edged Tongue; hath imposed severe Laws, invented cruel Punishments, hath sent abroad Fire and Sword and Faggot, to ravage, burn, depopulate and enslave Nations. Lastly, hath injuriously bowed the conquer'd Father down to, and bred up the slavish Son in an Estimation and Honour of those Men

3. Charles Sackville, sixth earl of Dorset (1638–1706), Restoration poet and wit, was described in these words by his friend John Wilmot, earl of Rochester, in "An Allusion to Horace, the 10th Satyr of the 1st Book," l.60.
4. *Macbeth* 1.4.
5. Shining faults.

and those Actions, which are the just Objects of Contempt, Abhorrence, and Detestation.

I know not so great, so glorious, so lovely an Idea of the benevolent Creator of the Universe, as that which is affixed to him by the noble Author whom we have so often quoted, and shall quote. He is (says he) *The best-natured Being in the Universe*;[6] the more therefore we cultivate the sweet Disposition in our Minds, the nearer we draw to Divine Perfection; to which we should be the more strongly incited, as it is that which we may approach the nearest to. All his other Attributes throw us immediately out of Sight, but this Virtue lies in Will, and not at all in Power.

Nor can the selfish Man want Incentives to this Virtue; for as it is more easily and safely satisfied than Ambition, Revenge, or any of those pernicious Passions, so are its Joys more exquisite, and less interrupted. Ambition is seldom satisfied without Fear, or Revenge without Remorse; but the good natured Man can never carry his Enjoyments too far, this being the only Affection of the human Mind which can never be sated.

[The Apology for the Clergy]

Saturday, March 29, 1740

—ἠτίμης᾽ ἀρητῆρα. HOMER[1]

There is nothing so unjustifiable as the general Abuse of any Nation or Body of Men: For which Reason, I have always disliked those Sarcasms we are too apt to cast on a particular Part of His Majesty's Dominions,[2] whose Natives have been commonly censured by the *English* Mob for Blundering and Assurance, tho' it is notorious that several of our greatest Wits and best-bred Men have come to us from that Quarter.

In like Manner, I have already condemn'd the Custom of throwing Scandal on a whole Profession for the Vices of some particular Members. Can any Thing be more unreasonable than to cast an Odium on the Professions of Divinity, Law, and Physic, because there have been absurd or wicked Divines, Lawyers, and Physicians?

But there is an Error directly opposite to this, which may likewise deserve Correction. I mean that Protection which some Persons would draw from their Professions, who, when they are justly censured for their Actions, retreat (if I may so say) behind the Walls of their Order, and endeavour to represent our Attacks on the Individual to be levelled at the whole Body. Whereas, the Profession should give no more Security to the Man than the Man should bring a Disgrace on his Profession.

The Awe which the wiser and better Part of Mankind have of the Supreme Being, and consequently of every Thing which seems more

6. The earl of Shaftesbury (see p. 5, n. 7), in A *Letter Concerning Enthusiasm* (1708) 5.

1. "Dishonoured the priest" (*Iliad* 1.11.).
2. Ireland.

immediately to belong to his Service, hath encouraged some Clergymen to apply to the Dignity or Divinity of their Office, as a Security against all Accusation: It is well known, that a few Years since, if you had given a Hint that any particular Person in Holy Orders had misbehaved himself, a Cry would have been immediately raised that the Church was in Danger,[3] and you would have been arraigned for spreading such Invectives, with a malicious Design of bringing the whole Body of the Clergy into Contempt.

Now it seems to me a most apparent Truth that the greater Honour which we entertain for our Creator, the greater Abomination we shall have for those who pervert his holy Institutions, and have the Impudence to wear the Livery of his more immediate Service, whilst they act against it. In what Manner would a good subject of *Great-Britain* behave to one of his profligate Countrymen abroad, who should betray the Interest of his King, and at the same Time presume to call himself his Ambassadour?

I have heard of a Pamphlet, called *Reasons of the Contempt of the Clergy*.[4] If by the Clergy, the Author means the Order, I hope there is no such Contempt; nay, I will venture to say, there is not among sensible and sober Men, the only Persons whose ill Opinion is to be valued, or by any Argument to be removed. This Contempt, therefore, must be meant of particular Clergymen, and even this I should be unwilling to allow justifiable, or to assign any *Reason* for it. Human Frailty is indeed such, that it is very difficult, if not impossible, to preserve any Body (especially so large a one) from some rotten Members, but the utmost Care is here taken on that Regard. Numberless public Schools are instituted for the Instruction of our Youth, the Masters of which are prefered with proper Respect to their *Morals* as well as Learning. Hence the Scholars are remov'd to one or other of two excellent Universities, *alike* remark'd for their Erudition, Sobriety, and good Order. After which the strictest and most impartial Examination must be undergone before the Candidate will be admitted into Holy Orders, in which the young Divine can afterwards expect no Promotion but from his Merit, no ecclesiastical Preferments being by any Means whatever to be purchas'd; and as for the Mitre, it is always inscrib'd (or at least of late hath been so) with these Words, DETUR MAGIS PIO.[5]

If, notwithstanding all this Care, a few unworthy members *creep*[6] in, it is certainly doing a serviceable Office to the Body to detect and expose them; nay, it is what the Sound and uncorrupt Part should not only be pleas'd with, but themselves endeavour to execute, especially if they are suspicious of, or offended at Contempt or Ridicule, which can never fall

3. See above, p. 104, n. 3.
4. Either John Hildrop's *The Contempt of the Clergy Considered, in a Letter to a Friend* (1739), which advocated freeing the church from state control, or the often reprinted satire, *The Grounds and Occasions of the Contempt of the Clergy and Religion enquired into* (1670), by John Eachard.
5. "Let it be given to the more pious".
6. Probably an allusion to Milton's *Lycidas*: ". . . such as for their bellies' sake, / Creep and intrude and climb into the fold" (114–15).

with any Weight on the Order itself, or on any Clergyman, who is not really a Scandal to it.

Tho' I am, as I have before said, very far from acknowledging that sensible or sober Minds are tainted with any such general Contempt, as hath been intimated, yet as perhaps some idle and unthinking young Men, may express too little Respect (to use a common Phrase) for the *Cloth*, I shall here attempt to set a Clergyman in a just and true Light, which will, I believe, be sufficient to guard him from any Danger of a Treatment which such a Person can never suffer, but thro' the Ignorance of those who are guilty of it. Such Ignorance I shall therefore attempt to remove, since I do not recollect any modern Writings tending this Way, and it may require some Reflection and Parts to collect a true Idea of so amiable a Character from nice[7] Observations on the general Behaviour of the Clergy.

I shall therefore consider the Clergy in a twofold Light, first, as they appear to us in the Gospel; and, secondly, as they are regarded in the Law.

As to the first, we are to look on them as the Successors of those Disciples, whom Christ, as we are told in Mark ii.14. ordained, *That they should be with him, and that he might send them forth to preach*; or, as the *Greek* properly signifies, *to proclaim their Master*; which they, and their Successors, were *to perform in all the World, for a Witness to all Nations, 'till the End come*, Matt. xxiv.14, and Mark xiii.10. In which Sense, *Simon* was figuratively told he should be made a *Fisher of Men*. And in the 9th of Luke, the Disciples are sent abroad to *proclaim the Kingdom of God*. And we read in the 10th Chapter of the same Gospel, *That the Lord appointed other Seventy also, and sent them two and two before his Face into every City, saying to them, Go your Ways, behold I send you forth as Lambs among Wolves*.

The Office, therefore, of the Disciples, and their Successors, was to proclaim or * * * to *call* or *summon* Men into the Kingdom of God, and by spreading the Excellence of His Doctrine to induce Men to become Followers of Christ, and by that Means Partakers of his Salvation.

As the Souls of Men are therefore of infinite more Consequence and Dignity than their Bodies, as eternal and perfect, is infinitely more valuable than imperfect and finite Happiness; this Office which concerns the eternal Happiness of the Souls of Men, must be of greatly superior Dignity, and Honour to any of those whose Business is at most the Regulation or well Being of the Body only.

But here I would not be understood to mean what we vulgarly call Honour and Dignity in a worldly Sense, such as Pomp or Pride, or Flattery, or any of this Kind, to which indeed nothing can be so opposite, as will appear from examining into the Qualities which are laid down as absolutely necessary to form this Character, and indeed must be understood so, as they are no other than the Copies of their great

7. Careful, precise.

Master's. And in which, whoever is deficient, can never be esteemed a true Disciple or Minister of Christ.

The First I shall name is Humility; a Virtue of which he himself was so perfect a Pattern, and which he so earnestly recommended to his Disciples, that he rebuked them when they contended *who should be reckoned the greatest;*[8] and in another Place, exhorted them to *beware of the Scribes which desire to walk in long Robes, and love Greetings in the Markets, and the* HIGHEST SEATS *in the Synagogues, and the chief Rooms at* FEASTS *which* DEVOUR WIDOWS HOUSES, *and for* SHOW *make* LONG *Prayers, &c. Luke* 20.46,47. And St. *Paul* is frequent in the same Advice, forbidding any to *think high of himself,* for which he gives them this Reason, *that very few wise, or mighty, or noble,* in a worldly Sense, were called to the Ministry, but such as were reputed to be *the Filth of the World, and the Offscouring of all Things.*[9] Our Blessed Saviour himself, instead of introducing himself into the World in the Houses or Families of what we call the Great, chose to be born of the Wife of a Carpenter, his Disciples were poor Fishermen, and *Paul* himself no more than a Tent maker; he everywhere practised and taught Contempt of worldly Grandeur and Honours, often inculcating in his excellent Discourses that his Kingdom was not of this World, nor his Rewards to be bestow'd in it, intending to lay the Foundation of a truly noble, refined, and Divine Philosophy, and not of any Pomp or Palaces, any of the Show, Splendour, or Luxury of the Heathenish Religions, for his Disciples, or their Successors to enjoy.

As we have not Room for half the Virtues of a Clergyman in this Paper, we shall defer the further Prosecution of this Subject till next Saturday; on which Day, weekly, we shall endeavour to communicate something GOOD *to our Readers, for the Instruction of such as frequent Coffee-Houses on a Sunday.*

Saturday, April 5, 1740.

—*Movet tantæ Pietatis Imago.*[1]—VIRG.

The Apology for the CLERGY *continued*

CHAPTER II

The next Virtue which I shall mention is Charity, a Virtue not confined to Munificence or giving Alms, but that brotherly Love and friendly Disposition of Mind which is every where taught in Scripture. Thus the Word ἀγάπη, which some Versions render Charity, is better rendered by others Love, in which Sense it is described by the Apostle in the 13th Chapter of his first Epistle to the *Corinthians. Charity suffereth long, and is kind; Charity envieth not; Charity vaunteth not itself, is not puffed up. Doth not behave itself unseemly, seeketh not her own, is not easily*

---

8. Matthew 18:1–5; Mark 9:34–37; Luke 9:46–48; 22:24–27.
9. Romans 12:3; I Corinthians 1:26; 4:13.

1. "May such an image of piety move you" (*Aeneid* 6.405).

provoked, thinketh no Evil. Rejoiceth not in Iniquity; but rejoiceth in the Truth. Beareth all Things, believeth all Things, hopeth all Things, endureth all Things.

First, then, a Minister of the Gospel must forgive his Enemies; *Charity suffereth long, is not easily provoked, beareth all Things, endureth all Things.* Thus *Christ* himself saith, *If you do not forgive, neither will your Father in Heaven forgive your Trespasses.*[2] Indeed this is the Characteristic of a Christian Minister, and must distinguish him from the best of the *Heathens*, who taught no such Doctrine.

Secondly, *Charity is kind*; or, as the Greek signifies, *does good Offices, behaves kindly*; not confined to our Wishes merely, but our Actions, under which Head I shall introduce Liberality, a necessary Qualification of any who would call himself a Successor of *Christ's* Disciples. By this Virtue, which is generally called Charity itself, (and perhaps it is the chief Part of it) is not meant the ostentatious giving a Penny to a Beggar in the Street (an Ostentation, of which I do not accuse the Clergy, having to my Knowledge never seen ONE guilty of it), as if Charity was Change for Sixpence, but the relieving the Wants and Sufferings of one another to the utmost of our Abilities. It is to be limited by our Power, I say, only. And this *Christ* himself, in the 25th Chap. of *Matthew*, finely illustrates by a Parable: For it is not expected that he who hath received two Talents only, should render as much as he who hath received five; but, on the other Hand, the Man to whom no more than one is entrusted ought not to hide that one in the Earth, for it is *his Lord's Money*. I shall dwell no longer on this Head, than to observe that this ESSENTIAL Duty is not to be discharged at so easy a Rate as some think, by a Christian, much less a Christian Minister, and that it would be a shocking and dreadful Consideration, if many hungry, should find no Meat; many thirsty, no Drink, many Strangers, none to take them in, naked, none to clothe them, sick, and in Prison, none to visit them, in a Country where *Christ* hath upwards of 10,000 Disciples, on whom he hath bestowed so *many Talents*.

Thirdly, *Charity envieth not.* * * *

Fourthly, *It vaunteth not itself, is not puffed up, doth not behave itself unseemly.* By which we may be assured that all Pride is inconsistent with this Quality.* * *

Fifthly, *It seeketh not her own.* By these Words the Apostle plainly points out the Forgiveness of Debts, as before he hath done of Injuries (for this is the plain Meaning of the *Greek*, whatever forced Construction may be put upon it). Thus in the 10th Chapter of the same Epistle, *Let no Man seek his own Wealth.* I would not *be righteous over-much*,[3] or extend this Text too far; as it might perhaps unhinge Society: But I cannot dismiss this Branch without paying a Compliment to the Clergy, who are of all Men the most backwards to insist on a rigid Payment with

---

2. Matthew 6:15.

3. Ecclesiastes 7:16. The phrase had special currency at this time because of Joseph Trapp's anti-

Methodist sermon on this text (see above, p. 64, n. 1).

their Creditors; and in regard to their Tithes, which (whether of common Right or no, a matter we may perhaps handle hereafter) are certainly by the *present* Laws of *England* their own, are known to consider not only the Straitness of Men's Circumstances, but likewise of their Consciences as in the Case of the *Quakers*;[4] for the Truth of which, I appeal to common Experience.

Sixthly, *Charity thinketh no Evil*. It is void of Suspicion, not apt to censure the Actions of Men, much less to represent them in an evil Light to others. Hence we may judge how inconsistent that odious Malignity, which is the Parent of Slander, is with the Character of a true Christian Disciple; a cursed Temper of Mind fitter for the Devil and his Angels, than for a Professor of that Love which was taught by *Christ*, and which *Solomon* had long before told us *cover'd all Sins*.[5]

Seventhly, *Rejoiceth not in Iniquity*. By this the Apostle doth not, I apprehend, point at that Joy which Sin may be supposed to give to an evil Mind, in the same manner as Virtue delights a good one: But rather to caution us against that feigned Delight in Sin, which we sometimes put on from a Subserviency to great ones. By not rejoicing in Iniquity is meant, not taking the Wages of sinful Men, nor partaking of their Dainties at the Expense of flattering them in their Iniquity. This is a Virtue, which as it becomes every Christian, so more particularly a Minister of the Gospel, whose Business it is to rebuke and reprove such Men, not to fall in with, or flatter their Vices, but,

Eighthly, *To rejoice with the Truth*. To rejoice in the Company of good and virtuous Men, without the Recommendation of Titles and Wealth, or the Assistance of Dainties and fine Wines. To give God Thanks who hath revealed the Truth to us, and to rejoice in all those who walk in it.

Ninthly, *Charity believeth all Things, hopeth all Things*. It is inclined to maintain good and kind Thoughts of Men. It is a Stranger to all Sourness and Bitterness of Mind, that Moroseness of Temper which seduces us *to think Evil* of others; whereas, Charity always turns the Perspective,[6] with a friendly Care to magnify all good Actions, and lessen evil. It weights all Mankind in the Scales of Friendship, and sees them with the Eyes of Love.

Charity is all this, and he who falls short of any of these, falls short of Charity, without which, the Apostle tells us, *That the gift of Prophecy, the understanding Mysteries, all knowledge, all Faith, nay, even Martyrdom itself are nothing, profit nothing, nor will they make a Man a Christian, much less a Successor of Christ's Disciples*.[7]

As this Virtue of Charity, which I have open'd in so diffusive a Manner, comprehends almost the whole particular Duty of a Christian, I

---

4. Quakers refused to pay tithes because they rejected the idea of an ordained separate spiritual leadership and would not support a mode of worship they considered impure and idolatrous. Although many Anglican priests selectively refrained from collecting these fees, others brought writs for nonpayment and drove some conscientious refusers into debtors prison for years.

5. Proverbs 10:12.

6. Telescope.

7. I Corinthians 13:2–3.

shall not dwell on those Virtues which we have been taught by Morality, such as Patience, Fortitude, Temperance, Chastity, &c., which, tho' all Mankind are bound to the Observance of, yet a Minister of the Gospel is obliged to it in a more strict and exemplary Manner.

The last Qualification which I shall mention, and which is peculiar to the Clergy, is Poverty. Thus, when *Jesus* represented the Mischiefs attending Riches to his Disciples,*Peter*, in the Name of them all, answered him, *Lo, we have left all, and have followed thee.*[8] And the Terms on which the young Man, whom St. *Luke* calls a Ruler, and who had been a strict Observer of the Law, was to be admitted a Follower of *Jesus* and Inheritor of the Kingdom of Heaven, were, that he should first sell ALL he had, and give it to the Poor.[9] I shall not quote more Texts on this Occasion, as they are almost numberless, and as this Doctrine, I know, is not by some good Men received in a strict, literal, practical Sense: But without *being righteous over much,*[1] we may, I think, conclude, that if the Clergy are not to abandon all they have to their Ministry, neither are they to get immense Estates by it; and I would recommend it to the Consideration of those who do, whether they do not make a Trade of Divinity? Whether they are not those Buyers and Sellers who should be drove out of the Temple? Or lastly, Whether they do not in the Language of *Peter* to *Simon*, sell the Gift of God for Money?[2]

[Chapter III (Saturday, April 12, 1740) explains how the clergy are "regarded by the Law" as "a Body of Men set apart for the immediate Service of the Divine Being, not for their own sakes alone, but the universal Good of the whole." Fielding considers in turn how English law "hath wisely dignified" this office "with the highest Honours, indulged it with the freest Immunities, rewarded it with the most plentiful Revenues, and secured it by the most wholesome Restraints."]

Saturday, April 19, 1740

—*Procul, O procul este, Profani,*

Exclamat Vates, totq; absistite Luco.—VIRGIL.[3]

The Apology for the CLERGY *concluded*

Having explained the Particulars which compose the true Character of a Christian Minister, I shall now draw them closer together, that the Reader may at one View comprehend this amiable Picture.

A Clergyman is a Successor of Christ's Disciples: A Character which not only includes an Idea of all the moral Virtues, such as Temperance, Chastity[4], Patience, &c. but he must be humble, charitable, benevo-

---

8. Mark 10:28; Luke 18:28.
9. Luke 18:22.
1. See above p. 64, n. 1.
2. Acts 8:20
3. " 'Away, oh away, you profane ones,' shouts the prophetess; 'keep away from the whole sacred grove.' " (*Aeneid* 6.258–9). Fielding substitutes *exclamat* for Virgil's *conclamat*.
4. The 1741 reprint reads "Charity," an apparent error. "Chastity" is used in a similar context four paragraphs above.

lent, void of Envy, void of Pride, void of Vanity, void of Rapaciousness, gentle, candid,[5] truly sorry for the Sins and Misfortunes of Men, and rejoicing in their Virtue and Happiness. This good Man is entrusted with the Care of our Souls, over which he is to watch as a Shepherd for his Sheep: *To Feed the Rich with Precept and Example, and the Poor with Meat also.* To live in daily Communication with his Flock, and chiefly with those who want him most (as the Poor and Distress'd) nay, and after his Blessed Master's Example, to eat with *Publicans and Sinners;*[6] but with a View of reclaiming them by his Admonitions, not of fatning himself by their Dainties.

Can such a Man as this be the Object of Contempt? or can any be more entitled to Respect and Honour? Perhaps indeed Boys and Beaus, and Madmen, and Rakes, and Fools, and Villains, may laugh at this sacred Person, may shake those ridiculous Heads at him which would have been flung in the Face of a *Socrates* or a *Plato.* But can such Contempt as this which would have been *enjoyed* by a Heathen, be *felt* by a Christian Philosopher, while all the good, the sober, the virtuous and the sensible Parts of Mankind concur in paying him Honour and Respect?

But perhaps this will be denied to be the Case, and I shall be told that some of this latter Kind have lately not only spoke but writ against the Clergy. I answer, if there are any such, they are Enemies to the Men and not the Order: Nay, the Order cannot be wounded through a bad Man's Sides, for he is really not of it. It is not a particular Habit, nor mounting once a Week into a Pulpit, nor taking the Revenues of the Church, can make a Man a Minister of Christ, but the fulfilling his Precepts and following his Example.

As I have already therefore shewn what a Clergyman is, I will now shew what he is not; but to avoid Prolixity, I will throw the several particular Features into one general Picture.

Let us suppose then, a Man of loose Morals, proud, malevolent, vain, rapacious, and revengeful; not grieving at, but triumphing over the Sins of Men, and rejoicing, like the Devil, that they will be punished for them; deaf to the Cries of the Poor; shunning the Distress'd; blind to Merit; a Magnifier and Spreader of Slander; not shunning the Society of the Wicked for Fear of Contamination, but from Hypocrisy and Vain Glory; hating not Vice but the Vicious; resenting not only an Injury, but the least Affront with Inveteracy. Let us suppose this Man feasting himself luxuriously at the Tables of the Great, where he is suffered at the Expense of flattering their Vices, and often too, as meanly submitting to see himself and his Order, nay often Religion itself, ridiculed, whilst, that he may join in the Burgundy, he joins in the Laugh, or rather is laughed at by the Fools he flatters.——Suppose him going hence, (perhaps in his Chariot) through the Streets, and contemptuously overlooking a Man of Merit and Learning in Distress. *Proh Deum atque*

---

5. "Free from malice; not desirous to find faults,"   6. Matthew 9:11, Mark 2:16; Luke 5:30.
Johnson's Dicitonary.

Hominum Fidem![7] Is this a Christian?——Perhaps it will be said I have drawn a Monster, and not a Portrait taken from Life. God forbid it should; but it is not sufficient that the whole does not resemble; for he who hath but an Eye, a Nose, a single Feature in this deformed Figure, can challenge[8] none of the Honours due to a Minister of the Gospel.

*   *   *

What then can the most candid Man conclude of a Clergyman, whom he beholds pursuing the very Measures which the Gospel shews him lead to the incurring Eternal Misery, and avoiding that Road which would conduct him to infinite Happiness, unless, but that he is an Ideot or an Unbeliever?

And as a Clergyman cannot be supposed a Christian without being a good Man; so if he be a Deist or an Atheist he is infinitely worse than all others of that Kind; for he must be both a Hypocrite and a Cheat.

In what other Light can such a Wretch appear in the Pulpit, than that of a Quack-Doctor on the Stage, who trumpets over the Virtues of his Pills only to pick the Pockets of the Multitude, whilst he believes the direct contrary of what he says, and begs to be excused from taking any of them himself?

Let such Wretches therefore, if any such there be, assure themselves that it is as impossible for any Order or Dignity to wipe off Contempt from their Characters, as to strip Jet of the Idea of Blackness: But suppose they should happen to be in the Wrong, suppose (as they will most certainly find them) the Threats as well as Promises of the Gospel should be true, what an Account are they then to make? How trifling is the Contempt of the World to what they then will suffer?

> —Quàm vellent æthere in alto,
> Nunc & Pauperiem & duros perferre Labores![9]

When they will be forced to render up an Account of their Charge, and must suffer for the Sins of all those whom their Examples have led astray. They will then be taught that the Duty of a Shepherd is not fleecing only. And will find themselves obliged to account not only for the lost Souls, but the lost Tithes too, which they took of COMMON RIGHT[1] or, in other Words, without doing any thing for them.

I have thus finished what I intended, and what I begun with a good Design; for as nothing can hurt Religion so much as a Contempt of the Clergy, so nothing can justify or indeed cause any such Contempt but their own bad Lives. If there are any therefore among them who want Reformation in this Particular, it would be a truly Episcopal Office to attempt it. If I should awaken any such Enquiry, I have had large Amends

---

7. "By the faith of gods and men!" (Cicero, *Tusculan Disputations* 5.16.48).
8. Claim.
9. "How gladly now would they undergo poverty

and hard labor in the air above" (*Aeneid* 6. 436–37).
1. The legal right to a share of another's property.

for my Labour, and shall be very indifferent whether avowed Deists abuse me for having Religion, or Hypocrites for having none.

AN ESSAY
ON THE KNOWLEDGE OF THE
CHARACTERS OF MEN †

I have often thought it a melancholy Instance of the great Depravity of Human Nature, that whilst so many Men have employed their utmost Abilities to invent Systems, by which the artful and cunning Part of Mankind may be enabled to impose on the rest of the World; few or none should have stood up the Champions of the innocent and unde-signing, and have endeavoured to arm them against Imposition.

Those who predicate of Man in general, that he is an Animal of this or that Disposition, seem to me not sufficiently to have studied Human Nature; for that immense Variety of Characters so apparent in Men even of the same Climate, Religion, and Education, which gives the Poet a sufficient Licence, as I apprehend, for saying, that

Man differs more from Man, than Man from Beast,[1]

could hardly exist, unless the Distinction had some original Foundation in Nature itself. Nor is it perhaps a less proper Predicament[2] of the Genius of a Tree, that it will flourish so many Years, loves such a Soil, bears such a Fruit, &c. than of Man in general, that he is good, bad, fierce, tame, honest, or cunning.

This original Difference will, I think, alone account for that very early and strong Inclination to Good or Evil, which distinguishes different Dispositions in Children, in their first Infancy; in the most un-informed Savages, who can be thought to have altered their Nature by no Rules, nor artfully acquired Habits; and lastly, in Persons who from the same Education, &c. might be thought to have directed Nature the same Way; yet, among all these, there subsists, as I have before hinted, so manifest and extreme a Difference of Inclination or Character, that almost obliges us, I think, to acknowledge some unacquired, original Distinction, in the Nature or Soul of one Man, from that of another.

Thus, without asserting in general, that Man is a deceitful Animal; we may, I believe, appeal for Instances of Deceit to the Behaviour of some Children and Savages. When this Quality therefore is nourished and improved by Education, in which we are taught rather to conceal

---

† First published in Fielding's *Miscellanies*, 1743. The text is from the Wesleyan Edition, vol. 1, ed. Henry Knight Miller.
1. John Wilmot, earl of Rochester, "Satyr Against Mankind," 224.
2. Predication, assertion. Fielding's meaning may become clearer if the order of the statement is inverted: "It is no more proper to say of all men that they possess certain moral qualities than it would be to say of all trees that they will flourish in the same conditions or bear the same fruit."

Vices, than to cultivate Virtues; when it hath sucked in the Instruction of Politicians, and is instituted in the *Art of thriving*,[3] it will be no Wonder that it should grow to that monstrous Height to which we sometimes see it arrive. This *Art of thriving* being the very Reverse of that Doctrine of the Stoics; by which Men were taught to consider themselves as Fellow-Citizens of the World, and to labour jointly for the common Good, without any private Distinction of their own: Whereas *This*, on the contrary, points out to every Individual his own particular and separate Advantage, to which he is to sacrifice the Interest of all others; which he is to consider as his *Summum Bonum*,[4] to pursue with his utmost Diligence and Industry, and to acquire by all Means whatever. Now when this noble End is once established, Deceit must immediately suggest itself as the necessary Means: for as it is impossible that any Man endowed with rational Faculties, and being in a State of Freedom, should willingly agree, without some Motive of Love or Friendship, absolutely to sacrifice his own Interest to that of another; it becomes necessary to impose upon him, to persuade him, that his own Good is designed, and that he will be a Gainer by coming into those Schemes, which are, in Reality, calculated for his Destruction. And this, if I mistake not, is the very Essence of that excellent Art, called *The Art of Politics*.

Thus while the crafty and designing Part of Mankind, consulting only their own separate Advantage, endeavour to maintain one constant Imposition on others, the whole World becomes a vast Masquerade, where the greatest Part appear disguised under false Vizors and Habits; a very few only shewing their own Faces, who become, by so doing, the Astonishment and Ridicule of all the rest.

But however cunning the Disguise be which a Masquerader wears: however foreign to his Age, Degree, or Circumstance, yet if closely attended to, he very rarely escapes the Discovery of an accurate Observer; for Nature, which unwillingly submits to the Imposture, is ever endeavouring to peep forth and shew herself; nor can the Cardinal, the Friar, or the Judge, long conceal the Sot, the Gamester, or the Rake.

In the same Manner will those Disguises which are worn on the greater Stage, generally vanish, or prove ineffectual to impose the assumed for the real Character upon us, if we employ sufficient Diligence and Attention in the Scrutiny. But as this Discovery is of infinitely greater Consequence to us; and as perhaps all are not equally qualified to make it, I shall venture to set down some few Rules, the Efficacy (I had almost said Infallibility) of which, I have myself experienced. Nor need any

3. At least two manuals offering instruction in this art appeared in the seventeenth century. Thomas Powell's *The Art of Thriving, or the Plaine Pathway to Preferment* (1635) appeared originally as *Tom of All Trades. Or The Plaine Path-way to Preferment. Being a Discovery of a Passage to Promotion in All Professions, Trades, Arts, and Mysteries* (1631). In 1674 *The Art of Thriving or, The Way to Get and Keep Money* was published anonymously. Another work in the same vein,

William de Britaine's *Humane Prudence, or The Art by Which Man May Raise Himself and Fortune to Grandeur*, went through thirteen editions between its appearance in 1680 and the time of Fielding's writing.
4. The highest good, a term used by such moral philosophers as Aristotle and Saint Thomas Aquinas to designate the ideal of human activity or attainment.

Man be ashamed of wanting or receiving Instructions on this Head; since that open Disposition, which is the surest Indication of an honest and upright Heart, chiefly renders us liable to be imposed on by Craft and Deceit, and principally disqualifies us for this Discovery.[5]

Neither will the Reader, I hope, be offended, if he should here find no Observations entirely new to him. Nothing can be plainer, or more known, than the general Rules of Morality, and yet thousands of Men are thought well employed in reviving our Remembrance, and enforcing our Practice of them. But though I am convinced there are many of my Readers whom I am not capable of instructing on this Head, and who are indeed fitter to give than receive Instructions, at least from me, yet this Essay may perhaps be of some Use to the young and unexperienced, to the more open, honest and considering Part of Mankind, who, either from Ignorance or Inattention, are daily exposed to all the pernicious Designs of that detestable Fiend, Hypocrisy.

I will proceed therefore, without further Preface, to those Diagnostics[6] which Nature, I apprehend, gives us of the Diseases of the Mind, seeing she takes such Pains to discover those of the Body. And first, I doubt whether the old Adage of *Fronti nulla Fides*, be generally well understood: The Meaning of which is commonly taken to be, that *no Trust is to be given to the Countenance.* But what is the Context in *Juvenal?*[7]

> —*Quis enim non vicus abundat*
> *Tristibus obscœnis?*
> —*What Place is not filled with*
> *austere Libertines?*

Now that an austere Countenance is no Token of Purity of Heart, I readily concede. So far otherwise, it is perhaps rather a Symptom of the contrary. But the Satyrist surely never intended by these Words, which have grown into a Proverb, utterly to depreciate an Art on which so wise a Man as *Aristotle* hath thought proper to compose a Treatise.[8]

The Truth is, we almost universally mistake the Symptoms which Nature kindly holds forth to us; and err as grossly as a Physician would, who should conclude that a very high Pulse is a certain Indication of Health; but sure the Faculty would rather impute such a Mistake to his deplorable Ignorance, than conclude from it, that the Pulse could give a skilful and sensible Observer no Information of the Patient's Distemper.

In the same Manner, I conceive, the Passions of Men do commonly imprint sufficient Marks on the Countenance; and it is owing chiefly to

5. "Honest and undesigning Men of very good Understanding would be always liable to the Attacks of cunning and artful Knaves, into whose Snares we are as often seduced by the Openness and Goodness of the Heart, as by the Weakness of the Head. True Wisdom is commonly attended with a Simplicity of Manners, which betrays a worthy Man to a tricking Shuffler, of a much inferior Capacity' (*The Champion*, February 21, 1739/40).

6. Symptoms.
7. *Satire* 2.8–9.
8. The *Physiognomonica*, not by Aristotle but possibly by a member of his peripatetic school of philosophy, enumerates signs of mental and moral qualities to be inferred from movements, gestures, voice quality, hair, skin, and body proportions, as well as facial expressions.

want of Skill in the Observer, that Phsyiognomy is of so little Use and Credit in the World.

But our Errors in this Disquisition would be little wondered at, if it was acknowledged, that the few Rules which generally prevail on this Head are utterly false, and the very Reverse of Truth. And this will perhaps appear, if we condescend to the Examination of some Particulars. Let us begin with the Instance given us by the Poet above, of Austerity; which, as he shews us, was held to indicate a Chastity or Severity of Morals, the contrary of which as himself shews us, is true.

Among us, this Austerity, or Gravity of Countenance, passes for Wisdom with just the same Equity of Pretension. My Lord *Shaftsbury* tells us, that *Gravity is of the Essence of Imposture.*[9] I will not venture to say, that it certainly denotes Folly, though I have known some of the silliest Fellows in the World very eminently possessed of it. The Affections which it indicates, and which we shall seldom err in suspecting to lie under it, are Pride, Ill-nature, and Cunning. Three Qualities which when we know to be inherent in any Man, we have no Reason to desire any further Discovery to instruct us, to deal as little and as cautiously with him as we are able.

But though the World often pays a Respect to these Appearances which they do not deserve; they rather attract Admiration than Love, and inspire us rather with Awe than Confidence. There is a Countenance of a contrary Kind, which hath been called a Letter of Recommendation;[1] which throws our Arms open to receive the Poison, divests us of all kind of Apprehension, and disarms us of all Caution: I mean that glavering,[2] sneering Smile, of which the greater Part of Mankind are extremely fond, conceiving it to be the Sign of Good-Nature; whereas this is generally a Compound of Malice and Fraud, and as surely indicates a bad Heart, as a galloping Pulse doth a Fever.

Men are chiefly betrayed into this Deceit, by a gross but common Mistake of Good-Humour for Good-Nature. Two Qualities so far from bearing any Resemblance to each other, that they are almost Opposites. Good-Nature is that benevolent and amiable Temper of Mind which disposes us to feel the Misfortunes, and enjoy the Happiness of others; and consequently pushes us on to promote the latter, and prevent the former; and that without any abstract Contemplation on the Beauty of Virtue, and without the Allurements or Terrors of Religion.[3] Now Good-Humour is nothing more than the Triumph of the Mind, when reflecting on its own Happiness, and that perhaps from having compared it with the inferior Happiness of others.

If this be allowed, I believe we may admit that glavering Smile, whose

9. A *Letter Concerning Enthusiasm* 2 (*Characteristics*, ed. J. M. Robertson [London: 1900] 1.10). Shaftesbury argues that the only way to determine true gravity from false is to submit it to the test of ridicule.

1. In his anecdotal *Lives and Opinions of Eminent Philosophers*, the third-century Greek writer Diogenes Laertius ascribed to Aristotle or Diogenes the saying that beauty is "a greater recommendation than any letter of introduction" 5.18, R. D. Hicks trans.).

2. Deceitful, flattering.

3. Compare the definition of good nature in *The Champion*, p. 310 above.

principal Ingredient is Malice, to be the Symptom of Good-humour. And here give me Leave to define this Word Malice, as I doubt whether it be not in common Speech so often confounded with Envy, that common Readers may not have very distinct Ideas between them. But as Envy is a Repining at the Good of others, compared with our own, so Malice is a rejoicing at their Evil, on the same Comparison. And thus it appears to have a very close Affinity to that malevolent Disposition, which I have above described under the Word Good-Humour: for nothing is truer than the Observation of *Shakespear*;

—*A Man may smile, and smile, and be a Villain.*[4]

But how alien must this Countenance be to that heavenly Frame of Soul, of which *Jesus Christ* himself was the most perfect Pattern; of which blessed Person it is recorded, that he never was once seen to laugh, during his whole Abode on Earth.[5] And what indeed hath Good-Nature to do with a smiling Countenance? It would be like a Purse in the Hands of a Miser, which he could never use. For admitting, that laughing at the Vices and Follies of Mankind is entirely innocent, (which is more perhaps than we ought to admit) yet surely their Miseries and Misfortunes are no Subjects of Mirth: And with these, *Quis non vicus abundat?*[6] the World is so full of them, that scarce a Day passes without inclining a truly good-natured Man rather to Tears than Merriment.

Mr. *Hobbes* tells us, that Laughter arises from Pride, which is far from being a good-natured Passion.[7] And though I would not severely discountenance all Indulgence of it, since Laughter, while confined to Vice and Folly, is no very cruel Punishment on the Object, and may be attended with good Consequences to him; yet we shall, I believe, find, on a careful Examination into its Motive, that it is not produced from Good-Nature. But this is one of the first Efforts of the Mind, which few attend to, or indeed are capable of discovering; and however Self-Love may make us pleased with seeing a Blemish in another which we are ourselves free from, yet Compassion on the first Reflection of any Unhappiness in the Object, immediately puts a Stop to it in good Minds. For Instance; suppose a Person well drest should tumble in a dirty Place in the Street; I am afraid there are few who would not laugh at the Accident: Now what is this Laughter other than a convulsive Extasy, occasioned by the Contemplation of our own Happiness, compared with the unfortunate Person's! a Pleasure which seems to savour of Ill-nature: but as this is one of those first, and as it were, spontaneous Motions of the Soul, which few, as I have said, attend to, and none can prevent; so it doth not properly constitute the Character. When we come to reflect

4. *Hamlet* 1.5.108.
5. The earliest source for this idea is apparently the Greek church father, St. John Chrysostom (345–407).
6. See Fielding's translation of Juvenal, p. 323 above.
7. "The passion of laughter is nothing else but *sudden glory* arising from some sudden *conception* of some *eminency* in ourselves, by *comparison* with the *infirmity* of others, or with our own formerly" (Hobbes, *Human Nature, or the Fundamental Elements of Policy* 9. 13 [*English Works*, ed. W. Molesworth, 4. 46]). The idea is reiterated in his *Leviathan* 1. 6.

on the Uneasiness this Person suffers, Laughter, in a good and delicate Mind, will begin to change itself into Compassion; and in Proportion as this latter operates on us, we may be said to have more or less Good-Nature: but should any fatal Consequence, such as a violent Bruise, or the breaking of a Bone, attend the Fall, the Man who should still continue to laugh, would be entitled to the basest and vilest Appellation with which any Language can stigmatize him.

From what hath been said, I think we may conclude, that a constant, settled, glavering, sneering Smile in the Countenance, is so far from indicating Goodness, that it may be with much Confidence depended on as an Assurance of the contrary.

But I would not be understood here to speak with the least Regard to that amiable, open, composed, cheerful Aspect, which is the Result of a good Conscience, and the Emanation of a good Heart; of both which it is an infallible Symptom; and may be the more depended on, as it cannot, I believe, be counterfeited, with any reasonable Resemblance, by the nicest[8] Power of Art.

Neither have I any Eye towards that honest, hearty, loud Chuckle, which shakes the Sides of Aldermen and 'Squires, without the least Provocation of a Jest; proceeding chiefly from a full Belly; and is a Symptom (however strange it may seem) of a very gentle and inoffensive Quality, called Dulness, than which nothing is more risible: for as Mr. *Pope*, with exquisite Pleasantry, says;

—Gentle Dulness ever loves a Joke.[9]

i.e. one of her own Jokes. These are sometimes performed by the Foot; as by leaping over Heads, or Chairs, or Tables, Kicks in the B——ch,[1] &c. sometimes by the Hand; as by Slaps in the Face, pulling off Wigs, and infinite other Dexterities, too tedious to particularize: sometimes by the Voice; as by hollowing, huzzaing, and singing merry (*i.e.* dull) Catches, by *merry* (*i.e.* dull) Fellows.

Lastly; I do by no means hint at the various Laughs, Titters, Tehes, &c. of the Fair Sex, with whom indeed this Essay hath not any thing to do; the Knowledge of the Characters of Women being foreign to my intended Purpose; as it is in Fact a Science, to which I make not the least Pretension.

The Smile or Sneer which composes the Countenance I have above endeavour'd to describe, is extremely different from all these: but as I have already dwelt pretty long on it, and as my Reader will not, I apprehend, be liable to mistake it, I shall wind up my Caution to him against this Symptom, in Part of a Line of *Horace*:

—Hic niger est; hunc tu caveto.[2]

There is one Countenance, which is the plainest Instance of the general Misunderstanding of that Adage, *Fronti nulla Fides*. This is a fierce

8. Most discriminating or skillful.
9. *The Dunciad Variorum* (1729) 2.30.
1. Breech (buttocks). See above, p. 196, n. 8.

2. "That man is black of heart; of him beware" (*Satires* 1.4.85, H. R. Fairclough trans.).

Aspect, which hath the same Right to signify Courage, as Gravity to denote Wisdom, or a Smile Good-Nature; whereas Experience teaches us the contrary, and it passes among most Men for the Symptom only of a Bully.

But I am aware, that I shall be reminded of an Assertion which I set out with in the Beginning of this Essay, *viz. That Nature gives us as sure Symptoms of the Diseases of the Mind as she doth of those of the Body.* To which what I have now advanced may seem a Contradiction. The Truth is, Nature doth really imprint sufficient Marks in the Countenance, to inform an accurate and discerning Eye: but as such is the Property of few, the Generality of Mankind mistake the Affectation for the Reality: for as Affectation always over-acts her Part, it fares with her as with a Farcical Actor on the Stage, whose monstrous over-done Grimaces are sure to catch the Applause of an insensible Audience; while the truest and finest Strokes of Nature, represented by a judicious and just Actor, pass unobserved and disregarded. In the same Manner, the true Symptoms being finer, and less glaring, make no Impression on our Physiognomist; while the grosser Appearances of Affectation are sure to attract his Eye, and deceive his Judgment. Thus that sprightly and penetrating Look, which is almost a certain Token of Understanding; that cheerful, composed Serenity, which always indicates Good-Nature; and that fiery Cast of the Eyes, which is never unaccompanied with Courage, are often over-looked: while a formal, stately, austere Gravity; a glavering, fawning Smile, and a strong Contraction of the Muscles, pass generally on the World for the Virtues they only endeavour to affect. [3]

But as these Rules are, I believe, none of them without some Exceptions; as they are of no Use but to an Observer of much Penetration: Lastly, as a more subtle Hypocrisy will sometimes escape undiscovered from the highest Discernment; let us see if we have not a more infallible Guide to direct us to the Knowledge of Men; one more easily to be attained, and on the Efficacy of which we may with the greatest Certainty rely.

And surely the Actions of Men seem to be the justest Interpreters of their Thoughts, and the truest Standards by which we may judge them. *By their Fruits you shall know them,* [4] is a Saying of great Wisdom, as well as Authority. And indeed this is so certain a Method of acquiring the Knowledge I contend for, that at first Appearance, it seems absolutely perfect, and to want no manner of Assistance.

There are, however, two Causes of our Mistakes on this Head; and which lead us into forming very erroneous Judgments of Men, even while their Actions stare us in the Face, and as it were hold a Candle to us, by which we may see into them.

The first of these is when we take their own Words against their Actions. This (if I may borrow another Illustration from Physic) is no less ridiculous, than it would be in a learned Professor of that Art, when he perceives his light-headed Patient is in the utmost Danger, to take his Word that he is well. This Error is infinitely more common than its extream Absurdity would persuade us was possible. And many a credulous Person hath been ruined by trusting to the Assertions of another, who must have preserved himself, had he placed a wiser Confidence in his Actions.

The Second is an Error still more general. This is when we take the Colour of a Man's Actions not from their own visible Tendency, but from his public Character:[5] when we believe what others say of him, in Opposition to what we see him do? How often do we suffer ourselves to be deceived, out of the Credit of a Fact,[6] or out of a just Opinion of its Heinousness, by the reputed Dignity or Honesty of the Person who did it? How common are such Ejaculations as these? 'O 'tis impossible HE should be guilty of any such Thing! HE must have done it by Mistake; HE could not design it. I will never believe any Ill of HIM. So good a Man, &c.!' when in Reality, the Mistake lies only in his Character. Nor is there any more simple, unjust, and insufficient Method of judging Mankind, than by public Estimation, which is oftner acquired by Deceit, Partiality, Prejudice, and such like, than by real Desert. I will venture to affirm, that I have known some of *the best sort of Men in the World*, (to use the vulgar Phrase,) who would not have scrupled cutting a Friend's Throat; and *a Fellow whom no Man should be seen to speak to*, capable of the highest Acts of Friendship and Benevolence.

Now it will be necessary to divest ourselves of both these Errors, before we can reasonably hope to attain any adequate Knowledge of the true Characters of Men. Actions are their own best Expositors; and though Crimes may admit of alleviating Circumstances, which may properly induce a Judge to mitigate the Punishment; from the Motive, for Instance, as Necessity may lessen the Crime of Robbery, when compared to Wantonness or Vanity; or from some Circumstance attending the Fact itself, as robbing a Stranger, or an Enemy, compared with committing it on a Friend or Benefactor; yet the Crime is still Robbery, and the Person who commits it is a Robber; though he should pretend to have done it with a good Design, or the World should concur in calling him an honest Man.

But I am aware of another Objection which may be made to my Doctrine, *viz.* admitting that the Actions of Men are the surest Evidence of their Character, that this Knowledge comes too late; that it is to caution us against a Highwayman after he hath plundered us, or against an Incendiary, after he hath fired our house.

To which I answer, That it is not against Force, but Deceit, which I am here seeking for Armour; against those who can injure us only by obtaining our good Opinion. If therefore I can instruct my Reader from what sort of Persons he is to withhold this Opinion, and inform him of all, or at least the principal Arts by which Deceit proceeds to ingratiate itself with us, by which he will be effectually enabled to defeat its Purpose, I shall have sufficiently satisfied the Design of this Essay.

---

5. Reputation.   6. Credence in a criminal act.

And here, the first Caution I shall give him is against FLATTERY, which I am convinced no one uses, without some Design on the Person flattered.

✻   ✻   ✻

Next to the Flatterer is the Professor,[7] who carries his Affection to you still farther; and on a slight or no Acquaintance, embraces, hugs, kisses, and vows the greatest Esteem for your Person, Parts, and Virtues. To know whether this Friend is sincere, you have only to examine into the Nature of Friendship, which is always founded either on Esteem or Gratitude, or perhaps on both. Now Esteem, admitting every Requisite for its Formation present, and these are not a few, is of very slow Growth; it is an involuntary Affection, rather apt to give us Pain than Pleasure, and therefore meets with no Encouragement in our Minds, which it creeps into by small and almost imperceptible Degrees: And perhaps, when it hath got an absolute Possession of us, may require some other Ingredient to engage our Friendship to its own Object. It appears then pretty plain, that this Mushroom Passion here mentioned, owes not its Original to Esteem. Whether it can possibly flow from Gratitude, which may indeed produce it more immediately, you will more easily judge: for though there are some Minds whom no Benefits can inspire with Gratitude; there are none,[8] I believe, who conceive this Affection without even a supposed Obligation. If therefore you can assure yourself it is impossible he should imagine himself obliged to you, you may be satisfied that Gratitude is not the Motive to his Friendship. Seeing then that you can derive it from neither of these Fountains, you may well be justified in suspecting its Falshood; and if so, you will act as wisely in receiving it into your Heart, as he doth who knowingly lodges a Viper in his Bosom, or a Thief in his House. FORGIVE THE ACTS OF YOUR ENEMIES hath been thought the highest Maxim of Morality; FEAR THE PROFESSIONS OF YOUR FRIENDS, is perhaps the wisest.

The Third Character against which an open Heart should be alarmed, is a PROMISER, one who rises another Step in Friendship. The Man who is wantonly profuse of his Promises ought to sink his Credit as much as a Tradesman would by uttering[9] great Numbers of Promissory Notes, payable at a distant Day. The truest Conclusion in both Cases is, that neither intend, or will be able to pay. And as the latter most probably intends to cheat you of your Money, so the former at least designs to cheat you of your Thanks; and it is well for you, if he hath no deeper Purpose, and that Vanity is the only evil Passion to which he destines you a Sacrifice.

---

7. Not the academic title, as the subsequent description confirms.

8. Present editor's emendation. Following the first edition and all subsequent reprints, the Wesleyan Edition reads "more," producing an assertion inconsistent both with the logic of Fielding's argument in this sentence and the next and with the sceptical view of human behavior inculcated in the essay. Under the pressure of proofing the *Miscellanies* for a publication twice previously promised and postponed, Fielding apparently failed to catch the printer's plausible misreading of his handwriting.

9. Issuing.

I would not be here understood to point at the Promises of political Great Men, which they are supposed to lie under a Necessity of giving in great Abundance, and the Value of them is so well known, that few are to be imposed on by them. The Professor I here mean, is he who on all Occasions is ready, of his own Head, and unasked, to promise Favours. This is such another Instance of Generosity, as his who relieves his Friend in Distress, by a Draught on *Aldgate* Pump.[1] Of these there are several Kinds: some who promise what they never intend to perform; others who promise what they are not sure they can perform; and others again, who promise so many, that like Debtors, being not able to pay all their Debts, they afterwards pay none.

* * *

I fear the next Character I shall mention, may give Offence to the grave Part of Mankind; for whose Wisdom and Honesty I have an equal Respect; but I must, however, venture to caution my open-hearted Reader against a Saint. No honest and sensible Man will understand me here, as attempting to declaim against Sanctity of Morals. The Sanctity I mean is that which flows from the Lips, and shines in the Countenance. It may be said, perhaps, that real Sanctity may wear these Appearances; and how shall we then distinguish with any Certainty, the true from the fictitious? I answer, That if we admit this to be possible, yet as it is likewise possible that it may be only counterfeit; and as in Fact it is so Ninety Nine Times in a Hundred; it is better that one real Saint should suffer a little unjust Suspicion, than that Ninety Nine Villains should impose on the World, and be enabled to perpetrate their Villainies under this Mask.

But, to say the Truth; a sour, morose, ill-natured, censorious Sanctity, never is, nor can be sincere. Is a Readiness to despise, to hate, and to condemn, the Temper of a Christian? Can he who passes Sentence on the Souls of Men with more Delight and Triumph than the Devil can execute it, have the Impudence to pretend himself a Disciple of one who died for the Sins of Mankind? Is not such a Sanctity the true Mark of that Hypocrisy which in many Places of Scripture, and particularly in the twenty third Chapter of St. *Matthew*, is so bitterly inveighed against?[2]

1. A mercantile Phrase for a bad Note [*Fielding's note*]. The location of this ancient pump near the commercial center of the old City of London prompted the pun on two meanings of "draught": a drawing of water and an order for payment of money, like a check.
2. Fielding next devotes a fourth of the essay to "ripping up" those who equate religion and virtue with "Austerities and Severities" instead of following "the Total of all Christian Morality," the Golden Rule, cautioning the reader against those who display ostentatious piety and scrupulous observance of "the least Matters in Religion" while neglecting the basic duties of charity, honesty, and justice. He then goes on to recommend observation of men's behavior toward those close to them as a guide to their true characters and ends by extending his remarks to public life.

PREFACE TO *THE ADVENTURES OF DAVID SIMPLE*[†]

*   *   *

I have attempted in my Preface to *Joseph Andrews* to prove, that every Work of this kind is in its Nature a comic Epic Poem, of which *Homer* left us a Precedent, tho' it be unhappily lost.

The two great Originals of a serious Air, which we have derived from that mighty Genius, differ principally in the Action, which in the *Iliad* is entire and uniform; in the *Odyssey*, is rather a Series of Actions, all tending to produce one great End. *Virgil* and *Milton* are, I think, the only pure Imitators of the former; most of the other *Latin*, as well as *Italian*, *French*, and *English* Epic Poets, chusing rather the history of some War, as *Lucan* and *Silius Italicus*; or a Series of Adventures, as *Ariosto*, &c. for the Subject of their Poems.[1]

In the same manner the Comic Writer may either fix on one Action, as the Authors of *Le Lutrin*, the *Dunciad*, &c. or on a Series, as *Butler* in Verse, and *Cervantes* in Prose have done.[2]

Of this latter kind is the Book now before us, where the Fable[3] consists of a Series of separate Adventures detached from, and independent on each other, yet all tending to one great End; so that those who should object want of Unity of Action here, may, if they please, or if they dare, fly back with their Objection, in the Face even of the *Odyssey* itself.

This Fable hath in it these three difficult Ingredients, which will be found on Consideration to be always necessary to Works of this kind, *viz.* that the main End or Scope be at once amiable, ridiculous and natural.

If it be said, that some of the Comic Performances I have above men-

† *The Adventures of David Simple: Containing An Account of his Travels Through the Cities of London and Westminster, In the Search of a Real Friend* (1744), by Fielding's sister Sarah (1710–68), was attributed to him. In a signed preface to the second edition later that year, he declined "the Honour of this Performance" except for "the Correction of some small Errors" and went on to remark "some of the Beauties of this little Work." The text is from this edition.

1. The first-century Roman poets Marcus Annaeus Lucanus and Silius Italicus wrote epics about, respectively, the war between Caesar and Pompey (*Pharsalia*) and the Second Punic War between Rome and Carthage (*Punica*). In *Orlando Furioso* (1532), the Italian poet Ludovico Ariosto traced the multifarious adventures of knights and princesses in the context of the war between Charlemagne and the Saracens.

2. The mock-epic poem *Le Lutrin* (1674), by the eminent French critic Nicolas Boileau-Des-

préaux, depicts the battle between two groups of clergy over the desk or lectern referred to in the title. Alexander Pope's *Dunciad* (1728; 1743) incorporates its extensive satire of contemporary culture within the mock-epic framework of the coronation of Cibber and the triumph of Dullness (stupidity). In *Hudibras* (1663;1664;1678), Samuel Butler (1612–80) satirized the Puritan dissenters who deposed Charles I and flourished under the Commonwealth (1648–60) through the rambling adventures of a Presbyterian knight and his Independent (Congregationalist) squire. Eight years later Fielding maintained that the "loose unconnected Adventures in Don Quixote" fell far short of "that Epic Regularity which would give it the Name of an Action" (*The Covent Garden Journal*, March 24, 1752, ed. G. E. Jensen [New Haven: Yale, 1915; reissued New York: Russell and Russell, 1964] 1.281).

3. Plot.

tioned differ in the first of these, and set before us the odious instead of the amiable; I answer, that is far from being one of their Perfections; and of this the Authors themselves seem so sensible, that they endeavour to deceive their Reader by false Glosses and Colours, and by the help of Irony at least to represent the Aim and Design of their Heroes in a favourable and agreeable Light.

I might farther observe, that as the Incidents arising from this Fable, tho' often surprising, are every where natural, (Credibility not being once shocked through the whole) so there is one Beauty very apparent, which hath been attributed by the greatest of Critics to the greatest of Poets, that every Episode bears a manifest Impression of the principal Design,[4] and chiefly turns on the Perfection or Imperfection of Friendship; of which noble Passion, from its highest Purity to its lowest Falsehoods and Disguises, this little Book is, in my Opinion, the most exact Model.

*   *   *

4. In *Poetics* 8, Aristotle praises Homer for selecting incidents from "all that ever befell his hero" to create in the *Odyssey* as well as in the *Iliad* "a complete whole, with its several incidents so closely connected that the transposal or withdrawal of any one of them will disjoin and dislocate the whole" (Bywater trans.).

BACKGROUNDS AND SOURCES

SAMUEL RICHARDSON

From *Pamela, or Virtue Rewarded* †

[This episode occurs more than a third of the way through the novel, after Pamela has been abducted to her master's Lincolnshire estate and confined in the custody of the villainous housekeeper, Mrs. Jewkes. Prevented from corresponding with her parents as she has up to now, she records her experiences in a journal addressed to them. The text is from the second edition, February 1741.]

TUESDAY *Night*

For the future, I will always mistrust most, when Appearances look fairest. O your poor Daughter! what has she not suffer'd since what I wrote of Sunday Night!—My worst Trial, and my fearfullest Danger! O how I shudder to write you an Account of this wicked Interval of Time! For, my dear Parents, will you not be too much frighten'd and affected with my Distress, when I tell you, that his Journey to *Stamford* was all abominable Pretence? for he came home privately, and had well nigh effected all his vile Purposes, and the Ruin of your poor Daughter; and that by such a plot as I was not in the least apprehensive of: And Oh! you'll hear what a vile and unwomanly Part that wicked Wretch, Mrs. *Jewkes*, acted in it!

The Maid *Nan* is a little apt to drink, if she can get at Liquor; and Mrs. *Jewkes* happen'd, or design'd, as is too probable, to leave a Bottle of Cherry-brandy in her way, and the Wench drank some of it more than she should; and when she came in to lay the Cloth, Mrs. *Jewkes* perceiv'd it, and fell a rating at her most sadly; for she has too many Faults of her own, to suffer any of the like Sort in any body else, if she can help it; and she bid her get out of her Sight, when we had supp'd, and go to bed, to sleep off her Liquor, before we came to bed. And so the poor Maid went muttering up Stairs.

About two Hours after, which was near Eleven o'Clock, Mrs. *Jewkes* and I went up to go to-bed; I pleasing myself with what a charming Night I should have.[1] We lock'd both Doors, and saw poor *Nan*, as I thought, (for Oh! 'twas my abominable Master, as you shall hear by-and-by) sitting fast asleep, in an Elbow-chair, in a dark Corner of the Room, with her Apron thrown over her Head and Neck. And Mrs. *Jewkes* said, There is that Beast of a Wench fast asleep, instead of being a bed! I knew, said she, she had taken a fine Dose. I'll wake her, said I, No, don't, said she, let her sleep on; we shall lie better without her. Ay, said I, so we shall; but won't she get Cold?

† By permission of the British Library (shelfmark 12614.3bbb.9.)
1. Temporarily relieved of the imminent threat of rape.

Said she, I hope you have no Writing to-night. No, reply'd I, I will go to-bed with you, Mrs. *Jewkes*. Said she, I wonder what you can find to write about so much; and am sure you have better Conveniencies of that kind, and more Paper, than I am aware of; and I had intended to romage[2] you, if my Master had not come down; for I 'spy'd a broken Tea-cup with Ink, which gave me a Suspicion; but as he is come, let him look after you, if he will; and if you deceive him, it will be his own Fault.

All this time we were undressing ourselves. And I fetch'd a deep Sigh! What do you sigh so for? said she. I am thinking, Mrs. *Jewkes*, answer'd I, what a sad Life I live, and how hard is my Lot. I am sure the Thief that has robb'd, is much better off than I, 'bating the Guilt; and I should, I think, take it for a Mercy, to be hang'd out of the way, rather than live in these cruel Apprehensions. So, being not sleepy, and in a prattling Vein, I began to give a little History of myself, as I did once before to Mrs. *Jervis*,[3] in this manner:

Here, said I, were my poor honest Parents; they took care to instil good Principles into my Mind, till I was almost twelve Years of Age; and taught me to prefer Goodness and Poverty to the highest Conditions of Life; and they confirm'd their Lessons by their own Practice; for they were of late Years remarkably poor, and always as remarkably honest, even to a Proverb; for, *As honest as Goodman Andrews*, was a Bye-word.

Well then, said I, comes my late dear good Lady, and takes a Fancy to me, and said, she would be the making of me, if I was a good Girl; and she put me to sing, to dance, to play on the Spinnet, in order to divert her melancholy Hours; and also learnt me all manner of fine Needlework; but still this was her Lesson, *My good* Pamela, *be virtuous, and keep the Men at a Distance*: Well, so I was, I hope, and so I did; and yet, tho' I say it, they all loved me and respected me; and would do any thing for me, as if I was a Gentlewoman.

But then, what comes next?—Why, it pleased God to take my good Lady; and then comes my Master: And what says he?—Why, in Effect, it is, *Be Not virtuous*, Pamela.

So here have I lived about Sixteen Years in Virtue and Reputation, and, all at once, when I come to know what is Good, and what is Evil, I must renounce all the Good, all the whole Sixteen Years Innocence, which, next to God's Grace, I owed chiefly to my Parents and my Lady's good Lessons and Examples; and chuse the Evil; and so, in a Moment's Time, become the vilest of Creatures! And all this, for what, I pray? Why truly, for a Pair of Diamond Ear-rings, a Necklace, and a Diamond Ring for my Finger; which would not become me: for a few paltry fine Cloaths; which when I wore, it would make but my former Poverty more ridiculous to every body that saw me; especially when they knew the base Terms I wore them upon. But indeed, I was to have a great Parcel of Guineas beside; I forget how many; for had there been ten

2. Search.
3. The virtuous housekeeper of Squire B——'s Bedfordshire estate, from whose protection Pamela has been removed.

times more, they would have been not so much to me, as the honest Six Guineas you trick'd me out of, Mrs. *Jewkes*.[4]

Well, forsooth! but then I was to have I know not how many Pounds a Year for my Life; and my poor Father (there was the Jest of it!) was to be the Manager for the abandon'd Prostitute his Daughter: And then (there was the Jest again!) my kind, forgiving, virtuous Master, would pardon me all my Misdeeds!

Yes, thank him for nothing, truly. And what, pray, are all these violent Misdeeds?—Why, they are for daring to adhere to the good Lessons that were taught me; and not learning a new one, that would have reversed all my former: For not being contented when I was run away with, in order to ruin me; but contriving, if my poor Wits had been able, to get out of Danger, and preserve myself honest.[5]

Then was he once jealous of poor *John*,[6] tho' he knew *John* was his own Creature, and helped to deceive me.

Then was he outrageous against poor Parson *Williams*,[7] and him has this good, merciful Master thrown into Gaol; and for what? Why truly, for that being a Divine, and a good Man, he had the Fear of God before his Eyes, and was willing to forego all his Expectations of Interest, and assist an oppressed poor Creature.

But to be sure, I must be forward, bold, saucy, and what not? to dare to run away from certain Ruin, and to strive to escape from an unjust Confinement; and I must be married to the Parson, nothing so sure![8]

He would have had but a poor Catch of me, had I consented; but he, and *you* too, know, I did not want to marry *any body*. I only wanted to go to my poor Parents, and to have my own Liberty, and not to be confined to such an unlawful Restraint; and which would not be inflicted upon me, but only that I am a poor, destitute, young Body, and have no Friend that is able to right me.

So, Mrs. *Jewkes*, said I, here is my History in brief. And I am a very unhappy young Creature, to be sure!—And why am I so?—Why, because my Master sees something in my Person that takes his present Fancy; and because I would not be undone.—Why therefore, to chuse, I must, and I shall be undone!—And this is all the Reason that can be given!

She heard me run on all this time, while I was undressing, without any Interruption; and I said, Well, I must go to the two Closets, ever since an Affair of the Closet at the other House, tho' he is so far off.[9] And I have a good mind to wake this poor Maid. No, don't, said she, I

---

4. She has just rejected her master's formal proposals to give her five hundred guineas and an estate with a two hundred and fifty-pound annual income to be managed by her father, in addition to the aforementioned jewelry, on the implicit condition that she become his mistress. Mrs. Jewkes has taken Pamela's money under the pretense of borrowing it.
5. Chaste.
6. A servant friendly to Pamela whom the master employs to gain access to her correspondence.

7. Parson Williams, Squire B——'s young chaplain, has attempted to help her escape, although he is dependent on the squire for a promised clerical living. His patron retaliates by imprisoning him for debt, as in *Shamela*.
8. As a ruse, the squire offers to make Pamela Williams's bride.
9. Early in the novel, the master hides in a closet (a small room off a bedchamber for reading, writing, or prayer) to assault Pamela.

charge you. I am very angry with her; and she'll get no Harm there; but if she wakes, she may come to-bed well enough, as long as there is a Candle in the Chimney.

So I looked into the Closets, and kneeled down in my own, as I used to do, to say my Prayers, and this with my under Cloaths in my Hand, all undrest; and passed by the poor sleeping Wench, as I thought, in my Return. But, Oh! little did I think, it was my wicked, wicked Master in a Gown and Petticoat of hers, and her Apron over his Face and Shoulders. What Meannesses will not *Lucifer* make his Votaries stoop to, to gain their abominable Ends!

Mrs. *Jewkes*, by this time, was got to-bed, on the further Side, as she used to be; and, to make room for the Maid, when she should awake, I got into Bed, and lay close to her. And I said, Where are the Keys? tho', said I, I am not so much afraid to-night. Here, said the wicked Woman, put your Arm under mine, and you shall find them about my Wrist, as they used to be. So I did, and the abominable Designer held my Hand with her Right-hand, as my Right-arm was under her Left.

In less than a quarter of an Hour, I said, There's poor *Nan* awake; I hear her stir. Let us go to sleep, said she, and not mind her: She'll come to-bed, when she's quite awake. Poor Soul! said I, I'll warrant she will have the Head-ach finely tomorrow for it! Be silent, said she, and go to sleep; you keep me awake; and I never found you in so talkative a Humour in my Life. Don't chide me, said I; I will say but one thing more: Do you think *Nan* could hear me talk of my Master's Offers? No, no, said she; she was dead asleep. I'm glad of that, said I; because I would not expose my Master to his common Servants; and I knew *you* were no stranger to his *fine* Articles.[1] Said she, I think they were fine Articles, and you were bewitch'd you did not close in with them: But let us go to sleep. So I was silent; and the pretended *Nan* (O wicked, base, villainous Designer! what a Plot, what an unexpected Plot, was this!) seem'd to be awaking; and Mrs. *Jewkes*, abhorred Creature! said, Come, *Nan*!—what, are you awake at last? Pr'ythee come to-bed; for Mrs. *Pamela* is in a talking Fit, and won't go to sleep one while.

At that the pretended She came to the Bed-side; and sitting down in a Chair, where the Curtain hid her, began to undress. Said I, Poor Mrs. *Ann*, I warrant your Head aches most sadly! How do you do?—She answer'd not one Word. Said the superlatively wicked Woman, You know I have order'd her not to answer you. And this Plot, to be sure, was laid when she gave her these Orders, the Night before.

I heard her, as I thought, breathe all quick and short: Indeed, said I, Mrs. *Jewkes*, the poor Maid is not well. What ails you, Mrs. *Ann*? And still no Answer was made.

But, I tremble to relate it! the pretended She came into Bed; but quiver'd like an Aspen-leaf; and I, poor Fool that I was! pitied her much—But well might the barbarous Deceiver tremble at his vile Dissimulation, and Base Designs.

1. See above, p. 337, n. 4.

What Words shall I find, my dear Mother, (for my Father should not see this shocking Part) to describe the rest, and my Confusion, when the guilty Wretch took my left Arm, and laid it under his Neck, as the vile Procuress held my Right; and then he clasp'd me round my Waist!

Said I, Is the Wench mad! Why, how now, Confidence? thinking still it had been *Nan*. But he kissed me with frightful Vehemence; and then his voice broke upon me like a Clap of Thunder. Now, *Pamela*, said he, is the dreadful Time of Reckoning come, that I have threaten'd.—I scream'd out in such a manner, as never any body heard the like. But there was nobody to help me: And both my Hands were secured, as I said. Sure never poor Soul was in such Agonies as I. Wicked Man! said I; wicked, abominable Woman! O God! my God! this *Time*, this *one* Time! deliver me from this Distress! or strike me dead this Moment. And then I scream'd again and again.

Says he, One Word with you, *Pamela*; one Word hear me but; and hitherto you see I offer nothing to you. Is this *nothing*, said I, to be in Bed here? To hold my Hands between you? I will hear, if you will instantly leave the Bed, and take this villainous Woman from me!

Said she, (O Disgrace of Womankind!) What you do, Sir, do; don't stand dilly-dallying. She cannot exclaim worse than she has done. And she'll be quieter when she knows the worst.

Silence! said he to her; I must say one Word to you, *Pamela*; it is this: You see, now you are in my Power!—You cannot get from me, nor help yourself: Yet have I not offer'd any thing amiss to you. But if you resolve not to comply with my Proposals, I will not lose this Opportunity: If you do, I will yet leave you.

O Sir, said I, leave me, leave me but, and I will do any thing I ought to do.—Swear then to me, said he, that you will accept my Proposals!— and then (for this was all detestable Grimace)[2] he put his Hand in my Bosom. With Struggling, Fright, Terror, I fainted away quite, and did not come to myself soon; so that they both, from the cold Sweats that I was in, thought me dying—And I remember no more, than that, when, with great Difficulty, they brought me to myself, she was sitting on one side of the Bed, with her Cloaths on; and he on the other with his, and in his Gown and Slippers.

Your poor *Pamela* cannot answer for the Liberties taken with her in her deplorable State of Death. And when I saw them there, I sat up in my Bed, without any Regard to what Appearance I made and nothing about my Neck; and he soothing me, with an Aspect[3] of Pity and Concern, I put my Hand to his Mouth, and said, O tell me, yet tell me not, what I have suffer'd in this Distress! And I talked quite wild, and knew not what; for, to be sure, I was on the Point of Distraction.

He most solemnly, and with a bitter Imprecation, vow'd, that he had not offer'd the least Indecency; that he was frighten'd at the terrible manner I was taken with the Fit: That he would desist from his Attempt; and begg'd but to see me easy and quiet, and he would leave me directly,

---

2. Pretense.   3. Look.

and go to his own Bed. O then, said I, take from me this most wicked Woman, this vile Mrs. *Jewkes*, as an Earnest that I may believe you!

And will you, Sir, said the wicked Wretch, for a Fit or two, give up such an Opportunity as this?—I thought you had known the Sex better.—She is now, you see, quite well again!

This I heard; more she might say; but I fainted away once more, at these Words, and at his clasping his Arms about me again. And when I came a little to myself, I saw him sit there, and the Maid *Nan*, holding a Smelling-bottle to my Nose, and no Mrs. *Jewkes*.

He said, taking my Hand, Now will I vow to you, my dear *Pamela*, that I will leave you the Moment I see you better, and pacify'd. Here's *Nan* knows, and will tell you, my Concern for you. I vow to God, I have not offered any Indecency to you. And since I found Mrs. *Jewkes* so offensive to you, I have sent her to the Maid's Bed, and the Maid shall lie with you to-night. And but promise me that you will compose yourself, and I will leave you. But, said I, will not *Nan* also hold my Hand? And will not she let you come in again to me?—He said, By Heaven! I will not come in again to-night. *Nan*, undress yourself, go to-bed, and do all you can to comfort the dear Creature: And now, *Pamela*, said he, give me but your Hand, and say you forgive me, and I will leave you to your Repose. I held out my trembling Hand, which he vouchsafed to kiss; and I said, God forgive you, Sir, as you *have been* just in my Distress; and as you *will be* just to what you promise! And he withdrew, with a Countenance of Remorse, as I hoped; and she shut the Doors, and, at my Request, brought the Keys to-bed.

This, O my dear Parents! was a most dreadful Trial. I tremble still to think of it; and dare not recal all the horrid Circumstances of it. I hope, as he assures me, he was not guilty of Indecency; but have Reason to bless God, who, by disabling me in my Faculties, enabled me to preserve my Innocence; and when all my Strength would have signified nothing, magnified himself in my Weakness.

*   *   *

CONYERS MIDDLETON

From the Dedication to *The History of the Life of Marcus Tullius Cicero* [†]

To the Right Honourable JOHN LORD HERVEY,
Lord Keeper of His Majesty's Privy Seal.

My LORD,

The public will naturally expect, that in chusing a Patron for *the Life of* CICERO, I should address myself to some person of illustrious rank,

The Reverend Conyers Middleton's *Life of Cicero* was published in February 1741. Fielding parodied this dedication in *Shamela* and derided its subject in the figure of Beau Didapper in *Joseph Andrews*. For Middleton and Hervey, see n. 2, p. 186 and n. 2, p. 245, above. The text is from the first edition.

distinguished by his parts and eloquence, and bearing a principal share in the great affairs of the Nation; who, according to the usual stile of Dedications, might be the proper subject of a comparison with the Hero of my piece. Your Lordship's name will confirm that expectation, and Your character would justify me in running some length into the parallel; but my experience of your good sense forbids me the attempt. For Your Lordship knows, what a disadvantage it would be to any character, to be placed in the same light with that of CICERO; that all such comparisons must be invidious and adulatory; and that the following History will suggest a reason in every page, why no man now living can justly be compared with him.

* * *

You see, my Lord, how much I trust to your good nature, as well as good sense, when in an *Epistle dedicatory*, the proper place of Panegyric, I am depreciating your abilities, instead of extolling them: but I remember, that it is an History, which I am offering to Your Lordship, and it would ill become me, in the front of such a work, to expose my veracity to any hazard: and my head indeed is now so full of antiquity, that I could wish to see the dedicatory stile reduced to that classical, simplicity, with which the ancient writers used to present their books to their friends or Patrons, at whose desire they were written, or by whose authority they were published: for this was the first use, and the sole purpose of *a Dedication*; and as this also is the real ground of my present address to Your Lordship, so it will be the best argument of my Epistle, and the most agreeable to the character of an Historian, to acquaint the public with a plain fact, that it was Your Lordship, who first advised me, to undertake *the Life of* CICERO; and when from a diffidence of my strength, and a nearer view of the task, I began to think myself unequal to the weight of it, Your Lordship still urged and exhorted me to persist, till I had moulded it into the form, in which it now appears.
* * * whatever censure it may draw upon Your Lordship, I cannot prevail with myself to conceal, what does so much honor to my work; that, before it went to the Press, Your Lordship not onely saw and approved, but, as the sincerest mark of Your approbation, corrected it. * * * You must pardon me therefore, my Lord, if * * * I cannot forbear boasting, that some parts of my present work have been brightened by the strokes of Your Lordship's pencil.
It was the custom of those *Roman* Nobles, to spend their leisure * * * in conversing with the celebrated wits and Scholars of the age * * * and here Your Lordship imitates them with success, and for love of letters and politeness may be compared with the Noblest of them. For Your house, like theirs, is open to men of parts and merit; where I have admired Your Lordship's agreeable manner of treating them all in their own way, by introducing questions of literature, and varying them so artfully, as to give every one an opportunity, not onely of bearing a part, but of leading the conversation in his turn. In these liberal exercises You drop

the cares of the Statesman; relieve Your fatigues in the Senate; and strengthen Your mind, while You relax it.

Encomiums of this kind, upon persons of Your Lordship's quality, commonly pass for words of course, or a fashionable language to the Great, and make little impression on men of sense, who know learning, not to be the fruit of wit or parts, for there Your Lordship's title would be unquestionable, but an acquisition of much labor and study, which the Nobles of our days are apt to look upon, as inconsistent with the ease and splendor of an elevated fortune, and generally leave to men of professions and inferior life. But Your Lordship * * * has learnt from Your earliest youth, that no fortune can exempt a man from pains, who desires to distinguish himself from the vulgar. * * * What time therefore others bestow upon their sports, or pleasures, or the lazy indolence of a luxurious life, Your Lordship applies to the improvement of Your knowledge; and in those early hours, when all around You are hushed in sleep, seize the opportunity of that quiet, as the most favorable season of study, and frequently spend an usefull day, before others begin to enjoy it.

I am saying no more, my Lord, than what I know, from my constant admission to Your Lordship in my morning visits, before good manners would permit me to attempt a visit any where else; where I have found You commonly engaged with the Classical writers of *Greece* or *Rome*. * * * I have seen the solid effects of Your reading, in Your judicious reflections on the policy of those ancient Governments, and have felt Your weight even in controversy, on some of the most delicate parts of their History.

There is another circumstance peculiar to Your Lordship, which makes this task of Study the easier to you, by giving You not onely the greater health, but the greater leisure to pursue it; I mean that singular temperance in diet, in which Your Lordship perseveres with a constancy, superior to every temptation, that can excite an appetite to rebel; and shews a firmness of mind, that subjects every gratification of sense to the rule of right reason. Thus with all the accomplishments of the Nobleman, You lead the life of a Philosopher; and while You shine a principal ornament of the Court, You practice the discipline of the College.

In old *Rome* there were no hereditary honors; but when the virtue of a family was extinct, it's honor was extinguished too; so that no man, how nobly soever born, could arrive at any dignity, who did not win it by his personal merit: and here again Your Lordship seems to have emulated that ancient spirit; for, though born to the first honors of Your country * * * You were not content with inheriting, but resolved to import new dignities into Your family; and after the example of Your Noble Father, to open Your own way into the supreme council of the Kingdom. In this august Assembly, Your Lordship displays those shining talents, by which You acquired a seat in it, in the defence of our excellent Establishment; in maintaining the rights of the people, yet asserting the prerogative of the Crown; measuring them both by the equal balance of the laws. * * *

In a nation like ours, which, from the natural effect of freedom, is divided into opposite parties, though particular attachments to certain principles, or friendships with certain men will sometimes draw the best Citizens into measures of a subordinate kind, which they cannot wholly approve; yet whatever envy Your Lordship may incur on that account, You will be found, on all occasions of trial, a true friend to our constitution   * * * if there be any, who know so little of You, as to distrust Your principles, they may depend at least on Your judgment, that it can never suffer a person of Your Lordship's rank, born to so large a share of the property, as well as the honors of the nation, to think any private interest an equivalent, for consenting to the ruin of the public.

But I ought to ask Your Lordship's pardon for dwelling so long upon a character, which is known to the whole Kingdom, as well as to myself; not onely by the high Office, which You fill, and the eminent dignity that You bear in it, but by the sprightly compositions of various kinds, with which Your Lordship has often entertained it. * * *

Next to that little reputation, with which the public has been pleased to favor me, the benefit of this subscription is the chief fruit, that I have ever reaped from my studies. I am indebted for the first to CICERO, for the second, to Your Lordship: it was CICERO, who instructed me to write; Your Lordship, who rewards me for writing: the same motive therefore, which induced me to attempt the history of the one, engages me to dedicate it to the other; that I may express my gratitude to you both, in the most effectual manner, that I am able. * * *

* * * Your Lordship's accumulated favors have * * * made it my perpetual duty, as it had always been my ambition, to profess myself with the greatest truth and respect,

MY LORD, Your Lordship's

Most obliged and
Devoted Servant,

CONYERS MIDDLETON

MIGUEL DE CERVANTES SAAVEDRA

From *The Life and Atchievements of the Renown'd Don Quixote*

[*El Ingenioso Hidalgo Don Quixote de la Mancha* by Miguel de Cervantes Saavedra was published in 1605; part 2 appeared in 1615. Between 1612 and 1742 various English versions went through dozens of editions. Phrases in *Don Quixote in England* suggest that Fielding relied on the version done by "several hands" under the direction of Peter Motteux (1700), as revised by John Ozell in 1725. The following excerpts are reprinted from the 1733 edition, as it would have looked to Fielding, with occasional regularizing of

spelling and punctuation, the insertion of quotation marks, and one alteration of a wording that obscures Cervantes's facetious narration (noted on
p. 352). The interpolated stories of Cardenio, Anselmo, and the other characters Fielding cites in book 3, chapter 1, are too lengthy to reproduce here.
Each of the incidents selected has some direct bearing on Fielding's conception of the novel. Quixote's first adventure after having himself "knighted"
by an innkeeper is a rare instance in which he encounters something like a
real wrong to be righted; the account of the battle with the Biscayan is Cervantes's most extended play on the posture of "true historian"; the Maritornes incident is the prototype of Fielding's final night scene; and Quixote's
eloquent defense of poetry anticipates Adams's discourse on Homer in a
parallel context. Together they may give some notion of what Fielding took
to be "the Manner of Cervantes."]

Part I, Book 1, Chapter 4

What befell the Knight after he had left the Inn.

Aurora began to usher in the Morn, when Don *Quixote* sally'd out of
the Inn, so well pleas'd, so gay and so overjoy'd to find himself knighted,
that he infus'd the same Satisfaction into his Horse, who seem'd ready
to burst his Girths for Joy. But calling to mind the Admonitions which
the Inn-keeper had given him, concerning the Provision of necessary
Accommodations in his Travels, particularly Money and clean Shirts,
he resolv'd to return home to furnish himself with them, and likewise
get him a Squire, designing to entertain as such a labouring Man his
Neighbour, who was poor and had a Charge of Children, but yet very
fit for the Office. With this Resolution he took the Road which led to
his own Village; and *Rozinante*, that seem'd to know his Will by Instinct,
began to carry him a round Trot so briskly, that his Heels seem'd scarcely
to touch the Ground. The Knight had not travelled far, when he fancy'd
he heard an effeminate Voice complaining in a Thicket on his right
Hand. "I thank Heaven, (said he when he heard the Cries) for favouring
me soon with an Opportunity to perform the Duty of my Profession, and
reap the Fruit of my Desires! For these Complaints are certainly the
Moans of some distressed Creature who wants my present Help." Then
turning to that Side with all the Speed which *Rozinante* could make, he
no sooner came into the Wood but he found a Mare ty'd to an Oak, and
to another a young Lad about fifteen Years of Age, naked from the Waist
upwards. This was he who made such a lamentable Outcry; and not
without Cause, for a lusty Country-fellow was strapping him fondly with
a Girdle, at every Stripe putting him in mind of a Proverb, *Keep your
Mouth Shut and your Eyes open, Sirrah.* "Good Master," cry'd the Boy,
"I'll do so no more, as I hope to be sav'd, I'll never do so again! Indeed,
Master, hereafter I'll take more Care of your Goods." Don *Quixote* seeing
this, cry'd in an angry Tone, "Discourteous Knight, 'tis an unworthy
Act to strike a Person who is not able to defend himself: Come, bestride
thy Steed, and take thy Lance," (for the Farmer had something that
look'd like one resting upon the same Tree to which his Mare was ty'd)

"then I'll make thee know thou hast acted the Part of a Coward." The
Country-fellow, who gave himself for lost at the Sight of an Apparition
in Armour brandishing his Lance at his Face, answered him in mild
and submissive Words: "Sir Knight," cry'd he, "this Boy, whom I am
chastising is my Servant, employ'd by me to look after a Flock of Sheep,
which I have not far off; but he is so heedless that I lose some of 'em
every Day. Now, because I correct him for his Carelesness or his Knavery, he says I do it out of Covetousness to defraud him of his Wages; but
upon my Life and Soul he belies me." "What! the Lie in my Presence,
you saucy Clown,[1] (cry'd Don *Quixote*;) by the Sun that shines I have a
good Mind to run thee through the Body with my Lance. Pay the Boy
this instant without any more Words, or, by the Power that rules us all,
I'll immediately dispatch and annihilate thee: Come, unbind him this
Moment." The Country-man hung down his Head, and without any
further Reply unbound the Boy; who being ask'd by Don *Quixote* what
his Master ow'd him, told him 'twas nine Months Wages, at seven Reals
a Month. The Knight having cast it up, found it came to sixty three
Reals in all; which he ordered the Farmer to pay the Fellow immediately, unless he intended to lose his Life that very Moment. The poor
Country-man trembling for Fear, told him, that, as he was on the Brink
of Death, by the Oath he had sworn (by the by he had not yet sworn at
all) he did not owe the Lad so much; for there was to be deducted for
three Pair of Shoes which he had bought him, and a Real for his being
let Blood twice when he was sick. "That may be," reply'd Don *Quixote*;
"but set the Price of Shoes and the Bleeding, against the Stripes which
you have given him without Cause: For if he has us'd the Shoe-leather
which you paid for, you have in Return misus'd and impair'd his Skin
sufficiently; and if the Surgeon let him blood when he was sick, you
have drawn Blood from him now he is in health; so that he owes you
nothing on that Account." "The worst is, Sir Knight," cry'd the Farmer,
"that I have no Money about me; but let *Andrew* go home with me, and
I'll pay him every Piece out of hand." "What! I go home with him,"
cry'd the Youngster, "the Devil a-bit, Sir! Not I truly, I know better
things, for he'd no sooner have me by himself, but he'd flea me alive
like another St. *Bartholomew*."[2] "He will never dare to do it," reply'd
Don *Quixote*; "I command him, and that's sufficient to restrain him:
Therefore provided he will swear by the Order of Knighthood, which
has been conferred upon him, that he will duly observe this Regulation,
I will freely let him go, and then thou art secure of thy Money." "Good
sir, take heed what you say," cry'd the Boy; "for my Master is no Knight,
nor ever was of any Order in his Life: He's *John Haldudo*, the rich
Farmer of *Quintinar*." "This signifies little," answered Don *Quixote*,
"for there may be Knights among the *Haldudo*'s; besides, the brave Man
carves out his Fortune, and every Man is the Son of his own Works."
"That's true, Sir," quoth *Andrew*; "but of what Works can this Master

1. Peasant.
2. One of Jesus' disciples, martyred by being skinned alive.

of mine be the Son, who denies me my Wages, which I have earn'd with the Sweat of my Brows?" "I do not deny to pay thee thy Wages, honest *Andrew*," cry'd the Master; "be but so kind as to go along with me, and by all the Orders of Knighthood in the World, I swear, I'll pay thee every Piece, as I said, nay and sweet scented to boot." "You may spare your Perfume," said Don *Quixote*, "do but pay him in Reals and I am satisfy'd; but be sure you perform your Oath, for if you fail, I my self swear by the same Oath to return and find you out, and punish you, though you should hide your self as close as a Lizard. And if you would be informed who 'tis that lays these Injunctions on you, that you may understand how highly it concerns you to observe 'em, know, I am the valourous Don *Quixote de la Mancha*, the Righter of Wrongs, the Avenger and Redresser of Grievances; and so farewel; But remember what you have promis'd and sworn as you will answer the Contrary at your Peril." This said, he clapped Spurs to Rozinante, and quickly left the Master and the Man a good Way behind him.

The Country-man, who followed him with both his Eyes, no sooner perceived that he was pass'd the Wood, and quite out of Sight, but he went back to his Boy *Andrew*. "Come, Child," said he, "I will pay thee what I owe thee, as that Righter of Wrongs and Redresser of Grievances has ordered me." "Ay," quoth *Andrew*, "on my word, you'll do well to fulfil the Commands of that good Knight, whom Heaven grant long to live; for he is so brave a Man, and so just a Judge, that adad if you don't pay me he'll come back and make his Words good." "I dare swear as much," answer'd the Master; "and to shew thee how much I love thee, I am willing to increase the Debt, that I may enlarge the Payment." With that he caught the Youngster by the Arm, and ty'd him again to the Tree; where he handled him so unmercifully, that scarce any Signs of Life were left in him. "Now call your Righter of Wrongs, Mr. *Andrew*," cry'd the Farmer, "and you shall see he'll ne'er be able to undo what I have done; though I fansy 'tis but a Part of what I am to do, for I have a good Mind to flea you alive, as you said I would, you Rascal." However he unty'd him at last, and gave him Leave to go and seek out his Judge, in order to have his Decree put in Execution. *Andrew* went his Ways not very well pleas'd you may be sure, yet fully resolv'd to find out the valorous Don *Quixote de la Mancha*, and give him an exact Account of the whole Transaction, that he might pay the Abuse with sevenfold Usury: In short, he crept off sobbing and weeping, while his Master staid behind laughing. And in this Manner was this Wrong redressed by the valorous Don *Quixote de la Mancha*.[3]

* * *

3. Much later in the novel, Andrew finds Quixote, but the knight is prevented from helping him by his prior vow to rescue an imaginary princess—a hoax perpetrated by his friends to get him home. " 'Sir Knight-Errant,' " the lad taunts in parting, " 'if ever you meet me again in your Travels, which I hope you never shall; though I were torn to pieces, don't trouble me with your plaguy Help, but mind your own Business' " (1.4.4).

Part I, Book 1, Chapter 8

Of the good Success which the valorous Don Quixote *had in the most terrifying and never-to-be-imagin'd Adventure of the Wind-mills; with other Transactions worthy to be transmitted to Posterity.*

*   *   *

[Shortly after his losing encounter with a set of windmills he takes for giants, Quixote "rescues" a lady traveling in a coach by attacking the monks accompanying it and in return asks only that she redirect her journey to acknowledge his triumph to his imaginary mistress, Dulcinea del Toboso.]

To this extravagant Talk, a certain *Biscayan* Squire, Gentleman-Usher, or what you'll please to call him, who rode along with the Coach, listen'd with great Attention; and perceiving that Don *Quixote* not only stopp'd the Coach, but would have it presently go back to *Toboso*, he bore briskly up to him, and laying hold on his Lance, "*Get gone*," cry'd he to him in bad *Spanish*, and worse *Biscayan*, "*Get gone thou Knight, and Devil go with thou; or by he who me create, if thou do not leave the Coach me kill thee now so sure as me be a* Biscayan." Don *Quixote*, who made shift to understand him well enough, very calmly made him this Answer: "Wert thou a Knight or Gentleman,[4] as thou art not, ere this I would have chastis'd thy Insolence and Temerity, thou inconsiderable Mortal." "What! me no Gentleman?" reply'd the *Biscayan*; "I swear thou be Liar, as me be Christian. If thou throw away Lance and draw Sword, me will make no more of thee than Cat does of Mouse. Me will shew thee me be *Biscayan*, and Gentleman by Land, Gentleman by Sea, Gentleman in spite of Devil; and thou lie if thou say contrary." "I'll try Titles with you, as the Man said," reply'd Don Quixote; and with that throwing away his Lance; he drew his Sword, grasp'd his Target,[5] and attack'd the *Biscayan* fully bent on his Destruction. The *Biscayan* seeing him come on so furiously, would gladly have alight'd, not trusting to his Mule, which was one of those scurvy Jades that are let out to Hire; but all he had Time to do was only to draw his Sword, and snatch a Cushion out of the Coach to serve him instead of a Shield; and immediately they assaulted one another with all the Fury of mortal Enemies. The By-standers did all they could to prevent their Fighting; but 'twas in vain, for the *Biscayan* swore in his Gibberish he would kill his very Mistress, and all those who presum'd to hinder him, if they would not let him fight. The Lady in the Coach being extremely affrighted at these Passages, made her Coachman drive out of Harm's-way, and at a Distance was an Eye-witness of the furious Combat. At the same time

4. The Spanish word *caballero* has both meanings. Quixote means the former; the Biscayan   angrily thinks he means the latter.
5. Shield.

the *Biscayan* let fall such a mighty Blow on Don *Quixote's* Shoulder over his Target, that had not his Armour been Swordproof he would have cleft him down to the very Waist. The Knight feeling the Weight of that unmeasurable Blow, cry'd out aloud, "Oh! Lady of my Soul, *Dulcinea*! Flower of all Beauty, vouchsafe to succour your Champion in this dangerous Combat, undertaken to set forth your Worth." The breathing out of this short Prayer, the griping fast of his Sword, the covering of himself with his Shield, and the charging of his Enemy, was but the Work of a Moment; for Don *Quixote* was resolv'd to venture the Fortune of the Combat all upon one Blow. The *Biscayan*, who read his Design in his dreadful Countenance, resolv'd to face him with equal Bravery, and stand the terrible Shock, with uplifted Sword, and cover'd with the Cushion, not being able to manage his jaded Mule, who defying the Spur, and not being cut out for such Pranks, would move neither to the Right nor to the Left. While Don *Quixote*, with his Sword aloft, was rushing upon the wary *Biscayan*, with a full Resolution to cleave him asunder; all the Spectators stood trembling with Terrour and Amazement, expecting the dreadful Event of those prodigious Blows which threaten'd the two desperate Combatants; The Lady in the Coach, with her Women, were making a thousand Vows and Offerings to all the Images and Places of Devotion in *Spain*, that Providence might deliver them and the Squire out of the great Danger that threaten'd them.

But here we must deplore the abrupt End of this History, which the Author leaves off just at the very Point when the Fortune of the Battle is going to be decided, pretending[6] that he could find nothing more recorded of Don *Quixote's* wondrous Atchievements than what he had already related. However the second Undertaker of this Work could not believe, that so curious a History could lie for ever inevitably buried in Oblivion; or that the Learned of *La Mancha* were so regardless of their Country's Glory, as not to preserve in their Archives, or at least in their Closets, come Memoirs as Monuments of this famous Knight; and therefore he wou'd not give over inquiring after the Continuation of this pleasant History till at last he happily found it, as the next Book will inform the Reader.

Part I, Book 2, Chapter 1

The Event of the most stupendious Combat between the brave Biscayan *and the valorous Don* Quixote.

In the First Book of this History, we left the valiant *Biscayan* and the renowned Don *Quixote* with their Swords lifted up, and ready to let fall on each other two furious and most terrible Blows, which had they fall'n directly, and met with no Opposition, would have cut and divided the

6. Claiming, declaring.

two Combatants from Head to Heel, and have split 'em like a Pomgran-
ate: But, as I said before, the Story remain'd imperfect; neither did the
Author inform us where we might find the remaining Part of the Relation. This vex'd me extremely, and turn'd the Pleasure which the Perusal of the Beginning had afforded me into Disgust, when I had Reason
to despair of ever seeing the rest. Yet, after all, it seem'd to me no less
impossible than unjust, that so valiant a Knight should have been destitute of some learned Person to record his incomparable Exploits; a
Misfortune which never attended any of his Predecessors, I mean the
Knights-Adventurers, each of whom was always provided with one or
two learned Men, who were always at hand to write not only their wondrous Deeds, but also to set down their Thoughts and childish petty
Actions, were they never so hidden. * * * I cou'd not induce my self to
believe that so admirable a History was ever left unfinish'd, and rather
chose to think that Time, the Devourer of all things, had either hid or
consum'd it. On the other Side, when I consider'd that several modern
Books were found in his Study[7] * * * I had Reason to think that the
History of our Knight, could be of no very ancient Date; and that, had
it never been continu'd, yet his Neighbours and Friends could not have
forgot the most remarkable Passages of his Life. Full of this Imagination,
I resolv'd to make it my Business to make a particular and exact inquiry
into the Life and Miracles of our renown'd *Spaniard*, Don *Quixote*, that
refulgent Glory and Mirrour of the Knighthood of *La Mancha,* and the
first who in these deprav'd and miserable Times devoted himself to the
neglected Profession of Knight-Errantry, to redress Wrongs and Injuries,
to relieve Widows, and defend the Honour of Damsels; such of them, I
mean, who in former Ages rode up and down over Hills and Dales with
Whip in Hand, mounted on their Palfreys, with all their Virginity about
them, secure from all Manner of Danger, and who, unless they happen'd to be ravish'd by some boistrous Villain or huge Giant, were sure,
at fourscore Years of Age, (all which Time they never slept one Night
under a Roof) to be decently laid in their Graves, as pure Virgins as the
Mothers that bore 'em. For this Reason and many others, I saw, our
gallant Don *Quixote* is worthy everlasting and universal Praise: Nor ought
I to be deny'd my due Commendation for my indefatigable Care and
Diligence, in seeking and finding out the Continuation of this delightful
History; though after all I must confess, that had not Providence, Chance,
or Fortune, as I will now inform you, assisted me in the Discovery, the
World had been depriv'd of two Hours Diversion and Pleasure, which
'tis likely to afford to those who will read it with Attention.

* * *

[The narrator's curiosity about a pile of Arabic papers hawked in a market
discloses the history of Don Quixote "written by Cid Hamet Benegeli, an
Arabian Historiographer"; he has it translated.]

---

7. Earlier Quixote's friends review the contents of the library that is the source of his chivalric mania.

Don *Quixote's* Fight with the *Biscayan* was exactly drawn on one of the Leaves of the first Quire in the same Posture as we left them, with their Swords lifted up over their Heads, the one guarding himself with his Shield, the other with his Cushion. The *Biscayan's* Mule was pictur'd so to the Life, that with half an Eye you might have known it to be an Hir'd Mule. Under the *Biscayan* was written Don *Sancho de Aspetia*, and under *Rozinante* Don *Quixote*. *Rozinante* was so admirably delineated, so slim, so stiff, so lank, so lean, so jaded, with so sharp a Ridgebone, and altogether so like one wasted with an incurable Consumption, that any one must have owned at first Sight that no Horse ever better deserved that Name.[8] Not far off stood *Sancho Panza* holding his Ass by the Halter; at whose Feet there was a Scroll, in which was written *Sancho Cancas*: And if we may judge of him by his Picture, he was thick and short, paunch-belly'd, and long-haunch'd; so that in all Likelihood for this Reason he is sometimes called *Panza* and sometimes *Cancas* in the History.[9] There were some other Niceties to be seen in that Piece, but hardly worth Observation, as not giving any Light into this true History, otherwise they had not pass'd unmention'd; for none can be amiss so they be authentick. I must only acquaint the Reader, that if any Objection is to be made as to the Veracity of this, 'tis only that the Author is an *Arabian*, and those of that Country are not a little addicted to lying: But yet, if we consider that they are our Enemies,[1] we shou'd sooner imagine that the Author has rather suppress'd the Truth, than added to the real Worth of our Knight; and I am the more inclinable to think so, because 'tis plain that where he ought to have enlarg'd on his Praises, he maliciously chooses to be silent; a Proceeding unworthy of an Historian, who ought to be exact, sincere, and impartial; free from Passion, and not to be biass'd either by Interest, Fear, Resentment, or Affection to deviate from Truth, which is the Mother of History, the Preserver and Eternizer of Great Actions, the professed Enemy of Oblivion, the Witness of Things pass'd, and the Director of future Times. As for this History, I know 'twill afford you as great Variety as you cou'd wish, in the most entertaining Manner; and if in any Point it falls short of your Expectation, I am of Opinion 'tis more the Fault of the unworthy Author than the Subject: And so let us come to the Second Book, which, according to our Translation, began in this Manner.

Such were the bold and formidable Looks of the two enraged Combatants, that with up-lifted Arms, and with destructive Steel, they seem'd to threaten Heaven, Earth, and the infernal Mansions; while the Spectators seem'd wholly lost in Fear and Astonishment. The cholerick *Biscayan* discharg'd the first Blow, and that with such a Force, and so desperate a Fury, that had not his Sword turn'd in his Hand, that single Stroke had put an End to the dreadful Combat, and all our Knight's

8. In Spanish, *rocin* means "hack" or "worn-out horse."
9. *Panza* means "paunch"; *cancas* (*zancas*) means "shanks" or "legs."

1. Spain and the neighboring region of North Africa had been a battleground between Christians and Moslems since the eighth century.

Adventures. But Fate, that reserv'd him for greater things, so order'd it, that his Enemy's Sword turn'd in such a Manner, that tho' it struck him on the left Shoulder, it did him no other Hurt than to disarm that Side of his Head, carrying away with it a great Part of his Helmet and one Half of his Ear, which like a dreadful Ruin fell together to the Ground. Assist me ye Powers! But it is in vain: The Fury which then engross'd the Breast of our Heroe of *La Mancha* is not to be express'd; Words wou'd but wrong it for what Colour of Speech can be lively enough to give but a slight Sketch or faint Image of his unutterable Rage? Exerting all his Valour, he rais'd himself upon his Stirrups, and seem'd even greater than himself; and at the same Instant griping his Sword fast with both Hands, he discharg'd such a tremendous Blow full on the *Biscayan's* Cushion, and his Head, that in spite of so good a Defence, as if a whole Mountain had fallen upon him, the Blood gush'd out at his Mouth, Nose, and Ears all at once; and he totter'd so in his Saddle, that he had fallen to the Ground immediately had he not caught hold of the Neck of his Mule: But the dull Beast itself being rous'd out of its Stupidity with that terrible Blow, began to run about the Fields; and the *Biscayan*, having lost his Stirrups and his Hold, with two or three Winces the Mule shook him off, and threw him on the Ground. Don *Quixote* beheld the Disaster of his Foe with the greatest Tranquillity and Unconcern imaginable; and seeing him down, flipp'd nimbly from his Saddle, and running to him, set the point of his Sword to his Throat, and bid him yield, or he would cut off his Head. The *Biscayan* was so stunn'd that he could make him no Reply; and Don *Quixote* had certainly made good his Threats, so provok'd was he, had not the Ladies in the Coach, who with great Uneasiness and Fear beheld these sad Transactions, hasten'd to beseech Don *Quixote* very earnestly to spare his Life. "Truly, beautiful Ladies," said the victorious Knight, with a great deal of Loftiness and Gravity, "I am willing to grant your Request; but upon Condition that this same Knight shall pass his Word of Honour to go to *Toboso*, and there present himself in my Name before the peerless Lady *Donna Dulcinea*, that she may dispose of him as she shall see convenient." The Lady, who was frighted almost out of her Senses, without considering what Don *Quixote* enjoyn'd, or enquiring who the Lady *Dulcinea* was, promised in her Squire's Behalf a punctual Obedience to the Knight's Commands. "Let him live then," reply'd Don *Quixote*, "upon your Word, and owe to your Intercession that Pardon which I might justly deny his Arrogance."

Part I, Book 3, Chapter 2

What happen'd to Don Quixote in the Inn which he took for a Castle.

The Inn-keeper, seeing Don *Quixote* lying quite a-thwart the Ass, ask'd Sancho what ail'd him? *Sancho* answer'd, " 'Twas nothing, only his Master had got a Fall from the Top of a Rock to the Bottom, and

had bruis'd his sides a little."[2] The Inn-keeper had a Wife, very different
from the common sort of Hostesses, for she was of a Charitable Nature,
very compassionate of her Neighbour's Affliction; which made her
immediately take care of Don *Quixote*, and call her Daughter, (a good
handsom Girl,) to set her helping hand to his Cure. One of the Servants
in the Inn was an *Asturian* Wench, a Broad-fac'd, Flat-headed, Saddle-
nos'd Dowdy; blind of one Eye, and t'other almost out: However, the
Grace[3] of her Body supply'd all other Defects. She was not above three
Foot high from her Heels to her Head; and her Shoulders, which somewhat loaded her, as having too much Flesh upon 'em, made her look
downwards oftner than she could have wish'd. This charming Original
likewise assisted the Mistress and the Daughter; and with the latter, help'd
to make the Knight's Bed, and a sorry one it was; the Room where it
stood was an old gambling Cock-loft, which by manifold Signs seem'd
to have been, in the days of Yore, a Repository for chopt-Straw. Somewhat further, in a Corner of that Garret, a Carrier had his Lodging; and
tho' his Bed was nothing but the Pannels and Coverings of his Mules,
'twas much better than that of Don *Quixote*; which only consisted of
four rough-hewn Boards laid upon two uneven Tressels, a Flock-bed,
that, for Substance, might well have pass'd for a Quilt, and was full of
Knobs and Bunches; which had they not peep'd out thro many a hole,
and shewn themselves to be of Wool, might well have been taken for
Stones: The rest of that extraordinary Bed's Furniture, was a Pair of
Sheets, which rather seem'd to be of Leather than of Linen Cloth, and
a Coverlet whose every individual Thread you might have told, and
never have miss'd one in the Tale.

In this ungracious Bed was the Knight laid to rest his belabour'd Carcase, and presently the Hostess and her Daughter anointed and plaister'd
him all over, while *Maritornes* (for this was the Name of the *Asturian*
Wench) held the Candle. * * *

[In the ensuing dialogue, Sancho acquaints the women with his master's
knight-errantry and his hopes of acquiring a kingdom, and Quixote pays
courtly tribute to the landlady and her daughter, who are "quite at a Loss
for the Meaning of this high-flown Language, which they understood full as
well as if it had been Greek."]

* * * And so, having made him such Returns as Inn-keeper's Breeding cou'd afford, they left him to his Rest; only *Maritornes* staid to rub
down *Sancho*, who wanted her Help no less than his Master.

Now you must know, that the Carrier and she had agreed to pass the
Night together; and she had given him her Word, that as soon as all the
People in the Inn were in Bed, she wou'd be sure to come to him, and
be at his Service. And 'tis said of this good-natur'd thing, that whenever
she had pass'd her Word in such Cases, she was sure to make it good,

2. Quixote and Sancho have been soundly thrashed   attempted to molest their mares.
by several wagon drivers after Rozinante has   3. "Activity" in the Motteux version.

tho' she had made the Promise in the midst of a Wood and without any Witness at all. For she stood much upon her Gentility, tho' she under-valu'd her self so far as to serve in an Inn, often saying that nothing but Crosses and Necessity cou'd have made her stoop to it.

Don *Quixote's* hard, scanty, beggerly, miserable Bed was the first of the four in that Wretch'd Apartment; next to that was *Sancho's* Kennel; which consisted of nothing but a Bed-Mat and a Coverlet, that rather seem'd shorn Canvas than a Rug. Beyond these two Beds was that of the Carrier, made, as we have said, of the Pannels and Furniture of two of the best of twelve Mules which he kept, every one of 'em goodly Beasts and in special good Case,[4] for he was one of the richest Muleteers of *Arevalo*, as the Moorish Author of this History relates, who makes par-ticular mention of him, as having been acquainted with him, nay, some don't stick to say he was somewhat a-kin to him. However it be, it appears that *Cid Mahomet Benengeli* was a very exact Historian, since he takes care to give us an Account of Things that seem so inconsiderable and trivial. A laudable Example which these Historians should follow, who usually relate Matters so concisely, that they seem scarce to have dipp'd in 'em, and rather to have left the most essential Part of the Story drown'd in the bottom of the Inkhorn, either through Neglect, Malice, or Igno-rance. A thousand Blessings then be given to the curious Author of *Tablante de Ricamonte*, and to that other indefatigable Sage who recorded the Atchievements of Count *Tomilla*,[5] for they have describ'd even the most minute and trifling Circumstances with a singular Preciseness. But, to return to our Story, you must know that after the Carrier had dress'd his Mules and given 'em their Night's Provender, he laid him down on his hard Bed, expecting the most punctual *Maritornes's* kind Visit. By this Time, *Sancho*, duly greas'd and anointed, was crept into his Sty, where he did all he could to sleep but his aching Ribs did all they could to prevent him. As for the Knight, whose Sides were in as bad Circum-stances as his Squire's, he lay with both his Eyes open like a Hare. And now was every Soul in the Inn gone to Bed, not any Light to be seen, except that of a Lamp which hung in the Middle of the Gate-way. This general Tranquillity setting Don *Quixote's* Thoughts at work, offer'd to his Imagination one of the most absurd Follies that ever crept into a distemper'd Brain, from the Perusal of Romantick Whimsies. Now he fansy'd himself to be in a famous Castle, (for, as we have already said, all the Inns he lodg'd in, seem'd no less than Castle's to him) and that the Inn-keeper's Daughter (consequently Daughter to the Lord of the Castle) strangely captivated with his graceful Presence and Galantry, had promis'd him the Pleasure of her Embraces, as soon as her Father and Mother were gone to rest. This Chimera disturb'd him, as if it had been a real Truth. So that he began to be mightily perplex'd, reflecting on the Danger to which his Honour was expos'd. But at last his Virtue

---

4. Condition.
5. A character in the chivalric romance *Historia de Enrique fi de Oliva* (1498). *Tablante de Rica-* *monte* (1513) is a prose version of a medieval Arthurian romance.

overcame the powerful Temptation, and he firmly resolv'd not to be guilty of the least Infidelity to his Lady *Dulcinea del Toboso*; tho' queen *Genever* her self, with her trusty Matron *Quintaniona*[6] should join to decoy him into the alluring Snare.

While these wild Imaginations work'd in his Brain, the gentle *Maritornes* was mindful of her Assignation, and with soft and wary Steps, barefoot and in her Smock, with her Hair gather'd up in a Fustian Coif,[7] stole into the Room, and felt about for her beloved Carrier's Bed. But scarce had she got to the Door, when Don *Quixote*, whose Ears were on the Scout, was sensible that something was coming in; and therefore having rais'd himself in his Bed, sore and wrapt up in Plaisters, as he was, he stretch'd out his Arms to receive his fancy'd Damsel, and caught hold of *Maritornes* by the Wrist, as she was, with her Arms stretch'd, groping her way to her *Paramour*; he pull'd her to him, and made her sit down by his Bed's-side, she not daring to speak a Word all the while: Now, as he imagin'd her to be the Lord of the Castle's Daughter, her Smock which was of the coarsest Canvas, seem'd to him of the finest Holland,[8] and the Glass-Beads about her Wrist, precious Oriental Pearls; her Hair that was almost as rough as a Horse's Mane, he took to be soft flowing Threads of bright curling Gold; and her Breath that had a stronger *Hogoe*[9] than stale Venison, was to him a grateful Compound of the most fragrant Perfumes of *Arabia*. In short, flattering Imagination transform'd her into the likeness of those Romantick Beauties, one of whom, as he remember'd to have read, came to pay a private Visit to a wounded Knight, with whom she was desperately in Love; and the poor Gentleman's obstinate Folly had so infatuated his outward Sense, that his Feeling and his Smell could not in the least undeceive him; and he thought he had no less than a balmy *Venus* in his Arms, while he hugg'd a fulsom Bundle of Deformities that would have turn'd any Man's Stomach but a sharp-set Carrier's. Therefore clasping her still closer, with a soft and amorous whisper, "Oh! thou most lovely Temptation," cry'd he, "Oh! that I now might but pay a warm Acknowledgment for the mighty Blessing which your extravagant Goodness would lavish on me; yes, most beautiful Charmer, I would give an Empire to purchase your more desirable Embraces: But Fortune, Madam, Fortune, that Tyrant of my Life, that unrelenting Enemy to the truly Deserving, has maliciously hurry'd and rivetted me to this Bed, where I lie so bruis'd and macerated, that tho' I were eager to gratify your Desires, I should at this dear unhappy Minute be doom'd to Impotence: Nay to that unlucky Bar, Fate has added a yet more invincible Obstacle; I mean my plighted Faith to the unrival'd *Dulcinea del Toboso*, the sole Mistress of my Wishes, and absolute Sovereign of my Heart. Oh! did not this oppose my present Happiness, I could never be so dull and insensible a Knight as to lose the Benefit of this extraordinary Favour which you have now condescended to offer me."

---

6. Spanish versions of Arthurian legend assigned Queen Guinevere a *duenna* or chaperone.
7. Coarse cloth cap.
8. Linen.
9. Stench.

Poor *Maritornes* all this while sweated for Fear and Anxiety, to find her self thus lock'd in the Knight's Arms; and without either understanding or willing to understand his florid Excuses, she did what she could to get from him, and sheer off, without speaking a Word: On the other side, the Carrier, whose lewd Thoughts kept him awake, having heard his trusty Lady when she first came in, and listen'd ever since to the Knight's Discourse, began to be afraid that she had made some other Assignation; and so without any more ado, he crept softly to Don *Quixote*'s Bed, where he listen'd a while to hear what would be the end of all this Talk, which he could not understand: But perceiving at last, by the struggling of his faithful *Maritornes*, that 'twas none of her Fault, and that the Knight strove to detain her against her Will, he could by no means bear his Familiarity; and therefore taking it in mighty Dudgeon, he up with his Fist, and hit the enamour'd Knight such a swinging blow in the Jaws, that his Face was all over Blood in a Moment. And not satisfy'd with this, he got o'top of the Knight and with his splay Feet betrampled him as if he had been treading a Hay-mow. With that the Bed, whose Foundations were none of the best, sunk under the additional Load of the Carrier, and fell with such a noise that it wak'd the Inn-keeper, who presently suspected it to be one of *Maritornes*'s nightly Skirmishes; and therefore having call'd her aloud, and finding that she did not answer, he lighted a Lamp and made to the Place where he heard the Bustle. The Wench, who heard him coming, knowing him to be of a passionate Nature, was fear'd out of her Wits, and fled for shelter to *Sancho*'s Sty, where he lay snoreing to some Tune: There she pigg'd in, and slunk under the Coverlet, where she lay snug, and truss'd up as round as an Egg. Presently her Master came in, in a mighty heat. "Where's this damn'd Whore?" cry'd he; "I dare say this is one of her Pranks." By this, *Sancho* awak'd; and feeling that unusual Lump, which almost overlaid him, he took it to be the Night-Mare,[1] and began to lay about him with his Fists, and thump'd the Wench so unmercifully, that at last Flesh and Blood were no longer to bear it; and forgetting the Danger she was in, and her dear Reputation, she paid him back his Thumps as fast as her Fists could lay 'em on, and soon rous'd the drousy Squire out of his Sluggishness, whether he would or no. Who finding himself thus pommell'd, by he did not know who, he bustled up in his Nest, and catching hold of *Maritornes*, they began the most pleasant Skirmish in the World. When the Carrier perceiving by the Light of the Inn-keeper's Lamp, the dismal Condition that his dear Mistress was in, presently took her Part; and, leaving the Knight whom he had more than sufficiently mawl'd flew at the Squire, and paid him confoundedly. On the other hand, the Inn-keeper, who took the Wench to be the Cause of all this hurly-burly, cuff'd and kick'd, and kick'd and cuff'd her over and over again: And so there was a strange Multiplication of Fisticuffs and Drubbings. The Carrier pommel'd *Sancho*, *Sancho* mawl'd the Wench, the Wench belabour'd the Squire, and the Inn-keeper thrash'd

---

1. A female spirit supposed to press down on and suffocate sleepers.

her again: And all of 'em laid on with such Expedition, that you would have thought they had been afraid of losing Time. But the best Jest was that in the Heat of the Fray, the Lamp went out, so that being now in the dark, they ply'd one another at a Venture, they struck and tore, all went to Rack, while Nails and Fists flew about without Mercy.

*   *   *

Part II (1615), Chapter 16

What happen'd to Don Quixote with a sober Gentleman of La Mancha.

*   *   *

[On the road, Quixote and Sancho are overtaken by a horseman whose "Mien and Appearance spoke him a Man of Quality." Discerning the gentleman's puzzlement at his own appearance, Quixote informs him of his knightly mission and the success of the first volume of his history, leaving the stranger "no less surpriz'd and amaz'd than ever."]

"For, is it possible there should be at this time any Knights-Errant in the World, and there shou'd be a true History of a living Knight-Errant in Print? I cannot persuade my self there is any body now upon Earth that relieves Widows, protects Damsels, or assists Married Women and Orphans; and I should still be of the same Mind, had not my Eyes afforded me a sight of such a Person as your self. Now Heaven be prais'd, for this History of your true and noble Feats of Arms, which you say is in Print, will blot out the Memory of all those idle Romances of pretended Knights-Errant that have so fill'd and pester'd the World, to the detriment of good Education, and the Prejudice and Dishonour of true History." "There is a great deal to be said," answer'd Don Quixote, "for the Truth of Histories of Knight-Errantry, as well as against it." "How!" return'd the Gentleman in Green "Is there any Body living who makes the least Scruple but that they are false?" "Yes, Sir, my self for one," said Don Quixote; "But let that pass: If we continue any time together on the Road, I hope to convince you that you have been to blame in suffering your self to be carry'd away with the Stream of Mankind that generally disbelieves 'em." The Traveller at this Discourse began to have a Suspicion that Don Quixote was distracted, and expected the next Words would confirm him in that Opinion; But before they enter'd into any further Conversation, Don Quixote begg'd him to acquaint him who he was, since he had given him some Account of his own Life and Condition.

*   *   *

[The gentleman describes his modest, humane, and pious way of life, prompting Sancho to salute him as a "Saint on Horse-back"; he then vents his disappointment at his son's pursuit of poetry instead of the law or divinity for which he had intended him.]

"Sir," reply'd Don *Quixote*, "Children are the Flesh and Blood of their Parents, and, whether good or bad, are to be cherish'd as part of our selves. 'Tis the Duty of a Father to train 'em up from their tenderest Years in the Paths of Vertue, in good Discipline and Christian Principles, that when they advance in Years they may become the Staff and Support of their Parents' Age, and the Glory of their Posterity. But as for forcing them to this or that Study, 'tis a thing I don't so well approve. Persuasion is all, I think, that is proper in such a case; especially when they are so Fortunate as to be above studying for Bread, as having Parents that can provide for their future Subsistence, they ought in my Opinion to be indulged in the Pursuit of that Science to which their own Genius gives them the most Inclination. For though the Art of Poetry is not so profitable as delightful, yet it is none of those that disgrace the ingenious Professor.[2] Poetry, Sir, in my Judgment, is like a tender Virgin in her Bloom, Beautiful and Charming to Amazement: All the other Sciences are so many Virgins, whose Care it is to Enrich, Polish and Adorn her, and as she is to make use of them all, so are they all to have from her a grateful Acknowledgement. But this Virgin must not be roughly handl'd, nor dragg'd along the Street, nor expos'd to every Market-place, and Corner of great Men's Houses. A good Poet is a kind of an Alchymist, who can turn the Matter he prepares into the purest Gold and an inestimable Treasure. But he must keep his Muse within the Rules of Decency, and not let her prostitute her Excellency in lewd Satires and Lampoons, nor in licentious Sonnets. She must not be Mercenary, though she need not give away the Profits she may claim from Heroick Poems, deep Tragedies, and Pleasant and Artful Comedies. She is not to be attempted by Buffoons, nor by the Ignorant Vulgar, whose Capacity can never reach to a due Sense of the Treasures that are lock'd up in her. And know, Sir, that when I mention the Vulgar, I don't mean only the common Rabble; for whoever is ignorant, be he Lord or Prince, is to be listed in the Number of the Vulgar. But whoever shall apply himself to the Muses with those Qualifications; which, as I said, are essential to the Character of a good Poet, his Name shall be Famous, and valu'd in all the polish'd Nations of the World. And as to what you say, Sir, that your Son does not much esteem our Modern Poetry; in my Opinion, he is somewhat to blame; and my Reason is this: *Homer* never wrote in *Latin*, because he was a *Grecian*; nor did *Virgil* write in *Greek*, because *Latin* was the Language of his Country. In short, all your Ancient Poets wrote in their Mother-Tongue, and did not seek other Languages to express their lofty Thoughts. And thus, it wou'd be well that Custom shou'd extend to every Nation; there being no Reason that a *German* Poet shou'd be despised, because he writes in his own

---

2. Practitioner, devotee.

Tongue; or a *Castilian* or *Biscayner*, because they write in theirs. But I suppose, your Son does not mislike Modern Poetry, but such Modern Poets as have no Tincture of any other Language or Science, that may adorn, awaken, and assist their Natural Impulse. Though even in this too there may be Error. For, 'tis believ'd, and not without Reason, that a Poet is naturally a Poet from his Mother's Womb, and that, with the Talent which Heaven has infus'd into him, without the help of Study or Art, he may produce these Compositions that verify that Saying, *Est Deus in nobis*, &c.[3] Not but that a natural Poet, that improves himself by Art, shall be much more accomplished, and have the advantage of him that has no Title to Poetry but by his Knowledge in the Art; because Art cannot go beyond Nature, but only adds to its Perfection. From which it appears, that the most perfect Poet is he whom Nature and Art combine to qualify. Let then your Son proceed and follow the Guidance of his Stars, for being so good a Student as I understand he is, and already got up the first Step of the Sciences, the Knowledge of the Learned Tongues, he will easily ascend to the Pinnacle of Learning, which is no less an Honour and an Ornament to a Gentleman, than a Mitre is to a Bishop, or the Long Robe to the Civilian.[4] Shou'd your Son write Satires to lessen the Reputation of any Person, you wou'd do well to take him to Task, and tear his defamatory Rhimes; but if he studies to write such Discourse in Verse, to ridicule and explode Vice in general, as Horace so elegantly did, then encourage him: For a Poet's Pen is allow'd to inveigh against Envy and Envious Men, and so against other Vices, provided it aim not at particular Persons. But there are Poets so abandon'd to the Itch of Scurrility, that rather than lose a villaninous Jest, they'll venture being banish'd to the Island of *Pontus*.[5] If a Poet is modest in his Manners, he will be so in his Verses. The Pen is the Tongue of the Mind; the Thoughts that are formed in the one, and those that are traced by the other, will bear a near Resemblance. And when Kings and Princes see the wonderful Art of Poetry shine in Prudent, Vertuous, and Solid Subjects, they honour, esteem, and enrich them, and even crown them with Leaves of that Tree,[6] which is ne'er offended by the Thunderbolt, as a Token that nothing shall offend those whose Brows are honour'd and adorn'd with such Crowns". The Gentleman hearing Don *Quixote* express himself in this manner, was struck with so much Admiration, that he began to lose the bad Opinion he had conceiv'd of his Understanding. As for *Sancho*, who did not much relish this fine Talk, he took an Opportunity to slink aside in the middle of it, and went to get a little Milk of some Shepherds that were hard by keeping their Sheep.

*   *   *

---

3. "There is a god in us" (Ovid, *Fasti* 6.5).
4. Someone learned in civil law; the long robe was the emblem of the legal profession.
5. A confused reference to Ovid's banishment from Rome to Tomi on the west coast of the Black Sea (*Pontus Euxinus*) for some offense to the Emperor Augustus.
6. The laurel.

PAUL SCARRON

From *Le Roman comique*

[Scarron published the first two parts of *Le Roman comique* in 1651 and 1657; he died in 1660 before completing a third part, which never appeared. Two inferior seventeenth-century conclusions were frequently reprinted, and one of these, attributed to Jean Girault, was included as Scarron's in the popular 1700 English translation of Tom Brown and a Mr. Savage. In translating the excerpts reprinted below, I have followed this version when it was not at variance with the original, but I have divided Scarron's uninterruped narration into paragraphs and modernized capitalization and punctuation.

The novel recounts the fortunes of an itinerant acting troupe and their camp followers: a poet, Roquebrune; a provincial officer, La Rappinière; and, most prominently, a dwarfish advocate, Ragotin, "the greatest little fool to traverse the field since Roland." Within the framework of the company's present knockabout misadventures, the principal players relate their romantic histories. Chief among these is the story of Le Destin (Destiny) and L'Étoile (Star), a supposed brother and sister who have recently become actors out of necessity. The mystery surrounding these lovers, their past vicissitudes, and the present attempts of their persistent enemy to abduct L'Étoile sustain the novel's main thread of dramatic suspense. The first excerpt follows the reunion of the divided troupe after their flight from a performance broken up by the provincial police.]

Part I, Chapter 12

Combat in the Night

I am too much a man of honor not to advise the good natured reader, that if he be offended at all the silly banter he has already seen in the present book, he will do well not to go on with the reading of it; for, upon my conscience, he must expect nothing else, although the book should become as fat as the *Grand Cyrus*.[1] And if from what he has already seen, he has trouble surmising what he will see next, it may be that I am in the same predicament, that one chapter leads to another and I do with my book as those who leave the bridle on the neck of their horses and let them go in good faith. It could also be that I have a fixed plan and that without filling my book with examples to imitate, by portrayals of actions and things sometimes ridiculous, sometimes blameworthy, I will instruct while amusing in the same fashion that a drunkard creates aversion for his vice while sometimes giving pleasure by the impertinences caused by his drunkenness. Let us end the moral lesson and return to our actors whom we left in the inn.

* * *

---

1. See above, p. 4.

After supper, Destiny alone remained in thee actresses' chamber. Cave loved him as her own son; Mademoiselle Star was no less dear to her; and Angelica, her daughter and her sole heir, loved Destiny and Star as her brother and sister. She did not yet know who they in truth were nor why they became players; but she had recognized that though they called each other brother and sister they were greater friends than near relations. She observed, that Destiny behaved toward Star with the greatest respect, that she was extremely virtuous and that if Destiny was a man of wit and evident good breeding, Mademoiselle Star seemed a young lady of quality rather than a strolling actress. If Destiny and Star were loved by Cave and her daughter, the reciprocal affection which they had for them merited it; and they did not find this very difficult since they deserved to be beloved as much as any actresses of France, though through bad luck rather than lack of talent they had never had the honor to appear on the stage of the Bourgogne or the Marais, which are both the *non plus ultra* of players.[2] Those who do not understand these three little Latin words (which I could not refuse a place here since they came so pat in my way) may explicate them as they please. To end the digression, Destiny and Star did not seclude themselves from the two actresses to caress each other after their long separation. They expressed as well as they could the anxieties they had had for one another. Destiny told Star that the last time they had performed at Tours he believed he saw their inveterate persecutor; he had caught sight of him in the audience although he had tried to hide his face in his cloak, and for this reason the actor had put a patch on his Face in leaving Tours to conceal himself from his enemy, not then being in a position to defend himself if he were attacked. * * * While Destiny spoke, poor Star could not refrain from shedding some tears. Destiny was extremely touched and, after having consoled her as well as he could, he added that, if she would permit him to exercise the same care in seeking their common enemy as he had until then to avoid him, she would soon see herself freed from his persecution or he would lose his life in the attempt. These last words afflicted her still more. Destiny did not have a strong enough mind to avoid being moved as well, and Cave and her daughter, very compassionate by nature, grieved out of complaisance or by contagion and I believe that they even wept. I do not know if Destiny cried, but I do know that the actresses and he said nothing for a long time, and meanwhile whoever wished to cried.

At last Cave ended the tearful pause and reproached Destiny and Star that since they had been together they could have recognized how much she was their friend; nevertheless, they had so little confidence in her and her daughter that they were still ignorant of their true condition. She added that she had been persecuted enough in her life to counsel unhappy persons such as they seemed to be. To which Destiny answered

2. The Hotel de Bourgogne and the enclosed tennis court in the Marais district housed the first permanent professional acting companies in Paris and dominated French theatre in Scarron's lifetime.

that it was not at all out of distrust that they had held back, but because
he had thought the account of their misfortunes could only be very
tedious; he offered to entertain her with it whenever she wished and had
some time to waste. Cave did not put off satisfying her curiosity any
longer, and her daughter, who ardently wished the same thing, having
seated herself next to her on Star's bed, Destiny was going to begin his
story when they heard a great noise in the next chamber. Destiny stood
listening a little while but instead of ceasing, the noise and the squabble
increased, and somebody even cried out, "Murder! Help! I am being
killed!" In three leaps Destiny got out of the chamber, at the expense of
his doublet, which Cave and her daughter tore in trying to detain him.
He went into the chamber whence the clamor came, where he could
see nothing and where the fisticuffs, boxes on the ears, and confused
voices of battling men and women, together with the hollow noise of
naked feet stamping on the floor, made a dreadful uproar. He rashly
mingled amidst the combatants and straightaway received a cuff on one
side and a box on the ear on the other. This changed his good intention
of parting these hobgoblins into a violent desire for revenge. He set his
hands in motion and twirled his two arms, which mistreated more than
one jaw, as it afterwards appeared from his bloody fists. The scuffle lasted
long enough for him to receive twenty cuffs more, which he returned
with double the number. In the heat of the fight, he felt himself bitten
in the calf of the leg; he put his hands there and lighting upon something
hairy, he thought he had been bitten by a dog; but Cave and her daughter, who appeared at the chamber door with a candle, like Saint Elmo's
fire after a storm, saw Destiny and enabled him to see that he was amidst
seven persons in their nightshirts who were very cruelly demolishing one
another and who let go of one another as soon as the light appeared.
The calm was not of long duration. The innkeeper, who was one of the
seven white penitents,[3] started in again with the poet; Olive,[4] who was
also among them, was attacked by the innkeeper's man, another penitent. Destiny tried to part them, but the hostess, who was the animal
who had bitten him and whom he took for a dog because she had a bare
head and short hair, leaped at his eyes, assisted by two maids as unclothed
and bare-headed as she. The cries began again; the cuffs and boxes rang
out more than ever and the conflict grew still more heated than it had
been. At last several persons who were awakened by the noise came into
the field of battle, pulled the combatants apart, and procured the second
armistice.

Now the question was to know the cause of the quarrel, and what
dispute had brought seven naked persons into the same room. Olive,
who seemed the least upset, said that the poet had left the room, and
that he had seen him return as fast as he could run, followed by the
innkeeper, attempting to beat him; that the innkeeper's wife had fol-

3. The combatants in their nightclothes are likened to members of one of the numerous religious
societies devoted to works of penance; these societies were commonly distinguished by the color of
their hooded robes.
4. One of the actors.

lowed her husband and threw herself on the poet; that as he was going to part them, a servant and two maids fell upon him; and that the light going out at the same time made them fight longer than they would have. Now it was the poet's turn to plead his case. He said that he had made the two finest stanzas heard since stanzas were in fashion, and fearing to lose them he had gone to ask for a candle from the maids of the inn, who had jeered at him; that the innkeeper called him a rope dancer and rather then remain without a retort he had called him cuckold.

He no sooner let loose that word anew than the host, who was in reach, gave him a box on the ear. You would have thought that they acted in concert, for as soon as the blow was given, the innkeeper's wife, his man and his maids rushed upon the strollers, who received them with sound cuffs. This last encounter was more fierce and sustained than the other two. Destiny, having hotly pursued a stout wench whose skirts he tucked up, gave her more than a hundred slaps on the buttocks. Olive, who saw this made the company laugh, did the same to another maid. The innkeeper was busy with the poet, and the hostess, who was the most furious, had been seized by some of the spectators, which threw her into such great anger that she cried out, "Thieves." Her cries awakened La Rappinière, who lodged opposite the inn. He ordered the inn doors unlocked and, judging by the noise that there could be no less than seven or eight people dead on the field, he put a stop to the fight in the name of the king. Having learned the cause of all the confusion, he exhorted the poet not to make any more verses at night and was on the verge of beating the innkeeper and his wife for chanting a hundred insults at the poor players, calling them mountebanks and buffoons and swearing to turn them out of doors the next day. Instead La Rappinière, to whom the innkeeper owed money, threatened to arrest him and by this threat closed his mouth. La Rappinière went home again, the others returned to their chambers and Destiny to that of the actresses, where Cave asked him not to defer any longer telling her his adventures and those of his sister. He said he was delighted to do so, and began his relation in the manner you shall see in the next chapter.

Part I, Chapter 19

Some Reflections which are not out of Place. A new Disgrace for Ragotin and other Things that you may read if you please.

Love, which makes the young undertake everything and the old forget everything, which has been the cause of the Trojan War and of many others which I do not wish to take the trouble to remember, would then have it known in the city of Mans that he was no less formidable in a wretched inn than in any other place he might be. He did not content himself, therefore, with ruining the amorous Ragotin's appetite. He inspired a hundred thousand wild desires in La Rappinière, who was very susceptible, and made Roquebrune enamored of the wife of the medicine show man, adding to his vanity, gallantry and poesy a fourth folly, or rather making him commit a double infidelity; for he had spoken of love a long time earlier to Star and to Angelica, who had both counselled him not to take the trouble to be in love with them. But all this is nothing alongside what I am about to say. Love triumphed as well over the callousness and misanthropy of Rancor, who became enamored of the mountebank's wife; and thus the poet Roquebrune, for his sins and as atonement for the damned books he had brought to the light, had as his rival the most mischievous man in the world.[5]

❊   ❊   ❊

[Ragotin fancies himself in love with Star. Borrowing a horse to impress her, he waits at an inn to accompany the actresses on their way to perform at a wedding in the country.]

He was scarce set down to eat his dinner when he was informed that the coaches were approaching. He flew to his horse on the wings of his love, with a great sword at his side and a carbine slung around his neck. He has never been inclined to say why he went to a wedding with such a great array of offensive weapons, something even Rancor, his dear confidant, has not been able to learn. By the time he had untied his horse's bridle, the coach was so near that he had no time to find an advantageous place from which to set himself up as a little Saint George. As he was neither a very good horseman nor prepared to display his aptitude before so many people, he acquitted himself very awkwardly, the horse being as long in the legs as he was short. Nevertheless, he hoisted himself valiantly in the stirrup and swung his right leg on the other side of the saddle; but the girth being a bit slack did great harm to the little man, for the saddle turned on the horse when he expected to perch on top of it. Still all might have been well but for the accursed carbine which hung from his neck like a horse collar and unhappily got between his legs without his realizing it, so that he fell so far short that his bottom did not touch the seat of the saddle, for it was not very flat and the carbine stretched across from the pommel to the crupper. Thus he did not find himself at ease, unable even to touch the stirrups with the tips of his toes. Thereupon the spurs which armed his short legs made themselves felt by the horse in a place never before touched by a spur. This made it start up in a more lively fashion than necessary for a little man resting only on his carbine. He clamped his legs, the horse raised his hindquarters and Ragotin, following the natural disposition of heavy bodies, found himself on the horse's neck, bruising his nose on it, the horse having raised his head in response to a furious jerk that the rash fool gave him. Hoping to correct his error, he let go of the bridle. The horse leaped forward, which made the backside of the condemned man clear the whole area of the saddle and put him on the crupper, still with the carbine between his legs. Unaccustomed to carrying anyone there, the horse made a *croupade*[6] that put Ragotin back in the saddle. The wretched rider again clenched his legs and the horse raised its rump still more forcefully, and then the poor man found himself with the pommel between his buttocks, where we will leave him as on a spindle while we rest ourselves for a while; for, on my honor, this description has cost me more than all the rest of the book and I am still not too well satisfied with it.

Chapter 20

The shortest in the present Volume. The Sequel of Ragotin's tottering, and Something similar that happened to Roquebrune.

We have left Ragotin seated on the pommel of his saddle, looking very perplexed and very anxious as to how to get down from there. I do not believe that the late Phaethon of unhappy memory had been more at a loss concerning his father's four fiery steeds[7] than our little lawyer then was on his horse as docile as an ass; and if it did not cost him his life as it had that celebrated reckless one, the blame must be assigned to fortune, whose caprice I would have a fine field to expatiate on if I were not obliged in conscience to extract him quickly from the peril in which he finds himself; for we will have plenty to do whilst our theatrical troupe remains in the city of Mans. As soon as the unfortunate Ragotin felt only the pommel under the two parts of his body which were the fleshiest and on which he was accustomed to sit, as are all other rational animals—I mean as soon as he felt himself seated on very little, he let go of the bridle like a man of discretion and seized the mane of the horse, which at once bolted. Thereupon the gun went off. Ragotin thought he was shot through the body; his horse believed the same thing and stumbled so roughly that Ragotin lost the pommel which had served him for a seat, insomuch that he hung for some time from the horse's mane, one foot caught by the spur in the saddle and the other foot and the rest of his body awaiting the freeing of the entangled foot to hit the ground in company with the carbine, sword, belt and bandolier. At last the foot was free, his hands let loose the mane, and he tumbled off, which he did more adroitly than he had mounted.

* * *

[The performance is aborted when Angelica is kidnapped. Failing to find her, Destiny returns to the company, leaving his servant to continue the search. Some time later, the bride and groom and the groom's mother, Madam Bouvillon, stop at the inn where the players are staying. When their coach breaks down the next day, Madam Bouvillon sends the newlyweds to visit a nearby relative.]

6. An equestrian maneuver in which the horse plants its forefeet and raises its hindquarters, lifting its hind legs under its body.
7. In Greek myth, when Helios, the sun god, allowed his mortal son to drive his chariot, the youth's inability to control the horses threatened to incinerate the earth until Zeus struck him down with a thunderbolt.

Part II, Chapter 10

How Madam Bouvillon could not resist a Temptation and got a Lump on her Forehead.

*   *   *

* * * thus Madam Bouvillon was the only one of her party to remain at the inn, finding herself a little fatigued or feigning to be, not to mention that her plump figure would not allow her to mount even a donkey, if one could have been found strong enough to carry her. She sent her servant to Destiny to request him to dine with her, and whilst dinner was being prepared she redressed her hair, curled and powdered, put on an apron and a laced peignoir and from her son's Genoa lace collar made a cap. She took from a case one of her daughter-in-law's wedding gowns and decked herself out in it; in short she transformed herself into a little nymph, albeit a stoutish one. Destiny would much rather have been free to dine with his comrades, but how could he refuse his very humble servant Madam Bouvillon, who had sent for him for dinner as soon as it was served? He was surprised to see her dressed like a hussy. She received him with a smiling countenance, took his hands to wash them and squeezed them in a manner that was meant to tell him something. He thought less about dining than about why he had been invited, but Madam Bouvillon reproached him so often for not eating that he could not refrain.

He did not know what to say, besides being naturally a man of few words. As for Madam Bouvillon, she was only too ingenious at finding topics of conversation. When a person who talks much meets another who says little and does not answer her, she always talks the more, for, judging others by herself, and perceiving that someone has not responded to what she has advanced as she would have done on a similar occasion, she believes that what she has said was not pleasing enough to her indifferent auditor, and tries to make amends for her fault by saying something which is often worth even less than what she has already said, never ceasing as long as she has her listener's attention. One is severely taxed to disengage, because it happens that these indefatigable talkers continue the conversation by themselves when they are in a companionable mood. I believe the best one can do with them is to speak as much as or more than they do, if possible; for all the world together will not keep a great talker next to another who will disrupt the game and make her an auditor by force. I base this reflection on much experience, and indeed I am not at all sure that I am not one of these whom I censure. As for the incomparable Bouvillon, she was the most immoderate reciter of nothings ever known, and she not only talked by herself but also answered herself. Given free play by Destiny's silent disposition and aiming to please him, she rambled over a large territory. She told him all that happened in the town of Laval, where she resided, making a scandalous story of it, and never ripped up an individual or a whole family of whom she could only speak ill but she opened a topic on which she could say something good about herself, protesting at each defect that she remarked in her neighbors that though she had many faults, she did not have this one. Destiny was extremely mortified at the beginning of her discourse, and made no answer; but at last he felt obliged to smile from time to time and to say occasionally either "That is very amusing" or "That is very strange," and more often than not he said them both at the wrong time.

The table was cleared as soon as Destiny finished eating; Madam Bouvillon made him sit next to her on the foot of the bed and her servant, who let the inn waiters out of the room before her, closed the door after her. Madam Bouvillon, who thought Destiny might have observed this, said to him: "See this scatterbrain has shut the door on us!" "I will go and open it, if you like," Destiny replied. "I am not saying that" responded Bouvillon, stopping him, "but you know very well that as two persons locked up alone together can do as they please, so people will believe of them what they wish." "It is not upon persons like yourself that such rash judgments are made," answered Destiny. "I am not saying that," said Bouvillon, "but one cannot have too much caution against slander." "It must have some foundation," replied Destiny, "and as regards you and me, people are well aware of the inequality between a poor actor and a woman of your station. Would you like me to go open the door?" "I am not saying that," said Bouvillon, going to lock it; "for," she added, "perhaps no one will notice whether it is locked or not, and as long as it is closed, it would be better if it could not be opened without our consent." Having done as she said, she approached Destiny, her fat face aglow and her little eyes sparkling, and gave him reason to consider how he could retreat with his honor from the battle in which she so evidently intended to engage him. The corpulent sensualist removed her handkercheif from her neck, and exposed to the eyes of Destiny, who took no great pleasure therefrom, at least ten pounds of breasts, that is, a third of them, the rest being distributed in equal portions under her two armpits. Her wicked intention made her blush (for a shameless person may also blush), her neck being no less red than her face, the two together resembling from a distance a scarlet stormhat with its earflaps down. Destiny also reddened, but out of modesty, whereas Madam Bouvillon, who had none, colored from what I leave you to guess. She cried that she had some little creature down her back, and wriggling in her harness as if she felt an itch, she asked Destiny to stuff his hand in there. The poor lad did so trembling and meanwhile Madam Bouvillon touched his sides through the openings in his doublet, asking him if he was not in the least ticklish. He was at the point of having to fight or surrender, when Ragotin was heard on the other side of the door, striking it with his feet and hands as if he wished to break it down and calling for Destiny to open it at once. Destiny withdrew his hand from the sweaty back of Madam Bouvillon to let in Ragotin (who all the while kept up a devilish noise), and, wishing to pass between her and the table agilely enough not to touch her, he stubbed his toe on something which made him fall and bump his head against a bench hard enough to be stunned a while. Madam Bouvillon meanwhile, having hastily replaced her handkerchief, went to admit the impetuous Ragotin, who, by pushing the door at the same time from the other side with all his might, made it affront the poor lady's face so forcefully that she had her nose flattened and in addition got a lump on her forehead as big as a fist. She screamed that she was dead. The little fool made not the least apology, but jumping up and down repeated: "Mademoiselle Angelica is found! Mademoiselle Angelica is here!," almost angering Destiny, whose calls for Madam Bouvillon's servant to help her mistress could not be heard because of Ragotin's noise. At last this servant brought water and a clean napkin. As well as they could, she and Destiny repaired the damage that the door, so rudely forced, had done to the poor lady. Impatient though he was to know if Ragotin was telling the truth, Destiny did not follow his impulse and leave Madam Bouvillon until her face had been washed and wiped and the bump on her forehead bandaged, not without his often calling Ragotin fool, who, for all this, never ceased tugging at him to go where he wished to convey him.

[Angelica has been mistaken for Star and released when the villain's men discover their mistake and capture their intended victim (hence the next chapter is titled "The Least Diverting in the Present Volume"). But the success is short-lived; Destiny and his friend rescue Star in the chapter after that (ironically titled "Which Will Entertain Perhaps as Little as the Preceding"). This is as far as Scarron carried the story of Destiny and Star.[8]]

* * *

ALAIN-RENÉ LESAGE

From *Histoire de Gil Blas de Santillane*

[Perhaps the most loosely episodic of the continental comic romances, *Gil Blas* records the adventures and observations of its narrator from his initial victimization as a country boy en route to the city through a series of liberally educational experiences with a variety of eccentric masters to confidential service at the highest levels of the Spanish court. As Gil Blas resiliently picks and stumbles his way through a maze of pretension and intrigue above stairs and cheating below, the center of comic interest is less the hero and his fortunes than the deceptions, delusions, and follies of the world he encounters.

8. For a reconstruction of Scarron's plan for completing their story, and its relation to Fielding's conception of Joseph and Fanny's story, see Goldberg, *The Art of* Joseph Andrews (Chicago and London: U of Chicago P, 1969) 46–50. Some of Scarron's other characteristic chapter titles are: "Which Does Not Contain Much"; "In Which Will Be Seen Many Things Necessary to Know to Understand the Present Book"; "Which Contains What You Will See if You Take the Trouble to Read It"; "Which Serves Only to Introduce the Others"; and "Which Has No Need for a Title."

The novel was published in three widely spaced installments. The first (vols. 1 and 2, books 1–6) appeared in 1715; the second (vol. 3, books 7–9) in 1724; and the third (vol. 4, books 10–13) in 1735. The following episode, cited by Fielding in *Joseph Andrews*, book 3, chapter 1, is from volume 3, book 7, in a 1725 translation. Gil Blas has just been driven from his comfortable post as steward to a young nobleman by the hostility of a fifty-year-old duenna whose advances he has spurned. In Grenada he meets the nobleman's relative, Don Fernando de Leyva, who promises to find him employment.]

Chap. II.

What befel Gil Blas *after his leaving the Castle of* Leyva; *and with what good Fortune his unsuccessful Amours were follow'd.*

* * *

Accordingly the first time I saw him, he said, The Archbishop of *Grenada*, my Friend and Relation wants a young Man of some Learning, who writes a good Hand, to copy his Writings over fairly, for he is a great Author. He has compos'd I don't know how many Homilies, as he continues to do every Day, which meet with great Applause. As I thought you a proper Person, I propos'd you, and he has promis'd to take you; go to him in my Name, you may judge by the Reception he gives you, whether I have spoken to your Advantage or not.

The Offer was as good as I could desire; wherefore having prepar'd my self to appear in the best manner possible before the Prelate, I went one morning to the Archbishop's. If I were to imitate the Makers of Romances, I should make a pompous Description of the Episcopal Palace of *Granada*; I should enlarge upon the Structure of the Building, and extol the Richness of the Furniture; I should speak of the Statues and Pictures therein, and should not spare the Reader the least of the Stories they represented; but I will rest satisfied with saying that it equal'd the Palaces of our Kings in Magnificence.

I found in the Apartments, a number of Ecclesiasticks and Swordsmen, most part whereof were his Grace's Officers, as Chaplains, Gentlemen, Masters of the Horse, or *Valets de Chambre*. The Laymen had almost all of them sumptuous Clothes, one should rather have taken them for Lords than Servants. They were haughty, and aimed at being thought Men of Importance. I could not forbear laughing at them within my self, Faith, (said I) these Fellows are very happy in bearing the Yoke of Servitude without feeling it, for if they felt it, methinks they should not be so stiff and proud. I address'd my self to a grave fat Gentleman who stood at the Archbishop's Closet-Door, to open and shut it according as was necessary. I ask'd him civilly if it was not possible to speak with his Grace. Stay a little, (says he, with a stiff Air) his Grace is coming out to go to Mass, he will give you a Moment's Audience *en passant*. I answer'd not a Word, but arm'd my self with Patience, and resolv'd to enter into Conversation with some of his Officers; but they began to

examine me from Head to Foot, without vouchsafing to answer me a
Word. After which, they look'd upon each other with a scornful Smile,
at the Liberty I had taken in intruding into their Discourse.

I was (I own) entirely confounded at seeing my self so treated by *Valets*. I had not well recover'd my self, when the Closet-Door open'd, and
the Archbishop appear'd. Immediately there was a profound Silence
among the Officers, who laid at once aside their insolent Behaviour, to
appear respectful before their Master. This Prelate was in his 69th Year,
and was made almost like my Uncle the Canon *Giles Perez*, that is to
say thick and short. He was besides very bow-leg'd, and so bald, that he
had only one tuft of Hair left behind, which oblig'd him to cover his
Head with a fine Linen Cap with long Ears. In spite of all this I thought
he had the Air of a Man of Quality, undoubtedly because I knew him
to be one. We Persons of an inferior Rank look upon great Men with a
Prepossession which often gives them an Air of Grandeur that Nature
has denied them.

The Archbishop came up to me immediately, and ask'd me, with a
Voice full of Softness, what was my Business. I told him that I was the
young Man of whom Don *Fernando de Leyva* had spoken to him. He
gave me not Time to say any more, but cried out, What you are the
Man whom he extoll'd so much! I take you into my Service; you are a
Person of Consequence to me, you need only stay here. At these Words
he went out leaning upon two Gentlemen of the Horse, after having
given Audience to some Ecclesiasticks who had something to impart to
him. He was hardly got out of the Chamber, but the same Officers who
had before disdain'd my Conversation, now sought after it. They immediately surrounded me, shew'd me all manner of Civility, and express'd
their Joy at my being become one of the Archbishop's Household. They
had heard the Words their Master had spoken to me, and impatiently
desir'd to know upon what footing I was to be with him; but I had the
Malice not to satisfy their Curiosity, to revenge my self for their Contempt.

His Grace was not long ere he return'd, and call'd me into his Closet
to discourse me in private. I judg'd that he had a Design to try my
Genius, wherefore I was upon my guard, and prepar'd my self to weigh
every Word. At first he examin'd me in the learned Languages; I answer'd
him very pertinently to his Questions, and he found that I was conversant with the *Greek* and *Latin* Authors. Then he tried me in *Logick*;
'twas what I expected; and he found me a perfect Master. Hereupon,
your Education (said he, with some Surprize) has not been neglected;
now let me see your Writing. I drew a Sheet out of my Pocket which I
had brought on purpose, wherewith the Prelate was not ill pleas'd. I am
satisfied with your Hand, (said he) and yet more with your Wit; I will
thank my Nephew Don *Ferdinand* for having procured me such a pretty
Servant; he has made me a valuable Present.

We were interrupted by the Arrival of some Noblemen of *Grenada*,
who came to dine with the Archbishop. I left them together, and with-

drew amongst the Officers, who overwhelm'd me then with their Civilities. When it was time to dine, I went to eat with them, and if they observ'd me during our Repast, I was not behind-hand with them. What an outward Shew of Wisdom was there in the Ecclesiasticks! they all seem'd to me like Saints, so great a Respect I paid to the Place where I was. It never so much as came into my Head that it might all be counterfeit; as if there were not Examples of the like amongst the Fathers of the Church.

I sat next an old *Valet de Chambre* call'd *Melchior de la Ronda*, who took care to serve me with the best Bits. The Regard he had for me, made me have the same for him, and my Politeness charm'd him. Signior Cavalier (said he shortly after Dinner) I should be glad of a private Conversation with you; at the same time he led me into a retir'd Part of the Palace, where no body could overhear us, and there he began this Discourse. My Son, I have found in my self an Inclination for you, from the first Moment I saw you; I will give you a certain Proof of it, by reposing in you a Confidence which will be of great Service to you. You are here in a House where the real good Men and the Hypocrites live promiscuously together; it would cost you an infinite Time to know what Ground you walk upon, I am going to spare you such a long and disagreeable Study, by discovering to you both the one and the other. By this means you may easily know how to behave your self.

I will begin (continued he) with his Grace. He is a very pious Prelate, who is incessantly employ'd in edifying the People, and in inciting them to Virtue, by Sermons full of excellent Morals, which he composes himself. He has abandon'd the Court these twenty Years, to give himself entirely up to the Zeal which he has for his Flock. He is a Man of Learning, and a great Orator; his whole Delight is in Preaching, and his Audience are ravish'd when they hear him. Perhaps there may be some Vanity in his way of acting; but besides its not being in the Power of Men to penetrate the Heart, it would very ill become me to scan the Faults of a Person whose Bread I eat. If I were allow'd to reprehend any thing in my Master, I should blame his Severity; instead of having an Indulgence for the Weaknesses of Ecclesiasticks, he punishes them with too much Rigour. Above all, he persecutes, without Mercy, such as, relying upon their Innocency, undertake to justify themselves legally, in Contempt of his Authority. I find also another Fault in him, which he has in common with many Persons of Quality: Altho' he loves his Domesticks, he has not any Regard to their Services; and he lets them grow old, without thinking of procuring them any Settlement. If he sometimes makes them a Present, they only owe it to the Goodness of somebody that has spoken for them; of himself he would never think of doing them the least Service.

This is what the old *Valet de Chambre* told me of his Master. After this, he disclos'd to me his Thoughts of the Ecclesiasticks with whom we had dined. He painted them after a manner very different from their Countenances. He did not indeed describe them as dishonest Persons, but only as sorry Priests: However, he excepted some, whose Virtue he extoll'd very much. I was no longer at a loss after what manner to behave my self. That very Evening, at Supper, I provided my self, like them, with a grave Outside, that costs nothing; one need not wonder that there are so many Hypocrites.

Chap. III.

Gil Blas *becomes the Favourite of the Archbishop of* Grenada *and the Person through whose Means his Favours are granted.*

I had been after Dinner to fetch my things, and my Horse from the Inn where I lodg'd; afterwards I return'd to Supper to the Archbishop's, where I had a very handsom Chamber, and a Down-Bed. The next Day his Grace had me call'd early in the Morning; 'twas to give me a Homily to transcribe, but he order'd me to do it with the utmost Exactness. I did not fail: I forgot neither Accent, nor Stop, nor Comma; accordingly he express'd a Joy thereat mingled with Surprize. Good God! (said he in a Transport, when he had cast his eyes over every Leaf of my Copy) did one ever see any thing so correct? You are too good a Transcriber, not to be a Grammarian. Speak freely to me, Friend, did you find nothing in my Writings that shock'd you? Was there no Negligence in the Stile, no improper Term? O, my Lord (replied I with a modest Air) I have not Understanding enough to make critical Observations; and if I had, I am persuaded your Grace's Works would escape my Censure. The Prelate smil'd at my Answer, and made no Reply; but he let me see, through all his Piety, that he was not an Author for nothing.

I compleated my getting into his good Graces by this Flattery. I became dearer to him from Day to Day; and I was inform'd by Don *Ferdinand*, who came to see him very often, that he had such a Value for me, that I might depend upon my Fortune's being made. This was confirm'd to me a little after by my Master himself, and on this Occasion; one Night in his Closet he repeated to me in a Rapture a Homily which he was to speak the next Day in the Cathedral. Not satisfied with asking me my Thoughts in general, he oblig'd me to tell him, what Places had touched me most. I had the good Fortune to name those which he esteem'd most himself, his favourite Pieces. By this I pass'd in his Opinion for a Man who had a delicate Taste of the real Beauties of a Work: This (cried he) is what is call'd having a Taste and Judgment. Go, Friend, I'll assure you you have not got Midas's Ears.[1] In a word, he was so well pleas'd with me, that he said with a lively Air, *Gil Blas*, make your self easy about your Fortune for the future, I will take care to render it perfectly agreeable to you; I love you, and to convince you of it, I will make you my Confident.

1. When Midas, legendary king of Phrygia, chose Pan over Apollo in a musical contest, the offended god of music gave him an ass's ears. The French text reads "*l'oreille Béotienne*" (Boeotian ear), another traditional expression for musical or literary insensitivity, from the ancient Athenians' contempt for their rustic northern neighbors.

I had no sooner heard these Words, than I fell at his Grace's Feet, quite overcome with Acknowledgement; I embrac'd his bow'd Legs with all my Heart, and I look'd upon my self as a Man who was in a fair way to be rich. Yes, my Child, (continues the Archbishop, whose Discourse had been interrupted by my Action) I will intrust you with my most secret Thoughts; listen with Attention to what I am going to tell you: I take a Pleasure in Preaching; the Lord blesses my Homilies; they strike Sinners, make them return to their Duty, and have recourse to Repentance. I have the Satisfaction of seeing the Miser, terrify'd with the Images I draw of his Covetousness, open his Treasures, and distribute them with a lavish Hand; of drawing a voluptuous Man from his Pleasures; of filling Hermitages with ambitious Men; and of confirming in her Duty a Wife that has been stagger'd by her deluding Lover. These Conversions, which are frequent, ought alone to incite me to continue my Labours. Nevertheless, I will confess my Weakness to you; I propose another Reward to my self, a Reward which the Delicacy of my Virtue reproaches me with in vain; 'tis the Regard which the World pays to fine polish'd Writings. The Honour of passing for a perfect Orator, has Charms worth my courting. My Works are thought equally expressive and delicate; but I would fain avoid the Fault of those good Authors who write too long; and go off the Stage with all my Reputation unsully'd.

Therefore my dear *Gil Blas* (continues the Prelate) I require one thing of your Zeal; whenever you find my Pen savours of old Age, when you find me flag, don't fail to apprize me of it. I don't trust my self in that respect, my Self-love might deceive me; this Observation requires a disinterested Judgment; I make choice of yours, which I know to be good; I refer my self to you. Thank Heaven, my Lord (replied I) you are yet at a great distance from that time; besides a Genius of your Grace's Stamp will preserve it self much better than any other; or, to speak more justly, you will be always the same. I look upon you like another Cardinal *Ximenes*,[2] whose superior Genius, instead of decaying as he advanced in Years, seem'd to recover new Strength. No Flattery, Friend (said he, interrupting me) I know I may sink all at once. People at my Age begin to feel Infirmities, and the Infirmities of the Body impair the Mind. I repeat it once more, *Gil Blas*, as soon as ever you shall judge my Senses to be declining, give me immediate Notice of it; don't fear being too free and sincere, I shall receive this Admonition as a Mark of your Affection for me. Besides, your Interest is concern'd therein; If unluckily for you, I should hear that they say in the City my Discourses have no longer their usual Energy, and that I ought to take my Rest, I declare fairly to you, that you will lose both my Friendship, and the Fortune I have promis'd you; this would be the Fruits of your foolish Discretion.

My Patron stopp'd here, to hear my Answer, which was a Promise to do as he desired. From that time he conceal'd nothing from me, and I

---

2. Francisco Ximenes de Cisneros (1436–1517), the most powerful churchman and statesman in Spain during the reign of Ferdinand and Isabella, was most active and productive as a statesman, scholar, and ecclesiastical reformer in the last two decades of his life.

became his Favourite. All the Domesticks, except *Melchior de la Ronda*, could not perceive it without Envy. 'Twas a thing worth seeing to observe the manner in which the Gentlemen and Masters of the Horse liv'd with his Grace's Confident. They were not asham'd to cringe to get into my Favour; I could hardly believe they were *Spaniards*. However I did not fail to do them Services, without falling a Victim to their selfish Civilities, The Archbishop, at my Desire, made use of his Interest for them. He got a Company for one, and put him in a way to make a Figure in the Army. He sent another to *Mexico*, to take Possession of a considerable Place which he procur'd him; and as for my Friend *Melchior*, I obtain'd a handsom Gratuity for him. I found by this, that if the Prelate did not prevent [3] them in his Grants, at least he seldom refused what was ask'd of him.

But what I did for a Priest I think deserves to be recounted. One Day our Steward brought me a certain Licentiate,[4] whose Name was *Lewis Garcias*, a young Man of a very good Mien: Signior *Gil Blas* (said he) this honest Eclesiastick is one of my best Friends; he has been Chaplain to a Convent of Nuns, whence his Character has not escap'd Slander. In short, they have blacken'd him so to his Grace, that he has suspended him; and unfortunately he is so much prejudic'd against him, that he will not give Ear to any Solicitations in his Favour. We have in vain employ'd Persons of the first Rank in *Grenada* to get him re-establish'd; our Master is inflexible.

Gentlemen (replied I) here is an Affair very wrongly manag'd; they had better have spared their Solicitations for Mr. Licentiate; they have done him an ill Office in endeavouring to serve him. I know his Grace; Intreaties and Recommendations only aggravate a Clergyman's Fault in his Opinion. It is not long since I heard him say, the more a Priest, who has been irregular, engages Persons to intercede for him, the more it increases the Scandal, and I am the more inexorable. This is unfortunate (said the Steward) and my Friend would be very much at a Nonplus if he did not write a good Hand. Fortunately for him he writes to Perfection, and by that means he extricates himself from Trouble. I was desirous to see whether his Writing, which was so much extoll'd, was better than mine; whereupon Mr. Licentiate, who had some about him, shew'd it me, and I admir'd it; it seem'd to me a Copy of a great Master's. Upon viewing so fine a Hand, a Thought came into my Head; I begg'd *Garcias* to leave the Paper with me, telling him, it might be of some Service to him; that I would not explain my self any farther then, but that next Day I would tell him more. The Licentiate (who undoubtedly had heard my Genius very much cried up by the Steward) withdrew as well satisfied as if he had been already re-instated in his Function.

I had indeed a mind he should be so; and that very Day I attempted it, after the following manner. Being alone with the Archbishop, I shew'd him *Garcias*'s Writing; my Patron seem'd charm'd with it: then, taking

3. Anticipate.
4. Holder of a university degree beyond the baccalaureate.

hold of that Opportunity, I said to him, My Lord, since you will not suffer your Homilies to be printed, I cou'd at least wish that they were written in such a Hand as this. I am satisfied with your Writing, replied the Prelate, but I confess that I should not be sorry to have a Copy of my Works in this Hand. Your Grace, answer'd I, need only speak; the Person who writes so finely is a Licentiate of my Acquaintance. He will be the more joyful at being so employed, because he will hope by that means to prevail upon your Goodness to extricate him from the Difficulties wherein he is at present intangled.

The Prelate ask'd what was the Licentiate's Name. He is call'd *Lewis Garcias*, replied I; he is almost desperate at having incurr'd your Displeasure. This *Garcias*, (said he, interrupting me) if I am not mistaken, was Chaplain to a Nunnery; He is fall'n under the Censure of the Church; I remember the Representations that have been made to me against him; his Behaviour has not been very good. My Lord (said I, interrupting him in my turn,) I won't undertake to justify him; but I know he has Enemies. He pretends [5] that the Authors of the Accounts you have of him, have taken more pains to do him ill Offices, than to represent the Truth. That may be (replied the Archbishop;) there are Persons in the World of a dangerous Temper. Besides, granting his Conduct has not been always irreproachable, he may have repented, and in short one ought to forgive all Offenses: Bring the Licentiate to me, I take off the Suspension.

Thus Persons of the greatest Severity will abate something of it, when 'tis contrary to their dearer Interest: The Archbishop willingly granted, for the vain Pleasure of having his Works well written, what he had refus'd to the Solicitations of Men of the first Rank. I immediately carried the News to the Steward, who inform'd his Friend *Garcias* of it. The next Day the Licentiate came to thank me proportionably to the Favour I had obtain'd him. I presented him to my Master, who contented himself with giving him a slight Reprimand, and gave him his Homilies to write over fair. *Garcias* acquitted himself so well of his Commission, that he was reinstated in his Ministry; and even obtain'd the Living of *Gabia*, a large Town in the Neighbourhood of *Grenada*.

Chap. IV.

The Archbishop falls into an Apoplexy. The Perplexity Gil Blas is in, and the manner he extricates himself.

*   *   *

Two Months after this * * *, whilst I was in the height of my Favour, we had a terrible Alarm at the Archiepiscopal Palace: His Grace was seiz'd with an Apoplexy. He was reliev'd so speedily, and such sovereign Remedies were applied, that in a few Days there was no more sign of it. But his Head receiv'd a terrible Shock; I observ'd it the first Sermon he compos'd. Nevertheless the Difference was not so great between that and

5. Claims.

his other Works, as to enable me to conclude that the Orator flag'd. I waited yet for another Homily, to know better what I was to think. O! as for that, it put it beyond Question. At one time the good Prelate tautolo-giz'd, at another he soar'd too high, or sunk too low. 'Twas a long-winded Oration, and Rhetorick of a wornout School-master, a *Capu-chinade*.[6]

I was not the only one who took notice of it; most part of the Auditors, (as if they likewise had been retained to examine it) whisper'd to each other, as he was delivering it, This Sermon smells strong of the Apo-plexy. Hereupon I said to my self, come Mr. Arbiter of the Homilies, prepare to do your Office, you see my Lord flags, you ought to apprize him of it, not only as being his Confident, but also for fear some of his Friends should be frank enough to prevent[7] you therein. If that should happen, you know what would be your Fate, you will be blotted out of his Will, where without doubt there is a better Legacy for you, than the Library of the Licentiate *Sedillo*.[8]

After these Reflections, I made others quite contrary. The Part I was to act seem'd to me very ticklish. I judg'd that an Author, who was opinionated[9] of his own Works, might receive such an Information but coldly; but rejecting this Thought, I represented to my self that 'twas impossible he should take it ill, after having exacted it of me after so pressing a manner. Besides this I rely'd upon my speaking to him with Address, and thought to gild the Pill so well as to make him swallow it. In short, finding that I ran a greater Risque in keeping Silence than in breaking it, I resolv'd upon the latter.

I was now only perplex'd about one thing; I did not know how to break the Ice. Happily for me the Orator himself assisted me at this plunge, by asking me what the World said of him, and if they were pleas'd with his last Discourse. I replied that they always admir'd his Homilies; but that I thought the Hearers were not so much affected with the last, as with the others. How Friend, (says he with some surprize) had they an *Aristarchus*[1] amongst them? No, my Lord, answer'd I, no; such Works as yours are not to be criticiz'd; there was no Body but what was charm'd with it. However since you have charg'd me to be free and sincere, I will take the Liberty to tell you that your last Discourse does not seem to have the Energy of the rest. Are not you of the same Opinion your self?

These Words made my Master turn pale; he said to me with a forc'd Smile, What Mr. *Gil Blas*, this Piece then is not to your Taste? I do not say so Sir (interrupted I, quite in a Confusion) I think it excellent, tho' a little inferior to your other Works. I understand you (replied he) I seem

---

6. A banal and flat moral exhortation, from the plain preaching espoused by the austere Capuchin order of Franciscans.
7. Anticipate.
8. Gil Blas's first master, an aged gluttonous priest, on his deathbed inserts a provision in his will leaving him "all my Books and Manuscripts, with-out exception"—a cookbook, a treatise on indiges-tion, a moth-eaten breviary, and some scraps of

legal paper.
9. Conceited.
1. A great critic of the time of Ptolemy Philadel-phus [*Lesage's note*]. Aristarchus of Samothrace, head of the legendary library at Alexandria in the second century B.C., edited and wrote commentar-ies on Homer and other classical authors. Because he rejected many Homeric lines as spurious, his name became a generic term for a severe critic.

to flag, don't I? Speak the Word out. You think it high time for me to think of retiring. I shou'd not have been so bold (answer'd I) to have spoken so freely, if your Grace had not commanded me. I only do it in Obedience to you, and I humbly beg your Grace not to take my Boldness amiss. God forbid (interrupted he with Precipitation) God forbid that I should reproach you with it. I don't take it at all ill that you tell me your Opinion, I only think your Opinion erroneous. I have been prodigiously deceiv'd in your narrow Understanding.

Tho' I was confounded, I would have found some Expedient to qualify Matters; but what way is there to pacify an exasperated Author? and more, an Author who is used to hear himself prais'd? Speak no more Friend, said he, you are too young yet to distinguish Truth from Falshood. Know that I never compos'd a finer Homily, than that which you don't approve of. My Understanding, thank Heav'n, has as yet lost nothing of its Vigour. For the future, I will choose my Confidents better; I will have those who are abler Judges. Go (continues he, thrusting me out of the Closet by the Shoulders) go tell my Treasurer to pay you an hundred Ducats; and Heaven direct you with that Sum. Farewel, Mr. *Gil Blas*, I wish you all manner of Prosperity, with a little better Taste.[2]

PIERRE CARLET DE CHAMBLAIN DE MARIVAUX

From *Le Paysan parvenu, ou les Memoirs de M* * * *

[*Le Paysan parvenu* was published in five parts between 1734 and 1736. Three additional parts of doubtful authorship appeared two years after Fielding's death. The excerpts reprinted are from a modern translation by Benjamin Boyce, *The Upstart Peasant* (Durham: 1974, published by the translator).

The novel recounts the adventures of Jacob, a shrewd young country lad, as he makes his way upward in Parisian society. In his first post as a servant, he attracts the interest of his mistress as well as a young chambermaid named Geneviève, who finds it profitable to cooperate with her master's amorous desires. In the scene preceding this excerpt from part 1, Jacob tactfully declines Geneviève's offer of marriage—with the gold her master has given her as dowry—on the grounds that the master would not approve. The next day the master summons Jacob to an interview.]

Part I

*   *   *

"I know," he said, "that Madame has taken you under her protection, and I am glad of that; but you do not tell me all; I have already heard

---

2. In the next chapter, Gil Blas meets the reinstated priest, Garcias, whose effusions of gratitude, flattery, and hospitality suddenly cease when he understands his benefactor has lost his influence.

about you; you're a sly fellow; why, you have been here only two or three months, and you have made a conquest already. As soon as you land you turn the pretty girls' heads; Geneviève is mad about you, and it seems that you love her in return?"

"Alas, Monsieur," replied I, "what would she have done to make me hate her, the poor child?" "Oh," said he, "speak boldly; you can open your mind to me; your father has been in my service for many years, I am pleased with him, and I should be delighted to do a favor to the son since the occasion presents itself; it is lucky for you that you appeal to Geneviève, and I approve your choice; you are young and well built, prudent and lively, they say; on her side, Geneviève is a likable girl, I am protector to her family, and I had her brought into our house only in order to be at hand to help her and to settle her well. (He was lying.) The design she has taken disconcerts my measures a little; you have nothing yet; I would have arranged for her a more advantageous marriage; but she loves you and wants only you. Very well. I am thinking that my good offices can take the place of what you lack and will be a substitute for a patrimony from you. I have already made a present to her of a considerable sum of money which I will tell you how to use; I will do more, I will furnish a little house for you for which I will pay the rent to relieve you until you may be better established; as to the rest you need not worry, I promise you lucrative commissions;[1] live well with the wife I give you, she is sweet and virtuous; above all, remember that you have at least a half share in all I do in this affair. Whatever good will I have for Geneviève's relatives I should not have gone so far if I hadn't had still more for you and yours. Say nothing about it here; your mistress's women would never let me rest, and all would want me to arrange marriages for them also. Request your dismissal quietly, say that someone offers you a better and more suitable position; Geneviève for her part will feign the necessity of a journey to see her mother, who is old, and as soon as you leave here you two will get married. Good-by. No thanks needed; I am busy; only go acquaint Geneviève with what I have said, and take from my table that little roll of money with which you will wait in an inn until Geneviève can leave here."

I stood like a statue at this discourse, for on one hand all the advantages that he offered to me were considerable.

I saw that from the first leap I made to Paris, I who didn't have any skill, any advantages, who was merely a poor peasant and who was prepared to labor all my life to acquire something (and that something in my farthest hopes was nothing in comparison with what was offered to me), I saw, I say, a sure establishment thrown at me.

And what an establishment! A house all furnished, plenty of ready money, profitable commissions which I could ask to be provided with immediately, finally the patronage of a powerful man, and in a position to be at my ease the very first day and grow rich later.

---

1. Assignments, duties.

Wasn't this Adam's apple returned for me?

I savored the proposition; that sudden fortune put my spirit in a flutter; my heart beat and my eyes sparkled.

To have only to hold out one's hand to be happy—what a seductive opportunity! Wasn't this enough to quiet my sense of honor?

On the other hand, that Honor pleaded its case within my troubled heart while my avarice pleaded its own. "To which shall I yield?" said I; I didn't know which to listen to.

Honor said to me, "Be firm; scorn these miserable benefits that are offered to you; they will lose all their charm when you have married Geneviève; the remembrance of her frailty will make her unbearable, and since you carry me in your breast, mere peasant that you are, I shall be your tyrant; I shall torment you all your life; you will find that your infamy is known to everybody; you will hold your house in horror, and you two, your wife and you, will make a Devil's household; all will be in disorder; her lover will avenge her for your scorn; she can destroy you with the influence he possesses. You will not be the first to whom this happens; think of that, Jacob. The wealth that your bride brings you is a present from the Devil, and the Devil is a cheat. One fine day he will take it all away from you in order to damn you with despair after having trapped you by his merchandise."

Perhaps these representations that Honor made to me will be found a trifle long, but he needs to speak at length, he does, in order to make an impression, and he has more difficulty in persuading than the passions.

For example, Avarice replied to all this in a mere word or two, but her eloquence, however laconic, was vigorous.

"It is just like you, you nobody," she said to me, "to be stopped by this chimera of honor! Doesn't it suit you wonderfully to be so delicate about that, you miserable bumpkin! Well, you are right; betake yourself to the alms-house, you and your honor; you will both find great favor there!"

"Not such great favor," said I to myself; "it is burying honor to take it to an alms-house; it won't shine much there."

"But does honor always lead you there?" "Yes, often enough, and if not there, at least thereabouts."

"But is one happy when he is ashamed of being so? Is it a pleasure to live comfortably with a bad conscience? What a quandary!"

This was the whole of what presented itself in an instant to my mind. To the increase of my confusion, I was looking at the roll of money which lay on the table; it seemed to be so full! What a pity to lose it!

Meanwhile Monsieur, surprised that I didn't say anything to him and that I didn't take the purse which he had put there to support his discourse, asked me what I was thinking about. "Why don't you say something to me?" he added.

"Ho, Monsieur," replied I, 'I am considering, and there is much to consider. Wait, let us speak candidly; suppose that I were you and that you were I. There you are, a poor man. But do poor men like to be cuckolds? You will be one nevertheless if I give Geneviève to you in marriage. Well, that is the subject of my pondering."

"What," said he in return, "is Geneviève not a good girl?" "Very good," replied I, "in making a compliment or bow; but in reference to what is needed in the wife of a husband, I do not think the goodness she possesses is proper for that."

"Why, what is there to reproach her for?" he asked. "Ho, ho, ho," replied I, laughing, "you know better than I the particulars and lengths in that affair; you were there and I wasn't; but one knows almost exactly what would happen. Wait, Monsieur; tell me the truth frankly: does a gentleman have need of a chambermaid? And when he has one, is it she who undresses him? I believe it is the other way around!"

"Oh, this time," he said to me, "you speak plainly, Jacob, and I understand you; peasant as you are, you don't lack wit. Now listen attentively to what I am going to tell you in my turn.

"All that you imagine of Geneviève is false; but suppose that it were true: you see the people who come to visit me; these are people of position who are rich, who have a great train.

"Do you know that among them are some who need not be named who owe their fortunes only to marriage with Genevièves?

"Now do you think yourself superior to them? Is it the fear of being laughed at that deters you? And who would do it? People know you, but are you someone of importance in the world? Will they think about your honor? Will anyone imagine that you have any, silly fellow that you are? You hazard only one thing—that is, having as many people envy you as there are people of your station who know you. Go, my boy; the honor of such as you is to have the wherewithal to live and the wherewithal for rising above their low condition; do you understand? The lowest of men is he who has nothing."

"No matter for that, Monsieur," I replied to him with an air between sadness and mutiny; "I had still rather be the meanest of those others than the unhappiest of all. The meanest of those others always finds his bread good when it is given to him, but the unhappiest man has no appetite for anything; no morsel will benefit him even if it is a partridge; and, i' faith, the appetite is worth keeping: but I should lose it, in spite of my good living, if I should marry your chambermaid."

"Your decision is made, then?" replied Monsieur. "I' faith, yes, Monsieur," replied I, "and I am very sorry, but how can I help it? In our village it is our custom to marry only maids,[2] and if there were one who had been chambermaid to a Monsieur, she would have to be content to have a lover; but for a husband, not a chance! If it rained husbands, none would drop for her; that's the rule with us, and especially in our family. My mother was a maid when she married, her grandmother the same, and from grandmother to grandmother I have descended directly as you see, with the obligation to make no change in that particular."

2. Virgins.

I had struggled to explain myself in so decisive a tone that he, frowning with pride and anger, said to me, "You are a knave. In my house you have publicly made love to Geneviève; you didn't aspire to anything, she told me, except the good fortune of being able to marry her some day. Madame's other women knew this; on the contrary, you dare accuse her of not being a girl of honor; your head is captured by that impertinent idea, and I don't doubt that in consequence you utter it when you speak of her; you are a man who would not spare her in your talk; and it is I, it is my simple good will towards her which may be the innocent cause of all the wrong you could do her. No, Monsieur Jacob, I shall put things in order, and since I have gone so far as to become involved and since you have already taken money upon the footing of a person who was to be her husband,[3] I do not propose to let you make a fool of her. I shall not allow you the liberty of injuring her, and if you do not marry her I tell you it is with me you will have to deal. Make up your mind; I give you twenty-four hours; choose her hand or prison; that is all I have to say. Go, get out, you scoundrel!"

This command and the epithet which strengthened it frightened me, and I made one leap from the chamber to the door.

* * *

[Jacob is rescued from this predicament and deprived of employment by the sudden death of his master. Disgusted with country crudeness after his taste of Parisian society, he is seeking a way to remain in the city when he encounters a woman taken ill and helps her to her home. Mademoiselle Haberd and her older sister are sanctimonious middle-aged spinsters. Marivaux' untranslatable term for such persons is *devotes*.]

The devotes offend the world, and pious people edify it; the former are devout only on their lips; the latter are so in their hearts: the devotes go to church simply to go there, to have the pleasure of being there, but the pious go to address God in prayer; these latter have humility, the devotes only want others to have it. One group are truly servants of God; the others merely seem so and pray in order to say "I pray"; carry to church some books of devotion in order to handle them, to open and read them; retire into a corner to crouch there in order to enjoy proudly the attitude of meditation; excite themselves to pious ecstasies in order to believe, if they catch some, that they have a very distinguished soul; feel some in fact which ardent vanity has produced and which the Devil, who doesn't let people lack any means of self-deception, has supplied. They come home from church all puffed up with respect for themselves and insolent pity for ordinary souls, and imagine in consequence that they have acquired the right to moderate their spiritual exercises by a thousand little luxuries which support a delicate health.

* * *

3. Jacob has accepted six gold pieces from Geneviève in full knowledge of how she earned them.

[Part I ends with Jacob's description of his first evening in their service.]

* * * Plague on it, what a juicy little dinner! See what they call a soup, not to mention a little platter of roast of such delicacy, of such perfect cooking—! A man's soul would have to be utterly indifferent to the pleasures given by these morsels not to succumb to the sin of epicurism when eating that roast and also the ragout, for it was more exquisitely seasoned than anything I have ever met elsewhere. If one ate in Heaven, I shouldn't wish to be served anything better; Mahomet in that repast would have been able to count one of the joys of his paradise.

Our ladies ate none of the boiled meat; it only made an appearance on the table and then was removed to be given to the poor.

Catherine[4] in her turn passed it by, she said, for charity, and I agreed at once to become as charitable as she. There's nothing like a good example!

I learned later that my predecessor[5] had not had, like me, any part in alms-giving, because he was too much a free-thinker to have the grace to do it and to be reduced to roast and ragout.

I didn't understand, moreover, how our two sisters managed in eating, but assuredly there was legerdemain in eating thus.

Never did they have an appetite; at least one never saw that they did; they ate by sleight of hand; food vanished without their appearing to touch it.

One saw these ladies use their forks negligently; scarcely did they make the effort to open their mouths; they cast looks of indifference over the good fare: "I have no appetite at all today." "Nor I either." "I find everything insipid." "It is all too salty for me."

These remarks threw dust in my eyes so that I imagined I saw the most squeamish creatures in the world, and yet the result of all this was that the dishes were so noticeably lightened when one removed them that I didn't know, the first days, how to reconcile all this.

But finally I perceived by what I had been duped those first days. It was the air of aversion which our mistresses displayed and which had hidden from me the secret busyness of their teeth.

Yet what is most amusing is that they imagined themselves to be small, temperate eaters; and because it was not proper for devotes to be gourmands, for one should eat to live, not live to eat, and since in spite of that reasonable and Christian maxim their gluttonous appetite did not want to lose anything, they had found the secret of indulging it without getting soaked in gluttony; it was by means of these pretences of scorn for food, it was by the indolence with which they touched it, that they convinced themselves of their temperance while preserving the pleasure of not being so; it was under the protection of that trick that their devotion innocently abandoned the field to intemperance.

4. The cook, who shares her mistresses' religiosity.   5. Their former servant.

One must acknowledge that the Devil is very cunning but also that we are truly fools.

The dessert was of a piece with the dinner: sweets both dry and liquid, and, to top them off, some small liqueurs to aid digestion and to refresh so mortified a palate.

After this, the elder Mlle. Haberd said to the younger, "Come, sister, let us return thanks to God." "That is very proper," answered the other with a fullness of gratitude, for assuredly she would then have been in the wrong to deny God.

"That is very proper," said she at once, and then the two sisters, rising from their chairs with the best-intentioned composure in the world and which they believed to be as meritorious as legitimate, gravely put their hands together to make a joint prayer in which they responded in alternate verses in tones which consciousness of their own well-being rendered very touching.

After this the cloth was removed; they let themselves sink into an armchair, the softness and depth of which invited repose; and there one occupied oneself with some reflections that had been made on godly readings, or perhaps on a sermon of the day or the day before whose topic they found wonderfully applicable to Monsieur or Madame such-and-such.

That sermon was made only for them; avarice, worldliness, pride, and other imperfections had been so well discussed in it.

"But," said one of them, "how could one hear the holy word of God and not come home with the intention of reforming oneself? Sister, do you understand a thing like that?

"Madame such-and-such, who during Lent came constantly to the sermon—how does she understand it? I always observe in her the same air of coquetry; and apropos of coquetry, Heavens, how scandalized I was the other day by the immodest manner in which Mlle.——— was dressed! Could one come to church in that condition? I tell you that she distracted me so much that I ask God's pardon, and she kept me from saying my prayers. Really it was frightful!"

"You are right, sister," replied the other, "but when I see such things I lower my eyes; because of the anger I feel, I refuse to look at them, and I praise God for the goodness he has shown me in having at least preserved me from those sins, and I pray to him heartily to wish to enlighten with his grace the people who commit them."

You say to me, how did you hear these conversations in which their neighbors sustained the digestion of these ladies?

It was while clearing the table and arranging the room where they sat.

The younger Mlle. Haberd, after I had cleared the table, summoned me as I was going to dinner and, speaking to me in a low voice because of a light drowsiness which began to close the eyes of her sister, said to me what you will see in the Second Part of this history.

[When the women's spiritual director disapproves of their taking an attractive young stranger into the household, the sisters quarrel and the younger leaves with Jacob. Within a few days, the insouciant youth, now known as Monsieur de la Vallée, has convinced her that he is "the one whom God wishes me to join myself to"; but their plan to wed secretly is shattered when the priest recruited to conduct the ceremony proves to be her former director. The elder sister then brings Jacob before a magistrate, but he prevails in defending the match, in the process attracting the interest of another middle-aged *devote*, Madame de Ferval. On the day after his marriage to her friend, this comely widow receives him "lying on a sofa, her head resting on one hand, and in a dishabille which was handsome but rather carelessly arranged" and "allowed one to see a little of the most beautiful leg in the world." In a flirtatious interview in which she assures herself of his ability to keep their liaison a secret and presses money on him, she arranges to meet him at the out-of-the-way house of a Madame Remy, "a woman whom I can command."]

Part V

I have said in the last Part that I hastened to go to Mme. Remy's, where Mme. de Ferval was awaiting me. It was nearly 5:30 in the evening when I arrived. I found the place at once. And I saw Mme. de Ferval's carriage in the little street which she had mentioned to me and where the back door was by which she had told me she entered; then following my instructions I entered by the other door after making sure that it was there that Mme. Remy lived. First of all I saw a rather narrow passageway, which led to a small courtyard at the end of which one entered a parlor, and it was from that parlor that one passed into the garden which Mme. de Ferval had mentioned.

I had not yet crossed the courtyard when someone opened the door from the parlor (for apparently someone heard me coming); then out came a tall elderly woman, thin, pale, dressed like a servant but nicely nevertheless, with a sedate, cunning air.

This was Mme. Remy herself.

"What do you want, Monsieur?" she said when I approached her. "I come," I replied, "to speak with a lady who should have arrived a few minutes ago or who will be here soon."

"And her name, Monsieur?" she said. "Madame de Ferval," I replied; immediately, "Come in, Monsieur."

I entered; there was nobody in the parlor. "She has not come yet?" I said. "You're going to see her," she replied, drawing from her pocket a key with which she opened a door which I hadn't noticed and which was that of a room where I found Mme. de Ferval seated near a little bed, reading.

"You are very late, Monsieur de la Vallée," she said, rising. "I have been here at least a quarter of an hour."

"Alas, Madame, do not blame me," I said; "it isn't at all my fault. I come this very moment from Versailles, where I was obliged to go, and I was very impatient to be here."[6]

6. In part 4, Jacob is sent to the court under the sponsorship of still another admiring lady to seek a position from her kinsman, a prominent official.

While we spoke, our accommodating hostess, without appearing to listen to us and with a preoccupied air, moved here and there in the room and then withdrew without saying anything. "You are going, then, Madame Remy?" cried Mme. de Ferval, approaching an open door that faced on to the garden.

"Yes, Madame," replied she. "I have business upstairs for a few minutes, and besides you perhaps wish to speak to Monsieur; shall you need me?"

"No," said Mme. de Ferval; "you may stay if you wish, but don't inconvenience yourself." Upon which, the Remy woman bowed, left us, closed the door on us, took the key, which we heard her withdraw, though very quietly.

"That woman must be a fool; I believe she has locked us in," said Mme. de Ferval, smiling with an air that opened the subject, that amorously invited conversation, and that said to me, "Do you see that we are alone?"

"What does it matter," said I (we were on the threshold of the door into the garden); "we have no need of the Remy woman to talk together; she would be worse than the chambermaid back there; didn't we make a bargain that we should be left undisturbed?"[7]

And while I engaged her in this conversation I held her hand, whose grace and whiteness I was noticing, and kissed it sometimes, "Is it thus that you tell me your history?" she said. "I'll certainly tell it to you," I said; "but that story is less urgent than I am." "Oh you!" she said, putting her other hand on my shoulder; "and for what are you so urgent?" "To tell you that your charms have made me dream of them all day," I replied. "I haven't dreamed about you any less," she said, "and dreamed so much that I thought of not coming here."

"Ah, why so, mistress of my heart?" I replied. "Oh, why?" she said; "because you are so young and so disturbing; I remember your vivacities of yesterday, altogether troubled as you were; and since you are now no longer so, will you reform yourself? I can't quite believe it." "And I likewise," said I, "for I am more in love than I was yesterday because it seems to me that you are still more beautiful."

"Very good, very good," she said with a smile, "here are fine preparations which reassure me greatly; to be alone with a giddy fellow like you, without being able to escape; for where has she gone, that stupid woman who left us? I should wager that we are perhaps the only ones here; ha, if she would only return I shouldn't quarrel with her; see, I pray you, what she exposes me to."

"Od's my life," I said to her, "it's easy enough for you to talk; you don't know what it is to be in love with you; is it just a matter of saying to people, 'Be still'? I should like to see you in my place to know what you would do." "Go, go, be quiet," she said jokingly. "I have had enough about me." "And yet?" I insisted in the same tone. "Very well; in your place," she replied, "I should try visibly to be reasonable." "And if it did

7. In their previous interview, Madame de Ferval arranges this secluded rendezvous because she fears being detected by her maid.

not help you at all to try," I continued, "what would come of it?" "Oh, what would come of it," she said, "I don't know at all; you demand too much of me; I am not there; but what matter if you love me, can't you do as I do? I am reasonable although I love you too; and I ought not to tell you, for you will only do more foolishness, and this will be my fault, little rebel that you are; see how he looks at me! Where has he learned that expression, the rogue? One can't endure it. Let us talk about Versailles."

"Oh, no," I replied, "let us talk about what you said—that you love me; that word is so pleasant, it's a charm to hear it, and it ravishes me, it transports me; what delight! Ah, how enchanting is your dear self!"

In making these remarks, I raised my eyes eagerly toward her; she was a little less covered than ordinarily. "There's nothing so sweet as that pretty bodice," I cried. "Now, now, little one; don't think of that any more, I don't want you to," she said.

At that she readjusted her costume rather badly. "Oh, my gracious lady, that is so well arranged, do not touch it." I took her hands then; her eyes were full of love; she sighed and said to me, "What do you want of me, La Vallée; I have done badly not to keep Remy here; another time I shall keep her; you don't at all listen to reason; move away a little; people can see us through those windows."

And in fact there was a view of us from the other side. "We only need to go into that room," I said. "We should," she replied, "but restrain yourself, my dear child, control yourself; I came here in good faith and you disquiet me with your love."

"I have, however, only what you have given me," I replied. "But you stand there, and that is tiring; sit down, do; seat yourself in that place where you were when I came." "What, there?" she said. "Oh, I wouldn't dare; I should be too much hemmed in, at least if you don't summon Remy. Call her, I beg you." What she said was in a tone lacking any stubbornness, and unknowingly we approached the spot where I had first found her. "Where are you leading me?" she asked in a languid and tender way. None the less she sat down, and I was throwing myself to my knees when we suddenly heard talking in the parlor.

Then the noise grew louder; it was like a dispute.

"Ah, La Vallée, what is that? Get up!" cried Mme. de Ferval. The noise increased. We distinguished the voice of a man in anger, against whom Mme. Remy, whom we heard also, appeared to defend herself. Finally the key was put in the lock, the door opened, and we saw a man enter, about thirty or thirty-five years old, very well built and handsome, who appeared to be extremely upset. I was holding the hilt of my sword, and I advanced to the middle of the room, much upset by this occurrence but resolved to repel the insult, supposing that this was what was meant toward us.

"Whom do you wish to see, Monsieur?" say I quickly. The man, without replying, casts his eyes on Mme. de Ferval, calms himself immediately, respectfully removes his hat, not without revealing great astonishment, and addressing himself to Mme. de Ferval: "Oh, Madame, I beg a thousand pardons," says he. "I am in despair for what I've just done; I was expecting to see another lady in whom I'm interested, and I had no doubt that it was she whom I should find here."

"Ah, truly," Mme. Remy said to him; "it is indeed time to demand apologies, and this is a well concocted one which you have just offered; Madame, who comes here for family business, to speak to her nephew whom she can see only in secret, has very real need of your excuses, and so have I!"

"You are in the wrong more than I," said the man, "for you had never warned me that you received other people here than the one I sought and myself. I return from dining in the country; I pass, I see a carriage in the little street; I suppose that it is that of the lady I know. But I haven't made an appointment with her; this surprises me; I even see at a distance a footman whose livery deceives me; I stop my carriage to know what the lady does here; you tell me she isn't here; I see that you are embarrassed; who in my place wouldn't imagine that there was a secret? As for the rest, forget the uneasiness that this could have given to Madame; it's as if nothing had happened, and I beg her once more to pardon me," he added, moving nearer to Mme. de Ferval with a very gallant gesture which had some tenderness in it.

Mme. de Ferval blushed and wished to withdraw the hand that he had taken and was kissing briskly.

At that I stepped forward, thinking I ought not to remain mute. "Madame doesn't appear to me to be angry," I said to the gallant; "the most discreet make mistakes; you have mistaken her for another; it's not a vast wrong; she excuses you; all that remains is to go away; that's the simplest course, now that you see what the situation is, Monsieur."

Then he turned around and stared at me attentively. "It seems to me that you are not a stranger," he said to me; "haven't I seen you at the home of Madame such-and-such?"

He was speaking, if you please, of the wife of the late seignior of our village. "That could be," I said, blushing in spite of all I could do, and indeed I began to restore him to himself. "Ho, it is Jacob," he cried to himself then, "I recognize him, it's he! Why, egad, my child, I'm delighted to see you here so well situated; your fortune must have changed considerably to have put you in reach of being intimate with Madame; man of quality as I am, I should like very much to have that honor as you do; for four months I have longed to be a humble one of her friends; she could perceive this even if I have encountered her only three or four times; my glances have told her how lovely she is; I was born with the tenderest inclination for her; and I'm sure, my dear Jacob, that my love is older than yours."

Mme. Remy was not present during this discourse; she had moved into the parlor and had left to us the problem of extricating ourselves from the intrigue.

As for me, I had lost all assurance, and like a real booby I bowed to the man at each word he addressed to me; sometimes I drew my foot back, sometimes I bowed my head, and I no longer knew what I did; I was undone; that disagreeable period in our acquaintance, his addressing me as a servant,[8] this sudden descent from the state of a man of good fortune in which he had found me to the state of Jacob to which he returned me—all this overwhelmed me.

In respect to Mme. de Ferval, it would be difficult to describe the expression on her face.

You recall that the Remy woman had spoken of me as a nephew of that lady; consider that she was a devote, that I was young, that her costume this day was more worldly than usual, her bodice gayer, less confining, and her bosom consequently freer; consider that we were found shut up at the house of Mme. Remy, a woman of convenience accustomed to lending her house (as we were learning); don't forget that the gallant who discovered us knew Mme. de Ferval, was a friend of her friends, and on top of all these matters that I've just mentioned to you, see the curious revelation one had of Mme. de Ferval's behavior, exhibiting the fine interior of her conscience—what miserable things exposed, and what miserable things they were, those that especially disgrace a devote, that declare her a hypocrite, an arrant cheat; for though she might be malicious, vindictive, proud, and scornful, she performs her duties and has therefore no less right to look haughty; all that does not in the least clash with the imperious austerity of her trade.

But to find herself convicted of being amorous, to be discovered in a gallant rendezvous—oh, all is lost! Behold the devote hissed; there is no clever turn to give to that.

Mme. de Ferval tried nevertheless to give one and said something in defense of herself, but this was with so noticeable an air of confusion that it was obvious her cause seemed to her desperate. Furthermore, she lacked the courage to plead very long.

"You are mistaken, Monsieur, I assure you that you are mistaken; I am here quite innocently; it is only to speak to him about a favor I wished to do him." After these few words the tone of her voice altered, her eyes were moistened with some tears, and a sigh broke off her speech.

On my part, I didn't know what to say. The name of Jacob by which he had remembered me held me in subjection; I kept fearing that he would resume the reproach, and I thought only of escaping in the best way possible; for what to do there with a rival before whom one could only be called Jacob, and that in the presence of a lady whom such an excess of familiarity humiliated no less than me? To have a lover, that already was a disgrace for her, and to have one with that name was a double disgrace; there was no possibility of a very delicate affair of the heart between her and a Jacob.

*   *   *

8. This is clearer in the French, where on recognizing Jacob the gentleman shifts to the familiar second-person singular used with servants in addition to demeaningly calling him by his first name.

[The flustered Jacob leaves but eavesdrops on their ensuing conversation long enough to hear Madame de Ferval succumb to the intruder's addresses in "a tone which granted what she was still rather denying in words." Disgusted with her, Jacob returns to his wife. The next day a new prospect of advancement opens when he rescues a young nobleman under attack. The novel as Fielding knew it ends with the two young men going off to the theatre.]

POLITICAL AND RELIGIOUS BACKGROUND

Joseph Andrews was written in the closing months of Sir Robert Walpole's unprecedented ascendancy as first commissioner of the treasury, chancellor of the exchequer, and *de facto* prime minister. Through imaginative financial management, adroit parliamentary maneuvering, and shrewd distribution of favors, he effectively controlled Parliament and influenced two monarchs over more than two decades (April 1721–February 1742). For much of this time, he and the "Court-side" were attacked by a vocal "Country-side" parliamentary opposition, a loose coalition of tories (Stuart loyalists and other conservative defenders of traditional authority in church and state) and several factions of disaffected "Patriots" from Walpole's own whig party whose common championing of "liberty" and "public interest" against "tyranny" and "corruption" barely concealed their divergent political agendas. Some sought a reconstituted whig ministry while a larger number advocated an administration transcending parties and reducing the overextended authority of the Crown. In the final years of Walpole's regime, leaders of the latter group suspected the former officeholders who were principal parliamentary managers of the coalition, William Pulteney (1684–1764) and John Lord Carteret (1690–1763), of using it to advance their own personal ambitions.

Fielding, who satirized Walpole in his theatrical farces as early as 1731, had been aligned with the whig opposition at least since 1735; his particular friends and patrons were among those leaders mistrustful of Carteret and Pulteney. His attacks on the ministry in *Pasquin* (1736) and *The Historical Register for the Year 1736* (1737) led Walpole to put through a theatrical licensing act that closed Fielding's Little Theatre in the Haymarket in June 1737. In November 1739, the dispossessed playwright-manager began his most sustained effort against the ministry as founding editor and part-owner of the thrice-weekly newspaper *The Champion; or British Mercury.* For the next two years, *The Champion* was in the forefront of the abusive battles between opposition and ministry-sponsored newspapers, focusing particularly on Walpole's half-hearted pursuit of the war against Spain, which he had sought to avoid. Fielding, however, gave up his part in the enterprise in June 1741 and may have stopped writing for it several months before that. In February of that year, the opposition had sustained an especially embarrassing defeat on a poorly managed motion to remove Walpole "from His Majesty's presence and counsels forever" when many tories supported the minister. That fiasco, alluded to in *Shamela* (see p. 302 n. 2), followed in April by the leadership's suspiciously conciliatory gestures toward the Court, may have persuaded Fielding to concentrate his energies elsewhere. Whatever the cause of his departure from *The Champion*, neither the opposition's significant reduction of the ministerial majority in the parliamentary elections a few months later nor the concerted plan of his patron and friend George Bubb Dodington (1691–1762) to exploit this opportunity in the new parliament were sufficient to sustain Fielding's commitment to opposition journalism.

By December, when the embattled Walpole was making his last parliamentary stand, Fielding was sufficiently disenchanted with the opposition, or some of its leaders or factions, to publish a scathing attack on the antiministerial politicians. In a cartoonlike satirical pamphlet entitled *The Opposition. A Vision*, he portrayed the anti-Walpole forces as a motley disarray of drivers and passengers in an overloaded wagon stalled by a confusion of leaders, ill-conceived tactics (including, prominently, the bungled February "motion"), and, above all, personal ambitions parading as patriotism. Expressing disillusionment with his own efforts on behalf of the opposition, he depicted himself and his fellow *Champion* editor James Ralph as starved asses who in pulling the overloaded wagon were "used to such purposes as the honesty of even an ass would start at." In contrast, the Walpole figure, with "one of the pleasantest, best-natured countenances I ever beheld," was shown releasing the asses and turning them out to feed—perhaps Fielding's figurative acknowledgment that he had recently received some government favors.

Near the end of this little allegory, he depicted the leadership, bouyed by their recent election victory, redirecting the wagon from "the great country road" to "St. James's [the seat of the Court], as fast as possible," a reflection of his friends' fears that Carteret and Pulteney would employ the electoral gains to strike a bargain with the ministry. The event confirmed these fears. When Walpole was forced to resign in February, Pulteney negotiated an arrangement with the Court that brought a few members of the larger tory and whig factions as well as Carteret, himself, and others from his small faction into the government but left much of the old ministry in place. For a short time, Pulteney held the "Patriot" alliance together with a promise of gradually wider participation in the government; but by early March, the king's resistance to admitting more malcontents and the failure of Pulteney's group to support an investigation of Walpole's administration drove the tories and most of the whigs back into open opposition.

This was the situation when Fielding—who had already satirized the Patriots' enthusiasm for the Spanish war and the "Country" candidates' inconstancy in the episode in which Parson Adams encounters the patriotic hunter and recounts his political history (2.7–9)—added two references to opposition opportunism in revising the second edition (see above, pp.

88, 110).[1] In June 1742, most readers would readily identify the "very honest Men" who had rescued their country "out of the hands of one Rifler, in order to rifle her" themselves. Now installed as secretary of state, Carteret, who had moved the removal of Walpole in the House of Lords, supported the measures he had formerly opposed. Pulteney's adjutant, Samuel Sandys (1695–1770), the Commons' inveterate mover of antiministerial measures (including the mismanaged Walpole removal motion and bills to restrict government pensioners and officeholders in parliament), now held Walpole's post as chancellor of the exchequer. But the most reviled object of public outrage was Pulteney himself, who had enhanced his reputation by a long-standing pledge to accept no government office. Although he adhered to the letter of that promise, he did take a seat in the king's cabinet council, and it was by then generally known that he had agreed to accept a peerage.

The politics of the time were reflected in the established Church of England. The Court appointed bishops who shared its whig sentiments, and their votes in the House of Lords helped sustain Walpole. One of the most political churchmen was Benjamin Hoadly, whose aggressive advocacy of the principles of the 1688 Revolution Settlement and the Hanoverian succession was rewarded with rapid preferment to successively wealthier episcopal sees. His most provocative arguments for the political subordination of the church had been made in A *Preservative against the Principles and Practices of the Non-Jurors both in Church and State* (1716) and in a related sermon preached before the king (1717). To counter the claim to an apostolic authority independent of the state put forth by the nonjurors (clergy who forfeited their church positions by refusing to transfer to the Hanoverian monarchs the loyalty sworn to the deposed Stuarts), he went so far as to deny the church's authority to legislate matters of conscience and salvation and even its corporate institutional existence. Arguing that Christ had delegated no "viceregents" or "judges" between His supreme authority and the individual conscience, he defined the Church as an "invisible society" of Christ's "equal subjects."

This radical view provoked a storm of clerical protest and rebuttals in what came to be known as the Bangorian controversy, Hoadly then being bishop of Bangor as well as chaplain to the king. The respondents represented not only nonjurors but a broad range of opinion within the church; but it was the tory "high-church" advocates of sacerdotal authority who sought to censure Hoadly in the Canterbury Convocation, prompting the government to suspend that deliberative church assem-

1. For a full discussion of these elements of the novel, see Martin Battestin, "Fielding's Changing Politics and *Joseph Andrews*," *Philological Quarterly* 39 (1960): 39–55. Battestin's interpretation of Fielding's attitude toward the opposition at this time and particularly the claim that he had accepted money from Walpole are supported by Bertrand

A. Goldgar, *Walpole and the Wits* (Lincoln: U of Nebraska P, 1976) 197–208, and disputed by William B. Coley, "Henry Fielding and the Two Walpoles," *Philological Quarterly* 45 (1966): 157–78, and Thomas R. Cleary, *Henry Fielding, Political Writer* (Waterloo: Wilfred Laurier UP, 1984) 152–62.

bly. Since nonjurors and other high church partisans had been Hoadly's favorite targets and antagonists since early in his career, this is probably the "Party" of "designing factious Men" to which Parson Adams consigns critics of Hoadly's later controversial view of the Sacrament (p. 65), although it too drew fire from a cross-section of churchmen. Their "favourite Schemes" were to increase clerical authority, to restrict protestant dissenters' rights, and, as confirmed by the implication of the high church leader Francis Atterbury, bishop of Rochester, in a 1722 plot, to restore the Stuarts. In the same speech, Adams voices the common fear that this event, with its associated revival of the doctrine of divine monarchical right, would imperil the "Liberty" secured by the 1688 Revolution Settlement and the 1714 Hanoverian succession.

Despite Hoadly's extensive political service to Walpole, Fielding held him in high esteem; he cited him as the clerical example of "True Greatness" in a poem on that subject published in January 1741, before he broke with the opposition. Beside sharing his whig animosity toward the high church Jacobites (supporters of the Stuarts), he concurred in his broad religious outlook. For extreme as were Hoadly's views on the institution of the church and the nature of the Sacrament, in most respects he espoused the prevailing liberal orthodoxy of the time. Called latitudinarian for its tolerance of a latitude of belief on doctrinal questions that had exercised zealous disputants in the previous age, this orientation fostered by Tillotson (p. 60, n. 3) and the prelates who succeeded him in the late seventeenth and early eighteenth centuries eschewed complexities of dogma in favor of a plain rationalist belief centered in the fatherhood of God and the brotherhood of man. "Persuaded of the centrality of this cardinal tenet of the beneficence of the Creator toward his creatures, the men of Latitude deduced the obligation on the part of mankind to imitate the divine charity by the performance of good works towards each other." [2] As Hoadly defined it in the Bangorian sermon, religion was "virtue and charity under the belief of a Supreme Governor and Judge." The same view is presented in Parson Adams's defense of Hoadly's interpretation of the Sacrament: men fulfill "the noble Purposes of Religion" by promising "in the Service of the supreme Being" to be "good, friendly and benevolent to each other" (p. 65).

Except for its insistence on the scriptures as divine revelation, this reasonable religion was not very far from the deism its orthodox proponents feared and denounced (see above, p. 166, n. 1). So it appeared to John Wesley and George Whitefield, young Oxford University clergymen whose preaching of the mystical doctrine of a "new birth" in Christ led a movement of spiritual revival within the church. Called Methodists for their rigorous habits of devotion and study, these fervent evangelists regarded the current liberal orthodoxy as spiritually shallow, complacent, and worldly. They held that its optimistic vision of a universe rationally ordered by a beneficent deity ignored the central fact of

2. Norman Sykes, *Church and State in England in the Eighteenth Century* (Cambridge: Cambridge UP, 1934) 257.

fallen man's sinful nature; preoccupied with virtuous conduct and charitable works, it had lost sight of the essential protestant tenet of salvation from that natural state through faith in Christ's redeeming grace, as stated in the Anglican Church's guiding Articles of Religion. Given man's sinful state, righteousness could only come from Christ; it was therefore vain to rely on good works or virtuous conduct to be justified (absolved from sin) before God. As Whitefield typically expounded this doctrine in a sermon preached in 1739 and published in 1740, since Christ has "fulfilled all Righteousness for us . . . all that we have to do, is to lay hold of this Righteousness by Faith . . . in that very Moment shall we be assured that the Blood of *Jesus Christ* has cleansed us from all Sin." Anticipating the objection made by others before Parson Adams (p. 65) that this was "a licentious Doctrine . . . opening a Door for Encouragement in Sin," he conceded in the same sermon that it might be "abused by Men of corrupt Minds," but far from "decrying all good Works" he insisted that the doctrine taught men how to do them "from a proper Principle." For his conception of the requisite faith was not assent "of the Head only" but a "living Principle wrought in the Soul by the Spirit of the ever-living God" which incites its possessors "out of a Principle of Love and Gratitude, to shew forth the same" by their works.[3]

Several things made Whitefield the favorite target of early critics of the revival. Less tactful than Wesley in attacking his fellow clergy, more flamboyant in his preaching, readier to resort to the unconventional (and technically illegal) practice of open air preaching when denied access to church pulpits, and more exploitive of his own spiritual crisis and conversion, he resembled the earlier dissenting puritan ministers whose "enthusiasm" (religious mania) had been a stock satiric target since the Restoration. Doctrinally he also departed farther than Wesley from the dominant liberal theology on mankind's eligibility for God's saving grace. He reasserted the church's original Calvinist belief that God had predestined individual souls to be saved or eternally damned; since salvation depended on faith in Christ, all who lived before or beyond the dissemination of Christianity were condemned. This puritan doctrine of absolute reprobation had been rejected by the earliest latitudinarians as inconsistent with God's omnipotent love and mercy, and by the time of the novel their view had prevailed even with Wesley and his followers. When Parson Adams denounces belief in the damnation of the virtuous unbeliever as "derogatory to the Honour of God" (p. 65), he is voicing one of the principal arguments repeatedly employed in the seventeenth and early eighteenth centuries against the Calvinist view.[4]

---

3. *What Think Ye of CHRIST?* A Sermon Preached at Kennington-Common, In the Year MDCCXXXIX. London, 1740.

4. See Philip Harth, *Contexts of Dryden's Thought* (Chicago and London: U of Chicago P, 1968) 148–73.

CRITICISM

Contemporary Responses and Early Criticism

LETTERS

George Cheyne to Samuel Richardson, March 9, 1742 [†]

* * * had Feilding's [sic] wretched Performance, for which I thank you. It will entertain none but Porters or Watermen. * * *

Thomas Gray to Richard West, April 1742 [‡]

* * * I have myself, upon your recommendation, been reading Joseph Andrews. The incidents are ill laid and without invention; but the characters have a great deal of nature, which always pleases even in her lowest shapes. Parson Adams is perfectly well; so is Mrs. Slipslop, and the story of Wilson; and throughout he shews himself well read in Stage-Coaches, Country Squires, Inns, and Inns of Court. His reflections upon high people and low people, and misses and masters, are very good. However, the exaltedness of some minds (or rather as I shrewdly suspect their insipidity and want of feeling or observation) may make them insensible to these light things, (I mean such as characterize and paint nature) yet surely they are as weighty and much more useful than your grave discourses upon the mind, the passions, and what not. * * *

William Shenstone to Richard Graves, 1742 [*]

* * * —Indeed, as to the little parody you send, it would fix your reputation with men of sense as much as (greatly more than) the whole tedious character of Parson Adams. I read it half a year ago; the week after I came to town: but made Mr. Shuckburgh[1] take it again, imagin-

† From *Samuel Richardson: Printer and Novelist*, ed. Alan McKillop (Durham: U of North Carolina P, 1936) 77. Cheyne (1671–1743) was a physician and friend of Richardson, whose writing Fielding had ridiculed (see above, p. 301, n. 7).
‡ From *The Correspondence of Thomas Gray*, ed. Paget Toynbee and Leonard Whibley (Oxford: Clarendon Press, 1935). Gray (1716–71), the poet,

is best known for his "Elegy Written in a Country Churchyard" (1751).
* From *Letters of William Shenstone*, ed. D. Mallam (Minneapolis: U of Minnesota P, 1939) 44. Shenstone (1714–63), a poet and essayist, was a friend of Fielding's patron, George Lyttleton.
1. A bookseller.

ing it altogether a very mean performance.—I liked a tenth part pretty well; but, as Dryden says of Horace (unjustly), he shews his teeth without laughing:[2] the greater part is *unnatural* and *unhumourous*. It has some advocates; but I observe, those not such as I ever esteemed tasters. Finally, what makes *you endeavour* to like it? * * *

William Shenstone to Lady Henrietta Luxborough, March 22, 1749 †

* * * I return your two first volumes of Tom Jones which I have read with some Pleasure, tho' I see no Character yet y^t is near so striking as Mr Abraham Adams. *That* was an *original*, I think; unattempted before, & yet so natural y^t most people seem'd to know ye Man. * * *

Elizabeth Carter to Catherine Talbot, January 1, 1743 ‡

* * * I must thank you for the perfectly agreeable entertainment I have met in reading Joseph Andrews, as it was your recommendation that first tempted me to enquire after it. It contains such a surprizing variety of nature, wit, morality, and good sense, as is scarcely to be met with in any one composition, and there is such a spirit of benevolence runs through the whole, as I think renders it peculiarly charming. The author has touched some particular instances of inhumanity which can only be hit in this kind of writing, and I do not remember to have seen observed any where else; these certainly cannot be represented in too detestable a light, as they are so severely felt by the persons they affect, and looked upon in too careless a manner by the rest of the world.

It must surely be a marvellous wrongheadedness and perplexity of understanding that can make any one consider this complete satire as a very immoral thing, and of the most dangerous tendency, and yet I have met with some people who treat it in the most outrageous manner. * * *

Samuel Richardson to Lady Dorothy Bradshaigh, 1749 *

* * * Has not the world shewn me, that it is much better pleased to receive and applaud the character that shews us what we are (little of

2. "The delight which Horace gives me is but languishing. * * * Where he barely grins himself, and * * * only shows his white teeth, he cannot-provoke me to any laughter." A *Discourse concerning the Original and Progress of Satire* (1693), *Essays of John Dryden*, ed. W. P. Ker, 2.84.

† From *Letters of William Shenstone*, ed. D. Mallam (Minneapolis: U of Minnesota P, 1939) 138.

‡ From A *Series of Letters Between Mrs. Elizabeth Carter and Miss Catherine Talbot* (London, 1809) 1.23–24. Admired by Dr. Johnson for her Greek scholarship, Carter (1717–1806) was one of the learned "Blue Stocking Ladies," who regularly conducted evenings of literary conversation.

* From *The Correspondence of Samuel Richardson* (London, 1804) 4.285–86.

novelty as one would think there is in that) than what we ought to be?[1] * * * So long as the world will receive, Mr. Fielding will write. Have you ever seen a list of his performances? Nothing but a shorter life than I wish him, can hinder him from writing himself out of date. The Pamela, which he abused in his Shamela, taught him how to write to please, tho' his manners are so different. Before his Joseph Andrews (hints and names taken from that story, with a lewd and ungenerous engraftment) the poor man wrote without being read, except when his Pasquins, &c. roused party attention and the legislature at the same time. * * * But to have done, for the present, with this fashionable author. * * *

PIERRE FRANÇOIS GUYOT DESFONTAINES

From *Observations sur les ecrits modernes* †

There appeared in England last summer a work that the English place above all the novels that have ever existed, or at least that they rank equal to the Adventures of D. Quixote and Scarron's Roman comique. It is entitled The History of the adventures of Joseph Andrews. * * * It is a judicious and moral novel, full of wit and amusement unsullied by libertine thought or sentiment, one which fosters a love of virtue and is infinitely affecting. The complications and episodes are delightful. The denouement, prepared from the beginning, is only realized in the last chapter, and cannot be predicted, so that before that the uncertain reader does not know what will be the outcome of the ingenious *imbroglio*. Moreover, nothing is so simple as the plot contrivance. The style is comic throughout, except where it is a tender and lawful love that provides the interest. Joseph Andrews is the brother of Pamela, who appears on the scene near the end of the second volume with the English nobleman who has married her; this creates the most pleasant situations. In short, I have no fear of affirming that England has never before produced anything so perfect of this kind. What is more, this is not a vain and frivolous fiction; it instructs the reader in the customs of the English which are not at all known in France, and it apprises us of a hundred curious particulars worthy of the attention of the most serious persons. The author is Mr. Feilding [*sic*], one of the best comic poets of England. The dialogue is also an excellent part of this book. Throughout, there are lively, unaffected, subtle, even delicate touches, always amusing and sometimes burlesque.

* * *

1. Richardson refers to his plans for *Sir Charles Grandison* (1754), the story of a model Christian gentleman, and to the popularity of Fielding's *Tom Jones*, then competing for acclaim with his own *Clarissa*.

† Volume 33, 1743, translated from the French. The Abbe DesFontaines (1685–1745), editor of this Parisian periodical review of current literary and intellectual developments, translated *Joseph Andrews* in 1744.

From *The Student, or, The Oxford and Cambridge Monthly Miscellany*, January 20, 1750

*   *   *

I have heard the character of Mr. ADAMS the clergyman, in an inge-nious work of FIELDING's, highly condemn'd, because, it seems, he *knew not the world*; and I am sorry to find that many of our divines are of the same opinion, and for the same reason.—But how much more laudable and agreeable figure does he now make, than he wou'd have done, had he been represented as ready to impose, as he is now liable to be impos'd upon? I know not what may be the opinion of others, but to me, his innocent ignorance of this world and its ways, demonstrates him not to have been a child of it, and if so, what they, his brothers of the cloth, who are so thoroughly knowing in this point, are, who is not able to guess?

*   *   *

SARAH FIELDING [AND JANE COLLIER?]

[Parson Adams Not an Object of Ridicule] †

*   *   *

That the chief personage of the comic should be endued with virtue and excellence, seems most palpably evident, in order to gain the atten-tion of the reader; as also to give him the opportunity of energizing the pleasing sensation of love and affection. Whatever of the ridiculous is to be admitted into such works should be found amongst the under char-acters, or what is properly called episodes. The principal figures in our view should give us leave to exercise our esteem; otherwise by what means can we be concerned for their distress, rejoice at their prosperity, or be anxious for the event of their story?

To travel through a whole work only to laugh at the chief companion allotted us is an insupportable burthen. And we should imagine that the reading of that incomparable piece of humour left us by Cervantes can give but little pleasure to those persons who can extract no other enter-tainment or emolument from it than laughing at Don Quixote's reveri-es, and sympathizing in the malicious joy of the maid at the inn, when she had confined the poor knight in painful durance, by tying him up to the window by the hand, and letting the weight of his whole body hang on that small hold:[1] and that strong and beautiful representation

---

† From *The Cry: A New Dramatic Fable*, Pro-logue to Part the Fifth (Dublin: 1754) 2.168–70.
1. Near the end of part 1, the mischievous Mari-tornes tricks Quixote into extending his hand to the supposedly lovestruck daughter of the innkee-per [*Editor*].

of human nature, exhibited in Don Quixote's madness in one point, and extraordinary good sense in every other, is indeed very much thrown away on such readers as consider him only as the object of their mirth. Nor less understood is the character of parson Adams in Joseph Andrews, by those persons, who, fixing their thoughts on the hounds trailing the bacon in his pocket (with some oddnesses in his behaviour, and peculiarities in his dress) think proper to overlook the noble simplicity of his mind, with the other innumerable beauties of his character; which, to those who can understand THE WORD TO THE WISE,[2] are placed in the most conspicuous view.

That the ridiculers of parson Adams are designed to be the proper objects of ridicule (and not that innocent man himself) is a truth which the author hath in many places set in the most glaring light. And lest his meaning should be perversely misunderstood, he hath fully displayed his own sentiments on that head, by writing a whole scene, in which such laughers are properly treated, and their characters truly depicted.[3] But those who think continual laughter, or rather sneering, to be one of the necessary ingredients of life, need not be at the trouble of travelling out of their depths to find objects of their merriment: they may spare themselves the pains of going abroad after food for scorn, as they may be bless'd with a plenteous harvest ever mature and fit for reaping on their own estates, without being beholden to any of their neighbors.

The greatest men, 'tis true, may have some oddnesses and peculiarities, which are indeed food for mirth and pleasantry: but the honest laughs which they create in the judicious and benevolent mind are such, as their own candor[4] (if they are truly great men) will readily excuse; and their good humour, if they have any, will then induce them to join the mirthful chorus; and the result must be the charm of universal chearfulness and innocent mirth. We are very apt to do as manifest an injury to comic writers, as we do the characters they represent; and because they here and there properly embellish their pictures with risible figures, we want to turn the whole into farce, by desiring to see nothing but the grotesque: we expect in every page to meet with such jests as shall distort our features into a broad grin; otherwise, let them paint the most agreeable images of human nature, let them ever so accurately search the inmost recesses of the human heart, there is a general outcry set up against them, that they are spiritless and dull.

But indignation at the malicious rather than ignorant absurdities, which we have heard vented on honest parson Adams, hath led us into a much wider digression than we at first intended.

*　　*　　*

2. A refrain in *The Cry* [*Editor*].
3. Book 3, chapter 7 [*Editor's* contraction of
author's note].
4. Fairness [*Editor*].

JAMES BEATTIE

[The New Comic Romance] †

* * *

The second species of the New Comick Romance is that which, in the arrangement of events, follows the poetical order; and which may properly enough be called the Epick Comedy, or rather the Comick Epick poem: *Epick*, because it is narrative;[1] and *Comick*, because it is employed on the business of common life, and takes its persons from the middle and lower ranks of mankind.

This form of the Comick Romance has been brought to perfection in England by Henry Fielding; who seems to have possessed more wit and humour[2], and more knowlege of mankind, than any other person of modern times, Shakespeare excepted; and whose great natural abilities were refined by a classical taste, which he had acquired by studying the best authors of antiquity: though it cannot be denied, that he appears on some occasions to have been rather too ostentatious, both of his learning, and of his wit.

Some have said, that Joseph Andrews is the best performance of Fielding. But its chief merit is parson Adams; who is indeed a character of masterly invention, and, next to Don Quixote, the most ludicrous personage that ever appeared in romance. This work, though full of exquisite humour, is blameable in many respects. Several passages offend by their indelicacy. And it is not easy to imagine, what could induce the author to add to the other faults of his hero's father Wilson the infamy of lying and cowardice; and then to dismiss him, by very improbable means, to a life of virtuous tranquillity, and endeavour to render him upon the whole a respectable character. Some youthful irregularities, rather hinted at than described, owing more to imprudence and unlucky accident than to confirmed habits of sensuality, and followed by inconvenience, perplexity, and remorse, their natural consequences, may, in a comick tale, be assigned even to a favourite personage, and, by

† From *On Fable and Romance*, 1783. Beattie (1735–1803) was a Scottish poet, critic, and professor of moral philosophy.

1. Beattie makes the neoclassical distinction between two kinds of narrative order, the "historical" (a "continued narrative of the life of some one person from his birth * * * till his adventures may be supposed to have come to an end") and the "poetical," which "begins in the middle of the story." The latter was considered the true epic arrangement, after the practice of Homer. As examples of the "historical" species of the new comic romance, Beattie cites *Gil Blas*, the novels of Marivaux, and Smollett's *Roderick Random* [Editor].

2. The great Lord Lyttelton, after mentioning several particulars of Pope, Swift, and other wits of that time, when I asked some question relating to the Author of Tom Jones, began his answer with these words, "Henry Fielding, I assure you, had more wit and more humour than all the persons we have been speaking of put together." This testimony of his Lordship, who was intimately acquainted with Fielding, ought not to be forgotten.

proper management, form a very instructive part of the narration: but crimes, that bring dishonour, or that betray a hard heart, or an injurious disposition, should never be fixed on a character who the poet or novel-writer means to recommend to our esteem. * * *

WILLIAM HAZLITT

[A Perfect Piece of Statistics in Its Kind] †

* * * without going so far as the celebrated French philosopher, who thought that more was to be learnt from good novels and romances than from the gravest treatises on history and morality, yet there are few works to which I am oftener tempted to turn for profit or delight, than to the standard productions in this species of composition. We find there a close imitation of men and manners; we see the very web and texture of society as it really exists, and as we meet with it when we come into the world. If poetry has 'something more divine in it,' this savours more of humanity. We are brought acquainted with the motives and characters of mankind, imbibe our notions of virtue and vice from practical examples, and are taught a knowledge of the world through the airy medium of romance. As a record of past manners and opinions, too, such writings afford the best and fullest information. For example, I should be at a loss where to find in any authentic documents of the same period so satisfactory an account of the general state of society, and of moral, political, and religious feeling in the reign of George II. as we meet with in the Adventures of Joseph Andrews and his friend Mr. Abraham Adams. This work, indeed, I take to be a perfect piece of statistics in its kind. In looking into any regular history of that period, into a learned and eloquent charge to a grand jury or the clergy of a diocese, or into a tract on controversial divinity, we should hear only of the ascendancy of the Protestant succession, the horrors of Popery, the triumph of civil and religious liberty, the wisdom and moderation of the sovereign, the happiness of the subject, and the flourishing state of manufactures and commerce. But if we really wish to know what all these fine-sounding names come to, we cannot do better than turn to the works of those, who having no other object than to imitate nature, could only hope for success from the fidelity of their pictures; and were bound (in self-defence) to reduce the boasts of vague theorists and the exaggerations of angry disputants to the mortifying standard of reality. Extremes are said to meet: and the works of imagination, as they are called, sometimes come the nearest to truth and nature. Fielding in speaking on this subject, and vindicating the use and dignity of the style of writing in which he excelled against the loftier pretensions of professed historians, says, that in their productions nothing is true but the names and dates, whereas in his

† From *Lectures on the English Comic Writers*, London, 1819. *Works*, ed. P. G. Howe (London: J. M. Dent, 1931) 6:106–7, 112–13, 115.

every thing is true but the names and dates. If so, he has the advantage on his side.

I will here confess, however, that I am a little prejudiced on the point in question; and that the effect of many fine speculations has been lost upon me, from an early familiarity with the most striking passages in the work to which I have just alluded. Thus nothing can be more captivating than the description somewhere given by Mr. Burke of the indissoluble connection between learning and nobility; and of the respect universally paid by wealth to piety and morals.[1] But the effect of this ideal representation has always been spoiled by my recollection of Parson Adams sitting over his cup of ale in Sir Thomas Booby's kitchen. Echard 'On the Contempt of the Clergy'[2] is, in like manner, a very good book, and 'worthy of all acceptation:'[3] but, somehow, an unlucky impression of the reality of Parson Trulliber involuntarily checks the emotions of respect, to which it might otherwise give rise: while, on the other hand, the lecture which Lady Booby reads to Lawyer Scout on the immediate expulsion of Joseph and Fanny from the parish, casts no very favourable light on the flattering accounts of our practical jurisprudence which are to be found in Blackstone or De Lolme. The most moral writers, after all, are those who do not pretend to inculcate any moral. The professed moralist almost unavoidably degenerates into the partisan of a system; and the philosopher is too apt to warp the evidence to his own purpose. But the painter of manners gives the facts of human nature, and leaves us to draw the inference: if we are not able to do this, or do it ill, at least it is our own fault.

*　*　*

There is very little to warrant the common idea that Fielding was an imitator of Cervantes, except his own declaration of such an intention in the title-page of Joseph Andrews, the romantic turn of the character of Parson Adams (the only romantic character in his works), and the proverbial humour of Partridge,[4] which is kept up only for a few pages. Fielding's novels are, in general, thoroughly his own: and they are thoroughly English. What they are most remarkable for, is neither sentiment, nor imagination, nor wit, nor even humour, though there is an immense deal of this last quality; but profound knowledge of human nature, at least of English nature; and masterly pictures of the characters of men as he saw them existing. This quality distinguishes all his works, and is shown almost equally in all of them. As a painter of real life, he was equal to Hogarth; as a mere observer of human nature, he was little inferior to Shakspeare, though without any of the genius and poetical qualities of his mind. His humour is less rich and laughable than Smol-

---

1. Edmund Burke, *Reflections on the Revolution in France*, vol. 2 of *Edmund Burke: Selected Works*, ed. E. J. Payne (Oxford: Clarendon P, 1921) 92–93 [Editor].

2. See above, p. 313, n. 4 [Editor].

3. 1 Timothy 1:15 [Editor].

4. A barber who becomes the hero's traveling companion in *Tom Jones*; his effusion of proverbs resembles the comic speech of Quixote's squire, Sancho Panza [Editor].

lett's; his wit as often misses as hits; he has none of the fine pathos of Richardson or Sterne; but he has brought together a greater variety of characters in common life, marked with more distinct peculiarities, and without an atom of caricature, than any other novel writer whatever. The extreme subtlety of observation on the springs of human conduct in ordinary characters, is only equalled by the ingenuity of contrivance in bringing those springs into play, in such a manner as to lay open their smallest irregularity. The detection is always complete, and made with the certainty and skill of a philosophical[5] experiment, and the obviousness and familiarity of a casual observation. The truth of the imitation is indeed so great, that it has been argued that Fielding must have had his materials ready-made to his hands, and was merely a transcriber of local manners and individual habits. For this conjecture, however, there seems to be no foundation. His representations, it is true, are local and individual; but they are not the less profound and conclusive. The feeling of the general principles of human nature operating in particular circumstances, is always intense, and uppermost in his mind; and he makes use of incident and situation only to bring out character.

*   *   *

There is nothing at all heroic, however, in the usual style of his delineations. He does not draw lofty characters or strong passions; all his persons are of the ordinary stature as to intellect; and possess little elevation of fancy, or energy of purpose. Perhaps, after all, Parson Adams is his finest character. It is equally true to nature, and more ideal than any of the others. Its unsuspecting simplicity makes it not only more amiable, but doubly amusing, by gratifying the sense of superior sagacity in the reader. Our laughing at him does not once lessen our respect for him. His declaring that he would willingly walk ten miles to fetch his sermon on vanity, merely to convince Wilson of his thorough contempt of this vice, and his consoling himself for the loss of his Æschylus, by suddenly recollecting that he could not read it if he had it, because it is dark, are among the finest touches of *naiveté*. The night-adventures at Lady Booby's with Beau Didapper, and the amiable Slipslop, are the most ludicrous; and with the huntsman, who draws off the hounds from the poor Parson, because they would be spoiled by following *vermin*, the most profound.

5. Scientific [*Editor*].

Modern Criticism

MARK SPILKA

Comic Resolution in Fielding's *Joseph Andrews* †

I

Though the night adventures at Booby Hall are among the most memorable scenes in *Joseph Andrews*, many scholars tend to ignore them or to minimize their importance. Generally speaking, they pluck the adventures out of context and file them away—out of sight, out of mind—among even more colorful bedroom antics within the picaresque tradition. Thus J. B. Priestley writes:

> Such chapters of accidents are very familiar to students of the *picaresque*, and all that need be said of this one is that there is some slight relation to character in it . . . but that it is not enough to make the episode anything more than a piece of comic business of a very familiar type. Smollett could bustle through such rough-and-tumble business just as well, if not better. . . .[1]

Priestley is right as far as he goes, but he forgets that *Joseph Andrews* is more novel than picaresque tale and that the novel requires special handling. In the picaresque tale there is little or no dramatic connection between one episode and the next, and the critic can lift things out of context to his heart's content. But with the more fully developed novel form he must show how an episode—lifted *from* a tradition—has been fitted *into* the scheme of a given book. Certainly this is the proper approach to the escapades at Booby Hall, the last major comic scenes in *Joseph Andrews*—scenes which involve all the major characters in the book and both aspects of the central theme, the lust-chastity theme.

Yet with all this in mind it may still be argued that the Booby Hall affair is a simple comic interlude, or diversion, which Fielding inserted at the most crucial point in the novel to increase suspense and at the same time to vary the fare. On the surface there is some truth to this assertion: the night adventures are sandwiched between the all-important

† From *College English* 15 (1953): 11–19.
1. *The English Comic Characters* (New York: Dodd, Mead, 1931), p. 113.

chapters in which the incest problem is first introduced then happily solved. But the argument breaks down before a simple comparison: in the famous knocking-at-the-gate scene in *Macbeth*, the commonplace is used (according to De Quincey) to offset and heighten the essential strangeness and horror of murder; if the "diversion" argument holds true, the same function should be performed by the bedroom scenes in *Joseph Andrews*; but as any honest reader will admit, these scenes perform precisely the opposite function—that is, they neither increase nor heighten the dramatic intensity of the incest plot; rather, they lessen its seriousness and achieve a special importance of their own. In the next chapter, for example, the company are "all very merry at breakfast, and Joseph and Fanny rather more cheerful than the preceding night"; it becomes obvious that some sort of emotional purgation has occurred and that the resolution of the main plot will be anticlimactic.

All this seems normal enough for a comedy based on character rather than on situation. As Aurelien Digeon points out, "The ending is necessarily the weak point in works of this kind. It is almost always engineered from without; for passions never stop working nor come to an 'end.' "[2] Unfortunately, Digeon fails to add here that if passions never stop working, they are sometimes resolved, and that it is the business of a good comic writer to resolve them. In the night adventures at Booby Hall, Fielding has done just that; with the aid of condensed, violent action, he has stood his book on its head, shaken out all the themes and passions, and resolved them through warmhearted laughter. If this interpretation seems far-fetched, its essential soundness may become evident as we pay more attention to the lust-chastity theme, to Fielding's theory of humor, to the role of nakedness in the novel, and, finally, to two of the most comic figures in the book, Parson Adams and Mrs. Slipslop. As for the other relevant characters—Joseph Andrews, Fanny Goodwill, Lady Booby, and Beau Didapper—we need only note here that the first two embody all the natural health, goodness, and beauty which Fielding admired, while the last two embody much of the vice and artificiality he deplored.

II

In order to parody Richardson's *Pamela,* Fielding built *Joseph Andrews* around a central moral problem: the preservation of (and the assault upon) chastity. On the one hand, Joseph Andrews must protect his virtue from such lustful creatures as Lady Booby, Mrs. Slipslop, and Betty the chambermaid; on the other, Fanny Goodwill must withstand the attacks of a beau, a squire, a rogue, and a servant. But as most writers have observed, the scope of the novel is much broader than this. Fielding saw affectation in two of its forms, vanity and hypocrisy, as the "only source of the true Ridiculous," and he hoped to expose these qualities

2. *The Novels of Fielding* (London: Routledge, 1925), p. 60.

wherever he found them. Accordingly, he also designed his novel along more general lines: three virtuous, good-natured persons—Joseph, Fanny, and Adams—must be thrust through every level of society as exemplars or as touchstones and instruments for exposing vanity and hypocrisy, and, just as important, goodness and kindness, in whomever they meet. Adams will be the foremost touchstone, since his religious position and his personal traits—innocence, simplicity, bravery, compassion, haste, pedantry, forgetfulness—will always pitch him into a good deal of trouble; yet, once in trouble, his virtues will make him stand out in complete contrast to those who take advantage of him. Finally, in his perfect innocence he will always be the main instrument for exposing his own mild affectations.

But, as these remarks indicate, Adams' position is somewhat ambiguous with regard to Fielding's formula for the ridiculous in humor. Like his predecessor, Don Quixote, he cuts a bizarre figure outwardly, but, at the same time, his inner dignity remains unassailable: as Joseph Andrews tells us, true virtue can never be ridiculed, and we know that Adams, however outlandish, is truly virtuous—so that he stands half within Fielding's theory of humor and half without.[3] But this theory is, after all, static and reductive rather than organic. Through shrewd analysis Fielding has called attention to the affectations, the *particular* qualities which make men appear in a ridiculous light. But through his admiration for Cervantes he has unconsciously seized on the principle of the *comic figure*—the whole man who is at once lovable and ridiculous, whose entire character is involved in each of his humorous actions, and whose character must be established through time and incident, in the reader's mind, before he becomes "wholly" laughable. To put it in different terms, when someone we know and like is involved in a ridiculous action, then the humor of the situation broadens and quickens to include our identification with and sympathy for that person. A sudden or prolonged juxtaposition of his inner dignity with his outer "awkwardness" produces a state of mixed emotions in us—love, sympathy, and identification, as well as condescension—and this state is released or resolved, in turn, through laughter.[4] The point can be made clearer perhaps through a modern analogy: the amorphous Keystone Cops amuse us (at least they used to) in accord with Fielding's theory of the ridiculous—that is to say, they lose their false outer dignity in falls and madcap fights; yet when Charlie Chaplin puts up a magnificent bluff in the boxing ring (as in *City Lights*), our laughter becomes much warmer and far more sympa-

---

3. In Book III, chap. vi, Joseph says, "I defy the wisest man in the world to turn a good action into ridicule. . . . He, who should endeavour it, would be laughed at himself, instead of making others laugh."

4. Fielding's (and Hobbes's) theory of humor depends upon the reader's feeling of superiority toward the person ridiculed. But in practice Fielding tapped a second psychological source by working upon our sympathies: all of us know how it feels to be misunderstood or defeated, and such feelings help us to maintain a close identification

with likable comic figures—Adams, Quixote, Chaplin. If, as Maynard Mack insists (in *Joseph Andrews*, ed. Maynard Mark [New York: Rinehart, 1948]), we view comedy from the outside, as a spectacle, this is only our conscious point of view; at the deeper emotional level we are actively engaged in the spectacle. Of course, all art demands some form of audience participation at this level, but the point deserves re-emphasis, since, in our current (and much-needed) passion for analysis, we have partially deadened our sense of the unity of aesthetic experience.

thetic in quality—Chaplin's bluff may be ridiculous, but the man who bluffs is brave, and we have learned something of this through time, situation, and the development of character; we are prepared, that is, for his simultaneous display of inner dignity and outer vanity in the boxing ring, and our laughter is accordingly that much richer. One Keystone Cop is much like the next, but Chaplin has become a unique and appealing figure in our eyes—and in a similar manner so has Parson Adams. Our respect, love, and admiration for Adams continue to grow through the length of *Joseph Andrews*. And only when his character has been firmly established in our minds (and in the same vein, only when the lust-chastity theme has been worked for all it is worth) can the night scenes at Booby Hall occur. Place these scenes earlier in the book and they will strike us as meaningless horseplay; but at the end of the book we are prepared for them—Parson Adams is now familiar to us as a well-developed comic figure, and his nakedness strikes us with symbolic force.

As a matter of fact the spectacle of nakedness is significantly common (though not always symbolic) in *Joseph Andrews*. Fanny, Joseph, Adams, Lady Booby, Mrs. Slipslop, Beau Didapper, Betty the chambermaid, Mr. Tow-wouse—all appear at one time or another and for various reasons, in a state of partial or complete undress. In the early chapters, for example, Joseph is beaten and stripped by robbers and left on the road to die; when a carriage passes, Fielding "tests" each of the passengers by his willingness to accept Joseph *as he is*, for what he is—a defenseless human being. And late in the book, when Adams appears in a nightshirt (the usual eighteenth-century equivalent for nakedness), Fielding tests, in effect, *our* willingness, as good-natured readers, to take Adams for what he is. It should not surprise us, therefore, that a definite symbolic equation between nakedness, on the one hand, and innocence and worth, on the other, occurs in other portions of Fielding's work: Squire Allworthy also appears in his nightshirt, for example, in the opening pages of *Tom Jones*; and in *The Champion* for January 24, 1740, Fielding even cites Plato to the effect that men would love virtue if they could see her naked. This platitude is put to good use in *Joseph Andrews*, though the problem there is to "expose" or "lay bare" both virtue and affectation, often in the same man.

With regard to affectation, Fielding's theory of the ridiculous fits in well with our "nakedness" theme. Affectations are "put on," and it is the humorist's job (or more properly the satirist's) to "strip them off." This much Fielding knew by rote from his earliest published work, a poem against masquerades, to his attack on masquerades in his last novel, *Amelia*: take off the mask, remove the outer pretense, and expose the "bare facts" which lie beneath—vanity, hypocrisy, smugness. But his chief accomplishment, as well as his chief delight, was to distinguish between a man's defects and his essential goodness; and we think in this respect of Adams, Tom Jones, Captain Booth,[5] and dozens of the minor

---

5. The errant and ultimately reformed husband of Amelia, heroine of Fielding's novel of that name (1752) [*Editor*].

creations. If a man is good-natured "at bottom," then the problem for the novelist is how to get to the bottom. Fielding usually arrives there by playing off the man's faults against his virtues, as when Adams first cautions Joseph against immoderate grief, then grieves immoderately, like any compassionate man, at the news of his son's supposed drowning. But a more pertinent example occurs in one of the inn scenes in *Joseph Andrews*, when Fanny faints and Adams in his haste to rescue her, tosses his precious copy of Aeschylus into the fire. Here Adams has literally stripped off an affectation while revealing his natural goodness—the book is a symbol, that is, of his pedantry, of his excessive reliance upon literature as a guide to life, and this is what is tossed aside during the emergency. Later on, when the book is fished out of the fire, it has been reduced to its simple sheepskin covering—which is Fielding's way of reminding us that the contents of the book are superficial, at least in the face of harsh experience. Thus the whole incident underscores the fact that Adams' faults, like his torn, disordered clothes, are only the outward, superficial aspects of his character and that the essential Adams, a brave, good man, lies somewhere underneath; his heart—not his Aeschylus, not his harmless vanity—is his true guide in all things of consequence.[6]

Mrs. Slipslop is another matter. She is usually praised by critics as the well-rounded comic foil to Lady Booby. But she is something more than this, since her lust for Joseph, and for all manner of men, is more natural and appealing than Lady Booby's hot-and-cold passion. To begin with, Mrs. Slipslop is an unbelievably ugly maidservant, who, after an early slip, has remained virtuous for many years. Now, at forty-five, she has resolved to pay off "the debt of pleasure" which she feels she owes to herself. Though Fielding heavily ridicules her vanity and hypocrisy through the book, he also brings out the pathetic strain in her makeup, and at times he even reveals an author's fondness for a favorite creation. Mrs. Slipslop may rail at Joseph, for example, but unlike Lady Booby she will never turn him out into the street; in fact, she saves or aids him on several important occasions; but, more than all this, there is something almost touching, as well as ridiculous, about her faulty speech, her grotesque body, and her foolish dream of becoming "Mrs. Andrews, with a hundred a-year." All in all, she is a comic figure in her own right, as well as a comic foil, and if Fielding deals her a sound drubbing in the night scenes at Booby Hall, he also "deals" her a last warm laugh.

III

Fielding beds down his entire cast at Booby Hall in preparation for the night adventures. Then, when the household is asleep, he sends

6. Consider in this respect what a poor showing Partridge makes as a comic figure in *Tom Jones*; like Adams he is vain, pedantic, and superstitious, but he lacks the nobility of heart which great comic figures—at least in the quixotic tradition—must possess.

Beau Didapper off to ravish Fanny through trickery, and the round of fun begins. By mistake, Didapper enters Mrs. Slipslop's pitch-dark room and, posing as Joseph, tells her that the incest report was false, and that he can delay the enjoyment of her charms no longer; then he climbs into bed with her. She receives him willingly enough—her dream comes true—but the two of them soon discover their mutual error. Ever-prudent, Mrs. Slipslop now sees her chance to win back her reputation for chastity, which she had damaged through recent conduct with Lawyer Scout; so she hugs Didapper even more firmly, calls out for help, and Parson Adams comes running to her rescue from the next chamber. But in his haste Adams has forgot to put on any clothes, and this action is far more characteristic of him than any we have yet seen in the novel. For Adams has now become his own true symbol: he stands there as God made him, all courage and kindness, with his affectations, his clothes, left in a heap behind him. He is now the naked truth, quite literally and lovably, and he is never more himself than at this moment, not even while throwing his Aeschylus into the fire to save Fanny. He is brave, true virtue on the march now, stripped clean of all encumbrance and far beyond the reach of ridicule—for true virtue, as we have already seen, can never be ridiculed. Of course, Adams is laughable because he is naked and imprudent and we are not; but mainly he arouses those feelings to which we have been conditioned, with regard to him, from the beginning of the novel. For as Fielding and Plato have told us, men will love virtue if they see her—or in this case him—naked. We see him naked now, and we laugh, to a great extent, out of love. But let us return for a moment to the going-on in Mrs. Slipslop's bedroom.

Obeying, of all things, the dictates of common sense, Adams now passes over the small, whimpering body—obviously the woman—and proceeds to grapple with the large bearded one—obviously the man. Here Fielding ridicules, in Slipslop and Didapper, that vanity by which one poses as a seducible woman and the other as a virile man. For the small body (Beau Didapper) escapes, and Slipslop receives an almost fatal beating. But Lady Booby, attracted by all the noise, enters the room in the nick of time with lighted candle in hand. At which point Adams discovers both his error and his nakedness and leaps under the covers with Mrs. Slipslop. We have then, in one corner of the bed, Vice posing as Virtue, which is hypocrisy; and in the other corner, Virtue hiding its "lovable" nakedness and apparently acting as Vice—which is false, foolish modesty at the very least. And we also have, as Lady Justice with the Lighted Candle, Lady Booby, the far from blinded villainess of the novel.

Shall we stop a moment to straighten things out? We have already seen that vanity has been exposed to ridicule—a normal enough procedure. But now we can see that virtue itself has been exposed to some sort of laughter; moreover, it has been exposed in a worthless cause—until Adams arrived and began pummeling Mrs. Slipslop, no one was in any real danger. This reminds us at once of Don Quixote, and the comparison enables us to see that virtue has been confounded rather than ridiculed and that we laugh once more, in the main, out of sympathy for a brave man in an awkward fix.[7]

There is more to it than this, however. We have been neglecting Mrs. Slipslop, who at long last has had not one but two men in her bed (simultaneously!), but who has been forced by circumstance to reject them both. The sex-starved maiden, with her mountainous breasts and her spur-of-the-moment virtue, has been soundly trounced. In a very real sense this is Waterloo for the prudent gentlewoman, and for the lust half of the lust-chastity theme as well. All, all is resolved through a burst of laughter, though again through laughter of a special kind. In a parody on *Pamela*, one of two lusting ladies (both foils for Richardson's clumsy Mr. B) was bound to receive a severe comeuppance. Fielding, the sure comic artist, chose the more comic figure; but the very condition which makes Slipslop appear so ridiculous in our eyes—the extreme distance between her desires and her qualifications—also makes her appeal to the warm side of our (and Fielding's) sense of humor. She is a far less harsh figure than Lady Booby and therefore the more proper bed companion for the equally harmless, "sexless," but virtuous Parson Adams.

Nevertheless, we must return to Lady Booby, at the scene of the alleged rape, for the key to all these resolutions and reversals. After berating Adams as a wicked cleric, the stern hostess spies Didapper's telltale cuff links on the floor. Then, when she hears Adams' story, when she takes in "the figures of Slipslop and her gallant, whose heads only were visible at the opposite corners of the bed," she is unable to "refrain from laughter." For once, then, Lady Booby appears in a good light: until now she has behaved in a completely selfish manner, but the kind of laughter which we cannot withhold, *in spite of ourselves*, stems more from the heart than the ego. Even the opinionated Mrs. Slipslop now checks her tongue, and it becomes apparent that evil itself has been dissolved by some strange power. We can say, of course, that Lady Booby laughs at a maid and a parson who are far too old and ridiculous for zealous modesty; but, more to the point, she laughs at Adams' lovable innocence, and perhaps she laughs at herself as well, at her own defeat; for, as we have observed, Mrs. Slipslop is in part her comic foil, and Parson Adams now lies in the place where Joseph Andrews might have lain, if her own hopes had been fulfilled.

At any rate, a general absolution has obviously just occurred: through elaborate contrivance (the creation of Beau Didapper as catalytic agent, the convenient rainstorm, the crisis in the main plot, Slipslop's affair with Lawyer Scout, and so on) Fielding has brought Adams before us in all his nakedness. The good parson has never seemed so ridiculous, nor has he ever been burdened so heavily with the guilt which rightfully

---

7. This is also Adam's first "real" windmill and therefore the most quixotic moment in the book. Until now Adams' rescues have been much to the point and more or less successful, since Fielding always attempted to show that virtue can be a successful way of life—hence Adams' vigor, his robust strength, his eventual muddling through. As a knight-errant, he is generally far more effective than the gallant Quixote.

belongs to those around him—to Slipslop, to Didapper, to Lady Booby, and even to you and me, as we stand behind the bold hostess in judgment of the scene and see our own sins revealed by flickering candlelight—yet Adams emerges untarnished from under this double burden of guilt and ridicule, and, like the true comic hero, he absolves us all with his naïve triumph over circumstance: for good and bad men alike have a common stake in that perfect, naked innocence which can force a Lady Booby, or even a Peter Pounce, to grin or laugh from some buried store of benevolence.[8] All this is nicely underscored, I think, when the lady retires once more and the scene at hand, which opens with naked Adams running characteristically to the rescue, now closes with naked Slipslop sliding lustfully, pathetically, characteristically, and as Fielding puts it, "with much courtesy," across the bed toward Parson Adams, who takes the hint and quickly leaves the room. One can't help thinking that at long last, among all those thorns, Fielding has placed a rose for Mrs. Slipslop—for the last warm laugh is hers, in a madcap world where virtue is masked as vice, and vice as virtue, while, in the unmasking, warmheartedness prevails over all morality.

In the next half of the chapter things begin to settle down. Adams, in his haste, inadvertently takes the wrong turn; he climbs quietly into what he thinks is his own bed and prepares for sleep. But in reality the poor man has moved directly from the bed of the ugliest, most indiscriminately lustful woman in the book to that of the loveliest and most chaste. On the other side of him lies Fanny "Goodwill" Andrews (not yet Joseph's wife but his supposed sister) in profound, peaceful, naked slumber; and Fielding promptly reminds us that Adams has done what every red-blooded man in the novel has been trying to do, unsuccessfully, since Book II, chapter ix: he has climbed into bed with Fanny:

> As the cat or lap-dog of some lovely nymph, for whom ten thousand lovers anguish, lies quietly by the side of the charming maid, and, ignorant of the scene of delight on which they repose, meditates the future capture of a mouse, or surprisal of a plate of bread and butter, so Adams lay by the side of Fanny [writes Fielding], ignorant of the paradise to which he was no near.

The book has now come full circle, for not only Fanny's incomparable charms but her priceless chastity as well are treated with the utmost indifference by the one man who has succeeded, so far, in sharing her bed; nor is she in any real danger, for this man, this cat or lap dog, neither knows nor cares, nor would care if he knew, about the "paradise" beside him; he simply wants to go to sleep. We can safely say, then, that

8. In Book III, chap. xii, the normally severe Peter Pounce is also forced to grin at the sight of Adams' bedraggled figure. In the same manner, a misanthrope might grin at a mud-spattered child: the outer ridiculousness is reinforced by inward innocence in both Adams and the child, and the responsive grin or laugh is basically sympathetic.

the lust-chastity theme has been fully and ironically resolved or, if you will, stood on both its ears.

But it is daybreak now, and Joseph Andrews has come for an innocent rendezvous with Fanny. When he raps at the door, the good-natured, hospitable parson calls out, "Come in, whoever you are." Consternation follows, and for the first time in the novel the three paragons of virtue, the three touchstones, are at complete odds with one another. Adams is again burdened with undeserved guilt and can only blame the affair on witchcraft; but, once he recounts his story, Joseph explains to him that he must have taken the wrong turn on leaving Slipslop's room. Then Fielding makes a significant emendation: he has already told his readers that the naked Adams is wearing a nightcap; now he reminds them that he is also wearing the traditional knee-length nightshirt—all this in deference, perhaps, to Fanny's modesty but nevertheless a sign that things are back to normal once more and that the naked truth no longer roams through the halls of night. Fanny and Joseph forgive the parson with the indulgence one shows to an innocent child, and again the scene ends on a benevolent note.

What are we to make of night adventures which serve as a kind of parody on the whole novel; which apparently involve no real problems but in which lust and self-love appear, momentarily, in an almost friendly light; in which chastity is ignored, brave virtue confounded, and a whole comic method thrown thereby into reverse? One solution seems obvious: by sending his beloved parson from bed to bed, Fielding has put a kind of comic blessing upon the novel; he has resolved the major themes and passions through benevolent humor. Or to push on to a more inclusive theory, the comic resolution in *Joseph Andrews* depends for its warmth upon the flow of sympathy which Fielding creates between his readers and his comic figures; for its bite, upon his ridicule and deflation of those figures; and for its meaning, upon the long-range development of character and theme, as well as the local situation at Booby Hall. Apparently Fielding, like Parson Adams, did not always practice the simple theories he preached. But as Adams insists at the close of the night adventures, there is such a thing as witchcraft, and perhaps this is what Fielding practiced upon Adams and upon his readers, and with a good deal of awareness of what he was doing.

DICK TAYLOR, JR.

Joseph as Hero in *Joseph Andrews* †

Commentators have generally recognized that Fielding's Tom Jones develops maturity of character and depth of insight through his experi-

† From *Tulane Studies in English* 7 (1957): 91–109. Some author's notes have been omitted.

ences and that Booth at the end of *Amelia*, albeit a trifle suddenly, attains a deeper vision of life. But they have not bestowed on Joseph Andrews his due meed of honor for his considerable increase in dignity and stature in the progress of the novel; and consequently they have failed to assess properly his real significance in Fielding's design. Probably the burlesque of *Pamela* and the forceful presence of Parson Adams have been mainly responsible for deflecting attention from Joseph's serious role. Possibly, too, Fielding's quiet method of portraying his hero set him at a disadvantageous balance with Adams. However, Joseph was clearly intended by Fielding to occupy a significant place in the total design. He is certainly as important as Adams and well justifies his name as title of the novel.

In the early part of *Joseph Andrews* it is true that Fielding has contrived to make Joseph somewhat of a joke in the frame of the burlesque of *Pamela*. There is, however, a clearly discernible point at which Joseph manifests a decided change in appearance on the stage and begins to show a noticeable elevation in character, personality and general status in the thought and action of the novel. This turning point occurs in the scene at the inn in Book II, chapter 12, which is focused on a song that he sings in one room, while unknown to him, Fanny and Adams sit in the next and listen to the unknown singer. This scene, amusing and adroitly done within itself, is one of the best bits of light ironic writing in the novel and can stand independently as such; but Fielding uses it in addition as the basis for further irony and further fun in the plot and for important thematic development and character portrayal. At first glance it appears that the song serves merely as a musical interlude used as a means of recognition, but actually Fielding initiates threads which are woven out until the end of the novel, as he lays the basis for following scenes which parody the song in action and language. The broad context of this current of action is the burlesque of *Pamela*, particularly as the wholesome, natural, headlong affections of Joseph and Fanny which become evident after the song contrast so markedly with the calculated scheming of Pamela in her love life. The threads of plot and theme which Fielding develops out of this scene are also related to the jocular side of his treatment of Adams, for Adams figures prominently in the later scenes which parody the song and its enveloping action. Most important, however is Joseph's emergence from the episode in II, 12 no longer a male Pamela but the hero of *Joseph Andrews*, who becomes increasingly the Master of the Event. Since this scene is so important for the currents of action and theme which it initiates—and is so good in itself—it seems best here to analyze it in some detail as a basis for further discussion.

I

On their journey back down to the country, Parson Adams is separated from Joseph who must travel by coach with Slipslop because of an injury to his leg. As Adams goes along, he rescues a young lady in distress, who turns out to be Joseph's sweetheart Fanny (II, 10). Temporarily detained in a justice's court by circumstances arising from this rescue (II, 11), Adams and Fanny are soon freed and continuing on their way are driven into a handy alehouse by a sudden shower of rain. Adams immediately finds a place by the fire, orders a toast and ale and a pipe, and devotes himself to his Aeschylean meditations, while Fanny also takes a place by the fire, possibly to dream of Joseph, who she thinks is far, far away. Fielding, then, after advising readers "of an amorous hue" to skip the forthcoming paragraph, gives a long, full and lusciously detailed portrait of Fanny and her beauties, which might indeed affect readers of an amorous hue. At this point Fanny's attention is suddenly engaged by a song which begins in the next room. The lyric of this song is a smooth sliding pastoral, telling of the love of the shepherd Strephon and the nymph Chloe.

As Fanny listens perhaps she is too intent upon identifying the strangely familiar voice of the singer, or perhaps she lacks the polish of the town ladies to interpret the various puns as the song trills on to its exciting climax, or perhaps she has never been to the plays, whose gay songs so delighted the sophisticated. However, a close inspection of its lines reveals that this is a very, very naughty little piece, in the manner of Dryden's "Whilst Alexis lay pressed," from *Marriage à la Mode,* or "After the pangs of a desperate lover," from *An Evening's Love,* or many other similar plaints which gayly toy with amorous innuendos, such as the word "die,"[1] and the like. Pamela might well have noticed that something was wrong and commented primly; and Shamela could always spot a "paw word." But Fanny is intent on the singer.

The song begins innocuously enough as it movingly describes Strephon's distraction because of Chloe. But the second and third stanzas produce suspicion of what is to come by their prominently placed use of several dangerous words, which had developed quite specific double meanings in the poetry of witty ribaldry of the stage or in the drolleries, or the amorous fiction of Mrs. Manley. "Rapture," "possess," "joy," "torment," and "smart" in such a context bode ill. In the fourth stanza the absent Chloe herself is brought on the scene by a bevy of Loves and Graces, with Zephyrus speeding to greet her and lead her to Strephon:

> A thousand Loves dance in her train
>   And Graces around her all throng.
> To meet her soft Zephyrus flies,
>   And wafts all the sweets from the flowers.

The last two stanzas bring about a remarkable reversal in Strephon's frustrated situation:

> My *soul,* whilst I gaze, is on *fire:*
>   But her looks were so tender and kind

1. A common double entendre for sexual climax [*Editor*].

My hope almost reach'd my *desire*,
    And left lame Despair far behind.
Transported with madness, I flew,
    And eagerly seiz'd on my *bliss;*
Her bosom but half she withdrew,
    But half she refus'd my fond kiss.

Advances like this made me bold,
    I whisper'd her,—Love, we're alone—
The rest let immortals unfold:
    No language can tell but their own.
Ah, Chloe, *expiring*, I cried
    How long I thy *cruelty* bore!
Ah, Strephon, she blushing replied,
    You n'er was so pressing before.

The song thus concludes with a high flown version of the common innuendo, *expiring for dying*, to describe Strephon's triumph, but this conclusion has been cleverly led up to by the prominent and bountiful use of key words in the previous stanzas, "Rapture," "joy," "on fire," the apparently harmless but deceptive word "soul," "transported," and "bliss," all related to the same innuendo—Fielding has sprinkled his song liberally with these *outré* words not only for the ironic effect of the present scene but to leave them in the reader's attention in preparation for effects he intends to achieve later. Thus we must conclude that here is a very wicked and wanton song, whose lyrical narrative plays an adroitly arranged crescendo to a lamentable incident, which is a violation of all that Pamela Andrews risked her virtue to uphold, or Shamela her "vartue."

But, lo! when the identity of the hitherto anonymous singer of such a song is discovered, he is none other than Joseph Andrews, that same Pamela's brother, who so far has distinguished himself by his Pamelian conduct in his firm repulse of three pressing females. The incident of recognition thus constitutes an ironic reversal. But Fielding is to develop the irony further almost in a double reversal. As soon as Fanny has recovered from her swoon, while Adams, subsuming the roles of the Loves and the Graces and Zephyrus, capers vigorously around the room (wafting the strong whiff of pipe and ale instead of "all the sweets from the flowers"), Joseph and she enact an ecstatic amorous scene of fervent kisses and embraces, which comes near to matching that of Strephon and Chloe. Fanny, however, recovers herself and restraining "the impetuousity of her *transports*," pushes him decorously from her and refuses any further kisses or embraces for the time. In this scene Joseph has demonstrated himself to be as fiery and pressing as Strephon, and Fanny has been momentarily yielding but properly coy as Chloe had remained for a long time. Fielding has previously noted their warm affection in I, 11, but has given only the slightest hint of Joseph's fiery impetuousity. A second more definite hint of Joseph's high natural spirits occurs in the second letter to Pamela, reporting Lady Booby's second attempt, as he remarks that "I am glad she turned me out of the chamber as she did, for I had almost forgotten every word parson Adams had ever said to me" (I, 10). Both of these hints, however, Fielding has carefully submerged in the context of the burlesque of Pamela.

Coming as it does between the luscious and warming description of Fanny and the luscious and warming love scene of Joseph and Fanny, the song is adroitly and amusingly ironic in its sly reflections of their own situation, feelings, and actions. Joseph's impetuous rush upon Fanny reveals that he has more than a touch of Strephon's smarting pain and more than a little of Strephon's fiery nature. Joseph has sung his song of longing even as Strephon the thwarted shepherd, and just as Chloe suddenly appears to Strephon so does Fanny suddenly reappear into Joseph's life led, of course, by Adams. Further, the scene at the inn, song and all, sets the pattern for the amorous behavior between Joseph and Fanny in the rest of the novel; and in the numerous love scenes which ensue, to the amusement of readers and at times to the discomfiture of Adams, they reenact, up to a critical point, the drama and the emotions of the song, the critical boundary being rigorously set by the convention of matrimony. Fielding casts the love scenes very much in the manner of the song, in Joseph's Strephon-like impetuosity, and in Fanny's coy but compulsive response; and his language describing these scenes echoes the language of the song in the romantic highly pitched emotion, in the mock pastoral manner, and in the sly use of some of the dangerous words applied to their innocent situation. Their love affair follows closely, then, the pattern of the song and the mood of the song, up to the critical point. Our Strephon will not press his Chloe as far as the shepherd in the song did beyond the convention of marriage, but he is very pressing to get this convention out of his way.

In effect, the first parody of the witty song comes in the love scene which immediately follows the lovers' recognition through the song. The second parody follows shortly. With eager warmth Joseph is so pressing with Fanny that only a few hours after their re-union, he has persuaded her, under the nose of the slumbering Adams to a marriage right then and there on the spot (II, 13), and the passage describing this action echoes the song, sometimes in very specific words:

> Let it suffice then to say, that Fanny, after a thousand entreaties, at last *gave up her whole soul to Joseph*; and almost fainting in his arms, with a sigh infinitely softer and sweeter too than any Arabian breeze, she whispered to his lips, which were then close to hers, 'O, Joseph, you have won me; I will be yours forever.' Joseph having thanked her on his knees, and embraced her with an eagerness which she now almost returned, *leapt up in a rapture*, and awakened the parson, earnestly begging him that he would that instant join their hands together.

Adams, however, less tolerant than the Loves, the Graces and Zephyrus, is scandalized by such impetuosity and such disregard for the forms of the Church. He rebukes Joseph strongly, lectures him characteristically on the serious aspects of matrimony, and insists, with Fanny's complete agreement, that they must observe the ceremony of the publication of the banns. Rapture is near for our Strephon, but it must await the third bann.

Various other love scenes between Joseph and Fanny then follow, some of which Fielding coyly hints at, suggesting to the reader, from the background of the song and the previous descriptions, the full warmth generated, as in II, 15, when he comments on their passing the time while Adams is visiting Trulliber, and then in II, 16, as "they solaced themselves with amorous discourse," while Adams is arguing with the kindly host. These scenes are innocently reminiscent of "I whisper'd her,—Love we're alone—" Then when they are travelling along after leaving this hospitable inn, they must stop for rest as nightfall overtakes them (III, 2); and as they tarry, Adams sits apart lost in his meditations, so they are "alone" again:

> This was a circumstance, however, very favorable to Joseph; for Fanny, not suspicious of being overseen by Adams, gave a loose to her passion which she had never done before, and, reclining her head on his bosom, threw her arm carelessly round him, and sufered him to lay his cheek close to hers. All this infused such happiness into Joseph, that he would not have changed his turf for the finest down in the finest palace in the universe.

After they reach Somersetshire, Joseph and Fanny do not have much time together, and so the love scenes cease.

At the end of the novel the story of Joseph and Fanny just as that of Strephon and Chloe at the end of the song finally culminates in joy and rapture, as they are married with much merry making at which Adams, now a genially approving amalgam of the Loves, the Graces, and Zephyrus, whose spirits have been borne aloft by the happiness of the occasion and by an abundance of ale and pudding, gives "a loose to more facetiousness than was usual to him." The final note of the song is echoed as Fanny in the bloom of beauty is taken to bed, and Joseph rushes "with the utmost eagerness to her," and a "minute carried him to her arms." So Strephon finally wins his Chloe—and the rest let immortals unfold.

II

The scene of the song at the inn not only establishes the pattern for one line of action which parodies the song in such a way as to allow for further strokes in the enrichment of the portrayal of Adams, to develop the contrasts with Pamela, and to afford the emergence of Joseph's amorous fire and impetuosity; more importantly it also marks the point of change in the appearance of Joseph in the thought and action so that he is treated on more serious levels of meaning, and it initiates a line of action which is to carry him to a dignity and a stature and an elevation of personality far beyond the original limitations imposed by the burlesque mode. After the scene at the inn, Joseph begins to appear with a poise, dignity, shrewdness and wisdom, and a courteous independence, which show up more and more in the novel leading to the conclusion when he settles down to run his estate, happily married to Fanny but without the false notions about himself that his erstwhile sister Pamela has developed upon her rise in the social scale. Still deferential to Adams, he nevertheless comes to maintain his own views against him in the discussion of ideas and in the making of arrangements, and he is used by Fielding to comment upon Adams' foibles. Since he is not selfish, acquisitive, or hypocritical himself, but displays much of the innocence of the good-natured man, he is a good agent to comment upon Adams' unworldliness, an unworldliness which in most people would be fatal.

Fielding at times also uses Joseph to express his own views, as he could not have used Adams. In his actions Parson Adams exemplifies much of the view of life that Fielding is expounding, but he could not remain in character and be a mouthpiece. But in his later appearances Joseph is an excellent agent and is so used to some extent. Fielding's portrayal of the good-natured man was to change considerably in his later novels, so that he laid less emphasis on innocence, naiveté, or eccentricity and more on the wisdom and realism that should accompany goodness. Squire Allworthy is a wiser man than Parson Adams, and Dr. Harrison a wiser man than both.[2] In the latter part of *Joseph Andrews*, Joseph shows a measure of the realistic, practical wisdom and social balance that Fielding must have come to consider necessary before he created Allworthy and Harrison.

Joseph's new appearance is no sudden inartistic trick of the author's, for Fielding has actually laid down several quiet hints and clues along in the early chapters. But these hints are not immediately striking, and it is only by reading back and disregarding the burlesque of *Pamela* that the reader sees their full import. Further, Joseph's increase in dignity and stature always remains within the frame of the mock heroic manner and in the ironic context of the satire. He is so inextricably enmeshed in the activities of Adams and in the rollicking treatment of this great character that he is unavoidably touched or colored by the episodes, mock heroic or picaresque, as in the mock epic Battle of the Canines. Thus as Fielding raises Joseph in stature, he nevertheless still has some fun at his expense; his treatment is not so serious as to deaden the fun.

In Book I and the early chapters of Book II, Joseph, either from the situation, action, or Fielding's comments, always appears in a laughable light, which, however, is not pejorative, as is true in the case of Shamela, or Pamela in her later appearance in this novel. Whatever one thinks of Joseph as a paragon of male chastity (and I suspect that the usual explanation that his affections are already fixed on Fanny is not a

2. Allworthy is the foster parent and benefactor of Tom Jones. The reverend Dr. Harrison is friend and counselor to the hero and heroine of *Amelia* [Editor].

good one), he is not portrayed as a hypocrite like Shamela or Pamela, and his change into a young man of high physical spirits is an amusing but wholesome natural phenomenon. After all Parson Adams has six children, and Mrs. Adams openly avers that she has never had any complaints about his affection for her (IV, 8). At the first of the novel, Joey, because of the sweetness of his voice, fails as birdkeeper and kennel whipper-in, and is translated to stable boy, where he is so successful that upon becoming seventeen he is made footboy to Lady Booby and entrusted with such manly duties as standing behind her chair, carrying her prayerbook to church and singing psalms with the beautiful voice that had charmed the birds and the dogs into ruining the hunt. The description of Joseph's singing here has some function and articulation in the plot, too, as a preparation for his song later by the inn fireside, so that his beautiful singing should be no surprise, nor Fanny's recognition, since she has heard it so often before; and although jocularly treated here this gift could not be one of the graces of a gentleman.

Joseph has attracted the interest of Parson Adams in the course of his instruction by the parson, and in the early part of the novel he is so deferential to Adams as to be subservient. Later it will be one of the signs of his growth that, still deferential except for one instance of extreme provocation, he will nevertheless dare to support his own opinions against this forceful and venerable man. Fielding gives a hint of his future plans for Joseph amid the early irony and jocularity at his expense in I, 3, when Joseph gives Adams an account of his independent and self-directed reading, amusing at the time in its inclusion of the *Whole Duty of Man* (which we recall was a favorite of Shamela) but still giving a hint of Joseph's independence of mind and of his search for a wider view of things and laying the basis for his sense and balance on later occasions. Next, in London Joseph is amusingly presented as he attends so closely yet so innocently upon Lady Booby with the scandalous whispers of Ladies Tittle and Tattle hissing in the background. However, he has been getting experience in his town sojourn, which later will help him to interpret action and character, as in the case of the generous gentleman—and he has had enough sparkishness to learn the popular wittily naughty songs of the day. And then after the death of Sir Thomas Booby, Joseph appears in an even more laughable light as he resists Lady Booby's first advances and immediately writes Pamela a horrified letter, of whose tone she might well have been proud, and soon after he is nearly so rudely forced by Slipslop. Then Lady Booby returns to the game in I, 8, when Joseph in desperation—and to her shock and amazement—proclaims his "virtue," as he reports in another horrified letter to Pamela, in which he admits, however, his awareness of Lady Booby's charms; and it seems to be not his faithfulness to Fanny as much as his loyalty to Pamela and fear of Adams that has stood him in stead here.

Joseph, then, through the wrath of Lady Booby is started on his journey from London to the country, a mildly and comically allegorical journey, which is to result in his triumph. There is still left some of the phase wherein he is an object of laughter. The ironic satire still includes him in its fun, and he still carries on as a male Pamela. On the road he is beaten and left for dead, naked beside the road—later he will give a much better account of himself in fights, but here it is necessary that he lose. There follows some amusing action, the horror of the young lady at the sight of a naked man, the activity about getting him clothed, the remarks of the wit which embarrass Joseph more than they do any of the other occupants of the coach, his inhospitable reception at the Dragon (I, 12), his affirmation of male chastity and of his loyalty to his sister's ideals in a monologue which leads Parson Barnabas to think that he is out of his mind (I, 13), and finally the assault by Betty which so vigorously threatens his virtue (I, 18). The burlesque of *Pamela* is still evident in this last scene not only in the assault but in the device of lofty moral statement which accompanies it. After Joseph has successfully repulsed Betty and locked her out of his room, Fielding interpolates the remark, "How ought a man to rejoice, that his chastity is always in his own power; that if he hath sufficient strength of mind, he hath always a competent strength of body to defend himself, and cannot like a poor weak woman, be ravished against his will." This interpolation is a parody of the occasional moralistic pronouncements or sayings of Pamela about the ways of the world in Richardson's novel. After one of Squire B——'s attempts at her virtue has failed, Pamela (Letter XI) writes, "O how poor and mean must those actions be, and how little must they make the best of gentlemen look when they offer such things as are unworthy of themselves, and put it into the power of their inferiors to be greater than they." In *Shamela* Fielding parodies these sayings by putting some of Shamela's best remarks into this form. With the incident of Betty, the parody of Joseph as a male Pamela ceases, and the ridiculous tone treating his actions almost disappears. He is caught with the bill for the horse's feed, which Adams has forgotten to pay, and he has a clumsy fall from a horse, which injures his leg. Although the fall from the horse is a comic episode, this injury is mainly a plot device to keep him separated from Adams for a time and thus to motivate the surprise meeting later in the inn. One small incident in their departure from the Dragon, however, is of some significance. It is Joseph who discovers that Adams does not have his sermons with him. This incident gives the first hint of Joseph's later change of status in relation to Adams.

Joseph begins to show a markedly different appearance soon after they leave the inn where he sang the song, and this is illustrated in the next incident. At the next stop they meet an apparently generous gentleman who offers Adam a three hundred pound living, lodgings for them all in his house for a couple of days, and the use of his coach and horses for a part of their journey (II, 16). In a burst of enthusiasm for such rare Christian charity, Adams accepts these offers, but in a series of events the gentleman eases out of every promise and in addition, it turns out, leaves them a score to pay for drinks. Adams is completely deceived, but Joseph soon realizes that they are being duped; and generally throughout this episode he displays good sense, good humor, and even wit.

The gentleman suddenly recollects first, just as he is leaving for home, that he cannot lodge them because his housekeeper has locked up all of his rooms and all of the linen, but he promises them his horses the next morning. When the travelers arise early to await the horses, Joseph has a difference of opinion with Adams as to whether Fanny should ride behind himself (II, 16), or as Adams demands, behind the gentleman's servant, since he says that Joseph is not to be trusted, "being weaker than he imagined himself to be"—Adams has not forgotten Joseph's fiery haste to have the marriage ceremony performed on the spot without benefit of banns. Although Adams is firm, Joseph is equally firm with his old preceptor that Fanny should be his riding partner. The dispute, which becomes more and more fierce, is saved from catastrophic developments by the arrival of a message from the gentleman that his groom unknown to himself had put his whole stable under a course of physic, so that he could not furnish the horses. Whereupon Adams, bursting into expressions of sympathy for this good-natured man who is so badly treated by his servants, further wonders if in addition his butler had not locked up his cellar the night before and thus forced him to visit the inn. But Joseph realistically is concerned as to how they can depart from the inn without any money to pay their bill. Taking one more chance on the gentleman, he advises Adams to write him for a loan. The messenger's long delay in returning leads Joseph ironically to venture that the gentleman's steward may have locked up his purse; but Adams does not notice the irony. When the news comes that the gentleman has gone away for a month and Adams bemoans his failure to borrow the money the night before, Joseph "smiling" answers that he was very much deceived "if the gentleman would not have found some excuse to avoid lending it." Joseph then explains some of the tricks that gentlemen use to forestall suitors and callers whom they wish to avoid. Adams, horrified by such chicanery, begins against these dishonest practices a lecture which might have detained their party for an untold time if Joseph had not realistically called him back to the problem of getting out of the inn. On this occasion the innkeeper kindly helps them, and eventually they set on their way. Throughout this whole episode Joseph's new bearing is noteworthy.

In the next incident at Mr. Wilson's Joseph is inconspicuous, presumably because Fielding did not want to connect Joseph and Wilson at this time in any fashion which might tip off the surprise ending. His sleeping through Wilson's story and missing the clue of the strawberry birthmark is necessary for the plot, and as a matter of verisimilitude, he is normally weary and in need of sleep and further is lacking the incentive to stay awake since Fanny is asleep in the bedroom with Mrs. Wilson. When they get back on the road the next morning, Adams produces a tirade against the public schools for their breeding of wickedness and proclaims that Wilson's troubles all came from his having a public school education rather than the morally straightening private schooling (III, 5). Joseph, although deferential, disagrees with him by defending the public schools, cites the example of his own good master, Sir Thomas Booby, as a fine type of public school man, and, on the other hand, recalls several privately taught country gentlemen who were nevertheless "as wicked as if they had known the world from their infancy." Joseph is probably thinking of some of the prototypes of the squire in Gay's *Birth of the Squire.*[3] Adams is in forceful talking fettle; consequently, Joseph retires, but on the plane of reasonable argument and truth to society and nature, he has made an excellent case, impervious as Adams may be. That Fielding is siding with Joseph here is confirmed by the immediately following episode,[4] for he introduces in close juxtaposition the story of the merry squire, who plays nasty jokes on Adams (still nasty even if Adams maintains his dignity) and later tries to kidnap Fanny in order to seduce her, or rape her, if persuasion fails (III, 6,7,9). Fielding makes a special point in III, 7 of giving a detailed character sketch of the squire in which he explicitly describes his private education "at his own home under the care of his mother and a tutor," and he follows the character sketch with the lengthy account of the squire's irresponsible and at times evil actions against Adams and Fanny. Thus it is clear that he intends Joseph's arguments with Adams to have a serious significance in the thought of the novel, and that Joseph's intellectual stature is growing. It is also clear that Joseph is gradually taking over the guidance and direction of the expedition, for it is he who brings them to a stop for eating, and after Adams has found the gold piece which Wilson had quietly slipped into their basket of provisions, he convinces him that it was not a mistake but an intentional gift to help them and thus persuades him not to make a trip back to return it.

As they sit after their refreshment, so generously supplied by Wilson, Joseph, with an assurance not previously displayed in Adams' presence, is fittingly led to deliver a discourse on charity (III, 6). His discourse, although at times somewhat illiterately expressed (as his calling Veronese "Varnish," Carraci "Scratchi," and Hogarth "Hogarthi," and his referring to "Squire Pope"), is nevertheless intended by Fielding to be read on a serious level. With feeling and good sense, Joseph expounds Fielding's own views about charity and its manifestation in charitable acts. He touches briefly upon the expressed subject of the novel, as he exclaims "I defy the wisest man in the world to turn a good action into ridicule. I defy him to do it." But Joseph's discussion of charity as it includes also reaches beyond Affectation and the Ridiculous as they were defined in the author's preface. He defines charity, gives instances of it, criticises its lack in rich people and their misuse of their wealth in false taste and bad spirit. The theme of *charity* is a dominant one in *Joseph Andrews,* which Fielding develops throughout with considerable complexity, in numerous aspects and gradations, usually in the actions or statements, charitable or uncharitable, of the characters. Although, in accordance

3. This 1720 satiric imitation of Virgil's Fourth Eclogue depicts a life devoted to hunting, wenching, and drinking [Editor].

4. Cross, *History of Henry Fielding,* I, 42, ff. has described Fielding's life at Eton, his happiness there and its lasting effect upon himself and his views of education which are pertinent here.

with the preface, Affectation, Hypocrisy, or the Ridiculous, are important springs of action and appearance in the novel, Fielding has developed the concept of charity in its own independent entity, even if often he treat it in relation to these other traits. He has developed his theme of charity in many strands both positively, by the postillion, by Betty, by the friendly innkeeper, by Wilson, by the pedlar, and of course, by Adams, and antithetically by various of the riders in the first coach, by Mrs. Towwouse, Trulliber, Slipslop, the merry squire, and others. Thus he is making Joseph the explicit spokesman for an important theme which elsewhere he has been presenting in action and has generally been rendering rather than expounding. The seriousness and depth of Joseph's discourse are further revealed as Fielding puts into his mouth praise of people whom he himself considered examples of the noblest practice of charity. When Fanny asks whether all the great folks are wicked (we are beginning to wonder if they are not), Joseph answers:

> Some gentlemen of our cloth report charitable notions done by their lords and masters; and I have heard Squire Pope, the great poet, at my lady's table, tell stories of a man that lived at a place called Ross, and another at Bath, one Al-Al- I forget his name, but it is in the book of verses. The gentleman hath built up a house, too, which the squire likes very well; but his charity is seen farther than his house, though it stands on a hill,—, ay, and brings him more honour too. It was his charity that put him in the book, where the squire says he puts all those who deserve it. . . .

The two examples of charity are, of course, John Kyrle, the Man of Ross and Ralph Allen, whom Pope praised for their charity, respectively, in *Moral Essays*, III, 250–90, and *Epilogue to the Satires*, Dial. I, 135–36. Fielding, who had good reason to know of Allen's vast charities, later used him as a partial model for Squire Allworthy.

Then in the immediately following mock heroic battle with the pack of hunting dogs, although Adams as usual is the focus for this kind of rough high jinks, Fielding has some fun with Joseph, too, describing in epic detail the provenance, career, and appearance of his staff with which he depletes the squire's kennel so terribly and narrating with ironic color his heroic actions in the fray. Even so, in the mock heroic frame Joseph acquits himself solidly and effectively without losing stature, and the squire retreats because of his performance. At the squire's dinner Joseph retires from the limelight for Adams, and we only see him upon their departure as he brandishes his illustrious staff menacingly at the servants. Next in the abduction of Fanny by the captain and his helpers, there is a *bona fide* fight in which he performs admirably, albeit with a touch of picaresque slapstick in some of the weapons he uses, and he is quelled only by a lucky blow which renders him unconscious, so that the captain escapes with Fanny.

After he has regained his consciousness in the next scene (III, 11), as

he talks with Adams, he reveals a natural turmoil and anxiety about
Fanny and despair at losing her, possibly forever, but Fielding does not
joke with his disconsolation or make it ridiculous, except that in addition
to the loss of his beloved he must listen to a long lecture by Adams on
the use of reason to learn patience and submission in these circumstances. He is not comforted by Adams' dilatation upon the beauties and
virtues of the girl whom he has lost or upon the dangers to which she is
now exposed, but he shows up well during the scene, endeavoring out
of deference to Adams to overcome his despair. This scene looks forward
to the later episode during which he is listening to another lecture on,
among other things, submission to adversity, when the news is brought
of the drowning of Adam's youngest child. A comparison of these two
scenes shows Joseph's growth during the interim.

In the meantime Fanny is rescued and the captain apprehended, and
they are brought to the inn, where Joseph exhibits proper manhood by
beating up the captain. When all three resume their journey to Somersetshire, it is noteworthy that Joseph now has Fanny as his riding partner
without any fuss, while Adams quietly gets into the coach with Pounce.

III

Down in the country, Joseph shows further poise, balance, dignity,
and good sense, which gain force in his now higher social status. Here
he meets his severest pressures from experience, primarily in the most
serious obstacles encountered yet to his marriage with Fanny and in the
possible temptation in his new status to break with old acquaintances
and submit to the Booby's plans for his social advancement. His behavior in all of these circumstances is admirable. In Book IV Fielding keeps
the frame of the mock heroic and the ironic satire, still introduces scenes
of picaresque hurly-burly, and returns to the burlesque of *Pamela* with
some rare touches at the expense of Pamela and the Squire, but he
almost entirely discards these techniques as regards Joseph and Fanny,
except for the episode with Didapper's servant, and possibly Joseph's
blow at Didapper in Adams' house. Nor is Joseph so enmeshed in Adams'
activities as before; consequently, the hurly-burly does not affect him
much. Joseph and Fanny figure only slightly in the nocturnal rumpus
involving Didapper, Slipslop and Adams, except that after Adams is found
in Fanny's bed Joseph behaves toward him with a restraint and understanding which reflect his own balance and good sense. However, Fielding is not over-serious with Joseph in Book IV, occasionally presenting
him in an amusing light to keep the fun going, but without using him
to burlesque Richardson.

First, through Lady Booby's scheming, which Lawyer Scout carries
to greater lengths than she had intended, Joseph and Fanny are both
arrested, brought before the justice and sentenced to Bridewell, with
particularly dire prospects for Fanny as well as the possibility of separation for them both. Beyond the justice's attraction toward Fanny, Field-

ing makes no attempt to make fun of Joseph and Fanny, as he had done in previous scenes even when they were in trouble. The happy arrival of Squire Booby and Pamela in Somersetshire saves them, for the squire gets them released under his guardianship. Booby then brings his own clothes to dress Joseph, and although Joseph (unlike Pamela) is careful to select "the plainest dress he could find," he nevertheless "looked so genteel, that no person would have doubted its being adapted to his quality as his shape." Joseph has now become a gentleman outwardly as well as inwardly, and, without the snobbery of Pamela, distinguishes himself by the bearing and dignity that a gentleman should have (he lapses from this dignity notably when he swats Didapper for making advances to Fanny!). He is so prepossessing in his new fashion that Lady Booby bursts into new flames so fierce that now she even considers him as a matrimonial possibility.

Next, in a significant interview, Mr. Booby and Pamela bring heavy pressure upon Joseph to give up Fanny for a match more suitable to his new station. But he refuses their demands, avowing his love, respect, and loyalty for Fanny and his determination to have her only. In this interview his manners are dignified and courteous; although firm, he is not clumsy or boorish in his refusal. This scene is a counterpart of the interview which Adams has held with Lady Booby about the banns, wherein with dignity and courtesy he refuses to deny the banns whatever his earthly jeopardy. When Joseph leaves the interview with the Boobys, he comes by accident upon Fanny in the evil grip of Didapper's servant, whom he routs after a fierce battle, in which he acquits himself nobly even if a few teeth are shaken.

The circumstances of the interview with the squire and Pamela and the ensuing perilous escape of Fanny give Joseph a deep concern about her, on the one hand from a fear of the interference of the Boobys and on the other a fear of future incidents like the attempt of Didapper's servant. His prophetic fears are justified soon after, too, by Didapper himself who undertakes a nocturnal excursion after Fanny, which, however, leads him instead into Slipslop's bed and concludes with the surprising discovery of Parson Adams in Fanny's bed the next morning. In his illuminating analysis of this episode, Professor McKillop, *Early Masters*, p. 114, has said that "Joseph and Fanny are as usual innocently passive."[5] Professor McKillop's comment is in the main true as regards Fanny but it seems to me that Fielding gives Joseph increased force of personality and increased stature. He holds Joseph from participating in the hurly-burly to keep him from being ridiculous, because he wants to maintain Joseph's dignity—Joseph is definitely out of the frame of either the Pamelian burlesque or picaresque high jinks. When Joseph does come into the episode the next morning in Fanny's room where Adams is discovered slumbering peacefully, he is far from innocently passive but is quite positive and dominating. He first strongly interrogates Adams how he came into Fanny's room, then 'in a rage" he sharply questions Fanny "hath he offered any rudeness to you." Back in II, 13, Fanny was overwhelmed by Adams and shifted ground from her support of Joseph's desire for immediate matrimony to her agreement with Adams that this was a most improper request, and Joseph at this point was somewhat humbled by Adams and could not push her farther. But now when she sees Joseph holding a strong line toward Adams, she holds a mighty prim one herself. However, Joseph's old respect for Adams and his own balance and good sense which he has been displaying increasingly prevent him from any headlong conclusions, so that he allows Adams to give his own version of what has happened. But it is Joseph who comprehends what has actually happened and how Adams made his mistake, and he explains to Adams that "It was plain that he had mistaken, by turning to the right instead of the left." Adams, for once, agrees immediately without arguing, and the scene is over. When Joseph leads him away to his room, this action symbolizes Joseph's ascendency. Throughout this incident Joseph has held the upper hand, and Adams is on the down side and backing up.

After this incident, motivated now not just by his strong physical passion for Fanny but also by his genuine concern for her safety, Joseph asks Adams if he might obtain a license and have the marriage performed at once. Adams, of course, misses the point and, now recovered from his psychological dip of the early morning, begins a strong and lengthy lecture on the evils of carnality in marriage and of the necessity for curbing one's passions and for learning patience and submission to the divine will. At the height of his exhortations, the news that his youngest child has been drowned throws him into a tantrum of grief, from which his own teachings now warmly expounded by Joseph cannot relieve him. Upon the discovery that the child is alive, Adams immediately resumes, as if without interruption, his lecture to Joseph, whose patience is now exhausted so that he argues stoutly with Adams, protesting the propriety of his devotion to Fanny and of love between man and wife. Adams is setting off on another lecture on the evils of over-fondness for a wife, but Mrs. Adams comes to Joseph's aid by roundly berating her husband for preaching such doctrine and threatening to burn any such sermon that he has in the house. She strongly proclaims that Adams has loved her satisfactorily. This argument is going very much Joseph's way against Adams, but it is interrupted by a visit from Lady Booby.

The next unfortunate turn for Joseph comes when it appears that he and Fanny are brother and sister. This blow he bears with stoic dignity, although with the keenest pain, and again Fielding narrates this part straight without joking at him. But, as we know, all ends happily, and we get our last glance of him living in bliss with Fanny and refusing to publish any account of his new high life.

Thus it is clear that Fielding, however much fun he has at Joseph's expense, particularly in the early stages of the Pamelian burlesque, is treating him in a serious manner and with serious aims. He gives Joseph his share of the serious burden of the novel as well as the jocular, and in some instances Joseph is his spokesman as well as a counterbalance to Parson Adams, such as was lacking in *Don Quixote* for the Don. Whatever his original plan for Joseph was, in the actual fabric of the novel he describes in Joseph a noticeable and sympathetic change and development of character into maturity. From Joey, the beautiful singer, and from Joseph the footman who is a paragon of male chastity, Fielding has brought Joseph Andrews a long way. Even against the engrossing figure of Adams, he has given Joseph a personality of his own, a stature and force and meaning in the novel, which contribute to its thought and richness of characterization.

MARTIN C. BATTESTIN

[Thematic Meaning and Structure] †

*   *   *

The characters and plot of *Joseph Andrews* mutually function to illustrate the dominant thematic motifs of the novel, namely, the exposure of vanity and hypocrisy in society, and the recommendation of their antithetical virtues—charity, chastity, and the classical ideal of life. The journey in *Joseph Andrews* is not a mere picaresque rambling, a device solely for the introduction of new adventures such as we find in the *Roman comique*, *Gil Blas*, or *Don Quixote*. The wayfaring of Fielding's heroes is purposeful, a moral pilgrimage from the vanity and corruption of the Great City to the *relative* naturalness and simplicity of the country.[1] In this respect Fielding, despite the hilarity of his comedy and his mock heroics, reminds us more of Bunyan or Fénelon than of Scarron, Le Sage, or Cervantes.

The two heroes of *Joseph Andrews*, furthermore, are more than merely a prudish young footman and a naïve parson. They embody the essential virtues of the good man—chastity and good nature. In accord with the preference for Christian heroes found both in the tradition of the biblical epic and in the homilies (especially Barrow's[2] "Of Being Imitators of Christ"), the careers of Joseph Andrews and Abraham Adams comprise brilliantly comic analogues to those of their Scriptural namesakes, likewise patterns, according to the divines, of the good man's basic virtues. Joseph chastely resists the charms of his mistress and is at last reunited with the father from whom he had been kidnapped as a child. Brandish-

† From *The Moral Basis of Fielding's Art: A Study of Joseph Andrews* (Middletown: Wesleyan, 1959) 88–95, 98–99, 101–18. Some author's notes are omitted.

1. In his excellent introduction to the Rinehart edition (New York, 1952), Maynard Mack has noticed that "the two poles of value in *Joseph Andrews* (as later in *Tom Jones*) are the country-

world and the city, neither perfect, but the former superior to the latter because more honest" (p. xii).

2. Isaac Barrow (1630–77), mathematician and latitudinarian divine whose sermons Battestin claims influenced Fielding's conception of the novel [*Editor*].

ing his crabstick like a pilgrim's staff, Adams, the good patriarch and priest, travels homeward through strange and idolatrous countries, and is "tempted" by the near drowning of his son. The use of biblical analogues here, like the adaptation of the *Aeneid* in *Amelia*, is surprisingly subtle, contributing to the mock-heroic character of the novel while at the same time reminding readers of the function of Joseph and Adams as exemplars. Finally, Adams as the true Christian minister has a more specific role in Fielding's efforts to correct a growing popular contempt of the clergy.

Again, I do not mean to suggest by these remarks and those that follow that Fielding was writing, not a great comic novel after all, but rather a book of Christian apologetics that now and then stoops to laughter. Fielding's good humor fills every page of *Joseph Andrews*, and we would be cheerless souls indeed who could not respond to it. But laughter and morality, as Fielding used to insist, are not incompatible. In *The Covent-Garden Journal*, No. 18 (March 3, 1752), he in fact spoke out against those who reject this proposition, who deny that wit and humor can be meant in earnest. His own practice is a case in point. As satirist, Fielding wrote both with a respect for his craft and with a sense of responsibility for the manners and morals of his age.

As we have already remarked, the theme of *Joseph Andrews* is implicit in its structure, the symbolic pilgrimage of its good men from the Great City to Parson Adams' country parish. For its titular hero the movement of the novel is, in effect, a quest to regain a rural paradise lost after the arrival in London. * * *

* * *

In *Joseph Andrews* this conventional symbolic polarity of city versus country most evidently informs the Wilson episode, which comprises the philosophical core of the novel, but it functions as well in the process of Joseph Andrews' education. Fortified by Adams' "many Admonitions concerning the Regulation of his future Conduct, and his Perseverance in Innocence and Industry" (I, 3), Joseph could withstand the solicitations of his Mrs. Potiphar and preserve his chastity even in the hostile environment of Mayfair. But while "his Morals remained entirely uncorrupted" (I, 4), the innocence and simplicity of his manners were at once tainted much to the delight of Lady Booby, by exposure to the vanities of London: "She plainly saw the Effects which the Town-Air hath on the soberest Constitutions." Encouraged by "his party-coloured Brethren, who endeavoured to make him despise his former Course of Life," Joseph affected the latest fashions, led the opinion of the footmen at the opera and their rioting at the playhouses, and—clearest sign of the danger of a more serious moral aberration—seldom attended church, where "he behaved with less seeming Devotion than formerly." Assisted, however, by Adams' "good Advice and good Example" (I, 10), Joseph resists temptation and recognizes the thorough degeneracy of "the great City," which the good parson, following his namesake, later compares to Sodom,[3] and where the highest precept of morality goes unobserved. "London is a bad Place," Joseph writes to Pamela, "and there is so little good Fellowship, that next-door Neighbours don't know one another" (I, 6). The flight from London, its affectation and fornication, toward reunion in the country with Adams[4] and Fanny thus acquires, especially after the establishment of the classical ideal in the Wilson episode (III, 4), broadly allegorical connotations. To use the language of the homilies, it is a moral pilgrimage through a world of vanity and vexation to a better country.

The major thematic motif of *Joseph Andrews*, the doctrine of charity, principally informs Part II of the novel (Book I, chapter 11, through Book III), containing the adventures on the road and dominated, appropriately enough, by the figure of the good patriarch and priest, Abraham Adams. The theme of Christian charity is sounded at the start of Joseph's journey by the dramatic recasting of the Good Samaritan parable. Though the episode (I, 12) is often adduced as an example of Fielding's hearty humanitarianism, its specific thematic implications have not been explored. The parable of the Good Samaritan (Luke X: 25–37)—prompted by the lawyer's questions, "What shall I do to inherit eternal life?" and "Who is my neighbour?"—was frequently cited by such divines as Benjamin Hoadly as inculcating "the great Duty of universal Charity, and a most comprehensive Compassion."[5] This also is the Pelagian message of *Joseph Andrews*, which asserts that salvation is the reward of an active, universal benevolence.[6] The account of Joseph's falling among the thieves in his passage from London is meant, quite deliberately, to recall both the parable and its Christian message. At the outset of his pilgrimage Fielding's hero is literally thrown naked upon the world. Robbed, beaten, stripped, and left for dead by the roadside, Joseph is grudgingly rescued by the self-interested passengers of the stage and given lodgings at the Dragon Inn. His only real comfort, however, comes from the Samaritan offices of two social outcasts, a postilion "since transported for robbing a Henroost" and a chambermaid, who clothe his nakedness in a traditional gesture of charity.[7] The dramatic enactment of this parable of Christian benevolence is a perfect introduction to the dominant ethical theme of the novel.

*   *   *

3. See Adams letter to *The True Patriot*, No. 7 (December 17, 1745).

4. Joseph reveals to Pamela that, the moment he is discharged by Lady Booby, he "shall return to my old Master's Country-Seat, if it be only to see Parson Adams, who is the best Man in the World" (I, 6).

5. Sermon XVI, "The Good Samaritan," *Twenty Sermons*, p. 323.

6. Following the doctrine of Pelagius (ca. 360–ca. 420), who denied man's innate depravity (original sin) and affirmed his free will to choose good or evil, diminishing the role of God's grace in salvation [*Editor*].

7. It is notable how often Fielding's Samaritans

may be found among the lower classes of society. In *Joseph Andrews*, besides the postilion and Betty, we may recall the fellow servant who clothed Joseph at the start of his journey (I, 10) and the pedlar who gave his last penny to enable Adams to discharge his account with the alehouse hostess (II, 15) and who later rescued the parson's son from drowning (IV, 8). One explanation may well be disclosed in Booth's remark to Amelia: "Compassion, if thoroughly examined, will, I believe, appear to be the fellow-feeling only of men of the same rank and degree of life for one another, on account of the evils to which they themselves are liable" (*Amelia*, X, 9).

From Adams' frequent discussions of charity there emerges a definition of the concept that corresponds precisely to that of the liberal divines examined earlier. True charity, which merits salvation, is not a matter of mere knowledge or profession or inclination, nor is it that self-centered, mercenary generosity cynically described by Hobbes and Mandeville.[8] Rather, it is rooted in a good-natured, disinterested compassion, actively relieving the distresses and promoting the welfare of mankind. Fielding's satire of the Hobbesian man, whose altruism is constrained and selfishly motivated, is clearly implied in the "Good Samaritan" episode. By persuading the other passengers of the stage that Joseph must be rescued lest they be held legally responsible for his death, the lawyer—a "mean selfish Creature . . . who made Self the Centre of the whole Creation, would give himself no Pain, incur no Danger, advance no Money, to assist or preserve his Fellow-Creatures" (III, 1)—perfectly exemplifies the moral worthlessness of a merely politic philanthropy. Similarly inadmissible is the self-interested charity of Mrs. Tow-wouse, who extends hospitality to Joseph only when she believes he can afford it (I, 15), or of Mrs. Slipslop, who discharges Joseph's debt so that he will be a more accessible target for her lust (II, 3). This is that Mandevillean charity that Fielding later explicitly condemns in *The Covent-Garden Journal*, No. 21 (March 14, 1752), and which he here traces to Vanity (or self-love): "O Vanity! . . . Sometimes thou dost wear the Face of pity, sometimes of Generosity" (I, 15). "Now true Charity," as Adams remarks in a letter to *The True Patriot*, No. 7 (December 17, 1745), "is of another kind, it has no self-interested Motives, pursues no immediate Return nor worldly Good, well knowing that it is laying up a much surer and much greater Reward for itself."[9]

* * *

The distinctively Christian character of this virtue, furthermore, is indicated by the obligation to extend its energies even to the forgiveness of injuries. "Forgive the acts of your enemies hath been thought the highest maxim of morality," Fielding wrote in *An Essay on the Knowledge of the Characters of Men*, and he asserted in *The Champion* (March 27, 1740) that this exalted Christian precept surpassed the instinctive altruism of simple good nature. Despite his integrity and goodness, Joseph Andrews, under the incompetent guidance of parson Barnabas, is unable to attain that pitch of charity. Advised by Barnabas to forgive the thieves who had robbed and beaten him, Joseph answered:

> 'He feared that was more than he could do; for nothing would give him more Pleasure than to hear they were taken.'—"That," cries Barnabas, "is for the sake of Justice."—"Yes," said Joseph, "but if I was to meet them again, I am afraid I should attack them, and kill them too, if I could."—"Doubtless," answered

8. See above, p. 66, n. 4, and p. 166, n. 3 9. See no. 3, p. 269 [*Editor*]. [*Editor*].

Barnabas, "it is lawful to kill a Thief; but can you say you forgive them as a Christian ought?" Joseph desired to know what that forgiveness was. "That is," answered Barnabas, "to forgive them as—as—it is to forgive them as—in short, it is to forgive them as a Christian." Joseph replied, 'He forgave them as much as he could.'—"Well, well," said Barnabas, "that will do." (I, 13)

Unlike Barnabas, Adams, the authentic clergyman, insists upon the performance of this Christian obligation. Dueling and imprisonment for debt were for Adams, as well as for Fielding, egregious violations of this duty. The good parson is quick to censure the conduct of the elderly gentleman who, "out of pure Charity," offered to arrange a duel between Mr. Wilson and a captain of the guards (III, 3), and he speaks out vehemently against the tailor who had Wilson committed to prison for being unable to discharge his account:

"He may expect Mercy," cries Adams, starting from his Chair, "where he will find none! How can such a Wretch repeat the Lord's Prayer; where the Word, which is translated, I know not for what reason, 'Trespasses,' is in the Original, 'Debts'? And as surely as do not forgive others their Debts, when they are unable to pay them, so surely shall we ourselves be unforgiven when we are in no Condition of paying." (III, 3)

*   *   *

But the man of charity is truly honorable; he is heroic for virtue's sake. And this is so even if in his ardent pursuit of the good his simplicity sometimes makes us smile. An important limitation in Fielding's theory of the Ridiculous is that it is an account of *satiric* laughter only; as Arthur Murphy long ago pointed out, it does not explain the pure, warmhearted *comedy* of Parson Adams.[1] We must be careful to distinguish between the simply comic aspects of Fielding's good men and the Ridiculous, which is the target for exposure and correction. "I defy the wisest Man in the World," says Joseph Andrews, "to turn a true good Action into Ridicule" (III, 6). Adams' innocence or Joseph's militant chastity may excite laughter, but never the moral castigation and contempt implicit in Fielding's definition of the Ridiculous,[2] which consists principally in the deviation from "the most golden of all Rules, no less than that *of*

1. *The Gray's-Inn Journal*, No. 96 (August 17, 1754).

2. Only if we credit Hobbes' narrow notion that all laughter is an expression of contempt can we mistake Adams for the object of his author's derision. It is instructive to keep in mind George Meredith's observation: "You may estimate your capacity for comic perception by being able to detect the ridicule of them you love without loving them less." Meredith continues by distinguishing between the modes of Satire, Irony, and Humor, the last of which he describes as follows: "If you laugh all round [the ridiculous person], tumble him, roll him about, deal him a smack, and drop a tear on him, own his likeness to you, and yours to your neighbor, spare him as little as you shun, pity him as much as you expose, it is a spirit of Humor that is moving you." "Parson Adams," he declares, "is a creation of humor." ("An Essay on Comedy," in *Comedy*, intro. Wylie Sypher [New York: Doubleday Anchor Books, 1956], pp. 42–43.)

doing to all Men as you would they should do unto you"—the deviation, in other words, from the rules of charity and good breeding.[3] A lack of charity, indeed, is the criterion of the Ridiculous. It is remarkable how often Fielding's satiric method is to oppose, in a given situation, the selfish and social passions and to direct our critical laughter against those whose avarice or lust or ambition or vanity subdues the requirements of compassion. Although expressed more subtly, or not openly expressed at all, the sentiments of the satirized in Fielding's novels may be finally reduced to Mrs. Tow-wouse's exclamation—"Common charity, a f—t!" (I, 12). In *Joseph Andrews*, Fielding's Christian heroes, patterns of the comprehensive virtues of chastity and charity, constitute, like the *vir bonus* of classical satire, a salutary alternative to this controlling satiric motif.

Behind the conception of Parson Adams in his capacity as exemplar— his origin in fiction must be traced to Don Quixote—lies the whole homiletic tradition of the good man, whose biblical prototype, it will be recalled, was Abraham—father of the faithful, whose faith was proved (according to St. James) by good works; a pilgrim "adhering stedfastly to the *True Religion*, in the *midst* of idolatrous and corrupt Nations."[4] Adams' name, character, and vocation, for example, combine Samuel Clarke's two examples of the good man, the patriarch Abraham and the true clergyman. And, with due acknowledgment of the bathetic adaptation of the epic in *Joseph Andrews*, Fielding's Christian hero as militant champion of truth and innocence ingeniously conforms to contemporary theories of the biblical epic and, in particular, to Isaac Barrow's preference for the "lives and examples of holy men" over the imaginary exploits of pagan heroes.

After his charity and goodness of heart, perhaps the most meaningful aspect of Adams' character as exemplar is his embodiment of Fielding's ideal of the true clergyman. As we shall see, it was a persistent aim of Fielding's writings both to rectify a widespread contempt of the clergy and to reform by ridicule the flagrant abuses within the Church that were the causes of that contempt. The "Apology for the Clergy," appearing in four numbers of *The Champions* (March 29, April 5, 12, and 19, 1740),[5] is an important indication that the representation of Adams in contrast to Barnabas, Trulliber, and the other ignorant, pleasure-loving, hypocritical parsons of *Joseph Andrews* was prompted by precisely these reforming motives.

*   *   *

The opening paragraphs of *Joseph Andrews*, we will recall, establish the importance to society of the examples of good men, and the novel itself, by the dramatic expansion of a suggestion in Isaac Barrow's "Of Being Imitators of Christ," presents as heroes Abraham, father of the

---

3. *The Covent-Garden Journal*, No. 55 (July 18, 1752); Jensen ed., II, 63.
4. Samuel Clarke, Sermon IV, "The Character

of a Good Man," *Sermons*, III, 86.
5. Selections from the *Apology* are reprinted above, pp. 312–21 [*Editor*].

faithful, and Joseph, pattern of virtue. In confirmation of the ideal conception of the clergyman in *The Champion*, furthermore, Fielding's Preface explains the choice of Adams' profession: "No other office could have given him so many Opportunities of displaying his worthy Inclinations." The true pastor, whose function is ultimately social as well as religious, was pre-eminently in a position to shape and amend public morality. In describing a good clergyman and his family in *The Champion* (February 26, 1739/40), Fielding added that "the whole parish is by their example the family of love," and in *Amelia* (III, 12) Dr. Harrison's constant supervision and example have a similar effect on his parish. In *Joseph Andrews* the beneficial influence that Adams' good counsel and practice have exerted upon his cure further underscores the social function of the clergy. In contrast to the ill example of Trulliber, whose parishioners "all lived in the utmost Fear and Apprehension of him" and imitated his uncharitableness (II, 15), Adams' benevolence and careful attention to the spiritual needs of his community produce fruits of charity (II, 15) and discipline rooted in love: "Indeed his Word was little less than a Law in his Parish; for as he had shown his Parishioners, by a uniform Behaviour of thirty-five Years' duration, that he had their Good entirely at heart, so they consulted him on every Occasion, and very seldom acted contrary to his Opinion" (I, 11). Later, Fielding contrasts the joy inspired in Adams' parishioners by the return of Lady Booby and the parson:

> How much more forcibly did the Affection which they bore Parson Adams operate upon all who beheld his Return? They flocked about him like dutiful Children round an indulgent Parent, and vyed with each other in Demonstrations of Duty and Love. The Parson on his side shook every one by the Hand, inquiring heartily after the Healths of all that were absent, of their Children and Relations; and exprest a Satisfaction in his Face which nothing but Benevolence made happy by its Objects could infuse. (IV, 1)

In order to achieve this ultimate objective of social order, Fielding felt, the Christian minister must have a proper sense of the qualifications and obligations of his calling. "What fine things," exclaimed Joseph in gratitude to Adams for enabling him to triumph over temptation, "are good Advice and good Examples!" (I, 10). Heavily burdened with responsibility under the egregious pluralistic system—as curate "with a handsome Income of twenty-three Pounds a-Year" (I, 3), he must preach at four churches (II, 8)—Adams, with his author, shares Whitefield's devotion to the example of Primitive Christianity. In reproof of Barnabas he vigorously opposes the corruption of the superior clergy:

> "Sir," answered Adams, "if Mr. Whitefield had carried his Doctrine no farther than you mention, I should have remained, as I once was, his Well-Wisher. I am, myself, as great an

Enemy to the Luxury and Splendour of the Clergy as he can
be. I do not, more than he, by the flourishing Estate of the
Church, understand the Palaces, Equipages, Dress, Furniture, rich Dainties, and vast Fortunes, of her Ministers. Surely
those things, which savour so strongly of this World, become
not the Servants of one who professed his Kingdom was not of
it." (I, 17)[6]

In his subsequent dispute with the pragmatical alehouse-keeper, Adams—
something of an anomaly in an age of widespread clerical ignorance,
indolence, and luxury—proudly discloses his exalted conception of his
office:

"There is something more necessary than Life itself, which is
provided by Learning; I mean the Learning of the Clergy. Who
clothes you with Piety, Meekness, Humility, Charity, Patience,
and all the other Christian Virtues? Who feeds your Souls
with the Milk of brotherly Love, and diets them with all the
dainty Food of Holiness, which at once cleanses them of all
impure carnal Affections, and fattens them with the truly rich
Spirit of Grace[?]" (II, 17)

Spoken in the interest of the moral welfare of "his Children"—"He
looked on all those whom God had entrusted to his Cure to stand to
him in that Relation" (II, 16)—Adams' frequent exhortations to charity,
patience, justice, truthfulness, and temperance, reinforced by the general conformity of his life, establish him indeed as a "valuable Pattern"
of the Christian hero, wayfaring in a land of vanity and vexation. As a
man and not a stiff and lifeless paragon like Dr. Harrison, his successor
in *Amelia*, Adams has his weaknesses—such as his pride in his sermons
(III, 3) and in his ability as a schoolmaster (III, 5)—but even these are
the product of his idealism and dedication to the public welfare. And
though the impractical side of his Christian Stoicism is amusingly revealed
in the episode of his son's "drowning" (IV, 8), Adams' inability to follow
his own advice on this occasion only sharpens our awareness of his compassionate nature. In a situation intentionally analogous to Abraham's
resigned relinquishment of his son Isaac, Adams' paternal tenderness in
this instance prevents his imitating the admired example of his namesake.[7]

In all other matters, however, where theory does not conflict with the

6. In *The Champion* (April 5, 1740), Fielding
similarly insisted on "poverty" as the final qualification of the true clergyman, and, by reference to
the Trapp-Whitefield controversy, indicated that
his sympathies—in this respect at least—were with
the Methodist: "Without being righteous over-
much, we may, I think, conclude, that if the
clergy are not to abandon all they have to their
ministry, neither are they to get immense estates
by it; and I would recommend it to the consideration of those who do, whether they do not make a
trade of divinity?" [Reprinted above, p. 318,

Editor.]
7. Fielding clearly intended this well-known incident to recall Genesis XXII: 1–18, the account of
the sacrifice of Isaac. Adams advises Joseph that
"we must submit in all things to the Will of
Providence, and not set our Affections so much
on anything here as not to be able to quit it
without Reluctance." Then, as preparation for the
analogy shortly to follow, he remarks: "Had Abraham so loved his Son Isaac as to refuse the Sacrifice required, is there any of us who would not
condemn him?" (IV, 8).

generous impulses of his heart, Adams practices what he preaches. He is charitable (I, 15), forgiving (III, 7), hospitable (IV, 1), chaste (I, 10), truthful (II, 3), just in rewarding merit (II, 11), and courageous in defense of the weak and oppressed (II, 5, 9, and III, 9). As a true disciple of Christ, "who made no distinction, unless, peradventure, by preferring the Poor to the Rich" (III, 2), he benefits the penniless and distressed by his constant counsel and attendance. Although he concurs with Hoadly's attempts to purge the Church of its misconceptions concerning the nature and purpose of ritual,[8] he is diligent in observing "the Forms of the Church" in the matter of marriage (II, 13); in this respect, Fielding's contemporaries would have contrasted him with the notorious parsons of the Fleet[9] who, before the Marriage Act of 1753, made a profitable business of illegal marriages. He is no time-serving clergyman, but maintains his integrity despite intimidation from his superiors (II, 8, and IV, 2).[1] And remembering, perhaps, Chillingworth's celebrated declaration—"The Bible, I say, the Bible only, is the religion of the Protestants"[2]—he is learned in the Scriptures to the point of emending the King James translation (III, 3, 8). Of nearly equal significance to his character as a clergyman, moreover, is his function as an educator: "He thought a Schoolmaster the greatest Character in the World" (III, 5). For, as we have already noticed, Fielding believed that much of the Ridiculous in society was owing to the prevalence of inadequate standards of education, promoting immorality by the indulgence of vanity and the encouragement of hypocrisy.

Joseph Andrews, and especially the character of Adams, is the first full dramatization of the concept of good nature that Fielding had enunciated in some detail in *The Champion* (March 27, 1740). There are moments in the novel when Fielding, like the school of sensibility, emphasizes the pleasurable transports of tenderness, pure and simple— as when, after her abduction, Fanny and Joseph are reunited: "O Reader! conceive if thou canst the Joy which fired the Breasts of these Lovers on this Meeting; and if thy own Heart doth not sympathetically assist thee in this Conception, I pity thee sincerely from my own; for let the hard-hearted Villain know this, that there is a Pleasure in a tender Sensation beyond any which he is capable of tasting" (III, 12); or when, upon their first meeting, Adams is shown "dancing about the Room in a Rapture of Joy . . . for the Goodness of his Heart enjoyed the Blessings which were exulting in the Breasts of both the other two, together with his own" (II, 12). Indeed, as Fielding later observes with reference to Captain Booth, tenderness and goodness are identical[3] Joseph Andrews' greater

---

8. See above, p. 65, n. 3 [*Editor*].
9. A London prison. Clergy imprisoned for debt there performed clandestine marriages without licenses or banns [*Editor*].
1. In a note Battestin also cites Adams's rebuke of Mr. Booby and Pamela during the marriage ceremony and the narrator's comments on it (see above, p. 268) [*Editor*].
2. William Chillingworth (1602–44), anti-catholic clergyman who maintained the sole authority

of the scriptures and the freedom of the individual conscience in interpreting them [*Editor*].
3. Booth "had a tenderness of heart which is rarely found among men; for which I know no other reason than that true goodness is rarely found among them; for I am firmly persuaded that the latter never possessed any human mind in any degree without being attended by as large a portion of the former" (*Amelia*, IX, 4).

concern on his "deathbed" for Fanny's grief than for his own danger (I,
13), or Fanny's compassion for the hare wantonly torn by the squire's
dogs (III, 6), or Adams' openhearted gratitude to the pedlar who rescued
his son (IV, 8), are random instances of this strain of sentimentalism in
the novel. Fielding's primary criterion for true good nature, however, is
its more palpable manifestation in an active social benevolence—that
"generous Disposition to relieve the distressed" translated into deeds.
Good nature in this sense is truly "that amiable quality, which, like the
sun, gilds over all our virtues."[4] The possession of this quality by one of
Fielding's characters is an infallible indication of his author's sympathy.
Like Tom Jones, for example, Betty the chambermaid's warm animal
spirits render her chastity tenuous at best, but her "Good nature, Generosity, and Compassion" more than atone for her indiscretions; on the
other hand, Mrs. Tow-wouse's self-interested insensibility to human misery
deserves the castigation of Fielding's irony, "though she was as true to
her Husband as the Dial to the Sun" (I, 18).

Of all Fielding's heroes, Parson Adams is the fullest personification of
good nature. It is Adams' embodiment of the essential characteristics of
this concept that permits Fielding to declare in his Preface—despite his
hero's apparent likeness to Don Quixote[5]—that "the Character of Adams
. . . is not to be found in any Book now extant." The theory of good
nature formulated in *The Champion* provided an ethical, rather than
literary, basis for Adams' distinctive traits: his compassion, charity, and,
above all, his simplicity. Even his gravity of countenance (I, 14) may be
traced to the empathic disposition of the good-natured man.[6] Instances
of the "Goodness of his Heart" and "his worthy Inclinations" (Preface)
are too frequent and obvious to require discussion here. Along with his
moral idealism learned from the classics and primitive Christianity,
however, the dominant feature of Adams' good nature, his simplicity, is
consciously manipulated by Fielding to serve the ethical purpose of his
satire. Adams, Fielding writes, was

> . . . as entirely ignorant of the ways of this World as an Infant
> just entered into it could possibly be. As he had never any
> Intention to deceive, so he never suspected such a Design in

4. *The Champion* (March 27, 1740). [Reprinted
above, p. 311, *Editor.*]
5. It was only natural that Fielding should fashion
Parson Adams, the incarnation of good nature,
after the model of Don Quixote. As early as *The
Coffee-House Politician* (1730), Fielding tended to
identify good nature and quixotism. Consider, for
instance, Constant's soliloquy:

> I begin to be of that philosopher's opin-
> ion, who said, that whoever will entirely
> consult his own happiness must be little
> concerned about the happiness of oth-
> ers. Good nature is Quixotism, and every
> Princess Micomicona will lead her
> deliverer into a cage.

6. In *An Essay on the Knowledge of the Characters*

of Men, for example, Fielding carefully distinguished between good humor and good nature,
which is

> . . . that heavenly frame of soul, of
> which Jesus Christ Himself was the most
> perfect pattern; of which blessed person
> it is recorded, that He never was once
> seen to laugh, during His whole abode
> on earth. And what indeed hath good-
> nature to do with a smiling counte-
> nance? . . . For . . . the world is so full
> of [the miseries and misfortunes of man-
> kind], that scarce a day passes without
> inclining a truly good-natured man rather
> to tears than merriment. [Reprinted
> above, p. 325, *Editor*]

others. He was generous, friendly, and brave to an Excess; but Simplicity was his Characteristic. (I, 3)

The "inoffensive Disposition of his own Heart" (III, 7) not only makes the parson slow to discover the impositions practiced upon him by the malicious and hypocritical, such as the false promiser or the confederates of the practical-joking squire—"a sort of People," writes Fielding with reference to Peter Pounce, "whom Mr. Adams never saw through" (III, 12)—but it also makes vivid by contrast the moral decadence and corruption of the world through which he moves. As revealed in *The Covent-Garden Journal*, No. 42 (May 26, 1752), an important but neglected essay on the *vanitas vanitatum* theme that locates the sources of the Ridiculous, Fielding conceives of Adams' innocence and idealism as an effective vehicle for exposing the folly and vice of society. Speaking here of the kind of scholar who derives his knowledge of the world from the classics rather than from experience—we may compare Adams' dispute with the widely traveled alehouse-keeper (II, 17)—he writes:

> In solemn Truth, Gentlemen who obtain an early Acquaintance with the Manners and Customs of the Antients, are too apt to form their Ideas of their own Times, on the Patterns of Ages which bear not the least Resemblance to them. Hence they have fallen into the greatest Errors and Absurdities.

He imagines "a Man, possessed of this Jaundice of Literature"—and, in Adams' case, we might add the jaundice of good nature—in his bewildered exposure to the vanities of the age: the levees of great men, country hunting matches and horse races, drums and routs, beaus and coquettes. We are reminded of Adams' amazed and outraged interpolations ("Good Lord! what wicked Times these are!") during Wilson's account of his rake's progress through London society: "A Scholar when he first comes to this Town from the University comes among a Set of People, as entirely unknown to him, and of whom he hath no more heard or read, than if he was to be at once translated into one of the Planets; *the World* in the Town and that *in the Moon* being equally strange to him, and equally unintelligible." We may laugh at the parson's good-natured innocence and bookish idealism, but his honest bewilderment and shock at the great world imply a standard by which to measure the moral degeneracy of his age.

Pilgrim, priest, and patriarch, Abraham Adams maintains his faith in strange and idolatrous lands. Apparently following another of Barrow's suggestions, Fielding chose as his representative of chastity, symbolic of the rational discipline of the passions, a virtuous footman named Joseph, whose initial situation was not only sure to amuse by evoking the absurdities of *Pamela*, but was, in accord with the theories of the biblical epic, precisely parallel to the story of his "namesake" and Potiphar's wife.

This, of course, was an age of the "double standard," when, as Sarah Fielding's Miss Baden says in *The History of Ophelia*, chastity "was even

made the Subject of Ridicule in such Men as were possessed of it,"[7] and
it would be scarcely conceivable that the author of *Tom Jones* seriously
undertook his first novel in defense of male chastity. Joseph's forcible
expulsion of the warm-spirited Betty from his room at the Dragon Inn
(I, 18) is certainly continence carried to a ludicrous extreme. "How ought
Man to rejoice," Fielding facetiously comments, "that his Chastity is
always in his own power; that, if he hath sufficient Strength of Mind,
he hath always a competent Strength of Body to defend himself, and
cannot, like a poor weak Woman, be ravished against his Will!" In *The
Champion* (March 15, 1739/40) he had warned against allowing even
"Virtue itself" to grow "too exuberant": "Men often become ridiculous
. . . by over-acting even a laudable part." And we have seen that Betty's
good nature, like that of Tom Jones and the narrator of *A Journey from
this World to the Next*, more than compensates for her indiscretions.

At the same time, however, it would be a mistake to underestimate
the importance of chastity—even male chastity—in Fielding's morality.
The "Character of Male-Chastity," he declares in the opening chapter
of *Joseph Andrews*, is "doubtless as desirable and becoming in one Part
of the human Species as in the other." Adultery, he feels, is "a Catastrophe, common enough, and comical enough too perhaps, in modern
History, yet often fatal to the Repose and Well-being of Families, and
the Subject of many Tragedies, both in Life and on the Stage" (I, 17).
Although Betty's slip with Mr. Tow-wouse is a subject more for mirth
than tears, the nearly tragic complications of Captain Booth's inconstancy pose a grave problem in *Amelia*, and even Tom Jones must repent
and learn to discipline his passions before he is accepted by Sophia. In
The Covent-Garden Journal, No. 20 (March 10, 1752), Fielding's
spokesman, the good-natured Axylus, regrets that the fashionable literature of the period has made adultery—"so execrable a Vice"—seem a
matter of jest and gallantry; and two later numbers of the *Journal*, Nos.
67 and 68 (October 21 and 28, 1752), urge the enactment of a law
against it. Fielding says:

> I may venture, without apprehending the Imputation of
> Pedantry or Moroseness to encounter the present general
> Opinion, and to question whether Adultery be really that Mat-
> ter of Jest and Fun which it is conceived to be, and whether it
> might not be decent and proper to contrive some small Pun-
> ishment for this Vice in a civilized (much more in a Christian)
> Country.

Twenty years earlier, Fielding had similarly criticized the loose marital
standards of the day in his bitter comedy, *The Modern Husband* (1732).
But perhaps his position with regard to male chastity is best shown in

---

7. Quoted in Richard P. Scowcroft's unpublished
Ph.D. dissertation, "Anti-*Pamela*: The Problem
of Retribution as it Affected Women in the Eighteenth Century Novel" (Harvard, 1946), p. 168.
Scowcroft's sixth chapter, "Chastity," discusses the
double standard in considerable detail.

The Wedding-Day (1743), as Heartfort upbraids Millamour for his incontinence and defines his own attitude toward the double standard:

> My practice, perhaps, is not equal to my theory; but I pretend to sin with as little mischief as I can to others: and this I can lay my hand on my heart and affirm, that I never seduced a young woman to her cwn ruin, nor a married one to the misery of her husband. . . .
>
> Custom may lead a man into many errors, but it justifies none; nor are any of its laws more absurd and unjust than those relating to the commerce between the sexes: for what can be more ridiculous than to make it infamous for women to grant what it is honourable for us to solicit, nay, to ensnare and almost compel them into; to make a whore a scandalous, a whoremaster a reputable appellation! Whereas, in reality, there is no more mischievous character than a public debaucher of women.

With regard to incontinence, as well as immorality in general, Fielding equally recognizes mitigating circumstances and motives; Captain Booth, for example, "though not absolutely a Joseph . . . yet could . . . not be guilty of premeditated inconstancy."[8] Upon occasion Fielding may excuse weakness in sexual matters, but he does not justify it. He stands squarely with Tom Jones, who remonstrates with Nightingale:

> "Lookee, Mr. Nightingale," said Jones, "I am no canting hypocrite, nor do I pretend to the gift of chastity more than my neighbors. I have been guilty with women, I own it; but am not conscious that I have every [*sic*] injured any. Nor would I, to procure pleasure to myself, be knowingly the cause of misery to any human being."[9]

Joseph Andrews' chastity, however, has wider implications than merely the preservation of his virginity. Like their biblical prototypes, Abraham and Joseph, Fielding's good men exemplify the sum of the individual's duty to God, society, and himself. Adams' personification of true faith expressed through charity comprehends the first two and Joseph's chastity the last. Tillotson, we recall, had thus defined the head of our duty to ourselves: "That we govern our passions by reason, and moderate our selves in the use of sensual delights, so as not to transgress the rules of temperance and chastity."[1] In *The Champion* for February 2, 1739/40, an essay of much interest in anticipating certain aspects of the characterization of Lady Booby, Fielding accordingly maintains the temperate ordering of the passions by reason and recommends the fulfillment of "that glorious precept *vince teipsum*":[2]

8. *Amelia*, X, 2.
9. *Tom Jones*, XIV, 4.
1. Sermon 101, "Of the Work Assign'd to Every Man, and the Season for Doing It," *Sermons on*

Several Subjects and Occasions (London, 1757) 6. 283, cited earlier in Battestin's book. For Tillotson, see above, p. 60, n. 3, and p. 391 [*Editor*].
2. "Conquer thyself."

> The conquest of one's self is justly preferred by wise men to
> that of armies and kingdoms. This is that courage which is so
> ardently recommended in our religion, and which, however
> passive it may be in regard to others, is extremely active with
> respect to one's self. Whoever carefully surveys his own mind,
> will find sufficient enemies to combat within; an army of obsti-
> nate passions that will hold him in tight play, will often force
> his reason to retreat; and if they are at length subdued, it will
> not be without much labour and resolution.

At several points in *Joseph Andrews*, Fielding dramatizes this psycho-
machy[3] in depicting the conflict between lust and hate and pride in the
mind of the rejected lady Booby (e.g., I, 9, and IV, 4, 13). Before learning that Joseph and Fanny may be brother and sister, for example, Lady
Booby rationalizes her disappointment at their forthcoming marriage:

> "What am I doing? How do I suffer this Passion to creep
> imperceptibly upon me? . . . To sacrifice my Reputation, my
> Character, my Rank in Life, to the Indulgence of a mean and
> a vile Appetite! How I detest the Thought! How much more
> exquisite is the Pleasure resulting from the Reflection of Vir-
> tue and Prudence than the faint Relish of what flows from
> Vice and Folly! Whither did I suffer this improper, this mad
> Passion to hurry me, only by neglecting to summon the Aids
> of Reason to my Assistance?" (IV, 13)

Although throughout Joseph's second interview with Lady Booby, Fielding is poking fun at Pamela's ostentatious flaunting of her "virtue," the
message of *vince teipsum*, more seriously presented in *The Champion*,
plainly underlies the exchange:

> "Would you be contented with a Kiss? [asks Lady Booby] Would
> not your Inclinations be all on fire rather by such a Favour?"
> "Madam," said Joseph, "if they were, I hope I should be able
> to control them, without suffering them to get the better of my
> Virtue." (I, 8)

Assisted by the good advice and good example of Parson Adams—
"(for he was a great Enemy to the Passions, and preached nothing more
than the Conquest of them by Reason and Grace)" (IV, 8)—and inspired
by his love for the chaste Fanny Goodwill, Joseph is able to resist the
temptation of his Mrs. Potiphar. It would, of course, be absurd to suggest that Fielding's principal objective in describing Joseph's encounters
with Lady Booby, Mrs. Slipslop, and Betty is not comedy, but the recommendation of a militant chastity. As with the innocence and idealism
of Adams, Joseph's chastity is amusing because extreme; but it functions
nonetheless as a wholesome antithesis to the fashionable lusts and intrigues
of high society.

3. Conflict of soul.

SHELDON SACKS

[Fielding's Guidance of the Reader's Attitudes in Book 1, Chapters 1–11] †

The Split Commentator

This chapter does not exhaust the topic of the narrator's function in Fielding's work, or even in *Joseph Andrews*, the novel chosen for close study. It is concerned primarily with delineating those structural devices, especially ethical agents, capable of conveying judgments crucial to the power realized in each of Fielding's novels. It is necessary, however, to consider the complex character of the narrator, for initially his comments control our attitudes toward characters who usurp evaluative tasks which were originally solely his own; his subsequent comments convey judgments either independently or, far more frequently, in concert with his creations.

In *Joseph Andrews* we first meet the narrator in his role as explicit commentator. Throughout the first chapter, he maintains this role consistently, yet with surprising complexity considering the brevity of the chapter. The complexity is the result of the ironic tone, of the subtle and rapid movement from serious to ironic comment and back again—in short, the result of the fact that, as explicit commentator, the narrator plays two roles almost simultaneously. He is free to, and does, assume the role of either serious or ironic commentator throughout the novel. He can, within certain limitations, drop or assume either at will. The nearly simultaneous use of both roles is typically reserved for special occasions once the pattern is established. As the novel progresses we have many structural clues as to which role he is playing, but in the beginning we have only rhetorical clues to rely on.

The first two paragraphs seem serious enough and there is no reason to doubt that they are. The sentiments are commonplaces not only of Fielding's time but of Fielding's writings, both earlier and later: [1] examples work more forcibly on the mind than precepts; the writer, in describing good men, does a service to mankind by communicating a valuable pattern to the world.

In the third paragraph, however, the serious commentator begins to smile, to introduce us to the burlesque element of the novel. He begins seriously enough by praising biographies that give patterns of worthy persons to the world—but then, ostensibly with a straight face, takes unmistakable pot shots at his own age, partially by donning the mask of

†From *Fiction and the Shape of Belief: A Study of Henry Fielding, with Glances at Swift, Johnson and Richardson* (Berkeley and Los Angeles: U of California P, 1964) 70–73, 76–94, 207–8, 214–16. Some author's notes have been omitted.

1. Nevertheless, Fielding was not always convinced that a worthy example was rhetorically effective. See *The Champion*, June 10, 1740.

ignorance and identifying himself with the ignorance of his own times. He admires not only contemporary biographers but also "those ancient writers which of late days are little read, being written in obsolete, and, as they are generally thought, *unintelligible languages* such as Plutarch, Nepos, *and others which I heard of in my youth.*" [Sacks's italics]

We are immediately put on guard by the author's professing ignorance of standard works in a field about which he has been discoursing more or less learnedly for two paragraphs and by the qualification of the ancient languages as "unintelligible." Our "guard" will extend tentatively to the writers in English discussed in the context of assumed ignorance. (The commentator's first two paragraphs prevent our assuming that his ignorance is real and it is important that they do, since, if the narrator cannot be trusted, if we laugh at instead of with him, his function as direct ethical commentator is destroyed. We cannot then take his word for anything and in *Joseph Andrews* we must take his word for a good deal.)

In his description of works in English which are "finely calculated to sow the seeds of virtue in youth, and very easy to be comprehended by persons of moderate capacity," Fielding reinforces our "suspicion" of the works in English that ostensibly fit the formula of the first two paragraphs as they relate to "biography." Knowledge of the works themselves helps, of course, to emphasize the disparity between the exemplary virtue of the first two paragraphs, the romantic, perhaps childish, virtue of John the Great, etc., and the false virtue of Cibber's *Apology* and of *Pamela*. But if we had no knowledge of these works, the commentator's position would still be relatively clear because of the terms in which he describes the "biographies": ". . . John the Great, who, by his brave and heroic actions against men of *large and athletic bodies* . . . that of an earl of Warwick, *whose Christian name was Guy. . . .*" [Sacks's italics]

In his last two paragraphs the commentator can, from one point of view, play it straight. His encomiums on *Pamela* and Cibber cannot be mistaken for real compliments, even though there is no stylistic indication that the commentator does not mean for us to take him seriously. The very incongruity of the comparisons is a clear signal to the reader: the works of Plutarch and Nepos (written in "unintelligible languages") are compared with *John the Great* and *Guy of Warwick* (exemplifying virtues such as "heroic actions against men of large and athletic bodies"), which are, in turn, compared with the *Apology* and *Pamela*.

With our present knowledge of Fielding and his attitudes toward Cibber and the early Richardson, it is easy to assume that the burlesque element is self-explanatory, that the exaggerated encomiums on the two works would automatically appear ridiculous to Fielding's contemporaries. This, of course, is not true. The *Pamela* hailed from the pulpit itself, the widely read autobiography of the poet laureate, were ridiculous only to some of the wits of the time. Fielding himself, in his letter to Richardson, was later to praise *Clarissa* in terms as laudatory as those he uses mockingly here in reference to *Pamela*.

We might assume that the effect of Pamela on Joseph, as described in the last paragraph, is innately funny; that it was, especially for the eighteenth century, ludicrous in itself for a young man "to preserve his purity in the midst of such great temptations" by "keeping the excellent pattern of his sister's virtues before his eyes." There is no evidence, however, that an eighteenth-century audience found it necessary to snicker at Malcolm when he announces to Macduff as one of the virtues that will fit him for kingship the fact that he is "yet unknown to woman."[2] Shakespeare's treatment of Malcolm is, of course, quite different from Fielding's treatment of Joseph, but that is essentially the point. It is the treatment of a general situation, its particularization, that tickles our risibility or stimulates our admiration, seldom the situation *per se*. We do not necessarily laugh *because* a man named Joseph Andrews is maintaining his purity against odds; we are inclined to laugh, even before we meet him, at Joseph Andrews' attempt to maintain his purity because a narrator acting in a subtly defined role as ironic commentator has already affected our attitude toward the pattern on which the as yet uncharacterized young man has molded himself.

* * *

Our introductory impression of the book is of great importance, for it establishes our attitudes toward the characters we are to meet—including our attitude toward that elusive and protean Narrator. Still more important, the pattern by means of which the commentator has tentatively conveyed certain generalized value judgments (Joseph Andrews' attempt to preserve his purity is amusing) is a recurrent pattern. The serious comment juxtaposed to the ironic comment becomes important at many places in the novel. * * *

* * *

* * * We begin with a commentator whom we take seriously; when he puts tongue in cheek, we do not lose confidence in him as a serious commentator; when he makes his mocking thrust at Cibber and, more important for his later London episodes, at *Pamela*, his ability to convey serious judgments is not compromised.[3] It is by comparison to the serious aesthetic frame established for "biography" in the first two paragraphs, by their inadequacy as examples worthy of perpetuation, that Cibber's *Apology* and *Pamela* and the "romances" too are seen to be ridiculous, rather than because they have measured up to a set of criteria which the narrator has labeled as ridiculous. As the pattern is repeated we know that, unless we have some rhetorical or structural clue to the contrary, the commentator means what he is saying, though he may, in a moment, begin to poke fun at something which is not apposite to his serious remarks or which is especially funny in the light of his serious remarks.

* * *

2. *Macbeth* 4.3.125–26 [*Editor*].
3. The learned preface adds weight to our acceptance of the serious commentator and to our knowledge that he has tongue in cheek when he talks of classical biography as being written in "unintelligible languages."

From Comment to Character

Once he has introduced himself in chapter i it is a relatively simple matter for the complex commentator to make use of our knowledge of his character in a number of ways: he can, on the one hand, continue the pattern already set up and, by the almost simultaneous use of his two roles, make barbed thrusts without destroying the validity of interspersed serious comments, or vice versa; he can, on the other hand, maintain either one of the roles for a relatively long time by making use of stylistic qualities to identify his role to the reader or, more important still in the next few chapters, by making use of his previous serious or mocking treatment of any subject. He can, for example, pay as many stylistically unqualified compliments as he wishes to *Pamela* or to Cibber's *Apology* without running the risk of our taking him at his word. At the opening of chapter iii after an initial complimentary description of Parson Adams, we learn: "He was generous, friendly, and brave to an excess; but simplicity was his characteristic: he did not more than Mr. Colley Cibber apprehend any such passions as malice and envy to exist in mankind, which was indeed less remarkable in a country parson than in a gentleman who hath passed his life behind the scenes. . . ." We have no difficulty in making the transition between the serious comments, which are just beginning to establish the character of Adams, and the thrusts at Cibber, which partially derive their destructive power from the implied discrepancy between the serious standard (here Adams' simplicity) and the thing mocked (Cibber's simplicity). Reliance on the commentator, in either or both of his roles, remains an important factor in conveying judgments before the removal to London. With one crucial exception, the burden of establishing characters in chapters ii and iii is his.

* * *

* * * When we consider that Joseph's quest for purity has already been defined as amusing in chapter i, that his ancestry has been described in ludicrous terms, that his position in the house of a family known as Booby has been treated lightly, it is not surprising that we expect the young man to take part in comic adventures and are prepared even for "burlesque." What is surprising is the fact that, within the comic frame, his essentially serious characteristics are revealed and his virtues are not (at this point) portrayed as ridiculous. These traits are taken seriously enough to survive a descent into absurdity that would normally destroy a fictional character for even a semiserious role—a descent that would normally take the young man's virtues, mocked in one frame, and make them perpetually ridiculous. As it is, Fielding must do some difficult rescue work after the London scenes, but that rescue work is made possible later by the care with which he handles tone and value judgment now, when he introduces us to his character proper.

* * *

In spite of the occasional aside directed at contemporary institutions, the commentator is at his most serious in his initial description of Adams. The areas in which Adams *may* become ridiculous are carefully defined, but not even the most loving kind of ridicule is offered the good parson at this time by the commentator. He is described as an excellent scholar, a man who knows many languages, and who "had treasured up a fund of learning rarely to be met with in a university."

> He was, besides, a man of good sense, good parts, and good nature; *but was at the same time as entirely ignorant of the ways of this world as an infant just entered into it could possibly be. As he had never any intention to deceive, so he never suspected such a design in others.* He was generous, friendly, and brave to an excess; but simplicity was his characteristic. . . . [Sacks's italics]

The traits italicized define the area in which we may expect Adams to get into situations with which he is incompetent to deal and which, in keeping with the basic tone of the book, will probably turn out to be amusing—with qualifications. The plethora of good traits assigned to Adams, and soon displayed in action, leaves a wide margin in which the good parson's word is to be trusted, his remarks taken seriously, his actions seen as more or less exemplary. As long as our faith in the serious commentator is to be maintained, he must keep faith with us. As long as Adams is foolish only in ways the narrator has led us to expect, he retains our complete faith in his competence to act wisely. If Fielding wishes to cross the line of definition (as he does, for example, with Adams' vanity about his sermon on vanity) he must cross it after we have had ample opportunity to witness Adams' general competence; all we need do, then, is add another limitation to the character's competence rather than shatter all notions of it. At this point, however, Adams' virtues are accented; ridicule is carefully avoided, since the general ironic tone makes us prone to it in any event, and Adams must not only help the commentator rescue the values of the London incidents but must also assume serious commentative functions later in the novel.

*   *   *

Once the bare bones of Adams' character are articulated, we immediately see the good man in action, questioning Joseph. He is amazed at such learning in a footman and, after discovering how Joseph was educated, asks him if he doesn't resent his lack of a liberal education. Joseph's emphatic "no" involves a certain amount of philosophizing: ". . . 'He hoped he had profited somewhat better from the books he had read than to lament his condition in this world. That, for his part, he was perfectly content with the state to which he was called; that he should endeavor to improve his talent, which was all required of him, but not repine at his own lot, nor envy those of his betters.' " The serious commentator need make no remarks about Joseph's theorizing; he can now use his new creation to do the job for him so that, at one stroke, he gives significance to Joseph's virtue, tentatively establishes Joseph's "philosophical" acceptance of his position as one of the acceptable parts of the value scheme of the whole novel,[4] and reinforces by example what the serious commentator has previously told us about Adams.

It is Adams, not the serious commentator, who evaluates Joseph's remark, though it was the serious commentator's word that indicated the degree of credit we are to give to Adams' evaluation: " 'Well said, my lad,' replied the curate; 'and I wish some who have read many more good books, nay, and some who have written books themselves, had profited so much by them.' " The narrator has momentarily delegated his role as serious commentator to Adams, but he now reassumes his own evaluative prerogative in creating other characters, though he makes good use of our absolute sympathy with Adams' goodness—Adams' foibles have not yet been exploited for purposes of ridicule—as a touchstone by which we can form our attitudes to the new characters he creates. Our attitudes toward these new creations are a result of the interaction between what the serious commentator tells us about their traits and what he tells us about their attitudes toward and treatment of Adams.

Immediately following the passage quoted above, the serious commentator begins to sketch the characters of the Boobys: "*Adams had no nearer access to Sir Thomas or my lady than through the waiting-gentlewoman*; for Sir Thomas was too apt to estimate men merely by their dress or fortune; *and* my lady was a woman of gayety, who had been blessed with a town education, and never spoke of any of her country neighbors by any other appellation than that of the brutes." [Sacks's italics] The commentator's method is readily apparent: the few traits of the Boobys—all unflattering—that he chooses to describe for us are ascribed as causes for their poor treatment of the good man. Fielding makes good use of his agents even as he creates them. In portraying the Boobys according to their treatment of Adams, the commentator reinforces Adams' ability to characterize others. He informs us that the unpleasant Boobys "both regarded the curate as a kind of domestic only, belonging to the parson of the parish, who was at this time at variance with the knight."

*   *   *

Parson Adams, toward the end of the chapter, tries through Slipslop to persuade Lady Booby to provide Joseph with an education which would qualify him "for a higher station than that of a footman." Slipslop's mangled refusal, involving unconscious ridicule of the ignorance of gentlemen, particularly London gentlemen, is amusing and in keeping with the tone of absurdity, soon to become dominant in the London chapters; but Joseph and the serious commentator have the final word before the removal to London and the temporary disappearance of Adams

---

4. Extreme manifestations of Stoicism are ridiculed later in the novel; such ridicule does not reflect on Joseph's moderate statement here.

before the first adventures of the book: "However, Andrews behaved very thankfully and gratefully to him for his intended kindness, which he told him he never would forget, and at the same time received from the good man many admonitions concerning the regulation of his future conduct, and his perseverance in innocence and industry." Adams showed us that Joseph's virtue was not to be considered ridiculous; now Joseph is able to use the credit he has gained from the good parson's words seriously to compliment Adams before his own departure and to leave us with a picture—in no way portrayed as ridiculous—of Adams giving him serious advice.

By removing Adams from the scene now, by keeping him entirely apart from the subsequent London chapters after he has been established in the role of serious evaluator of people and actions, Fielding has left a bridge by means of which Joseph can be rescued after the latter fulfills the destiny promised in chapter i—that of a young man in a ridiculous struggle to keep his virginity. By his refusal to laugh now at Adams' foibles, despite the fact that laughter is our general expectation from the first chapter, the narrator has seen to it that Joseph's virtue is not made ridiculous *per se*. The result is that, after it is seen as ridiculous in one kind of frame, the "burlesque," it can be moved later into another kind of frame; it is then subtly modified so that it constitutes a positive antidote to the standards ridiculed in the London scenes, but an antidote which does not act simply to reverse the values seen as absurd. Overindulgence in virginity is ridiculous, but in the scheme of values in *Joseph Andrews* promiscuity never becomes virtuous; sexual incontinence is no virtue, but loss of chastity does not indicate that its loser is a villain.

London: Old Friends in a New Frame

The London episodes continue from chapter iv through xi; allusions to *Pamela* are strongly resumed with the appearance of Pamela and Mr. Booby toward the end of the novel. It is, however, in the earlier chapters that Joseph's ordeal, promised in the first chapter, takes place. Fielding makes use of the situation, already characterized as ridiculous, of a young man using Pamela Andrews as a model for the defense of his virtue. In the later chapters it is not Joseph who is portrayed as ridiculous; his honest virtue, his healthy love for Fanny, his willingness to defend the heroine against the rudeness of Beau Didapper are then, though still in a humorous frame, seen as admirable. The ridiculous pretensions of Pamela and the dangerous arrogance of Lady Booby temporarily threaten the expected resolution; defeated, they give increased force to the desirability of the union of Joseph and Fanny blessed by a courageous Adams.

But even in chapters iv through xi, although the double attack on Joseph's virginity by Lady Booby and Mrs. Slipslop is emphasized, the ridicule directed at Joseph is actually of shorter duration than one might suppose: long comic scenes between Mrs. Slipslop and Lady Booby, comic analyses of Lady Booby's passion, the introduction of Lady Tittle and Lady Tattle, receive much of our attention.

The fact that, by the end of the novel, Joseph's virtues become a standard by means of which his sister's virtues are mocked indicates how carefully Fielding must have handled his materials and manipulated our attitudes, since at this point in the novel, ridicule of virtues similar to those the "hero" posseses at the end is itself the tool by which Pamela's ethical deficiencies are revealed. That he has been able to achieve this is a testimony to Fielding's artistry.

Before we even learned of the Boobys' impending removal to London, the city had been tentatively categorized for us so that we do not approach it without prejudice. In the very creation of the two female characters who are to take the greatest part in the London incidents our attitudes toward the city has—whether we remember the source of our bias as we read is unimportant—been formed: it is her being "blessed with a town education" that causes Lady Booby to refer to her country neighbors by no "other appellation than that of the brutes," that prevents her from having any social intercourse with Adams except through Slipslop. And it is as a result of the fact that "she had been frequently at London" and therefore "knew more of the world than a country parson could pretend to" that Slipslop engages in her incomprehensible arguments about theology with the learned, bewildered Parson Adams. London is their world, and it is a world removed not only geographically but also in tone and value from the world in which we have seen Adams and Joseph act in semiserious roles; it is no accident that before he again meets Adams, Joseph leaves the metropolis—where we never see the two men together in action.

To add to these distinctions of tone and value, to help isolate London as a separate world which only accidentally, and always negatively, impinges on that wider, freer world of "the road"—where even the ridiculous and the vicious take more direct, less insidious forms—the mocking thrusts of the ironic commentator are woven into the very texture of the book. We can see now how these thrusts, ostensibly relevant only to actual objects outside the novel, can be employed to affect its value scheme at a later time. Note, in the passage quoted previously on page 444, how, in the very act of establishing Adams' character, the thrust at Cibber, "a gentleman who hath passed his life behind the scenes," has tentatively suggested (London does not have to be mentioned by name) an essential difference between Adams' world and the "behind the scenes" world we enter in these chapters.

What is more important, however, is that when we enter that world, by virtue of which both the predatory females claim their distinction, we do not have to make any shifts in our judgments of either of them. The tentative hostility already directed at Lady Booby is reinforced by our hostile laughter and need in no way be counteracted later; similarly, while we learn more about the lusty elements in Slipslop's nature, they do not surprise us; we do not particularly care whether she is successful or unsuccessful in her attempt on Joseph's virtue; her love-making advances are couched in the same malapropisms as her disputes with Adams—she remains ridiculous and our attitude toward her is entrenched rather than modified.

As a result of fulfilling rather than modifying our expectations about the two female predators whom Joseph frustrates, Fielding is able to modify the implications of our laughing at Joseph, who, though he has fulfilled the expectations established by the commentator's promise in chapter i, steps slightly out of the character established in chapter iii in that what was previously seen as commendable is now exaggerated to the point of the ridiculous. Ridiculous or not, even when we laugh at him most, Joseph retains more of our sympathy than either of the two women he frustrates, largely because our initial attitudes toward the two women are reinforced. Joseph may appear ridiculous, but we are glad that the arrogant Lady Booby cannot have her wish; he may misinterpret Slipslop's advances, but the spotlight is focused on her vanity, on her malapropisms, so that she, rather than Joseph, becomes the object of our laughter.

It is easy to underestimate the importance of this in the whole scheme of the novel unless we realize that, if Fielding intended the London scenes only as destructive burlesque of *Pamela* unconnected to the rest of his novel, he has not made as much of his "satiric" tools as he might have. By keeping our sympathy with Joseph stronger than with those he frustrates and by focusing his attack on characters other than Joseph and on incidents which have only the most tenuous analogy to those in *Pamela*, Fielding makes the burlesque secondary to an exposé of the ridiculous that takes our attention away from Richardson's work. No one knew better than the Fielding who wrote the *Champion* of Tuesday, December 25, 1739, and was to write *Jonathan Wild*, the destructive effect to be achieved in satire by an absolute reversal of values: what is condemned is what you really mean most to praise; what you praise is to be most condemned.[5] More important still, the author of *Shamela* was well aware that, for a full destructive attack on Richardson's values—or what he took to be Richardson's values—nothing could match the effectiveness of directing sympathy toward that which Richardson attacks and great hostility toward the virtuous embodiment that Richardson admires.

> Well; at Dinner Mr. *Booby* was very civil to Mr. *Williams*, and told him he was sorry for what had happened, and would make him sufficient Amends, if in his power, and desired him to accept of a Note for fifty Pounds; which he was so *good* to receive, notwithstanding all that had past; and told Mr. *Booby*, he hop'd he would be forgiven, and that he would pray for him.

5. In *Jonathan Wild* (1743), Fielding pays sustained ironic tribute to the "greatness" of his criminal hero. The *Champion* essay decries the "pernicious" effects of classical learning upon divinity, law, and medicine [Editor].

> We made a charming Fool of him, i'fackins; Times are finely
> altered, I have entirely got the better of him, and am resolved
> never to give him his Humour.[6]

Think what we will of Mr. Booby, booby that he is, how can we help
feeling sorry for him?

I do not mean to imply that there is only one effective way of satirizing
Pamela, or that the exposure of the ridiculous in *Joseph Andrews* is ineffectual: we certainly can see that the predatory Lady Booby may be meant
as the female analogue of Mr. B. in *Pamela* just as Joseph is the male
analogue of Pamela; the humor then derives from the treatment of the
reversed situation. And yet, laugh as we will at Lady Booby, are we
laughing at Mr. B. or at *Pamela* itself? How do the discussions between
Mrs. Slipslop and Lady Booby make us laugh at *Pamela* or at Joseph
Andrews? As we laugh at their vanity, at the essential similarity of their
desires despite the nugatory difference in their modes of attack on Joseph,
is not Fielding exposing the ridiculous in areas far more central to the
whole of *Joseph Andrews* than to a burlesque of *Pamela*?

Fielding is essentially accurate when he tells us, of *Joseph Andrews*,
that while he has "sometimes admitted this [burlesque] in our diction,
we have carefully exclude it from our sentiments and characters; for
there it is never properly introduced, unless in writings of the burlesque
kind, which this is not intended to be."[7] This does not imply that Fielding had in mind such distinctions as those made in the present work
among satire, apologue, and action when he wrote this sentence or when
he wrote *Joseph Andrews*.[8] But the distinctions are useful in explaining
why, despite the special qualities which distinguish the London episodes
from most of the others in the novel, we do not regard them as digressive
in anything like the degree we do Mr. Wilson's tale later in the novel.

According to these distinctions, any true burlesque is a subtype of
satire. That is, it is a work organized to ridicule an external object, in
this case a particular literary production or a type of literary production.
Viewed in this way, the burlesque London scenes are extremely deficient. Fielding has not only failed to exploit all the resources of relevant
ridicule; he has included an inordinate number of elements irrelevant
to ridicule of *Pamela*. Judged merely as works organized to ridicule
Richardson's novel, *Shamela* must be regarded as infinitely superior to
the later *Joseph Andrews*. But * * * Fielding's satiric deficiencies disappear when we consider the London episodes as parts of the rich comic
action. The form of *Joseph Andrews* easily accommodates any number
of occasional mocking remarks about characters who exist apart from the

---

6. P. 301 above [Editor].
7. P. 4 above [Editor].
8. Earlier Sacks distinguishes three types of fiction: *satire*, "organized so that it ridicules objects
external to the fictional world created in it"; *apologue*, "organized as a fictional example of the
truth of a formulable statement or a series of such

statements"; and *represented action* (or novel),
"organized so that it introduces characters, about
whose fates we are made to care, in unstable
relationships which are then further complicated
until the complication is finally resolved by the
removal of the represented instability." He places
Joseph Andrews in the last category [Editor].

fictional world of the novel. * * * As parts of the action such ironic thrusts frequently help ensure an appropriate ethical response to portrayed characters and events, as some of the remarks about Cibber cooperate in characterizing the "behind-the-scenes" world of London and those who derive their prestige from it—the Boobys and Slipslop. More extensively and directly the "burlesque frame" of the London chapters performs the same service. The attempts of Lady Booby and of Slipslop on Joseph's virtue, in fact the whole sequence of events that lead to Joseph's dismissal, when viewed apart from any consideration of *Pamela*, make perfectly comprehensible contributions to the complication of relationships among characters about whose fates we have been made to care. They are well-organized parts of the action. The "burlesque frame," except for one passage, consists of no more than a choice of diction (including the names of characters) that so successfully alludes to *Pamela* as to give us a hilarious contrast between the standard by which sexual and other activities are regarded in *Joseph Andrews* and in the work which immortalized the hero's sister.

To sum this up, in the subtype of satire known as burlesque, of which *Shamela* is a perfect example, the artistic end is the ridicule directed at the work parodied. In *Joseph Andrews* the ridicule of *Pamela* is incorporated as part of the language of the novel in such a way as to make a vital and spirited contribution to both our expectations about and our desires for the represented characters; even the episodes in which the allusive language is most strongly operative are organized not as parts of a satire but as parts of an action.

Nevertheless, the framework is there; when Fielding does concentrate on Joseph's fondness for his virginity, some of our reactions depend upon allusions to *Pamela*—i.e., upon our understanding the language—since the pungency of the humor depends at least in part, on the reader's knowledge of Richardson's novel. (Joseph's letter to Pamela would make rather slim comedy to a reader who had never heard of *Pamela*; but the scenes which concentrate on the analysis of Lady Booby's passion, on Slipslop's hilarious attempt on Joseph's virtue, on Lady Booby's fear of Slipslop's knowledge of her attempted indiscretion, would be as pungent or as ridiculous if *Pamela* had never been written.)

Since Joseph, unlike the females who appear in the burlesque scenes, is to be seen in a new light in the new London world, it is useful to see him in a new dress, to show him developing new characteristics which, while not incompatible with his virtues, are ridiculous (they have already been "defined" as London has been "defined") and better fit him for his role as buffoon. Since these ridiculous elements constitute no more than a superficial change in taste, an acceptance of certain aspects of London fashion, they can be doffed at the moment he rejects and leaves London without doing violence to his character, as easily as they were donned when he entered the city and accepted its fashions.

*   *   *

By ascribing to Joseph the nonserious vices of the footman-fop, he has made him temporarily ridiculous. The superficial follies of London, which can easily be dropped, are not the "vices" which constitute the main analogue to *Pamela*, the focal point of the "burlesque episodes." It is the very virtues Joseph has retained, especially his refusal to indulge in—that magnificent euphemism—"any other genteel vice the town abounded with," which enables Fielding to incorporate ridiculed virtues of *Pamela* in such a way as to ensure an appropriate reaction to sexual and other activities and attitudes of characters in *Joseph Andrews*. By dressing his character in a set of superficial and removable London follies, Fielding has set his very virtues in a ridiculous frame—one perfectly appropriate for incorporating such ridicule; when the removal of the frame, in combination with other rescue devices, restores dignity to the young man's virtues as he returns from the footman-fop to the "Joey" we originally met, he can perform his role in the comic adventures on the road. The rescue is complete enough to permit his "virtue" ostensibly mocked here to become a standard of virtue later in the book.

*   *   *

Immediately after the death of Sir Thomas Booby, Lady Booby, nearly naked, invites the newly dressed and curled London Joseph into her bedroom, and at this point Fielding has the first real fun with Joseph's virtue. Much of the humor of the scene evolves from Joey's seriously construing the transparent, hypocritical veil in which Lady Booby couches her proposals; so, after quizzing Joseph about whether his virtue of secrecy (" 'a very commendable quality, and what I am far from being angry with you for' ") would persist in a "hypothetical" love affair with a lady, she ends by asking, " 'Can you keep a secret, my Joey?' " In spite of the new London spirit the Lady has discerned in him, "my Joey" interprets the question as being a general inquiry into his character as footman: " 'Madam,' says he, 'I hope your ladyship can't tax me with ever betraying the secrets of the family; and I hope, if you was to turn me away, I might have that character of you.' " If Joseph ever steps out of character it is not in the passages in which he waxes eloquent about life in formal language; he does this from the time we meet him and continues doing it after the burlesque scenes. His sharpness, occasional wisdom, and eloquence are part of the character of Joseph Andrews, though they are not characteristics one might expect of the generalized concept "footman." It is in the London scenes that we depart from the character of Joseph Andrews we have met before and will meet again. The departure, brief and in the isolated frame of London values, will not bother us when the footman again becomes Joseph Andrews.

Joseph's obtuseness in the scene, his inability to comprehend his mistress' devious purpose, elicits further humor as, in all honesty, his remarks become, in view of his lady's uncomprehended purpose, the quintessence of tactlessness. When the veil in which her intentions are couched has been withdrawn farther and farther until intention and lady have both reached the point of approximate nudity, and the lady with some justification bursts into a fury at Joseph's blindness, Joseph defends himself as follows:

> "Madam," said Joseph, "I would not have your ladyship think any evil of me. I have always endeavored to be a dutiful servant both to you and my master." "O thou villain!" answered my lady, "why didst thou mention the name of that dear man, unless to torment me, to bring his precious memory to my mind?" (And then she burst into a fit of tears.)[9]

Joseph's very "innocence," ridiculously as it is portrayed, turns the tables so that our laughter is directed at the hypocritical lady. The reader, it is presumed, is not quite so innocent as Joseph and is aware that the remarks he makes in all innocence could not better deflate the lady if they had been contrived for that purpose by a shrewd antagonist.

We see this pattern, too, when Slipslop attacks the hero's virtue. His innocence makes her just as angry as it made her mistress and, though her intentions are not veiled, the parallel to her lady's attack adds greatly to the humor of the scene; the similarity of the operation of the "passion" of lust in lady and maid adds to our laughter at the expense of the proud Lady Booby:

> "Yes, madam!" replied Mrs. Slipslop with some warmth, "do you intend to result my passion? Is it not enough, ungrateful as you are, to make no return to all the favors I have done you; but you must treat me with ironing? Barbarous monster! How have I deserved that my passion should be resulted and treated with ironing?" "Madam," answered Joseph, "I don't understand your hard words; but I am certain you have no occasion to call me ungrateful, for, so far from intending you any wrong, I have always loved you as well as if you had been my own mother." "How, sirrah?" says Mrs. Slipslop in a rage; "your own mother? Do you assinuate that I am old enough to be your mother? . . ."[1]

Poor Joseph! To emphasize the situation of the comic martyr the narrator uses, for the first time in the novel, a stylistic device which he later employs frequently for comic purposes, the mock-heroic[2] simile in which Mrs. Slipslop is compared to "a hungry tigress" and "a voracious pike," Joseph to a lamb and "a roach or gudgeon." * * *

Joseph has, however, between the two attempted seductions, written a letter to his mock-exemplary sister which, while revealing him at his most naïve and ridiculous, prepares us for the dropping of the "burlesque" frame by revealing his rejection of what London stands for and

9. P. 24 above [Editor].
1. P. 27 above [Editor].
2. In "Henry Fielding's Theory of the Comic Prose Epic," *University of Wisconsin Studies in Language and Literature*, No. 30 (Madison: U of Wisconsin P, 1931), Ethel Margaret Thornbury more accurately suggests that Fielding does not employ the mock heroic but a comic analogue of epic paraphernalia.

his honest desire to see Adams again. * * * Here, for a brief moment, the insistent male virgin is back with Parson Adams, is attacking what the novel attacks—is again on the side of those angels who have never undergone the misfortune of a temporary descent into absolute absurdity.

In the adventure with Slipslop, our attention is centered on her ridiculous antics, to the parallel between her attack on Joseph and her lady's. Our attention then is completely withdrawn from Joseph to scenes in which Slipslop and Lady Booby have a go at each other, other scenes in which the comic commentator has a field day with mock-heroic apostrophes to love, with interspersed thrusts at Cibber and Richardson, with comic analyses of the Lady's psychological state, and with Slipslop's and Lady Booby's false and wavering condemnations of Joseph's lack of virtue. But there follows one more interview with Joseph, terminated by his unfortunate "tenderness for his virtue" and ending in his discharge. A final letter to Pamela employs the absurd qualities in Joseph a little longer and, at the same time, indicates that he is potentially virile: " 'But I am glad she turned me out of the chamber as she did, for I had once almost forgotten every word Parson Adams had ever said to me.' " Even the commentator shows some concern at the beginning of the chapter for his protagonist's future reputation: "The disconsolate Joseph would not have had an understanding sufficient for the principal subject of such a book as this if he had any longer misunderstood the drift of his mistress; and indeed, that he did not discern it sooner, the reader will be pleased to impute to an unwillingness in him to discover what he must condemn in her as a fault." The reader may or may not follow the commentator's injunction—it will not matter. No explanation can give us the kind of retroactive knowledge that, in other comic actions, can sometimes make us say, "We've misjudged the man—he was not a fool; we didn't know why he was acting that way." Joseph has been ridiculous and, no matter what we learn about him later in a re-reading of the apposite scenes, he remains ridiculous in the London episodes. The craftsmanship employed in creating his "burlesque frame" enables Fielding to switch frames again so that Joseph appears in a new light, judged by another, though not a retroactive, set of laws by which his virtue is not judged ridiculous. The contrast between evaluations in the two frames helps establish the values of the novel and prevents us from simply reversing Richardson's ridiculed standards.

The removal begins immediately after Joseph's final letter to Pamela— and it is not initially a geographical removal: "Joseph having received his little remainder of wages, and having stripped off his livery, was forced to borrow a frock and breeches of one of the servants (for he was so beloved in the family that they would all have lent him anything). . . ." The serious commentator's remark reminds us of another world in which we have seen Joseph and, in the next chapter, as Joseph leaves London, he expends much of his time in stimulating that memory.

We are immediately told about Fanny and again our old standard for measuring character is reintroduced as Parson Adams is further entrenched in the exemplary and evaluative roles we have seen him perform previously:

> This young creature [Fanny] (who now lived with a farmer in the parish) had been always beloved by Joseph, and returned his affection. She was two years only younger than our hero. They had been acquainted from their infancy, and had conceived a very early liking for each other, which had grown to such a degree of affection that Mr. Adams had with much ado prevented them from marrying, and persuaded them to wait till a few years' service and thrift had a little improved their experience, and enabled them to live comfortably together.
>
> They followed this good man's advice, as indeed his word was little less than a law in his parish; for as he had shown his parishoners, by an uniform behavior of thirty-five years' duration, that he had their good entirely at heart, so they consulted him on every occasion, but very seldom acted contrary to his opinion.

It is a familiar world now and one in which we can expect future actions to take place. And yet the ingredients of the love of Joseph and Fanny, approved by Adams, certainly do cause a backward glance at the previous scenes: "Though her modesty would only suffer her to admit his eager kisses, her violent love made her more than passive in his embraces, and she often pulled him to her breast with a soft pressure, which, though perhaps it would not have squeezed an insect to death, caused more emotion in the heart of Joseph than the closest Cornish hug could have done."

Lest we miss the application, the narrator's remark that Fanny could not write and therefore did not correspond with Joseph definitely directs our attention back to *Pamela* and its letter-writing heroine and, by implication, to the ridiculed standard. This is a different Joseph, perhaps, from the one mocked; but if his healthy manhood has been restored, he has not become a roué, and his slightly impatient chastity is not mocked in the new frame. When we compare the values of the two frames and look at the Tow-wouse–Betty incident it is clear that even George Sherburn's mild statement, in reference to *Tom Jones*, to the effect that "Undoubtedly Fielding underrated chastity as a moral virtue," may be too strong to apply to the value scheme of *Joseph Andrews*; the negative view of Richardson exaggerates because, as with most undesirable notions in *Joseph Andrews*, its absurdity is stressed; the positive values of the nonallusive frame subtly modify our notions of the place of sexual propriety in the world of the novel.

*   *   *

[Wilson's Tale]

*   *   *

In Mr. Wilson's tale * * *, value judgments are again the result of the interaction of an important ethical agent with the narrator of the digressive tale; as in the tale just discussed,[1] the ethical agent initially indicates his interest in the narrator's life and actually requests the tale. The interaction, though, is far simpler than in the old man's narrative. Mr. Wilson, the strayed lamb, has found his way back to the path of virtue and is trustworthy both in the narration and in the interpretation of the events of his life. Adams is limited to emphasizing Wilson's own judgments, though this emphasis is important not only in itself, but occasionally, by indicating a difference in the degree to which Wilson and Adams condemn a given action, it places that action in a perspective it would not otherwise have had. Simple emphasis is achieved in a variety of obvious, though often comically effective, ways: Adams groans repeatedly as Wilson describes his "course of doing nothing" in London, and is in essential agreement with the strayed lamb when he points out to him, "Sir, this is below the life of an animal hardly above vegetation."[2] But when the serious transgressions are described, Wilson's self-condemnation cannot prevent Adams from reproaching him further; when Wilson describes how he "debauched" a young woman, his insistence that "it will never be sufficiently repented of in my own opinion" only mitigates the displeasure of Adams, who fervently hopes that "heaven grant you may sincerely repent of this and many other things you have related!"[3]

The purpose of Adams' interspersed comments is clear. What is far less clear is the purpose of the whole digression, a tale in which a sketchily characterized young man is shown as participating in and almost ruined by a variety of forms—represented in detail—of the folly, villainy, and madness fashionable in London, from which he finally escapes to a rural paradise only slightly, though significantly, marred by a dog-killing squire. The tale is obviously not represented, as the old man's tale is in *Tom Jones*, as an alternative way of life rejected by the protagonist, who has slept through much of the narration.

*   *   *

To descend from the theoretical, we can see that, in his role as a strayed lamb, Mr. Wilson has made a series of foolish, even horrendous, choices which have had the consequences of almost engulfing him in vices represented as typical of London; if Joseph's tenderness for his virginity, as it manifests itself in his relations with Lady Booby in the burlesque London adventures, is ridiculed, Fielding makes ample restitution to the cause of sexual continence when, not by discursive invective, but by neat juxtaposition of ethical agencies, he condemns, in one of the

---

1. The story of the Man of the Hill, *Tom Jones* 8.
11–14 [*Editor*].

2. P. 160 above [*Editor*].

3. P. 162 above [*Editor*].

most vigorous ways possible to the value structure of the novel, Mr. Wilson's serious participation in those "other genteel vices" with which London is shown to abound.[4] That Mr. Wilson, sketchily characterized as essentially a good man who has found the path which leads, both geographically and morally, away from London and what it has, in precise terms, come to represent (largely by virtue of his own tale) emphasizes the discrepancy between his present and past modes of life; his narrow escape has the effect of establishing the condemned vices as not merely the pursuits of the hopelessly corrupt, but as embedded social institutions capable of corrupting decent men.[5] Nor is Mr. Wilson's tale concerned solely or even primarily with sexual vice. The triviality, hypocrisy, and sexual laxness seen as laughably characteristic of London during Joseph's sojourn there are seriously subsumed in Mr. Wilson's tale, but comprise only a few of the threats which his virtue encounters. Embodied institutions that engender false ethics, philosophical ideas that cater to the whims of spurious virtue, corrupt business practices, disregard of literary merit, and such social aberrations as dueling figure prominently in Wilson's early misadventures.

London, unpeopled and largely undefined, has from the very beginning of the novel been closely associated with the follies and vices of all the major characters, excluding Adams, who appear both in the first and final sections of *Joseph Andrews*. But the association has defined London only as a geographical tag for what is unacceptable and, partially because of Joseph's burlesque adventures, ludicrously rather than viciously unacceptable. As a result of Mr. Wilson's straying down paths artistically difficult of access to Joseph or Adams, London has been condemned for specific forms of foolishness and vice, and has been condemned with a variety of unvirtuous characters seen participating in a carefully selected variety of unsavory affairs.[6] As a further result of Mr. Wilson's tale, the scope of Adams' value judgments has, with considerable economy of means, been extended to include what is represented as an insidiously influential urban culture with which he has had no first-hand experience but which seriously affects the world in which he lives. This extension of the area in which Adams' ethical evaluations are seen as applicable significantly though loosely expands the ethical frame in which we see the marriage of Joseph and Fanny as an important ethical victory for the comic world they inhabit;[7] it is not only Lady Booby, Lawyer Scout,

4. The consistent agreement of the paragon figure with one defined as a good man is especially emphatic; Adams' inability to comprehend some of the refinements of the vices Wilson describes * * * indicates the absolute degree to which the vice is condemned.

5. Mr. Wilson does not, of course, escape to an ideal world when he leaves London; the dog-killing squire attests to the fact that rural life is capable of producing its own forms of vice.

6. The fate of the Wilsons' lost child, strawberry mark and all, prepares us for the discovery that the Wilsons are Joseph's parents; at the very least, we know we will meet the Wilsons again after Adams,

Joseph, and Fanny leave their country retreat. But there is no integral connection between the expectations thus aroused and the strayed-lamb adventures of which Mr. Wilson's tale largely consists.

7. The ironic fact that the happy ending is brought about partly through Mr. Booby's intercession with a corrupt judge and that he, who stands opposed to what Adams represents, is also the agent who rewards Adams with a living of 130 pounds a year mocks the hostile elements in society, not the virtues of Fanny, Joseph, or Adams. The irony increases the special comic pleasure when they receive their final rewards despite an antagonistic world.

Pamela, and their ilk who are seen as eventually overcome by Adams, Fanny, and Joseph, but also the retinue of vicious and foolish characters whose values are indirectly hostile to those that proclaim the two innocents deserving of the particular brand of happiness they win; it is as if they had won this happiness in spite of a hostile world—including the vicious London world depicted primarily in the digression—whose direct agents happen to be Lady Booby, Pamela, Lawyer Scout, *et al.*

Finally, though most of Mr. Wilson's early difficulties, unlike Joseph's, have stemmed at least partially from his own participation in the vices and follies which threaten his virtue, his discovery of the path from London and what it represents to rural bliss with the former Harriet Heartfree constitutes a perceptible analogue to the struggles and final victory of Joseph and Fanny. But the digressive narrative facilitates more economical expansion of values because the particular forms of obstacles the Wilsons overcome, the terms in which their passion for each other is expressed, and even the minimum material rewards necessary for their happiness are those consonant only with the traits of characters of a different social class from that to which Joseph and Fanny belong. The substance of the obstacles both couples overcome, the nature of the virtuous passion they feel, and the rewards they desire are just similar enough to suggest that the problem of footman and milkmaid has a wider pertinence; despite the jocular, and probably ironic, sleight-of-hand involved in the discovery that the Wilsons are Joseph's parents, it is appropriate that the last two paragraphs of the novel reveal: "Lady Booby . . . returned to London . . . where a young captain of dragoons, together with eternal parties at cards, soon obliterated the memory of Joseph," while the "happiness of this couple [Joseph and Fanny] is a perpetual fountain of pleasure to their fond parents [the Wilsons]."[8]

*   *   *

MORRIS GOLDEN

[Fielding's Psychology and Its Relation to Morality][†]

*   *   *

From the beginning of his writing career, Fielding sees the aim and reward of the good life as happiness, a purely psychological condition consequent on one's awareness of one's own benevolence, on a Shaftesburian harmony with one's kind. But harmony with one's kind requires a wide-ranging awareness of, and responsiveness to, its variety; and yet

---

8. Gaffer and Gammer Andrews conveniently disappear; it is the Wilsons with whom Joseph and Fanny live and on whom they shower their happiness.

† From *Fielding's Moral Psychology* (Amherst: U of Massachusetts P, 1966) 17–19, 42–43, 53–55, 76–80, 92–95, 124–31. Some author's notes have been omitted.

happiness is lodged within the mind. In an effort to resolve part of this enduring paradox, Fielding argues that the mind must send emissaries to external reality and rove among other human beings, but that it can naturally recognize only those moral qualities in man and society that correspond to what is within itself. On the question of whether, through experience, the mind can develop an intellectual awareness of what is not within it, Fielding vacillates. He is eager for the achievement of such awareness, attempts to teach it in all his writings, but can be certain of no mechanism capable of providing it. Weak or inexperienced good men, like Heartfree,[1] respond only to virtuous signals, with which they are in sympathy, and so they can easily be made victims. Fielding's sad tendency, from the beginning of his career as a writer of fiction, is to see his function as that of providing elements of romance to prevent the reality of contemporary life from destroying the good.

With pain and pleasure our only stimuli and our only rewards, it seems at first inexplicable that some people still engage in violent evil, disturbing others and themselves. The cause, Fielding suggests, is a misreading of the signals—the assumption that "greatness" really means prestige in the world—coupled with a self-enclosed refusal to grant humanity to others. Essentially, it is the substitution of competition for sympathy and self-approval. As punishment, the evil, like Jonathan Wild, live within their own delusive creation, a permanent hell of selfish competition. Unable to defer any gratification, self-enclosed evil men aggressively attack society, from which they tear the joys that poison them.

Fielding's ideal is the "great and good" men, who have formed intellectual conceptions of the evil which they cannot feel, and can move out benevolently, forcing sympathetic communication and recognizing its signals. The great and good should be provided with prudence as well as energy, but the former is a dubious quality. Very often the bad for Fielding (as for Aristotle) is the good perverted, and he fears the consequences of power even in the best. He fears that with power the movement outward will too often become exploitive. His great horror, therefore, is aroused by hypocrisy, which he sees as a deliberate distortion of reality, a deliberate blow to our only hope, sympathetic understanding of a world in which we have to do good almost blindly. Reputation is a most important concomitant; it should be our key to the apprehension of the real moral condition of others, but through vanity, hypocrisy, and calumny it becomes another medium of confusion.

As a consequence, Fielding usually points to the *actions* of men, since if these are observed long enough we can approach men's motives, their casts of mind, through all the distortions which the artificialities of society, the lies of others, and their own pretensions have introduced. Virtuous actions usually—though not always—look virtuous; but vice also seeks the appearance of virtue, imposing lies on others as one means of denying them equal humanity. In love lie the greatest capacities for the

---

1. The exemplar of virtue in *Jonathan Wild*, whose trust is betrayed by the unscrupulous Wild [*Editor*].

fulfilment of virtue, since an intense conviction of the humanity of another is combined with an intense concentration of the self outward and an intense satisfaction of the self within. Since love is the greatest good, the perversion of love (as with Wild and his Laetitia)[2] is the worst evil, and it most denies the humanity of another as it most tortures the self.

Briefly, Fielding's central vision of man as enclosed within the self, experiencing happiness or discontent exclusively within the mind, and yet needing to get out of it for the exercise of goodness, has a number of corollaries in his thought. It permeates Fielding's epistemology and psychology, limiting both how people know the world around them and what their reactions to it will be; it tends to combine optimism about the possibilities of happiness within the mind with pessimism about the destinies of the insulated virtuous unless they are miraculously protected from the consequences of their innocence; it combines something of a deterministic approach to human character with a hope that the improvement of environment will allow cultivation of the widespread seeds of goodness.

* * *

In the famous preface to *Joseph Andrews* the derivation of the ridiculous from affectation, which in turn is derived from vanity or hyprocrisy, immediately relates Fielding's subject and technique to his sense of psychological enclosure. Vanity is a distorted view of the self and of outer reality arising from an inability to see oneself in proper perspective; hypocrisy, an attempt to mislead others—who are also assumed to be masqueraders—as they try to compare themselves with us. In either case, preoccupation with the self causes, and manifests itself in, limited ways of knowing: we can know mainly elements outside ourselves which correspond to elements within.

All through *Joseph Andrews* major plot issues depend on the enclosure of the self and the consequent comic lack of communication. The first significant episode, Lady Booby's attempted seduction of Joseph, involves three failures to see outside the self: her failure to recognize that she is subject to an animal desire which levels her with others of her species; her inability to communicate her feelings clearly to Joseph, at least in the first scene; and hilarious problems of communication with her serving woman Slipslop, who recognizes the animal lust and snobbery—since she shares both in cruder form—but cannot tell which element is dominant in Lady Booby. In turn, Lady Booby is unable to imagine for Joseph any orientation notably different from her own, any response to sex but the exploitive one which would make her a highly desirable conquest for a footman. At the end of the novel, when the peddler tells the story that makes Joseph and Fanny brother and sister, everyone believes him, except Pamela, who had never heard her parents mention another child, "and except the Lady Booby, who suspected the falsehood of the

2. Before their fathers arrange their marriage, the sluttish Laetitia Snap repels Wild's sexual assaults while enjoying other lovers [Editor].

story from her ardent desire that it should be true; and Joseph, who feared its truth from his earnest wishes that it might prove false" (IV, xiii).

Between beginning and end, incident after incident shows that our knowledge of the outside world reflects what is within ourselves. In one sequence, for example, Parson Trulliber, at the moment eager to sell hogs, unhesitatingly accepts his wife's identification of Adams as a hog buyer. Besides the Lockean associationist psychology, we are also presented with the pervasive moral issue of seeing others simply as ministrants to our needs and desires. Trulliber is taken up with his own "greatness and importance," which is fed both by his wealth and by his wife's willingness to yield her identity to serve and admire him. But the yielding is not so slavish and self-effacing as it at first seems. He is evidently sexually prodigious, so that he serves her lust while she satisfies his pride. In Fielding's novels, such a modus vivendi is often routine humanity's parody of the unusual felicity of the heroes. We rub along, he shows, substituting the exhibition of parallel passions for the intersection of good dispositions which constitutes true communication.

* * *

As I have suggested earlier, sex is a major medium by which Fielding symbolically demonstrates both morality and psychology. In each of the novels, the completely communicative love of the hero and heroine is contrasted, in the framework and details of the action, with the self-enclosed lusts of others. All of the heroes are given opportunities to make sexual conveniences of willing women in sequences on which the plots of the novels turn. All the heroines are the objects of male lust.

In *Joseph Andrews*, Lady Booby's appetite for Joseph, which is complicated by her high-bred neuroses, is largely mental, made up of fantasies of his beauty and nourished by scandals of the lovers of great ladies. While Mrs. Slipslop's tigerish lust is completely animal, expressing itself in treats of food and drink, Lady Booby intellectually assumes that social conventions are on her side, and is shocked when Joseph speaks to her of preserving his virtue. Though this is supposed to be and is hilarious, it nonetheless reaffirms Joseph's insistence on his individual humanity and forces Lady Booby, toward the end of the book, to think of him as a person rather than as a generic handsome footman from whom his mistress can fairly demand sexual adventure. Though Lady Booby is not sensitive to the purport of his arguments, a good deal of her later perplexity is caused by Joseph's popping out from anonymity to personality.

Fanny's attractions, which Fielding describes in gastronomical terms, arouse in various men the sexual hunger that at times forms the basis of the plot. She enters the novel on the edge of rape, where Fielding balances her, sometimes pathetically and always absurdly, through encounters with the vicious roasting squire, Didapper's servant, and minor dangers like the justices before whom she appears. So obviously is she a symbol of sexual convenience to surrounding society that Beau Didapper, plainly effeminate, tries to use her as a device by which to assert manly potency. And so powerful and mysterious is beauty for Fielding at this stage that even Abraham Adams, in Lady Booby's enchanted castle, finds himself magically in bed with her. At the end, sexual activity is directly and amusingly contrasted to the central message of Christianity: Adams's sermon to the assembled company "concluded with strongly asserting that there was no such thing as pleasure in this [world]. At which Pamela and her husband smiled on one another" (IV, xiii).

But the relations among the central trio are completely opposite to such self-enclosure. While Joseph and Fanny both seek the pleasure of sex (which is neutral rather than bad), they are willing to subordinate their desires to social law, to the church's codification of divine law, and, above all, to the loving guidance of Adams. In all of Joseph's rescues of Fanny it is her welfare he is centrally concerned with, and when Fanny heard that Joseph was sick at an inn, she "that instant abandoned the cow she was milking" and went off to find him (II, x). Though Adams is less divorced from this world than he would admit—witness his vanity and his earthly concern for his child—in his responsiveness to the needs of all people he shows a deeper outgoing love than his final sermon suggests.

* * *

In the preface to *Joseph Andrews*, Fielding admits that he has introduced black vices despite his program of ridiculing only foibles. Since he is following real human nature, he says, he cannot omit vices: humanity cannot be faithfully imitated without reproducing the consequences of violent passions. For that matter, his practice suggests that the springs of action—or at least of plot in fiction—are violent passions, not foibles. Though rewards and punishments are registered within the mind, man must act in the world outside, where his preoccupations must inevitably conflict with those of others. Plot is a series of such conflicts. Though Cervantes is one of Fielding's models, Molière is his master in drama; conflict of passions, not the exhibition of one deluded consciousness, constitutes his imitation of the real world. Adams' absentmindedness would be insignificant without his argumentative dogmatism, which brings him to the verge of battle with various equally violent acquaintances. And there would be no novel at all without Lady Booby's lust and Joseph's passionate chastity.

Vanity, the master passion of the comic psychology which dominates the first novel and influences considerably the themes and structures of the other two, is basic in the moral statement of *Joseph Andrews*. Vanity, the source of all passional violence—"All our passions are thy slaves"— is the most confining of all passions for Fielding and the most widespread. No one is safe from some tincture of vanity; even Sophia and Amelia[3] love to look in mirrors. The virtuous and experienced Wilson,

---

3. The exemplary heroines of *Tom Jones* and *Amelia* [*Editor*].

in the course of narrating his own tale (his journey from indifference to a sense of another, his cousin Harriet who saves him socially and becomes the object of his morally saving love) says for Fielding that "vanity is the worst of passions, and more apt to contaminate the mind than any other. . . ." Selfishness, he says, is widespread, and "it is natural to hate and envy those who stand between us and the good we desire." In lust, ambition, even avarice, comparatively few persons stand between us and our desires, "but the vain man seeks pre-eminence; and everything which is excellent or praiseworthy in another renders him the mark of his antipathy" (III, iii). Even Parson Adams, the most unworldly of Fielding's creations, has his share of vanity, which is centered in the subjects of learning, the ministerial function, and the qualities of the schoolmaster.

In general, Fielding finds that vanity is a tractable vice. Wherever we are vain others can conveniently manipulate us. In small matters, vain people like Lady Booby or Slipslop or Pounce can be appeased by flattery. On a larger scale, vanity can lead to great acts of public usefulness, such as the establishment of colleges and hospitals. Joseph, in a lecture on charity, argues that the path to this virtue can be the vanity of the giver (III, vi), an argument which the author was to present in his own person in *Amelia:* "Nay, give me leave to wonder that pride, which is constantly struggling, and often imposing on itself, to gain some little preeminence, should so seldom hint to us the only certain as well as laudable way of setting ourselves above another man, and that is, by becoming his benefactor" (IV, iv).

Because passages of this sort clearly connect vanity and charity (following Mandeville, and perhaps Pope on the master passion),[4] Mr. Battestin can plausibly argue that the thematic unity of the first novel lies in the balance achieved between a satiric thesis of vanity and a positive antithesis of charity. Such a view, I think, slightly blurs the focus of the book. In his preface Fielding says that vanity and hypocrisy are his subjects, and it is evident that everything in the novel is explicable by these qualities, not by their opposites. If we consider charity a theme equal to vanity, we cannot sufficiently excuse the absurdity of Adams; if vanity is predominant, then Adams becomes the perfect illustration of inevitable imperfection in even the best human character. In the first case, we must make central the narrative of Wilson, thereby giving structural primacy to an inactive stretch (which I grant that Fielding is using symbolically, as he uses the Man of the Hill's account in *Tom Jones*), an unlikely arrangement for a confirmed Aristotelian. In the other, the encounter with the vicious squire—the extreme in that self-enclosed vanity which poses the greatest threat to all the virtuous—is the central climax. If we abandon the issue of climax and argue instead for thematic iteration as the source of unity, then the story of Leonora the flirt is irrelevant to charity but directly concerned with vanity. While charity is clearly

4. *An Essay on Man* 2. 131–32, 175–76, 245–46. In *An Essay on Charity and Charity-Schools,* Bernard Mandeville accused the promoters of these new schools (see above, p. 19 n. 8) of religious hypocrisy and concern for their own reputations [*Editor*].

the positive answer to the follies exposed, the actual exposure of those follies across the spectrum of human nature is, as Fielding said, the substance of the novel.

But vanity and its subordinate passions do not always work alone, nor is their operation uniform. The scene between Lady Booby and Mrs. Slipslop early in *Joseph Andrews* is constructed on the principle "that passions operate differently on the human mind, as diseases on the body, in proportion to the strength or weakness, soundness or rottenness, of the one and the other"; hence "the different operations of this passion of love in the gentle and cultivated mind of the Lady Booby, from those which it effected in the less polished and coarser disposition of Mrs. Slipslop" (I, vii). Despite the irony—the moral difference between the two "operations" is only that between psychological and physical rape— the distinction is meaningful. Environment—particularly social educa- tion—can help to repress the overt aggression of violent passions by transferring it from the realm of unthinking action (Mrs. Slipslop) to that of conscious imagination (Lady Booby). As in Pope's famous lines, social pressures can here act the part of reason.[5] Furthermore, a favorite practice of Fielding as novelist, hinted at in *Tom Jones* when he speaks of the variety which he has created within the same social strata and occupations, is to combine the various atoms—passions, reflective abil- ity, disposition, social position, education, habit, occupation—in differ- ent ways, to see what the resultant may be. In the Lady Booby–Joseph case, the power which society gives to aristocrats over footmen can sup- port the passions in achieving their desires; later in the novel, the vicious squire can count on much of society's approval in his wish to rape Fanny. Indeed, society itself can abet certain kinds of passions, as Fielding iron- ically observes: he says that Lady Booby is sorely tempted by Joseph's beauty, and hopes that his women readers, when he describes his hero, will "bridle their rampant passion for chastity, and be at least as mild as their violent modesty and virtue will permit them" in judging her (I, viii). As a social satirist, Fielding is notable for his early insistence that comstockery can be as unsavory as the motives for excess.

The most extended study of passion in the novel is Lady Booby. Early and late, her mind is a battlefield, in which vanity always wins. Within this mind, the outgoing passions, Love, Honour, and Pity, are on Joseph's side; self-enclosed Pride and Revenge are against him, "and thus the poor lady was tortured with perplexity, opposite passions distracting and tearing her mind different ways" (I, ix). Her dismissal of Joseph is for therapeutic, not moral reasons; she thinks her mind will be more at rest with him away, and finds it convenient to think also that she is pushing aside temptation. When we meet her later, we find that she again is subjected to mental disturbances by a succession of various passions, which returned the day after she dismissed Joseph (IV, i). Evidently her disposition is itself made up of a confused conflict of passions.

---

5. In Epistle 2 of the *Essay on Man*, Pope defines reason's part as restraining the individual's self- love or passions. In Epistle 3, 269–82, he argues that men form societies and adopt laws for the same purpose [Editor].

Her imaginative wallowing in sensual pleasures does not permit direct, outward joys of the sort which Joseph and Fanny can have. Joseph, who has caused the fancies, has also put her pride in great public danger: such acts as attempting to send Fanny to a bridewell are beneath her as an aristocrat, and through them she has completely committed herself to the pursuit of a footman. There is no peace for her, as Fielding suggests in the title of Book IV, Chapter xiii, where her absurd similarity to a tragic heroine is alluded to: "The history, returning to the Lady Booby, gives some account of the terrible conflict in her breast between love and pride." And her single case is no more than a critical example of the mind affected by a mixture of passions. As generally in Fielding's psychology, where a variety of passions dominates a mind over a long period of time, their combination constitutes the character; in such a mind the disposition must be selfishly indrawn.

The relations between the basic disposition and the overlay of different passions allow for the permanence within variety which Fielding claims as his province in his comment on the universality of the Tow-wouses: "where extreme turbulencey of temper, avarice, and an insensibility of human misery, with a degree of hypocrisy, have united in a female composition, Mrs. Tow-wouse was that woman; and where a good inclination, eclipsed by a poverty of spirit and understanding, hath glimmered forth in a man, that man hath been no other than her sneaking husband" (III, i). Disposition, as I have earlier noted, is something antecedent to the passions but deducible from them, "given," and not subject to destruction, though it may be modified and camouflaged by education. Mrs. Tow-wouse's passions, all connected with her presumably selfish disposition, seem to reinforce each other, though they must be kept within acceptable limits by her social and economic condition. Her husband, whose good disposition is constantly checked by a bad passion (cowardice) and who is unable to see the world clearly, is inevitably a butt of comic frustrations. While Fielding is centrally concerned to reveal vanity and hypocrisy in *Joseph Andrews*, he does not stop with these elements of character, but goes on to make a serious attempt to support the comic actions with "nature": a coherent system of psychology made up of passional building blocks.

* * *

Though the basic disposition of the good man is benevolent—a corollary of his necessary religious feelings—nonetheless the right use of reason teaches him to protect himself and society against evil where he sees it. * * * As all his social pamphlets show, both from his analytical observation of life and by training as lawyer and magistrate, Fielding refused to fall into the trap of easy and universal benevolism; he insisted that evil was a reality and not an illusion, and that it had to be dealt with severely. Only the exercise of reason—which involves the assessment of how life develops in society—can guide the responsible judge.

* * *

In addition to reason, the other factor that shapes the passions toward right action is religion. Reason is a restraining power which keeps vicious passions under control; but when it is their sole guide, it destroys the wish to act outside the self. Christianity, by contrast, is a motivating power, causing its subject to act in a charitable and well-disposed way, leading him out of himself to love others and work selflessly for them. The religious impulse is usually personal and absolute, whereas reason is predominantly social and relative. The disposition is largely affected by or allied with the private force of religion, while the relations of the passions and society are mediated through reason. The two animate, modify, and enforce each other in a serene mind. The formal Christian system is the perfect union of the two in society.

A good many times Fielding indicates how the demands of religion—nebulously, like reason, intermediate between a disposition and a passional appetite—conflict with the largely selfish passions; and sometimes the religious system, like any system, is not applicable to actual society. At least in *Joseph Andrews* and *Tom Jones*, though Fielding advocates religion he delights in showing that even the finest man will forget that earthly joy is vanity when he loves a beautiful woman. Sometimes the conflict is impossible to solve, just as in practice reason's advice to examine the objects of passion before acting may be impossible to follow.

In *Joseph Andrews*, when religion is in conflict with powerful social or emotive values, Fielding never opposes the religious truth though he sometimes emphasizes its irrelevance in the responses of ordinary people. In the argument between Truilliber and Adams, Mrs. Truilliber "begged him not to fight, but show himself a true Christian, and take the law of him" (II, xiv). After Fanny has been abducted, Adams lectures Joseph on his duty, as a Christian, to accept the blows of life with thanks; Joseph says he knows it is his duty, but he is nonetheless heartbroken. In both cases short-sighted individual passions have repelled the universal rules of religion; but in the first the motive is vanity, while in the second it is primarily love, the good disposition, a deep concern for the well-being of another. By implication, where the good disposition seems to come into conflict with the religious system, it is at least supportable, since it is fundamentally in accord with the spirit which underlies the system. Indeed, Fielding uses Adams himself to illustrate the human impossibility of following formal religious rules literally in practice: as Joseph points out, Adams' sermon on moderation, on not doting on others passionately, is immediately disproved by his own responses to the news of his son's drowning and his safety. While there is no question that in *Joseph Andrews* Fielding, as Mr. Battestin says, endorses the liberal church views of Barrow and Clarke,[6] his ridicule of otherworldliness as an alternative to the warm facts of human feeling suggests a preference for the good disposition and its passions to systematic religion. No better

6. See above, p. 166, n. 1 and p. 427, n. 2 *[Editor]*.

system exists, but any system is intellectual and therefore no more than a form for feeling, which is primary.

* * *

Despite Fielding's hopes for reform and the buoyancy of *Joseph Andrews* and *Tom Jones,* his novels often have sad implications, as is inevitable when happiness is seen as residing only within the mind. He provides us with gloriously triumphant fantasies—the deliberate substitution of the ideal for the actual—but frequently forces us to abandon them, or at least subordinate them to sane awareness of surrounding actuality. Pervasively, he opposes the romance, the fairy tale, the myth or reverie, the self-indulgence of the mind, with the actuality which seems to give it the lie.[7]

Sometimes the actuality is dramatically active; sometimes it is strongly implied. In the jolliest book, *Joseph Andrews,* the checks of reality are relatively minor, though too evident to overlook. * * *

* * *

In the preface to *Joseph Andrews,* Fielding regretfully asserts the impossibility of staying within the limits of comic fantasy if the constituents of it are to be people as one knows them in life. Though follies are the proper substance of the ridiculous, the vices inevitable in drawing "nature" are too serious for amusement. Despite his assurances that these vices will not triumph, the novel itself inescapably implies that without authorial intervention virtue would be destroyed. In London, Joseph's fellow-servants at once subject him to temptation, and though he resists pretty well, he dresses gaudily and participates in theater riots; ideal as Joseph's appearances before us show him to be, Fielding implies that the actual condition of being a footman forbids completely virtuous behavior. On the road at night after Joseph has been dismissed, he is robbed, beaten, stripped, and tossed into a ditch for dead. Through the element of romance, "story," a coach stops after his groans are heard, and again we see that normally the postilion would overlook the groans, or, if he were kind and adventurous, that the passengers would insist on driving past. We are to understand that an actual person in Joseph's situation would die.

The grimness of the alternatives to fantasy is communicated largely through implication in *Joseph Andrews,* since in that novel Fielding is not concerned to work out as limiting a series of events as in *Tom Jones,* where he insists on giving us "natural" situations and complications. That is, the first novel is much more than the others the fairy-tale adventures of odd, even unique people, highly exaggerated over whatever living models they could be based on. At the beginning, Joseph is a male version of what Fielding believes to be a wildly improbable character,

---

7. In *Fielding's Art of Fiction,* Maurice Johnson writes illuminatingly of this characteristic of Fielding's technique, particularly as it appears in *Joseph Andrews.*

Richardson's Pamela. The delightful Adams is an intellectual conception of the combination of perfect active goodness with complete innocence. Fanny, like Gilbert's Patience,[8] is a caricature of the quintessential milkmaid. In their actions in the plot, they do not have the moral significance of typicality or presumed normality. The encounter between Joseph and the predatory Mrs. Slipslop early in the novel means no more than a good joke, whereas the reactions of Tom in similar situations have evident moral implications about the behavior of inexperienced but good-natured youth when faced with sexual temptation. Joseph's beauty so powerfully affects Betty the chambermaid (who is as much Cervantes' Maritornes as she is Good Samaritan) that he is forced to throw her out of the room to protect his chastity—a burlesque of Pamela's troubles, a deliberately exaggerated fantasy of male attractiveness, but not an exemplum. Tom Jones, a much less fabulous hero, attracts the promiscuous Molly and Jenny, but both engagements are affected by his social position, and both reflect his moral nature and his realistic opportunity to choose. Booth, in the last novel, is brought into Miss Matthews' bed after a long train of circumstances that provide her actions with a context and an analysis of her character that makes the result likely. Fielding moves steadily from a novel in which exaggeration implies the realistic alternative to one in which not only the possible but the probable and perhaps even the inevitable take place, according to his late view that a life is a consistent pattern of actions.

In *Joseph Andrews* the contrast between the likely danger of the outer world of action and the self-enclosed world of fantasy is epitomized in the adventures of the heroes and the leisurely journey of Lady Booby's entourage, which Fielding makes available for indifferent rescues. When Joseph is held hostage for the feed bill for Adams' horse, Mrs. Slipslop conveniently comes along to pay his ransom. At another time, Peter Pounce's coach saves Fanny from certain rape and the men from an embarrassing and possibly dangerous imprisonment. While Joseph, Fanny, and Adams are properly brave and buoyant in their travels through the English countryside, the natives (acting on the selfish principles of "nature") are not generally friendly, and the actual workings of the social system are most threatening.[9] A real trip of this sort would certainly end in exploitation or prison, and possibly in death. If the journey epitomizes the movement out of the self into right action in the world, Fielding makes no guarantees of easy success. The only assured reward is internal.

Even the inserted Leonora romance, which in the tradition Fielding inherited from Cervantes would be divorced from its realistic context, is at times used for direct or implied comment on social actuality. During

8. The heroine of the Gilbert and Sullivan operetta of that name [*Editor*].

9. Mr. Battestin, in *The Moral Basis of Fielding's Art*, pp. 30 ff., convincingly places Adams within a contemporary homiletic tradition which made the wanderings of Abraham in exile models of faith and good works; but he tends to minimize the likelihood that at this stage Fielding is using Isaac Barrow for allusive humor, as he elsewhere in the novel uses such favorite authors as Sophocles and Homer.

one of its interruptions, Miss Grave-Airs, a prudish passenger, refuses to allow the limping Joseph to ride in the same coach with her because he is a footman, the sort of treatment which he might have met regularly outside a novel. An exchange between Adams and the narrator sharply indicates the stupidity and ignorance of judges of courts of sessions. In the romance itself, when Leonora's father avariciously refuses to give Bellarmine a fortune with her, he abandons his suit and runs off to Paris, she immures herself in a lonely great house, and Horatio, staying a bachelor, soberly sticks to business and grows rich. Again, Leonora's aunt seems much more appropriate to a satire on society than to a romantic tale; she urges Leonora to break her word to Horatio for the sake of a richer match, has taken bribes, and is a religious hypocrite. All of this is dismayingly realistic for a romantic insert, in which we might expect at least a suicide or two for love. Compare, for example, the heroics in the inserted tales in *Don Quixote*, Fielding's model.

To allow for this pervasive contrasting of the actual with the fabulous, Fielding arranges for Adams not to keep his clerical gown clean or, at times, even visible; consequently, he can be involved in uncensored English life of a sort that might not be available to an actual pastor in full bloom. In their first contact with the legal system, Adams, Joseph, and Fanny are saved by pure luck, an indication of what their fates might have been in the ordinary course of life. Only the coincidental presence of a gentleman who recognized Adams saved him and Fanny from commitment on the spot by an ordinary justice of the peace. Without help from the gentry, such poor as depart from the normal—a man in a dirty cassock accompanied by a disheveled dairy maid, for example—are in danger from Fielding's society.

From time to time, as in the discussion of the quarter-session, the contrasts are made overtly. After a congenial innkeeper damns the false-promising squire (a conscious and therefore dishonest Don Quixote) and cites the damage that he has done, Adams observes that since he has the appearance in his face of "that sweetness of disposition, which furnishes out a good Christian," he may still reform (II, xvii). The host argues that this is nonsense. If one has traveled in the world, he says, the only thing one expects to learn from a stranger's face is whether he has had the smallpox. Adams, at this point absurd, heatedly pursues his argument that the classics teach more about human character than does experience. Just in time to prevent violence, Joseph arrives, to demonstrate again the deliberate doubleness of Fielding's view. In the normal course of the argument, Adams would have seriously annoyed the host, who surely would have revoked his cheerful assumption of the cost of their meals as an unrecoverable debt. The best of men, if he is eccentric and therefore enclosed against others on certain issues, will alienate even his friends in the actual world.

In the background of the jolly events, but visible to all of us, is the immense danger in which the poor in England find themselves, the immense power of the squires. A young neighbor shoots the harmless dog of Wilson's daughter, and there is nothing to be done about it. The vicious squire who captures the wandering trio on the hare hunt is angry over the damage done by Joseph and Adams; and while he and his lackeys ponder what to do we realize that they can do practically anything. The actions of the squire take the form of folly and practical jokes—an indication of the triviality to which idleness and power and ignorance lead—but he also organizes the abduction of Fanny and the beating of her escorts. He and his "curs" are available for any viciousness, and are consequently utterly dangerous to any weaker people, who have no recourse against them without the unlikely help of Peter Pounce and his men.

Pounce's hypocritical fantasy about the wastefulness of charity in such a mild and fertile land as England is another crisp indication of the difference between the dream as some would like it and the actuality. We know that he lies, and so does Adams, who soon leaves the coach. But his argument is no more absurd than the continual rescuing of the main characters, which equally forces on us the contrasting truth. Lady Booby's threats to turn Adams from his curacy if he publishes the banns for Joseph's wedding a second time again point up the conflict of actuality and fantasy. Adams, as he must, says that he cannot deviate from the church's rules no matter what the cost, and the novel is so arranged that her threat is not carried out. But we know that actually he and his family are at her mercy. Lest we miss the point, Fielding earlier had him tell us that all his hopes for preferment had been destroyed time and again by his refusal to sell his nephew's vote at elections. Moreover, while his courageous stands indicated his integrity and contributed to his mental peace, their beneficiaries in a corrupt system were as bad as his tempters. The political actuality was shameful, perhaps hopeless; the only good was in the ideal political myths in Adams's mind.

At the end, all the complications are settled miraculously and happily, as they should be in a comic epic. But the effect is different from, say, a Roman comedy, where a number of implausible, stylized people run through a plot which is not a comment on contemporary life even though it exhibits a good many "realistic" details and the issues (marriage, the freeing of a slave, the son's rebellion against the father) are part of everyday life. *Joseph Andrews* also differs significantly from such English versions of the classical comic tradition as Jonson's *Alchemist* and *Bartholomew Fair*. In those, the characters and their actions are primarily comments on the consequence of folly and vice; while everything is providentially made right in the end, there has been no danger for decent, good-natured, reasonable people like ourselves. All we need do is mind our business and avoid the complacent folly of Littlewit or the wild pride of Sir Epicure Mammon[1] and we will be all right. In contrast, all the fortuitous escapes of the central trio in *Joseph Andrews*,

---

1. A foolish sensualist who believes the alchemist will provide him the "philosopher's stone" to turn base metal to gold. In *Bartholomew Fair*, Littlewit allows or encourages other men to take freedoms with his wife *[Editor]*.

as well as the breakneck plotting of the conclusion, persuade us that without the conscious intervention of the author our chances of survival, if we were in their place, would not be good. The fantasy and the actuality comment on each other. Outer actuality—which must be faced—can very possibly be murderous. In an escape to the fantastic lies some safety; but one cannot always live in fantasy (or an ideal estate in the country). Adams can reason in the purity of his mind wherever he is. But less saintly figures like Joseph, Fanny, and pre-eminently Wilson, must demonstrate the goodness of their dispositions in the world before they can retire to serenity.

HOMER GOLDBERG

The Reasoning Behind the Form of *Joseph Andrews* †

Most readers of *Joseph Andrews* have found the novel's distinctive substance in the adventures of Parson Adams. Although he yielded primacy of place on the title page to Joseph's story as the object of long-range expectation and the focus of the novel's resolution, from Fielding's Preface, which contains no reference to the young footman or his fortunes, one might infer that the running encounter between his "Character of perfect Simplicity" and a "copious Field" of the vain and hypocritical lay closer to his central preoccupations in conceiving the book. Obviously it was through this strain that it derived most significantly from the work of which it proclaimed itself an imitation. Whatever the actual process by which Fielding arrived at his eventual conception of the novel's distinctive form, the hypothesis that the work as it stands represents his solution to problems posed by his adaptation of Cervantes' general formula is at least as plausible as the hard-dying notion that he set out to write a second *Shamela* and wandered astray. As good a place as any, then, to begin reconstructing the thinking behind the finished structure is with the definition of the nature of that imitation and the problems it entailed, commencing with "the most glaring [character] in the whole."

I

The essential formula Fielding perceived at the heart of Cervantes' novel was a character set off from the other inhabitants of his fictional world by a persistent tendency to misconstrue that world in a certain way, yet exhibiting, for all his error and oddity, moral and intellectual qualities that earn the reader's affection and admiration. The most obvious modification he made in devising his own particular version of this for-

† From *The Art of* Joseph Andrews (Chicago and London: U of Chicago P, 1969) 73–92. Text has been slightly revised, roman numerals added, book and chapter numbers substituted for page references; some footnotes are revised, some added, and others omitted.

mula was to narrow the scope of his comic hero's misapprehension. Whereas Quixote's obsession works its transformations upon all aspects of reality, Parson Adams' mistakes are confined to the characters of men.[1] Fielding may have seen the path of his deviation marked out by Cervantes himself in the "most fortunate and noble Beginning" of Quixote's "Feats of Arms." The adventure of the whipped serving lad's rescue involves no wild metamorphosis of the situation.[2] The joke turns upon Quixote's error in assuming that the peasant will honor his pledge to pay the lad and refrain from punishing him; while the knights rides off exultant at having "redressed the greatest Wrong and Grievance that ever Injustice could design or Cruelty commit," the reader remains to see the farmer take out his resentment on the boy's hide. Cervantes' primary point, underlined in the episode's long-delayed sequel, is that by intervening on the boy's behalf, the great avenger has only made him suffer more. For Fielding, the greater interest of the episode may have been in the knight's idealistic expectations concerning the master's adherence to his oath, an error acknowledged by Quixote himself in the sequel: "I might, by Experience, have remembered, that the Word of a Peasant is regulated, not by Honour, but Profit."[3] Coming at the very outset of Quixote's adventures, this atypical mistake might well have impressed Fielding. He also had before him the model of Gil Blas's repeated disillusionments to suggest the general direction of the adventures of his parson-errant. But though Adams was to undergo even more disappointing discoveries than Lesage's mistreated hero, his habitual assumption that the men he meets are as good as they profess was to be incorrigible by experience.

Obviously influenced by Fielding's specific ethical preoccupations, this concentration of Adams' Quixotism in the realm of character may also have been affected by his concern to make his adventures more "natural" than those of his master. He later praised Mrs. Lennox for similarly confining her heroine's folly to "mistakes [of] one Man for another," avoiding "the Absurdity of imagining Windmills and Wine-Bags to be human Creatures, or Flocks of Sheep to be Armies."[4] The *donnée* of these "much less extravagant and incredible" adventures also seemed to him more probable than that of the original: that "the Head of a very sensible Person is entirely subverted by reading Romances" was a "Concession . . . more easy to be granted in the Case of a young Lady than of an old Gentleman." In his own revision of the Cervantean formula, he did away altogether with the artificial subversion of mind; the premise that a country parson immersed in ancient learning and Christian teaching might be "as entirely ignorant of the ways of this World as an Infant" required no comparable special "concession." In keeping with his praise of the "perfect Judgment and Art" with which the "Subversion

---

1. Two exceptions are Adams' belief that the sheepstealers are ghosts (3:2) and his taking Slipslop for the devil or a witch (4:14).
2. See above, pp. 344–46.

3. *Don Quixote*, part II, chapter 31.
4. In a review of *The Female Quixote* by Charlotte Lennox (1720–1804) in *The Convent Garden Journal*, March 24, 1752; Jensen ed., I. 281–82.

of the Brain in Arabella is accounted for by her peculiar Circumstances, and Education," he provided his own comic hero a background against which his failure to "apprehend any such Passions as Malice and Envy to exist in Mankind" was, as he sardonically understated it, "less remarkable" than from the worldly perspective of a Colley Cibber.

By giving his hero's mistakes a more "natural" genesis, Fielding deprived himself of the abnormal fixation which, once conceded, "accounted for" Quixote's persistence in fantasy in the face of a hundred potentially disabusing adventures, and for his retention of amiable and noble qualities in the midst of his folly. He thus faced, in peculiarly aggravated form, the problem of combining the "difficult ingredients" of the "amiable, ridiculous, and natural" to which he referred, in full awareness of his own recent experience of their difficulty, in the Preface to *David Simple*.[5] He had to persuade his reader that a mature, genuinely learned, and sane man of "good Sense" and "good Parts" could credibly persist in mistaking the characters of his fellow men after repeated exposure to their meanness and fraud; and to preserve affection for him in the face of his persistence in error.

He was able to do this without violating his own canons of fictional "Truth" by conceiving his "Character of perfect Simplicity" in accordance with notions about the constitution of character which he stated in his essays and gave dramatic embodiment in his novels. Adams' exclamations on the wickedness of the times and his suspicion that "he was sojourning in a Country inhabited only by Jews and Turks" do not really affect his perception of his fellow creatures, because this peculiar defect of vision stems from a more fundamental element of his character than "good Sense" or "good Parts." This is made apparent in the "very curious Adventure" of the false promising gentleman (2:16) "in which Mr. *Adams* gave a much greater Instance of the honest Simplicity of his Heart than of his Experience in the Ways of this World." Inexperience might account for the parson's original delusion; but his sustained failure to suspect the fraud in the face of mounting evidence must be traced to another source, the same characteristic which prompts him, even after he is convinced that his deceiver "is indeed a wicked Man," to detect "in his Countenance sufficient Symptoms of that *bona Indoles*, that Sweetness of Disposition which furnishes out a good Christian." The irony is not simply that Adams mistakenly projects onto the psuedo-benevolent his own disposition: it is this very constitution which is the source of his habitual error. Like the pattern priest Fielding describes in the "Apology for the Clergy," he is "void of suspicion" and "not apt to censure the actions of men" because he exercises to an extraordinary degree the virtue which "comprehends almost the whole particular duty of a Christian":

> . . . "charity believeth all things, hopeth all things." It is
> inclined to maintain good and kind thoughts of men. It . . .

<hr />

5. See above, p. 331.

always turns the perspective, with a friendly care to magnify all good actions, and lessen evil. It weighs all mankind in the scales of friendship, and sees them with the eyes of love.[6]

Though this "brotherly love and friendly disposition of mind" is "everywhere taught in Scripture," in Adams it is not the product of instruction. It is the manifestation of the most important of the "goods" with which he is endowed—"good Nature." In an essay "On the Knowledge of the Characters of Men," probably written about the same time as *Joseph Andrews* and closely related to the preoccupations of the novel, Fielding offered a definition of this quality which, if it was not drawn with Adams specifically in mind, certainly describes accurately the central principle of his character.

Good-nature is that benevolent and amiable Temper of Mind, which disposes us to feel the Misfortunes, and enjoy the Happiness of others; and consequently pushes us on to promote the latter, and prevent the former; and that without any abstract Contemplation on the Beauty of Virtue, and without the Allurements or Terrors of Religion.[7]

The incorruptible, and therefore incorrigible, "honest Simplicity" of Adams' heart is clearly of this order: this is the force behind his impulsive intercession at the sound of a woman's cries, his groans at the misfortunes of Leonora and the follies of the young Wilson, and his dance of joy at the reunion of Joseph and Fanny. In all these responses, as in his benevolent misappraisals of his fellowmen, his behavior is the unmediated product of the deepest impulse of his *nature*, a term through which Fielding expressed his concept of the primordial and essentially unchangeable individuating principle of character—that "unacquired, original distinction, in the nature or soul of one man, from that of another" which he infers from the "very early and strong inclination to good or evil, which distinguishes different dispositions in children, in their first infancy."

Although the essential determinant of Adams' comic behavior is thus radical to his character, Fielding adapted another element of Cervantes' conception by relating the peculiarity of his protagonist's vision to his reading, which, if it is not the ultimate source of his characteristic error, serves to reinforce it. Adams' amazement at "the Wickedness of this World" stems not only from his own open nature ("As he had never any Intention to deceive, so he never suspected such a Design in others") but from his related tendency to assume that the noble sentiments of the ancient poets and philosophers and the virtuous conduct enjoined by the scriptures delineate human nature as it is, rather than as it might be or ought to be. Hence, even as he persists in misreading men's characters, he remains convinced of his superior knowledge of humanity, for "Knowledge of Men is only to be learnt from Books, *Plato* and *Seneca* for that" (2:16).

6. P. 317 above.   7. P. 324 above.

This erroneous equation of learning with practical wisdom is paralleled by a corresponding overestimation of all that is to be drawn from books—precept, doctrine, rational argument—as influences upon the direction of behavior and the formation of character. (In this respect Adams is the unlikely vehicle for Fielding's derision of the views expounded and dramatized in *Pamela*.) Emblematically, the anecdote the parson cites in his argument with the innkeeper (2:17) as an example of the invaluable knowledge to be gained from books defines the character of Socrates as one in which a "Disposition . . . naturally . . . inclined to Vice" was "corrected . . . by Philosophy." At the heated close of this debate, unaware how his very contention contradicts what he contends, he declares the learning of the clergy "more necessary than Life it self," for it "clothes you with Piety, Meekness, Humility, Charity, Patience, and all the other Christian Virtues." Thus Adams' "Blind side" extends from his ignorance of the failings of others, through his overestimation of the pedagogue as "the greatest Character in the World," to an incomprehension of the nature of his own spontaneous goodness, an irony Fielding is at pains to bring out in the immediately succeeding portion of the novel and again, most tellingly, near its close.

The particular doctrines of rational stoicism, submission to providence, and reliance on grace that Adams has drawn from his reading of classical philosophy and Christian scripture are contravened by his own impulsive humanity. But when Fielding, in the memorable episode of his son's supposed drowning, dramatically contrasts the parson's practice with his preaching, he is not exposing him as one "who *is* the very Reverse of what he would *seem* to be (Preface)." His lack of self-knowledge is the antithesis of conscious dissimulation. If he is vain enough to envisage the publication of his sermons and to aspire to the role of Socrates (3:7); if, believing the schoolmaster "the greatest Character in the World," he regards himself as "the greatest of all SchoolMasters" (3:5); if he prides himself on his learned insight into the characters of men, the area of his most essential blindness—he cannot be said to affect a false character in order to purchase applause. Because of his essential innocence and lack of selfish egoism, even these secondary and less appealing aspects of his character cannot be traced to Fielding's "only Source of the true Ridiculous."

Fielding might justly claim at the end of his preface that this "Character of perfect Simplicity" was "not to be found in any Book now extant." By taking as his starting point the fundamental paradox he remarked in the Quixote character—the wondrous mingling of sagacity and madness repeatedly emphasized in Cervantes' narrative—he set his comic hero above the dreary run of one-trait imitation Quixotes, from Sorel's extravagant shepherd to Smollett's Launcelot Greaves.[8] By compounding and intensifying his own version of this central irony, he created a figure

---

8. The hero of *Le Berger extravagant* (1627) by Charles Sorel (1599–1674) loses his wits reading pastoral romances; his bucolic adventures mock d'Urfé's *Astree* (see above, p. 4, n. 5). In *The Life* and *Adventures of Sir Launcelot Greaves* (1762) by Tobias Smollett (1721–71), a young man crazed by disappointment in love sets out accompanied by a cowardly squire to right wrongs.

whose internal complexity and life rival the richness of their great original. In place of Cervantes' single, endlessly fruitful source of comic error and mischance, he conceived a set of naturally related but amusingly inconsistent attributes out of which he was able to multiply comic ironies within a work of much briefer scope.[9] At the same time, he supplanted the often rather arbitrary concatenation of the ludicrous and noble in Quixote with a fusion of the amiable and ridiculous at the very heart of his protagonist. Fielding's remarks in the *Convent Garden Journal* and his own theatrical adaptation[1] suggest that he saw Quixote, like Mrs. Lennox's Arabella, as a mixture of distinct elements deriving from independent sources—the good qualities of the sane Senor Quesada persisting amidst the follies generated by his delusion. There are numerous incidents in Cervantes' novel that convey this impression: in the episode of the puppet show (pt. 2, chap. 26), for example, the quiet gentleman who comments critically on the narrator's management of his tale seems to have no necessary connection with the furious madman who suddenly begins hacking up the puppets whom he takes for real Saracens. If at other times Fielding saw the knight's obsession engendering flights of brilliance and nobility beyond the potential of the uncrazed hidalgo, there is no evidence that he ever found the knight's delusion itself amiable or appealing. In his own conception he heightened the paradox by making the very root of Adams' comic error the principal source of his amiability. Though his "good Parts," like Quixote's, merit respect and admiration, his good nature makes the strongest appeal to the reader's affections. Even as Fielding found innocence and "the greatest benevolence" among Quixote's "much more endearing" traits, so he would have his readers cherish Adams' good heart, and that simplicity which provokes their laughter.

II

This convergence of "difficult ingredients" was facilitated by an accompanying alteration of the context in which he placed his comic hero. Although Don Quixote describes his as a "degenerate Age, Fraud and a Legion of Ills infecting the World,"[2] except for such isolated vignettes as the galley-bound criminals this image is not reflected in the persons and situations he encounters. Were it not for his obsession, his life would be quiet and uneventful. If Adams traversed a prevailingly innocuous world like that which Quixote's imagination transforms into the stuff of "adventures," his perfect simplicity would not lead him into surprises and embarrassments. Demonstrating that "Life every where furnishes an

---

9. The character of Adams is rounded out by a set of secondary and less idiosyncratic foibles. Of these, the belief in the science of physiognomy which he articulates in his argument with the ex-sailor host (2:17) and the pedantic impulse to correct minor errors are most directly related to his central peculiarities, but his absentmindedness and perpetual hurry, the motley costume which deteriorates as the journey progresses, and even his belief in ghosts are consonant with the primary conception of his character.

1. *Don Quixote in England*, 1734.

2. *Don Quixote* 1.2.3.

accurate Observer with the Ridiculous," Fielding created a fictional universe answerable to his description of contemporary society as "a vast masquerade, where the greatest part appear disguised under false vizors and habits; a very few only showing their own faces, who become, by so doing, the astonishment and ridicule of all the rest." [3] Adapting Lesage's conception of a protagonist whose adventures serve to expose a range of foibles, he went beyond Lesage and Marivaux in peopling his actions with a parade of lascivious prudes, savage Christians, cowardly heroes, and learned illiterates. Even Joseph and Fanny have their innocent vanities and pretenses, [4] but none of the good-natured characters is driven, as are most persons they encounter, by an overriding self-love that seeks to satisfy itself at the expense of others.

Indeed, ill nature or a lack of feeling for one's fellows seems as important a component in defining the antipathetic side of Fielding's comedy as affectation. The callous indifference of Gil Blas's lordly masters and Jacob's "betters" [5] is extended to the world in general. When Joseph is found wounded by the roadside, he is given aid only after debate on the propriety of such action, and then only for reasons of prudence. Adams, asking directions, is bid *"follow his Nose and be d—n'd."* When Joseph strikes Didapper for pawing Fanny, Squire Booby reprimands him for impropriety; when Adams rescues her from a ravisher, the jealous Slipslop tells him such actions do not become a clergyman. Whenever a company gathers—at the sign of the Dragon, at the justice's, or at the squire's—there is someone ready to pounce upon and ridicule those in distress, or to show up the simple and the innocent. Among the knowledgeable citizens of this world, the fashion is to deny or sneer at tender feelings, and the highest virtue is a calculating prudence which inclines to suspicion. In *Don Quixote*, the judge, recognizing the captive as his long-lost brother, "flew into his Arms with such Affection, and such abundance of Tears, that all the Spectators sympathiz'd in his Passions." [6] In *Joseph Andrews*, the long separated friends, Paul and Leonard, embrace "with a Passion which made many of the Spectators laugh, and gave to some few a much higher and more agreeable Sensation" (4:10).

Consequently, Adams' frequent involvement in battles or near-battles is another likeness with a difference. Though quick to clench a fist or brandish a crabstick, he never converts a peaceful situation into an arena out of manic belligerency. He is drawn into fights to protect himself and other bedeviled innocents. Only in the whipping of the servant lad does Quixote encounter a real wrong to be righted by the might of his arm (an exception underscored by the knight's pursuit of the chimerical res-

3. "Character of Men," p. 322 above.
4. In the aftermath of his second interview with Lady Booby, Joseph retires to his garret to lament "the numberless Calamities which attended Beauty, and the Misfortune it was to be handsomer than one's Neighbours" (1:10). Barely out of the hands of her first would-be ravisher, Fanny responds to

Adams' disclosure that Joseph is homeward bound thus: "La! Mr. *Adams* . . . what is Mr. *Joseph* to me? I am sure I never had any thing to say to him, but as one Fellow-Servant might to another" (2:10).
5. In *Le Paysan parvenu*.
6. *Don Quixote* 1.4.15.

cue of the "Princess Micomicona" instead of avenging Andrew or even being acquainted with the real grievance of the betrayed maiden who plays the princess).[7] Fielding's world abounds in particular wrongs and general injustice. In contrast to the isolated betrayal of Dorothea, Fanny Goodwill must constantly fear for her virtue; the object of four attempted rapes, she arouses even the money-obsessed Peter Pounce and the effeminate Didapper. Whereas all the company at the inn join in persuading Ferdinand to do right by the injured girl, the ladies and gentleman of Booby Hall try to persaude Joseph to abandon his beloved for a more "suitable" match. In this milieu, law serves the whims of the powerful, and justice obtains by accident; modesty is usually its own and only reward; the postilion who gives the victimized Joseph his coat is reproved for swearing and transported for stealing chickens; and the "worthiest, best-natured creature" wears a ragged cassock, while the self-serving Barnabas and the hypocritical Trulliber thrive.

Thus it was not only the Quixote character that underwent a "sea change," as Cross[8] put it, in Fielding's conception. Retaining the comic hero's essential goodness while altering the nature and source of his mistakes, combining them with the exposure of affectation found in Lesage and Marivaux, and making the persecution of innocent "low people" by inhumane "high people" (a theme diversely developed by Lesage, Marivaux, and Richardson) a central circumstance of his fictional universe—Fielding converted Cervantes' benign and relatively self-contained comedy into a more abrasively ironic mode, redirecting its satiric impact from the isolated target of the accursed romances to the more immediate foibles of his own society and mankind at large. If Adams, like Quixote, is a freak in the world he traverses, he is so not because of any bizarre aberration but because of his abnormal goodness, his unselfish, impulsive feeling for others. If, like Quixote, he mistakenly takes his books as reliable guides to the reality he encounters, his reading is not extravagant fantasy but the wisdom of antiquity and the teachings of Christianity. However nobly transfigured he may appear to some modern readers, Quixote acts on premises which the normative figures of the novel recognize as plainly absurd.[9] But many of Adams' difficulties result from his living or expecting others to live according to precepts which his fellow creatures (and Fielding's contemporary readers) profess to believe. Adams has not had his mind subverted by books; the denizens of his world have been subverted from the noble humanity whose image he retains.

As a consequence of the more clearly drawn moral disparity between

---

7. In *Don Quixote* 1.4, the knight and his squire meet Dorothea, who has been seduced and abandoned by Don Ferdinand. She helps Quixote's friends lure him home by pretending to be the princess of a remote kingdom terrorized by a giant. Quixote's commitment to the fanciful mission of rescuing her prevents him from aiding the real victim of his first exploit who appears to claim his promised vengeance. See above, p. 346, n. 3.

8. Wilbur L. Cross, *The History of Henry Fielding* (New Haven: 1918) 1.323.

9. See Oscar Mandel, "The Function of the Norm in *Don Quixote*," *Modern Philology* 55 (1958): 154–63.

the hero and most of the persons he encounters, the amusement of Fielding's comedy is qualified by other feelings even more than Marivaux's. Each time Adams is duped or guyed there is an increment of comic indignation, and there is a complementary satisfaction when the antipathetic figures are exposed and discomfited. In the long run, Fielding could count on the reader's accumulated sense of the world's injustice to generate a desire to see affectation and vice put down and virtue and innocence rewarded. Yet he would have the reader realize that, given the state of the world, Adams' innocent good nature, unqualified by a measure of prudence, is a weakness. He wrote his essay on "Knowledge of the Characters of Men" about the same time as the novel explicitly to "arm . . . against imposition" the "innocent and undesigning" whose "open disposition, which is the surest indication of an honest and upright heart . . . principally disqualifies" them to detect falsehood in others.[1] In the *Champion* (March 15, 1739/40) he had remarked that "men often become ridiculous or odious by overacting even a laudable part: for Virtue itself, by growing too exuberant . . . changes its very nature, and becomes a most pernicious weed of a most beautiful flower"; and in another essay roughly contemporaneous with the novel he saw "Good-Nature itself, the very Habit of Mind most essential to furnish us with true Good Breeding," as a potential source of error and opprobrium.[2] By manipulating the reader's sympathies and reservations concerning the comic hero in the service of his "one great end," Fielding made the sequential articulation of this complex view a crucial mechanism of the novel's structure.

III

The obvious structural weakness of the kind of episodic comedy Fielding envisaged in the adventures of Abraham Adams was its lack of a narrative goal. The reader would be carried from one encounter between the character of perfect simplicity and the world of affectation to the next with no more specified expectation than further adventures of the same general kind. In Fielding's conception, as in Cervantes', the radical peculiarity of the protagonist's vision precluded a "learning" plot; the reader must soon sense that it is vain to wonder when the hero will discover his error or what it will take to open his eyes. Even in part 2, Cervantes had not made the uncoiling of his comic mainspring an object of long-range suspense, erecting instead the framework of expectation concerning Saragossa and the return of Samson Carrasco.[3] Given the

---

1. Pp. 321, 323 above.
2. "An Essay on Conversation" (1743), *Miscellanies, Vol. I*, ed. H. K. Miller (Middletown: 1972) 124–25.
3. In Cervantes' sequel, Quixote sets out with the long-range goal of attending a jousting tournament in Saragossa. After his young friend Carrasco is

defeated in his early effort to abort this new sally, the reader is told he contemplates revenge and "in due time the History will speak of him again." He eventually reappears in armored disguise and after defeating Quixote in single combat compels him to terminate his expedition.

particular etiology of Adams' error, Fielding could not even resolve his narrative with a dramatic change of outlook comparable to Quixote's terminal cure without arbitrarily destroying the "natural" character he had so carefully constructed. Nor would Adams' loss of innocence be as satisfying as Quixote's return to pious sanity.

The most common way of dealing with this generic problem of episodic fixed-character comedy was to import an external source of specified suspense and dramatic resolution from the conventional staple of serious romance, the trials and triumphs of one or more pairs of lovers. Cervantes pursued this strategy for a time in part 1, when he intertwined the adventures of the knight and his friends with the stories of Cardenio and Dorothea. In generally similar fashion, Lesage made the happy ending of the interpolated history of Don Alphonse and the fair Seraphine, with the attendant elevation of Gil Blas into a secure stewardship, serve as conclusion to the original (1715) version of his novel. But it was Scarron, whose comedy was dispersed among a "demi-douzaine de héros," who offered Fielding the most cogent demonstration of this narrative strategy, carrying it to its logical commencement and incorporating the whole novel within the sustained mystery and suspense concerning Destin and Étoile.[4]

The advantages of embedding the adventures of his parson-errant within a similar structure of expectation focused on an innocent and amiable youth and maiden were not likely to have escaped Fielding, who had regularly employed the fortunes of lovers in a similar fashion in his theatrical comedies—particularly since it avoided another difficulty peculiar to his revision of the Quixote formula. Whereas there could be no more fitting opening for *Don Quixote* than the old gentleman's sallying forth in obsessive quest of adventures, for Fielding to show his selfless priest setting out for London to sell his sermons, or on any comparable mission outside the parish to whose service he is devoted, would be to launch his story on a slightly false note. Beginning with Joseph's story permitted him to account for Adams' presence on the road "naturally"—as the result of a characteristic naïvely vain expectation—without focusing attention on the atypically worldly enterprise itself.

Some such reasoning might have produced a narrative resembling *Joseph Andrews*, except for the peculiarities of construction that support the tradition of its improvisatory development: the love between Joseph and Fanny is not disclosed until the eleventh chapter, and in the interim the eventual object of romantic expectation is cast in a mock-Pamelian role. If Fielding did not simply start to write a parody and then change his mind, it would seem that he was willing to sacrifice the consistency of the whole for the sake of the parodic introduction, which would be radically weakened if the figure of male chastity were presented as a faithful lover. But if we concede to Fielding the same awareness of what he was about in constructing his own narrative that he later attributed to

4. See above, pp. 359 and 367, n. 8.

Richardson's composition of *Clarissa*,[5] the abortive seduction of Pamela's brother can be seen as an ingenious improvement upon either plunging Adams directly into adventures in the manner of Cervantes or establishing Joseph as a conventional romantic hero in the fashion of Scarron. Placing his titular hero in a broadly humorous situation would establish unmistakably that his was to be a comically qualified version of the standard romance plot. At the same time this preliminary bout between innocence and hypocrisy would prefigure the central comic interaction between the amiable parson and his antipathetic antagonists. By defaulting, after only two interviews between mistress and servant, on his initially promised story of how "the excellent Pattern of his Sister's Virtues" enabled Joseph to "preserve his Purity," Fielding could foster the desire to see this conflict resume, thereby establishing a stronger arc of *comic* expectation over the whole narrative than Cervantes had developed in part 2 from the scheme of Samson Carrasco. Such a beginning would also function, like the anticipatory opening chapters of part 2, to make the very commencement of the central line of comic adventures a satisfying event. Having named Adams as coprotagonist on the title page, and given teasing glimpses of his character in the Preface and third chapter, he would make the reader wait a dozen chapters to see him in action, whetting his appetite the while by beginning and suspending another comedy of innocence and affectation and displaying the "Ways of this World" of which his innocent is so "entirely ignorant." Adding to these reasons the obvious dividends in taking off the still-current talk of the town, Fielding might well have considered the appearance of makeshift construction a small enough price to pay—especially since the sudden redefinition of Joseph's situation would serve to establish emphatically that his was no "simple Book," "*easily to be seen through*" (1:11).

For this opening strategy was part of an overall narrative scheme which, while it may have been influenced by Marivaux's fusion of comic and romantic and Scarron's manipulation of the reader's knowledge for effect, was essentially different from any structure he had seen in earlier comic romances. Starting with two lines of action more closely and "naturally" related than the converging histories of a troupe of comedians or a parcel of chance-met travelers, he combined them in a dynamic synthesis in which the reader's expectations concerning each would be significantly modified in the course of the narrative. Going beyond Scarron's interweaving of strands to generate suspense and produce surprising turns, he conceived a system of actions in which what happened in one line would affect the reader's opinions and desires concerning the other, and expectations aroused in one would be satisfied in the other. As the comic anticipations aroused by the promised parody of *Pamela* were to be transferred from Joseph's story to Adams' adventures, so in the second half of the novel desires for moral satisfaction generated by the good parson's

5. In 1748, Fielding wrote to Richardson, praising his skillful management of the reader's emotions and attitudes in the sequence encompassing the rape of his heroine. See E. L. McAdam, "A New Letter from Fielding," *Yale Review* 38 (1948): 300–310.

misadventures in a world of vanity and hypocrisy would be redirected to the renewal of Joseph's conflict with Lady Booby. The result would be an integrated "series of actions" in which the peculiarity of the beginning would heighten the effect of the central sequence of misadventures, and developments in that sequence would make the eventual resumption of the transformed original conflict a satisfying completion of an emotional process controlled by the comic intent Fielding defined in the preface as the determinant principle of his composition.

To achieve the benefits of his peculiar beginning, Fielding had only to suppress the knowledge of Joseph's love until the parodic episode was over. The reader would need no persuasion this early in the narrative to transfer his vague anticipation of certain kinds of comic incidents from a rather meagerly defined character whose adventures had scarcely begun to one whose description promised a broader range of actions. The greater problem would lie in reestablishing Joseph's story as the primary focus of the narrative two hundred pages later: how could the reader be led to accept the renewal of the conflict between the erstwhile male Pamela and his former mistress as a satisfying alternative to further adventures of one of the most extraordinary comic figures in literature? Fielding's strategy for effecting this more difficult transition was complex. It involved modifying the reader's view of both Adams and Joseph and gradually altering their relationship while intensifying the menace of their environment. Without blurring the novel's fundamental distinction between the amiable protagonists and the many antipathetic ridiculous persons they meet, he would guide the reader to a progressively more sympathetic view of Joseph and a somewhat less appealing impression of his old teacher. In the middle of the novel he would shift the emphasis of Adams' comedy from his endearing natural simplicity to his vanity, from his misestimates of individual character to his mistaken beliefs and misapplied doctrines, at the same time altering the perspective in which his perfect simplicity was to be viewed. Instead of the affected and ill-natured, he would now be contrasted with Mr. Wilson and his undiscovered son, good-natured men of generous inclination and pure motive who have nonetheless learned through experience the world's true moral state and the circumspection required to cope with it. In the light of their practical wisdom, his innocence would seem more of a flaw, especially as the inimical world's threats to the "innocent and undesigning" were intensified.

The complementary process of Joseph's emergence from a parodic role into a modest (and admittedly unparticularized) heroism, prepared early in the novel, would reach its most important development in a sporadic series of exchanges with his old master. In this structurally functional adaptation of the running disagreement between Don Quixote and Sancho Panza over the interpretation of the phenomena they encounter, the contrast between Joseph's worldly prudence and Adams' impulsive ineptitude would be reinforced by the pupil's display of the sounder understanding of moral character and its formation (2:16; 3:5) and the teacher's pedantically doctrinaire responses to his young friend's sufferings as a lover (3:11; 4:8).[6] In a coordinated development, the cumulative sense of the world's injustice would be sharpened by the depredations of the vicious "hunter of men," the impact of which would be heightened by juxtaposition with the immediately preceding idyll at Wilson's cottage—a more sharply drawn version of Cervantes' implicit contrast between Quixote's entertainment in turn by the soberly wise and modest "knight of the green coat" and the pranking duke and duchess.[7] As a result of these converging developments, the reader's desire for moral satisfaction would mount as Adams was made to appear less worthy of serving as its principal agent or object, thereby facilitating the reemergence of Joseph's story as the vehicle through which virtue would be rewarded and villainy routed. At the same time, the progressive emphasis on the less appealing aspects of Adams' complex character, together with his subjection, in the final stage of the journey, to treatment whose nastiness comes uncomfortably close to the boundaries of comedy, would make the reader relinquish more willingly the prospect of his further adventures. Thus when the curtain rose on the reassembled principals at Booby Hall, the renewal of the now redefined conflict between Lady Booby and Joseph would serve as a satisfactory dramatic and comic climax to the novel.

Such reasoning about the form of the novel, capitalizing on hints from Cervantes' improvement on the structure of part 1 in part 2, would not be out of character for the analytic admirer of *Clarissa* and the creator of *Tom Jones*. The best available evidence that he thought in this way six years earlier is to be found in the "judgment and art" with which he disposed the elements of *Joseph Andrews* in the service of this hypothesized conception.[8]

6. Dick Taylor, Jr. "Joseph as Hero of *Joseph Andrews,*" *Tulane Studies in English* 7 (1957) 3: 91–109, claims a "noticeable and sympathetic change and development of character into maturity" for Joseph, citing as "signs of his growth" some of the same evidence I have used in the subsequent analysis of the protagonists' realignment. In my view, neither Joseph nor Adams undergoes any substantive character change. Their roles and relationship are modified by manipulating the reader's knowledge of the two characters and their situations, through ordering and emphasizing the representation of their various traits, and by changing the circumstances in which they interact and the context in which they are viewed. Despite Taylor's ingenuity in educing Joseph's "personality," and his "stature and force" as "the

Master of the Event," he remains a less particularized figure than Adams or Tom Jones, and the reader is not intended to respond to his fortunes with the same degree of seriousness as to Tom's.
7. In *Don Quixote,* part 2, Quixote and Sancho are hospitably entertained by a model Christian gentleman leading a retired life similar to Wilson's; he is converted from suspicion to admiration by Quixote's discourse on poetry (see above, pp. 356–58) as Wilson is by Adams's dissertation on Homer. Later they encounter the hunting party of a duke and duchess who invite them to their residence for a lengthy stay during which they and their underlings play a series of elaborate tricks upon the knight and squire.
8. The next chapter develops a detailed analysis of the novel's sequential structure.

BRIAN McCREA

Rewriting *Pamela*: Social Change and Religious Faith in *Joseph Andrews* †

Joseph Andrews today stands as a kind of literary endangered species—a text that critics have dared to "close." This is not to say that Martin C. Battestin, Homer Goldberg, Mark Spilka, and Sheldon Sacks (to name just a few of the novel's interpreters) share one critical method or one version of what the story is about. Rather it is to point out the remarkable comprehensibility of the work. Whether approached via the history of ideas (Battestin), the study of continental literary models (Goldberg), analysis of formal features (Spilka), or of rhetoric and genre (Sacks), *Joseph Andrews* makes sense; its interpreters do not hesitate to use the words "moral," "truth," and "resolution" when they discuss it. The initial popularity of the novel may indicate that Fielding's contemporaries responded similarly. Frederick T. Blanchard has shown that, except for a few Richardsonian complaints about lowness and vulgarity, no one in the 1740s attacked *Joseph Andrews* as subversive or confusing. Whether or not they approved of the book, its first critics (like its later) felt they understood it.

Blanchard records this response with some surprise because, following Lord Byron, he finds in Fielding a "democratic spirit" at odds with eighteenth-century notions of social rank and place.[1] A mere aside in his massive history of the critical response to Fielding's work, Blanchard's surprise goes uninvestigated. But I want to raise again the question of Fielding's "democratic spirit" because by addressing it we can discover sources for both the comprehensibility of *Joseph Andrews* and for Fielding's stormy but ultimately profitable literary relationship with Samuel Richardson. Of course, the Richardson-Fielding contrast has been around since the days of Dr. Johnson, but it has lent itself to such confident and clear descriptions of the differences between the two that it has stopped most critics from going on to an important question.[2] What exactly did

†From *Studies in the Novel* 16 (1984): 137–49. Parenthetical page references in the text and some author's notes have been omitted.

1. *Fielding the Novelist* (1926; rpt. New York: Russell and Russell, 1966), pp. 351–52. Byron derived his sense of Fielding's political radicalism principally from *Jonathan Wild*. Blanchard extends Byron's claim to other works. See pp. 365, 449, 556.

2. Johnson claimed that, "There is all the difference in the world between characters of nature and characters of manners; and *there* is the difference between the characters of Fielding and those of Richardson. Characters of manners are very entertaining; but they are to be understood by a more superficial observer than characters of nature, where a man must dive into the recesses of the human heart" (James Boswell, *Life of Johnson*, ed. R. W. Chapman and J. D. Fleeman [London: Oxford Univ. Press, 1970], p. 389). In a later, equally famous and equally resounding contrast, Samuel Taylor Coleridge claimed, "There is a cheerful, sunshiny, breezy spirit that prevails everywhere [in Fielding] contrasted with the close, hot, day-dreamy continuity of Richardson" (Blanchard, p. 320). The difference here is more in connotation than observation; Coleridge pro-

Fielding see in *Pamela* that helped him to organize an extended prose narrative? He had vented his dislikes in *Shamela*, attacking what he took to be the prudery and moral complacency of *Pamela*, but *Shamela* did not depart from the satiric vein in which he had worked as a dramatist and journalist, did not become a novel. With *Shamela* behind him, Fielding returns to the character of Pamela Andrews, indicating, I think, that there was a part of *Pamela* that he could not handle to his satisfaction by merely travestying Richardson, a problem so sticky that he had to reintroduce a character he had discredited and consider her once more. In doing so Fielding was not making amends to Richardson; that would come later. Rather, he was rewriting him, taking an issue that he felt Richardson had mishandled, and showing him how it might better be treated. The issue was class conflict, and Fielding's means for dealing with it was the birth-mystery plot.

By hiding the true identities of Joseph Andrews and Frances Goodwill, Fielding takes the confusions about rank in *Pamela* and tries to sort them out, in effect closing a question that Richardson had left open. Fielding's amelioration of the conflicts he found in Richardson, however, finally depends upon the character of Abraham Adams, upon a religious faith as powerful as it is special. Thus the confidence *Joseph Andrews* has inspired in its interpreters is not misplaced, but Fielding's novel, even in the mid-eighteenth century, is a special case. In the terms of Ronald Paulson, Fielding takes the "popular" and socially subversive achievement of Richardson and attempts to render it "polite."[3] But as eighteenth-century society moved closer to political democracy and literary romanticism, Richardson's values would undergird the new standards, while Fielding's age was passing as he wrote.[4]

Critics like Blanchard and Byron err when they describe Fielding's spirit as democratic, but their mistake is an easy one to make. At first glance, *Joseph Andrews* does appear to be strongly egalitarian. It opens with an attack on concern for genealogy, one which concludes by asking rhetorically: "Would it not be hard, that a Man who hath no Ancestors should therefore be render'd incapable of acquiring Honour, when we see so many who have no Virtues, enjoying the Honour of their Forefathers?" (I.ii). It challenges elitist attitudes by introducing Joseph and Fanny as characters of low birth whose physical charms and Christian virtues far outshine those of their social superiors. Joseph, in particular,

---

tests against precisely the inwardness and recessiveness that Johnson admires. My point is that these contrasts, while insightful and memorable, are descriptive. They do not analyze how Fielding's response to Richardson led him to write a novel. Even if Fielding consciously (or unconsciously) decided to open Richardson's "close, hot, day-dreamy" world, that decision would not have written his book for him. But his decision to recast Richardson's treatment of class conflict was one that suggested characters, incidents, and techniques—provided, that is, the basis for an extended narrative.

3. *Popular and Polite Art in the Age of Hogarth and Fielding* (Notre Dame and London: Univ. of Notre Dame Press, 1979), pp. 69, 96, 102.
4. This point is made most economically by Margaret A. Doody in her Introduction to the Penguin edition of *Pamela* (New York, 1980), p. 8: "the novels of Richardson, homegrown as they are, were to have considerable influence in the development of European literature. *Pamela*, which we with hindsight can see presages the era of the French Revolution and of Romanticism, was to influence Rousseau, Diderot, Goethe, and Pushkin."

continually passes for a gentleman and has, as the narrator pointedly observes, "an Air, which to those who have not seen many Noblemen, would give an idea of Nobility" (I.viii). Fanny has "a natural Gentility, superior to the Acquisition of Art, and which surprized all who beheld her" (II.xii). The handsomeness of Joseph and Fanny, which subverts at least one correlation between virtue and rank, finds its ethical counterpart in Abraham Adams's fearless challenges of his social betters: Lady Booby, when she tries to prevent the marriage of Joseph and Fanny; Mr. Booby and Pamela, when they laugh during the marriage ceremony (IV.xvi). Even the narrator appears to share this egalitarianism. When he accounts for Slipslop's superior airs by noting that social distinctions vary "according to Place and Time," he treats lightly, satirically the metaphor of the Great Chain of Being. He reduces it to "a kind of Ladder" whose different rungs have no intrinsic worth (II.xiii) and thus attacks the philosophical basis for the elitism of a writer like Pope.

When Joseph boxes Beau Didapper for insulting Fanny (IV.xi), however, revolution is not at hand. The moment is comic not climactic, for Fielding's story ultimately is not one that exalts the humble poor, nor is it one whose spirit is democratic. We discover that Joseph is, after all, a gentleman, and that Fanny is of better birth than we thought. With the blessing of her aristocratic brother-in-law, she brings a fortune to Joseph, and their marriage no longer is the affront to social class that it briefly appeared to be. Adams is spared a final conflict with Lady Booby and accepts from Mr. Booby (the man he publicly rebuked) a living of one hundred thirty pounds a year, hiring a curate to tend it. Of course, this resolution of the "birth-mystery" has many precedents in the romance tradition, and Joseph's acquisition of money and social status fits the requirements of what Northrop Frye has called "New Comedy."[5] But while literary conventions are served, so equally is the class structure of English society, once seemingly under attack.

How does Fielding, given the democratic tendency of his earlier descriptions of Joseph, Fanny, and Adams, make this conclusion work? Why do we not feel that he contradicts himself? Recall that in *Pamela* Richardson faced a similar problem. For almost two-thirds of the novel Pamela asserts her value, writing her parents that "your *poverty* is my *pride*" and telling Mr. B that "my *soul* is of equal importance with the soul of a princess." She persistently justifies her "disobedience" of Mr. B by reminding him that all men and women are equal in the eyes of God. Mrs. Jewkes, who takes a less exalted view, describes Pamela's behavior as "downright rebellion," and, in one sense, she is right. Throughout Pamela's tribulations, she refuses her master privileges he claims to be due his rank. She asserts another standard—a spiritual, egalitarian one. Mr. B summarizes the logic of this portion of the novel when he claims, "How, then, with the distance between us, in the world's judgment, can I think of making *you* my wife? Yet I must have you." In

5. See *The Anatomy of Criticism* (Princeton: Princeton Univ. Press, 1957), p. 51 (for discussion of "birth-mystery plots") and p. 44 (for the definition of "New Comedy").

the face of Pamela's intransigence and rebellion, Mr. B seemingly must commit a revolutionary act and marry her.[6]

Once Mr. B's decision is made, however, Richardson sets about defusing the social time bomb he has constructed. He does so in a manner significantly different from Fielding's—a manner Fielding will call attention to and satirize. Rather than discovering a true identity that has been lost (as Joseph and Fanny do), Pamela changes her identity. The girl who, besieged by her master, found strength in the lessons and examples of her parents, suddenly finds a new parent, telling Mr. B "it will be a pleasure to me to shew every one, that, with respect to my happiness in this life, I am entirely the work of your bounty." Having replaced her parents as the authors of her being and happiness, and having shifted her focus to "this life" from eternal life, Pamela even goes so far as to compare Mr. B to "the Creator," and to describe his beneficence as "God-like."

Her identity changed by Mr. B's generosity, Pamela turns down an opportunity to have her parents live with her and tells a servant "times . . . are much altered with me. I have of late been so much honoured by better company, that I can't stoop to yours." The extent of her change becomes clear when she turns to her old enemy Mrs. Jewkes, and the once ogre-like Colbrand for protection from Lady Davers. The ultimate rationalization for the change, however, comes from its author, as Mr. B asserts that a man admits his wife "into his own rank, be it *what* it will." The post-marriage Pamela is a new person, metamorphosed by the beneficence of her Godlike master-husband, not by her own pluck and luck. Richardson nips a budding attack on the status quo, but only by reversing his earlier characterizations of Pamela, her master, and even of Colbrand and Mrs. Jewkes.[7]

The phenomenal popularity of *Pamela* may reflect its social schism. The story that, in its first part, provided wish fulfillment for every humble servant, in its second flattered aristocrats; lowly villagers and great poets all could find something to like in it.[8] But the conclusion of *Joseph Andrews* reveals Fielding's doubts about Richardson's resolution. In his portrayal of Pamela Booby, he focuses intently, almost single-mindedly on Richardson's handling of her social rise. He places Pamela and her husband in the palpably false position of trying to argue Joseph out of a match like theirs. When Fielding has his Pamela say of Fanny, "She was my Equal . . . but I am no longer *Pamela Andrews*, I am now this Gentleman's Lady, and as such am above her" (IV.vii), he is echoing Richardson, not travestying him. The echo becomes satiric not because

6. See Doody, Introduction, pp. 9, 14 for discussion of the social revolution in *Pamela*, as the work demands "new assumptions about class, property, authority and identity."

7. The shift in Pamela's descriptions of Mr. B is particularly stark. The man she once describes as a votary of Lucifer and then as "Lucifer himself" becomes, once he offers marriage, "this *now* wholly good gentleman," "the dear gentleman," "the most generous of men."

8. For a concise summary of the range of the appeal of *Pamela* (from the humble villagers at Slough to Alexander Pope), see Martin C. Battestin's introduction to Henry Fielding, *Joseph Andrews* and *Shamela* (Boston: Houghton Mifflin, 1961), p. vii.

it is inaccurate, but because of the situation in which it occurs. Similarly, when Mr. Booby claims that his "Fortune" permitted him to please himself in a wife, while Joseph's does not, his words ring hollow. Again Fielding does not distort Richardson, but rather, through Joseph and Fanny, suggests that Pamela's metamorphosis and marriage have not resolved the conflict triggered by her earlier rebellion.

Pamela, then, resurfaces in the conclusion of Fielding's novel so that he can criticize Richardson's attempt to mute the revolutionary implications of her progress. Richardson ameliorates class conflict by elevating Pamela, by changing her creator and her rank; Fielding accomplishes the same end, but does so by restoring Joseph and Fanny to their true identities and thus to their rightful places. Although he seemingly attacks it through much of his story, Fielding finally implies that the social hierarchy, by and large, has value. Richardson's attack is not so easily suspended. Until her elevation, Pamela's character and rank never bear any relation to each other, and she remains, even after her marriage, a social anomaly. With almost painful regularity, onlookers marvel at the accomplishments of a girl of such humble origin. Beau Didapper to the contrary (and he is rendered comically impotent), once Fielding straightens out his characters' identities, their ranks and natures roughly correspond. Joseph's fair skin and good looks do, indeed, belong to a gentleman. He discovers his parents and eventually lives next to them, rather than cutting himself off from them. That he is not Pamela's brother protects him from the confusion that her rise has caused; that the unlettered Fanny is her sister suggests how overreaching the resolution of Pamela's dilemma actually is. Joseph, of course, does profit from Pamela's good fortune, but even here Fielding blunts the revolutionary thrust of his work. The "Fortune" Mr. Booby gives to Fanny, and which Joseph lays out in "a little Estate" (IV.xvi), is owing to "unprecedented Generosity." Joseph and Fanny come to their rightful place through the good auspices of a great aristocrat; they do not stage a long, protracted rebellion prior to their reward.

The contrast between resolution-through-restoration and resolution-through-transmutation sustains other important differences between Fielding's treatment of social conflict and Richardson's. Throughout *Joseph Andrews*, even as characters discredit notions of rank and class, Fielding suggests the need for them. In the novel's opening scenes, for example, Joseph (whom Lady Booby sees as a walking challenge to class distinctions) relies for protection upon the distance between himself and his mistress. When his lady hypothetically suggests a liaison, his response reveals how fully, if implausibly, he has internalized the standards he seems to overturn: "Madam . . . I should think your Ladyship condescended a great deal below yourself" (I.viii). The bloody quarrel at the inn in Book II, Chapter 5 takes place after Joseph finds the host's treatment of Adams unacceptable and bids him "know how to behave himself to his Betters" (II.v). Mrs. Slipslop, who once thinks her knowledge of her mistress's "Secret had thrown down all Distinction between them"

(I.ix), soon recognizes the limits to her power and displays a sensitivity to rank as finely developed as that of the haughtiest aristocrat. In her argument with Miss Grave-airs, she actually relies upon her mistress's status, at one point noting that "her Lady was one of the great Gentry, and such little paultry Gentlewomen, as some Folks who travelled in Stage-Coaches, would not easily come at her" (II.v). Mr. and Mrs. Towwouse, Betty the chambermaid, and the magistrate who tries Adams and Fanny are only a few of the other characters in the novel who act on the basis of social distinctions and who, although inhabiting different rungs on the "Ladder of Dependence," accept the standards of those higher up.

Of course, Mrs. Slipslop is not the moral center of *Joseph Andrews*, and her espousal of elitist views offer some satire of them. Similarly, Lawyer Scout's craven submission before Lady Booby (IV.iii) clearly is an attitude that Fielding scorns. But these and other instances[9] do not change the essential point: Fielding, in his treatment of Joseph and Slipslop, and throughout the novel, persistently and subtly links the two attitudes that Richardson so abruptly (two-thirds through his novel) collapses together. In *Joseph Andrews* social status is challenged and cherished almost simultaneously. Consider again Fielding's travesty of the Great Chain of Being (II.xiii). Even though he reduces the importance of rank (really, he says, it is merely a matter of timing), he also relies upon the distinctions he comically makes. Not as noble as Pope's divinely constructed chain, the ladder nonetheless brings order and scope to human activity.

In *Pamela* characters share a sensitivity to rank, and Pamela herself hopes that the distance between her and Mr. B will protect her. But because she changes her identity, rather than discovering her true identity, all the characters (whether virtuous or vicious) who rely on social distinctions have their expectations disappointed. Lady Davers cannot believe that Mr. B has married his mother's maidservant; Goodman Andrews shares her assumption and fears his daughter has been ruined. While their reactions to proof of the marriage differ, both the great lady and the failed schoolteacher are surprised by it. In trying to reconcile the social variances he has created, Richardson confounds all conventional social wisdom. This confusion is largely responsible for Fielding's negative reaction—for his viewing Pamela's marriage as an unsuccessful attempt to resolve the conflicts initiated by her rebellion.

The contradictions latent in his portrayal of Adams reveal Fielding both attempting to improve upon Richardson and relying on a particular religious faith to achieve that end. Adams, who once attacked "the Luxury and Splendour of the Clergy" (I.xvii), accepts from Mr. Booby a profitable living and hires a curate to tend it. Can Fielding's figure of moral rectitude be guilty of pluralism? Similarly, while Adams is famous

---

9. Most particularly, Leonora and Bellarmine in "The History of Leonora, or the Unfortunate Jilt" reveal the falsity, hypocrisy, and danger of unqualified commitment to social distinctions.

for his sermons on submission—a fact of which his long-suffering wife reminds him—he refuses to follow Lady Booby's orders concerning Joseph and Fanny (IV.viii). Finally, Adams himself splits his personality, declaring that "Mr. *Adams* at Church with his Surplice on, and Mr. *Adams* without that ornament, in any other place, were two very different Persons" (IV.xvi). One Adams challenges and rebukes the elite; the other is their servant, sometimes their victim. One Adams stands (in clerical garb so tattered it barely identifies him) as a Christian of simple virtue, following Benjamin Hoadly in the belief that Anglican ritual must be demystified (I.xvii); the other insists that Joseph and Fanny marry in accord with church law (IV.xvi). But while he shares in both the spiritual egalitarianism and social submission that rive *Pamela*, Adams never has struck readers as self-contradictory, let alone schizophrenic. Dualities which, in a twentieth-century novel, would lead to meditations upon the void have little effect on Adams or on our estimation of him. He remains, to most readers, totally admirable; he remains, to himself, totally righteous.

Adams's rising above loyalties that, taken in isolation, appear self-contradictory depends on some careful work by Fielding. In relation to the question of pluralism, Fielding's elaborate descriptions of Adams's poverty—particularly of his family's worn clothes, humble fare, and limited opportunities—prepare us to see the parson's final financial boon as long overdue. In balance with this evidence, doubts about Adams's hiring a curate do not weigh very heavily. Similarly, Adams's penchant for physical violence, although he never strikes first, gives us an indelible image of his aggressiveness, strength, and courage, even as we learn that he preaches submission. In an action typical of him, he tolerates with due respect the insults of the company of the roasting country squire, but, having discovered the squire's brutal motive, he defends himself (and Joseph and Fanny) with impressive force. We are not, then, surprised to see Adams, a man whose fist we know to be massive (I.xv) and often clenched, rebuke the Boobies from the pulpit in which "he had always preached up Submission to Superiours" (IV.viii). Finally, Fielding's characterization of Adams during his journey hides the division between the parson's assertive and submissive halves. Like Joseph, Adams (outside the pulpit) is a gentleman in disguise. His clothes, his eating and drinking habits, and his spontaneous benevolence all hide his rank. They open him to contact with all social types and place him in situations in which he suffers from injustice and hypocrisy within the social order. But Adams too, however unwittingly, relies on the definitions of place and privilege that his character seems to overturn. Facing unjust imprisonment, he is rescued by the discovery not of his virtues but of his rank (II.xi). Unable to pay the bill he ran up because of the lying gentleman's promises, he is pardoned by an innkeeper who honors "the Clergy too much to deny trusting one of them for such a Trifle" (II.xvi). While he finds no charity in his fellow clergyman Trulliber, he praises the good that Lady Booby has done in the parish. His sense of her religious failings in no way blinds him to her social virtues (II.iii).

Throughout Adams's journey, shifts in his garb cause shifts in the perception of his rank by others. So also Adams himself moves between Christian and social standards, judging Trulliber by Christ's model, but praising Lady Booby for her community service. By orchestrating these shifts, Fielding tempers the divisions in Adams. They exist and are important, but they do not rend his character asunder. The basis for Adam's wholeness is his religious faith, the particular orientation of his Christianity toward social involvement and good works. Underlying both his challenges to his superiors and his submission to the status quo is his unflagging conviction that "he was a Servant of the Highest" (IV.xvi)— a belief that combines humility and deference to rank ("Servant of")with an egalitarian assertion of quality ("the Highest").

To argue that Adams's faith is the source of his special strength, one first must take into account recent work by Donald Greene in which he attacks the notion, introduced by R. S. Crane and elaborated by Martin C. Battestin,[1] that the latitudinarian divines of the late seventeenth and early eighteenth centuries were distinguished by a modified Pelagianism, emphasizing good works at the expense of faith, benevolent feelings at the expense of grace. Greene argues that, except for their latitude in "questions of church government, discipline, liturgy, and ritual," the latitudinarians were conventional Anglicans, that latitudinarianism "is nothing more than general Protestantism of the time." On the important question of good works—the basis upon which Battestin asserts the distinctiveness of the latitudinarians and classifies Adams as one—Greene offers this conclusion: "For the Anglican there can be no 'bitter debate' about 'the relative importance of faith or works' [as Battestin claims], for there is nothing to debate about. It is faith that saves; the possession of saving faith inevitably results in the performance of good works; the absence of good works is proof of the absence of saving faith; yet the mere fact of 'good' works, mechanically performed, is no proof of its presence. This does not really seem hard to grasp."[2]

Greene's argument is both correct and specious. Clearly, all forms of Christianity, back to those practiced by Saint Paul and Saint James, call for both strong faith and good works. This is not hard to grasp or prove. But the day offers all Christians only twenty-four hours, and they must decide how to spend them. Will they emphasize individual or communal activities, private prayer or public acts? There is room here for tremendous difference in emphasis and approach. While the volumes of sermons that Adams has left behind him might include ones on the

1. R. S. Crane, "Suggestions Toward a Genealogy of the 'Man of Feeling.'" *ELH*, 1 (1934), 205–30; Martin C. Battestin, *The Providence of Wit: Aspects of Form in Augustan Literature* (Oxford: Oxford Univ. Press, 1974), pp. 223, 257, and *The Moral Basis of Fielding's Art*, pp. 14–25,

74–81.
2. "Latitudinarianism and Sensibility: The Genealogy of the 'Man of Feeling' Reconsidered," *Modern Philology*, 75 (1977), 176. See also pp. 167, 180.

importance of faith, on the impossibility of salvation other than by means of grace, his life clearly emphasizes works—the performance of charitable acts. Similarly, I suspect that further investigation of the latitudinarian divines,[3] while taking into account their calls for faith and their descriptions of man as depraved (as cited by Greene), will vindicate Crane and Battestin to this extent: while remaining Anglicans, Protestants, Christians, and thus calling for both faith and works, the latitudinarians gave more importance to works than did their contemporaries. And this doctrinal emphasis distinguishes them as surely as their latitude in matters of church government.

A summary of latitudinarianism and its history is not possible here, but the salient point is that this version of Christianity, at least as Fielding embodies it in Adams, emphasizes the good actions that follow from faith; it defines true Christians as those who, unlike Parsons Barnabas and Trulliber, are acting charitably within their society. Fielding's latitudinarianism combines the two tendencies—Christian valuing of all souls equally and recognition of social imperatives—between which Richardson awkwardly shifted. Without this special faith, Parson Adams in the pulpit and Parson Adams on the road would conflict inevitably and violently. With it Adams (and we) hardly notice the contradictions in his characters and roles.

By understanding how Fielding uses Adams to mediate between submission and defiance, we can establish an analogy between the treatments of class conflict in *Pamela* and *Joseph Andrews* and the treatments of "providential promise" in *Clarissa* and *Tom Jones*. Mary Poovey has shown how Richardson and Fielding, despite their sharing a religious faith, offer different literary renderings of future reward. Richardson's "rigorously realistic conception of the temporal world" permits no compromise between that world and the virtuous Clarissa; her reward can come only in heaven and to achieve it she must die. Fielding, on the other hand, sees the "relationship between this world and the next" as "metaphorical."[4] He can reward Tom Jones in this world and use that reward to represent, to figure, a coming heavenly reward. In *Pamela* and *Joseph Andrews* the point at issue is as much social as religious, but Poovey's distinction holds. Both writers share a loyalty to the social status quo and affirm the power and virtue of England's ruling class (just as both share Christianity). Fielding quarrels with Richardson not for trying to defuse social conflict, but for drawing it so starkly, so uncompromisingly. He tries to right Richardson's work by subtly and persistently joining those attitudes—defiance and conformity—that Richardson forces together. We may guess that Richardson argues much less carefully for the status quo than Fielding does because the upwardly mobile virtuous apprentice could not curb his democratic impulses as easily as the sec-

3. Frans De Bruyn, "Latitudinarianism and Its Importance as a Precursor of Sensibility," *Journal of English and Germanic Philology*, 80 (1981), 349–68.

4. "Journeys from This World to the Next: The Providential Promise in *Clarissa* and *Tom Jones*," *ELH*, 43 (1976), 314.

ond cousin of the fourth Earl of Denbigh.[5] Speculation aside, Richardson's uncertain handling of social conflict clearly makes his novel more difficult to close than Fielding's. Questions about irony in his descriptions of Pamela's motives and actions, most notably her "chance" meetings with Mr. B and long delays in leaving his house, have been debated for years without resolution. The contradictions in Fielding's work, while apparent, are less confusing. Few have begrudged Adams his final prosperity and his lectures from the pulpit; few have felt that Joseph's virtues are not appropriate for his final place.

The comprehensibility of *Joseph Andrews*, then, in part derives from Fielding's attempting to avoid what he felt was a confusing and unsuccessful resolution in *Pamela*. But in recognizing this comprehensibility, we also should recognize that it depends on a faith inexplicable, rare, and strong. Adams's rising above a seemingly classic split personality is a miracle. When his wife points to the disparity between his sermons and his deeds (IV.viii), he makes no response. The division cannot be debated or investigated, only observed. His personal righteousness here spares Adams the torment of psychomachia[6]—the torment that Lady Booby (she of social virtue but little faith) feels so acutely, once Joseph's charms set her democratic and aristocratic loyalties at odds. We wonder how Adams can be one person in church and another out; he does not. We note the potential hypocrisy of his accepting a living from Booby; he does not. When these seeming moral dilemmas arise, his faith blesses Adams with a saving obtuseness, an obtuseness Fielding makes credible by describing its less beneficial counterparts: Adams's naiveté in his dealings with villainous, deceitful men and his inability to recognize the strength and virtue of arguments that his opponents use.[7] Adams is blind to his weakness because he is sure of his virtue. Convinced that God orders all for the best, he believes with equal fervor that he is God's "Servant."

While Joseph grows from Adams's pupil to his guide,[8] he always remains Adams's student in this one regard. His faith also blinds him to any incongruities that his virtues and gifts may suggest. Clothes too big for Mr. Booby fit Joseph perfectly (IV.v), but this and numerous other suggestions of his quality never cause him to seek a higher place. At the story's opening he is "perfectly content with the State to which he was called" and feels no "envy . . . of his Betters" (I.iii). At the story's end, although the discovery of his true identity elevates him, he retains his submissiveness. He has learned to practice what Adams preaches, even as his life's course testifies against the sermon's doctrine. He too sees no conflict.

While Blanchard could see a "democratic spirit" in Fielding's work,

5. The son of a woodworker, Richardson was apprenticed to a printer at seventeen; Fielding came from an aristocratic country family [*Editor*].
6. Conflict of soul [*Editor*].
7. Adams loses an argument about education with Joseph (III.v) and an argument about learning with a virtuous innkeeper (II.xvii). But he refuses to give any credence to their telling points or to modify his views.
8. Dick Taylor, Jr., "Joseph as Hero of *Joseph Andrews*," *Tulane Studies in English*, 15 (1953), 11–19.

Joseph Andrews finally calls for submission to (and benefit from) the elite. The faith of Joseph and Adams means that they never feel conflicts that we experience today—conflicts that emerged full force once the faith that informs Fielding's novel weakened. As clergymen in both gothic and sentimental novels lose Adams's righteousness, their democratic impulses become both stronger and more confusing. A clergyman in *A Sentimental Journey*, with no apparent duties, Parson Yorick finds disappointment among the French elite and turns to the poor for nature and love.[9] He also is prey to conflicting emotions (unable to decide how to treat the Monk, unable to commit himself to Augustan standards of rational control, but not uninhibited enough to seduce the *fille-de-chambre* or to join the peasant dance). In Matthew Lewis's *Monk*, Ambrosio loses both his religious faith and his social bearings. The ensuing confusion and violence reveal that the conflict between submission and striving, deferred in the works of Richardson and Fielding, has come due with a vengeance. In one sense, however, the deferment of conflict practiced by Fielding and Richardson continued. Walpole, Radcliffe, and Lewis all portray social and political upheaval taking place in foreign countries at a different time, not in eighteenth-century England.[1] Regicide and street violence are offered by these gothic novelists, but only with oblique reference to English life. In the definitive sentimental novel, Henry Mackenzie's *Man of Feeling*,[2] attention is directed away from the source of injustice or oppression to the feelings that the injustice evokes. Mackenzie closes by asking his readers to "pity the men" of the world, not to change the world itself.

Strong of faith, Fielding in 1742 affirms social, religious, and literary standards (witness the classicism of his Preface to *Joseph Andrews*). But the conflicts latent in Adams's double personality and the "natural Gentility" of Joseph and Fanny could not be put off forever. The emergence of political revolution and literary gothicism awaited only the weakening, the attenuation of the faith that Adams embodied. Richardson, although less accomplished than Fielding, was more successful. His abrupt shift from egalitarianism to elitism (and the large scope he gave to democratic themes) better fit the political and literary worlds aborning. Fielding's righting of Richardson's resolution actually set him apart from great historical and literary trends. Having built his work on a special version of Christianity whose day was passing, he stands, in his own age, somewhat like Parson Adams—marvelous but outdated, possessed of latent conflicts whose importance and scope later writers will limn.

9. Laurence Sterne, *A Sentimental Journey Through France and Italy* by Mr. Yorick, ed. Gardner D. Stout, Jr. (Berkeley and Los Angeles: Univ. of California Press, 1967), pp. 261–67.

1. The gothic novels of Horace Walpole (*The Castle of Otranto*, 1764), Mrs. Ann Radcliffe (*The Mysteries of Udolpho*, 1794, among others), and Matthew Lewis (*The Monk*, 1796) are set in medieval or renaissance Italy or Spain [*Editor*].

2. Published in 1771 [*Editor*].

Selected Bibliography

Asterisks indicate books from which excerpts are reprinted in this edition. Articles reprinted in this edition are not included in this bibliography.

BIBLIOGRAPHIES

Battestin, Martin C. "Fielding." *The English Novel: Select Bibliographical Guides*. Ed. A. E. Dyson. London: Oxford UP, 1974. 71–89.
————. "Henry Fielding." *The New Cambridge Bibliography of English Literature*. Ed. George Watson. Cambridge: Cambridge UP, 1971. 2: 925–48.
Morrisey, L. J. *Henry Fielding, A Reference Guide*. Boston: G. K. Hall & Co., 1980.
Stoler, John A., and Richard D. Fulton. *Henry Fielding: An Annotated Bibliography of Twentieth-Century Criticism, 1900–1977*. New York and London: Garland Publishing Co., 1980.

BIOGRAPHIES

Cross, Wilbur. L. *The History of Henry Fielding*. 3 Vols. 1918. New York: Russell & Russell, 1963.
Dudden, F. Homes. *Henry Fielding: His Life, Works, and Times*. 2 Vols. 1952. Hamden: Archon Books, 1966.

GENERAL STUDIES

Alter, Robert. *Fielding and the Nature of the Novel*. Cambridge, MA: Harvard UP, 1968.
Baker, Ernest. Vol. 4 of *The History of the English Novel*. 1930. New York: Barnes & Noble, 77–196.
Blanchard, Frederic T. *Fielding the Novelist: A Study in Historical Criticism*. New Haven: Yale UP, 1926. (An account of the critical reception and reputation of Fielding and his work from his own time into the early twentieth century.)
Booth, Wayne C. *The Rhetoric of Fiction*. 2nd ed. Chicago: U of Chicago P, 1983.
————. "The Self-Conscious Narrator in Comic Fiction Before *Tristram Shandy*." *Publications of the Modern Language Association of America* 67 (1952): 163–85.
Braudy, Leo. *Narrative Form in History and Fiction: Hume, Fielding, and Gibbon*. Princeton, Princeton UP, 1970.
Butt, John. *Fielding*. Writers and Their Work 57. London: Longmans, Green & Co., 1954.
Cleary, Thomas R. *Henry Fielding, Political Writer*. Waterloo: Wilfred Laurier UP, 1984.
Digeon, Aurelien. *The Novels of Fielding*. 1925. New York: Russell and Russell, 1962. (Translation of *Les Romans de Fielding*. Paris: 1923.)
* Golden, Morris. *Fielding's Moral Psychology*. Amherst: U of Massachusetts P, 1966.
Hatfield, Glenn. *Henry Fielding and the Language of Irony*. Chicago: U of Chicago P, 1968.
Hunter, J. Paul. *Occasional Form: Henry Fielding and the Chains of Circumstance*. Baltimore and London: Johns Hopkins UP, 1975.
Johnson, Maurice. *Fielding's Art of Fiction: Eleven Essays on Shamela, Joseph Andrews, Tom Jones and Amelia*. Philadelphia: U of Pennsylvania P, 1961.
McKillop, Alan Dugald. *The Early Masters of English Fiction*. Lawrence: U of Kansas P, 1956. 98–146.
Maresca, Thomas. *Epic to Novel*. Columbus: Ohio State UP, 1974. 181–231.
Paulson, Ronald. *Satire and the Novel in Eighteenth-Century England*. New Haven: Yale UP, 1967. 100–64.
————, and Thomas Lockwood. *Henry Fielding: The Critical Heritage*. London and New York: Routledge & Kegan Paul; Barnes & Noble, 1969. (A comprehensive anthology of eighteenth-century responses to Fielding's works.)

Price, Martin. *To the Palace of Wisdom: Studies in Order and Energy from Dryden to Blake.* 1964. New York: Doubleday, 1965. 286–312.

* Sacks, Sheldon. *Fiction and the Shape of Belief: A Study of Henry Fielding, with Glances at Swift, Johnson, and Richardson.* 1964. Chicago: U of Chicago P, 1980.

Sherbo, Arthur. *Studies in the Eighteenth-Century English Novel.* East Lansing: Michigan State UP, 1969. 1–84, 104–27.

Sherburn, George. "Fielding's Social Outlook." *Philological Quarterly* 35 (1956): 1–23.

Tave, Stuart M. *The Amiable Humorist: A Study in the Comic Theory and Criticism of the Eighteenth and Early Nineteenth Centuries.* Chicago and London: U of Chicago P, 1960. 140–63.

Thornbury, Ethel. *Henry Fielding's Theory of the Comic Prose Epic.* University of Wisconsin Studies in Language and Literature 30. 1931. New York: Russell and Russell, 1966. (Reprints the sale catalogue of Fielding's library.)

Watt, Ian. *The Rise of the Novel: Studies in Defoe, Richardson, and Fielding.* Berkeley and Los Angeles and London: U of California P, 1957. 239–89.

Williams, Aubrey. "Interpositions of Providence and the Design of Fielding's Novels." *South Atlantic Quarterly* 70 (1971): 265–86.

Wright, Andrew. *Henry Fielding: Mask and Feast.* Berkeley and Los Angeles and London: U of California P, 1965.

DISCUSSIONS OF *JOSEPH ANDREWS* AND *SHAMELA*

Amory, Hugh. "*Shamela* as Aesopic Satire." *ELH: A Journal of English Literary History* 38 (1971): 239–53.

Baker, Sheridan. "Fielding's Comic Epic-in-Prose Romances Again." *Philological Quarterly* 58 (1979): 63–81.

———. "Henry Fielding's Comic Romances." *Papers of the Michigan Academy of Science, Arts, and Letters* 45 (1959): 411–19.

———. "Introduction." *An Apology for the Life of Mrs. Shamela Andrews.* Henry Fielding. Berkeley and Los Angeles: U of California P, 1953. xi–xxiv.

Battestin, Martin. "Fielding's Changing Politics and *Joseph Andrews*." *Philological Quarterly* 39 (1960): 39–55.

———. "Fielding's Revisions of *Joseph Andrews*." *Studies in Bibliography* 16 (1963): 81–117.

———. "Lord Hervey's Role in *Joseph Andrews*." *Philological Quarterly* 42 (1963): 226–41.

* ———. *The Moral Basis of Fielding's Art: A Study of Joseph Andrews.* Middletown: 1959.

Brooks, Douglas. "The Interpolated Tales in *Joseph Andrews* Again." *Modern Philology* 65 (1968): 208–13.

Coley, William B. "The Background of Fielding's Laughter." *ELH: A Journal of English Literary History* 26 (1959): 229–52.

Donovan, Robert A. "*Joseph Andrews* as Parody." *The Shaping Vision.* Ithaca: Cornell UP, 1966. 68–88.

Evans, James E. "Fielding, *The Whole Duty of Man, Shamela*, and *Joseph Andrews*." *Philological Quarterly* 61 (1982): 212–19.

* Goldberg, Homer. *The Art of Joseph Andrews.* Chicago and London: U of Chicago P, 1969.

———. "Comic Prose Epic or Comic Romance: The Argument of the Preface to *Joseph Andrews*." *Philological Quarterly* 43 (1964): 193–215.

———. "The Interpolated Stories in *Joseph Andrews*, or 'The History of the World in General' Satirically Revised." *Modern Philology* 63 (1966): 295–310.

Jenkins, Owen. "Richardson's *Pamela* and Fielding's 'Vile Forgeries.'" *Philological Quarterly* 44 (1965): 200–210.

Paulson, Ronald. "Models and Paradigms: *Joseph Andrews*, Hogarth's *Good Samaritan*, and Fénelon's *Télémaque*." *MLN* 91 (1976): 1186–1207.

Reed, Walter L. "*Joseph Andrews* and the Quixotic: The Politics of the Classic." *An Exemplary History of the Novel.* Chicago and London: U of Chicago P, 1981. 117–36.

Rothstein, Eric. "The Framework of *Shamela*." *ELH: A Journal of English Literary History* 35 (1968): 381–402.

Spacks, Patricia Meyer. "Some Reflections on Satire." *Genre* 1 (1968): 22–30.

Weinbrot, Howard D. "Chastity and Interpolation: Two Aspects of *Joseph Andrews*." *Journal of English and Germanic Philology* 69 (1970): 14–31.

Weinstein, Arnold. "The Body Beautiful: *Joseph Andrews*." *Fictions of the Self: 1550–1800.* Princeton: Princeton UP, 1981. 114–28.

Woods, Charles. "Fielding and the Authorship of *Shamela*." *Philological Quarterly* 25 (1946): 248–72.